The Psychotherapist's
Own Psychotherapy

THE PSYCHOTHERAPIST'S OWN PSYCHOTHERAPY

Patient and Clinician Perspectives

Edited by
JESSE D. GELLER
JOHN C. NORCROSS
DAVID E. ORLINSKY

OXFORD
UNIVERSITY PRESS

2005

OXFORD

UNIVERSITY PRESS

Oxford   New York
Auckland   Bangkok   Buenos Aires   Cape Town   Chennai
Dar es Salaam   Delhi   Hong Kong   Istanbul   Karachi   Kolkata
Kuala Lumpur   Madrid   Melbourne   Mexico City   Mumbai   Nairobi
São Paulo   Shanghai   Taipei   Tokyo   Toronto

Copyright © 2005 by Oxford University Press, Inc.

Published by Oxford University Press, Inc.
198 Madison Avenue, New York, New York 10016

Oxford is a registered trademark of Oxford University Press

www.oup.com

Library of Congress Cataloging-in-Publication Data
The psychotherapist's own psychotherapy : patient and clinician perspectives /
edited by Jesse D. Geller, John C. Norcross, David E. Orlinsky.
p.   cm.
Includes bibliographical references and index.
ISBN-13 978-0-19-513394-3
ISBN 0-19-513394-3
1. Psychotherapists—Counseling of.   2. Psychotherapists—Mental health.   3.
Psychotherapy patients.   I. Geller, Jesse D.   II. Norcross, John C., 1957–   III. Orlinsky,
David E. (David Elliot), 1936–
RC451.4.P79P786 2004
616.89'14'023—dc22   2004049243
Rev.

Chapter 7 first appeared in the *International Review of Psychoanalysis*, Vol. 2, 1975, 145–156.
© Estate of Harry Guntrip.

Portions of Chapter 10 were adapted from the *Journal of Humanistic Psychology*, Vol. 36, No. 4,
Fall 1996, 31–41. © 1996 Sage Publications, Inc.

Portions of Chapter 12 first appeared in the *Family Therapy Networker*, now the *Psychotherapy
Networker*. © 1999, *Family Therapy Networker*. Used by permission.
www.psychotherapynetworker.org

1 3 5 7 9 8 6 4 2

Printed in the United States of America
on acid-free paper

PREFACE

More than three-quarters of mental health professionals have undergone personal psychotherapy on at least one occasion. Proportionally speaking, psychotherapists are probably the largest consumers of long-term psychotherapy. Many therapists relate that their own experience in personal treatment has been the single greatest influence on their professional development. Furthermore, research indicates that identifications with their own therapists are a key determinant of the ways in which therapists-in-training understand and apply therapeutic principles.

Yet, until recently, little professional attention and scant empirical research has been devoted to the psychotherapist's personal therapy. Consequently, there is no organized body of knowledge that summarizes what is known about psychotherapy with mental health professionals and that effectively guides the work of "therapist's therapists." Even less is published about conducting treatment with fellow therapists or the linkages between receiving and conducting psychotherapy. The taboo against open examination of the psychotherapist's own treatment is both revealing and troubling.

This book is designed to realize two primary aims. The first is to synthesize and explicate the accumulated knowledge on psychotherapy with psychotherapists. The second and interrelated aim is to provide clinically tested and empirically grounded assistance to psychotherapists treating fellow therapists, as well as to those clinicians who seek personal treatment themselves.

In this respect, the intended audience for the book is large and diverse. The book is intended as a treatment reference for clinicians, of all professions and persuasions, who treat or intend to treat therapist-patients. It is also intended for graduate students who are contemplating or currently involved in personal therapy, for seasoned clinicians returning to personal therapy, and for educators who are responsible for training future therapists. Those who do not have specialized knowledge in this area but are intrigued by the inner workings of our profession will also be interested.

STRUCTURE OF THE BOOK

This edited volume brings together personal experiences, research findings, and clinical wisdom from "both sides of the couch." For the sake of clarity, the book addresses separately receiving personal psychotherapy and conducting personal therapy. This structure allows us to embrace the perspectives of both patient and therapist, in contrast to previous literature that addressed only a single perspective.

The Psychotherapist's Own Psychotherapy is integrative in another sense. Multiple theoretical orientations are evident in the coeditors, the contributors, and the chapter contents. Both the patient and the clinician narratives traverse the theoretical landscape. Ideological diversity prevails throughout.

The book is divided into four parts: The Therapist's Therapy in Different Theoretical Orientations; Being a Therapist-Patient; Being a Therapist's Therapist; and Epilogue.

Part I presents the spectrum of theoretical viewpoints that have shaped the profession's attitudes regarding personal therapy. It consists of five essays about the diverse theoretical orientations that have guided the practice of psychotherapy with psychotherapists.

Part II features the experiences of distinguished psychotherapists undergoing psychotherapy. Six firsthand accounts by therapist-patients are followed by five research reviews on the experience of undergoing personal treatment. In this and the subsequent part, the book moves from personal knowledge through systematic research and toward clinical wisdom. This structure reflects the way knowledge of personal therapy has itself progressed—tacit knowledge via participation in undergoing and conducting personal therapy, through empirical research, and back to clinical wisdom. In the best scientist-practitioner tradition, first-person narratives are interwoven with contemporary research data on psychotherapists' own psychotherapy.

All of the autobiographical chapters in part II were written specifically for this book, with one exception—Guntrip's first-person account of his analyses with Fairbairn and Winnicott. It is an inspiring example of how one might write in a scholarly yet personal voice about the linkages among receiving personal therapy, selecting a theoretical orientation, and developing a personal style of conducting therapy.

Part III turns to the therapist's therapist, again from both personal experiences and research reviews. Seven colleagues representing diverse theoretical orientations share their lessons, mistakes, and recommendations in treating fellow mental health professionals. The three subsequent chapters are coauthored research reviews on the extant research on conducting personal therapy. Chapter 25 reports on a new study, specifically commissioned for this book, on psychotherapists' experiences in treating fellow clinicians.

Both the contributing therapist-patients and therapists' therapists followed common guidelines in preparing their psychobiographical chapters. The guidelines were formulated to (1) promote continuity among the chapters in the book; (2) afford convergence between the first-person accounts and the subsequent research-oriented chapters; and (3) permit comparative analyses between the complimentary experiences of therapists conducting personal therapy (part III) and those receiving it (part II). The guidelines for the firsthand accounts are reproduced in the appendix.

Our epilogue presents our efforts to synthesize the collective wisdom found in this volume and to advance the ultimate integration of the experiential, theoretical, and research perspectives on the psychotherapy of therapists. As is evident in the structure of the book, we attempt to integrate the experiences of, and linkages between, being a therapist-patient and being a therapist's therapist.

ACKNOWLEDGMENTS

We want to thank Joan Bossert, our editor at Oxford University Press, for her superb advice and untiring patience in seeing this project to fruition. In editing a large book, one comes to appreciate that the Muses are not always on schedule. We are grateful to the contributors to this book for taking time from their busy schedules to write their chapters and for their willingness to take our editorial suggestions seriously. A very special thanks to those authors who accepted the challenge to write about their very private life experiences.

Jesse Geller owes an immense debt to the following people for their varied help: Ruth Geller, Kenneth Pope, and Edie Wolkovitz. Each made contributions that were crucial and well timed. The Guntrip essay has been reprinted here with the kind permission of the *International Review of Psychoanalysis*.

John Norcross gratefully acknowledges the research collaboration of Elizabeth Kurzawa, the internal funding of the University of Scranton, and the clerical assistance of Melissa Hedges and Dennis Reidy. As always, he appreciates his family's loving tolerance of his writing commitments.

David Orlinsky thanks his coeditors, Jesse Geller and John Norcross; his friends and colleagues in the SPR Collaborative Research Network (especially but not only Professor M. Helge Rønnestad, Dr. Hadas Wiseman, and Dr. Ulrike Willutzki); and, as always, his wife, Marcia Bourland.

Jesse D. Geller   John C. Norcross   David E. Orlinsky
New Haven, Connecticut   Clarks Summit, Pennsylvania   Chicago, Illinois

CONTENTS

Contributors   xiii

1.   The Question of Personal Therapy:
Introduction and Prospectus   3
JESSE D. GELLER, JOHN C. NORCROSS, & DAVID E. ORLINSKY

PART I. THE THERAPIST'S THERAPY IN DIFFERENT THEORETICAL ORIENTATIONS

2.   The Training Analysis in the Mainstream
Freudian Model   15
RICHARD LASKY

3.   The Role of Personal Therapy in the Formation
of a Jungian Analyst   27
THOMAS B. KIRSCH

4.   Personal Therapy and Growth Work in
Experiential-Humanistic Therapies   34
ROBERT ELLIOT & RHEA PARTYKA

5.   Personal Therapy in Cognitive-Behavioral Therapy:
Tradition and Current Practice   41
ANTON-RUPERT LAIREITER & ULRIKE WILLUTZKI

6.   The Role and Current Practice of Personal Therapy
      in Systemic/Family Therapy Traditions   52
      JAY LEBOW

             PART II. BEING A THERAPIST-PATIENT

Personal Experiences: Firsthand Accounts by Therapist-Patients

7.   My Experience of Analysis with Fairbairn
      and Winnicott: How Complete a Result Does
      Psychoanalytic Therapy Achieve?   63
      HARRY GUNTRIP

8.   My Experiences as a Patient in Five Psychoanalytic
      Psychotherapies   81
      JESSE D. GELLER

9.   The Personal Therapy Experiences of a
      Rational Emotive-Behavior Therapist   98
      WINDY DRYDEN

10.   The I and the Self: Reminiscences of
      Existential-Humanistic Therapy   114
      BRYAN WITTINE

11.   The Role of Individual and Marital Therapy
      in My Development   129
      CLARA E. HILL

12.   A Shamanic Tapestry: My Experiences with Individual,
      Marital, and Family Therapy   145
      WILLIAM M. PINSOF

Research Findings: Undergoing Personal Therapy

13.   The Prevalence and Parameters of Personal Therapy
      in the United States   165
      JOHN C. NORCROSS & JAMES D. GUY

14.   The Prevalence and Parameters of Personal Therapy
      in Europe and Elsewhere   177
      DAVID E. ORLINSKY, M. HELGE RØNNESTAD, ULRIKE WILLUTKI,
      HADAS WISEMAN, JEAN-FRANCOIS BOTERMANS, AND THE SPR
      COLLABORATIVE RESEARCH NETWORK

15.   Psychotherapists Entering Personal Therapy:
      Their Primary Reasons and Presenting Problems   192
      JOHN C. NORCROSS & KELLY A. CONNOR

16.   The Selection and Characteristics of Therapists'
      Psychotherapists: A Research Synthesis   201
      JOHN C. NORCROSS & HENRY GRUNEBAUM

17.   Outcomes and Impacts of the Psychotherapists'
      Own Psychotherapy: A Research Review   214
      DAVID E. ORLINSKY, JOHN C. NORCROSS,
      M. HELGE RØNNESTAD, & HADAS WISEMAN

PART III. BEING A THERAPIST'S THERAPIST

Personal Experiences: Firsthand Accounts by Therapists' Therapists

18.   On Analyzing Colleagues (Trainees Included)   235
      EMANUEL BERMAN

19.   Treating Psychotherapists with Cognitive Therapy   254
      JUDITH S. BECK & ANDREW C. BUTLER

20.   Feminist Therapy with Therapists: Egalitarian and More   265
      LAURA S. BROWN

21.   Listening to the Listener: An Existential-Humanistic
      Approach to Psychotherapy with Psychotherapists   282
      MYRTLE HEERY & JAMES F. T. BUGENTAL

22.   Conducting Marital and Family Therapy with Therapists   297
      HARRY J. APONTE

23.   Group Therapy for Therapists in Gestalt Therapy
      Training: A Therapist-Trainer's Perspective   307
      PHILIP LICHTENBERG

24.   Treating Impaired Psychotherapists and
      "Wounded Healers"   323
      GARY R. SCHOENER

Research Findings: Providing Personal Therapy to Other Therapists

25.   Research on Conducting Psychotherapy with
      Mental Health Professionals   345
      JESSE D. GELLER, JOHN C. NORCROSS, & DAVID E. ORLINSKY

26.   Training Analyses: Historical Considerations
      and Empirical Research   365
      REBECCA C. CURTIS & MAZIA QAISER

27.   Boundaries and Internalization in the Psychotherapy
      of Psychotherapists: Clinical and Research Perspectives   379
      JESSE D. GELLER

                        EPILOGUE

The Patient Psychotherapist, the Psychotherapist's
Psychotherapist, and the Psychotherapist as a Person   405
DAVID E. ORLINSKY, JESSE D. GELLER,
& JOHN C. NORCROSS

                        APPENDIX

Guidelines for Firsthand Accounts   417

Index   421

CONTRIBUTORS

HARRY J. APONTE, Couples and Family Therapy Program, Drexel University, Philadelphia, Pennsylvania

JUDITH S. BECK, Beck Institute for Cognitive Therapy and Research, Department of Psychiatry, University of Pennsylvania, Philadelphia, Pennsylvania

EMANUEL BERMAN, Department of Psychology, University of Haifa, Israel Psychoanalytic Institute, Haifa, Israel

JEAN-FRANCOIS BOTERMANS, Faculty of Psychology, Centre de Guidance de Louvain-la-Neuve, Brussels, Belgium

LAURA S. BROWN, Department of Psychology, Argosy University, Seattle, Washington

JAMES F. T. BUGENTAL, Emeritus Clinical Faculty, Stanford University School of Medicine, Stanford, California

ANDREW C. BUTLER, Beck Institute for Cognitive Therapy and Research, Department of Psychiatry, University of Pennsylvania, Philadelphia, Pennsylvania

KELLY A. CONNOR, Department of Psychology, University of Scranton, Scranton, Pennsylvania

REBECCA C. CURTIS, Department of Psychology, Derner Institute of Advanced Psychological Studies, Adelphi University, Garden City, New York

WINDY DRYDEN, Department of Psychology, Goldsmiths College, London, England

ROBERT ELLIOT, Department of Psychology, University of Toledo, Toledo, Ohio

JESSE D. GELLER, Department of Psychiatry, Yale University School of Medicine, New Haven, Connecticut

HENRY GRUNEBAUM, Department of Psychiatry, The Cambridge Hospital, Cambridge, Massachusetts

HARRY GUNTRIP, Deceased

JAMES D. GUY, Headington Institute, Pasadena, California

MYRTLE HEERY, Department of Psychology, Sonoma State University, Rohnert Park, California

CLARA E. HILL, Department of Psychology, University of Maryland, College Park, Maryland

THOMAS B. KIRSCH, C. J. Jung Institute, San Francisco, California

ANTON-RUPERT LAIREITER, Center for Clinical Psychology, Psychotherapy, and Health Psychology, Institute of Psychology, University of Salzburg, Salzburg, Austria

RICHARD LASKY, New York University Postdoctoral Program in Psychoanalysis, Institute for Psychoanalytic Training and Research, New York, New York

JAY LEBOW, Family Institute at Northwestern University, Northwestern University, Evanston, Illinois

PHILIP LICHTENBERG, Graduate School of Social Work and Social Research, Gestalt Therapy Institute of Philadelphia, Bryn Mawr, Pennsylvania

JOHN C. NORCROSS, Department of Psychology, University of Scranton, Scranton, Pennsylvania

DAVID E. ORLINSKY, Department of Psychology, University of Chicago, Chicago, Illinois

RHEA PARTYKA, Department of Psychology, University of Toledo, Toledo, Ohio

WILLIAM M. PINSOF, Family Institute at Northwestern University, Center for Applied Psychological and Family Studies, Northwestern University, Evanston, Illinois

MAZIA QAISER, Derner Institute of Advanced Psychological Studies, Adelphia University, Garden City, New York

M. HELGE RØNNESTAD, Department of Psychology, University of Oslo, Oslo, Norway

GARY R. SCHOENER, Walk-In Counseling Center, Minneapolis, Minnesota

ULRIKE WILLUTZKI, Department of Psychology, Ruhr University, Bochum, Germany

HADAS WISEMAN, Faculty of Education, University of Haifa, Haifa, Israel

BRYAN WITTINE, C. G. Jung Institute, San Francisco, California

The Psychotherapist's Own Psychotherapy

1

THE QUESTION OF PERSONAL THERAPY

Introduction and Prospectus

JESSE D. GELLER, JOHN C. NORCROSS,
& DAVID E. ORLINSKY

Personal treatment for psychotherapists—receiving it, recommending and conducting it—is at the very core of the profession of psychotherapy. Personal therapy or analysis is, in many respects, at the center of the mental health universe. Our training, our identity, our health, and our self-renewal revolve around the epicenter of personal therapy experience. In their early classic *Public and Private Lives of Psychotherapists*, Henry, Sims, and Spray (1973, p. 14) concluded: "In sum, the accumulated evidence strongly suggests that individual psychotherapy not only serves as the focal point for professional training programs, but also functions as the symbolic core of professional identity in the mental health field."

The vast majority of mental health professionals, independent of professional discipline, have undergone personal treatment, typically on several occasions (see chapters 13 and 14). The overwhelming bulk of evidence, with the exception of its inconclusive effects on subsequent patient outcomes, supports the effectiveness of personal treatment. Fully 85% of therapists who have undergone therapy report having had at least one experience of great or very great benefit to themselves personally, and 78% relate that therapy has been a strong positive influence on their own professional development (chapter 17).

At the same time, upward of three-quarters of psychotherapists have themselves treated a psychotherapist colleague or psychotherapist-in-training (see chapter 25). Moreover, a substantial number of clinicians occupy the special status known as "therapist's therapist" (Norcross, Geller, & Kurzawa, 2000), a position that provides unique gratifications and profound satisfactions. The corresponding perils entail increased evaluation anxieties, ambiguous boundaries, and the danger of turning one's therapist-patients into disciples or supervisees (chapters 26 and 27).

Perhaps most frequently cited are satisfactions—and problems—stemming from the clinician's "match" or "fit" with his or her personal therapist. According to our authors, the foundation of favorable matches seems to be built on reciprocal role expectations (Dryden, chapter 9), compatible styles and professional philosophies (Geller, chapter 8), converging cultural and social values (Brown, chapter 20), and congruence of reciprocal personality dynamics (Berman, chapter 18; Lictenberg, chapter 23; Lasky, chapter 2).

Psychotherapists do not receive extensive training and supervised experience in working with therapist-patients, as they do with other "types" of patients. In actuality, therapists have traditionally received little formal training in the conduct of psychotherapy with fellow therapists. In many (perhaps, most) instances, the only training therapists receive is that which comes from having been patients themselves. Training institutions do not typically provide guidelines to their therapists of the therapists-in-training and provide little or no monitoring of these relationships. Complicating matters further, there is still no organized body of knowledge that guides the work of therapists' therapists. Consequently, much of what therapists do when the patient is a therapist is premised on unsystematized, often unverbalized, assumptions about the similarities and differences between the psychotherapy of therapists and the psychotherapies offered to other "types" of patients.

There is no simple answer to the question: What distinguishes the psychotherapy of therapist-patients from the psychotherapy of nontherapist patients? As this book makes clear, there are deep similarities, and there are important differences too. For example, it is self-evident that the situations in which the psychotherapy of mental health professionals occurs are potentially much different from those encountered during and after treatment with patients who are not mental health professionals. Although therapists differ in the importance they assign to such differences, there is widespread agreement that there is a genuine and unambiguous need to advance our understanding of the therapeutic challenges that are more or less particular to the psychological treatment of patients who are themselves therapists or therapists-in-training.

As was mentioned in the preface, this book brings together theoretical, clinical, experiential, and research perspectives to bear on the question: What distinguishes the psychotherapy of patients who are themselves therapists or therapists-in-training?

This brief opening chapter introduces the "question of personal therapy." Specifically, we review the integrative structure of the book, proffer a working definition of personal therapy, trace its evolution, and review its multiple and yet singular purpose(s).

INTEGRATIVE STRUCTURE

We have structured this book in an integrative fashion, in at least three distinct ways. First, the book concerns itself with psychotherapists both receiving personal therapy (part II) and conducting it (part III). The research literature and the therapist's therapists' accounts demonstrate the direct relevance of each to the other. Second, in both parts II and III of the book, we integrate personal experiences with research findings. The narrative and empirical perspectives have not productively interacted with each other when it comes to the psychotherapy of therapists. It is only when clinical experiences and empirical research are in close dialogue with one another that true progress is made in understanding therapeutic change.

The third integrative structure of this book reflects the traditional meaning of psychotherapy integration: the synthesis of different psychotherapy systems or theoretical orientations (Norcross & Goldfried, 2005). The authors in this volume were chosen to reflect the diverse theoretical traditions that inform clinical practice. An entire section (part I) of the book is dedicated to the therapist's therapy in different theoretical orientations.

DEFINING PERSONAL THERAPY

In this book, *personal therapy* is a broad and generic term encompassing psychological treatment of mental health professionals (or those in training) by means of various theoretical orientations and therapy formats. Personal therapy can thus refer to 12 sessions of group therapy for a social work graduate student, a year of couples therapy for a psychiatric resident, or three years of intensive individual psychotherapy for a licensed psychologist. However, we reserve the term *training analysis* for the more specific case of individual psychoanalysis required by a formal, postgraduate psychoanalytic institute. An entire chapter is devoted to the special case of the training analysis (chapter 2).

For our purposes, *personal therapy* refers to psychological treatment that is either voluntary or required. In most European countries, a requisite number of hours of personal therapy is obligatory in order to become accredited or licensed as a psychotherapist. In the United States, by contrast, only analytic training institutes and a few graduate programs require a course of personal therapy.

EVOLUTION OF PERSONAL THERAPY

Much has changed about the practice of psychotherapy since psychoanalytic theory and method were conceived. But two of Freud's original ideas continue to exert a powerful influence on the ways therapy is practiced and therapists are trained. From the beginning, Freud proposed that personal therapy was the deepest and most rigorous part of one's clinical education.

Freud (1937/1964, p. 246) rhetorically asks in "Analysis Terminable and Interminable": "But where and how is the poor wretch to acquire the ideal qualification which he will need in this profession? The answer is in an analysis of himself, with which his preparation for his future activity begins." Freud (1926, p. 126) also had this in mind when he wrote:

> No one who is familiar with the nature of neurosis will be aston-
> ished to hear that even a man who is very able to carry out an
> analysis on other people can behave like any other mortal and be
> capable of producing the most intense resistances as soon as he
> himself becomes the object of analytic investigation. When this
> happens, we are once again reminded of the dimension of depth in
> the mind, and it does not surprise us to find that neurosis has its
> roots in psychological strata to which an intellectual knowledge of
> analysis has not penetrated.

A recurrent theme of this book is the acknowledgment that it is easier to be wise and mature for others then for ourselves. Berman (chapter 18), among others (e.g., Bridges, 1993; Fleischer & Wissler, 1985; Gabbard, 1995; Kaslow, 1984), has observed that therapists who cling to a sense of strength and mastery are threatened by the dilemma of "needing help." This is one of the identity conflicts and narcissistic wounds with which psycho-therapists are likely to struggle in personal treatment. These concerns are related to the desire to be self-reliant, the quest for perfectionism, and the deep fear of being an impostor.

Directly and indirectly, all of the therapist-patients in this book reported that no matter how intellectually prepared they were to collaborate, they could not "resist resisting." Dryden (chapter 9) concludes his chapter by saying that "I would not be a very easy client for most therapists. I have a clear idea of what is helpful to me and what is not, and I have a definite preference for self-help, which makes being in therapy a problematic expe-rience for me if that therapy is not focused sharply on encouraging me to help myself."

Freud also recommended returning to psychotherapy as a means of alleviating the burdens inherent in the practice of psychoanalysis. Freud (1937/1964, p. 249) proposed that "every analyst should periodically—at intervals of five years or so—submit himself to analysis once more, without feeling ashamed of taking this step." As the chapters in part I make clear, this view is compatible with those of other mainstream schools of psycho-therapy. Existential, humanistic, interpersonal, systemic, relational, and other models advocate personal therapy as an essential part of becoming a psychotherapist. Consequently, many generations of psychotherapists have been in their own personal therapy.

Their ranks have included many talented clinical writers who could have described their interactions with their therapists in ways that illuminated and clarified questions we are all obliged to think through as psychotherapists. But, for undoubtedly complex reasons, very few psychotherapists have written in a detailed and specific way about their experiences as patients in the first person. The profession has rarely embraced autobiography either as a methodology or as a source of knowledge. This trend has led psychotherapists to disguise and disavow their own patienthood when using material from their therapies as "evidence" on behalf of their theoretical convictions. Kohut is perhaps the most striking instance. It has been disclosed that in all likelihood Kohut, himself, was the patient under consideration in his famous article "The Two Analyses of Mr. Z." (Kohut, 1979), which signaled his turning away from classical analysis and toward self psychology.

Like clinical case reports, autobiographical accounts of therapy are neither publicly confirmable nor replicable. We make no claim that the psychotherapists' accounts of their treatment experiences are more accurate than those provided by lay patients. Perhaps more than any other group, therapists are aware of the unreliability and self-serving nature of remembering (and forgetting). Nevertheless, autobiographical narratives constitute a vital source of information about what is "helpful" and "harmful" about therapy. Moreover, by asking the authors to address certain questions in their autobiographical accounts (see the appendix), we sought to determine whether the themes reflected in their chapters converged with the research findings.

At the same time, for better and for worse, psychotherapists experience considerable pressure to be "good patients," probably more so than laypersons. In turn, the potentially burdensome pressure to be successful is felt more intensely by therapists when the patient is a colleague. The motivational thrusts of these pressures can be readily discerned in the chapters written by Aponte, Wittine, Geller, Hill, and Berman.

Psychotherapists have also been reluctant to write about their work with therapist-patients without resorting to "radical disguises" (Berman, chapter 18). Therapists' therapists have offered a variety of meaningful and rationalizing explanations as to why they would not write about therapist-patients. The majority revolved around protecting privacy. Some said it seemed "too personal" to write about psychotherapists as patients. Others said they would only write clinical or theoretical papers concerning therapist-patients in a distant, general, and abstract way.

Far more research attention has been devoted to the intellectual training and supervision of therapists than to the psychotherapy of therapist-patients. Only in the last 15 years have systematic efforts to conceptualize and research the psychotherapy of psychotherapists appeared regularly in the literature. These investigations have focused almost exclusively on the characteristics of therapist-patients and their experiences in receiving personal therapy. Many important questions about the psychotherapy of psychotherapists have not been answered or even asked by empirical investigators.

WHAT IS MISSING?

In this regard, it is noteworthy that two crucial questions about the psychotherapy of psychotherapists have not been answered or even asked by previous investigators. We only briefly touch upon these in this book as well. First, we cannot locate a single research study that assesses the logistics or effects of fee assessment on the psychotherapist's personal treatment. We simply do not know whether reduced payment, full payment, no payment, or managed care coverage materially influences the process and outcome. It is as though money has no place or significance in personal therapy, although it obviously does for both those seeking it and those rendering it.

Second, relatively little is known about the stage of life at which psychotherapists seek personal treatment. The firsthand accounts of patient therapists in part II of this book make it compellingly clear that therapists seek different therapeutic goals at different seasons of their professional and personal lives; yet there is little in the way of systematic study of the topic. In discussing his own odyssey of personal therapy over a 45-year career, Yalom (2002, p. 42) pointedly observes: "I entered therapy *at many different stages of my life.* Despite an excellent and extensive course of therapy at the onset of one's career, an entirely different set of issues may arrive at different junctures of the life cycle" (italics in original).

All of the therapist-patient accounts in this volume are grounded within their own developmental context. As predicted by adult development theory, the reasons for seeking personal treatment were frequently linked to anxieties about their ability to deal with age-associated tasks. Dryden (chapter 9) sought Jungian analysis to prevent a midlife crisis. Hill (chapter 11) entered therapy to deal with the opposing claims of family and career. Pinsof (chapter 12) initiated couples treatment to address the pressures of his work and marriage and then undertook a course of psychoanalysis analysis for individuation during a critical time in his personal and professional development. Normatively speaking, therapists enter personal treatment an average of two to three times during their careers—and probably for and during developmentally propitious crises.

Psychotherapists seeking personal treatment repeatedly during their careers supports Wiseman and Schetler's (2001, p. 140) conclusion: "Personal therapy is perceived not only as an essential part of the training phase, but as playing an important role in the therapist's ongoing process of *individuation* and in the development of the ability to use the self, to achieve moment-to-moment authentic relatedness with one's clients." Indeed, as reviewed in chapter 17, multiple studies consistently demonstrate that the enduring lesson taken by practicing clinicians from their own treatment concerns the importance of the therapeutic relationship and the centrality of nurturing interpersonal skills. This heightened awareness may well translate into clinical practice, at least according to self-reports.

THE MULTIPLE YET SINGULAR PURPOSE
OF PERSONAL THERAPY

Mental health professionals seek psychotherapy at different times in their lives for different purposes. Further, as we make clear in our epilogue, proponents of disparate theoretical orientations accord different value to the various purposes and parameters of personal treatment.

These pronounced and genuine differences, however, tend to obscure the overriding commonality of purpose. Namely, the goal of the psychotherapist's personal treatment is to alter the nature of subsequent clinical work in ways that enhance its effectiveness. The actual mechanism of this process is as complex and individualized as the number of psychotherapist-patients (and their therapists). But there are at least six recurring commonalities in the literature on how the therapist's therapy is said to improve his or her clinical work (Norcross, Strausser-Kirtland, & Missar, 1988).

Goal of Personal Therapy	Mechanism of Improved Clinical Work
• Improves the emotional and mental functioning of the psychotherapist	• Makes the clinician's life less neurotic and more gratifying
• Provides the therapist-patient with a more complete understanding of personal dynamics and interpersonal elicitations	• Enables the therapist to conduct treatment with clearer perceptions and reduced countertransference potential
• Alleviates the emotional stresses and burdens inherent in the "impossible profession"	• Deals more successfully with the special problems imposed by the craft
• Serves as a profound socialization experience	• Establishes conviction about the effectiveness of psychotherapy and facilitates the internalization of the healer role
• Places therapists in the role of the client	• Increases sensitivity to and respect for the patients' struggles
• Offers an intensive opportunity to observe clinical methods	• Models interpersonal and technical skills

The ostensible paradox is resolved: multiple purposes toward the singular goal of improving clinical work in a profession where one's own health and wholeness is an indispensable foundation.

IN CLOSING

This integrative book provides a state-of-the-art compendium of what is known about undergoing, recommending, and conducting psychotherapists' personal treatment. It is intended to be both descriptive and prescriptive, as the personal narratives and the research reviews both point to evidence-based practices.

At the same time, we hope the clinical accounts and research reviews will stimulate others to consider the fundamental, yet neglected, questions surrounding the psychotherapy of therapists. Such questions include: What particular aspects of their own personal therapies are therapists likely to repeat with their own patients? Do the payment arrangements for personal therapy materially impact its process or outcome? What distinguishes the treatment of mental health professionals who undergo therapy at different stages of their careers? What special considerations attend to the decision to medicate or hospitalize a mental health professional? What are the additional burdens and special problems posed by therapists mandated by professional authorities to receive treatment? What criteria can a therapists' therapist trust to distinguish countertransference-based doubts about professional competence from the reality of overextending oneself? Is treating a fellow mental health professional without specific training and supervision analogous to working outside of one's area of competence?

We extend a cordial invitation to study how one's efforts to master psychological problems and to find solutions to basic existential questions are reflected in one's treatment of patients, be they therapists or nontherapists. We hope to initiate a dialogue on what the therapy of therapists can teach us about the person of the therapist and how to more effectively treat all patients, therapists and nontherapists alike. This book is a beginning.

REFERENCES

Bridges, N. A. (1993). Clinical dilemmas: Therapists treating therapists. *American Journal of Orthopsychiatry, 63,* 34–44.

Fleischer, J. A., & Wissler, A. (1985). The therapist as patient: Special problems and considerations. *Psychotherapy, 22,* 587–594.

Freud, S. (1926/1959). The question of lay analysis: Conversations with an impartial person. In J. Strachey (Ed. and Trans.), The standard edition of the complete psychological works of Sigmund Freud (Vol. 20). London: Hogarth Press.

Freud, S. (1937/1964). Analysis terminable and interminable. In J. Strachey (Ed. and Trans.), *The standard edition of the complete psychological works of Sigmund Freud* (Vol. 23, pp. 216–253). London: Hogarth Press.

Gabbard, G. O. (1995). When the patient is a therapist: Special challenges in the psychoanalysis of mental health professionals. *Psychoanalytic Review, 82,* 709–725.

Guntrip, H. (1975). My experience of analysis with Fairbarn and Winnicott. *International Review of Psycho-analysis, 2,* 145–156.

Henry, W. E., Sims, J. H., & Spray, S. L. (1973). *The public and private lives of psychotherapists.* San Francisco: Jossey-Bass.

Kaslow, F. W. (Ed.). (1984). *Psychotherapy with psychotherapists.* New York: Haworth.

Kohut, H. (1979). The two analyses of Mr. Z. *International Journal of Psycho-analysis, 60,* 3–27.

Norcross, J. C., Geller, J. D., & Kurzawa, E. K. (2000). Conducting psychotherapy with psychotherapists: I. Prevalence, patients, and problems. *Psychotherapy, 37,* 199–205.

Norcross, J. C., & Goldfried, M. R. (Eds.). (2005). *Handbook of psychotherapy integration* (2nd ed.). New York: Oxford University Press.

Norcross, J. C., Strausser-Kirtland, D., & Missar, C. D. (1988). The processes and outcomes of psychotherapists' personal treatment experiences. *Psychotherapy, 25,* 36–43.

Wiseman, H., & Schefler, G. (2001). Experienced psychoanalytically oriented therapists—narrative accounts of their own personal therapy: Impacts on professional and personal development. *Psychotherapy, 33,* 129–141.

Yalom, I. (2002). *The gift of therapy: An open letter to a new generation of therapists and their patients.* New York: HarperCollins.

I

THE THERAPIST'S
THERAPY IN
DIFFERENT THEORETICAL
ORIENTATIONS

2

THE TRAINING ANALYSIS
IN THE MAINSTREAM
FREUDIAN MODEL

RICHARD LASKY

The clinical analysis of the candidate in training, known as *the train-ing analysis*, is usually considered to be the most important compo-nent of the tripartite model of psychoanalytic training. The other two components are didactic coursework, in both theory and technique, and conducting supervised analyses of a number of patients. Freud's early fol-lowers read his works avidly, and they made pilgrimages to Vienna from all over the world in order to be analyzed by him. From the very beginning being analyzed was as important as reading Freud's papers. The rush to be analyzed, preferably by the master himself, was not because it was a require-ment of some sort or because Freud's original students suffered particu-larly severe psychopathology themselves. It occurred because they were so taken by psychoanalysis as the only real method of knowing themselves. The idea that one has unconscious motives that play a greater role in mental life than do one's conscious intentions was both revolutionary and electrifying, and the first generation of analysts were eager to have firsthand experience. It is also probable that they flocked to analysis in identification with Freud, who made such prominent use of his own self-analysis in his discoveries about the unconscious.

It is likely that the first generation of analysts would have had some of the same kind of unconscious ambivalence about being analyzed that any present-day patient has. But whatever ambivalence may have given them pause, intense curiosity—combined with the high level of intellectual ex-citement surrounding psychoanalysis—drove those first-generation analysts forward. It was unthinkable that anyone wanting to become an analyst would not be analyzed as part of the process of becoming an analyst. Lack of interest in being analyzed or, especially, outright resistance to the idea, was a contradiction in terms that would have been incomprehensible to Freud and to the other early analysts. In that day there was never a problem getting reluctant aspiring analysts to go into analysis—there were no reluctant aspiring analysts; the problem was getting enough analysts to supply the continuously growing demand.

In Freud's view (1910/1957) the training analysis was in itself an education, albeit an unorthodox one. Freud thought that no unanalyzed person could possibly know how powerful and extensive the unconscious is. No amount of ordinary education—that is, no amount of book learning, supervision, or discussion—can adequately convey the immensity of the influence that the unconscious exerts over all of mental life. And, by definition, not just the reach but also the extent and the nature of the unconscious are incomprehensible outside an analysis. One cannot consciously know about the contents and functions of the unconscious because we have in place active psychological defenses that are specifically designed to prevent such knowledge. This is because most—not all, but almost all—of the unconscious is composed of forbidden wishes, unacceptable desires, and taboo ideas. In addition, narcissistic considerations also cause us to defend against knowing the power and extent of the unconscious. Most people like to think that they have free will, that they are in control of their destiny, that they know themselves well, that they are basically in charge of their thoughts, feelings, and actions. Learning how untrue this is can be a narcissistic injury, a serious insult to one's self-esteem. Because the motives for keeping the unconscious as fully unconscious as possible are so powerful, nothing less than an analysis itself, Freud thought, is capable of bringing it into the light.

In Freud's earliest model of psychoanalytic action, the whole work of analysis was to make the unconscious conscious. It was not until 1923 (*The Ego and the Id*), when Freud added the structural theory (the id, the ego, and the superego) to the earlier topographical theory (unconscious, preconscious, and conscious), that the famous dictum "Where there is unconsciousness, consciousness shall be" was changed to "Where there is id, ego shall be." Freud doubted (1912/1958b, 1915/1958a) that any analyst could help patients realize this goal if she or he could not do it for herself or himself. The problem for an unanalyzed analyst is obvious; aware of the fact that almost all of mental life is unconscious but unable to appreciate the vast scope of its influence with any personal immediacy or conviction, she or he will inevitably stop short of revealing to the patient the full extent of the patient's unconscious forces. Imagining that she or he has delved as deeply into the patient's unconscious as it is reasonably possible to go, an unanalyzed analyst can go only as far as her or his own limited experience with the unconscious permits her or him to go (Freud, 1915/1958a). Thus, Freud thought, the kind of education the analyst's analysis provides is not merely desirable, it is an absolute necessity if she or he is to do this kind of work with others.

In the very early days of psychoanalysis the training analysis was educational in another way, too. Unlike the way we practice today, in those days teaching as well as "analyzing" was common during analytic hours. Freud, his disciples, and their students commonly discussed theory and technique (and sometimes each other's patients) during analytic hours; this was in addition, of course, to their informal meetings among themselves (for example, at the famous Wednesday evening group). The "frame" was considerably looser in those days, and one even saw interpretations offered by letter and at professional meetings (if the folklore is true). In those early times, when the number of analysts could practically be counted on one's fingers and toes, didactic material was frequently discussed in analytic hours. The flexibility of the frame in those days, as now, was a byproduct of the times. Those teaching moments appear to have been rather impulsive and not intended be an intentional tool, a formal or specific technique, in the conduct of the analysis. It seems clear that when Freud described the training analysis as educational he meant it in the sense associated with the expansion of consciousness rather than in the sense associated with didactic teaching. However, it did take a long time for the practice of didactic teaching and supervising to be fully abandoned in the training analysis. Part of why this took so long may have been because the early analysts were so heavily identified with Freud. The thing that really shifted didactic teaching out of the training analysis, however, was the development of formal psychoanalytic training programs in the "Eitingon model" (Eitingon proposed his model for psychoanalytic training, and it was adopted at the 1912 meeting of the International Psycho-Analytical Association). In this model, personal analysis, supervision, and course work are formally and officially separated from each other. The training analysis, to be concurrent with the other components of the training, ends at the joint discretion of the candidate and training analyst.

With personal analysis part of the official curriculum of training, which is how it came to be known as the *training analysis,* a number of problems arose, some clinical and others political. The first model of a training analysis was, of course, Freud's self-analysis. At the start, he analyzed prospective analysts and told them if and when they were ready to treat patients of their own. Some were physicians who were already treating patients according to methods they gleaned on their own from Freud's early writings, and they came to Freud with a practice already in place. Unless they were totally crazy, Freud did not tell them to give up their work. But he did advise them quite directly about their capacity to continue to perform it, along with his analysis of their strengths and weaknesses. That generation of analysts, trained and analyzed by Freud, also practiced in a similar, informal manner with the next group of (mainly) physicians attracted to psychoanalysis. The analysts in the first wave of *formal* training programs, following where they thought Freud's original model led, routinely reported to the "institute" or to its "training" or "education" committee on the candidate's readiness to proceed in the curriculum and when she or he could begin to do supervised analytic work.

In the United States, doing just as Freud did with his original "professional" patients, this practice was common at most of the "medical" (American Psychoanalytic Association–affiliated) institutes and, to a lesser extent, at the independent "nonmedical" institutes, until comparatively recently, when pressures from candidates and many of the faculty forced a change in this policy.

Many candidates and faculty, including some training analysts, who were opposed to the *reporting* part of the training analysis requirement were convinced that it was mishandled by some training analysts and also by some of the institutes' education/training committees. Candidates with innovative ideas or those who were attracted to alternate or competing schools of analysis (the Kleinian model, for example, or the existential, cultural, or interpersonal schools) were labeled "insufficiently analyzed" and could not move forward in their training. Ultimately, they either toed the line, or they had to go elsewhere—some by choice, others by necessity. (And this is how some cities ended up with not one analytic institute but with two or three competing institutes.) Those opposed to *reporting* argued that it had a stultifying effect on the field.

Candidates with overly strong negative transferences as well as candidates with legitimate complaints against their analysts, their supervisors, or the institute were often lumped together by training/education committees, which reacted as if any and every complaint could be nothing more than a form of negative transference. And when the training analyst reported this to the training committee, candidates with legitimate grievances could be, and often were, held back in their educational progress. Candidates who were attracted to either theoretical or institutional "enemies" of their training analysts, which the analyst would learn about in the analysis, of course, "needed further analysis" before they were ready to move ahead in the program. Candidates were often assigned an analyst by the institute rather than being able to choose from the pool of training analysts themselves, a practice that still exists at some institutes today, hard as that is to imagine. Often, if candidates found themselves in a bad fit with their assigned analyst they were told the mismatch was their fault, that it was merely negative transference going unanalyzed, and they too were often held back in their training.

But even with many of the faculty also dissatisfied with reporting, changing the reporting system at the institutes was no easy task. There were, however, other faculty and candidates who did not think the potential for abuse required trashing the whole system of reporting. This was a significant minority, and without minimizing or ignoring the problems associated with politics and power, they raised some of the positive issues concerning the impact of reporting. They reminded everyone that the reporting analyst model served other, quite legitimate ethical and pedagogical issues.

Many of the problems and abuses of the system, the supporters of reporting argued, were created by the practice of reporting on the *specific content* of a candidate's analytic work. Most supporters agreed that *this* aspect of reporting was highly inflammatory and that it created more difficulties than it ever solved. They suggested instead that reports should be limited only to a yes or no answer (with no other elaboration) to the question: *Is the candidate ready to undertake the next stage of training?* (no matter which step was being considered). They assumed that this would have a limiting effect on the potential for abuse, but they certainly acknowledged that acting out would still be possible even under this more stringent policy. The point was not to guarantee that acting out would not occur, it was to make it as unlikely as possible. The vast majority of training analysts and education committees did not act out in this way, the minority argued, and jettisoning the system in its entirety just because a tiny minority could abuse it seemed, to them, like throwing out the baby with the bathwater. Given the fact that problems can still arise even with this kind of limited reporting, what did they think there was to be gained by continuing the practice?

Their argument rests on the premise that candidates come to training with unresolved neurotic conflicts and then the training itself throws candidates into considerable additional conflict. Given the extremely high level of conflict candidates experience, the training analyst, intimately aware of the nuances of the candidate's inner life, is in the best position to gauge the readiness of a candidate to go forward. Conversely, she or he is also in the best position to know when a candidate is swamped by inner turmoil— either original or induced by the training—and, thus, whether a candidate is ready to proceed. That may be so, argued the opponents of reporting, but still, why not leave it up to the candidate? Because, the supporters replied, candidates may not be sufficiently objective about themselves, particularly when their conflicts (or the defenses they employ in response to them) may be blinding them to their own condition. Why not just leave it, then, up to the supervisor? Because even supervisors may not be shown areas of difficulty, both intentionally and unintentionally. Why not leave it up to classroom instructors? Because classroom instructors also may not know enough about the candidate. It is one thing to know whether or not the candidate has passed the course and quite another to know whether or not she or he is ready to progress in all parts of the training program, most especially its clinical components.

An extremely bright, charming, charismatic narcissist, for example, can easily pass all of the required courses with flying colors, but in truth one really might not want to leave her or him alone in a room with a patient. A manipulative candidate can carefully show only her or his most winning side to supervisors, who, after all, see her or him for only 45 minutes once a week. But it is not likely that candidate-patients will be equally able to hide, say, a shallow capacity for object relationships or a tendency to use others—including patients—from their analysts. Such candidates, supporters argued, could, conceivably, pull themselves together enough both in class and during supervision so that the depth of the problem is essentially hidden to anyone who does not know them with sufficient intimacy. This, they argued, would pertain despite the fact that the teachers and supervisors are trained analysts.

Teachers and supervisors might notice a tendency of that sort, for example, but the analyst would have a realistic sense of just how deep the problem is and whether or not it presents insurmountable impediments to the work. Opponents to reporting have suggested the opposite: that the analyst may *not* know how the candidate works. That is, that the analyst, blinded by the candidate's conflicts, may not be aware of the candidate's higher level nonregressed functioning. Supporters considered this highly unlikely, but unfortunately neither group had any empirical support for their strongly held views.

In opposition to this point of view, however, we have considerable anecdotal material suggesting that analyses that involve reporting are compromised. That is, no "real" analysis takes place because candidate-patients will not open up sufficiently or will actively hide their conflicts because they fear the analyst's reaction. In other words: "I can't let the analyst really know what's going on inside me because, once knowing that, she or he will never let me progress in the training or graduate." Whether this is a paranoid concern or a reality, reports of "hiding" from the analyst are common. Whether this is a grandiose claim ("I can successfully keep hidden from the analyst that which I do not want her or him to see") or an actual ability, reports of participating in "false" analyses are also common. Given the stories of such abuse, one may wonder whether all of the anxiety about this is based only on reality considerations; after all, such ideas are consistent with the kind of transference paradigms and fantasies that typically arise in analysis, ideas in which the "powerful and dangerous" father or mother disapproves of, damages, attacks, withholds from, punishes or gives rewards, gratifies, satisfies, and loves the relatively helpless child. Whether today's training analysts could be trusted not to abuse the reporting system is an empirical question; it is a question that anecdotal evidence about the past cannot prove, but the psychic reality of such concerns, even today, is indisputable.

Being a training analyst myself, having served as both chairman of the faculty and of the committee that appoints training analysts at a psychoanalytic institute, and having discussed the experience of being a training analyst with a number of other training analysts, I can tell you that my experience does not support those fears. Training analysts just do not "lie in wait" for the "evidence" that will let them get their patients kicked out of the institute; I find the problem to be just the opposite. If anything, I think training analysts sometimes overlook and even minimize pathology that really exists because they often are overidentified with their candidate-patients. The unconscious fantasy generated by this identification brings about reaction formations against any reservations that might "unfairly" prevent their patient from progressing or graduating. Or they fear that a negative analytic report will be a reflection not on the patient, but on their own skills as a training analyst. This discussion of reporting versus nonreporting has not been just an interesting side issue; the question of the candidate's ability to get a real analysis in training has been and still is a central pedagogical concern.

Having described how the training analysis developed and having described some of the arguments for and against the practice of reporting, I will now say what is perhaps the single most important professional capacity the training analysis is intended to make available. I will begin by stating a problem; that is, that psychoanalysts are in a profession in which their personalities are constantly at risk. (This idea was first brought to my attention by Anna Freud [personal communication, 1964].) To express this in clinical terms, the problem is this: psychoanalysts (being myself a working analyst, I will now switch my stance to the first person in describing these things) are in a calling in which we hear what no one else wants to. The average doctor, traumatized by hearing the kinds of the things we have to hear, might be inclined to prescribe a couple of aspirins, or some Prozac or Zoloft, and then tell the patient to come back next month or, better yet (if the doctor is sufficiently traumatized), next year. Even many psychotherapists might be tempted to refer a patient elsewhere if they get a hint that the patient is going to make them quite uncomfortable. But we analysts don't have the luxury of turning away from anxiety-provoking patients in self-defense. If anything, when we say "Tell me more," we have to really mean it. And we don't just want to *hear* more about it, we don't just want to *intellectually understand it*, we want to let it *get inside of us*; that is, to have it resonate and reverberate, psychologically, inside of us, potentially aiding or doing damage, in order to properly do our work.

In this work we regularly make trial identifications with our patients, with their conflicts, and with their objects. In order to be able to do that, and to do it in a genuinely penetrating way, we have no choice other than to revive conflicts in ourselves that had previously been more or less laid to rest; laid to rest only after considerable work and struggle, and laid to rest to our great relief. Our conflicts are *revived*, not merely *remembered*, for three reasons: (1) because activated conflicts are an essential constituent of some of those identifications; (2) because only the unconscious, which comes into play when they are revived, can put us in a position to make interventions that strike the patient at multiple levels of psychic functioning simultaneously; and (3) because psychoanalysis is not an intellectual or an educational encounter—this work is not simply a clever exercise in deductive logic and inductive reasoning. Looked at in this way, we use our personality much more in this work than we ever do our intellect. And because that is the case—because we do not do psychoanalysis at a distance— I will put the problem in a nutshell. Is there any kind of work in this world where the tools never get dulled, chipped, or broken?

We walk a very fine line. We try to manage our identifications so that they constitute a temporary, one might say a trial, experience, and we go as deeply into it as we can while still maintaining it only as a trial. When reactive conflict is revived in us we do not try to *limit* it; instead, we try to *contain* it; and, in that condition, we then bring the residually autonomous aspects of our ego to bear upon it. When we are successful we develop a deep, empathic relation to our patients, and we are then able to transform that state of mind, even if it is also based on some of the most painful of our own inner experiences, into something useful for the treatment. When we are working well, really well, we do this over and over again, and my point is that it does not come without cost, sometimes a rather significant cost.

When we are unsuccessful at this, when we become fixated in identification or in counteridentification with our patients, their conflicts, or their objects, and when the conflicts revived in us by working with a patient get the upper hand, we become locked into some kind of countertransference; then we support, or even initiate, action and enactment instead of analysis. So you see, in each and every case, certainly when we are working badly but even when we are working at our very best, doing analysis can be extremely hard on the equipment.

Let me use the following issue to help explain what I mean—What is at work when boundary violations occur in an analysis? Do we simply assume that the analyst had an inadequate analysis and managed, somehow, to slip through the cracks? Do we assume that boundary violators are people who, at heart, are narcissists, that they *all* suffer from depression, impulse disorders, a lack of frustration tolerance, weak egos, and weaker superegos? Do we assume that all this simply escaped the attention of their analysts? One thing we can probably assume is that analysts who have violated a boundary almost certainly never expected it to happen. For many problem-free years they are likely to have thought, when they heard about an analyst overstepping the limits—just as you might be doing now—that such a thing could never happen to them.

No doubt there are some disturbed individuals who slip through the cracks, and individuals who fit our most negative stereotypes. But I think they are a tiny minority and, not counting them, most investigators who have reported on boundary violations (Gabbard, Peltz, and COPE Study Group, 2001; unpublished discussion on ethics and the impaired analyst, circulated on the internet to American Psychoanalytic Association listserv members, 2001) say that narcissism, depression, lack of impulse control, lack of frustration tolerance, and compromised ego and superego functioning, while present, were usually only latent in most analysts before they got themselves in trouble. That's interesting: only latent. They report a mixture of those factors, which tend to move from latent to active under the pressure of some crisis in the analyst's life while, at the same time, the analyst is in a highly pressured, directly complementary, transference environment with a particular patient. The emphasis in these reports (and in other as yet unpublished reports I am aware of) is always on how being the immediate instinctual target of the patient plays into some kind of crisis in the analyst's life. Thus, for example, an analyst with some of those latent problems, in the midst of an ugly and humiliating divorce, may fall in love, and act out, with a patient who absolutely worships him in a highly charged erotic transference. It takes a crisis in the analyst's life, not just doing this work, to revive his latent conflicts. But once those conflicts (differing, of course, from analyst to analyst) are revived, we can see how the pressures of doing this work can further compromise the analyst.

Now let me turn this a bit on its head, because it is not necessary to act out so grossly, or to be in a life crisis, in order to be sorely tried by our work. Nor is every case in which we are sorely tried a negative one. Very often even the most *constructive* analytic situations may trigger potentially disorganizing conflict and anxiety. Let me give you an example that will demonstrate how and why intense personal conflict is not exclusive to countertransference enactment; that is, I will show how anxiety can not only impair but can also facilitate empathy, depending on the circumstances. I want to tell you about a male patient in a training analysis, about whom I have reported elsewhere in much greater detail (Lasky, 1989). During the analysis he developed an intense, disturbing homosexual panic. He searched his fantasy life and the transference for an explanation of his powerful but repulsive wishes and fears, but without success. Like most men, he passed through a passive negative oedipal phase. He relinquished the wishes of that phase and buried the memory of them, also like most men, under the pressure of castration anxiety. Why did he not readily find the source of his homosexual panic specifically in the transference? It was, surely, a part of his psyche: but at that time it just wasn't a dominant feature of his transference to me (and we know that in psychoanalysis timing is crucial). Thus, having not resolved this through the transference, disagreeable ego-dystonic homosexual wishes continued to arise, initiating fantasies that made him feel "unmanned." We remained pretty much in the dark about this until he began to speak about a relatively new patient of his, a control case—a woman who began her analysis with him about three or four months before his homosexual panic started. It seems that her presenting problem was an intense fear of penetration while, at the same time, she also found being penetrated to be incredibly, almost unmanageably, exciting. This put her in a state of almost constant tension, and here is how the difficulty shaped up for my patient, her analyst. In order to appreciate what she was fearful about, and to understand the other side of her feelings, her intense excitement about penetration, my patient had to identify with her. But how, as a man, was he supposed to appreciate either the intensity of her excitement about being penetrated or the intensity of her fear, when his feminine identifications—and, most especially, the ones associated with sexuality—had been renounced or ruthlessly suppressed; that is, forced to exist exclusively in unconsciousness?

He was a good analyst, my patient, and very well suited for this work, for despite the panic it put him into, he was able to reactivate (not remember, but reactivate) his passive, negative, oedipal wishes and fears, in order to empathize with his patient. I am not suggesting that he was able to consciously make the decision to do this. He did it automatically, and unconsciously. My patient, as do all good analysts, pulled conflict-laden wishes and fears out of hibernation as the basis for the necessary identification with his patient and her concerns. The reemergence of those conflicts did not occur in the form of intellectualized memories of his past—that is, he did not remember those old wishes and fears in relation to his father, which was their original context. Instead, he experienced them as if they were brand new and occurring all over again in the present.

You may be thinking that, as a man, he would never be able to know—to know exactly—about those wishes and fears in precisely the way a grownup woman would. And, of course, you are right. In fact, well beyond the question of gender, we know that no one can ever really know exactly what someone else's experience is like. But if you want to get really close, as close to another human being's experience as you can, this kind of identification process, painful as it sometimes is, is the only way to do it. This is what we analysts do; we expose ourselves to serious conflict many times a day, every working day of our lives, in order to get into contact with our patients. And this carries over from our work; these conflicts, stimulated by our work, will often encroach on our play, disturb our sleep, and impose themselves—sometimes dreadfully—into many, if not most, other areas of our lives outside of the active work itself.

Not every identification is based on such thoroughly conflicted material, but despite this we still have to experience conflict many times over as we identify with our patients, their objects, and their specific conflicts. Every time we examine a countertransference enactment we take the presence of conflict in us for granted. But a high level of activated conflict is not limited to countertransference; remember that its presence is necessary just for us to be adequately related to our patients (that is, to have empathy for them at their most conflicted by experiencing *transient* identifications with them at our most conflicted levels). And if what I have thus far said is applicable to working with garden-variety neurotics, the ante is upped considerably in our work with the more disturbed kind of patient. You do not even begin to know anything about the inner life of a typical borderline patient, for example, without experiencing a certain amount of painfully regressed functioning in yourself during that person's treatment.

Constant exposure to conflict is traumatic even when it is someone else's conflict, and constant exposure to the reactivation of our own conflicts is even more traumatizing. It is a long-term strain, and it can erode even the strongest constitutions. It is exactly this that I meant when I said that the analyst's personality is constantly at risk. And this is why the training analysis has become so central in its importance.

My statement about the risk involved in doing this work is not a pessimistic harbinger (or a guarantee) of doom. Being "at risk" does not result in definitely being "damaged"; it is not the same as "already harmed," and it does not automatically imply that a negative outcome is a foregone conclusion. It is well known, for example, that countertransference and enactment are not necessarily permanent, and they can sometimes even be put to very good use—when one is no longer a slave to them. In fact, sometimes it is only from the dilemmas we get ourselves into that it is possible for us to see and appreciate subtle dimensions of the patient and of the transference that have, until then, eluded us. And there is an even more positive side to this. The value in experiencing revived personal conflict is not limited only to understanding the patient and the treatment better; incremental resolution of those conflicts brings about advances in the strengthening of our own psychic apparatus, and this kind of growth is based on a singular kind of self-knowledge that we can get in no other way (barring future returns to analysis ourselves).

We do our best work even though, and sometimes because, we are imperfect, conflicted people. As we help our patients, we ourselves continue to grow right alongside them. For analysts, remaining in a kind of psychological status quo is not possible except in the shortest of short runs; in the long run, our only choices are to regress or to move forward. If we run the risk of psychological damage by practicing this trade, it is more than balanced by this special opportunity for personal growth; opportunities for personal development that are unequaled by any other occupation I can think of.

And now I return a final time to the central importance of the training analysis, because the groundwork for this benefit is laid in the training analysis. Training analysts intuitively, if not intentionally, pay particular attention to establishing the kinds of ego and superego resources needed to withstand the constant onslaught of conflict experienced in a life of doing analysis professionally; as training analysts, we regularly work a little closer to the bone, one might say. The development of what we usually think of as an "analytic ego" and an "analytic superego," which we consider to be so crucial to this line of work, is not merely a simple, straightforward, identification with the training analyst's analytic ego and superego. If that were the case, it would only be (by common definition) a kind of transference cure. It is established only through particularly deep and thorough analysis—and then, and only then, do we see the development of those functions as evidence of a particularly high level of psychic structuralization that supports the work we do. No one ever reaches the level of being entirely conflict free, but the manifestations of infantile and fractional solutions to our conflicts are substantially diminished by the concentration and depth of our training analyses. Then, afterward, those psychic capacities are both challenged and reinforced by the work we live our lives through. Our psychic lives will continue to be constantly examined as we resonate, and not just during working hours, with material aroused in us by the analysis of our patients.

REFERENCES

Freud, S. (1957). Future prospects for psycho-analytic therapy. In J. Strachey (Ed. and Trans.), *The standard edition of the complete psychological works of Sigmund Freud* (Vol. 11, pp. 139–151). London: Hogarth Press. (Original work published 1910)

Freud, S. (1958a). Observations on transference love. In J. Strachey (Ed. and Trans.), *The standard edition of the complete psychological works of Sigmund Freud* (Vol. 12, pp. 157–171). London: Hogarth Press. (Original work published 1915)

Freud, S. (1958b). Recommendations to physicians practicing psycho-analysis. In J. Strachey (Ed. and Trans.), *The standard edition of the complete psychological works of Sigmund Freud* (Vol. 12, pp. 109–120). London: Hogarth Press. (Original work published 1912).

Freud, S. (1961). The ego and the id. In J. Strachey (Ed. and Trans.), *The standard edition of the complete psychological works of Sigmund Freud* (Vol. 19, pp. 12–66). London: Hogarth Press. (Original work published 1923)

Gabbard, G. O., Peltz, M. L., & COPE Study Group on Boundary Violations. (2001). Speaking the unspeakable: Institutional reactions to boundary violations by training analysts. *Journal of the American Psychoanalytic Association, 49*, 659–673.

Lasky, R. (1989). Some determinants of the male analyst's capacity to identify with female patients. *International Journal of Psycho-Analysis, 70*, 405–418.

3

THE ROLE OF PERSONAL THERAPY IN THE FORMATION OF A JUNGIAN ANALYST

Thomas B. Kirsch

A personal analysis is central to become a Jungian analyst; it is the aim of this chapter to describe the evolution of training analysis in analytical psychology and to present some issues which pertain to its practice.

HISTORICAL INTRODUCTION

Jung was the first to recognize the necessity of a training analysis and did so in 1912 while still collaborating with Freud, who acknowledged this important contribution when he wrote: "I count it one of the valuable services of the Zürich school of analysis that they have emphasized this necessity and laid it down as a requisition that anyone who wishes to practice analysis of others should first submit to be analyzed himself by a competent person" (Freud, 1912, p. 116).

After the break with Freud, Jung entered a long period of introversion, experiencing many images and fantasies that he could not explain using Freud's theories. At first he referred to them as "primordial images" (Jung, 1961), later as "archetypal images." These events, central to his self-analysis, and described in *Memories, Dreams, Reflections* in the chapter "Confrontation with the Unconscious," form the basis of all his subsequent theories (Jung, 1963). Jung then described a collective level to the unconscious, which he believed contained creative potential, extending Freud's picture of the unconscious as the repository of repressed infantile material. Within his own theoretical framework the personal analysis was the core of an analyst's professional training. In 1946 Jung wrote the following about the training analysis: "anybody who intends to practice psychotherapy should first submit to a 'training analysis,' yet even the best preparation will not suffice to teach him everything about the unconscious. . . . A complete emptying of the unconscious is out of the question if only because its creative powers are continually producing new formations" (1946, p. 177).

At the conclusion of World War I, people from around the world, especially English-speaking individuals, came to Jung for consultation and analysis. As a result of their analyses and their transference to Jung, many wished to become analysts. They had come out of personal need, but they literally were transformed into practitioners of a new profession. In addition to analysis, Jung offered a seminar in English during the academic year, to which he invited many of his analysands. The English seminars continued until 1939, when World War II intervened, and were never resumed because after his first heart attack in 1944 he went into semiretirement. Most of those who sought out Jung in the 1920s and 1930s also saw a second analyst during their stay in Zürich. Usually this was Toni Wolff, who served as Jung's main assistant. According to Joseph Wheelwright, one brought the "big dreams" to Jung, while Toni Wolff handled more personal material (Wheelwright, 1975). This practice was called "multiple analyses," with the analysand consulting more than one analyst concurrently. Those who spoke German could also attend Jung's weekly lectures at Zurich's Eigenosse Technische Hochschul (ETH, Switzerland's equivalent of MIT, where Jung was professor of psychology).

After an undetermined period of time an individual would receive a letter from Jung affirming that he or she was qualified to practice analysis according to Jung's methods; often the person returned to practice Jungian analysis in the home country. Jung's criteria for eligibility to receive this letter of approval were never made explicit. To some he suggested more education, a medical or psychological degree, while to others he made no such recommendation. As in the early days of Freud, many individuals lacking academic credentials became analysts on the basis of a personal analysis alone.

This was the state of affairs until 1948, when the C. G. Jung Institute in Zürich opened its doors to begin formal training, ending the period when a personal analysis with Jung or one of his immediate associates became the sole criterion to become an analyst. After 1948 an academic curriculum, in addition to the personal analysis, was required for graduation. These requirements were instituted worldwide in 1955 when the International Association for Analytical Psychology was established. Though now part of an institutionalized process, the personal analysis has remained central to training. Before going into greater detail, I would like to present some core concepts of analytical psychology.

Core Concepts

Dreams. The importance of working with dreams is paramount, with an emphasis on the manifest content. The dream is seen as an "interior drama," compensatory to the attitude of consciousness. Not only is the retrospective origin, the "where from" of the dream, examined but also its prospective "where to"—that is, the potential development to which the dream points.

Psychological type. Important factors influencing many analyses are Jung's two attitudes of introversion and extraversion, and his four functions: sensation, intuition, thinking, and feeling.

Transference and countertransference. Although borrowed from psychoanalysis, these terms have a different meaning for analytical psychology. The transference includes not only projections from past family figures but also potential for future development, still dormant in the unconscious, which is projected onto the analyst.

Dialectical relationship. The analysand and analyst are equally involved in the analytical relationship. The analyst's subjective reactions are an integral part of the therapy and are not seen only as neurotic countertransference. Nor is the Jungian analyst considered a blank screen.

Symbolic versus developmental. There is a basic divide between those Jungians who utilize a more developmental approach and include post-Freudian psychoanalytic theories in their orientation, and those who adhere closely to Jung's basic writings and his methods of working, as handed down by those who analyzed with him. The majority of Jungians fall somewhere between the two extremes. Depending on the approach, this will affect the frequency of sessions per week, the use of the couch versus chair, the emphasis on transference/countertransference interpretations, the importance of early development, and the nature of dream interpretation.

U.S. AND EUROPEAN TRAINING GUIDELINES

In addition to the theoretical and technical differences among Jungians, there are also political issues that account for wide variation in what constitutes the training analysis. For instance, in England the influence of Kleinian and British object relations theorists is very strong. In the United States, which lacks a national Jungian organization, the training situation is very different from all other countries, where a national organization determines training standards. In the United States, each locally accredited institute within the International Association for Analytical Psychology needs only to adhere to the basic minimal standards of the International Association and is free to set its own standards. There is wide variation among U.S. training institutes in the emphasis on developmental or classical Jungian theories and methods.

Another important issue is the category "training analyst." Most of the major training institutes have established such a category. The San Francisco

Institute, where I trained, makes no such distinction. Its founders believed that the category "training analyst" would create a problematic hierarchy; they also wished to provide the candidate-in-training a wide choice among personal analysts; however, they stipulated that to supervise control work with a candidate, the analyst must have been a member in good standing for five years. This policy seems to have promoted openness to both developmental and classically Jungian theory, and enabled the inevitable tensions that arise to be contained without divisive splitting.

A further political issue is the role of the personal analyst in evaluating an applicant during the admissions process or the candidate during training. In the early days of the Jung Institute in Zürich, the personal analyst was intimately involved in the evaluation process (Hillman, 1962b, p. 8). Until recently, many other major institutes followed this example. In the San Francisco Institute, the personal analyst was forbidden to participate in his or her analysand's admission or evaluation processes, so as not to overburden the already difficult work of analysis and to prevent potentially disturbing analytic material from being withheld by the candidate fearing that this information might prevent passage to the next phase of training.

CURRENT TRAINING ISSUES

Now, as we are aware of boundary issues in analysis, and what happens when they are transgressed, this policy has changed in every training institution around the world. The philosophy is to preserve the privacy of every candidate's personal analysis. The task of evaluating candidates has now fallen to reviewing committees that collect information from seminar leaders, supervisors, and control analysts.

In spite of these provisions, the analyst is still likely to regard the candidate in analysis differently from other analysands. First, the person who enters analysis with the idea of becoming an analyst has a definite aim or goal beyond his or her own therapy. This person wishes to have the analysis serve the ego aim of becoming an analyst, which means forming some kind of identity with the analyst, often raising unresolved issues for both the analyst and analysand. Such an aim is clearly different from that of a person who comes for the relief of symptoms. In the nontraining analysis, there is an endpoint at which the analyst and analysand separate, whereas in the training analysis there is a continued connection in their shared professional world. Another way to express this is in terms of the tension between individuality and collective responsibility. The personal training analysis must, on the one hand, honor the individual expression of the analysand; on the other, it has a collective responsibility to the Jungian community to affirm certain basic values. Each analyst has an individual relationship to the professional group, and the candidate must forge his or her independent relationship to the same professional community. Much of this work happens through the personal training analysis, but the question remains whether a truly independent relationship, free of transference residuals, is ever possible.

Academic knowledge helps orient the developing analyst, but personal analysis provides the model for his or her own professional work. With time and experience the new analyst develops a unique style, which continues to evolve over the course of his or her professional career.

THE TRAINING ANALYSIS

In my experience, most Jungian analysts acquire a great deal more analysis than is required for graduation or certification. The usual requirement is that the entering candidate have a minimum of 100 to 200 hours of personal analysis before beginning training. Most programs require candidates to be in analysis during the training period. Many trained Jungian analysts go back for further analysis as different life circumstances arise. In fact, analysts are encouraged to return for analysis at nodal points. Freud also believed that one should go back every five years for further analysis, although in those days the analyses were much shorter. As the Jungian community is relatively small, and members are likely to know each other, many analysts seek further analysis with non-Jungians. Furthermore, today there is much more crossfertilization between analytical psychologists and psychoanalysts than formerly, so that many Jungian analysts want the experience of having their personal material dealt with in the language and philosophy of another school.

Often a candidate in Jungian training is advised to have analysis with both a man and woman, or with an analyst of a particular psychological attitude or type, in the belief that gender and psychological type influence the nature of the dialectic in ways deemed desirable for that candidate's development. The practice of seeing more than one analyst concurrently, referred to above as *multiple analysis* and examined in greater depth elsewhere (Kirsch, 1976), has been much debated within Jungian circles. On the one hand, it dilutes and splits the transference; on the other hand, new and valuable material is evoked. Today, with our greater sensitivity to transference issues, this practice of seeing more than one analyst during training has become less common.

Fordham (1962) has provided a rationale for the many hours of personal analysis that Jungian analysts have today. He says that it is important for trainees to experience as many psychopathological states in themselves as possible. In fact, he encourages candidates to experience these psychopathological states in their training analyses, because then they will be able to cope with them more readily when they face the same issues as analysts. Equally, the trainees can learn to identify the parts of themselves that are healthy, not requiring analytic work, and serving as a source of strength (Fordham, 1962).

LIMITS OF PERSONAL ANALYSIS

Fordham also says that an unresolvable pathological nexus exists between any patient and his or her analyst, regardless of the length of analysis. This factor will also influence the training analysis. Full elucidation of infancy and childhood will minimize the influence of unresolved complexes upon the analytic relationships the new analyst will form with subsequent analysands. However, some traumatic experiences can be elucidated but not necessarily changed, hence the concept of the "wounded healer."

All too often a candidate's unresolved complexes are projected onto the local society in which he or she will practice. In this way the professional community, to some extent, is seen through the scrim of one's family of origin, in both its positive and negative lights. Concurrent with this are the many transference/countertransference residuals between individual members that are never fully resolved, and exist in every society, regardless of its philosophic school or analytic method; the extent and intensity of these differences, far more than any philosophical disagreement, determines whether a group will remain together or divide (Kirsch, 2000).

A lifelong pursuit of inner growth and personal development is the sine qua non of the Jungian analyst. Analytical psychology has undergone many changes in its evolution as a profession and a psychoanalytic discipline, yet throughout, a personal analysis remains at the core in shaping the present-day Jungian analyst.

REFERENCES

Edinger, E. (1961). Comment. *Journal of Analytical Psychology, 6*(2), 116–117.
Fordham, M. (1962). Reply. *Journal of Analytical Psychology, 7*(1), 24–26.
Fordham, M. (1971). Reflections on training analysis. In Joseph B. Wheelwright (Ed.), *The Analytic Process* (pp. 172–184). New York: Putnam.
Fordham, M. (1976). Comment. *Contemporary Psychoanalysis, 12*, 168–173.
Freud, S. (1958). Recommendations to physicians on the psychoanalytic method of treatment. In J. Strachey (Ed. and Trans.), *The standard edition of the complete psychological works of Sigmund Freud* (Vol. 12, pp. 109–120). London: Hogarth Press. (Original work published in 1912)
Guggenbühl-Craig, A. (1971). *Power in the helping professions.* New York: Spring.
Hillman, J. (1962a). A note on multiple analysis and emotional climate at training institutes. *Journal of Analytical Psychology, 7*(1), 20–22.
Hillman, J. (1962b). Training and the C. G. Jung Institute, Zurich. *Journal of Analytical Psychology, 7*(1), 3–18.
Jung, C. G. (1961). The theory of psychoanalysis. In F. C. Hall (Trans.), *Collected works* (Vol. 4, pp. 85–226). New York: Pantheon. (Original work published in 1913)
Jung, C. G. (1946). Psychology of the transference. In F. C. Hall (Trans.), *Collected works* (Vol. 16, pp. 163–321). New York: Pantheon. (Original work published in 1954)
Jung, C. G. (1961). Psychological types. In F. C. Hall (Trans.), *Collected works* (Vol. 6, p. 197). Princeton, NJ: Princeton University Press.

Jung, C. G. (1963). *Memories, dreams, reflections* (A. Jaffe, ed.; R. Winston & C. Winston, Trans.). New York: Random House.

Kirsch, T. (1976). The practice of multiple analyses in analytical psychology. *Contemporary Psychoanalysis, 12,* 159–167.

Kirsch, T. (1995). Analysis in training. In M. Stein, (Ed.), *Jungian analysis* (2nd ed., pp. 437–450). La Salle, IL: Open Court.

Kirsch, T. (2000). *The Jungians.* London: Routledge.

Marshak, M. O. (1964). The significance of the patient in the training of analysts. *Journal of Analytical Psychology, 9*(1), 80–83.

Newton, K. (1961). Personal reflections on training. *Journal of Analytical Psychology, 6*(2), 103–106.

Plant, A. (1961). A dynamic outline of the training situation. *Journal of Analytical Psychology, 6*(2), 98–102.

Samuels, A. (1985). *Jung and the post-Jungians.* Boston: Routledge and Kegan Paul.

Spiegelmann, M. J. (1980). The image of the Jungian analyst. *Spring,* 101–116.

Stone, H. (1964). Reflections of an ex-trainee on his training. *Journal of Analytical Psychology, 9*(1), 75–79.

Wheelwright, J. B. (1975). A personal view of Jung. *Psychological Perspectives, 6,* 64–73.

4

PERSONAL THERAPY AND GROWTH WORK IN EXPERIENTIAL-HUMANISTIC THERAPIES

Robert Elliott & Rhea Partyka

The experiential-humanistic tradition in psychotherapy subsumes several therapies that share core concepts and values. These therapies include classic approaches such as person-centered (e.g., Rogers, 1961), gestalt (e.g., Perls, Hefferline, & Goodman, 1951), and existential (e.g., Schneider & May, 1995), as well as neohumanistic approaches such as focusing-oriented (e.g., Gendlin, 1996), experiential (e.g., Mahrer, 1989), and process-experiential/emotion-focused (e.g., Greenberg, Rice, & Elliott, 1993) psychotherapies. While therapists in this tradition vary in how they work with clients, all share a set of common values (Elliott, Watson, Goldman, & Greenberg, in press), including support for immediate experiencing, client self-determination, personal and political pluralism/equality, wholeness, therapist presence or authenticity, and personal growth throughout the life span.

This last value means that, in these therapies, individuals are viewed as possessing a growth tendency, regarded as an ever-present developmental tendency that forms the basis of therapeutic change. This tendency involves a continual process of reorganizing experiences at increasingly higher levels of complexity, thus maintaining and enhancing the self, as well as attaining maximum creative flexibility in whatever environment persons find themselves (Greenberg et al., 1993). Two important resources that support this growth tendency are self-awareness and a lifetime of learning and experience. A therapist can and should support his or her own growth tendency through ongoing personal growth activities that foster self-awareness in a variety of contexts.

In this brief chapter, we provide an overview of therapist personal growth work that is vital to living these values and becoming competent as an experiential-humanistic therapist. Thus, we argue that personal therapy is valuable only insofar as it facilitates personal growth in the context of a therapy that emphasizes awareness of immediate experience and supports personal agency—all of which takes place within an egalitarian, authentic therapeutic relationship that pursues wholeness through integration of multiple, often conflicting, aspects of self.

In addition, this tradition recognizes (and has pioneered) other growth-facilitating practices besides formal psychotherapy. These other avenues include in vivo experiential workshop training, growth groups, personal journaling, and broadening life experiences. Many of these activities have multiple goals, including both education and personal growth, and, in some cases, dealing with problems.

FUNCTIONS OF PERSONAL THERAPY AND GROWTH WORK

Continuing therapist growth is vital because experiential-humanistic therapies require more than technical mastery. They depend on the person of the therapist being empathically attuned to the client's experiencing; prizing the client's strengths and vulnerabilities; tolerating the client's rough edges and interpersonal prickliness; and being authentically present. This means being self-aware, including awareness of one's blind spots and special sensitivities; being on good terms with the different aspects of one's self; and being able to handle conflict, inconsistency, and ambiguity—both in oneself and in others.

More specifically, personal therapy and other growth activities serve several important functions. First, they *provide experience-near learning*. Within the experiential-humanistic tradition, immediate lived experience is assumed to lead to richer, more useful learning (knowledge by acquaintance versus knowledge by description). Such "anchored instruction" (Binder, 1999) is more readily retained and thus more accessible for later use with clients. Second, personal therapy and other growth activities are held to *provide the basis for the therapist's genuineness or authenticity* with clients (although there is no formal research to support this claim). In any case, if the therapist has personally experienced the process that he or she is offering the client, the offer has greater moral weight. Third, these activities *enhance therapist empathy and prizing*. If the therapist has personally been through what is being offered to the client, he or she will also be better able to understand the client's experience, and that will help the therapist to be more responsive to the client's moment-to-moment experiencing. Fourth, personal therapy provides a means for *managing training-related stress and vulnerability*. Because mastering psychotherapy requires so much of the therapist as a person, and because therapists-in-training typically have so much of their self-identity tied up in the image of themselves as therapists, they approach the training process with considerable anxiety and vulnerability (Rennie, 1998).

Writers in the experiential-humanistic tradition have often strongly advocated that therapists-in-training take part in some form of personal growth work, including therapy. We will sample some of these arguments, organized into person-centered, gestalt, existential, and process-experiential orientations.

PERSON-CENTERED THERAPY

Personal therapy is often encouraged in person-centered therapies. For example, Garfield and Kurtz (1976) found that, when compared with therapists from a learning theory orientation, therapists from Rogerian, humanistic, and existential orientations held more positive views toward personal psychotherapy. However, their views were slightly less favorable than therapists from an analytical and neo-Freudian group.

A common theme in training client-centered therapists is that the trainee is engaged in a process of "personal becoming" (Patterson, 2000), which involves growing beyond self-consciousness and reactivity with clients and learning to become more open to one's own and the client's experiencing. For example, Rennie (1998) suggests that it is important to help trainees learn to feel comfortable working with their own inner experiences, particularly when these involve uncertainties, insecurities, and doubts.

In the development of client-centered therapy, an early emphasis on technique diminished during the 1940s and 1950s, as attention to the trainee's underlying experience and relational attitudes increased. Thus Pagell, Carkhuff, and Berenson (1967) found that while attending skills and summarization of feeling can be learned didactically, the ability to create and maintain an empathic relationship is better learned experientially.

In addition, Mearns and Thorne (1988) argue that the investment of the self of the therapist in the therapeutic process cannot be overemphasized. Concepts such as acceptance, empathy, and genuineness are not solely reserved for the therapist's relationship with his or her clients but must also be extended to self, if they are to be effective. Therefore, a therapist's willingness to give attention and care to self should be required, out of a sense of responsibility to clients.

Barrett-Lennard (1998) differentiated between two main reasons for which a therapist trainee may decide to enter personal therapy: for emotional healing, perhaps due to painful inner conflict or suffering; and for personal growth and learning. Rogers (1951) suggests that it should not be expected that personal therapy will permanently remove all likelihood of conflict or eliminate the possibility that the therapist's own needs may interfere with therapeutic work. However, a therapist's personal therapy should sensitize him or her to the types of attitudes or feelings the client may be experiencing. Personal therapy should also allow the therapist to become empathic at a deeper level. Nevertheless, the decision to engage in personal therapy should be dependent on the individual needs of the trainee. In fact, required individual therapy for trainees is not consistent with a client-centered approach. However, opportunities should be available so that the trainee is able to utilize them whenever he or she feels the need.

In addition to making personal therapy available, other growth-oriented educational and self-help experiences are typically built into person-centered training programs. For example, a therapist-in-training may experience personal growth while working with a supervisor on personal issues that are relevant to his or her effectiveness as a therapist. In addition, support groups can provide an environment in which therapists work to cultivate self-acceptance and a willingness to face the truth. Learning to listen to oneself is an important skill that can be developed through talking with others, prayer, meditation, journaling, or experiential focusing (Gendlin, 1996), all of which can be understood as forms of self-therapy (Mearns & Thorne, 1988). Finally, person-centered therapists also grow through working with clients. For example, after termination with a client, Mearns and Thorne (1988) encourage therapists to explore their experience of the therapy, asking themselves "What have I learned from this client?" and "How have I been affected by this experience?"

GESTALT THERAPY

Personal growth is regarded as an essential aspect of training and practice in Gestalt therapy. However, compared to client-centered therapy, the Gestalt tradition puts much more emphasis on personal therapy and organized personal growth within the context of training.

Clarkson (1989) argues that therapists have a professional and ethical responsibility to continue the process of self-development, including personal therapy. Korb, Gorrell, and Van De Riet (1989) and Clarkson (1989) argue that personal therapy should begin during training, before therapists begin seeing clients for themselves. Therapy is generally believed to reduce the possibility that the therapist's own dysfunctional processes will distort therapy, and Clarkson (1989) argues further that therapy helps counter the undue influence of charismatic teachers. Furthermore, these writers say that Gestalt therapists should continue in personal therapy with an expert therapist throughout their career, to process emotions, to obtain support, to prevent problems, and to maintain sensitivity to the vulnerability and anxiety typically experienced by clients.

On the other hand, Enright (1970) has argued that it may be inappropriate to require therapy of trainees, as it is expensive and tends to be narrowly focused on problems rather than playful exploration, which he argues is the essence of Gestalt work. Instead, he describes experiential training groups that resemble group therapy in many ways.

Much gestalt training takes place in experiential workshops or group formats. For example, the awareness training groups described by Enright (1970) are designed to help trainees unlearn their habits of suppressing immediate awareness. Such groups typically begin with a simple awareness exercise. After group members process their responses, the trainer asks one person to take part in a live demonstration of an unblocking exercise aimed at expanding awareness. Enright views the group format as the most effective setting for awareness training, as it allows trainees to see others work. Emotional safety issues are handled by allowing volunteers the opportunity to stop participation in an exercise at any time.

Daldrup, Beutler, Greenberg, and Engle (1988) describe a similar experiential workshop within their training protocol for focused expressive psychotherapy, a manualized version of Gestalt therapy. A form of group work, led by experienced therapists, the format includes an initial "check-in" time to allow group members the opportunity to identify their desire to work, personal work in the form of one or more in vivo demonstrations, and feedback and processing time to relate what has happened to theory. These authors emphasize the importance of balancing therapy with didactic elements, so that both learning and personal growth needs are met. The nature of the group work evolves over the course of training. In the initial phase of training, the group work is more therapeutic in nature; however, by the middle phase of training it has become a combination therapy-training group, as group members begin to assume the role of therapist in the group.

Writers in the Gestalt tradition have also noted that learning on one's own can be effective. In fact, the first half of the classic Gestalt text (Perls et al., 1951) consists of a sequence of 18 graduated experiments. The format consists of an initial theory presentation, followed by instructions for one or more exercises. Exercises begin with simple awareness ("feeling the actual"), progress to remembering and anxiety, and finally explore the classic gestalt contact boundary disturbances: retroflection, introjection, and projection. Throughout the focus is on processes that interfere with successful completion of the experiment, providing a kind of self-help format.

EXISTENTIAL THERAPY

There is virtually no information on either training in or the role of personal therapy in existential therapy. However, Schneider and May (1995) offer ordered sequences of skill-building exercises intended to help students experience the key therapeutic process, "existential liberation," for themselves. These exercises are intended for a small group or workshop context, and they consist of personal exercises and clinical exercises. The personal exercises include the Who Am I exercise, role-playing an intriguing but generally suppressed side of self, and writing one's obituary. The clinical exercises are fairly standard awareness and helping skill training exercises, in which students pair up and take turns in client and therapist roles.

PROCESS-EXPERIENTIAL THERAPY

Process-experiential therapy also emphasizes the importance of experiential learning and awareness training, particularly with regard to emotional experience, and draws parallels between training and therapy (Greenberg & Paivio, 1997). Greenberg and Goldman (1988, p. 701) note the debate between training the whole person versus training in specific skills. They hold that "training which leads to attitudinal change and personal growth is of great importance in experiential therapy because it allows trainees to know in a personal fashion how the experiential change process works."

Elliott and colleagues (2004) have developed an experiential training workshop format with therapeutic elements. Sessions include handling of group issues, minilectures, brief self-exploratory group exercises to identify possible therapeutic markers, live or video demonstrations, and practice in "client" and "therapist" roles. The sessions typically end with processing and discussion of the exercises.

In addition, Greenberg (2002) offers a series of self-led personal growth exercises for students to use on their own in order to develop skills of emotional awareness, emotion regulation, and changing emotion with emotion, essential elements in an "emotion coaching" approach to process-experiential therapy.

In focus group research carried out with 20 current and former students on their experience of learning process-experiential therapy, Elliott and colleagues (2004) found that informants commonly reported experiential workshop training as an important component of their training. Specifically, being in the client role was frequently mentioned as a helpful component. Informants reported the value of "seeing it work," "testing it out with oneself," "the experience of having tasks used on me," and "discovering that it works." Students also mentioned the value of trying things out in workshop first before using them with clients, and noted the importance of feeling safe in the workshop. In addition, many informants noted the value of being in personal therapy.

CONCLUSION

For experiential-humanistic therapists, work on the self is never complete. By viewing authenticity and personal growth as a continuous process of "becoming," therapists in this tradition dedicate themselves to a lifelong task of learning and growing. Within this tradition, therapists view a dedication to personal growth as a responsibility to one's client. A therapist cannot authentically ask a client to engage in a given therapeutic process unless he or she has also been through it!

REFERENCES

Barrett-Lennard, G. T. (1998). *Carl Rogers' helping system: Journey and substance.* London: Sage.

Binder, J. L. (1999). Issues in teaching and learning time-limited psychodynamic psychotherapy. *Clinical Psychology Review, 19*, 705–719.

Clarkson, P. (1989). *Gestalt counseling in action*. London: Sage.

Daldrup, R., Beutler, L., Greenberg, L., & Engle, D. (1988). *Focused expressive therapy: Freeing the overcontrolled patient*. New York: Guilford.

Elliott, R. Watson, J., Goldman, R., & Greenberg, L. S. (2004). *Learning emotion-focused therapy: The process-experiential approach to change*. Washington, DC: American Psychological Association.

Enright, J. B. (1970). Awareness training in the mental health professions. In J. Fagan & I. L. Shepherd (Eds.), *Gestalt therapy now: Theory, techniques, applications* (pp. 263–273). New York: Harper and Row.

Garfield, S. L., & Kurtz, R. (1976). Personal therapy for the psychotherapist: Some findings and issues. *Psychotherapy, 13*, 188–192.

Gendlin, G. T. (1996). *Focusing-oriented psychotherapy: A manual of the experiential method*. New York: Guilford.

Greenberg, L. S. (2002). *Emotion-focused therapy: Coaching clients to work through their feelings*. Washington, DC: American Psychological Association.

Greenberg, L. S., & Goldman, R. L. (1988). Training in experiential therapy. *Journal of Consulting and Clinical Psychology, 56*, 696–702.

Greenberg, L .S., & Paivio, S. (1997). *Working with emotions in psychotherapy*. New York: Guilford.

Greenberg, L. S., Rice, L. N., & Elliott, R. (1993). *Facilitating emotional change: The moment-by-moment process*. New York: Guilford.

Greenberg, L. S., & Sarkissian, M. G. (1984). Evaluation of counselor training in Gestalt methods. *Counselor Education and Supervision, 23*, 328–340.

Korb, M.P., Gorrell, J., & Van De Riet, V. (1989). *Gestalt therapy: Practice and theory* (2nd ed.). New York: Plenum.

Mahrer, A. R. (1989). *How to do experiential psychotherapy: A manual for practitioners*. Ottawa: University of Ottawa Press.

Mearns, D., & Thorne, B. (1988). *Person-centred counselling in action*. Newbury Park, CA: Sage.

Pagell, W. A., Carkhuff, R. R., & Berenson, B. G. (1967). The predicted differential effects of the level of counselor functioning upon the level of functioning of outpatients. *Journal of Clinical Psychology, 23*, 510–512.

Patterson, C. H. (2000). *Understanding psychotherapy: Fifty years of client-centered theory and practice*. Llangarron, UK: PCCS Books.

Perls, F. S., Hefferline, R. F., & Goodman, P. (1951). *Gestalt therapy*. New York: Julian.

Rennie, D. (1998). *Person-centred counselling: An experiential approach*. London: Sage.

Rogers, C. R. (1951). *Client centered therapy*. Boston: Houghton Mifflin.

Rogers, C. R. (1961). *On becoming a person*. Boston: Houghton Mifflin.

Schneider, K .J., & May, R. (1995). *The psychology of existence: An integrative, clinical perspective*. New York: McGraw-Hill.

5

PERSONAL THERAPY IN COGNITIVE-BEHAVIORAL THERAPY

Tradition and Current Practice

Anton-Rupert Laireiter & Ulrike Willutzki

Personal therapy or some other kind of experience focusing on the person of the therapist does not have a very long or deep tradition in cognitive-behavior therapy (CBT). However, the integration of person-related experience into the training of cognitive-behavior (CB) therapists has been intensively discussed during the last 15 to 20 years, especially in some European countries. Training is not the only context where personal therapy is of importance in CBT. Many cognitive-behavior therapists (about 50% to 60%) engage in personal therapy at least once during their professional lives (Norcross & Guy, chapter 13; Norcross & Connor, chapter 15; Orlinsky, Rønnestad, Willutzki, Wiseman, & Botermans, chapter 14). Because most of them do not engage in cognitive-behavioral therapies but prefer psychodynamic or humanistic orientations (Laireiter, 2000a), their therapeutic style as well as their therapeutic competence may be intensely influenced by these experiences. Until now it is not yet fully acknowledged whether this kind of eclecticism is positive or problematic for doing therapy in a cognitive-behavioral frame of reference. This brief chapter gives an overview of the personal therapy of CB therapists.

CURRENT STATUS OF PERSONAL THERAPY IN CBT

Historically, the requirement for trainees to undergo psychotherapy has a long tradition and goes back to Freud and other leading figures of early psychoanalysis. Behavior therapists did not view personal therapy as necessary, because therapy was not seen as a process of working through the unconscious and the transference neurosis but rather as a learning experience, in which one person, the client, learns with the help and technical support of another, the therapist, to change behaviors, attitudes, and cognitions. Within this framework it did not seem necessary for therapists to be deeply aware of their own unconscious feelings, fantasies, and countertransference reactions in the therapeutic process. On the contrary, behavior therapy stressed that change is due primarily to learning and to the sound and technically adequate application of therapeutic methods. Thus, neither undergoing a personal therapy nor completing some analogous experience had a place in training in early CBT.

In fact, the opposite conviction was held. The idea and requirement of a personal therapy were rejected (McNamara, 1986), mostly (as mentioned) because it was seen as contradictory to the theoretical and methodological principles of behavior therapy. Furthermore, it was believed that mandatory therapy for the therapist interferes with the principle of voluntary collaboration in CBT and thus may counteract the basic working factors of this orientation. It was also argued that empirical studies do not show any specific positive effect of personal therapy on the later effectiveness of a therapist. Importantly, empirical studies found that personal therapy does not always have positive effects but even may result in negative or harmful outcomes (Pope & Tabachnick, 1994). Personal therapy was also perceived as too expensive an experience for most training candidates. Last but not least, personal therapy was seen as necessary not for all and perhaps for only a few trainees (see DiGuiseppe, 1991; Gray, 1991; McNamara, 1986; Ramsay, 1980; Wright, 1991).

Although early behavior therapy firmly rejected the idea of requiring personal therapy for trainees, this view has changed during the last 20 years and is more balanced now. Today it is accepted that personal therapy may be necessary and helpful for some trainees, and it is also accepted that such an experience may be helpful in attaining important training goals in CBT. In this context, specific personal qualities and interpersonal competencies are sought, such as the development of a self-reflective working style, self-knowledge about "blind spots" and inappropriate feelings toward clients, knowledge of one's interpersonal style and sensitivity, and promoting empathy for the client (Laireiter & Fiedler, 1996). Some authors also underscore the importance of therapy and self-exploration for the correction of dysfunctional styles and for the development of personal, interactional, and therapeutic competencies; for example, acquiring a positive view of clients or adopting a resource-oriented and a problem-solving therapeutic style. At the very least, it is assumed that this training element may be helpful in the mediation of therapeutic competence by offering the trainee the possibility to observe a model and to learn from it (DiGuiseppe, 1991).

Although the usefulness of some kind of personal therapy is widely acknowledged in CBT today, it is not yet accepted as a standard training element. In line with this stance, most behavior therapists reject personal therapy as a training requirement, and in most countries the mandatory implementation of personal therapy is not seen as valuable. In most training programs the following position prevails: attending personal therapy or some other kind of personal growth work should be facilitated or recommended by the training program but never be obligatory (BABCP, 2000; EABCT, 2001; Gray, 1991; Wright, 1991). Personal therapy in the sense of treating the future therapist is not regarded as a model for the training situation in CBT (Kanfer, Reinecker, & Schmelzer, 1996).

There are some exceptions to this general position. In some European countries where government regulations on psychotherapy exist (Austria, Germany, Switzerland, the Netherlands, Ireland, Finland), personal therapy is obligatory in order to become accredited as a psychotherapist in the health care system and also as a CB therapist. In most of these countries, state laws require that every accredited psychotherapy orientation must develop its own training curriculum that includes a program of personal sensitivity work. While this is a formal training requirement, it must be underlined that, in most of these countries, especially in the German-speaking ones and the Netherlands, this tradition also has its roots within CBT.

REMARKS ON TERMINOLOGY

Because CBT does not require a personal therapy (in its classical sense) as a training component, other terms had to be selected to characterize it. Unfortunately, no consensual term has been developed within CBT. The German associations of CBT agreed to call it *Selbsterfahrung*, a term that is not easily translated into English. At best it may be called "self-centering experience," "self-related experience," "self-directed experience," or simply "self-exploration" (Laireiter, 1998). In the international literature, very different terms are used for this training element, such as "personal sensitivity work" (BABCP, 2000), "personal growth-work" (Rotary, 1992), "self-experiential work" (DiGuiseppe, 1991), or "self-reflection" (Bennett-Levy et al., 2001). In some countries, such as the Netherlands, it is called "training therapy" (Everts, 1991).

OBJECTIVES OF PERSONAL THERAPY IN CBT

In CBT, the international discussion of the relevant goals of personal sensitivity work is just beginning, with greater progress in the German-speaking countries. The following aims are seen as most important.

1. Identification and management of the personal involvement of the therapist in the process of therapy, and his or her contribution to it (BABCP, 2000)
2. Improvement of self-insight, self-knowledge, and sensitivity for one's own problematic behaviors, habits, and interpersonal schemata and patterns (Laireiter & Fiedler, 1996)

3. Reduction of negative, noxious effects of the therapist on the therapeutic process (Kanfer et al., 1996)
4. Development of desired personal and interpersonal skills such as self-monitoring, interpersonal sensitivity, social assertiveness, self-esteem, and so on (Bennett-Levy et al., 2001)
5. Acquisition of more specific therapeutic skills, such as empathy and perspective taking, developing the therapist-patient relationship effectively, and managing the therapeutic process (Laireiter & Fiedler, 1996)
6. Personal acquaintance with strategies and methods of CBT by observing the therapist as a model, and by experiencing the client role and conducting client behaviors (Bennett-Levy et al., 2001; Laireiter & Fiedler, 1996)
7. Related to this, as a general aim, the improvement of training effects and the personal identification of the future therapist with CBT (Laireiter & Fiedler, 1996)

Psychotherapy to resolve the candidate's behavioral disorders is not generally conducted in this kind of work. Candidates needing such treatment are either filtered out at the beginning of the training or they are obliged to engage in a personal (psycho)therapy outside the regular training context (Kanfer et al., 1996). In cases of extreme psycholgical disorder, trainees may be forced to interrupt training while they are undergoing treatment.

METHODS OF PERSONAL THERAPY IN CBT

In the absence of any generalized model of self-exploratory work in CBT, very different methods have been developed. The theoretical and practical convergences in these methods may be summarized as follows:

1. Self-exploration in CBT is intended primarily to facilitate the attainment of specific training goals and the development of specific professional competencies (Kanfer et al., 1996).
2. Theoretical and practical principles of CBT should form the basis of this training element (Kanfer et al., 1996; McNamara, 1986).
3. Practically, personal sensitivity work is not realized in personal (psycho)therapies of the trainees but in specific training courses (*self-exploration seminars*). Very often it is also a component of supervision (Gray, 1991; Lieb, 1994; Wright, 1991).
4. The prefered setting for self-exploration is the group rather than the dyadic setting.
5. The relevance of personal self-exploratory work for training and practice in psychotherapy cannot be established by tradition, or common sense, or clinical impressions. It has to be proven empirically; in addition, the concepts and methods of this kind

of work must be evaluated by empirical studies (Kanfer et al., 1996).

The concepts and models can be summarized in four protoypical categories with respect to their primary focus and to their methods (table 5.1).

Person-centered concepts concentrate on the person of the trainee without looking at his or her professional role or activities. Therefore, the person in his or her past, current, and future life is the object of self-exploration. In most of these programs sensitivity work takes place within cognitive-behavioral or thematically structured groups containing elements from the encounter tradition, psychodrama, and experiential learning groups (Fiedler, 1996). This kind of work typically focuses on themes of the person and his or her life, such as family background, specific biographical experiences, interactional and interpersonal schemata, bonding experiences, or stressful phases.

Table 5.1   Models and methods of sensitivity work in CBT training

1. **Person-centered concepts**
- *Cognitive behavioral oriented groups* or *thematically structured groups* related to:
    Own learning history and family background
    Own resources, potentials, and well-being
    Blind spots and problematic aspects of own personality
    Behavior and interactional plans and schemas, etc.
- Sometimes individual sessions and work in the dyadic setting in addition

2. **Practice-centered concepts**
- *Thematically structured self-reflection groups* or *self-exploratory practice groups* related to:
    The person of the therapist in his or her professional role
    Interpersonal aspects of the therapeutic relationship
    Personal involvement of the therapist in therapy
    Personal values and goals of the therapist and his or her relation to therapy
    Problematic interpersonal situations in therapy
- Self-exploration and self-reflection as a component of *supervision*

3. **Technique-related models ("self-practice")**
- *Groups*, either unguided or guided by a teaching therapist, related to:
    Self-application of cognitive-behavioral methods
    Self-application of treatment manuals
    Self-modification and self-management programs
- Sometimes *individual self-practice*

4. **Training therapy models**
- *Individual therapy*:
    Modified classical treatment
    Training therapy models
    Self-exploration therapy
- *Group therapy*:
    Interactional cognitive-behavioral-oriented groups
    Multimodal group therapy
    Functional-analytic group therapy

Although this kind of work normally takes place in the group setting, some authors have recently recommended the addition of individual sessions (up to 30 or 40) or the use of individual sensitivity work within the group setting, in order to deepen specific individual themes (Zimmer, Zimmer, & Wagner, 1994).

Practice-centered concepts concentrate on the experiences, behaviors, and interpersonal performances of the therapist within the therapeutic context. Therefore, their primary concern is not the development of an increased sensitivity of the therapist but the therapist's personal involvement in the process of therapy and his or her contribution to it (Kanfer et al., 1996; Lieb, 1994). Practically, these programs most often take place either in structured, goal-directed groups related to typical themes of professional life, such as preferences for specific clients, difficult interpersonal situations, and power in psychotherapy. These programs also take place in self-exploratory practice groups, where the trainee's personal and interpersonal experiences and involvement in therapy are the subject of reflection (e.g., Knickenberg & Sulz, 1999).

Practice-centered self-exploration often is integrated into supervision either as an optional element or as an explicit component of it. In the first case, self-exploration is an option that is chosen whenever it becomes obvious that personal or interpersonal factors play a role in the therapy process (e.g., Lieb, 1994). In the second case, self-exploration is a regular component of supervision that is realized in every supervisory process (Gray, 1991; Ramsay, 1980).

Technique-related models are concerned with the self-practice of therapeutic techniques, such as assertiveness training, and cognitive methods, or in some cases with specific treatment-manuals of CBT (Bennett-Levy et al., 2001; Fiedler, 1996). This kind of experience is either done in groups guided by a training therapist or is carried out by the trainee alone or in unguided groups. One important focus of this kind of work is self-modification of a trainee's problematic behavior, such as work behavior, smoking, or coping with stress. Self-management programs are sometimes used as a singular element of self-exploration (e.g., Pfingsten, 2000); more often they are either a component of person-centered programs (Lieb, 1998) or combined with person- and/or practice-centered models (e.g., Döring-Seipel, Schüler, & Seipel, 1995).

Training therapy models are rather complex, and very different concepts may be subsumed under this category. In some cases, slightly modified cognitive-behavioral treatments are applied (e.g., Bleijenberg & Schippers, 1990); in other cases (e.g., Barrett-Levy et al., 2001; Fiedler, 1996), therapy is combined with a reflective process concerning two perspectives: the person of the therapist and the teaching of technical and treatment aspects. Thus, this personal therapy model combines person- and technique-related elements of self-exploration. A third conception are "self-exploration therapies." In these programs, elements of functional analysis, cognitive-behavioral intervention techniques, and methods to intensify self-exploration are combined to work through personal life experiences, actual and past conflicts, interactional behaviors, and the cognitive-affective schemata and plans lying behind them (e.g., Zimmer et al., 1994). Because these protoypical models are very selective in relation to their goals, in practice most training programs use combinations of two or more of these models. Most often either person- and practice-centered models are combined with self-management projects (e.g., Bennett-Levy et al., 2001; Döring-Seipel et al., 1995).

PERSONAL THERAPY BEYOND TRAINING

Several studies and literature reviews show that psychotherapists utilize psychotherapy themselves intensively: about 85% of them attend at least one personal therapy during their professional career, and about 60% after having finished formal training. About 55% engage in two courses of therapy, about 20% three and more (Norcross & Guy, chapter 13; Norcross & Connor, chapter 15; Orlinsky et al., chapter 14; Pope & Tabachnik, 1994). Therapists with a cognitive-behavioral orientation do this to a lesser extent: estimates range from about 40% to 50% (Norcross & Prochaska, 1984) up to 60% (Orlinsky et al., chapter 14). Compared to personal therapies of humanistic or psychodynamic therapists with a mean of about 250 hours, the duration of therapy among CB therapists has only a mean of about 50 to 80 hours (Norcross & Prochaska, 1984; Pope & Tabachnick, 1994).

One very stable observation, however, is most important: CB therapists are the most likely to undergo personal therapy based on a theoretical orientation other than their own (Lazarus, 1971; Norcross & Prochaska, 1984; Pope & Tabachnick, 1994). Laireiter (2000a) found that CB therapists attend treatments of the following distribution: CBT, 10% to 15%; psychodynamic therapies, 50% to 60%; humanistic, 20% to 30%; and systemic, 10% to 15%. Therapists of other orientations are much more loyal to their own orientation when they undergo personal therapy (psychodynamic-oriented therapists, up to 90%; humanistic-oriented, up to 70%). Only systemic and family therapists seem to be as eclectic as CB therapists in their personal therapy choices.

An important question in this context concerns the consequences of these choices. It is particularly relevant, because it has been found empirically that attending personal therapy may have important effects on therapeutic style, information processing, and the interpersonal behavior of the therapist (Laireiter, 2000b). Being a patient in psychoanalysis or experiential therapy may therefore change the style of CB-trained therapists into a less directive one and into a preference for longer, more process-oriented therapies, as well as placing a stronger focus on interactional factors, such as transference and countertransference.

Should a change in this direction be evaluated as positive or problematic?

Empirical findings do not give clear answers to this question. On the one hand, Willutzki and Botermans (1997) found a positive correlation between the breadth of theoretical concepts a therapist relies on and his or her subjectively perceived therapeutic competence. On the other hand, Lieb (1998) found that therapists who were grounded firmly in CBT reported having gained more from their CBT-oriented sensitivity work.

Because the participants in these studies differ in their therapeutic experience, the results may be interpreted as follows. At the beginning of a therapeutic career, for novices, it seems important to attend self-exploratory programs that are compatible with the theoretical orientation the therapist is trained in. Conceptual homogeneity may be an important criterion for developing a sound and integrated personal identity as a therapist. Later in professional life, however, personal therapies from alternative theoretical orientations may be perceived as enriching one's own therapeutic style and competence and therefore may contribute to the further development of the therapist by broadening his or her professional competence (Willutzki & Botermans, 1997).

As these conclusions are built on just two studies, they must be regarded as tentative. Additional research, especially with objective methods, on the effects of attending therapies from alternative orientations is necessary.

CONCLUDING COMMENTS

The use of personal therapy and the development of specific programs to foster personal and interpersonal competencies have started in CBT during the last 20 years. The primary focus of these programs is the person of the therapist within and outside of his or her therapeutic practice. The central objectives are to make the CB therapists more sensitive to their own behaviors, cognitions, feelings, schemas, and interactional styles, as well as to develop sensitivity to interpersonal processes in therapy, empathy for the client, and a self-reflective style. In addition, knowledge and skills related to therapeutic processes should be effectively cultivated. Although empirical evidence is not compelling at present, it supports the notion that most of these goals may be attained by a combination of person- and practice-related self-exploration.

We believe the future development of personal sensitivity work in CBT should focus on several points.

- An international discussion should be started on the necessity and the effectiveness of self-exploratory work in training in CBT, not only in a few European countries.
- If it becomes generally accepted that personal sensitivity work is an important training requirement, then valid training standards regarding this matter should be established.
- A combined model that integrates the person of the therapist, his/her practice, and cognitive-behavioral techniques seems to

be of greatest advantage. To realize these multiple goals, the components should be systematically sequenced. Personal self-exploration integrating CBT techniques (e.g., in self-management programs) should be introduced at the beginning of the training to form a base of self-knowledge and a basic self-reflection competence. For an optimal transfer of this competence, however, it seems necessary to practice self-exploration parallel to therapeutic work by practice-related self-reflection. After having finished formal training, the reflection and controlled analysis of one's own therapeutic practice would contiue and would become a component of continuing supervision.

- Self-reflection is no luxury but a necessary component of therapeutic practice. Accordingly, it may be regarded as a criterion of the quality of therapeutic practice in CBT.

REFERENCES

BABCP, British Association of Behaviour and Cognitive Therapy. (2000). *Minimum training standards for members approaching personal accreditation as practitioners.* London: BABCP.

Bennett-Levy, J., Turner, F., Beaty, T., Smith, M., Paterson, B., & Farmer, S. (2001). The value of self-practice of cognitive therapy techniques and self-reflection in the training of cognitive therapists. *Behavioural and Cognitive Psychotherapy, 29*, 203–220.

Bleisenberg, J., & Schippas, G. (1990). Rationeel emotive leer therapie, evvar ingen eh wakwijzc [Rational emotive training therapy. Experiences and effects] *Tijdschrift voor Psychotherapie, 122*, 115–116.

DiGuiseppe, R. (1991). Should trainees undergo psychotherapy? Dr. Raymond DiGuiseppe responds. *Behavior Therapist, 14*, 258–259.

Doering-Seipel, E., Schüler, P., & Seipel, K. H. (1995). Selbsterfahrung für verhaltenstherapeuten: Konzept eines trainings zielorientierter selbstreflexion: Erste erfahrungen [Self-exploration for CB-therapists: A training-model in goal-directed self-reflection: Primary experiences]. *Verhaltenstherapie, 5*, 138–148.

EABCT, European Association of Behavior and Cognitive Therapy. (2001). *Minimum training standards.* London: EABCT. [Also available at: http://www.eabct.com/training.htm]

Everts, D. B. (1991). Leertherapie, een kwestie van effect of affect? [Training therapy: A question of effect or affect?] *Tijdschrift voor Psychotherapie, 16*, 3–11.

Fiedler, P. (1996). *Verhaltenstherapie in und mit gruppen. Psychologische psychotherapie in der praxis* [CBT in and with groups. Practicing psychological psychotherapy]. Weinheim: Beltz Psychologie Verlags Union.

Gray, J. (1991). Should trainees undergo psychotherapy? Dr. James Gray responds. *Behavior Therapist, 14*, 257.

Kanfer, F. H., Reinecker, H., & Schmelzer, D. (1996). *Selbstmanagement-therapie. Ein lehrbuch für die klinische praxis* [Self-management therapy. A training guide for clinical practice]. Berlin: Springer.

Knickenberg, R. J., & Sulz, S. K. D. (1999). Interaktionsbezogene fallarbeit in der verhaltenstherapeutischen fort- und weiterbildung [Interactional case work in the training of CBT]. *Verhaltenstherapie, 9*, 23–29.

Laireiter, A.-R. (1998). Self-directed experience and personal therapy: The situation in the Germain-speaking countries and the state of the art of empirical research. In E. Sanavio (Ed.), *Behavior and cognitive therapy today: Essays in honor of Hans J. Eysenck* (pp. 163–179). Oxford: Pergamon Press.

Laireiter, A.-R. (2000a). Selbsterfahrung in der psychotherapie: 1. Inanspruchnahme von psychotherapie durch psychotherapeutInnen. Ein literaturüberblick [Self-exploration in psychotherapy: 1. The attendance of psychotherapy by psychotherapists. A review of empirical findings]. In A.-R. Laireiter (Ed.), *Selbsterfahrung in psychotherapie und verhaltenstherapie—Empirische befunde* [Self-exploration in psychotherapy and CBT—Empirical results] (pp. 45–88). Tübingen: dgvt-Verlag.

Laireiter, A.-R. (2000b). Selbsterfahrung in der psychotherapie: 2. Evaluation. Effekte von eigentherapie und selbsterfahrung auf die person des therapeuten, seine therapeutische kompetenz und die prozess- und ergebnisqualität von psychotherapie [Self-exploration in psychotherapy: 2. Evaluation. Effects of personal therapy and self-exploration on the person of the therapist, his/her therapeutic competence and the process- and outcome-quality of psychotherapy]. In A.-R. Laireiter (Ed.), *Selbsterfahrung in psychotherapie und verhaltenstherapie—Empirische befunde* [Self-exploration in psychotherapy and CBT—Empirical results] (pp. 89–233). Tübingen: dgvt-Verlag.

Laireiter, A.-R., & Fiedler, P. (1996). Selbsterfahrung und eigentherapie [Self-exploration and personal therapy]. In M. Bruch & N. Hoffmann (Eds.), *Selbsterfahrung in der verhaltenstherapie?* [Self-exploration in CBT] (pp. 82–123). Berlin: Springer.

Lazarus, A. A. (1971). Where do behavior therapists take their troubles? *Psychological Reports, 28*, 349–350.

Lieb, H. (1994). Selbsterfahrung als selbstreferenz: Zur integration von selbsterfahrung in die verhaltenstherapeutische supervision. [Self-exploration as self-reference: Toward integrating self-exploration and supervision in CBT.] In A. R. Laireiter & G. Elke (Eds.), *Selbsterfahrung in der verhaltenstherapie. Konzepte und praktische Erfahrungen* [Self-exploration in CBT. Concepts and practical experiences] (pp. 80–105). Tübingen: dgvt-Verlag.

Lieb, H. (1998). Veränderungen und wirkvariablen in der selbsterfahrung aus sicht der teilnehmer: Resultate einer evaluationsstudie [Trainees' views on how and why they change as a result of self-experience in behaviour therapy: An evaluation study]. *Verhaltenstherapie, 8*, 270–278.

McNamara, J. R. (1986). Personal therapy in the training of behavior therapists. *Psychotherapy, 23*, 370–374.

Norcross, J. C., & Prochaska, J. O. (1984). Where do behavior (and other) therapists take their troubles? II. *Behavior Therapist, 7*, 26–27.

Pfingsten, U. (2000). Selbstmodifikation als einstieg in die verhaltenstherapieausbildung. Ein erfahrungsbericht [Self-modification as an entry into training in CBT. A research report]. In A.-R. Laireiter (Ed.), *Selbsterfahrung in psychotherapie und verhaltenstherapie—Empirische befunde* [Self-exploration in psychotherapy and CBT—Empirical results] (pp. 475–491). Tübingen: dgvt-Verlag.

Pope, K. S., & Tabachnick, B. G. (1994). Therapists as patients: A national survey of psychologists' experiences, problems and beliefs. *Professional Psychology: Research and Practice, 25*, 247–258.

Ramsay, R. W. (1980). Goals of a personal therapy for trainees considered from a behavioral viewpoint. In W. de Moor & H. R. Wijngaarden (Eds.), *Psychotherapy: Research and training.* (Proceedings of the Eleventh International Congress of Psychotherapy held in Amsterdam, August 27–31, 1979) (pp. 273–276). Amsterdam: Elsevier.

Rotary, N. (1992). Personal growth work in the training of counseling and clinical psychologists in Ireland. *Irish Journal of Psychology, 13,* 168–175.

Willutzki, U., & Botermans, J. F. (1997). Die ausbildung in psychotherapie in Deutschland und der Schweiz und ihre bedeutung für die psychotherapeutische kompetenz [Training in psychotherapy in Germany and Switzerland and its relation to therapeutic competence]. *Psychotherapeut, 42,* 282–289.

Wright, F. (1991). Should trainees undergo psychotherapy? Dr. Fred Wright responds. *Behavior Therapist, 14,* 257–258.

Zimmer, F. T., Zimmer, D., & Wagner, W. (1994). Selbsterfahrung in der verhaltenstherapeutischen Weiterbildung [Self-exploration in the training of CBT]. In A.-R. Laireiter & G. Elke (Eds.), *Selbsterfahrung in der verhaltenstherapie—Konzepte und praktische erfahrungen* [Self-exploration in CBT—Concepts and practical experiences] (pp. 17–31). Tübingen: dgvt-Verlag.

6

THE ROLE AND CURRENT PRACTICE OF PERSONAL THERAPY IN SYSTEMIC/ FAMILY THERAPY

Jay Lebow

The traditions of family therapy and systems therapies are diverse. This is nowhere more evident than in their approach to the role assigned to personal therapy for therapists.

The concept that unites family-centered approaches lies in the core importance assigned to interaction and to interaction in the family as a focus for and vehicle toward change. Gurman, Kniskern, and Pinsof (1986) offered the following classic definition of family therapy: "any psychotherapeutic endeavor that explicitly focuses on altering the interactions between or among family members and seeks to improve the functioning of the family as a unit, or its subsystems, and/or the functioning of individual members of the family."

Beyond the common goals and some notion of a systemic process in which the behaviors of family members affect one another, there is much that varies across couple and family therapies. Specifically, the role and salience accorded personal therapy also ranges enormously, from viewing personal therapy as at the very core of becoming and being a family therapist to regarding personal therapy as irrelevant or even possibly coercive.

THERAPY FOR THERAPISTS ACROSS THE MODELS OF FAMILY THERAPY

Underlying the many models of systemic and family therapy are a diversity of worldviews. The most radical set of concepts about personal therapy for therapists emanated from those family approaches that grew exclusively as extensions of general systems theory and were not grounded in any school of individual therapy or theory of personality. The developers of these approaches often were originally not psychotherapists but from other disciplines, such as anthropology (Gregory Bateson and John Weakland), engineering (Paul Watzlawick), or communication studies (Jay Haley). The models they created for promoting change radically deemphasized individual functioning, personality, and personal history and instead accented the circular processes that ultimately characterize all systems and the cybernetics of those systems. For those espousing such viewpoints, psychotherapy was primarily an engineering task, and personal therapy for therapists was at best an irrelevancy. The only way the therapist's personality was viewed as important lay in the therapist remaining uncontaminated and distant from processes raging within the system. Even here, the road to attaining such independence was seen as lying in the creation of better engineering plans rather than the therapist's personal growth.

A variation on this theme emphasized a position that was highly critical of therapy as traditionally practiced. The core writings of the early strategic family therapies, especially the members of the first (Bateson, Jackson, Haley, & Weakland, 1954) and second Palo Alto (Watzlawick, Weakland, & Fisch, 1974) groups, presented traditional therapies as ways of maintaining problems, through promoting what these groups regarded as first-order change, change that did not really change the system's fundamental properties. They argued that traditional therapy was ineffective and that even if one had the goal of personal change for therapists (and they did not), personal therapy as typically practiced would not be an effective road to this goal.

The culmination of this viewpoint about personal therapy for therapists came with the development in the 1970s and 1980s of problem solving therapy by Jay Haley (Haley, 1976). Haley began as a member of the first Palo Alto group and was well known during the time of that group for his humorous essays that poked fun at traditional therapy (Haley, 1963). In recounting the methods of problem solving therapy, Haley frequently reiterated a position suggesting that personal therapy was of no value to therapists in their development. He further argued vociferously against training program expectations that therapists should participate in their own therapies, contending that such methods were not only unhelpful but also coercive. Perhaps a response to the strong promotion of personal therapy in more traditional training programs, Haley's position signaled perhaps the most critical position by any person within the community of psychotherapists toward personal therapy for therapists.

Unfortunately, because of the radical nature of these tenets, the novel thoughts contained, and the powerful writing style of its proponents, these strategic viewpoints often came to be identified by those outside the family therapy community as representing typical family therapists' views of traditional therapy and of personal therapy for therapists. However, this vantage point always has been a minority viewpoint, and these models now have few proponents among couple and family therapists.

Structural therapy, developed by Salvatore Minuchin (1974) aims to create powerful intervention strategies to redistribute power, redraw boundaries, and recreate alliances within families. For this approach, personal psychotherapy for therapists is an irrelevance. Although therapists entering their own therapies are not viewed as threatening their clinical effectiveness by being coopted by older, more traditional viewpoint, there is no promotion of personal therapy either. In his early writing, Minuchin never referred to personal therapy for therapists, nor have his followers in variants of structural/strategic approaches that derive from his model. Interestingly, structural approaches do contain a strong emphasis on the development of a therapeutic alliance with families, but with almost no consideration of how therapists develop their own personalities so as to be capable of forming such alliances with a broad range of families. Instead, structural therapists were encouraged to learn a number of "joining" operations, with little sense that self-knowledge would aid in building this ability (Minuchin & Fishman, 1981).

Another prominent set of models for couple and family therapy grows out of the cognitive-behavioral tradition. These approaches also bring a silence to the role of personal therapy, neither arguing for or against its merits. The emphasis in behavioral marital therapy (Jacobson & Margolin, 1979; Stuart, 1980) and behavioral family therapy, with such problems as conduct disorder (Patterson, 1982) and adolescent delinquency, clearly has been on the active interventions employed, with little or no attention to the self of the therapist. Over the years, behavioral couple and family therapists have moved from ignoring the therapeutic alliance to acknowledging that therapies must attend to client engagement and cooperation (Alexander & Parsons, 1982; Patterson & Chamberlain, 1992) but have not changed in their disregard of a role for personal therapy for therapists. However, informal observation suggests that behavioral couple and family therapists always have been less negative about personal therapy than therapists who practice strategic or problem-solving models.

By contrast, several family therapy models have emphasized personal therapy for therapists. Several approaches accentuate therapists' participation in their own therapies, during which they examine their own family experiences, with the aim of changing both the ongoing interactions with family as well as the internal representation of those interactions. Other models more broadly highlight the value of therapists seeking therapy to allow them to most effectively work as therapists. Six of these models are considered here.

Carl Whitaker (Whitaker & Keith, 1981), in an early model that grew out of the experiential tradition, suggested that therapists would be most effective when they could remain grounded in work with families while fully experiencing their countertransferences. Whitaker strongly accented the development of therapists' authenticity and experience through their own therapies, as well as other life experiences. Given a model centered on authentic experience of the client with a therapist able to utilize her own unconscious processes toward therapeutic ends, personal therapy became the essential aspect of training for therapists. Strikingly, Whitaker also emphasized the therapeutic value of therapy for the therapist as well as the client. Whitaker was a therapist to many therapists and was principally responsible for popularizing family therapy for therapists.

A related approach was that of Virginia Satir (1986). Satir's work, which also heavily accented therapist authenticity, was influenced by the human encounter movement. Considerable focus was on the development of therapist's own experience, especially in group or family therapy formats.

Building on a quite different tradition, that of psychoanalytic psychotherapy, but also including many of the same themes as Whitaker and Satir, James Framo (1981) pioneered a method of family-of-origin sessions that had enormous impact on therapy for family therapists. Rather than conjointly treating the entire family (as would Whitaker), Framo conducted the majority of sessions with an individual or couple but would include sessions with the family-of-origin in the context of that therapy. These sessions, during which the original clients would take up issues with their families, were typically seen as pivotal events in the treatment, around which much of the rest of the therapy was organized. Given the importance most couple and family therapists assign to family connection, and given the relative ease of organizing such sessions with family-of-origin compared to logistically engaging in a full therapy with family, having such a session or sessions with family became a very common mode for family therapists in their own treatment.

Murray Bowen (1978) originated what perhaps is the most influential method for family therapists working with their own family-of-origin. Bowen's approach highlights individuals or couples focusing their therapy on ongoing efforts to engage with and process relationships with their families of origin. The families of these individuals typically are never seen in sessions but are continually in focus, as the therapist acts as a coach to help the clients process their reactions to their families and find what Bowen refers to as more highly "differentiated" ways of dealing with them. Bowen's therapy goals are to reexperience one's family from an observing position, to reconnect in a new and different way with family, and thereby to also change self. Bowen's description of his own efforts to explore his connection with his family-of-origin is one of the classic papers in family therapy (Bowen, 1978). Therapists' engaging in such therapy became a core part of training in the Bowen method, as well as in several related approaches influenced by Bowen (Kramer, 1980). Interestingly, such exploration also became an aspect of training in this method, so that training and personal therapy often had considerable overlap. Combining the therapy and training contexts, it is more typical than not for a contemporary family therapist to have experienced some form of doing both kinds of work.

Object relations–centered psychoanalytic family therapists (Scharff & Scharff, 1987) and other psychoanalytic family therapists share with Bowen the tendency to recommend individual therapy formats for therapists' therapy. The typical psychotherapies for these therapists are psychoanalysis or psychoanalytic psychotherapy. In these models, family interactions in clients are viewed as evoking powerful countertransference reactions in therapists. Therapists are therefore encouraged to learn to identify and manage their countertransferences through their own personal explorations.

A newer and increasingly popular tradition in family therapy has been narrative therapy (White & Epston, 1990). Growing out of a postmodern viewpoint emphasizing individual's voices, stories, and viewpoints, therapists from this orientation bring a major focus to understanding their own stories. With therapy conceived of as an exchange between equals in a conversation, therapists have been encouraged to examine their own narratives in their own treatment. Much as in the psychoanalytic approaches, this exploration is principally done in the context of the individual format of psychotherapy.

HOW FAMILY AND SYSTEMS THERAPISTS VIEW PERSONAL THERAPY

Moving to a position that is meta to the notions espoused by each of these schools, here are a few summary conclusions about how personal therapy for mental health professionals is viewed within family therapy.

1. Family therapy includes a diversity of viewpoints toward personal therapy. Advocates for personal therapy strongly suggest its value; other approaches regard it as irrelevant; yet others suggest it may be harmful. Basically, the psychoanalytic, Bowenian, narrative, and experiential approaches are most positive about personal therapy for therapists; the behavioral and structural approaches neutral; and the strategic approaches most negative. It might also be added that in the newer "empirically supported" family therapies, which derive primarily from the behavioral and structural approaches, personal therapy for therapists is rarely mentioned in the manuals that document these models.

2. Although powerful ideologies are put forth in these models, the practice of couple and family therapy often transcends the boundaries of the schools (Lebow, 1987). Most couple and family therapists describe themselves as integrative or eclectic in orientation, not as adherents to a specific model. Further, most couple and family therapists have been influenced by traditions in individual therapy as well as those of family therapy (Lebow, 1997). Therefore, for most couple and family therapists, just as for most other therapists, it is typical for a major focus in their development to be centered on the value of their own therapy and to continue to utilize it throughout their lives at times when they believe it will be helpful. Most couple and family therapists remain positive about personal therapy and are as likely to participate in it as are individual therapists. Indeed, it should be highlighted that increasingly couple and family therapy is a format offered by a wide array of

therapists with varying backgrounds, and that the day of the ideologically centered family therapist seems to be giving way to that of the practitioner who utilizes couple and family therapy when most appropriate. With this change, those doing couple and family therapy come to be much the same people who engage in individual therapy and are likely to be more influenced by the general zeitgeist about personal therapy.

3. A pivotal choice for couple and family therapists lies in the format for their own therapies; that is, whether their personal therapy features individual, couple, or family sessions. Some models, particularly those of early family therapists, have strongly suggested the special value of therapists participating in their own family therapies, particularly with family-of-origin. For other approaches, particularly in the psychoanalytic and narrative traditions, individual therapy has primarily been viewed as the primary format for the personal development of family therapists.

4. A pragmatic difference separating family therapists from others is that it is far more common for family therapists to experience a wider array of formats for therapy than their individual therapist counterparts, and to participate in individual, couple, and family therapies at some time in their lifetimes. The multiple formats to consider and the distinct goals of these formats leads couple and family therapists to often participate in many different therapies both simultaneously and serially and, typically, to accrue many years in therapy over their lifetimes.

5. Despite the openness of most family therapists to personal therapy, a culture among the adherents to some models (such as strategic and problem solving) has been created that has made it atypical for those therapists to participate in their own therapies. Furthermore, because these family therapists work within a somewhat insular community, in which practice, training, and professional development are frequently away from the traditional structures of psychiatry, psychology, or social work, those trained in these models of family therapy might never be exposed to a context where personal therapy for therapists is common.

6. Couple therapy is probably the most frequent conjoint format in which couple and family therapists participate in psychotherapy. The openness of family therapists to conjoint therapies, the ready accessibility of therapists who specialize in this modality, and the nearly universal value of this modality for couples all add to a high utilization of couple therapy among couple and family therapists.

REFERENCES

Ackerman, N. W. (1958). *The psychodynamics of family life*. New York: Basic Books.
Alexander, J. F., & Parsons, B. (1982). *Functional family therapy: Principles and procedures*. Carmel, CA: Brooks/Cole.
Bateson, G., Jackson, D., Haley, J., & Weakland, J. (1954) Toward a theory of schizophrenia. *Behavioral Science, 1*, 251–264.
Bowen, M. (1978). *Family therapy in clinical practice*. Northvale, NY: Aronson.

Framo, J. L. (1981). The integration of marital therapy with sessions with family of origin. In A. S. Gurman & D. P. Kniskern (Eds.), *Handbook of family therapy* (pp. 133–158). New York: Brunner/Mazel.

Gurman, A. S., Kniskern, D. P., & Pinsof, W. M. (1986). Research on marital and family therapies. In S. L. Garfield & A. E. Bergin (Eds.), *Handbook of psychotherapy and behavior change* (3rd ed., pp. 565–624). New York: Wiley.

Haley, J. (1963). *Strategies of psychotherapy.* New York: Grune and Stratton.

Haley, J. (1976). *Problem-solving therapy.* San Francisco: Jossey-Bass.

Jacobson, N. S., & Margolin, G. (1979). *Marital therapy: Strategies based on social learning and behavior exchange principles.* New York: Brunner/Mazel.

Kramer, C. (1980). *Becoming a family therapist.* New York: Human Sciences Press.

Lebow, J. L. (1987). Integrative family therapy: An overview of major issues. *Psychotherapy, 40,* 584–594.

Lebow, J. (1997). The integrative revolution in couple and family therapy. *Family Process, 36,* 1–20.

Minuchin, S. (1974). *Families and family therapy.* Cambridge, MA: Harvard University Press.

Minuchin, S., & Fishman, C. (1981). *Family therapy techniques.* Cambridge, MA: Harvard University Press.

Patterson, G. R. (1982). *Coercive family process.* Eugene, OR: Castalia.

Patterson, G. R., & Chamberlain, P. (1992). A functional analysis of resistance (A neobehavioral perspective). In H. Arkowitz (Ed.), *Why don't people change? New perspectives on resistance and noncomplicance* (pp. 220–242). New York: Guilford.

Satir, V. (1986). *Conjoint family therapy.* Palo Alto, CA: Science and Behavior Books.

Scharff, D., & Scharff, J. S. (1987). *Object relations family therapy.* New York: Aronson.

Stuart, R. (1980). *Helping couples change.* New York: Guilford.

Watzlawick, P., Weakland, J., & Fisch, R. (1974). *Change.* New York: Norton.

Whitaker, C. A., & Keith, D. V. (1981). Symbolic-experiential family therapy. In A. S. Gurman & D. P. Kniskern (Eds.), *Handbook of family therapy.* New York: Brunner-Mazel.

White, M., & Epston, D. (1990). *Narrative means to therapeutic ends.* New York: Norton.

II

BEING A THERAPIST-PATIENT

Personal Experiences:
Firsthand Accounts
by Therapist-Patients

7

MY EXPERIENCE OF ANALYSIS
WITH FAIRBAIRN
AND WINNICOTT

How Complete a Result Does
Psychoanalytic Therapy Achieve?

Harry Guntrip

I t does not seem to me useful to attempt a purely theoretical answer to the question forming the subtitle. Theory does not seem to me to be the major concern. It is a useful servant but a bad master, liable to produce orthodox defenders of every variety of the faith. We ought always to sit light to theory and be on the lookout for ways of improving it in the light of therapeutic practice. It is therapeutic practice that is the real heart of the matter. In the last resort good therapists are born not trained, and they make the best use of training. Maybe the question "How complete a result can psychoanalytic therapy produce?" raises the question "How complete a result did our own training analysis produce?" Analysts are advised to be open to postanalytic improvements, so presumably we do not expect "an analysis" to do a "total" once-for-all job. We must know about postanalytic developments if we are to assess the actual results of the primary analysis. We cannot deal with this question purely on the basis of our patients' records. They must be incomplete for the primary analysis and nonexistent afterwards. As this question had unexpected and urgent relevance in my case, I was compelled to grapple with it; so I shall risk offering an account of my own analysis with Fairbairn and Winnicott, and its aftereffects: especially as this is the only way I can present a realistic picture of what I take to be the relationship between the respective contributions of these two outstanding analysts, and what I owe to them.

The question "How complete a result is possible?" had compelling importance for me because it is bound up with an unusual factor: a total amnesia for a severe trauma at the age of three and a half years, over the death of a younger brother. Two analyses failed to break through that amnesia, but it was resolved unexpectedly after they had ended, certainly only because of what they had achieved in "softening up" the major repression. I hope this may have both a theoretical and a human interest. The long quest for a solution to that problem has been too introverted an interest to be wholly welcomed, but I had no option, could not ignore it, and so turned it into a vocation through which I might help others. Both Fairbairn and Winnicott thought that but for that trauma, I might not have become a psychotherapist. Fairbairn once said: "I can't think what could motivate any of us to become psychotherapists, if we hadn't got problems of our own." He was no superoptimist and once said to me: "The basic pattern of personality once fixed in early childhood, can't be altered. Emotion can be drained out of the old patterns by new experience, but water can always flow again in the old dried up water courses." You cannot give anyone a different history. On another occasion he said: "You can go on analyzing for ever and get nowhere. It's the personal relation that is therapeutic. Science has no values except scientific values, the schizoid values of the investigator who stands outside of life and watches. It is purely instrumental, useful for a time but then you have to get back to living." That was his view of the "mirror analyst," a nonrelating observer simply interpreting. Thus he held that psychoanalytic interpretation is not therapeutic per se, but only as it expresses a personal relationship of genuine understanding. My own view is that science is not necessarily schizoid, but is really practically motivated, and often becomes schizoid because it offers such an obvious retreat for schizoid intellectuals. There is no place for this in psychotherapy of any kind.

I already held the view that psychoanalytic therapy is not a purely theoretical but a truly understanding personal relationship, and had published it in my first book before I had heard of Fairbairn; after reading his papers in 1949, I went to him because we stood philosophically on the same ground and no actual intellectual disagreements would interfere with the analysis. But the capacity for forming a relationship does not depend solely on our theory. Not everyone has the same facility for forming personal relationships, and we can all form a relationship more easily with some people than with others. The unpredictable factor of "natural fit" enters in. Thus, in spite of his conviction Fairbairn did not have the same capacity for natural, spontaneous "personal relating" that Winnicott had. With me he was more of a "technical interpreter" than he thought he was, or than I expected: but that needs qualification. I went to him in the 1950s when he was past the peak of his creative powers of the 1940s, and his health was slowly failing. He told me that in the 1930s and 1940s he had treated a number of schizophrenic and regressed patients with success. That lay behind his "theoretical revision" in the 1940s. He felt he had made a mistake in publishing his theory before the clinical evidence. From 1927 to 1935 he was psychiatrist at the University Psychological Clinic for Children, and did a lot of work for the N.S.P.C.C. One cannot be impersonal with children. He asked one child whose mother thrashed her cruelly: "Would you like me to find you a new kind Mummy?" She said: "No. I want my own Mummy," showing the intensity of the libidinal tie to the bad object. The devil you know is better than the devil you do not, and better than no devil at all. Out of such experience with psychotic, regressed and child patients, his theoretical revision grew, based on the *quality* of parent–child relations, rather than the *stages* of biological growth, a "personality-theory" not an impersonal "energy-control theory." He summed it up in saying that "the cause of trouble is that parents somehow fail to get it across to the child that he is loved for his own sake, as a person in his own right." By the 1950s when I was with him, he wisely declined to take the strains of severely regressing patients. To my surprise I found him gradually falling back on the "classical analyst" with an "interpretative technique," when I felt I needed to regress to the level of that severe infancy trauma.

Stephen Morse (1972), in his study of "structure" in the writings of Winnicott and Balint, concluded that they discovered new data but did not develop structural theory in a way that could explain them; which, however, he felt could be done by what he called the "Fairbairn–Guntrip metaphor." Having had the benefit of analysis with both these outstanding analysts, I feel the position is somewhat more complex than that. The relation between Fairbairn and Winnicott is both theoretically important and very intriguing. Superficially they were quite unlike each other in type of mind and method of working, which prevented their knowing how basically close they were in the end. Both had deep roots in classic Freudian theory and therapy, and both outgrew it in their own different ways. Fairbairn saw that intellectually more clearly than Winnicott. Yet in the 1950s Fairbairn was more orthodox in clinical practice than Winnicott. I had just over 1,000 sessions with Fairbairn in the 1950s and just over 150 with Winnicott in the 1960s. For my own benefit I kept detailed records of every session with both of them, and all their correspondence. Winnicott said, "I've never had anyone who could tell me so exactly what I said last time." Morse's article suggested a restudy of those records last year, and I was intrigued to find the light they cast on why my *two analyses failed to resolve my amnesia for that trauma at three and a half years, and yet each in different ways prepared for its resolution as a post-analytic development.* I had to ask afresh, "What is the analytic therapeutic process?"

In general I found Fairbairn becoming more *orthodox in practice* than in theory while Winnicott was more *revolutionary in practice* than in theory. They were complementary opposites. Sutherland in his obituary notice (1965) wrote:

> Fairbairn had a slightly formal air about him—notably aristocratic, but in talking to him I found he was not at all formal or remote.

Art and religion were for him profound expressions of man's needs, for which he felt a deep respect, but his interests revealed his rather unusual conservatism.

I found him formal in sessions, the intellectually precise interpreting analyst, but after sessions we discussed theory and he would unbend, and I found the human Fairbairn as we talked face to face. Realistically, he was my understanding good father after sessions, and in sessions in the transference he was my dominating bad mother imposing exact interpretations. After his experimental creative 1940s, I feel his conservatism slowly pushed through into his work in the 1950s. The shock of his wife's sudden death in 1952 created obvious domestic problems. Early in the 1950s he had the first attack of viral influenza, and these became more virulent as the decade advanced. For two years after his wife's death he worked hard on his fine paper, "Observations on the Nature of Hysterical States" (Fairbairn, 1954) which finalized his original thinking. He clarified his views on "psychoanalysis and science" in two papers (Fairbairn, 1952b, 1955). But there was a subtle change in his next paper, "Considerations Arising out of the Schreber Case" (Fairbairn, 1956). Here he fell back from his "ego and object relations" psychology, explaining everything as due to "primal scene" libidinal excitations and fears. Finally, in his last paper, "On the Nature and Aims of Psychoanalytical Treatment" (Fairbairn, 1958) his entire emphasis was on the "internal closed system" of broadly oedipal analysis, not in terms of instincts, but of internalized libidinized and antilibidinized bad-object relations. I went to him to break through the amnesia for that trauma of my brother's death, to whatever lay behind it in the infancy period. There, I felt, lay the cause of my vague background experiences of schizoid isolation and unreality, and I knew that they had to do with my earliest relations with mother, though only because of information she had given me.

After brother Percy's death I entered on four years of active battle with mother to force her "to relate," and then gave it up and grew away from her. I will call that, for convenience, the oedipal internalized bad-object relations period: it filled my dreams, but repeatedly sudden, clear schizoid experiences would erupt into this, and Fairbairn steadily interpreted them as "withdrawal" in the sense of "escapes" from internalized bad-object relations. He repeatedly brought me back to oedipal three-person libidinal and antilibidinal conflicts in my "inner world," Kleinian "object splits" and Fairbairnian "ego splits" in the sense of oedipal libidinal excitations. In 1956 I wrote to ask him to say exactly what he thought about the Oedipus complex, and he replied: "The Oedipus complex is central for therapy but not for theory." I replied that I could not accept that: for me theory *was* the theory of *therapy*, and what was true for one must be true for both. I developed a double resistance to him consciously, partly feeling he was my bad mother forcing her views on me, and partly openly disagreeing with him on genuine grounds. I began to insist that my real problem was not the bad relationships of the post-Percy period, but mother's basic "failure to relate at all" right from the start. I said that I felt oedipal analysis kept me marking time on the same spot, making me use bad relations as better than none at all, keeping them operative in my inner world as *a defence against the deeper schizoid problem*. He saw that as a defensive character trait of "withdrawness" (Fairbairn, 1952a, chap. 1). I felt it as a problem in its own right, not just a defense against his closed-system "internal world of bad-object relations."

But my oedipal analysis with Fairbairn was not a waste of time. Defenses have to be analyzed and it brought home to me that I had actually repressed the trauma of Percy's death and all that lay behind it, by building over it a complex experience of sustained struggle in bad-object relations with mother, which in turn I had also to repress. It was the basis of my spate of dreams, and intermittent production of conversion symptoms. Fairbairn for long insisted that it was the *real core* of my psychopathology. He was certainly wrong, but it did have to be radically analysed to open the way to the deeper depths. That happened. Steadily regressive and negative schizoid phenomena thrust into the material I brought to him, and at last he began to accept in theory what he no longer had the health to cope with in practice. He generously accepted my concept of "regressed ego" split off from his "libidinal ego" and giving up as hopeless the struggle to get a response from mother. When I published that idea, Winnicott wrote to ask: "Is your Regressed Ego withdrawn or repressed?" I replied: "Both. First withdrawn and then kept repressed." Fairbairn wrote to say:

> This is your own idea, not mine, original, and it explains what I
> have never been able to account for in my theory, Regression. Your
> emphasis on ego-weakness yields better therapeutic results than
> interpretation in terms of libidinal and anti-libidinal tensions.

When in 1960 I wrote "Ego-weakness, the Hard Core of the Problem of Psychotherapy" he wrote to say: "If I could write now, that is what I would write about." I knew my theory was broadly right for it conceptualized what I could not yet get analyzed. With I think great courage, he accepted that.

I shall complete my account of Fairbairn as analyst and man by illustrating the difference in "human type" between him and Winnicott, a factor that plays a big part in therapy. The setup of the consulting room itself creates an atmosphere which has meaning. Fairbairn lived in the country and saw patients in the old Fairbairn family house in Edinburgh. I entered a large drawing room as waiting room, furnished with beautiful valuable antiques, and proceeded to the study as consulting room, also large with a big antique bookcase filling most of one wall. Fairbairn sat behind a large flat-topped desk, I used to think "in state" in a high-backed plush-covered armchair. The patient's couch had its head to the front of the desk. At times I thought he could reach over the desk and hit me on the head. It struck me as odd for an analyst who did not believe in the "mirror-analyst" theory. Not for a long time did I realize that I had "chosen" that couch position, and there was a small settee at the side of his desk at which I could sit if I wished, and ultimately I did. That this imposing situation at once had an unconscious transference meaning for me became clear in a dream in the first month. I must explain that my father had been a Methodist Local Preacher of outstanding eloquence as a public speaker, and from 1885 built up and led a Mission Hall which grew into a Church which still exists. In all my years of dreaming he never appeared as other than a supportive figure *vis-à-vis* mother, and in actual fact she *never* lost her temper in his presence. I wanted Fairbairn in transference as the protective father, helping me to stand up to my aggressive mother, but unconsciously I felt otherwise, for I dreamed:

> I was in father's Mission Hall. Fairbairn was on the platform but he had mother's hard face. I lay passive on a couch on the floor of the Hall, with the couch head to the front of the platform. He came down and said: "Do you know the door is open?" I said: "I didn't leave it open," and was pleased I had stood up to him. He went back to the platform.

It was a thinly disguised version of his consulting room setup, and showed that I wanted him to be my supportive father, but that wish was overpowered by a clear negative transference from my severe dominating mother. That remained by and large Fairbairn's transference role "in sessions." He interpreted it as the "one up and the other down" bad parent–child "seesaw" relation. It can only be altered by turning the tables. I found that very illuminating, containing all the ingredients of unmet needs, smothered rage, inhibited spontaneity. It was the dominant transference relationship in sessions. After sessions Fairbairn could unbend in our theory and therapy discussion, the good human father.

This negative transference in sessions was, I feel, fostered by his *very intellectually precise interpretations.* Once he interpreted: "Something forecloses on the active process in the course of its development." I would have said: "Your mother squashed your naturally active self." But he accurately analyzed my emotional struggle to force mother to mother me after Percy died, and showed how I had internalized it. That had to be done first, but he held it to be the central oedipal problem, and could not accept till it was too late, that this masked a far deeper and more serious problem. Later Winnicott twice remarked: "You show no signs of ever having had an Oedipus complex." My family pattern was not oedipal. It was always the same in dreams and is shown by the most striking one of them.

> I was being beseiged and was sitting in a room discussing it with father. It was mother who was beseiging me and I said to him: "You know I'll never give in to her. It doesn't matter what happens. I'll never surrender." He said, "Yes. I know that. I'll go and tell her" and he went and said to her, "You'd better give it up. You'll never make him submit," and she did give up.

Fairbairn's persistence in oedipal interpretations I could not accept as final, cast him in the role of the dominating mother. It came to our ears that Winnicott and Hoffer thought my adherence to his theory was due to its not allowing him to analyze my aggression in the transference. But they didn't see me knock over his pedestal ashtray, and kick his glass door-stopper, "accidentally" of course, and we know what that means in sessions, as he was not slow to point out. They did not see me once strew some of his books out of that huge bookcase over the floor, symbolic of "tearing a response out of mother," and then putting them back tidily to make reparation *à la* Melanie Klein. But after sessions we could discuss and I could find the natural warmhearted human being behind the exact interpreting analyst.

I can best make this clear by comparison with Winnicott. His consulting room was simple, restful in colors and furniture, unostentatious, carefully planned, so Mrs. Winnicott told me, by both of them, to make the patient feel at ease. I would knock and walk in, and presently Winnicott would stroll in with a cup of tea in his hand and a cheery "Hallo," and sit on a small wooden chair by the couch. I would sit on the couch sideways or lie down as I felt inclined, and change position freely according to how I felt or what I was saying. Always at the end, as I departed he held out his hand for a friendly handshake. As I was finally leaving Fairbairn after the last session, I suddenly realized that in all that long period we had never once shaken hands, and he was letting me leave without that friendly gesture. I put out my hand and at once he took it, and I suddenly saw a few tears trickle down his face. *I saw the warm heart of this man with a fine mind and a shy nature.* He invited my wife and me to tea whenever we visited her mother in Perthshire.

To make the ending of my analysis with Fairbairn meaningful, I must give a brief sketch of my family history. My mother was an overburdened "little mother" before she married, the eldest daughter of 11 children, and saw four siblings die. Her mother was a feather-brained beauty queen, who left my mother to manage everything even as a schoolgirl. She ran away from home at the age of 12 because she was so unhappy, but was brought back. Her best characteristic was her strong sense of duty and responsibility to her widowed mother and three younger siblings, which impressed my father when they all joined his Mission Hall. They married in 1898 but he did not know that she had had her fill of mothering babies and did not want any more. In my teens she occasionally became confidential and told me the salient facts of family history, including that she breastfed me because she believed it would prevent another pregnancy; she refused to breastfeed Percy and he died, after which she refused further intimacy. My father was the youngest son of a High-Church and high Tory family, the politically leftwing and religiously Nonconformist rebel; and antiimperialist who nearly lost his position in the City by refusing to sign his firm's pro–Boer War petition. That passing anxiety gave my mother the chance to wean me suddenly and start a business of her own. We moved when I was one year old. She chose a bad site and lost money steadily for seven years, though everything was more than retrieved by the next move. *That first seven years of my life, six of them at the first shop, was the grossly disturbed period for me.* I was left to the care of an invalid aunt who lived with us. Percy was born when I was two years old and died when I was three and a half. Mother told me father said he would have lived if she had breast-fed him, and she got angry. It was a disturbed time. In her old age, living in our home, she would say some revealing things. "I ought never to have married and had children. Nature did not make me to be a wife and mother, but a business woman," and "I don't think I ever understood children. I could never be bothered with them."

She told me that at three and a half years I walked into a room and saw Percy lying naked and dead on her lap. I rushed up and grabbed him and said: "Don't let him go. You'll never get him back!" She sent me out of the room and I fell mysteriously ill and was thought to be dying. Her doctor said: "He's dying of grief for his brother. If your mother wit can't save him, I can't," so she took me to a maternal aunt who had a family, and there I recovered. Both Fairbairn and Winnicott thought I would have died if she had not sent me away from herself. All memory of that was totally repressed. The amnesia held through all the rest of my life and two analyses, till I was 70, three years ago. But it remained alive in me, to be triggered off unrecognized by widely spaced analogous events. At the age of 26, at the University, I formed a good friendship with a fellow student who was a brother figure to me. When he left and I went home on vacation to mother, I fell ill of a mysterious exhaustion illness which disappeared immediately I left home and returned to College. I had no idea that it was equivalent to that aunt's family. In 1938, aged 37, I became minister of a highly organized Church in Leeds, with a Sunday afternoon meeting of 1,000 men, an evening congregation of 800, and well-organized educational, social and recreational activities. It was too large for one minister and I had a colleague who became another Percy-substitute. He left as war clouds loomed up. Again I suddenly fell ill of the same mysterious exhaustion illness. It was put down to overwork, but by then I was psychoanalytically knowledgeable, had studied classical theory under Flugel, knew the stock literature, had an uncompleted M.A. thesis under supervision of Professor John Macmurray, seeking to translate Freud's psychobiology, or rather clinical data, into terms of "personal relations" philosophy, and had studied my own dreams for two years. So I was alerted when this illness brought a big dream.

> I went down into a tomb and saw a man buried alive. He tried to
> get out but I threatened him with illness, locked him in and got
> away quick.

Next morning I was better. For the first time I recognized the reeruption of my illness after Percy's death, and saw that I lived permanently over the top of its repression. I knew then I could not rest till that problem was solved.

I was drawn into wartime emergency psychotherapy by the Leeds Professor of Medicine, appointed to a lectureship in the Medical School, and went on studying my own dreams. I recently reread the record and found I had only made forced textbookish oedipal interpretations. Of more importance was that three dominant types of dream stood out: (1) a savage woman attacking me, (2) a quiet, firm, friendly father figure supporting me, and (3) a mysterious death-threat dream, the clearest example based on the memory of mother taking me at the age of six into the bedroom of my invalid aunt, thought to be dying of rheumatic fever, lying white and silent. In one dream:

> I was working downstairs at my desk and suddenly an invisible
> band of ectoplasm tying me to a dying invalid upstairs, was pulling
> me steadily out of the room. I knew I would be absorbed into her.
> I fought and suddenly the band snapped and I knew I was free.

I knew enough to guess that the memory of my dying aunt was a screen memory for the repressed dead Percy, which still exercised on me an unconscious pull out of life into collapse and apparent dying. I knew that somehow sometime I must get an analysis. In 1946 Professor Dicks appointed me as the first staff member of the new Department of Psychiatry, and said that with my views I must read Fairbairn. I did so and at the end of 1949 I sought analysis with him.

For the first few years, his broadly oedipal analysis of my "internalized bad-object relations" world did correspond to an actual period of my childhood. After Percy's death and my return home, from the age of three and a half to five, I fought to coerce mother into mothering me by repeated petty psychosomatic ills, tummyaches, heat spots, loss of appetite, constipation and dramatic, sudden high temperatures, for which she would make me a tent-bed on the kitchen couch and be in and out from the shop to see me. She told me the doctor said: "I'll never come to that child again. He frightens the life out of me with these sudden high temperatures and next morning he's perfectly well." But it was all to no purpose. Around five years I changed tactics. A new bigger school gave me more independence, and mother said: "You began not to do what I told you." She would fly into violent rages and beat me, from about the time I was five to the age of seven. When canes got broken I was sent to buy a new one. At the age of seven I went to a still larger school and steadily developed a life of my own outside the home. We moved when I was eight to another shop where mother's business was an outstanding success. She became less depressed, gave me all the money I needed for hobbies and outdoor activities, scouting, sport, and gradually I forgot not quite all the memories of the first seven bad years. It was all the fears, rages, guilts, psychosomatic transient symptoms, disturbed dreams, venting the conflicts of those years from three and a half to seven, that Fairbairn's analysis dealt with. In mother's old age she said: "When your father and Aunt Mary died and I was alone, I tried keeping a dog but I had to give it up.

I couldn't stop beating it." That's what happened to me. No wonder I had an inner world of internalized libidinally excited bad-object relations, and I owe much to Fairbairn's radical analysis of it.

But after the first three or four years I became convinced that this was keeping me marking time in a sadomasochistic inner world of *bad-object relations* with mother, as a defense against quite different problems of the period before Percy's death. This deeper material kept pushing through. The crunch came in December 1957 when my old friend whose departure from College caused the first eruption of that Percy-illness in 1927, suddenly died. For the third time exhaustion seized me. I kept going enough to work and travel to Edinburgh for analysis, feeling I would now get to the bottom of it. Then, just as I felt some progress was being made, Fairbairn fell ill with a serious viral influenza of which he nearly died, and was off work six months. I had to reinstate repression, but at once began to "intellectualize" the problem I could not work through with him in person. It was not pure intellectualization by deliberate thinking. Spontaneous insights kept welling up at all sorts of times, and I jotted them down as they flowed with compelling intensity. Out of all that I wrote three papers; they became the basis of my book *Schizoid Phenomena, Object-Relations and the Self* (1968): "Ego-Weakness, the Core of the Problem of Psychotherapy" written in 1960 (chapter 6), "The Schizoid Problem, Regression and the Struggle to Preserve an Ego" (chapter 2) written in 1961, and "The Manic-Depressive Problem in the Light of the Schizoid Process" (chapter 5) written in 1962. In two years they took me right beyond Fairbairn's halting point. He generously accepted this as a valid and necessary extension of his theory.

When he returned to work in 1959, I discussed my friend's death and Fairbairn's illness and he made a crucial interpretation: "I think since my illness I am no longer your good father or bad mother, but your brother dying on you." I suddenly saw the analytical situation in an extraordinary light, and wrote him a letter which I still have, but did not send. I knew it would put a bigger strain on him than he could stand in his precarious health. I suddenly saw that I could never solve my problem *with* an analyst. I wrote: "I am in a dilemma. I have got to end my analysis to get a chance to finish it, but then I do not have you to help me with it." Once Fairbairn had become my brother in transference, *losing him* either by ending analysis myself, or by staying with him till he died, would represent the death of Percy, and I would be left with a full-scale eruption of that traumatic event, and no one to help me with it. Could Fairbairn have helped me with that in transference analysis? Not in his frail state of health and I phased out my analysis in that year. I have much cause to be grateful to him for staying with me, in his increasingly weak state of health, till I had reached that critical insight. The driving force behind my theory writing in 1959–1962 was the reactivation of the Percy-trauma, causing a compelling spate of spontaneous ideas. I could contain it and use it for constructive research, partly because I was giving Fairbairn up gradually, partly because he accepted the validity of my ideas, and partly because I had resolved to seek analysis with Winnicott before Fairbairn died.

Fairbairn first introduced me to Winnicott in 1954 by asking him to send me a copy of his paper: "Regression within the Psychoanalytical Setup" (in Winnicott, 1958). He sent it and, rather to my surprise, a letter saying: "I do invite you to look into the matter of your relation to Freud, so that you may have your own relation and not Fairbairn's. He spoils his good work by wanting to knock down Freud." We exchanged three long letters on each side. I stated that my relation to Freud had been settled years before I had heard of Fairbairn, when studying under Flugel at University College, London. I rejected Freud's psychobiology of instincts, but saw the great importance of his discoveries in psychopathology. Regarding that correspondence I now find I anticipated Morse's (1972) conclusion almost in his words, 18 years earlier: that Winnicott's "true self" has no place in Freud's theory. It could only be found in the id, but that is impossible because the id is only impersonal energy. In fact I felt that Winnicott had left Freud as far behind in therapy as Fairbairn had done in theory. In 1961 I sent him a copy of my book *Personality Structure and Human Interaction* (Guntrip, 1961) and he replied that he had already purchased a copy. I was reading his papers as they were published, as also was Fairbairn who described him as "clinically brilliant." By 1962 I had no doubt that he was the only man I could turn to for further help. I was by then only free to visit London once a month for a couple of sessions, but the analysis I had had made it easier to profit by that. From 1962 to 1968 I had 150 sessions and their value was out of all proportion to their number. Winnicott said he was surprised that so much could be worked through in such widely spaced sessions, due I think in the first place to all the preliminary clearing that had been done by Fairbairn and to the fact that I could keep the analysis alive between visits; but most of all to *Winnicott's profound intuitive insights into the very infancy period I so needed to get down to.* He enabled me to reach extraordinarily clear evidence that my mother had almost certainly had an initial period of natural maternalism with me as her first baby, for perhaps a couple of months, before her personality problems robbed me of that "good mother." I had quite forgotten that letter I did not send to Fairbairn about the dilemma of not being able either to end analysis or go on with it, once my analyst became Percy in the transference. Ending it would be equivalent to Percy dying and I would have no one to help me with the aftermath. If I did not end it, I would be using my analyst to prevent the eruption of the trauma and so get no help with it, and risk his dying on me. My amnesia for that early trauma was not broken through with Winnicott either. Only recently have I realized that in fact, unwittingly, he altered the whole nature of the problem by enabling me to reach right back to *an ultimate good mother, and to find her recreated in him in the transference.* I discovered later that he had put me in a position to face what was a double trauma of both Percy's death and mother's failing me.

As I reread my records I am astonished at the rapidity with which he went to the heart of the matter. At the first session I mentioned the amnesia for the trauma of Percy's death, and felt I had had a radical analysis with Fairbairn of the "internalized bad-object defenses" I had built up against that, but we had not got down to what I felt was my basic problem, not the actively bad-object mother of later childhood, *but the earlier mother who failed to relate at all.* Near the end of the session he said: "I've nothing particular to say yet, but if I don't say something, you may begin to feel I'm not here." At the second session he said:

> You know about me but I'm not a person to you yet. You may go away feeling alone and that I'm not real. You must have had an earlier illness before Percy was born, and felt mother left you to look after yourself. You accepted Percy as your infant self that needed looking after. When he died, you had nothing and collapsed.

That was a perfect object relations interpretation, but from Winnicott, not Fairbairn. Much later I said that I occasionally felt a "static, unchanging, lifeless state somewhere deep in me, feeling I can't move." Winnicott said:

> If 100% of you felt like that, you probably couldn't move and someone would have to wake you. After Percy died, you collapsed bewildered, but managed to salvage enough of yourself to go on living, very energetically, and put the rest in a cocoon, repressed, unconscious.

I wish there were time to illustrate his penetrating insight in more detail, but I must give another example. I said that people often commented on my ceaseless activity and energy, and that in sessions I did not like gaps of silence and at times talked hard. Fairbairn interpreted that I was trying to take the analysis out of his hands and do his job; steal father's penis, oedipal rivalry. Winnicott threw a dramatic new light on this talking hard. He said:

> Your problem is that that illness of collapse was never resolved. You had to keep yourself alive in spite of it. You can't take your ongoing being for granted. You have to work hard to keep yourself in existence. You're afraid to stop acting, talking or keeping awake. You feel you might die in a gap like Percy, because if you stop acting mother can't do anything. She couldn't save Percy or you. You're bound to fear I can't keep you alive, so you link up monthly sessions for me by your records. No gaps. You can't feel that you are a going concern to me, because mother couldn't save you. You know about "being active" but not about "just growing, just breathing" while you sleep, without your having to do anything about it.

I began to be able to allow for some silences, and once, feeling a bit anxious, I was relieved to hear Winnicott move. I said nothing, but with uncanny intuition he said:

> You began to feel afraid I'd abandoned you. You feel silence is abandonment. The gap is not you forgetting mother, but mother forgetting you, and now you've relived it with me. You're finding an earlier trauma which you might never recover without the help of the Percy trauma repeating it. You have to remember mother abandoning you by transference on to me.

I can hardly convey the powerful impression it made on me to find Winnicott coming right into the emptiness of my "object relations situation" in infancy with a nonrelating mother.

Right at the end of my analysis I had a sudden return of hard talking in session. This time he made a different and extraordinary statement. He said:

> it's like you giving birth to a baby with my help. You gave me half an hour of concentrated talk, rich in content. I felt strained in listening and holding the situation for you. You had to know that I could stand your talking hard at me and my not being destroyed. I had to stand it while you were in labour being creative, not destructive, producing something rich in content. You are talking about "object relating," "using the object" and finding you don't destroy it. I couldn't have made that interpretation five years ago.

Later he gave his paper on "The Use of an Object" (in Winnicott, 1971) in America and met, not surprisingly I think, with much criticism. Only an exceptional man could have reached that kind of insight. He became a good breast mother to my infant self in my deep unconscious, at the point where my actual mother had lost her maternalism and could not stand me as a live baby any more. It was not then apparent, as it later became to me, that he had transformed my whole understanding of the trauma of Percy's death, particularly when he added:

> You too have a good breast. You've always been able to give more than take. I'm good for you but you're good for me. Doing your analysis is almost the most reassuring thing that happens to me. The chap before you makes me feel I'm no good at all. You don't have to be good for me. I don't need it and can cope without it, but in fact you are good for me.

Here at last I had a mother who could value her child, so that I could cope with what was to come, It hardly seems worth mentioning that the only point at which I felt I disagreed with Winnicott was when he talked occasionally about "getting at your primitive sadism, the baby's ruthlessness and cruelty, your aggression," in a way that suggested not my angry fight to extract a response from my cold mother, but Freud's and Klein's "instinct theory," the id, innate aggression. For I knew he rejected the "death instinct" and had moved far beyond Freud when I went to him. He once said to me: "We differ from Freud. He was for curing symptoms. We are concerned with living persons, whole living and loving." By 1967 he wrote, and gave me a copy of his paper, "The Location of Cultural Experience" (in Winnicott, 1971), in which he said: "I see that I am in the territory of Fairbairn: 'object-seeking' as opposed to 'satisfaction-seeking.'" I felt then that Winnicott and Fairbairn had joined forces to neutralize my earliest traumatic years.

I must complete this account with the one thing I could not foresee. Winnicott becoming the good mother, freeing me to be alive and creative, transformed the significance of Percy's death in a way that was to enable me to resolve that trauma, and my dilemma about how to end my analysis. Winnicott, relating to me in my deep unconscious, enabled me to stand seeing that it was not just the loss of Percy, but being left alone with the mother who could not keep me alive, that caused my collapse into apparent dying. But thanks to his profound intuitive insight, I was not now alone with a nonrelating mother. I last saw him in July 1969. In February 1970 I was told medically that I was seriously overworked, and if I did not retire "Nature would make me." I must have felt unconsciously that that was a threat that "Mother Nature" would at last crush my active self. Every time I rested I found myself under a compulsion to go back to the past, in the form of rehearsing the details of my ministerial "brother-figure's" leaving in 1938, and my reacting with an exhaustion illness. I soon saw that this was significant and it led on to an urge to write up my whole life-story, as if I had to find out all that had happened to me. By October I developed pneumonia and spent five weeks in hospital. The consultant said: "Relax. You're too overactive." I still did not realize that I was fighting against an unconscious compulsive regression. I had never linked the idea of "retirement" with the deep fear of losing my battle with mother to keep my active self alive, in the end. After a slow winter recuperation, I heard in the New Year 1971 that Winnicott had a 'flu attack.' Presently I enquired of Masud Khan how Winnicott was, and he replied that he was about again and liked to hear from his friends, so I dropped him a line. A little later the phone rang, and the familiar voice said: "Hallo. Thanks for your letter" and we chatted a bit. About two weeks later the phone rang again and *his secretary told me he had passed away. That very night I had a startling dream. I saw my mother*, black, immobilized, staring fixedly into space, *totally ignoring me* as I stood at one side staring at her and feeling myself frozen into immobility: the first time I had ever seen her in a dream like that. Before she had always been attacking me. My first thought was: "I've lost Winnicott and am left alone with mother, sunk in depression, ignoring me. That's how I felt when Percy died." I thought I must have taken the loss of Winnicott as a repetition of the Percy trauma. Only recently have I become quite clear that it was not that at all. I did not dream of mother like that when my college friend died or my ministerial colleague left. Then I felt ill, as after Percy's death. This time it was quite different. That dream started a compelling dream-sequence which went on night after night, taking me back in chronological order through every house I had lived in, in Leeds, Ipswich, College, the second Dulwich shop, and finally the first shop and house of the bad first seven years. Family figures, my wife, daughter, Aunt Mary, father and mother kept recurring; father always supportive, mother always hostile, but no sign of Percy. I was trying to stay in the post-Percy period of battles with mother. Then after some two months two dreams at last broke that amnesia for Percy's life and death. I was astonished to see myself in a dream clearly aged about three, recognizably me, holding a pram in which was my brother aged about a year old. I was strained, looking anxiously over to the left at mother, to see if she would take any notice of us. But she was staring fixedly into the distance, ignoring us, as in the first dream of that series. The next night the dream was even more startling.

> I was standing with another man, the double of myself, both
> reaching out to get hold of a dead object. Suddenly the other man
> collapsed in a heap. Immediately the dream changed to a lighted
> room, where I saw Percy again. I knew it was him, sitting on the
> lap of a woman who had no face, arms or breasts. She was merely a
> lap to sit on, not a person. He looked deeply depressed, with the
> corners of his mouth turned down, and I was trying to make him
> smile.

I had recovered in that dream the memory of collapsing when I saw him as a dead object and reached out to grab him. But I had done more. I had actually gone back in both dreams to the earlier time before he died, to see the "faceless" depersonalized mother, and the black depressed mother, who totally failed to relate to both of us. Winnicott had said: "You accepted Percy as your infant self that needed looking after. When he died, you had nothing and collapsed." Why did I dream of "collapsing" first, and then of going back to look after Percy? My feeling is that my collapse was my first reaction of terrified hopelessness at the shock of finding Percy dead on mother's lap, but in that aunt's family I quickly seized the chance of staying alive by finding others to live for.

That dream series made me bring out and restudy all my analysis records, till I realized that, though Winnicott's death had reminded me of Percy's, the situation was entirely different. That process of compelling regression had not started with Winnicott's death, but with the threat of "retirement" as if mother would undermine me at last. I did not dream of Winnicott's death, but of Percy's death and mother's total failure to relate to us. What better dream-evidence could one have of Winnicott's view that "There is no such thing as a baby": i.e. there must be a "mother and baby," and what better evidence for Fairbairn's view that the basic psychic reality is the "personal object relation"? What gave me strength in my deep unconscious to face again that basic trauma? It must have been because Winnicott was not, and could not be, dead for me, nor certainly for many others. I have never felt that my father was dead, but in a deep way alive in me, enabling me to resist mother's later active paralyzing in-hibiting influence. Now Winnicott had come into living relation with pre-cisely that earlier lost part of me that fell ill because mother failed me. *He has taken her place and made it possible and safe to remember her in an ac-tual dream-reliving of her paralysing schizoid aloofness.* Slowly that became a firm conviction growing in me, and I recovered from the volcanic up-heaval of that autonomously regressing compelling dream-series, feeling that I had at last reaped the gains I had sought in analysis over some 20 years. After all the detailed memories, dreams, symptoms of traumatic events, people and specific emotional tensions had been worked through, one thing remained: *the quality of the overall atmosphere of the personal re-lations that made up our family life in those first seven years.* It lingers as a mood of sadness for my mother who was so damaged in childhood that she could neither be, nor enable me to be, our "true selves." I cannot have a different set of memories. But that is offset by my discovery in analysis of how deeply my father became a secure mental possession in me, support-ing my struggle to find and be my "true self," and by Fairbairn's resolving my negative transference of my dominating mother on to him, till he be-came another good father who had faith in me, and finally by Winnicott entering into the emptiness left by my nonrelating mother, so that I could experience the security of being my self. I must add that without my wife's understanding and support I could not have had those analyses or reached this result. What is psychoanalytic psychotherapy? It is, as I see it, the pro-vision of a reliable and understanding human relationship of a kind that makes contact with the deeply repressed traumatized child in a way that enables one to become steadily more able to live, in the security of a new real relationship, with the traumatic legacy of the earliest formative years, as it seeps through or erupts into consciousness.

Psychoanalytic therapy is not like a "technique" of the experimental sciences, an objective "thing-in-itself" working automatically. It is a pro-cess of interaction, a function of two variables, the personalities of two people working together toward free spontaneous growth. The analyst grows as well as the analysand. There must be something wrong if an analyst is static when he deals with such dynamic personal experiences. For me, Fairbairn built as a person on what my father did for me, and as an analyst enabled me to discover in great detail how my battles for independence of mother from three and a half to seven years had grown into my personality makeup. Without that I could have deteriorated in old age into as awkward a person as my mother. Winnicott, a totally different type of personality, under-stood and filled the emptiness my mother left in the first three and a half years. I needed them both and had the supreme good fortune to find both. Their very differences have been a stimulus to different sides of my makeup. Fairbairn's ideas were "exact logical concepts" which clarified issues. Winnicott's ideas were "imaginative hypotheses" that challenged one to explore further. As examples, compare Fairbairn's concepts of the libidi-nal, antilibidinal and central egos as a theory of endopsychic structure, with

Winnicott's "true and false selves" as intuitive insights into the confused psychic reality of actual persons. Perhaps no single analyst can do all that an analysand needs, and we must be content to let patients make as much use of us as they can. We dare not pose as omniscient and omnipotent because we have a theory. Also Fairbairn once said: "You get out of analysis what you put into it," and I think that is true for both analyst and analysand. I would think that the development of clear conscious insight represents having taken full possession of the gains already made emotionally, putting one in a position to risk further emotional strains to make more emotional growth. It represents not just conscious understanding but a strengthening of the inner core of "selfhood" and capacity for "relating." So far as psychopathological material is concerned, dreaming expresses our endopsychic structure. It is a way of experiencing on the fringes of consciousness, our internalized conflicts, our memories of struggles originally in our outer world and then as memories and fantasies of conflicts that have become our inner reality, to keep "object relations" alive, even if only "bad-object relation," because we need them to retain possession of our "ego." It was my experience that the deeper that final spate of dreams delved into my unconscious, the more dreaming slowly faded out and was replaced by "waking up in a mood." I found I was not fantasying or thinking but simply feeling, consciously in the grip of a state of mind that I began to realize I had been in consciously long ago, and had been in unconsciously deep down ever since: a dull mechanical lifeless mood, no interest in anything, silent, shut in to myself, going through routine motions with a sense of loss of all meaning in existence. I experienced this for a number of consecutive mornings till I began to find that it was fading out into a normal interest in life: which after all seems to be what one would expect.

There is a natural order peculiar to each individual and determined by his history, in which (1) problems can become conscious and (2) interpretations can be relevant and mutative. We cannot decide that but only watch the course of the individual's development. Finally, on the difficult question of the sources of theory, it seems that our theory must be rooted in our psychopathology. That was implied in Freud's courageous self-analysis at a time when all was obscure. The idea that we could think out a theory of the structure and functioning of the personality without its having any relation to the structure and functioning of our own personality, should be a self-evident impossibility. If our theory is too rigid, it is likely to conceptualize our ego defenses. If it is flexible and progressive it is possible for it to conceptualize our ongoing growth processes, and throw light on others' problems and on therapeutic possibilities. Balint's "basic fault" and Winnicott's' "incommunicado core," since they regard these phenomena as universal, must be their ways of "intuitively sensing" their own basic reality, and therefore other people's. By contrast with Fairbairn's exactly intellectually defined theoretical constructs which state logically progressive developments in existing theory, they open the way to profounder exploration of the infancy period, where, whatever a baby's genetic endowment, the mother's ability or failure to "relate" is the *sine qua non* of psychic health for the infant. To find a good parent at the start is the basis of psychic health. In its lack, to find a genuine "good object" in one's analyst is both a transference experience and a real life experience. In analysis as in real life, all relationships have a subtly dual nature. All through life we take into ourselves both good and bad figures who either strengthen or disturb us, and it is the same in psychoanalytic therapy: it is the meeting and interacting of two real people in all its complex possibilities.

REFERENCES

Fairbairn, W. R. D. (1952a). *Psychoanalytic studies of the personality.* London: Tavistock.

Fairbairn, W. R. D. (1952b). Theoretical and experimental aspects of psycho-analysis. *British Journal of Medical Psychology, 25,* 122–127.

Fairbairn, W. R. D. (1954). Observations of the nature of hysterical states. *British Journal of Medical Psychology, 27,* 106–125.

Fairbairn, W. R. D. (1955). Observations in defence of the object-relations theory of the personality. *British Journal of Medical Psychology, 28,* 144–156.

Fairbairn, W. R. D. (1956). Considerations arising out of the Schreber case. *British Journal of Medical Psychology, 29,* 113–127.

Fairbairn, W. R. D. (1958). On the nature and aims of psychoanalytical treatment. *International Journal of Psychoanalysis, 39,* 374–385.

Guntrip, H. (1960). Ego-weakness, the hard core of the problem of psychotherapy. In Guntrip (1968).

Guntrip, H. (1961). Personality structure and human interaction. London: Hogarth Press.

Guntrip, H. (1968). Schizoid phenomena, object-relations and the self. London: Hogarth Press.

Morse, S. J. (1972). Structure and reconstruction: A critical comparison of Michael Balint and D. W. Winnicott. *International Journal of Psychoanalysis, 53,* 487–500.

Sutherland, J. (1965). Obituary. W. R. D. Fairbairn. *International Journal of Psychoanalysis, 46,* 245–247.

Winnicott, D. W. (1958). *Collected papers. Through paediatrics to psycho-analysis.* London: Tavistock.

Winnicott, D. W. (1971). *Playing and reality.* London: Tavistock.

8

MY EXPERIENCES AS A PATIENT IN FIVE PSYCHOANALYTIC PSYCHOTHERAPIES

Jesse D. Geller

I am currently 62 years old. I have become introspective again. I welcome reminiscing with old friends about the persons and events that have contributed significantly to our development. I approached writing this chapter about my experiences as a patient in five different psychoanalytic psychotherapies with hopes similar to the ones I bring to these intimate conversations. I was not disappointed. I took another look at what I learned about my symptoms, and my character pathology. Like my experiences in therapy, this effort yielded new self-discoveries. I will not dwell on these matters in this chapter; I have no interest in producing what Joyce Carol Oates (1999) would call an "exercise in pathography."

I also retrospectively evaluated whether and how each of my therapies contributed to my growth as a therapist and as a human being. What I realized is that I have no settled opinions about these matters. My understanding of the ways I have changed over time keeps changing. Moreover, my current estimates of how much I have benefited, personally, from my various therapies is different, in some important respects, from the remembered estimates I took in my forties and fifties. If I had written this retrospective report during those decades, my estimates would have been biased in a more negative direction.

Still, I strongly believe that the illustrative experiences related here would have been the same ones I would have included if I had written this chapter earlier in my life. For me, they represent the decisive moments that took place in each of my therapies. Memories of these critical incidents are somehow emblematic of something that stood at the emotional center of each of my therapies. I seem to return to them over and over again when reflecting on the continuing and particular roles each of my therapies have played in determining what I do and what I do not do as a therapist. The primary purpose of this chapter is to further explore these connections in some detail.

ON BECOMING A PSYCHOTHERAPY PATIENT

The gateway into my first therapy was by way of seeking "vocational guidance." I arrived at the City College of New York in 1956 poorly educated, learning disabled, and math phobic. I took a bus and the subway into Manhattan from Flushing, Queens, where I lived with my parents and shared a bedroom with my two younger brothers. I feared I would flunk out and would have to join the army like the majority of my friends. I have been ill prepared for every major undertaking in my life. I was convinced that I would have to perform well beyond my "intelligence" if I were to remain in college.

In the hopes that I would be told what my interests and talents were and what I should become, I went, at the beginning of my sophomore year, for "vocational guidance" at the college's counseling center. I was interviewed and took a battery of psychological tests. To my surprise, I was told that I needed "psychotherapy," not vocational guidance, and that the school would provide me with free psychotherapy if I chose to go.

I was assigned to Dr. A. I had very little idea of what to expect. I didn't know how to ask him for help. I was too proud to ask him for help. I was afraid of asking him for help. As I was to learn, I was searching for someone to help me develop what I would have called courage, in particular the courage to face and conquer my fears of failure, weakness, disease, accidents, an early death, and after death.

LEARNING HOW TO USE THERAPY

Dr. A introduced me to experiences that were previously unknown to me. I was the first person I knew who'd ever gone into therapy. I never knew anyone who dressed in three-piece tweed suits and smoked a pipe, as Dr. A did most hours. I had never had a productive conversation with an adult, in private, about matters that were important to me. My father and I had never had a "heart-to-heart" talk. He would become angry and impatient when his efforts to teach me how to tie my shoelaces or solve an arithmetical problem repeatedly failed. I estimate that by age six I had stopped asking him for help, reassurance, or instruction.

With Dr. A I took my first tentative steps toward learning how to learn with a "trusted companion" (Bowlby, 1973) through the medium of dialogue. I talked with Dr. A, as I could talk to no other adult, about the helpless terrors of early childhood. I owe my acute "sense of place" (Bachelard, 1994) to having grown up in a Bronx basement apartment whose foyer door opened onto the building's furnace, discarded furniture, garbage cans, and the superintendent's savage German shepherd. I had grown accustomed to feeling anxious and alone in an ugly environment.

Dr. A helped me to find names and metaphors for my feelings. He provided me with clarifying descriptions of my "unformulated" (Stern, 1983) experiences. He helped me translate what had been "fits of anxiety" into particular fears. Fears can be met with courage. Anxieties, having no definable object, cannot. Unfortunately, I experienced my fears as a form of cowardice. I was ashamed that my mind lacked the power to overcome my acute fears of an early death. Bravery was the preeminent value in my neighborhood.

My most vivid memory of therapy with Dr. A is the following communicative exchange: "Jesse, you've often spoken about feeling angry at your father, and the things that make you angry with him. Yet, you never talk about feeling angry with your mother. Is there anything that she does that gets you angry?" I shrugged my shoulders, hesitated, and then answered ". . . I can't think of anything." He replied, "How about her having poisoned your view of your father?" I doubt that this is what we actually said, but this representation of it has the feel of truth. He was right. I tended to see my father through my mother's often disrespectful eyes. With this remark, Dr. A opened me up to the possibility of revisioning how I was treated by each of my parents. With this primal insight Dr. A earned my respect. Nonetheless, I never felt deep affection for him. I reserved this feeling for my teachers.

MY DIFFICULTIES WITH BEING A PATIENT

I did not enjoy being Dr. A's patient and, as it turns out, wrongly assumed that I wasn't benefiting from therapy. In fact, to anticipate a later point, I might have dropped out of therapy if I hadn't concurrently been studying psychology, literature, and philosophy with teachers whom I admired and wished to emulate and whose approval meant a great deal to me. For the most part, I hated going to my weekly 50-minute sessions when I first began seeing Dr. A I had to overcome many obstacles in order to use my relationship with Dr. A for personal benefit.

My conception of what a patient is supposed to do was something like "I have to be a good soldier." A misguided sense of bravery required me to face unflattering truths about myself, however humiliating, while maintaining the facade of "taking it very well . . . like a man." I counterphobically revealed what I wished to conceal.

The idea that my self was intrinsically worthwhile was alien to me. I believed doctors only gave you "bad news" about yourself. I did not trust that Dr A would be nonjudgmental or respectful. In the absence of trust it takes courage to become aware of and to admit to the raw, unexpressed, and unknown aspects of one's personality.

I had trouble being the focus of Dr. A's "serious interest" and "sympathetic understanding" (Freud, 1912/1953). I was incapable of un-self-conscious consciousness of myself. I had trouble taking my own suffering seriously. It felt "weird" speaking with seriousness of purpose about myself. I was constantly watching him watching me. I rarely made eye contact with him. I especially dreaded it when we looked at each other during silences, and there were many.

I also dreaded his asking "What are you thinking?" to break a silence. I could usually be found taking inventory of whatever I felt I should be telling him—my pathetic vanities, my unkept promises, my mind-boggling grandiosity, my self-hatred, my sexual fantasies, and so on. It was particularly difficult when he asked this question while I was thinking that I preferred my psychology teachers to him. Like my unvoiced bad habits, this secret alienated me from Dr. A.

I hated it even more when he would ask me "What are you feeling (right now)?" as he was disposed to do. I often didn't know. The question left me speechless. He seemed to believe me when I said "Words fail me," but I assumed that he experienced me as a secretive and unrewarding patient. I didn't know if he really liked me.

In hindsight, it occurred to me that I was able to endure the hardships of being in therapy, stoically, because of what I was learning in the classroom, in the theater, at the movies, and in Greenwich Village. I persisted in therapy because my intellectual heroes advocated the view that self-understanding was intrinsically worth pursuing, whether or not it "cured" one's neurosis. My psychology professors taught me that being in an insight-oriented therapy would turn one into a better, smarter, more cultured person, if not a healthier one. This conviction was especially important to me because I felt I was failing to transform my "intellectual insights" into "emotional insights," to use the jargon of that time. Being concurrently a psychology major and a psychotherapy patient provided me with an "identity" (Erikson, 1963).

Psychoanalysis and psychotherapy offered the alienated/secular college students of my time and place, New York in the 1950s, standards and values regarding our unanswered questions regarding meaning and morality. I came to the study of psychology, and my first therapy, seeking guidance about masturbation, romantic love, premarital sex, conventional cultural mores, and the ethical conduct of life. Moreover, studying developmental and abnormal psychology reassured me that my "symptoms"—agonizing self-consciousness, vocational disorientation, rebellion, preoccupation with health, heightened ambivalence, elusive mood swings, and identity confusion—were regarded by the experts as the "typical" manifestations of adolescence. Studying Freud and the neo-Freudians reassured me that beneath the surface of socially acceptable behavior of even the most mature person existed patricidal and incestuous wishes. At the same time, I was becoming aware that the psychoanalytic theories of the day were molding the taste, opinions, language and lifestyles of serious, (e.g., intellectual, artistic and bohemian) New Yorkers. I wanted to be one of them. I saw psychoanalysis as an ally in my struggle to establish myself as a cultural rebel, a defiant individualist, an American existentialist. I was attracted to the tension between the pro- and antisocial forces found in the teachings of Freud. My studies, my psychotherapy, and the conversations that dominated my social life were being integrated into a way of being in the world.

I decided to go to graduate school to study clinical psychology while in therapy, but I believe this choice grew primarily out of my identifications with my teachers. Once this decision was made, I began to see psychotherapy as a way of sharpening the knowledge I required to be an outstanding student. I discovered that while paying close attention to what was on *my* mind I was learning how *the* mind works. As I have gotten older, it has become clearer to me that there is a direct continuity between the questions and concerns I have struggled with in therapy and my scholarly interests.

A BRIEF ENCOUNTER

After graduation and before starting graduate school, I was in a psychotherapy that I terminated unilaterally after six sessions. I had been referred to Dr. B by Dr A. Dr. A was opposed to transferring me into his private practice after having treated me "for free" for more than two and a half years. He told me that Dr. B was a Horneyian, as he himself was, and that he would see me for a reduced fee. At the time I terminated with Dr. A, there was still a possibility I would get into NYU's clinical Ph.D. program. My favorite college professors were all graduates of NYU. I didn't want to leave New York or my girlfriend, Ruth. As it turned out, I was rejected by NYU. I chose to go to the University of Connecticut (1960–66) because it was closer to New York than the other schools that had accepted me. And that has made all the difference.

Two things about my therapy with Dr. B stand out in my memory— the overall physicality of the therapeutic situation, and a particular piece of dialogue.

Dr. B sat eight to ten feet away from me. He felt too far away. I was distracted by the voices of his wife and children, who lived next door to his posh Upper West Side office. I felt he was oblivious to matters of taste and style, as was revealed by the furniture, paintings, and lamps that inhabited his consulting room. I couldn't see him clearly because of the glare and shadows created by the late afternoon sun that poured through the large windows located directly behind his chair. All in all, I was disappointed because I did not find signs of expertise and healing authority when I submitted his office to semiotic and aesthetic scrutiny.

I am, however, indebted to Dr. B in one respect. In the fifth session Dr. B said to me "You seem to be comparing me unfavorably to Dr. A." I replied "No, I think you are a very good *psycholoshits*." I dropped out of therapy at the next session, but I took away an unshakable conviction that parapraxes provide an especially compelling vantage point from which to explore conflicts and their transformations. My Freudian slip convinced me of the existence and creativity of unconscious processes.

THE DECISION TO BECOME A PSYCHOTHERAPIST

When I entered graduate school I had only the vaguest idea about how I was going to earn a living. The men in my family had jobs. I was going to be the first one that had ever had a career. During my second year at the University of Connecticut, I began to think that the practice of psychotherapy was a suitable and viable career aspiration. I could imagine of no higher calling than to free others from their suffering. But my principle motives for seeking training as a psychotherapist lay elsewhere. I was drawn to the field by the realization that becoming a therapist would essentially involve the professionalization of my interests and talents. I saw earning some of my living by doing psychotherapy as a valid response to various conflicts, for example, the practical versus the idealistic. I regarded the private practice of therapy as a way of being what the Dalai Lama and Cutler (1998) describe as "wisely selfish." The profession appealed to me because in the early 1960s psychotherapists were still seen as in the vanguard of social change.

THE CORNERSTONES OF MY APPROACH TO THERAPY

During my six years at the University of Connecticut all of my supervisors and psychotherapy teachers identified themselves, first and foremost, as "Kaiserians." They had all been treated or trained by Helmuth Kaiser. Kaiser had begun his career in Europe as a classically trained Freudian analyst. In his maturity, he arrived at a position that radically departed from psychoanalytic insight-seeking psychotherapy as it was practiced during the 1950s and early 1960s. Kaiser's theory is basically founded on the notion that what is healing about psychotherapy can be found in the degree of "communicative intimacy" that the participants have been able to achieve (1965).

Kaiser's teachings have been labeled in several ways—namely, as existential, humanistic, and interpersonal and as an extension of Reich's (1949) psychoanalytic writings about character analysis. Not surprisingly, my supervisors interpreted his ideas in various ways. Ross Thomas taught my first practicum. He instructed us: "See what happens when you make engaging in authentic dialogues with your patients your sole and exclusive concern." Harvey Wasserman emphasized the importance of being able to estimate the congruence between what a patient is feeling and avowing. For Wasserman, the basic intent of a Kaiserian therapist was to promote in patients a feeling of responsibility for their words and deeds. Alan Willoughby advocated a nondirective but highly interactive therapy that focused on the patient's immediate and concrete experience in the "here and now."

These broad and ambiguous mandates held for me what Yeats (1959) called "the fascination of the difficult." Although they were scary as hell, they suited my temperament and values. The Kaiserian point of view was for me a great place from which to begin training as a therapist. It appealed to me intellectually, emotionally, and aesthetically. Its emphasis on authenticity and personal responsibility was consistent with the existential values I embraced in college. It pleased me that Kaiser's key concepts anticipated what were to become the dominant concerns of the late 1960s and early 1970s. It was during my generation that authenticity became a virtue. Taking a revisionist position vis-à-vis psychoanalysis appealed to my need to see myself as irreverent and as a maverick. I received my graduate education in an era when psychotherapists essentially had two choices—you either followed or reacted against psychoanalysis. I resonated with Kaiser's use of artistic means to convey his scientifically based views about the effectiveness of psychotherapy. In an allegorical play called *Emergency* (1965), he called into question fundamental aspects of psychoanalytic therapy. From a distance it is clear to me that another crucial motive was at play. Identifying with a radical minority of Kaiserian therapists enabled me, at one and the same time, to remain an outsider and to join a community of believers.

THE QUEST FOR AUTHENTICITY

It was inevitable that I would go to see a Kaiserian when I decided to return to therapy, which I did during my third year of graduate school. I conceived of this choice as essential to my "initiation" into the group of therapists who were known to be Kaiserians, or who acknowledged being influenced by him (e.g., Shapiro, 1975). Although this "pseudo-community" existed only in my imagination (even Kaiser insisted he wasn't a Kaiserian), going into therapy with Dr. C felt like my idea of the "training analyses" offered within the context of psychoanalytic institutes. I entered treatment with Dr. C to grapple with the key choices I had made during my transition into early adulthood (e.g., marrying Ruth and starting a family), and to deal with my conflict between the need to succeed and my desire to be loving and loved. During an argument, without realizing the fullness of what she was saying, Ruth described me as becoming "ruthless" whenever I undertook a writing project.

I came to therapy with Dr. C wanting to reveal myself without artifice, without self-dramatization, without fictionalizing myself, or uglifying my past. I wished to reveal myself (as I really was). But I knew all too well that I would have to overcome a variety of obstacles in order to speak with Dr. C spontaneously, authentically, and expressively. To name a few: having grown up surrounded by people I experienced as "too pushy," "too vulgar," "too demonstrative," in effect "too much," inhibited me against speaking expressively. I had spent much of my youth "pretending" everything was all right, although I knew something was dreadfully wrong. At home I'd always kept my worries to myself. By the time I got to college, I had arrived at the Buddhist position that much of my suffering was caused by wishing and wanting. I tried, willfully, to disavow the desire to have what I didn't already have. I operated under the assumption that you were more likely to get what you wanted if you didn't let the other know what you wanted. I acted as if my hurts and disappointments were unimportant. To counteract my boyish and, so I was told, "cute" appearance, I developed the ability to assume the physiognomy of seriousness. In high school this required presenting an image of myself as "cool." In college, my preferred persona was that of a beatnik or a bohemian intellectual like the melancholy young men I admired in foreign films and existential novels.

DR. C AND HIS THERAPY STYLE

I was painfully aware of the myriad occasions in which my behavior was at variance with what I felt. With Dr. A I had learned how difficult it is to resist resisting. Not surprisingly, I began therapy with Dr. C feeling somewhat fearful about looking closely at the contradictions that existed between the "images" I sought to project and my insider's view of what was "really" going on.

Dr. C saw clearly those aspects of myself that I found difficult to accept. He seemed to emphasize, in a highly selective way, what was left unsaid but conveyed by my postures, gestures, facial expressions, and voice qualities. It was a therapy in which the "form" rather than the "content" of what I said was given priority. His approach with me seemed to conform most closely to the psychoanalytic notion of confronting and analyzing resistances. Bringing a patient's attention to the expressive behaviors that accompany speech requires considerable tact and must be done compassionately. From my own difficult firsthand experience with Dr. C, I know that focusing on the nonlinguistic aspects of a patient's utterances will provoke shame, and little else, if these qualities are lacking.

Sadly, Dr. C did not interpret and enact the principles of Kaiser in a style that was congruent with my sensibility. Dr. C prided himself on his sense of irony. I found him too glib, droll, and sarcastic. As a neophyte adult, embarking on an uncharted course, I needed to be taken seriously. Dr. C's approach seemed to be in the service of not taking what I said "too seriously." He did not give my suffering its due. I felt he did not acknowledge its magnitude. I felt caricatured by him. He seemed insufficiently grounded in a tragic perspective on the human condition. I felt he could have benefited from Paul Simon's (1973) advice "Try a little tenderness. There is no tenderness beneath your honesty."

During my one and a half years of therapy with Dr. C I took further steps toward learning how to say "I think . . .", "I feel . . .", "I believe . . .", "I want . . ." directly and straightforwardly. Not finding in Dr. C the idealized model of the Kaiserian therapist I hoped to become, I felt greater affection for and identified more with my teachers than my therapist, as I had in college. In fact, much of what I took away from my therapy with Dr. C was the conviction I would develop a therapy style that was gentle, kind, and nonironic.

COMING TO NEW HAVEN

In graduate school I was taught mainly what was wrong with psychoanalysis. When I arrived in New Haven in 1967, almost all of the therapy being practiced was derived from and judged against psychoanalysis. Here, the prevailing view was that psychoanalysis was the deepest and most thorough form of therapy.

New Haven is a city in which psychoanalytic theory and practice continues to flourish. Then, and to a lesser extent now, the most intellectually rigorous and admired figures were and are psychoanalysts. As an assistant professor in the Yale Department of Psychiatry, I was supervised by men such as Sid Blatt, Marshall Edelson, and Borge Lofgren, who persuasively argued that a four- or five-times-a-week psychoanalysis was inherently superior to all other therapies and a necessary training requirement. I read their typed manuscripts and sat in at seminars and lectures with Roy Schafer and Hans Loewald. I could say of Roy Schafer (1983, p. 284) what he said of his relationship to Erik Erikson:

> I was absolutely enamored of his way of thinking, his way of
> integrating social psychological, biological, and anthropological
> material with psychoanalytic material. I then found myself in a
> position of a kind that I think is not rare among young analysts. I
> was imitating my hero, thinking and talking like him. It was only
> when I tried writing like him that I became aware that it was as
> though I was trying to be Erikson himself.

It was practically and politically wise to think and speak in the vocabulary shared by therapists working in the psychoanalytic tradition. Concurrently, I had grown distrustful of the ways Kaiser's ideas were being interpreted by the handful of clinicians in New Haven who espoused this point of view. And so, when I felt the need to return to therapy, I decided to be psychoanalyzed. A friend who was being trained as a psychoanalyst recommended I see Dr. D. He described him as bright and unflappable and as having had a lot of experience treating hospitalized adolescents.

MY DISAPPOINTMENTS IN DR. D

I am aware of representing all of my therapists in a twofold manner. First, they are represented as the persons with whom I engaged in psychological development. In the second, they are the source of disappointments and negative transference reactions, perhaps originating in my troubles with significant others. The latter peaked during my psychoanalysis.

I took it as a matter of course that Dr. D would draw anger and disappointed reactions toward himself through no fault of his own. I was intellectually prepared for him to become the target of displacements from significant male authority figures of my past. But by the sixth or seventh month of analysis, I was beginning to fear that Dr. D and I were a poor fit. I felt at times that he was studying me like a "case." This suspicion was confirmed years after I terminated, when I stumbled on an article he had published. I was shocked when I found myself being described by him, "disguised" of course. He had never sought my permission.

Dr. D was a very proper, textbook analyst. With me he never seemed to deviate from "correct" technique. I felt his therapeutic stance and stratagems were unduly influenced by obeisance to orthodox interpretations of Freud's recommendations regarding anonymity, abstinence, and neutrality. However technically expert he may have been, he never said anything that I found evocative or exciting. He never dazzled me with the depth of his insights or led me to feel as if I had been enriched by new ideas. I wanted an analyst who had the qualities of inventiveness and originality. I felt he did not grasp the unpredictable specifics of my life. He did not have a creative edge about him. He seemed to value my efforts of arriving at interpretations of myself, but all too often I felt as if I was teaching myself what I had come to learn from and with him.

Like the film stereotype of the rigid analyst, he was not responsive to my "realistic" questions. By scrupulously avoiding all forms of self-disclosure, I felt he was duplicating my family's secrecy. He remained silent when I needed an empathic reflection of my feelings. Whereas Dr. C had delivered his confrontations in tones of irony, the tonal qualities of Dr. D's voice did not convey liveliness or vitality. I remember him as slouched over in a director's chair that seemed too small for his large and burly body.

Dr. D did not tell me if he agreed or disagreed with my interpretations, with one major exception. We disagreed about my interpretation of his management of the business aspects of our relationship. When my VA insurance benefits for outpatient therapy ran out, during the third year of my analysis, I asked if we could renegotiate the fee. We disagreed about what I should pay. I felt he wanted more than I could afford. I don't know if he bought into Menninger's (1962) then influential assertion that for therapeutic purposes the fee should be a "definite sacrifice" for the patient. I regarded my position as consistent with my commitment to the values of the community mental health center movement (Geller & Fierstein, 1974). In the Outpatient Department of the Connecticut Mental Health Center, where I worked, our mission was to offer long-term psychodynamic psychotherapy to people who could not afford the fees charged by therapists in private practice. A study published in 1977 by Pope, Geller and Wilkinson documented that neither the amount nor the source of the money paid for therapy bore a significant relationship to positive outcomes among the patients seen in our clinic. I was rooting for this finding.

Whatever their meanings, our conflicts over the economics of therapy were never resolved, and I left the analysis prematurely. The shocking discovery that he had made extensive use of material from my analysis to illustrate his theoretical convictions in a published article, without first consulting me, transformed my disappointments in him into disillusionment. I have forgiven my father, but I still have not forgiven Dr. D.

RECLAIMING MY PAST

In each of my therapies I have especially treasured the sessions during which I recovered memories that seemed to have been permanently lost. With Dr. A I learned that I pictured myself walking forward in a straight line. One step behind me, a tall, red brick wall was following me. It moved forward as I did. Its monolithic presence made it impossible for me to look to see where I had come from. We extracted many meanings from this metaphor. Doing so awakened me to the possibility of thinking historically about myself. Dr. A encouraged me to be curious about myself, and I took pleasure in identifying the "originators" of my problems-in-living.

I began my analysis in the hope of recovering many more formative childhood experiences. As my therapy with Dr. B was essentially focused on the here-and-now, I had not progressed very far in my quest to overcome my "childhood amnesia." With Dr. D I reconstructed far less of my childhood than I had hoped but perhaps no less than would have been predicted by Ernst Schactel (1959), one of my favorite authors.

On the other hand, as with all my therapies, analysis did bring about beneficial changes in unforeseen directions. One such unexpected, but greatly appreciated, change was the discovery of the constant flux of visual images that stream through my "inscape" (Hopkins, 1998). While lying on the couch I often closed my eyes in order to make contact with the kaleidoscopic flow of flickering, often grainy, and silent visual images. My memory medium is film montage, not the narratives found in novels. Psychoanalysis strengthened my ability to disallow the censorship of the images that are evoked during regressive and disorganizing experiences. As I was to learn, once one has achieved the ability to "stay with" objectionable fantasies, "an inescapable gap" (Berger, 1995) between imagery and spoken language still remains. Only a pale version of dreams as they are experienced can be reported.

THE LANGUAGE OF DREAMS

I do not think I am deceiving myself by suggesting that my therapies contributed to the transformation and extinction of a nightmarish dream that had tormented me since childhood. In its original form I am running away in fear from two anonymous men. Sometimes I find temporary sanctuary in the tenement apartment of a middle-aged African American woman. Just as I am about to fall asleep on the cot in her kitchen, the two men forcibly gain entrance into the apartment by climbing up the fire escape and by breaking in a window. The next generation of dreams was signaled by the disappearance of one of the men. I was still running away, but I interpreted the dream more optimistically as suggesting that the magnitude of my fears was diminishing.

The final dream in this series took place during my analysis. This time the action occurred at the front door of my house in New Haven. The man was banging on the door and yelling at me. We could see each other through the glass and oak door that separated us. He was wearing a navy blue suit, a white shirt, and a tie. I didn't know who he was. That night, instead of taking flight, I grabbed a baseball bat, opened the door, and said, "Come on in you motherfucker, I'm ready for you."

Obviously, this dream can be interpreted in multiple ways. I would like to think it meant I had developed the courage to face and conquer whatever fears "he" symbolized. Perhaps it signified that I was prepared to integrate into my sense of self the aggressive and destructive qualities that I had previously projected onto him. For me, all interpretations contain an irreducible element of fiction. What is important, though, is the fact that after that night, I no longer had dreams that were so scripted.

THE DEVELOPMENT OF BODY AWARENESS

During and after my psychoanalysis, I experienced the benefits of a variety of practices whose basic operating premise is that changes in personality can be brought about directly by modifying the body structure and its functional motility. These educative or growth-oriented approaches included Feldenkrais's (1949) system of postural and neuromuscular relearning, therapeutic massage, Rolf's (1963) structural integration, and yoga. I also began my ongoing participation in authentic movement groups (Pallaro, 1999) and my study of treatment modalities derived from the creative arts (Clarkson & Geller, 1996; Geller, 1974, 1978). These largely nonverbal, noncognitive practices have complemented and reinforced the benefits I have derived from the "talking cure."

In tandem with psychoanalysis, my involvement in these practices has taught me how to pay attention to the subtle and localized physical sensations that accompany various experiential states, including those altered states of consciousness that occur while free associating. They provided me with alternative modes of communicating the "truths" that even the poets find difficult to express in words. It was deeply reassuring to learn that artists' descriptions of the creative process closely resembled my struggles as a patient.

Singly, and in combination, these experiential approaches enabled me to "embody" the insights I derived from therapy. In psychoanalysis I explored conflicts between "the urge to let go" and the felt necessity to maintain self-control, but it required neuromuscular relearning for me to surrender to passive weight and to experience trust kinesthetically. I learned about the many meanings and functions served by my addiction to cigarettes in analysis, but I learned how to breathe naturally, and without the aid of cigarettes, by doing body-movement work. (I had unconsciously held my breath—a legacy of childhood fears—and thus paradoxically lit cigarettes in order to reinitiate the cycle of inhaling and exhaling). In analysis I sought further understandings of my hyperactivity, but I learned how to sit in stillness, without getting muscularly bound, by doing yoga and other forms of meditation. In psychoanalysis I examined the ways I was at one and the same time an amoral sensualist and a bashful prude, but it required direct body work to melt my "physical armor" (Reich, 1949) so that I could take unconflicted pleasure in sensory experiences.

WRITING AND PSYCHOTHERAPY

Each of my therapies can be characterized in terms of the developmental tasks I was dealing with when I entered treatment. For example, Dr. A accepted my adolescent pretensions while supporting my adult aspirations. He helped me to leave my home and New York City. There is, however, one theme that has recurrently surfaced in all of my psychotherapies—my relationship to writing academic papers, especially those concerning psychotherapy.

In my first therapy, I discovered that the obligation to write term papers within a specified period of time invariably awakened annihilation anxieties. Somehow I had acquired the view that I would perish before reaching my goals or because of my efforts to reach my goals. My inability to accept as valid comforting religious beliefs that could only be explained on the basis of faith intensified my acute fears of death, and what happens after death. As a youth, my deepest connection to other Jews was linked to an intense awareness of the Holocaust and the dangers of anti-Semitism. No one in my family accepted the faith of Judaism or ever went to a synagogue to pray. None of the men on either side of my family were bar mitzvahed. We did not participate in any organized aspects of Jewish life. My favorite uncles mocked the idea that the Jews were the chosen people of the most powerful God. I both envied and felt sorry for those who had a benign vision of the eternal and could apprehend a divine presence at work in the world. My parents were admirably principled but were analytically skeptical about the existence of God. They brought me up to believe in the classical "virtues"—courage, wisdom, justice, and temperance.

Although it is not the full explanation, I recognize a deep connection between having grown up as a nonobservant and unaffiliated Jew and the inchoate spiritual yearnings I brought to each of my therapies, my reluctance to join any school of therapy, and my ongoing struggle to find a theoretical vocabulary in which to write about therapy.

Dread of doing a dissertation figured prominently in my therapy with Dr. C. With him I dealt with the peculiar disappointment that I was not a "genius" and my fears of being mediocre. With him I dealt with my rebellious wish to challenge the strictures of academic formalism. I came to understand that my search for respect and self-worth depended too heavily on what and how much I wrote.

I am deeply committed to providing my patients with unconditional positive regard. But, for as long as I can remember, I have felt that my ultimate value as a man depended on the quality of what I created. Eight and a half- by eleven-inch lined, yellow pieces of paper have been the battleground on which I have struggled with this contradiction. I was compelled to publish so as not to "perish" at Yale. I broodingly anticipated that my productivity would be insufficient to get tenure. At the same time, I felt that I had chosen the wrong medium in which to express my imperious need to create. I considered going to drama school to become a theater director. These issues were an important focus of self-exploration during my analysis. Within this context I learned a great deal about the ways my perfectionism, competitiveness, aggressiveness, narcissism, and exhibitionistic motives complicated my efforts at writing.

DR. E AND VIOLATIONS OF DISTANCE

I deliberately chose Dr. E as my next therapist, in part, because I knew he, too, was conflicted about writing. It was rumored that he had a closet filled with unpublished manuscripts. While in therapy with Dr. E, to keep my ambivalences about continuing to write in the foreground of my awareness, I posted Yeats's (1959, p. 242) poem "The Choice" on our refrigerator door. It begins:

> The intellect of man is forced to choose,
> Perfection of the life, or of the work.

Dr. E was thought to be one of the premier psychoanalytically oriented therapists' therapists in my area. He was widely respected for his intelligence and his clarity of thought. At conferences that I attended, he spoke expertly and eloquently about his work. He impressed me as the kind of man I could respect. He is a European man and has maintained a European style. It pleased me that, like myself, he wore comfortable shoes, corduroy pants, cotton shirts without ties, and sweaters made of soft fabrics. There was a kind of aura about him that was not present in my American therapists, whether they were Jewish (Drs. A, B, and C) or Christian, psychologist or psychiatrist. Dr. D was the only psychiatrist. Dr. E's aura seemed to suggest that he had achieved "wisdom." I could imagine that he was a highly evolved, mature, unusually creative, scholarly, probing yet gentle therapist. I hoped to find in him the idealized model of the type of therapist I hoped I was becoming.

Sadly enough, being Dr. E's patient did not match the fantasy as much as I had hoped. He frequently seemed tired, distracted, inattentive, and melancholy. There were occasional flashes of brilliance and insight that renewed my hope that he was returning to the top of his game. I still meditate on the meanings of his koan-like interpretation: "Jesse, you don't pretend to be who you are not, you pretend you are not who you are." His finest moments seemed to take place when he said goodbye at the end of a session. His exit lines (e.g., "Till next time") had in them the promise that maybe next time things would get better.

When I felt Dr. E enjoyed my presence, I was able to relax and turn my attention to my inner life. If I felt his presence could not be taken for granted, I became preoccupied instead with our relationship. While in therapy with Dr. E, I belonged to an informal network of his current and former patients. We were all therapists. Comparing our experiences with him was reassuring. We admitted to one another that Dr. E seemed to fall asleep, occasionally, during therapy sessions. We compared the differing ways we reacted to his eyes glazing over and his unwillingness to acknowledge his obvious fatigue. Some feared that he found them boring. I deeply resented the times he acted as if I could not make impartial judgments about his lapses of interest.

We speculated about how his personal life was affecting his work. Some details were known to us. This knowledge softened our disappointments in Dr. E. There are no objective or absolute standards against which to judge the intensity, breadth, and persistence of a therapist's interest in a patient. Therefore, it is very difficult to locate the boundary beyond which the felt inability to take and show lively interest in a patient warrants an apology or an inquiry. Our inner circle of therapist-patients of Dr. E found these ambiguities a hardship.

In a previously published article (Geller, 1994) I used clinical material from my therapy with Dr. E (I disguised my identity) to illustrate how to understand the temptation to emotionally withdraw from a patient. What I wish to underscore here is the following proposition: Like getting "too close" to a patient, markedly diminished interest in a patient carries with it ethical as well as technical implications. I believe a boundary violation occurs when the depth and breadth of a therapist's interest falls below the levels a patient has a "right" to expect. Gross reductions of interest constitute a violation of distance (Katherine, 1991).

TERMINATION THERAPY WITH DR. E

During the second year of my therapy with Dr. E, I experienced a major episode of writer's block. I was trying to finish a paper on the role of separation and loss in psychotherapy (1987). My life was in turmoil because of the continuing crises triggered by our younger daughter's deafness (Geller, 1996) and the decision of the Yale Department of Psychiatry not to promote me. Dr. E gave me permission to stop writing. "Jesse, you don't have to finish this paper if you don't want to." But, for reasons I still only incompletely understand, I persisted. It therefore seemed fitting that Dr. E would say to me, in a dream that I took as a signal that I was moving toward termination, "Jesse, you can have a room of your own." In the dream, we are standing face-to-face in a well-lit but unfurnished attic. As you may recall, *A Room of One's Own* is the title of Virginia Wolff's (1927) essay on what is required for a writer's life.

CONCLUSION

I approached writing this chapter in the spirit of those who discover what they believe and wish to say in the act of writing. While writing this chapter, I made connections that were not evident to me before. I was surprised to see how much I had triangulated my teachers and therapists, thereby recreating a pattern that was laid down when I felt caught between my father and my uncles. Looking back and seeing from whence I came has deepened my appreciation of the ways identifications and counteridentifications with my therapists have shaped my attitudes toward those aspects of therapeutic practice that are not covered in formal training programs, and are not readily manualized. These include, but are not limited to, my conversational style, the fees I charge for my services, the importance I assign to embodying consciousness, and the centrality of presence.

Autobiographical accounts of therapists' experiences in therapy can be written in various genres. We don't need more confessionals. As a result of writing this chapter, I have come to the conclusion that it would be advantageous to set for ourselves the task of finding narrative formats that would enable therapists to explore the nonrational and irrational sources of their handling of the ambiguities and unscripted aspects of therapy.

Psychotherapy theories are, at best, skeletal and only loosely based on empirically grounded information. I would, therefore, recommend that writing an essay devoted to the question *How has my biography influenced my theoretical and clinical dispositions?* should become an integral part of the professional education of all therapists. Armed with this knowledge, therapists would, I believe, practice the "applied science" (Geller, 1998) of psychotherapy more effectively.

REFERENCES

Bachelard, G. (1994). *The poetics of space.* Boston: Beacon Press.

Berger, J. (1995). *Ways of seeing.* New York: Viking.

Bowlby, J. (1973). *Attachment and loss: Vol. 2. Separation.* New York: Basic Books.

Clarkson, G., & Geller, J. D. (1996). The Bonny Method from a psychoanalytic perspective: insights from working with a psychoanalytic therapist in a guided imagery and music series. *Arts in Psychotherapy, 23,* 311–331.

Dalai Lama, & Cutler, H. C. (1998). *The art of happiness.* New York: Riverbeach Books.

Erikson, E. H. (1963). *Childhood and society* (2nd ed.) New York: Norton.

Feldenkrais, M. (1949). *Body and mature behavior.* New York: International Universities Press.

Freud, S. (1912/1953). Recommendations on psychoanalytic technique. In J. Strachey (Ed. and Trans.), *The standard edition of the complete psychological works of Sigmund Freud* (Vol. 6). London: Hogarth.

Geller, J. D. (1974). Dance therapy as viewed by a psychotherapist. *American Dance Therapy Association Monograph, 3,* 1–23.

Geller, J. D. (1978). The body, expressive movement and physical contact in psychotherapy. In J. Singer & K. Pope (Eds.), *The power of the human imagination.* New York: Plenum.

Geller, J. D. (1987). The process of psychotherapy: Separation and the complex interplay among empathy, insight and internalization. In J. B. Feshbach & S. Feshbach (Eds.). *The psychotherapy of separation and loss.* San Francisco: Jossey-Bass.

Geller, J. D. (1994). The psychotherapist's experience of interest and boredom. *Psychotherapy, 31,* 3–16.

Geller, J. D. (1996). Thank you for Jenny. In B. Gerson (Ed.), *The therapist as a person.* New York: Analytic Press.

Geller, J. D. (1998). What does it mean to practice psychotherapy scientifically? *Psychoanalysis and Psychotherapy, 15,* 187–215.

Geller, J. D. & Fierstein, A. (1974). Professional training within community mental health centers. In G. Farwell, N. Gumsky, & P. Coughlan. (Eds.) *The education of counselors.* Gretna, LA: Pelican Press.

Hopkins, G. M. (1998). *The selected poems of Gerard Manley Hopkins.* New York: Oxford University Press.

Horney, K. (1966). *New ways in psychoanalysis.* New York: Norton.

Kaiser, H. (1965). *Effective psychotherapy* (L. B. Fierman, Ed.). New York: Free Press.

Katherine, A. (1991). *Boundaries.* New York: Hazelden.

Menninger, K. (1962). *Theory of psychoanalytic technique.* New York: Basic Books.

Oates, J. C. (1999, July 19). Writers on writing. *New York Times,* p. 10.

Pallaro, P. (1999). *Authentic movement: Essays by M.S. Whitehouse, Janet Adler and Joan Chodorow.* London: Kingsley.

Pope, K., Geller, J. D., & Wilkinson, L. (1977). Fee assessment and outpatient psychotherapy. *Journal of Clinical and Consulting Psychology, 1,* 11–14.

Reich, W. (1949). *Character analysis.* New York: Orgone Institute Press.

Rolf, I. P. (1963). Structural integration. *Systematics, 1,* 66–83.

Schactel, E. (1959). *Metamorphosis: On the development of affect, perception, attention and memory.* New York: Basic Books.

Schafer, R. (1983). *The analytic attitude.* New York: Basic Books.

Shapiro, D. (1975). Dynamic and holistic ideas of neurosis and psychotherapy. *Psychiatry, 33,* 218–226.

Simon, P. C. (1973) Tenderness. On *There goes rhymin' Simon,* BHI. Compact disk.

Stern, D. B. (1983). Unformulated experience. *Contemporary Psychoanalysis, 10,* 71–99.

Wolff, V. (1927). *A room of one's own.* London: Harcourt Brace.

Yeats, W. B. (1959). *The collected poems of W.B. Yeats.* New York: Macmillan.

9

THE PERSONAL THERAPY EXPERIENCES OF A RATIONAL EMOTIVE-BEHAVIOR THERAPIST

Windy Dryden

In Britain today, most professional bodies require psychotherapists to have had personal therapy before being registered or accredited. While professional bodies representing different therapeutic approaches specify the length and frequency of such personal therapy, this is not the case with more general professional bodies. Both the British Association for Counselling and the Division of Counselling Psychology of the British Psychological Society now specify that accredited (in the first case) and chartered (in the second case) practitioners have to have a minimum of 40 hours of personal therapy. What is so magical about 40 hours? Neither body has given a convincing argument for this figure and certainly not one that stems from the research literature.

When I began my training as a counsellor in Britain (in 1974), there were few general accrediting professional bodies and there was very little guidance (outside the analytic tradition) concerning whether to seek personal therapy, let alone what type one should seek and how long and how frequently one should seek it. What follows, then, is an account of my personal therapy experiences from my contemporary position strongly in the rational emotive-behaviour therapy (REBT) tradition.

In recounting my history of personal therapy I will cover experiences of individual and group therapy that I had before my training as a counselor and after I began training. I will also discuss the personal development groups that I attended, which were a mandatory part of three periods of my professional training. Finally, I will discuss instances of self-help because they illuminate why I derived so little help from consulting my fellow practitioners. After relating each episode (or related episodes) of personal therapy, I will comment on my experiences.

THREE FUNERALS AND A WEDDING

The first time I entered personal therapy was at the end of 1974. I had just started my professional training as a counselor and, at the age of 24 years, was suffering from general feelings of unhappiness, a sense that my life was something of an effort even though I had clear vocational goals and was pursuing them. Had I completed the Beck Depression Inventory at that time, I would have scored in the mild to moderate range of depression. So I decided to seek personal therapy partly to deal with state of unhappiness but also because I thought that I *should* be in personal therapy, given that I was training to become a counselor. Even though there was no edict at that time from any professional body that I was associated with, there was a "feeling" that being in personal therapy was "a good thing," a view that was expressed by the various psychoanalytic associations. In Britain at that time (and to a lesser extent today) counseling was dominated by psychoanalytic and person-centered practitioners. The person-centered school recommended the inclusion of personal development groups in the therapeutic curriculum, and the psychoanalytic school recommended personal therapy as a mandatory activity, which had to take place away from the training institution where one was being trained.

I do not recall why I chose to seek a psychoanalytic personal therapist, but I do remember at that time uncritically accepting what I now consider to be a myth: that psychoanalytic therapy is "deeper" than other approaches.

Funeral 1

I am being somewhat unkind to therapists in this account by referring to my experience with them as *funerals*. What I mean to convey is that they were more or less ineffective from the point of view of helping me overcome my malaise. My first therapist was a middle-aged, male Jewish therapist (as I am now) and, I think, a Kleinian. My uncertainty stems from the fact that the person who referred me to him only said he was psychoanalytic by persuasion. My therapist certainly didn't tell me anything directly about his therapeutic orientation, and I didn't ask because at that time it never occurred to me to ask.

This therapist was not austere in his demeanor but neutral and strictly interpretative. Whenever I was speaking he buried his head in his hands, and on the infrequent occasions when he was about to say something, he would rock forward, take his hands away from his mouth, make an interpretation—which I usually found puzzling—and then return to his normal pose. My attempts to seek clarification about his interpretations were met by silence or by a further interpretation, along the lines that I wanted him to feed me (hence my guess that he was Kleinian). Indeed, as I recall, this was his favorite interpretation.

This therapy was unstructured and open ended. I had the sense that I could talk about whatever I wanted and that I could see him for as long as I wanted. Actually, the therapy lasted for about six months of weekly sessions because I was moving away from London and was reluctant to make the weekly trips back to London to see him. While I was not sorry to end, I have always wondered how (and indeed if) it would have progressed had I stayed. One thing was clear at the end of this episode of personal therapy: I still experienced the same sense of unhappiness.

Funeral 2

My second venture into personal therapy was with a psychiatrist who taught a module on "psychiatry" in the counseling program I had finished in July 1975 and in which I made the transition to lecturer in August 1975. I asked this man for a recommendation of someone who might take me on, since I still wanted to get to the bottom of my unhappiness. He suggested that he could see me himself in his National Health Service clinic at the local psychiatric hospital. I should add in his defense that the issue of dual relationships was not as sharply drawn as is now the case. I was just pleased at his suggestion and gratefully accepted his offer.

I knew that this second therapist was also psychoanalytically oriented, but he was far more interactive than my previous therapist. He also practiced psychodrama, and we used several psychodrama techniques over the time that I saw him. About five or six months after I had started to see him, he told me that he had to end the therapy because he was leaving his practice to work full-time as a senior lecturer in psychiatry. I understood this and experienced a good sense of closure, since he also arranged for me to see a colleague in the same clinic. My abiding memories of this second episode of personal therapy was that my therapist took voluminous notes at the beginning, which I found off-putting. However, he was quite happy to stop doing so when I asked him to. I also remember the psychodrama techniques and found them quite useful in getting me out of my head and more into my experience. My most vivid memory, as I look back on this experience, was that we both smoked cigars during therapy sessions but that his were longer than mine!

There was again no therapeutic contract at the beginning and, like my first experience, it had an open-ended quality about it. My feelings of unhappiness persisted.

Funeral 3

I was then referred to a man who was one of the few fully trained psychoanalysts working in the Midlands. However, he did briefer work in the clinic, where I had been seeing the second therapist and he had agreed to take me on at the request of that person. In all, I had eight sessions with this man, and it was an experience I found quite frustrating. Again, there was no therapeutic contract and no agreed time limit as part of this contract. In my innocence I was operating on the assumption that again the therapy would be open ended. My third therapist was neutral and cold. Looking back, I never experienced my first therapist as cold, even though he was strictly neutral. Somehow I sensed that he did have a concern for my well-being. However, this was not the case with my third therapist. I also remember that on one occasion I asked him whether what I was experiencing was transference and received quite a sarcastic reply. No, this man didn't show any concern for me as I look back, and this was also how I felt at the time.

I am drawn to books on therapy that seek to explore key therapy moments—crucial sessions and turning points in the therapeutic process—for I can still remember quite vividly the eighth and final session that I had with this man. He began the session by announcing that this was to be our last session. I am very sure, looking back, that we had not agreed on an eight-session contract (or any other time-limited contract), and my sense of shock and bewilderment at the time strengthens me in my retrospective view on this point. He then said, casually, and this is really clear in my mind, that if I wanted to continue to see him then I could do so in his private practice. I can't recall how I responded to this, other than to decline the invitation and to get myself out of his office as soon as I could. The lasting impression that I have of this man is that he was arrogant. I recall him being late for one session and offering no apology or explanation for his behavior. When I brought this up in the session, he dismissed my legitimate complaint and proceeded to interpret my reaction.

I remember to this day feeling dazed as I made my way home after the final session. I just couldn't believe what had happened. Had I imagined it? Had I offended him in some way? I was given no explanation for this abrupt termination except that this was to be the last session.

. . . and a Wedding

Having been dismissed by this third psychoanalytic therapist, I decided to fall back on my own resources. Earlier in my life I had overcome my public-speaking anxiety, which I had developed due to my attitude toward a speech impediment, by implementing a technique that I heard described on the radio. In brief, I resolved to speak up at every opportunity—without recourse to the myriad of ways I had developed to prevent myself from stammering—while telling myself: "If I stammer, I stammer. Fuck it!!" Not only did I largely overcome my anxiety by this method, I stammered far less than previously.

Those who know anything about REBT will recognize this as an unschooled version of one of its major techniques: the rehearsal of a rational belief while simultaneously confronting one's fears. Consequently, it will not come as too much of a surprise to learn that in 1976 I turned for inspiration to *A New Guide to Rational Living*, an REBT self-help book written by Albert Ellis and Robert Harper (1975). We had briefly studied REBT during my counseling program a year or so earlier, and I remembered resonating to Ellis's ideas about the theory and practice of psychotherapy, but I didn't have time to study REBT in depth because we were mainly concerned with the work of Carl Rogers.

On reading about the REBT perspective on psychological problems and their remediation, I quickly saw that my unhappiness was due to feelings of inferiority about various personal issues. I further realized that the reason I suffered from such feelings was because I held a number of irrational beliefs about myself in relation to achievement and approval. At last I had found what I was looking for: an approach that spelled out for me a perspective that I could make sense of and relate to (that I was unhappy because of the rigid and extreme beliefs I had about myself) and a way of overcoming these feelings (by identifying, challenging, and changing these beliefs using a variety of cognitive, imaginal, behavioral, and emotive techniques).

So my self-help therapy gave me what my therapist-delivered therapy failed to—clear information about a conceptualization of my psychological problems that I accepted and specific guidelines of how to overcome these problems. Not one of my three individual therapists had given me any kind of account of how they conceptualized my problems, and none of them gave me any guidelines at all concerning how to remediate those problems. I am not saying that all clients require such clarity, but I certainly did. If they had given me specific directions about conceptualization and treatment, I could have given my informed consent to proceed or decided that I did not want to continue.

You may be wondering whether I was not given this information because I was expected to know it, being a trainee counselor. I doubt this because (1) openness was not a feature of my therapists' behavior in other areas and (2) they did not even inquire of me whether I wanted this information. At any rate, if any of my therapists decided not to give me information about conceptualization and treatment because they thought I would know this already, then they were sadly mistaken.

COMMENTS

None of my three therapists made any significant attempt to explain to me how they conceptualized psychological problems in general or my problems in particular. This is what Bordin (1979) considers a key therapist *task* and forms an important part of eliciting informed consent from the patient. Thus, none of my three therapists elicited my informed consent to proceed with therapy. While some would regard this as an ethical oversight, I will be charitable and say that my therapists were following the analytic tradition, where such explicit explanations are generally eschewed. Clearly, this lack of explanation did not meet my psychological "need" for explicitness. I am a person who likes to know clearly what help I am being offered so I can make my own mind up whether or not I wish to proceed. My attempts to elicit such clarity were either ignored, interpreted, or, in the case of my third therapist, ridiculed. Why did I not decide earlier that psychoanalytic therapy was not for me? Simply because I did not have the confidence in my judgment to do so.

Looking back, I thought that if I stayed in psychoanalytic therapy long enough, I would be helped by the process, despite evidence to the contrary. This taught me that clients may place too much faith in their therapists, who they think know what is best for them. As a therapist, I emphasize to my clients that what I have to offer them is one approach to understanding client problems and how to address them, and I stress that there are other approaches available. I tell them that if what I have to offer is not perceived as helpful to them then they are not to blame, and that I will make every effort to refer them to a practitioner who may be able to help them more effectively. As my friend and colleague Arnold Lazarus (Dryden, 1991) has said, making judicious referrals is a skill and a mark of therapist maturity. None of my individual therapists raised this as a possibility. Did they fail to do so because they knew I was a therapist-in-training and thought that I could be expected to know about their approach to the therapy they were practicing? Did they assume that I had already made an informed decision that I wished to proceed with therapy in each case? As I said earlier, I doubt that they had made such assumptions; even if they had, then they were in error. What I have learned from this is not to assume that therapists-in-training or even trained therapists have given informed consent to proceed without explicitly eliciting such consent first, unless there is powerful evidence to the contrary.

None of these three therapists discussed in this section explained to me what my tasks were in therapy or, for that matter, explained what tasks they were going to engage in during the therapeutic process. My guess is that either I was expected to know as a counseling trainee or, more likely, I was expected to just talk about whatever I was disturbed about at the time. It was all very unstructured and loose when I needed clarity and structure. The exception to this was the second therapist, who asked me if I wanted to try out some psychodrama techniques on several issues that I was exploring. My recollection was that this therapist introduced the possibility of using these techniques in a relaxed, nonpressuring way, and I was pleased with both the offer and how it was made.

Bordin (1979) has argued that it is important for therapist and client to agree on the latter's *goals* for change. This does not mean that the therapist uncritically accepts the client's goals. Rather, it means discussing openly the issue of goals so that agreed objectives emerge from such dialogue. It would have been helpful to me if my individual therapists had initiated such a discussion (for I do believe that it is the therapist's responsibility to do so). While I now understand the psychoanalytic position on goals, I did not realize this then, and therefore I was looking toward my therapists for guidance on this issue—guidance that never came. Even if I couldn't realistically have expected my therapists to change their practice to accommodate to my preference, was it too much to expect them to elicit my position so that they could judge whether I was suitable for their mode of treatment? I think not. Again, in my practice, I attempt to elicit my clients' views on this point, and I am clear with them concerning my position on eliciting goals for change.

It should be clear by now that none of my therapists understood what I thought might be most helpful to me from therapy. Such understanding forms one important part of what Bordin (1979) refers to as the *bond* component of the working alliance. Another aspect of the bond relevant to these personal therapies concerns the interpersonal connection between therapist and client. The relationship between the first therapist and myself was fairly neutral. Behind his steadfast interpretative stance, I sensed he was a fairly kindly man, but this was only a shadowy impression.

As I said earlier, I knew the second therapist in a different context, in that he taught in my counselor training program when I was a student and continued to teach this module during the time that I consulted him, when I was lecturing on the same course. So I knew him in other contexts and experienced him as someone who was reasonably caring. This side of him came to the fore after I had requested that he stop taking notes and give me greater face-to-face contact. Before this I sensed that he was hiding behind his psychiatrist role. He responded well to my request, and from that point I would characterize our therapeutic relationship as two colleagues, one senior and the other junior, working to help the latter toward some unspecified goal. Of all the individual therapists I consulted, he was the one who best understood my need to be active in therapy and suggested on occasion that we use psychodrama techniques. I would say that of the three therapists discussed in this section, I had the smoothest relationship with him and the most difficult relationship with the third therapist.

I didn't have the sense that the third therapist was listening attentively to me. He may have been, but as Rogers (1957) wisely said, for the core conditions to have a therapeutic impact on the client, the client has to experience their presence. If the therapist is listening attentively and the client does not experience this, then there will accrue no positive impact for the client. Indeed I experienced him as detached, uncaring, and somewhat arrogant. The way he abruptly and unilaterally terminated therapy, along with the offer that he could continue to see me as a patient in his private practice, showed the somewhat exploitative nature of this man's work with me and perhaps his greed. In brief, I didn't much care for him and sensed also that he didn't much care for me. By today's standards, I suppose one could argue that there were abusive elements to this relationship. I am thinking here of his unilateral announcement, without any prior warning, that he was terminating the therapy.

To be charitable, one might argue that in 1976 the importance of planning for termination was not as much appreciated as it is now, and the practice of moving patients from the National Health Service where therapy is free to the private (fee-paying) sector may not have been viewed as unethical, as it would be now. However, this man was a fully trained psychoanalyst, for goodness sake, and a full member of the Institute of Psychoanalysis, one of the most prestigious psychoanalytic institutes in the world. Even at that time, I am sure that his colleagues would have been shocked by his behavior toward me. The fact that I used this experience to very good effect should not be used to condone this behavior.

I described earlier how I gave up on therapist-delivered therapy and turned, with good results, to self-help. Why was this experience more effective for me than more than one year's therapy delivered by well-qualified practitioners? First, I resonated much more with the REBT explanatory model than with the psychoanalytic one, such as I understood it. I liked the fact that when I read Ellis and Harper's (1975) *A New Guide to Rational Living*, the authors, from the very outset, made perfectly clear how they conceptualized emotional disorders. However, even if my therapists had clearly stated the psychoanalytic view of psychopathology, I would still have favored the REBT view. Why? Because it emphasized the role of cognitive factors, which struck a real chord with me in helping me to understand not only my own problems but also those of my clients. Up to that time, I was still practicing person-centered therapy, but my encounter with this REBT self-help book and my subsequent successful self-help efforts led me to decide to retrain in REBT, a decision I have never regretted.

Second, I resonated with the REBT's direct, clearly understood, and, some would say, no-nonsense approach to dealing with one's emotional problems. It was never really clear to me how talking in an open-ended way, as in my psychoanalytic therapies, would help me to overcome my sense of unhappiness, but it was crystal clear to me on reading Ellis & Harper's (1975) book what I needed to do to free myself of these feelings. I needed to identify, challenge, and change my irrational beliefs and act in ways that were consistent with the rational alternatives to these beliefs. Simple, but not easy, as we say in REBT.

For me, one of the problems with these individual therapies was that they were too open-ended with respect to goals. None of my therapists asked me what I wanted to achieve from therapy. When I began to use REBT with myself, I not only asked myself what my problems were, I asked myself where I wanted to be with respect to each of these problems. I saw that my problems at the time were to do with feelings of inferiority, and I wanted to be more self-accepting. The REBT position on unconditional self-acceptance (Dryden, 1999b) was a revelation to me. It encouraged me to view myself as equal in humanity to all other humans, to fully acknowledge my weaknesses as well as my strengths, and to appreciate that the existence of the former did not mean that I was inferior and that I could address them nondefensively. Carl Rogers's (1957) notion of unconditional positive regard did not have a similar impact on me, since it was, as I saw it then, encouraging people to prize rather to accept themselves.

Having a clear idea where I was headed on this issue, as well as how to work toward getting there, were key ingredients to the progress I made in overcoming my unhappiness. I should add that in my overenthusiasm I did not appreciate at the time that it is not possible to achieve perfect self-acceptance. I realize now that this is a lifelong process and that whereas I am far more self-accepting now that I was then, I still have my vulnerabilities in this area. This fact, however, does not discourage me.

It is perhaps strange to think of developing a bond with yourself, but in self-help that is precisely what happens. In helping myself overcoming my malaise, I developed a more accurate understanding of myself than my personal therapists had shown toward me. This was because I used the REBT perspective to understand myself. Note that I could not use the psychoanalytic perspective to do this, nor was I helped to do so by any of my personal therapists.

Finally, an important aspect of the therapeutic bond is pacing. All of my therapists worked too slowly with me, another feature of the psychoanalytic approach with which I did not resonate. By contrast, when I used REBT to help myself, I was able to do so at my own, quicker rate.

From all these experiences, I have learned the following, which I routinely implement my practice as a therapist.

1. I explain to clients exactly what REBT is and outline broadly the kinds of tasks I am likely to implement and the kinds of tasks they will be called upon to engage in. I elicit their reactions and, if they indicate that REBT is not the type of therapy they are seeking, I refer them to a therapist who is likely to meet their treatment preferences—as long as these preferences do not perpetuate the clients' problems.
2. I help my clients to specify their problems and what they want to achieve with respect to each of these problems. Then I focus therapy on helping my clients to achieve their goals.
3. I strive to develop the kind of bond that will facilitate the treatment process and if I consider that any of my colleagues can better develop a stronger bond with any of the people that are seeking my help, I do not hesitate to effect a suitable referral. I am fortunate that financial considerations do not compromise my position on this issue, since I am not dependent on my practice for my livelihood.

Having described and commented on my experiences of both therapist-delivered and self-help therapy, let me move on to my experiences of being a member of a therapy group that I joined in the final year of my undergraduate degree—before I began to train as a counselor.

ONE YEAR OF GROUP THERAPY

The therapeutic experiences I have just related were not actually my first experience of being a client. In May 1970, toward the end of my second year of my undergraduate degree, I decided to stop working for my exams and to feign illness. I was sent to see the college psychiatrist, who decided that I needed to join a psychodynamic group that was being convened at the beginning of the next academic session in October 1970 that he was running with a psychiatrist colleague. In the interim, however, I finally got my act together and resat the exams in July, which I duly passed.

I dutifully joined the group, which was made up of about eight patients and two therapists, who both took a fairly inactive, interpretative role. I did admit to the group that I had feigned illness after about six months, but since I was well over my crisis by then, this disclosure didn't really help me.

Looking back, I think that my stopping working and feigning illness was an attempt to get out of something that I did not enjoy (second-year psychology topics are notoriously tedious), and I hoped that I could go into the final year of the course on the basis of my course work in lieu of passing the exams. Once I had tested the system and realized that I couldn't avoid the second-year examinations, I faced up to my responsibilities and studied hard from that point forward. My decision to take responsibility did not come from my participation in the group, since all this happened before I joined the group.

I did learn one thing from the group sessions that proved to be a valuable life lesson. I became friendly with one of the group members, and we started to meet socially (which, if I recall, was not prohibited by our group membership). This friendship turned out to be very one-sided; and if I did not contact him, he wouldn't contact me. Initially, I disturbed myself about this lack of reciprocity and even confronted him about it in the group. He apologized and promised to initiate contact, but didn't. At this point I remember changing my attitude about it. I reasoned that he was the person he was and not the person I expected him to be and if I wanted to be friends with him, I had to realize that I would have to initiate contact because he wasn't going to. Once I accepted this grim reality, I calmed down and decided to remain friends with the guy. He never did initiate contact, but I was undisturbed about it. Looking back on this episode, it occurs to me that I never shared my self-authored insight with the group since I tend to work things out in my head rather than through dialogue with other people.

So what else did I learn from being in the group? Precious little, other than that psychodynamically oriented groups were not for me. This was a lesson that I had to relearn several times, as I will presently discuss. Of course, some would say that being a member of the group helped me to come to this realization, and indeed this may be true, despite my protestations to the contrary. However, this hypothesis is impossible to disprove. All I can say is that it didn't seem to me either at the time or in retrospect that being in the group had a bearing on my adjustment to my friend's behavior.

COMMENTS

Looking back, I really don't know why I was referred to this psychodynamic group. Certainly, when I saw the psychiatrist for an assessment interview and he made the recommendation that I join the group, he did not give me any kind of rationale for my joining. My impression is that he needed to get sufficient numbers for the group to be viable and there were no strong contraindications that would rule me out as a group member. At the time I was in awe of this psychiatrist (because of his status rather than his personality); if he thought that I needed to join a group for one year, then he must be right. After all, he was the professional and I was a mere undergraduate. Now, of course, I know different. As a practitioner, I regard giving clients a clear rationale for treatment as paramount, and I make sure that they think carefully about my treatment recommendations before accepting them.

One of the features of this group experience was the inactivity of the group therapists. Much of the work was done by the group members, who often gave each other fairly inept advice. When the therapists did intervene, it was to make interpretations, and if these were ignored, as they generally were, they remained silent. From what I could see, very few of the group members derived much benefit from the year of group therapy.

This experience taught me that it was important for a group therapist not only to encourage interaction between members but also to intervene frequently in the group process. This helps group members focus on their goals and presents a corrective force when they give each other bad advice. The way I do this as an REBT group therapist is to highlight any helpful aspects of the proferred advice and then to focus on the psychological issues that group members often overlook when they advise one another (Dryden, 1999a). In this way I strive to preserve the motivation of the group members to be helpful to one another, while focusing their attention to what they need to do psychologically to achieve their goals. As an REBT group therapist, I see myself as having a gate-keeping role, whereby I encourage fruitful interaction between group members, and an educative role, whereby I encourage members to use REBT techniques to help themselves and one another. The two group therapists running the group I have just described were rather poor gate-keepers, often allowing unhelpful interactions between group members to develop unchecked, and were poor educators in that they did not provide explanations for their interpretations.

FOUR TEDIOUS YEARS OF PERSONAL DEVELOPMENT GROUPS

In all, I experienced four years of being in three personal development groups. Frankly, I found them something of a waste of time. Since they were composed of students who saw one another in other contexts (academic, supervisory, and social), most of us were on our guard concerning what we said in the group about our lives and about our feelings toward one another. Not that such groups were unhelpful for everyone. From what I could see, they especially helped socially inhibited members, who learned that they could talk about themselves and even confront other group members and that nothing terrible resulted from such disclosures and confrontations. Since I already knew this, I decided to knuckle down and play the game, which seemed to be that one talked about oneself at length every five or six weeks and said something in every other group when others were talking at length. It seemed that unless you did this, you became the focus of the other group members, who wanted to know why you were silent or distancing yourself from the group.

I make no apologies for sounding cynical about these groups, but I do apologize to my past students for making them a mandatory part of counseling programs that I have run. I did so not because I thought that they were of any value but because professional accrediting bodies expect them to be a part of the training curriculum, and I didn't want to disadvantage my students by depriving them of this "mandatory" experience.

COMMENTS

These personal development groups were, strictly speaking, not therapy groups but more like sensitivity groups. Group members were not seen as having personal problems for which they needed help but as developing professionals who needed to become more aware of themselves and their impact on other people. This is quite a reasonable activity for counselors-in-training to be engaged in, and I wouldn't have objected to attending one such group for a year. What I objected to was having to attend three such groups over a four-year period. My requests for exemption fell on deaf years, for a reason that I can understand, being a counselor trainer myself, but which ultimately cannot be justified, since the raison d'être of a personal development group (PDG) is the "personal development" of its individual members. It was thought that if trainees could exempt themselves from being a member of a personal development group, then this would produce a schism in the training cohort, which would split into "attenders" and "nonattenders." Trainers are very wary of permitting any practices that divide a training cohort and that deprive group members of a forum where they could discuss their feelings about the course and about other course members in a group facilitated by a person external to the course. However, I am not speaking against having a forum for course members to discuss the course, although in my view this needs to be done with the course director present.

It seemed, therefore, that my continuing membership in these personal development groups had more to do with promoting harmony (or at least minimizing conflict) in a cohort of trainees than with facilitating the personal development of individual trainees. My argument at the time was that my own particular personal development could have been better promoted outside the group setting, and I still hold to this view.

I mentioned that in my personal development groups many trainees were wary about what they said because they had to see their fellow trainees in other settings. If membership in a personal development group is to be a mandatory training experience, it would be more sensible if such groups were made up of students from different training courses so that each group member of a PDG would only meet with other members in the PDG setting. The practice of putting trainees in patient groups addresses this issue but raises a number of other issues, a discussion of which is beyond the scope of this chapter. My suggested alternative would also mean that trainees who had previously attended a PDG would not be obligated to attend another. If this practice had been in operation when I did my training, I would have been spared three tedious years of attending PDG groups and would only have had to put up with one such year!

PREPARING FOR A MIDLIFE CRISIS THAT NEVER HAPPENED: TWO MONTHS OF JUNGIAN THERAPY

As I approached my fortieth birthday, I decided to reenter personal therapy to prepare for my midlife crisis. I should say that I wasn't experiencing a crisis at the time, nor have I subsequently had the crisis, but I was persuaded by the idea that preparing oneself adequately for a crisis is better psychologically than responding to that crisis after it happens. This time I deliberately chose a Jungian therapist, on the basis that Jung's work seemed especially suited to midlife issues, and I wanted to see a female therapist, merely because all my previous therapists had been male.

I remained in this therapy for about two months. It became clear to me fairly quickly and, I believe, also to my therapist that I was not suited to a Jungian approach. For one thing, I couldn't remember any of my dreams, which I think my therapist found somewhat frustrating, since it seemed to me that she liked to work with dreams. In addition, I found talking more helpful than her interventions, which, to some degree, took me away from my train of thought, but not in a productive way. So I decided to terminate—an ending that was mutually agreed, well-planned, and amicable. This ending enabled us to work together on a collegial, professional level much later. These contacts revealed her to be much warmer and humorous than she ever was as my therapist!

COMMENTS

When I first entered individual therapy I had just begun to train as a counselor, and therefore it could have been said that I was naive in deciding to go into a psychoanalytic form of therapy. My knowledge of what was available in the therapeutic scene was fairly limited, and my major preoccupation was to find a therapist who came highly recommended. However, 16 or so years on, I could not be said to be naive. I had already had a good deal of therapy and had discovered that I was more suited to a cognitive-behavioral approach than a psychoanalytic one. So what possessed me to go into Jungian therapy? I have already given one explanation: Jung's approach was said to be particularly suited for those wishing to explore midlife conflicts and although I hadn't begun to be affected by such issues, I was taking preventative measures. I also wanted to see a woman.

But as I have engaged in writing this chapter, it is also clearer to me that I would not have made a very good client of cognitive-behavior therapy either, not in the early 1990s at any rate. If I had sought help from a cognitive-behavior therapist at this point, I would have had to curb my tendency (which, as I write, I see would have been clearly present) to supervise my therapist. If I may humbly say so, I have been a leading proponent of REBT in particular, and of cognitive-behavior therapy in general, for a number of years; I had obtained by the early 1990s a reputation in the field. I was probably Britain's leading REBT therapist and could not envisage consulting one of the very small band of trained British REBT therapists. First, I knew them all quite well and had trained most of them; second, I would have been sorely tempted to supervise them and correct their errors! In addition, I did not think of consulting a more generic CBT therapist, because that person would not have focused on my irrational beliefs but would have chosen instead to focus on my cognitive distortions and the like, which I would have found frustrating, as I did when I trained in Beck's cognitive therapy in 1981, after I had trained as an REBT therapist a few years earlier.

So it is a bit rich of me to criticize my Jungian therapist for practicing an approach which I must have known in my heart of hearts I would not resonate with. This, of course, turned out to be the case, and thus I do not feel inclined to be too critical of her.

I will only comment on one further thing. As I mentioned earlier, years after this therapy had ended, I met my ex-therapist in a professional activity and found her to be a charming, warm woman with a good sense of humor. These qualities were not apparent to me when I was her patient. This raises for me an interesting question. In adopting a fairly neutral therapeutic style, do psychodynamic therapists (and I include Jungians here) lose much of the therapeutic potency of their natural interpersonal style and qualities? My experience is that they probably do.

CONSULTING WITH ALBERT ELLIS

The final personal "therapy" experience concerns the consultations I have had over the years with Albert Ellis, the founder of REBT and the person I most consider a mentor. For over 20 years I have made annual visits to what is now known as the Albert Ellis Institute in New York City. Whenever I go I arrange to see Albert Ellis, in what are known as his lunchtime and suppertime sessions. These are, in effect, his breaks between therapy sessions. While for the most part I have used these sessions to discuss matters relating to (1) finer points of the theory and practice of REBT;

(2) problems I have had in my clinical practice of REBT; and (3) joint writing projects, I have on various occasions used these sessions to consult with Al on a number of personal issues. Normally, these have been issues where I have failed to identify a subtle factor that has eluded me and thus I have not been able to get to the heart of the matter. Invariably, Al has helped me to identify this factor and has trusted me to take remedial steps to deal with the clarified problem on my own.

COMMENTS

Of all the therapist-delivered treatment I have had—and when I put together all of them, I am shocked to learn how much therapy I have had (with so little return!)—Albert Ellis, in the sporadic times when I have discussed a personal issue with him has been, by far, the best therapist I have ever had. Why is this so? First, our therapeutic discussions over the years have been in the context of him being more of a mentor than a therapist. This for me challenges the wisdom of implementing overly strict boundaries between therapy and nontherapy discussions with the same person. Such boundaries would be constructive for some, but would not have been for me.

Another aspect of therapy with Al Ellis that I appreciated was his use of self-disclosure. I would discuss a personal issue with Al, and he would tell me about a relevant experience that he had had with the same issue. Sometimes he would tell me how he had helped one of his clients with a similar problem. Rarely, if ever, would he practice formal, active-directive REBT with me. While I have never discussed this point with him, my sense is that he was quite aware that I knew REBT theory and practice very well and could trust that I had tried to use it with myself before discussing the issue with him. He respected my position as a knowledgeable REBT therapist, and he sought to help me in ways that I had perhaps not thought of. His indirect approach here was most beneficial.

As I write this, I am reminded of a remark that one of my REBT colleagues made about supervisory feedback he had received on one of his therapy tapes by an REBT supervisor he had sought help from. "He treated me as if I knew nothing about REBT," claimed my colleague, who found this approach to supervision patronizing and unhelpful. Al Ellis never once treated me in our therapeutic discussions as if I did not know REBT.

The other helpful aspect of having "therapy" with Ellis was that his style with me did not change according to the issue we were discussing. I contrast this with the discrepancy between my Jungian therapist's "inside therapy" style and her "outside therapy" style. Al was his humorous, raunchy, interesting self no matter what we were discussing. In a phrase, I experienced him to be genuine in all his dealings with me, and this "genuine informality" is a therapist quality that I find particularly helpful as a client and that I strive to achieve in my own work. I contrast this with the "nongenuine formal" style of my other therapists.

It is fitting to close this chapter with my therapy experiences with Albert Ellis since I owe him so much as a professional. It is also fitting that I have ended with a discussion of my one positive therapist-delivered treatment that I have had. Although I have been critical of my previous therapists (with the exception of Albert Ellis), I want to end by saying that I would not be a very easy client for most therapists. I have a clear idea of what is helpful to me and what is not, and I have a definite preference for self-help, which makes being in therapy a problematic experience for me if that therapy is not focused sharply on encouraging me to help myself.

And yet, so many of my therapists failed to discover this. As a result I have learned to consistently ask myself whether or not my REBT practice best suits the needs of the person who is seeking my help. If it does, then we can proceed; if not, I am prepared to refer this person to someone else. This is the lasting legacy of my personal therapy experiences and one that helps to keep my feet on the ground and helps me to remain dedicated and humble.

REFERENCES

Bordin, E. S. (1979). The generalizability of the psychoanalytic concept of the working alliance. *Psychotherapy, Theory, Research and Practice, 16*, 252–260.

Dryden, W. (1991). *"It depends": A dialogue with Arnold Lazarus.* Buckingham: Open University Press.

Dryden, W. (1999a). Friend or therapist? In S. Greenfield (Ed.), *Therapy on the couch: A shrinking future?* London: Camden Press.

Dryden, W. (1999b). *How to accept yourself.* London: Sheldon Press.

Ellis, A., & Harper, R. A. (1975). *A new guide to rational living.* Hollywood, CA: Wilshire.

Rogers, C. R. (1957). The necessary and sufficient conditions of therapeutic personality change. *Journal of Consulting Psychology, 21*, 95–103.

10

THE I AND THE SELF: REMINISCENCES OF EXISTENTIAL-HUMANISTIC PSYCHOTHERAPY

BRYAN WITTINE

In their provocative study of personality theory, the psychoanalysts Atwood and Stolorow (1993, p. 5) argue that divergent theoretical approaches to the human psyche are not "theoretical models which can be tested against one another in a meaningful way, but rather [are] competing ideological and conceptual orientations to the problem of what it means to be human." The theories of different investigators are embedded in "irreconcilable, encapsulating structures of metapsychological suppositions," which stem from the subjective experiential worlds of the theorists themselves. Thus, Freudian, Jungian, existential-humanistic, and cognitive theories, to name but a few, arise from the subjective and personal influences of those who invented them, for "personality theorists tend to rely on their own lives as a primary source of empirical material" (p. 6).

If the metapsychological systems of the great psychologists are grounded fundamentally in the unconscious organizing principles of the theorists, can something similar be said of therapists and the particular theoretical orientations to which they gravitate? As a therapist, might not I be attracted to certain psychological theories that resonate with my own subjective experience, approaches that express something concerning my own unconscious design for living?

For me, the answer to these questions is an emphatic yes. As I look back on my 25-year career as a psychotherapist, I recognize that I have been drawn to theoretical systems that are personally meaningful and that address in definite ways certain lacunae in my psyche. In particular, I have needed depth psychology to help me address the reality of death, the in-

114

exorableness of change, and the ramifications of an absent father, issues that haunted me from childhood.

I have been drawn to three psychologies that specifically address these issues. They are existential-humanistic psychotherapy, psychoanalytic self psychology, and Jungian psychoanalysis. In this chapter, I concentrate primarily on my journey in existential-humanistic psychotherapy, which I undertook at the beginning of my career. This journey went to the very ground of my being and had such power that it shaped my subsequent development as a therapist. What I learned in it became the foundation of who I am and how I work.

A foundation, of course, is not the whole building, and I have since gone on to become a Jungian psychoanalyst. My existential-humanistic journey, however, remains the bedrock of my professional life.

I began therapy because of depression and a sense of failure after I separated from my first wife, with whom I was married for 10 years. In addition, I had just begun to teach at a nearby university, and I needed support from someone I admired who could soothe me when I made mistakes, encourage me to keep going, and act as a role model. My existential journey took place over a period of five years at two and three times per week with two different therapists. It continued until my second therapist's retirement. From there I began a Jungian analysis, enrolled in analytic training, and subsequently was certified as an analyst. My Jungian journey has been with two analysts for approximately 12 years, mostly twice a week.

My existential-humanistic therapist taught me a process of inner searching, which required me to turn inward and sense within myself the nuances of thought, feeling, and sensation that go on all the time just below the level of conscious awareness. Transference phenomena were explored, but exploration of the transference in depth took a back seat to the inner search.

THE INEVITABILITY OF DEATH

In classical Freudian psychodynamics, our aggressive and libidinal drives spawn conscious and unconscious anxieties, which propel us to adopt coping and defensive mechanisms. Existential psychotherapy (Yalom, 1980) replaces the Freudian view of psychodynamics. Here anxiety and subsequent defenses are triggered by our awareness of certain ultimate existential concerns: death, freedom, isolation, and meaninglessness. I shall begin by describing how the ultimate concern of death drew me specifically to the existential-humanistic orientation.

I became aware of the inevitability of death when I was a very young child. When my mother was nine, her eight-year-old sister was murdered on the streets of Cleveland. Early that morning on her way to mass my mother knew something was wrong. She found Elaine's rosary beads in a pool of blood on the sidewalk a block or so away from the church. "Little Girl Slain by Madman" read the headline in the *Cleveland Plain Dealer*. By the time I was born, 16 years later, this tragedy had become a central organizing event in the life of my mother's devout Roman Catholic family. Elaine had become a heroine and a martyr and her story had the numinosity of myth.

Later, when I was 12, my maternal grandmother died, and her corpse, lying in the casket with flowers all around it, fascinated me. I remember thinking to myself: "Her body is like a shellacked eggshell; the life has been sucked out of it like a yoke." My grandmother's death was the first of 11 deaths that took place in my extended family over the next two years. My father's father followed three weeks later; then, one by one, great-uncles and great-aunts died, wiping out an entire generation of my family. "She (or he) was young yet," the bereaved would say, as they looked at their beloved in the casket. And they *were* young—from late fifties to 72.

My parent's marriage was too tenuous to hold up under the impact of these deaths. A tumultuous breakdown took place in my family, which eventually resulted in their divorce when I was 16 and my own move to California to join the flower children two years later. Ending after ending, change after change scared me to my core and made me intimately aware of the fragility and impermanence of life. I thus began to question the meaning of life in the face of certain contingency.

What possible yearning might arise in a young man who had directly encountered death, the ultimate mystery, again and again? What might catch my interest in the face of a bewildering, inconsistent world of relationships irretrievably severed by death? I turned to Asian philosophies and meditation, where I hoped to find the deathless spirit, the unborn and undying, the changeless behind the ever-changing. I immersed myself in the practice of Eastern techniques of meditation, and I came to regard Western psychology, with the arguable exception of Jung's, as having little to do with spiritual enlightenment, the meaning of life, and other ultimate concerns. These matters, I believed, belonged to spiritual teachers in meditation halls and monasteries, not to psychotherapists in their consulting rooms. In that sense, I believed that what depth psychotherapy could achieve in terms of peace and happiness was decidedly inferior to the fulfillment I would experience if I realized the deathless spirit promised by the great contemplative traditions of the East. The stability of spirituality was what I wanted: the Atman of Vedanta, the Beloved of Sufism, the Buddhist's Buddha-nature, Kether on the Kabalistic tree of life, and the "Not I, not I, but the Christ who liveth in me" of Saint Paul. I read a lot of Jung as a young man but was not converted. His notion of the transpersonal Self seemed to point to the same spiritual reality the mystics sought, but I wanted the real thing, not some psychological substitute. Consequently, I had no idea I would become a psychotherapist and certainly no sense that I needed psychotherapy. Now, as I look back on those years, I recognize with tenderness and compassion the defensive grandiosity of an impetuous youth with his head in the heavens and his feet dangling far above the earth.

It was not until I separated from my first wife after a 10-year marriage that I thought I might need psychotherapy. While in graduate school I encountered the ideas of James F. T. Bugental, one of the best-known proponents of the existential-humanistic orientation in psychotherapy. In his books (Bugental 1978, 1981) I discovered how the existential-humanistic approach could become a vehicle that supported the realization of the spirit, which Bugental called the "true I" or the "I-process," as distinct from my "self," the system of identity-constructs with which I was unconsciously identified. This seemed familiar to me. It paralleled the distinction that Indian yogis make between the Atman, or Self (with a capital *S*), and the ego. The same distinction is found in Jung, who wrote extensively on the archetype of the Self and its relationship to the ego. Like Parsifal in the grail legend, who became transfixed upon his first sighting of a knight in shining armor and knew immediately he wanted to become one, my imagination was seized by the idea that I might become a psychotherapist. Although it was Jung who first taught me to regard the unconscious as a rich font of creative possibilities rather than a seething cauldron of instinctual drives, it was Bugental who taught me how to access this font and ultimately to differentiate between the true I and my constructed self.

Bugental also fathered me. Like many men of my generation, I grew up with a distant father, resulting in a zone of emptiness in my psyche where a paternal imago should be. I have no doubt that the absence of a stable father contributed to my feeling groundless and insecure, feelings I also associate with death and change. Quite unconsciously, I was searching for the good father I never had to replace the critical and distant father I did have. In my spiritual search, however, I was also looking for God the Father.

I had no idea of the transference implications of these images when I set about to find Bugental and go into therapy with him. "I'll need to see you at least three, preferably four times per week," he said on the phone. "My fee is $75 an hour." This was a hefty amount at the time.

Financially, this was a huge investment. Getting to him was also a major investment of time. He lived in Santa Rosa, a solid hour and a half drive from my home. Moreover, choosing to see him represented a psychological challenge. As I said, at that time I was very much identified with a grandiose persona, but inside I felt inferior. I also didn't trust men as mentor figures. I now see that I was in deep conflict between my mother, who needed me to be her shining star (thus my grandiose persona) and my father, who wanted a son like other boys and was disappointed to find that he had produced a creative, artistically inclined kid. We were never close, and I certainly felt rejected. I therefore had to overcame my suspicion of male authorities long enough to begin working with Bugental. I finally became his patient—yes, three times a week at first, although in time he made it easier by scheduling two of those sessions back to back.

THE ART OF INNER SEARCHING

Bugental was steeped in classical psychoanalysis, having had a five-times-per-week analysis of his own that went on for several years. He was not content, however, with the depth reached in his own analysis; consequently, he drew on the work of Wilhelm Reich and Fritz Perls to deepen and intensify Freud's technique of free association. His work became experience centered. The focus of the therapy session was the living moment—what was actually going on phenomenologically in me as I spoke to him about my life. Bugental began my therapy by instructing me in the art of searching:

> Here's what I'd like you to do when you come into the office,
> Bryan. Lie down on the couch, take some time to get comfortable,
> and think about what concerns you. Pay particular attention to
> how you experience that issue in your body and feelings. Then
> describe as openly and as freely as you can what goes on within you
> as you contemplate your issue. Tell me what it makes you think of,
> how you feel as you tell me about it, what your earlier life was like,
> and how you'd like your future to be. In doing so, keep one eye on
> the feelings and sensations in your body. The main thing is for you
> to disclose as openly and as freely as possible what goes on in your
> awareness while you're here. Don't wait for me to say much. Just
> keep going from within yourself.

In this way he taught me to use "feelingful awareness" in choosing, describing, and redescribing my concerns. I learned to keep focused on my feelings and the sensations in my body, which became triggers for accessing thoughts, images, memories, desires, hopes, fears, wishes, and all else flowing within my awareness from moment to moment.

For me, Bugental's initial instructions became the basic rule of existential-humanistic psychotherapy. I tried very hard to follow it because I wanted to please the father! Now, as I look back, his instructions seem mechanical and unwieldy. I rarely use them with my patients. I am inclined, however, to use the more subtle instructions Bugental offered (adapted from Bugental, 1978, pp. 29–31):

- "Bryan, tell me, what are you experiencing inside yourself as you tell me these things?"
- "Bryan, listen, will you try something for me? Let's stop conversing for a moment, so you can get in touch with what's going on inside you right now. Take your time. Then come on back and see if you can't tell me a little about what you find, okay?"
- "I have the sense, Bryan, that there's a lot going on inside of you right now as you tell me about this. Could you share some of that, too?"

To me, a novice psychotherapist, these were elegant communications, which had the effect of making it clear that Bugental believed in the primacy of the subjective, and that his first concern was to help me become as subjectively centered as possible during my sessions.

Looking back on it, I think he taught me most about inner searching by modeling the search process. Whenever I confronted him he took me seriously. He often searched within his own subjectivity and disclosed what he found, whenever it was appropriate to our work. I remember one hour in which his self-disclosure taught me more about searching than any instruction he gave. About a year into the therapy, life presented him with a major event and a choice, both of which irrevocably influenced my work with him. First, his friend Al Lasko, a psychologist in southern California, unexpectedly died. This was a profound loss for Jim, and everyone in the small existential-humanistic community around him knew it. Second, shortly before or after Lasko's death, I don't remember which, he decided to retire from private practice. This left me approximately two years time to complete my work.

I do not know whether his decision to retire and his friend's death were linked, but his decision was a blow to me. It was like being told that your long-lost father whom you recently found was now given a death sentence, just at the point where you were absorbing all the qualities you had missed for a lifetime. I shall comment at greater length on the ramifications of his decision for me later in this chapter. For now I will simply say that I was angry and saddened, but I buried the trauma. As I still had two years, I resolved to use the time as fully as I could. But the existential realities of death and of life's inevitable endings were part of my therapy with him from that day on.

One day he became ill and had to cancel my session. Largely due to an error on his part, the message didn't reach me, and I made the hour-and-a-half trek to Santa Rosa, *seemingly* for nothing. I was sympathetic toward Jim because he was ill, but I also felt angry that he overlooked my needs. "I think you're resisting being fully present with me," I complained at the start of our next session. Jim's response transported me into a dimension of depth and meaning that seemed entirely numinous. He closed his eyes, sat quietly for a few moments, turned to me, and said slowly and with great feeling, "You're right. I was caught up in my own concerns. . . . the end of my friendship with Al . . . the end of my private practice . . . approaching the end of my life . . ."

When he said this it was as if the floor beneath us sprang open, and Jim and I together plunged down a well that opened into a vast underground chamber. I was on holy ground, and I *knew* it.

"Do you think much about death, Jim?"

"Quite a bit, Bryan."

"Are you afraid of it?"

Again, silence as Jim made his way even further down into that mysterious chamber, and I with him. "No, not exactly. Not anymore. I used to be afraid. Now I'm more curious, very curious." And I knew that this was his truth because for me the energy in the room was positively electric.

This was not only the decisive moment in my discovery of the art of inner searching but one of the most healing moments of my therapy. No older male, no father figure, had ever given me the gift of self. I felt honored when he opened himself to me and showed me that I was worth his trust. I felt proud that this man whom I loved and admired would take me into his private world. I also felt the fullness of my own being. I felt large enough to receive him in his heaviness and depth. This was not an inflated, grandiose experience of myself. I felt solid and real. Perhaps for the first time I felt my legs underneath me, my feet on the ground, and my roots in the earth. This event also helped me to feel much safer to access and share in a less inhibited way what I found within myself. When Jim searched within his own subjectivity for his motives for forgetting my session, he opened and gave himself to me, and I felt ready to open myself to Jim.

The "Self"

From that moment when I dove in, I relaxed my social persona, contemplated my concerns, and disclosed what I found in my awareness. The most meaningful issues of my life—my feelings of deficiency and frustration as a psychotherapist, my turbulent relationship with my fiancée, my conflict between spirituality and worldliness, my fear of death—literally tumbled out.

One of the themes that concerned me most was my work as a psychotherapist, about which we often spoke. Bugental handled this concern like any other. It simply became the starting point for the search process. To illustrate: I might begin a session by describing my difficulties tolerating the rage of a female patient; that, in turn, reminded me of a similar problem I felt with women in general. I would then be reminded of, say, a dream I had had in which "my foundation is being gnawed by a rodent," which led me to wonder if I felt my patient was undermining to my self-esteem. Going deeper I might say, "Damn self-esteem. I'm so up-and-down, so vulnerable to what other people think and feel. I hate that about myself. Wish I could be myself, warts and all, and that it would be okay." That led me to acknowledge, "How much I wish I had enough self-possession to withstand my patient's angry attacks without flinching, without flying away." Then I might think of something with my mother, which would lead me to describing my relationship with my fiancée, then back again to my relationship with my patient.

At times I pulled on Bugental to give me advice about my patient, but he usually refused, knowing it would derail the search process. I remember him once asking why I needed him to take off his therapist hat and become my consultant. That led me to describing my loss of my father and how I therefore did not know how to handle the parts of my mother that frightened me.

As I spoke about each of my concerns, Bugental listened, not just to what I said, but to implicit meanings he heard between the lines. He placed great emphasis on *process*—the ways I spoke, the urgency or lack thereof, my shifting moods, my breathing patterns, my nuances of vitality and dysphoria, my unconscious choice of words, my Freudian slips of tongue. He used all of these to lay bare the structures of my subjectivity—my conscious and unconscious identities, which he called my self-construct.

For example, he repeatedly confronted the pressure I put on myself to inwardly search, my inability to simply allow myself to be a channel through which the content of my awareness could flow out of me in my own authentic way. He showed me this by identifying my pervasive tendency to split myself into a slave who needed prodding by a domineering internal object, which he called my master. At times I identified with the punitive master who demanded perfection in the art of searching; at others I identified with the anxious slave who couldn't do searching deeply and freely enough. We talked about the ways the master and slave replicated my image of my father and my relationship to him.

Inevitably this pattern also became visible in my transference relationship with Bugental. I projected the master onto him and, like a good student, strained to get in touch with my inner awareness out of a desire to please him and ultimately to receive his acceptance and confirmation. When it didn't work, my perception of him changed into my disapproving father, who withheld from me the love and affirmation I needed.

We uncovered the same complex at work in my relationships with my students. At the time I was clinical director for an agency, responsible for the training of 12 beginning therapists. They were a tough group. I often felt overwhelmed by their unruly rejection of such common psychotherapeutic frame issues as setting fees and requesting that clients pay for canceled hours. At times I felt like a stern, disciplining teacher who had to put the brakes on an eager, impulsive group of adolescents, while at other times I felt like a criticized child when they were upset with me for not meeting their expectations.

I also realized that dimensions of my meditation practice were similarly motivated. I was raised Roman Catholic and had thought my conversion into Buddhism was motivated by the purity of a longing for truth. I discovered that it was also motivated by a desire to feel special and to compensate for feeling deficient behind my grandiosity. I also found that my meditation practice was motivated by my need to appease a judging, withholding Father God, as if meditating would somehow make me into his perfect son, finally worthy enough for Him to cough up his good grace.

Another motivation for meditation was to seduce God as powerful authority to rescue me from death and uncertainty. Apparently my unconscious child-self had gotten it into his head that if I meditated God would swoop down at the last minute, just before I fell off the world into a dark and lonely abyss, and save me from death itself. Never mind that God never lifted a finger to help Jesus on the cross. Didn't Jesus, after all, ask, "My God, why hast thou forsaken me?" I felt crushed and humiliated to discover that my God-image, my father complex, and my transference to Bugental were all cut from the same cloth. I became increasingly aware of how small and insubstantial I felt underneath it all.

The I-Process

This procedure of exposing and deconstructing the unconscious constructs of my self and my world came to its inevitable apogee as Bugental and I focused on the paradigms underlying my spirituality. I will never forget one session in which I spoke about how I wanted the mystical Christ to rise up from the depths of my unconscious, take hold of me from the inside, and pull me down into his awesome depths. Jim looked at me incredulously and said, "Bryan, that's sixteenth-century spirituality!"

I was shocked and infuriated. For the first time I thought Bugental blew it. To me, this was an empathic failure, a violation of the therapeutic frame, and a technical error all rolled up into one. Certainly, I thought, his own countertransference was involved. Bugental was an existentialist, not a transpersonalist, and it seemed to me he was repressing the sublime in his own life and now was advocating that I repress the sublime in myself as well. I accused him of being unable to move from existential to transpersonal levels of consciousness, to move from his ultimate concern of death and finitude to my ultimate concern of enlightenment and unity with God. A Jungian analyst would certainly understand that I longed for the archetypal Self and would help me become aware of "its" presence, to help me organize my life around "it"—the still point at the center of the turning world, as T. S. Eliot put it.

But Bugental was insistent and would not let go. "That still point," he asserted, "is not an entity in your unconscious separate from you. The still point of being and awareness is who and what you are." He seemed stern, even awesome, as he confronted me with how I made my essence into an "other," how I persisted in seeing myself as a tiny force with everything good outside, how I reified the pure subject into an object to be worshiped rather than recognizing my essence as pure being and consciousness. "The mystical Christ as a Jungian archetype existing inside you is a *concept*," he pushed on, "another object in consciousness. It's an image of reality, not reality itself."

From this moment on, reality wasn't what it used to be. Bugental was now debunking a primary structure of my identity, an underlying concept of myself as small and inconsequential next to God as wholly other, altogether perfect, the sole source of grace. As this structure began to shake, I felt no still point of being and awareness. I looked inside and saw a terrible nothingness. I had no solid self. My identity and the identities of others were highly relative; my thoughts and feelings were like weather patterns—vaporous, shifting, and fluid.

The horror I felt came from my direct experience that my known self was simply nonexistent as something tangible and real. My self-identity was built out of subtle levels of thought that arose from unconscious memory traces starting in the first hours of life. These traces gradually became the building blocks of the superstructure of my identity. I had become identified with images of self as master, slave, small child needing the protection of a wholly beneficent Other, seeker after the mystical Christ, and any number of other constructs, all of which had as their basis a feeling of individuality rooted in identification with my physical body. In other words, the self-identity is first a bodyego, as Freud himself recognized. My identification as a body was the foundation of this entire superstructure. Underneath it, however, emptiness pervaded. I recognized my essence to be nothing. I, as a "something," simply did not exist.

I became restless. If I am not any of these identities, then "Who am I?" and "What is Other?" These questions flooded my consciousness. One day, as I described to Jim how I felt doomed to eternal nothingness, he said to me, "Bryan, you sense you are nothing now. But you also were nothing before you characterized yourself as something. What was that like?"

That question served like a Zen koan. At that moment my mind seemed to stop, and I had the subtle, but deeply powerful feeling that I, essentially nothing, existed as nothing, outside of time. This I, as nothing, witnessed the pharaohs of Egypt and all times past, present, and future. The *I* witnessed these, not an individual entity but as living presence that simultaneously seemed to be pure being/awareness. All content appeared to arise within this vast, cognizant, luminous being/awareness. Other than being awareness itself, this *I* had no form, no weight, no color, no substance, no locality. In those moments I tasted stillness and peace, along with feelings of pure joy.

This experience also seemed to alleviate my death anxiety. The pure *I* seemed to be deathless, present everywhere and at all times. Individual cycles circumscribed by birth and death seemed to occur within the *I*, but the *I* seemed transcendent to these cycles. Obviously I have no direct knowledge of the reality of life after death, but this and other experiences gave me greater faith that something about the human being survives death and is immortal.

Eastern mystics also describe experiences that are similar to what I experienced. For example, Bassui, a fourteenth-century Zen master, said: "Your Mind-essence is not subject to birth or death" (cited in Kapleau, 1967, p. 173). My impression was that I as living presence transcended birth and death. There is no death because the true *I* is never born. It stands completely outside of time. Manifestation throughout time takes place within the I-process, much as weather patterns appear and disappear against the clear sky. Thus, I as living presence and awareness could be said to exist at the time of the Egyptian pharaohs, not as an individual form but as an abiding witness.

Similarly, the Hindu sage Ramana Maharshi (1959, p. 30) wrote:

> Because the individual self [or self-construct], which is nothing but the mind, has lost the knowledge of its identity with the real Self [or I-process], and has enmeshed itself in bondage, its search for the Self, its own eternal primal nature, resembles that of the shepherd searching for a lamb which all the time he bears on his

own shoulders. During these moments, I realized the true *I* not in
the sense of attaining something new but simply in being that
which I always am and have always been, but didn't know it,
because my true *I* was overshadowed by the content of the self.
Now, after I had temporarily transcended the self, the *I* stood out
clear and shining, and it had been there all along. "Muddy water,
let stand, becomes clear" is the way the Chinese sage Lao Tse put
it. The self-construct is the silt in the water of the *I*, pure awareness. When the silt settles down, the water stands clear, but the
water was always there. This reminds me of something a meditation
master once told me: "Gradually, your mind will relax into enlightenment." For a few, brief, shining moments, then, I felt free from
my limited self, and I understood a saying attributed to Abu Sa'id,
a fourth-century Sufi mystic: "Inside this robe there is only God."
(cited in Vaughan-Lee, 1995, p. 204)

HOW PSYCHOTHERAPY HEALS: WHAT I LEARNED FROM THE EXISTENTIAL-HUMANISTIC PERSPECTIVE

It has been said that trainees learn how to do psychotherapy more by being
in their own therapy than in books and graduate school! This was certainly true for me. My current work as a psychotherapist has as its foundation certain postulates I learned from Bugental. In the intervening years
I made a thorough study of psychoanalytic self psychology and Jungian
psychology, which offer important teachings. But I have now come full
circle, and I believe the following points remain indelibly the foundation
of all my work.

1. The centrality of the inner search
2. The therapist's presence and concern as central to facilitating
   the inner search
3. The selfobject transferences, which serve as the background of
   the search process
4. The importance of distinguishing between the *I*, which is pure
   being and awareness, and the self, which is a construction of
   identity rather than a constitutional given

First, my journey in existential-humanistic psychotherapy taught me
to regard the inner search as central to how psychotherapy heals. The classical psychoanalytic approach is overly mental and divorced from what is
actually going on in the patient's subjectivity in the living moment. What
is truly going on in the therapist's office and what is most directly (almost
tangibly) available for the work is the present living moment, the patient's
and analyst's being in this very *now*. This means that the flow of the patient's
stream of consciousness, especially as it starts in somatic and affective experience and in the patient's feeling of genuine concern for his or her life,

is the primary focus of the therapeutic situation. The therapist's subjectivity is also central to facilitating the unfolding of the patient's inner search.

Helping my patients form a relationship with the depths of their own subjectivity remains the core of my work. I try to help my patients listen deeply within their larger awareness to all that is present within them. I contribute by immersing myself in the flow of their associations and amplifying whatever I perceive is "ascendant" in their experience, whenever they need me to do that. In this way, patients discover what is underneath their surface thoughts and emotional reactions and bring to consciousness whatever is implicit and deeply felt but dimly realized.

The physical and psychological presence and the responsiveness of the therapist are, of course, central to the creation of a therapeutic environment that facilitates the search process. With a safe, containing therapist, the inner search unfolds with greater freedom and ease; without the therapist's presence, searching is difficult if not impossible.

Presence was the primary quality of being that Bugental modeled. For example, no one with whom I have since worked has been more empathic and "experience-near" than he. I often felt him inside me, immersed in my subjectivity with me, as we flowed together down the river of my awareness like some Lewis and Clark on a journey to discover uncharted territories within my psyche. On this expedition he was usually quiet, never intrusive. But he was energetically potent, either as a helmsman when I needed help or as a steady, onlooking presence when I didn't. When he spoke, it was often because I became caught in some repetitive thinking pattern, or because he wanted to illumine something struggling for emergence from within me that I couldn't quite realize on my own, or to ask questions that took me deeper into my subjectivity.

Two related aspects of Bugental's presence stand out to me. First, he modeled very clear boundaries, which made it safe to search within myself. One of the most difficult aspects of being in therapy with him was his centrality in a small community of professionals who trained and consulted, and in some instances went into therapy, with him. Although he kept confidences strictly, I felt embarrassed on a few occasions to meet colleagues who passed me in the hall at the same time I arrived for or departed from my sessions. I remember one conversation I had with him in which I complained about feeling exposed. There was nothing we could do except to arrange for me to arrive for my sessions promptly and thus avoid meeting people I knew. Because I was a part of this small community, however, he urged me not to share my therapy sessions with members of our community and, if I wanted to discuss anything, to do so with people whom I trusted outside of our group.

Another quality that helped me feel safe to search was his willingness to disclose his own subjectivity when it seemed relevant to our work, as when he shared with me his feelings concerning his friend's death. This was such an important aspect of how therapy healed that I made it a point to read everything I could on therapist disclosure. For many years I believed

I needed to consciously know the structures of the patient's subjectivity into which the patient will absorb what I disclose and the fact of my disclosing it. Then I thought I could make a *conscious* choice and be certain that my disclosure would enhance the patient's individuation instead of derailing it. Now this process occurs intuitively inside me, below the threshold of my conscious awareness. Generally speaking, I do not self-disclose very often, but when I do it is directly relevant to the patient's search and often proves to be meaningful. This is clearly something I learned from Bugental, and it has served me well over the years.

Something else comes to mind concerning Bugental's presence. When I was in therapy with him, I felt enormous confidence in my own work as a therapist. At the beginning of their training and in the early years of their professional career, most novice therapists are struggling with underlying anxieties. They are usually worried about getting patients, and once they have them they are worried about losing them. This makes it difficult to relate to patients as the situation requires. Because of their anxiety they might be too nice and too understanding, or may feel insecure about holding a hard line when needed. By contrast, while I worked with Bugental I felt self-confident. I had no trouble setting fees, required prospective patients to come twice a week, insisted that they take their therapy seriously, and confronted when necessary. True, I did have my defensive grandiosity, but that was surface veneer. No, in retrospect I believe I was borrowing Bugental's stability and calm, his nonanxious manner, his strength and power, and incorporating them into myself. It became painfully obvious after my therapy was over that these qualities did not really belong to me.

Throughout the roller-coaster ride of disclosing my selves and discovering the living presence of the I-process, Bugental remained a still point in my emotionally chaotic universe—stationary, stable, and calm. His steadiness enabled me to relax my defenses and make the descent into the gaping nothingness I found myself to be. He was there when I needed him.

Today, having immersed myself in psychoanalytic self psychology, I understand that I had formed an "idealizing selfobject transference" with my therapist. My archaic developmental needs from childhood were reactivated, and Bugental responded optimally to those needs, thus enabling derailed processes of individuation to get back on course. Bugental identified my master-slave structure and illumined its operation in my thinking, my relationships, and in my transference with him. I believe this made up part of the repetitive dimension of the transference. In the background, however, an idealizing selfobject transference operated.

What is important is that the therapist be available for as long as it takes the patient to idealize, devour, and metabolize the therapist. As I have already said, my psychotherapy with Bugental ended prematurely. Bugental had ceased taking on new long-term patients two years previously, and now, at age 68, he was ending his practice and concentrating solely on writing and consultation. Consequently, my therapy did not have an organic end. I did not choose to terminate the therapy. Seven or eight months after I had tasted the pure livingness of the *I*, he closed his office. Gradually I realized how abandoned I felt and how traumatic this premature ending was.

When my therapy ended, then, this transference remained unresolved, and a restructuring of the self along positive lines had not taken place. Moreover, I was unable to speak to him about my feelings of abandonment because my idealization was holding. I couldn't conceive of letting him know of my feeling that he failed me. This was important because it meant that a major part of my father-complex concerning my abandonment had not been resolved, and the idealizing transference had not been worked through.

Within a year after therapy ended, I remarried, and so my capacity for interpersonal relationships improved significantly. Nonetheless, Bugental had exposed me to the self's relative reality and had opened me to the I-process. This satisfied many spiritual yearnings and helped me face my death anxieties, but I was left on the border between the emptiness of the pure *I* and the form of the self. It was not until I was firmly involved in Jungian analysis that I began to put my self back together, to feel equilibrium in the world, and to live as both the self and the pure *I*.

I have since discovered that my ontological insecurity is the intrinsic insecurity of the self when it feels separate and dissociated from its source, the I-process. I had only glimpsed the pure *I*; I hadn't found permanent residence there and certainly had no clue as to how to be intrinsically empty and in the world as an individual at the same time. I have learned that healing this fundamental dissociation in the human psyche requires intensive psychotherapy of several years duration as well as a long-term practice of meditation.

I am certain my therapy would have gone on for several more years had Bugental remained in private practice. I am also certain I would have outgrown my need for him and have found my own inner source of strength and wisdom to the degree that I let myself fully have him. As it was, our ending was traumatic, and I began searching for another therapist within months of our last session. This search was painful and disappointing, because no therapist was Bugental.

It took me many years to process this ending and to internalize and integrate Bugental's image. It took several years with Jungian analysts to help me metabolize him and to begin to practice psychotherapy in ways that seem creative and authentic to me and are not merely copies of him. I no longer mimic him, as I once did long ago, but now offer my own life-experiences and myself. Still, I sometimes imagine him sitting next to me as I sit behind the couch listening to my patients. But then, I also imagine inside me the presences of my Jungian analysts and case consultants. At times I think a council of ancestors surrounds me and guides the career of their younger professional colleague.

Even after several years of Jungian analysis, however, I regard those three years lying on Bugental's couch and engaging in the search process as watershed experiences in my personal and professional development. I cannot help but connect everything I have since learned about how psychotherapy heals back to those years of working with Bugental to get in touch with the ongoing flow of subjectivity and to emancipate the pure awareness and livingness of the *I* from the self-construct.

This emancipation of the pure *I* was profoundly healing. Over time, what I learned from those experiences was that my self-concepts are entirely arbitrary and are based not on reality in the here and now but upon memory traces that are formed from the earliest moments of life. Gradually, these memory traces coalesce into self- and object-representations, which shape and organize our view of the world and ourselves. Our known identities, therefore, are phantoms. They act as grids through which we see the world and ourselves in that world.

This realization resulted in a feeling of enormous freedom. It also resulted in a convincing impression that I create my world afresh from moment to moment and that I can choose to see it through my egoic grid or with wholly unmediated eyes. Thus, my perceptions became more immediate and less contrived, and seemed to convey reality itself rather than reality perceived through an egoic grid.

Of all the remarkable things I learned in existential-humanistic psychotherapy, this is the part of its legacy that remains for me the gist of this work and the foundation of my own: the self, apparently necessary for us to get about in life, is a construction of consciousness, by no means our essence. There is a power within us that is the very heart of the human being. It is something nonexistent in the ordinary sense, not an objective thing at all; yet this true *I*, the pure subject, the pure livingness, is very much the fathomless source of all human possibility.

REFERENCES

Atwood, G. E., & Stolorow, R. D. (1993). *Faces in a cloud: Intersubjectivity in Personality Theory.* Northvale, NJ: Aronson.

Bugental, J. F. T. (1978). *Psychotherapy and process: The fundamentals of an existential-humanistic approach.* Reading, MA: Addison-Wesley.

Bugental, J. F. T. (1981). *The search for authenticity: An existential-analytic approach to psychotherapy* (Enlarged ed.). New York: Irvington.

Bugental, J. F. T. (1987). *The art of the psychotherapist.* New York: Norton.

Kapleau, P. (1967). *The three pillars of Zen.* Boston: Beacon Press.

Ramana Maharshi. (1959). *The collected works of Ramana Maharshi* (A. Osborne, Ed.). London: Rider.

Vaughan-Lee, L. (Ed.). (1995). *Travelling the path of love: Sayings of Sufi masters.* Inverness, CA: Golden Sufi Center.

Yalom, I. (1980). *Existential psychotherapy.* New York: Basic Books.

11

THE ROLE OF INDIVIDUAL AND MARITAL THERAPY IN MY DEVELOPMENT

Clara E. Hill

One of my major lifelong goals has been to understand myself, who I am, and where I am going. I agree with Socrates that the unexamined life is not worth living. So I have engaged in many efforts to understand myself, my family, and almost everyone with whom I come into contact. Although I have trepidation about revealing myself in such a public forum, I have decided to do so because I hope that hearing about my experiences can help other people on their journey toward self-understanding. First I describe several nontherapy experiences that were influential in my development, to provide a context, and then I discuss the effects of long-term individual and marital therapy on my development.

My love of introspection probably came from my family, in that we all tried to figure out ourselves and each other. Unfortunately, these attempts to understand ourselves and others did not translate into clear and direct communication with one another but rather took the form of talking about (criticizing) other family members when they were not present. Furthermore, the family values were not toward seeking therapy for solving problems but toward turning to God and health food as the answers to all problems.

Religion was a strong influence in my childhood. My father had trained to be a Baptist minister, and my parents were devout Christians. According to my family, there was one true way, and the answers were all written in the Bible. There was a lot we could not do (dance, smoke, drink, play cards, premarital sex). We were encouraged to be different from others and to devote our lives to God. Although the church taught us not to think for ourselves, my parents did teach us to read and think for ourselves, which they regretted later, when my siblings and I all turned away from the church. I became disillusioned when I was in high school, when fighting among the church members caused the church to split and when my father could not provide convincing answers for my doubts. I have remained cautious and suspicious when people try to demand that I become a true believer and use charisma to sway emotions and convert me, as was the case in the Baptist church.

When I was 19 and a sophomore at Southern Illinois University, I went to the university counseling center because I was depressed, having trouble with the transition to a large public university from a restrictive, religious home, having difficulty choosing a major, and not knowing who I was or wanted to be. I did not know how to ask for help with my existential issues, though, so I asked for help with vocational problems. The counselor was not empathic; she did not ask me any questions about myself but just scheduled me for a vocational test. I never went back to take the test. It makes me angry even now thinking about how much I needed help but did not get it. I recall a comment an administrator in the counseling center later made to the effect that they did not need to do more to encourage students to use counseling facilities because waiting lists were already too long. My experience did spark my interest in what keeps people from seeking help, and I did my undergraduate honor's thesis on the topic. I remain convinced that we need to do a better job of teaching therapists to recognize unspoken client distress, and we need to do more to make therapy accessible to people.

I liked my introductory psychology class and did not like any other majors, so I decided to major in psychology. After a summer working at a mental hospital, I realized that I wanted to work with "normal" people. So I began graduate school in counseling psychology in 1970 at Southern Illinois University (SIU). It was the height of the student protests over Vietnam and the beginning of the women's movement. It was an exciting time to be in graduate school because so much was happening in the culture. The counseling psychology program at SIU was a wonderful place to be because the faculty were very client centered, treated us like colleagues, let us help change the curriculum, and fostered our having major input into our education.

A very important influence on me was that I met my future husband, James Gormally, during graduate school. We were two of the four students admitted to our graduate program in 1970 and the only two to graduate. Jim has been my best friend since we met and one of the most important positive influences in my life. He is gentle and easy to talk to about everything. Being in the same profession and learning how to do therapy has provided us with the skills necessary to listen to each other and work through problems.

A profound impact of graduate school for me personally as well as professionally was learning helping skills (e.g., reflection of feelings, interpretation). I had always been a listener, but I used listening primarily as a defense against revealing anything about myself. Learning helping skills taught me to use those listening skills as a first step in being empathic and caring about other people. The skills also gave me a sense of confidence in knowing what to do with clients. The theoretical foundation for the helping skills was client-centered theory, which fit well with my humanistic values. I was not, however, attracted to the dogmatic quality of the helping skills approach as we learned it. We were taught that there was a certain way to do therapy (e.g., that an empathic statement was a reflection of feelings, that 12 reflections should be used before attempting an interpretation, that if clients did not get better it was totally the fault of the therapist). I reacted strongly against being told that there was one right way to do therapy, especially given the weakness of the empirical evidence for the assertions. We were supposed to believe what we were taught without questioning it. These demands for loyalty felt too much like the demands of the Baptist church, that is, that I believe without questioning. Despite the dogmatism of the approach, I was able to take away good things from the experience of learning helping skills. In fact, I have spent much of my research career testing the effects of therapist techniques and have recently come back to revising the helping skills into what I think is a more flexible, theoretically sound, empirically based approach (Hill, 2004; Hill & O'Brien, 1999).

I was also influenced during graduate school by behavioral theory. We had a really good professor who was excited about and good at demonstrating behavioral techniques. Since leaving graduate school, I have also been influenced by psychodynamic theories. Furthermore, teaching all the different approaches has forced me to value the positive features in all of them. In fact, it is clear to me that an integrative approach makes the most sense.

In graduate school, I was also influenced by conducting research. It was fun, and I liked the challenge of thinking of ideas and then figuring out how to test them. I also liked the idea that therapy involves a personal scientific approach, where the therapist is always trying to be aware of how the client is responding and what is working.

I certainly had the required amount of supervision during graduate school, and it did help me to gain confidence in my therapy skills. But I do not have specific memories of any supervision experiences during graduate school that influenced my development. I do have specific memories of the helpfulness of supervision during my internship because my supervisor encouraged me to become more spontaneous and try out a number of different techniques. His encouragement freed me up to trust my intuition more as a therapist.

Another important influence on my development was encounter groups, which were very popular during the time that I was in graduate school. Encounter groups were used as a way of helping people learn about how they are perceived by others. Our first-year class of counseling and clinical psychology graduate students formed a leaderless encounter group.

I remember initially being terrified and sitting like a frozen statue, saying nothing. Fortunately, my classmates confronted me gently, and I began to open up somewhat. I realized that I was not the only one who had problems, even if the other students seemed to be so much more together than I. Throughout graduate school, I led a number of encounter groups with undergraduate students and was in a number of them. These encounter groups were incredibly beneficial in terms of giving me feedback about how I came across and in teaching me about group process.

I got my Ph.D. in counseling psychology, got married, began as an assistant professor in the counseling psychology program in the Department of Psychology at the University of Maryland, and started a small private practice in 1974. This was a time of many transitions, particularly into adulthood.

I continued my personal growth endeavors. I was in a women's consciousness raising group that met weekly for a few years right after graduate school. In addition, my husband and I were in a leaderless couples group with three other couples that met about once a month for about five years, starting two years after graduate school. Most of the members of the group were therapists who were all newly married and just beginning to have children, so we talked about marriages and transitions to becoming parents. We have remained close friends with two of the couples, who feel like our chosen family. Recently, we met again for several group sessions to talk about transitions to having our children leave home and to thinking about the next stages in our careers.

I was also involved in two different supervision groups for a couple of years early in my career, with two very different supervisors. My experience with one supervisor, a well-known, aggressive, dogmatic, confrontational man, was very negative. I recall bursting into tears a couple of times when he confronted me in a particularly cruel manner; he was very lacking in empathy and understanding. My other supervisor (a woman) was more benign but not particularly impactful or memorable.

INDIVIDUAL THERAPY

I decided to start individual therapy in 1975 after I was married and began my position at the University of Maryland. I cannot recall the initial stimulus for seeking therapy, but it probably had something to do with my pervasive anxiety, difficulty maintaining a separate identity, unhappiness with my job, weight control issues, and constant disputes with my mother. In retrospect, it makes sense that I sought therapy at this point in my life. Earlier in my life, I think I was too vulnerable to be able to tolerate therapy. By this point I had gained some self-confidence in myself both personally (I was in a relationship with a good person) and professionally (I had completed my doctorate and secured a very good professional position).

I wanted individual therapy rather than group therapy. I wanted a therapist all to myself. I had been the youngest of four children in a family with limited emotional goodies to go around, and I did not want to have to share my therapist. I wanted to see an experienced female psychologist who was relatively similar to me in terms of age and location, had a humanistic orientation, and was gentle and insightful. I wanted to see a therapist who was not dogmatic and who did not think that she had the right answer but who would listen to me and help me grow. It was also important to me that my therapist not be someone who was a therapist for anyone else I knew, and I did not want to see anyone who my colleagues knew. I knew a number of other people who all saw the same therapist, and I wanted no part of that type of incestuous community. I wanted someone who was mine alone. Finally, I wanted long-term therapy because I knew that it would take a while to work through my issues. It is important to note that long-term, depth-oriented therapy was the norm at that time, especially for therapists.

Of course, such requirements made it difficult to find a therapist because I could not rely on referrals. Luckily, I found a listing of therapists that Ralph Nader's group had compiled. (I have seen no such list since that time.) On that list, I found Dr. Rona Eisner, a clinical psychologist who fit all my criteria. Even more important, I liked Rona when I met her. I did not choose Rona for her reputation (which was considerable) but rather because I felt comfortable with her. In retrospect, I probably would not have felt comfortable discontinuing treatment if I had not liked her (she was the only therapist I called), so I am fortunate that she was so terrific, especially considering the rather impersonal way I went about selecting her. I have seen Rona off and on for individual therapy over the last 28 years for a total of 580 sessions.

I should note that I contacted Rona when I was first asked to write this chapter. She read an early draft of the chapter, gave me the dates of my sessions, verified the factual material, made suggestions for additions, and gave permission for me to use her name. She was supportive of my writing the chapter and liked the way I characterized her in the chapter.

Rona reminded me of my mother in terms of appearance. When we started, she looked the way my mother did when I was growing up. But, unlike my mother, Rona listened to me, was a consistent presence, and treated me as an individual. She was about 10 years older than me, Jewish, and married with two children. Her husband was an internist, and they lived in a very nice part of town, so I always assumed that she was quite wealthy. She had directed a clinic but had recently gone into a small private group practice when I first started seeing her. So we had some differences (Jewish versus Christian, 10 years age difference, socioeconomic status), but these did not seem as important to me as our similarities (gender, theoretical orientation).

My first episode of individual therapy lasted three years and involved one or two sessions per week. I vividly recall being so anxious talking about myself during the first year of therapy that I had to run out at least once during most sessions to go to the bathroom. I also recall vividly that Rona knitted during all the sessions. I felt wounded because I thought she could not possibly be listening to me. I was sure that she was knitting because I was boring, which was a familiar feeling for me. Very few people in my life had ever listened to me. When she seemed sleepy and occasionally even fell asleep, I added that evidence to my certainty that I was a boring client, which I probably was, because I was so defended and afraid of opening up for fear of rejection and being boring. I did not mention my feelings about her knitting or falling asleep in the therapy at the time.

I spent hours between sessions thinking about what Rona and I had talked about in therapy and planning what I wanted to talk about in the next session. I also talked endlessly about my therapy experiences with my husband and close friends, who were all also in therapy. Being in psychotherapy was a major part of my identity at the time. Therapy was very helpful, even though it was also anxiety-producing.

Rona did many things that were helpful. I remember clearly one of Rona's early self-disclosures. I was talking about how it was not possible to combine career and family. She reminded me that she had been able to combine career and family and so it was clearly possible. She did not disclose much over the years, but when she did, it was typically at an important point. Rona used self-disclosures to show me that we were similar and to serve as a model for something that I needed to think about or do.

Rona worked within a long-term psychodynamic orientation, where you look closely at family history, every part of the relationship, and transference and proceed carefully and slowly toward termination. Hence she offered many interpretations. She tried to help me understand what was going on and what caused me to act as I did. She would repeatedly come back to certain things from my childhood that were crucial in my formation (e.g., my younger sister dying when I was three). She would make connections between our therapy relationship and my relationship with my parents. I should note that her interpretations were done in a collaborative manner. She was not the expert telling me about myself, but rather we were working together to try to understand what was going on. She encouraged my introspection and independence.

At the same time that she was interpretive and sometimes even confrontive, Rona was supportive and empathic. I felt safe to talk about almost everything. I felt that she could understand my struggles. In fact, I felt that Rona was a repository for me of everything I thought and felt. She remembered what I had said. I knew I existed because she had heard me. I needed to tell her things so that I knew that they happened. And if I told her things, I knew that she was there to remind me that I existed. It is hard to express this feeling in words, but I felt very grounded knowing that Rona knew so much about me across so many years. She held me together when I felt unable to hold myself together.

Rona also had clear, consistent, reasonable boundaries about such things as fees, cancellation, and phone calls, but she was also humane and kind about the way she implemented these boundaries. She started and ended sessions promptly, and I felt very special when I could get a couple of extra minutes from her. I did not call her between sessions except to ask for an additional appointment when I was in crisis. I did run into her once in a store—she was very cordial when I said hello, and we chatted briefly. She came to see me once when I gave a talk at a convention, and I was proud, grateful, and a bit nervous that she was there. I should note that I did not really try to push any of her limits. In fact, I did the opposite. I tried to be the best client possible and follow all the rules so that she would not get angry at me.

We terminated the first episode of therapy about the time that I was pregnant with my first child. I felt much better and wanted to try to manage things on my own. We processed the termination carefully for several months, and when we stopped, Rona assured me that I could come back if and when I needed to. I remember giving her a gift of a picture I had taken of Niagara Falls, which she graciously accepted (and said recently that she still has).

I started individual therapy again with Rona about three years later. Being a parent of two young children was difficult and brought up many issues for me about what it had been like to be parented. I found myself doing things exactly as my parents had, and I often heard my mother's voice come out of my mouth. Being a parent has done more to teach me about the highs and lows of my personality than any other event in my life, and I needed help to deal with the feelings. I went to therapy this time about once a week for nine years. We went much deeper this time, and I would say that this was when I formed a strong, healthy attachment to Rona. It took a long time for me to work through my conflicts not only about raising children but also about combining work and family, individuating from my parents, developing my identity, and establishing my career.

I did not talk about my therapy as much with my friends during this second episode of therapy as I had previously. I had two small children, a busy career, and little time to spend with friends. But, more important, I do not think I needed to talk about therapy with friends as much at this point as I did earlier. I was in a different phase in which I was safe and comfortable working on my issues rather than being "into therapy."

Toward the end of this second therapy episode, I was able to tell Rona that her knitting bothered me. We talked about it, as we did everything in therapy. She told me that she knitted to keep her hands occupied so that she could focus more on me. I understood that intellectually, but emotionally I needed her to stop knitting. She did quit knitting, which made me feel good that she responded to my needs.

At some point, I felt a need to stop therapy again. I felt that I had gone as far as I could go. The time that it took to go to therapy and the cost became important factors, signifying to me that I was better because therapy was not the priority that it had once been. I knew that I could go back whenever I needed to, which reassured me that I was not losing contact with Rona.

Indeed, I have gone back several times for "tuneups" in the last few years. The third time I went back, Rona was knitting again. In contrast to my earlier reactions, though, I realized that her knitting no longer bothered me. I was able to see that Rona could pay attention to me just fine (she didn't even fall asleep any more) and that it helped her relax. I probably was less boring as time went on because I came to believe in myself more and was able to talk more openly about my feelings.

Our relationship has evolved over time. Initially, I was needy, vulnerable, dependent, defended, and reserved. I came to be more open and to perceive Rona as an equal with whom I consulted about my personal and career concerns. As an illustration of her serving in a consultant capacity, I recall talking with Rona a few years ago about my uncertainty about whether I wanted to write a book on dream work in therapy. I lacked confidence in my ideas. It seemed so bold to propose a new theory, to say how I thought dream work should proceed. After all, who was I to propose a new theory of dream work? Rona asked me to tell her about my dream model, and we talked about it as I would with a colleague. She reassured me that she liked my ideas and encouraged me to write the book (Hill, 1996). Her professional opinion and encouragement was very important to me, both as a therapist and as a colleague.

Rona recently retired from doing private practice full-time, which means that she closed her office and stopped accepting new patients, but she continued to see her long-term patients on an as-needed basis in her home office. I went back for a session while writing this chapter. I wanted to see her in her home office and be reassured that she was still there if I needed her. I also wanted to consult with her about the chapter and make sure that I was not violating any confidences or misrepresenting her. Rona reassured me about both things. It was good to see her and to fill her in on what had happened in the interim. One thing I was struck by is her memory for all the things that have happened to me over the years. It is truly comforting to know that she remembers so much of my history and can remind me of why I get stuck and anxious (e.g., she always remembers an image of me hiding under the table in the middle of the kitchen when I was a small child). Her reassurance and caring have kept me grounded.

An overall point that I think is important is that I have never really gotten angry at Rona. I got annoyed with the knitting and asked her to stop, and a few times I got annoyed if she was late starting a session, but I never felt or expressed anger to her. I attribute my not getting angry at her to both of us. On her part, she was really good, so there was not much need to get angry. She is a calm, centered person. In her reaction to a draft of this chapter, Rona said that few of her clients have ever gotten angry at her, which she attributed to the clarity of her boundaries, her not feeling guilty about setting limits but seeing it as a necessary way of taking care of herself, and her willingness to be honest and explain her decisions to patients. For myself, although I get angry at other people, I have trouble expressing anger to anyone other than my husband and children. There is a part of me that is still afraid that if I got angry at Rona, she would not like me and might reject me. However, given that I do not feel any anger at her at this point, I do not feel a need to work on this issue with her.

Another overall point is about the cost of therapy. Fees were low when I started therapy in 1975, and my health insurance paid for 50% of the cost, so the cost was very reasonable. And, because I really needed the therapy, cost was not an issue. Rona typically increased her fees by $10 to $15 every two or three years, so that her fees were quite high toward the end of my therapy experience. Because she did not join managed care panels and was therefore an out-of-network provider, my share of the fee was proportionally even higher toward the end. As I felt better and the costs skyrocketed, the costs as well as the hassle of getting every 10 sessions preauthorized became a factor in my thinking about whether to go back for sessions. I am very grateful that insurance was generous during the years when I really needed therapy.

I am not sure that being a psychotherapist myself has had much impact on me as a client in my individual therapy. I was more interested in getting help than in being treated in a special way because I was a therapist.

In retrospect, though, I can point to some positive and negative things about being a therapist in therapy. On the positive side, I knew what to expect from therapy and was firmly committed to it. I knew that I needed therapy, and I did not delude myself into thinking that I was doing it for training. I knew what the boundaries were supposed to be, and I did not try to challenge or change them. In addition, because Rona understood my job so well, I was able to talk about it at a depth that might not have been possible if I had been in another career.

One the negative side, I may have restrained myself more in therapy than I would have if I had not known the "rules." I did occasionally code or judge her techniques (e.g., "that was a good interpretation") or think about what theoretical approach she was using, but it did not seem to get in the way of the therapy too much. We were able to get past it to get to work.

Did Rona act any differently with me because I was a psychologist? I doubt it. She was very secure in who she was as a person and as a professional. She was very well regarded in the therapeutic community and never seemed threatened by my professional successes.

MARITAL THERAPY

At about the time I went back for my second episode of individual therapy, the pressures on my marriage were also escalating. My husband and I had two small children and two challenging careers, so we needed marital therapy in addition to our individual therapies. We were learning in our individual therapies about ourselves, but we were not learning how to communicate with each other and resolve problems.

But we wondered how we should go about it. Should it be his therapist or mine? I certainly did not want to go to his therapist. I had seen his therapist one time for some reason that I cannot remember, and his abrasive, confrontational style really turned me off and made me angry. Likewise, my husband did not want to go and see my individual therapist. We needed someone just for the marital therapy who had no allegiance to either of us individually. Jim broke the deadlock by getting a name from his individual therapist of a marital therapist, a clinical psychologist who had recently retired from working for the government. Despite my resistance to the referral having come from Jim's action (yes, we were definitely into power struggles) and from his individual therapist, I went because we truly needed outside help.

When we walked into the office, and I saw this older, portly, white-haired gentleman with diplomas from Catholic universities all over his walls, I freaked out. I immediately thought that there was no way that this old, Catholic guy could ever understand me. I should mention that I had somewhat reluctantly converted to Catholicism when we got married and still have never settled my conflicts related to religion. After my initial negative reaction, I did settle down and tried to get something out of the experience. I never trusted Dr. M (he has since died, so I could not secure permission to use his name) as much as I did Rona, and I always felt somewhat uncomfortable opening up to him. My transference to Dr. M made it difficult for me to see him accurately or trust him completely. I do not recall that Dr. M ever dealt with my transferences to him directly, which was okay with me at the time, because I wanted to work on the marriage and not on the therapy relationship. In retrospect, it might have been helpful to talk about the transference more, but I do not think I was ready to do so at the time.

We saw Dr. M for about 75 sessions spread out over about two years. It is hard to characterize Dr. M's orientation. Sometimes he was psychoanalytic. He would sit for entire sessions saying nothing and making us do all the work. It was helpful for us to be there, even though he was silent, because it provided a time and place for us to talk to each other. He would not rescue us but forced us to "stew in our juices." His hands-off policy was good for us, for the most part, because we did have the skills to communicate and needed the time and safety to be able to talk. At other times, Dr. M would become directive and tell us exactly what he thought. For example, he was directive in helping us work through our power struggles about childcare and was forthright in giving opinions and advice when he thought it was necessary. Dr. M was also very gentle, friendly, warm, and secure. His office was in his home, and he seemed open about his family. His wife would often chat with us for a few minutes before sessions.

One of the major things Jim and I learned through this course of marital therapy was about our transferences to each other. I was amazed to learn that Jim projected onto me that I was like his mother because I certainly could not see the similarities. I had just been angry that he was blaming me for things that seemed out of proportion to what I was doing or who I was. And I did the same with Jim. I treated him like he was my father and expected that he was acting out of the same motivations that I attributed to my father. I had a hard time separating the two of them. The therapist was able to help us sort out those transferences, see each other more realistically, and react to each other rather than to our transference figures. I learned to restrain myself for the most part and to try not to control Jim's life and change him.

An additional benefit of this therapy is that Jim and I were able to better negotiate dividing the chores of parenting. Given our different expectations stemming from our different family backgrounds, we had gotten quite stuck in expecting each other to play the roles that had obtained in our families of origin. The marital therapy helped us make it through those tough years of raising small children.

On the negative side, our marital therapist gave us several questionnaires to complete individually and together after the first session. Being good students, we did as we were told and spent hours completing these questionnaires. We got something out of completing the measures, but I was annoyed that Dr. M never referred to our responses in the sessions. He may have used them in understanding us more, but he did not tell us anything about what he gained from seeing our responses on the measures. I was annoyed that we had spent so much time completing them if he was not going to use them in the therapy.

Gender, age, and religion were all major factors in my not feeling as safe with Dr. M as I had with Rona. I trusted Dr. M enough to allow him to help Jim and me talk with each other, but I would not have wanted him as my individual therapist. And I was definitely ready to stop the marital therapy after two years, especially given that Jim and I were able to keep working on our issues on our own.

I learned that you can get something from therapy even if the relationship is not the absolute best. Furthermore, the relationship with the marital therapist did not seem as important to me as it was in individual therapy, because my relationship with my husband was more important. The therapist was there to help us work on our marital relationship, not to work on my relationship with him.

BENEFITS OF MY PSYCHOTHERAPY EXPERIENCES TO ME AS A PSYCHOLOGIST

In my traditional scientist-practitioner training as a counseling psychologist, I learned to value and be both a researcher and a therapist. During graduate school, I expected that I would be a therapist when I graduated, although I enjoyed doing research. I changed career paths when my advisor suggested that I would have more flexibility if I tried academia first. He said that I could always move from academics to practice but would be less likely to be able to move from practice to academics. I tried academia, and after a bumpy start, discovered that I loved most parts of an academic position.

I should note here that I no longer see private clients. I continued providing therapy in my small private practice out of my home for about the first 15 years after graduate school. It became increasingly difficult, however, to maintain my practice after I had children and professional activities intensified. I felt that I did not have enough time to seek out supervision, and it was difficult to find the hours to do therapy. Something had to give, and I found that I enjoyed doing other professional things more than I enjoyed doing therapy. So I have not seen private clients for the last 15 years.

I do, however, keep an active involvement in therapy in several ways. First, I occasionally see clients for research studies. Second, I teach helping skills and theories of psychotherapy to undergraduate and graduate students and often demonstrate the skills in class. Third, I advise undergraduate and graduate students, which involves a great deal of therapeutic skill. Fourth, I teach and demonstrate dream work to students and professionals. Fifth, I do research on psychotherapy. For this research, I have interviewed many therapists and clients about their therapy experiences. For example, I have interviewed therapists about how they deal with impasses in therapy (Hill, Nutt-Williams, Heaton, Thompson, & Rhodes, 1996) and how they manage their reactions to client anger directed toward them (Hill et al., in press). I have interviewed clients about their experiences in brief therapy involving dream work (Hill et al., 2000). I have also transcribed and watched many therapy sessions and coded them for therapist intentions and techniques (e.g., Hill, 1989). Finally, I listen to my husband talk about his experiences with clients and thus am able to maintain some empathy for real-world therapists.

I would say that my experiences of being a client in therapy have had an important influence on me as a psychologist. First of all, I disclose that I have been in therapy to model for students that being in therapy can be helpful and to encourage them to seek out therapy when they need it. We do not require that students seek out therapy in our graduate program because we do not think it is a good idea to legislate people getting help. I am very wary of proselytizing about anything, given my religious background, where we were supposed to go out and try to convert people.

My experiences have also influenced my theorizing about therapy. Because I benefited personally mostly from psychodynamic and humanistic approaches, I lean toward these approaches for therapy. But I also believe in the value of behavioral interventions, which I learned during graduate school. I think, however, that behaviors can be changed most easily once clients are motivated, have formed a good therapeutic relationship, and possess some understanding of why they behave as they do. In addition, my therapists tended to use a variety of different techniques depending on what they thought I needed at the time, modeling that rigid adherence to a theoretical approach is not therapeutic. Finally, teaching a variety of theoretical approaches has helped me look for what works in all of them. Hence my therapeutic approach can be characterized as an integration of humanistic, psychodynamic, and behavioral approaches (see Hill, 2004; Hill & O'Brien, 1999).

My experiences as a client have also influenced my research program. I have a better understanding of psychotherapy process from having been in my own therapy, as well as from having been a therapist. When I think of a topic I am interested in researching (e.g., therapist interpretations), I think about how I experienced my therapists' interpretations and then how I offered interpretations as a therapist. Both experiences give me a benchmark against which to evaluate theory and research findings. For example, I got interested in doing research on dreams from my teaching experiences, but then I worked on several dreams with Rona and got more invested in the value of conducting research on dream work in therapy. My dream model (Hill, 1996, 2003) was different from Rona's, which supports the idea that I felt empowered to develop my own ideas rather than make myself a clone of Rona.

My ideas for research projects have typically come as much from my teaching experiences as from my therapy experiences. Perhaps if my therapy experiences had been negative, I would have been more invested in studying them.

LESSONS LEARNED FROM MY THERAPY EXPERIENCES

1. The therapeutic relationship is important. Clients have to feel comfortable enough with their therapists before they will disclose deep secrets or allow their therapists to have much influence over them. Of course, even when the therapeutic relationship is close to ideal, clients choose what they are ready to disclose and what they think therapists can help them with. But clients can be helped even when the therapeutic relationship is less than ideal. They might not get as much out of the therapy as they would with a better relationship, and they may have to be more cautious with the therapist, but they can sometimes be helped in more limited ways. Furthermore, the therapeutic relationship is probably much more important for very long-term individual therapy than it is for short-term or marital work, although it has to be "good enough" in the brief modalities for clients to feel sufficiently safe to work.

2. Therapist techniques are also important in helping clients change. Therapists help clients explore, devise interpretations, challenge clients out of complacencies, educate clients, and teach specific skills. Specific techniques were useful in my therapy experiences. It was not enough that my therapists were just there; they had to do specific things to help me figure out what was going on with me and how to change. Of course, the dichotomy between the relationship and the techniques is simplistic. In fact, techniques are used to build and maintain the relationship, and the relationship is needed to potentiate techniques.

3. Clear, reasonable limits are essential in therapy to help clients feel safe and know what to expect. Equally important is that therapists are secure and comfortable setting and maintaining the limits.

4. Long-term psychodynamic therapy can be very useful to help clients make long-lasting personality changes. Furthermore, it is ideal for clients to be able to do several episodes of therapy with the same therapist over time to be able to deal with developmental transitions. We ought to be demanding that insurance companies pay for longer term therapy, and we ought to be doing more to study the specific effects of long-term therapy.

5. Change occurs through multiple forms of therapeutic interventions, both formal and informal. In my case, I had a good relationship with my husband and a supportive network of friends and colleagues. I was involved in individual therapy, marital therapy, encounter groups, a leaderless couples group, a consciousness-raising group, and supervision experiences. I was also fortunate enough to be in a professional career that involves reading about, teaching about, and doing research on psychotherapy. I was involved in many self-change efforts (e.g., working on my own dreams). Finally, I also have engaged in a healthy lifestyle in terms of diet and exercise, regularly see my medical doctor and dentist, and use chiropractors and massage therapists when appropriate. All of these therapeutic activities have helped me grow and develop who I am. It is not possible to isolate the unique effects of the individual and marital therapy from all of these other experiences.

6. We need to rethink how we measure outcome when we think about the effects of long-term psychotherapy. Long-term therapy can be thought of as one aspect of a lifelong educational process. We sometimes take a short course of brief therapy to resolve crises or reduce symptoms, just as we might take one course in college to learn a little bit about one subject. But 10 sessions of brief therapy is not a full therapeutic education. For the outcome of long-term therapy, we need to be looking at contentment, personal acceptance, personality reorganization, the ability to have successful relationships and careers, and the ability to resolve new crises and life transitions as they occur.

7. It is hard to change. Cognitive and behavior patterns are usually deeply rooted and difficult to alter. I have empathy for clients in their struggles to make changes in their lives.

8. Clients are very attentive to whether therapists are paying attention to them. Things like knitting and falling asleep are noted but are hard for clients to confront directly, perhaps because they feel like such a narcissistic wound. It is probably equally hard for therapists to bring these issues up because they feel vulnerable or like they did something wrong. But these are the very issues that may need to be talked about in therapy (see also Geller, 1994).

9. Transference can have a powerful influence in therapy. The influence can be positive, as was shown in my experiences with my individual therapist, or negative, as shown by my experiences with my marital therapist. In the long run, dealing with these transferences openly is undoubtedly important for learning how to confront difficult interpersonal situations.

10. Barriers to seeking therapy need to be reduced. Many people need therapy but do not seek it because of stigma, cost, or vulnerability. Many

who want therapy do not know how to choose a good therapist, and many who do seek therapy end up with someone they do not feel comfortable with but do not know how to switch.

CONCLUSIONS

Being a psychotherapist and a psychologist had minimal influence on my experiences as a client in therapy, at least as far as I am aware. Being a therapist and psychologist was helpful to me in that I understood what I was getting into, what was expected of me, and what I could hope to get out of therapy; but it did not have much impact on the therapy process. Of course, I was fortunate enough to have excellent therapists, who treated me as an individual who was in pain and needed help rather than being overly concerned about my being a therapist and a psychologist.

One could question whether my 580 sessions of individual therapy and about 75 sessions of marital therapy were necessary or whether they were an unnecessary luxury. After all, insurance companies will now only reimburse for brief, necessary therapy of diagnosable disorders and see no benefit to society of long-term therapy of "normal" people. I would assert that my therapy was not only very beneficial for me personally but also crucial for my development as a professional. The proof of the effectiveness of my therapy is in my life—I have been happily married for 29 years, have two well-adjusted grown children, and have had a successful career. I am grateful for my therapy experiences. I might have resolved some of my personal conflicts through other means (e.g., support groups), but therapy was a good method for me because it fit with my values, training, and beliefs.

ACKNOWLEDGMENT   I would like to express my appreciation to Rona Eisner, Jesse Geller, Charles Gelso, James Gormally, Misty Kolchakian, and John Norcross for giving me feedback on drafts of this chapter.

REFERENCES

Geller, J. D. (1994). The psychotherapist's experience of interest and boredom. *Psychotherapy, 31,* 3–16.

Hill, C. E. (1989). *Therapist techniques and client outcomes: Eight cases of brief psychotherapy.* Newbury Park, CA: Sage.

Hill, C. E. (1996). *Working with dreams in psychotherapy.* New York: Guilford.

Hill, C. E. (2003). *Dream work in therapy: Facilitating exploration, insight, and action* (2nd ed.). Washington, DC: American Psychological Association.

Hill, C. E. (2004). *Helping skills: Facilitating exploration, insight, and action* (2nd ed.). Washington, DC: American Psychological Association.

Hill, C. E., Kellems, I., Kolchakian, M., Nakayama, E. Y., Wonnell, T., & Davis, T. L. (in press). The therapist experience of being the target of hostile versus suspected-unassented client anger: Factors associated with resolution. *Psychotherapy Research, 14,* 475–496.

Hill, C. E., Nutt-Williams, E., Heaton, K. J., Thompson, B. J., & Rhodes, R. H.

(1996). Therapist retrospective recall of impasses in long-term psychotherapy: A qualitative analysis. *Journal of Counseling Psychology, 43,* 207–217.

Hill, C. E., & O'Brien, K. M. (1999). *Helping skills: Facilitating exploration, insight, and action.* Washington, DC: American Psychological Association.

Hill, C. E., Zack, J., Wonnell, T., Hoffman, M. A., Rochlen, A., Goldberg, J., Nakayama, E., Heaton, K. J., Kelley, F., Eiche, K., Tomlinson, M., & Hess, S. (2000). Structured brief therapy with a focus on dreams or loss for clients with troubling dreams and recent losses. *Journal of Counseling Psychology, 47,* 90–101.

12

A SHAMANIC TAPESTRY

My Experiences with Individual, Marital, and Family Therapy

WILLIAM M. PINSOF

The tradition of psychotherapists in psychotherapy is as old as the human species. The first psychotherapists were the shamans, who were chosen for their profession by virtue of their disorders, and who learned the secrets of their own underworld in order to cure their fellow tribesmen (Eliade, 1964; Lommel, 1967). In line with this ancient tradition, who I am today as a clinical psychologist and integrative psychotherapist is the product not only of my education, training, and personality but also, perhaps even more important, my experience as a patient in various psychotherapies over the course of my life. All of these experiences have become interwoven strands in the tapestry of my professional self.

FAILURE AND GROWTH

Without failure, there is no growth. Learning and failure are inextricably bound to each other in the evolution of our species, in the development of a person, and in the development of a psychotherapist. Failure drives the development of integrative psychotherapies. It also drives innovation within the therapy of any particular individual or family. In addition, the repeated and manageable failures of the therapeutic relationship drive the development of the selves of our patients. Embracing and understanding our failures is the key to the growth of our field, our therapies, and ultimately, our selves.

Resolving psychotherapeutic failures has been the key to my growth as a clinician and scholar. *Integrative problem-centered therapy* (Pinsof, 1983, 1995, 2002), a therapeutic model for integrating family, individual, and biological therapies, is the product of my failures and those of my students and colleagues over the last 30 years. The process of problem-centered therapy is failure driven. It utilizes relatively indirect, complex, and expensive interventions only when more direct, simpler, and less expensive ones fail to resolve the problems for which our patients seek help.

Much as I would like to claim that this model derives from a set of well-researched experiments, or a set of elegant, theoretically derived, and logically inexorable principles, I would not be truthful if I did. The model has three sources: my experience as a therapist with more than 30 years of experience; my knowledge as a psychotherapy researcher over the last 30 years; and, most profoundly, my experience as a person and patient. I have had approximately four extended formal episodes of therapy as I have struggled over the course of my life to resolve a variety of problems. My integrative problem-centered model reflects that experience as much, if not more, than my experience as a clinician and researcher. It is a model that I can sell, because I have bought it. I know it from the inside as well as the outside.

In this chapter I present, in roughly chronological order, a variety of therapeutic episodes, illustrating key failure and growth experiences. In some of them I am the patient and in some the therapist. These episodes delineate the major personal and professional strands that make up my psychotherapeutic self. I briefly present their integration into the coherent and cohesive model of psychotherapeutic practice that I call problem-centered therapy. I conclude with reflections on the normality as well as the extraordinary nature of therapists in psychotherapy.

THE FAILURE OF PSYCHOANALYSIS AND
THE DISCOVERY OF FAMILY THERAPY

I was born into the world of psychoanalysis in Chicago at the end of World War II. Members of my family had been in analysis before I was born, and the works of Freud occupied a central place in our family library. As the youngest of three, I did not understand the jokes and taunts about penis envy and Oedipal complexes that flew around the dinner table. But I did understand that there was a lot of pain in my family and that pain was not to be talked about. The dual refrains were "Talk to your doctor about that" or "My doctor thinks . . ."

My father, the head of a family business, spent much of his time at home in his basement study, cataloguing and expanding his art collections. His emotional withdrawal and periods of depression, never openly discussed, affected our entire family life. My own relationship with him was distant. I cannot remember him ever holding me, telling me he loved me, or offering himself as an educational or emotional mentor. However, he did step in at key points in my childhood and adolescence to support and promote my intellectual and cultural development. He also represented an ideal of intellectual and professional excellence that has sustained and inspired me.

By the time I was 13, the others in my family and I were islands of pain, each with our own psychoanalytic individual therapist. I yearned for my father's love and on Saturday mornings I often talked to my therapist about it. Then my father would pick me up at my therapist's office in downtown Chicago and drive me home. We sat silently so he could listen to the Metropolitan Opera on the car radio. My therapist never suggested a joint session with my father, nor did he coach me to speak directly to my father about my yearning for connection.

I entered psychodynamic individual therapy at the age of 13 and decided that I wanted to be a psychologist at 15. My junior theme in high school compared Freud and Jung. In college I majored in the history of religion. Prior to the middle of the nineteenth century, almost all "psychotherapy" occurred within a religious context, and therefore, for me, the history of religion became the history of psychotherapy. My college honors thesis articulated a model of psychotherapy that encompassed shamanism, psychoanalysis, and Zen Buddhism.

I attended graduate school in clinical psychology at York University in Toronto from 1970 to 1975. My "conversion" occurred the first month, upon meeting with my research supervisor. I noticed a book on his shelf called *Intensive Family Therapy* (Boszormenyi-Nagy & Framo, 1969). In response to my question "What's family therapy?" he replied, "That's where they put people together in the same room and have them talk to each other." I was shocked and enthralled. The idea of sitting in the same room with my family and speaking our true feelings and thoughts excited and frightened me. With terror and fascination, I plunged into family therapy.

After two years in graduate school reading everything I could find on family therapy and actually doing a little bit as well, I received a three-year Canada Council Fellowship that allowed me to become a part-time clinical fellow at the McMaster University Department of Psychiatry in Hamilton, Ontario, to learn family therapy. Nathan Epstein and his colleagues from Jewish General Hospital in Montreal established McMaster's Psychiatry Department in the late 1960s. Nate had originally been trained in New York with Nathan Ackerman and was the "father" of family therapy in Canada.

My first week at McMaster I watched Nate conduct a "live supervision interview" with a psychiatric resident who was treating a family with a sexually promiscuous and conduct-disordered adolescent daughter named Rene.[1] Her father, Tom, was disengaged from his wife and daughter, while Rene and her mother, Francine, were conflictually enmeshed. In the initial part of the interview with the resident, the parents complained that things were continuing to deteriorate. They complained that they had no control over Rene.

At this point Nate entered the session, having observed the first 20 minutes from behind a one-way mirror. Nate began by exploring what prevented the parents from creating a firm and consistent structure for Rene. Francine complained bitterly that she got no help from Tom, who just sat there as she spoke and shrugged. Nate turned to Tom and asked him what prevented him from getting involved. He said, "I try, but I just don't know what to do." Nate replied: "Okay, let's work on it now. I'll tell you what to do." Tom looked like a deer caught in the headlights of an oncoming car.

Nate asked Francine what she felt was the most pressing issue they needed to talk about pertaining to Rene. She replied: Rene respecting curfew. Rene immediately argued that curfew was not as important as her mother's racist attitudes toward her black Jamaican boyfriend. The mother became enraged, yelling that she, and not Rene, would decide what was to be talked about. At this point, Nate turned to Tom and said, "Get in there, man. Help your wife." The father turned his palms up and said helplessly, "I don't know what to do." Nate said, "I don't care what you do, but you better do something and do it now, cause they're heating up." Tom lamely said to his wife and daughter, "Be quiet. Stop yelling." They ignored him. Nate said: "Good start. Raise your voice this time and tell them what you'd like them to do, not just what they shouldn't do." The father pleaded, "I can't." Nate said "Come on man, do it."

Slowly increasing his voice to a low holler, Tom yelled, "Rene, shut up and listen to your mother." Rene looked incredulously at her father and said, "You stay out of it." Nate said to Tom, "Keep going, don't let her knock you off track." Not even glancing at Nate, Tom stared at Rene and said, "Don't tell me what to do, young lady. I said listen to your mother and I mean it. You'll listen or else." Rene mimicked: "Or else what?" Tom glanced at Nate, who sat stonefaced, staring at Rene. Tom hesitated, waiting for help from Nate or Francine. The silence grew. Finally Tom turned to Rene and said, very quietly, "Or else you'll just have to get out of our house. You've tried to be the boss of this family, and it's over. I won't have it." Nate clapped slowly twice and said, "Rene, your father's back."

Nate's intervention turned the tide for this family and their therapy. Within the session, Rene visibly calmed down. Francine looked flustered but soon expressed relief that the whole burden of dealing with Rene was no longer on her shoulders. It was clear that there was still more work to be done, but I had never observed such rapid and powerful change. By simply and unequivocally directing Tom, Nate had transformed the family's structure. I could not help thinking, as I sat behind the one-way mirror, *What would have happened to my family had we run into Nate Epstein? Why didn't my therapist or my sister's therapist, or my mother's therapist, challenge my father to get involved the way Nate did with Tom? Instead of sustaining the fragmentation of my family, instead of empathizing with our pain, why didn't the system of therapists working with us pull us together and take away some of the reasons for the pain?*

At McMaster I learned the power of direct intervention in families. I learned that some people could change without historical-genetic insight, and that sometimes that change was lasting and transforming, not just for the person transformed but also for everyone involved. I learned that sometimes you could say directly to people "Just do it," and they would do it. Sometimes, as the Strategic-Mental Research Institute therapists taught, it was necessary to be indirect, if not paradoxical, to achieve such change. But what became clear to me was that everyone did not need in-depth, psycho-analytically oriented interventions in order to change. In fact, such interventions, as was the case with my own family (I thought), could retard the change process and depotentiate the family. Nate and the other therapists at McMaster built on the strengths of patients, not their deficits. If change was possible with direct and powerful interventions, they achieved it.

WHEN FAMILY THERAPY FAILS:
FROM THE CHILDREN TO THE ADULTS

As I worked with more families at McMaster and observed other therapists, I saw that in a substantial number of cases, direct intervention would change the way the parents related to the children and would shift the boundaries and behavior patterns within the family, but the changes would not last. With these families the "first-order" (Watzlawick, Weakland, & Fisch, 1974) changes would endure for a while, but then the families would "cycle back" to their maladaptive ways. With these families, and with many families in which it was impossible to even achieve such first order-changes, more often than not marital issues were the primary constraints to change. With single-parent families, parental depression played a similar constraining role. The required shift in the treatment of these families was from a more behavioral, action-oriented approach with the family to a more affectively focused marital treatment with intact couples and individual therapy with single parents. The transitional work usually focused on how the marital conflict or parental depression interfered with the parents' abilities to consistently and/or appropriately coparent their child or adolescent.

WHEN MARITAL THERAPY FAILS:
BRINGING IN THE FAMILY-OF-ORIGIN

In 1975, I moved from Canada back to Chicago to take a job on the staff of the Family Institute of Chicago (which is now the Family Institute at Northwestern University), which had just become part of Northwestern Memorial Hospital and the Northwestern University Medical School. At McMaster most of the cases I treated presented as families with a child as the identified patient. At the Family Institute, most of the cases presented as couples, with their relationship as the problem. Initially, I tried to treat these cases as I had at McMaster when family treatment became marital treatment. I focused, in the here and now, on the directness and clarity of emotional expression between the partners, their problem-solving patterns, and the intensity and exclusivity of their involvement with each other.

   At that time my wife, Suzan, and I got into marital therapy. Since marrying in 1969, our relationship had been conflictual. We spent the first eight months of therapy addressing our relationship—how we solved problems and how we dealt with our feelings toward each other. One of the patterns that became clear was that I displaced much of my anger at my parents, particularly my father, onto Suzan. I would have a frustrating interaction with my parents and blow up at Suzan. Despite becoming aware of this pattern, I was unable to change it.

At this point our therapist recommended bringing my parents into our therapy. It was as though he shot adrenaline directly into my veins. I was frightened by primitive fears and emotions—it would kill them, or he (my father) would kill me. And I was excited—I was finally bringing my family therapy training home. Nate Epstein would finally work with my parents and me. After much talk and planning, Suzan and I invited my parents to join us for three sessions. Three eventually turned into ten of the most powerful therapy experiences of my life. Before each session I was a paranoid wreck—seeing insults everywhere and picking fights with Suzan for no reason. After each session, I was depleted and exhausted—spent.

The high point came in the sixth session. My mother was sick and could not attend, so it was just our therapist, Suzan, my father, and me. I had used the previous sessions to progressively work my way toward my father, exploring my fear of his anger and withdrawal. Growing up, I had been more comfortable fighting with my mother, and more recently with my wife, rather than doing battle with my much more distant and frightening father. In this session, with the support of Suzan and our therapist, I told my father that if he didn't start coming through for me as a father, I would not be there for him as a son. He responded defensively: "Then you won't be there as a son." I shot back: "Fuck you," and burst into tears. My father just sat there saying nothing. I sobbed and let go of an ocean of tears. I still have no recollection of how the session ended.

The next day my father called and invited me to have lunch with him. This invitation initiated a new phase in our relationship, in which he reached out to me as he never had before. I responded with enthusiasm and affection. At the end of the next session, we hugged and kissed each other for the first time in my memory. I was thrilled. At the age of 29, I finally had a father. I could now tell him what I was upset about in our relationship, and he listened and tried to change as much as he could. Now I was able to transact the business with him that was ours, rather then displacing it onto my mother or Suzan. Not surprisingly, the level of conflict in our marriage diminished.

After this experience in marital therapy with my parents, I started doing family-of-origin work and using family-of-origin sessions with couples when we were stuck at the level of their relationship. However, it soon became clear that not all families responded the way mine had. My story illustrates the *family-of-origin breakthrough*, in which the parents and the children respond constructively. Our interaction patterns changed, and the relationships between my parents and me improved. But parental responses frequently illustrate a second outcome scenario, *the family-of-origin wall*. In this scenario, the parents do not change, and the family-of-origin sessions consist of the adult-child banging his or her head against the parental wall to no avail. Ultimately, this failure experience facilitates the adult child letting go of the wished-for transformation of the parent-child bond, a painful but maturing experience.

CONFRONTING THE THERAPIST OF MY ADOLESCENCE: FAMILY-OF-ORIGIN ADDENDUM

An interesting side story to my experience in therapy with my parents concerns my "reunion" with the therapist I had worked with as an adolescent in Chicago. Upon returning to Chicago in 1975 and taking a position at the Family Institute, I received an appointment as an assistant professor in the Department of Psychiatry and Behavioral Sciences at Northwestern University. At my first faculty meeting of the Psychiatry Department, I was surprised to see the psychiatrist, whom I will call John Logan, with whom I had worked in my adolescence. He was also a member of the faculty. We said hello to each other, and he congratulated me on my appointment.

About a year later, after my experience with my family in couples therapy, I began to feel very angry at John. Why did I have to wait 15 years to have a relationship with my father, when John could have confronted my father or helped me confront my father when I was a teenager? Serendipitously, at that time, I received a call from John's wife, who was a doctoral student at Northwestern. I was teaching a very popular graduate seminar in family assessment and treatment in the Clinical Psychology Program in the Medical School, for which I had just closed enrollment. John's wife asked if she could get into the seminar. Without hesitating, I said "yes." That night I recounted this story to Suzan, who asked, "Why did you let her in after the course was closed?" I replied: "So I can teach her how her husband cheated me out of a relationship with my father." She responded sarcastically: "Oh, that's a good idea."

I realized that I needed to talk with John and not use his wife to communicate my thoughts and feelings about our therapy. I called him, and he suggested that we meet for coffee in his office. I told him that I deeply resented his passivity in the face of my father's neglect and asked why he hadn't intervened to try and stop the hurt that he saw my father inflicting on me. He said that in those days (1960–65) for a psychoanalytically oriented psychiatrist to call in the parents of a young adolescent patient and to recommend behavioral changes was the equivalent of an obstetrician recommending an abortion. It was illegal. He then apologized. I felt touched by his sensitivity and honesty in the face of my confrontation. We parted amicably. Fortunately, this meeting spared John's wife the experience of being the object of my wrath at the passivity of the psychoanalytic position, and ultimately, I suspect, the passivity of my father in the face of various threats to the happiness and well-being of myself and my family.

WHEN FAMILY-OF-ORIGIN WORK FAILS:
TOWARD OBJECT RELATIONS

In the early 1980s, 45-year-old Frank Harper, a cardiac surgeon, came to me to "to get rid of the son-of-a-bitch inside of him." He had just moved from New York to Chicago to take a senior position at a major hospital and was about to remarry. Frank and his fiancée, Helen, who would join him in Chicago in six months, had been in therapy in New York with a therapist who had focused extensively on their families-of-origin. That therapist had helped each of them to see the family-of-origin legacies that afflicted them currently, and Frank had been sent to me in Chicago with instructions from his therapist and Helen to work on himself in preparation for his impending marriage.

Our initial work addressed whose therapy this was: his fiancée's or his. Did he want to address the "son-of-a-bitch inside of him," or was that his fiancée's and/or his New York therapist's agenda? Who was driving our work? He said he wasn't sure what he wanted to work on, but he knew that something was wrong with him. It had screwed up his first marriage, and he wanted to make sure it would not screw up this one. We focused on his early experiences in his family-of-origin.

Frank's father was killed in an airplane accident when he was seven. His mother had sent Frank to a residential prep school when he was nine. They never lived at home on a permanent basis again. Frank became a quietly enraged, highly successful student, athlete, and now doctor. His previous therapy had made clear the irony of his work—aggressively fixing broken hearts. He felt his heart had been broken in his childhood, and the resulting chip on his shoulder had driven his first wife and children away from him, leaving him abandoned again. He was terrified he would drive Helen away and be alone forever.

When Helen would visit Chicago, she would join our sessions, but the bulk of our work was individual. After four months, it became apparent that although he had done a lot of insight-oriented family-of-origin work, he had never really expressed his feelings about what had happened directly with his mother. We decided to bring Frank's mother into therapy. She was living in Florida but agreed to fly up to Chicago for three sessions over a four-day period. The sessions were productive; Frank expressed his anger and grief to her about what had happened. She listened and was remorseful. She knew that she had sacrificed her son for herself, but even in retrospect she felt that he might well have been better off not living with her and her depression. She wished she had been a stronger and more resilient person.

This work was cathartic for Frank. He felt as if a burden had been lifted, and his relationship with his mother improved. They were more honest and open with each other, and felt closer. However, the chip on Frank's shoulder was clearly still there. He would blow up at nurses who did not follow his orders promptly, he felt flashes of anger at Helen, and he felt tense within himself—"like a coiled spring."

Since we could not bring his father in, we started working on his relationship with his father in his imagination. I had completed the three-year training program at the Gestalt Institute of Toronto while I was in graduate school, and I was comfortable doing empty chair work. We worked on his relationship with his father in a series of two chair dialogues. The man who emerged as his father was critical, rejecting, unreliable, and uncaring. I was struck by the archaic and partial quality of Frank's representations of his father. His mother also entered the dialogues. At times she would emerge as a selfish, uncaring, and very-angry-at-being-abandoned figure in one of the chairs. The difference between the inner mother of Frank's psyche and the mother who had come into therapy was striking.

As we were doing this work, I began to experience Frank's anger indirectly. He would say things to me in a way that felt angry but didn't sound angry. I was not sure my perception was accurate, but I felt increasingly uneasy. If I was late for a session, he'd accuse me of being angry with him and acting it out. I felt like he was turning the tables on me—he was the psychologist and I the patient. When I went to do a workshop in Seattle, he jokingly accused me of flying as far as I could in the continental United States to get away from him—because he was too much to take.

All of this came together serendipitously. On March 25, my birthday, I was in a shoe store in Chicago buying a new, much-too-expensive pair of shoes as a birthday present to myself. As I was trying the shoes on, Frank walked in. As we chatted, I commented that I was buying myself a birthday present. He looked stunned. I asked him what was wrong, and he replied: "Today is my father's birthday as well." At that moment I realized that despite the close to 15-year gap in our ages, despite my sense of myself almost as a kid in relationship to this man, I represented a father figure to him. The transference had emerged, and he was in the process of working out his unfinished business with his father with me.

In the subsequent sessions we began to explore my meaning to him, the ways that meaning changed over time, and the fears, anxieties and wishes that were getting played out with me. Through projective identification, I felt "his" uneasiness, with Frank as the object of my uncertainty. I felt "his" anger as I was judged and accused by him. He was clearly terrified that I would abandon him—that he was too much for me, as he must have felt that he was too much for his father and his mother. As we explored our relationship, the two-chair work ran out of steam. The energy was now in our relationship, and that was where the therapy focused.

Frank started to uncoil. As he realized that he was not too much for me and that I would not abandon him, he relaxed. He also started to understand his relationship with Helen, and to some extent his ex-wife, not just in the simplistic transferential terms of "she's my mother," but in terms of how they each took on different aspects of the internalized and transformed representations of his parents and himself. As he began to observe and manage this process within himself, his relationship with Helen improved. She commented that he seemed more mature and balanced.

Frank's therapy helped me go beyond transgenerational burdens and direct family-of-origin work in two ways. I realized that at times the here-and-now transformation of the family-of-origin does not substantially affect the internalized and transformed representations of the family and the self—the object relations. If the object relations were the primary constraints to change, they would have to be addressed in their own right. Second, I learned to appreciate how object relations could get played and worked out in the transference with me. Our relationship became the vehicle of understanding and transformation. As these realizations dawned, it struck me that I was coming back to where I had started—psychoanalysis. Not the classic psychoanalysis that my family had experienced but a new, more relational and active psychoanalytic method.

WHEN PSYCHODYNAMIC THERAPY FAILS: HEALING THE SELF

After a number of years in marital therapy, Suzan and I felt that our therapy was no longer helping. We had gained substantially, decreasing our conflict, balancing and equalizing our relationship, and focusing more on each other. We still had conflicts and spent long periods being distant, but our relationship was better. We decided to stop marital therapy. However, I still felt unfinished personally and started seeing our therapist individually.

My individual work focused primarily on the constructive use of my aggression at work and my projections and transferences with Suzan. My therapist was very supportive, encouraging me to "go for it," whatever "it" was. I was not used to having a man in my corner, encouraging and supporting me. This helped me enormously at work, where I was becoming more effective and successful. However, as we pushed on to deal with my relationship to Suzan, I hit a wall within myself. I could understand my transferences and how they played out with Suzan, and I could touch on my transferences to my therapist, but I was stuck. The closer we got to whatever was at the heart of my anxieties, the more anxious I became. After almost two years of twice-a-week therapy, my therapist recommended analysis. Economically and emotionally I was not ready and decided to stop therapy. Leaving that therapy was very sad for me. I felt like a grieving, bereft child. The final sessions were filled with my tears.

Three years later the circle closed, and I returned to the therapy that my unhappy family had embraced more than 40 years before. I decided, in my late thirties, to finally take the plunge into analysis. I felt stuck with myself and did not want to spend the rest of my life that way. I had tried virtually everything else, and analysis was the only thing left. I had achieved considerably, but I still felt frightened and driven about my work. My marriage was better, but intimacy still frightened me. After interviewing several analysts, I found an older "wise owl" who I felt could see through me. His orientation was primarily, but not exclusively, self psychology (Kohut, 1971, 1984). We began.

One of the most important experiences of the analysis was completely nonverbal. Regularly I would fly into a midafternoon analytic session in the midst of various work crises. I had taken over the reins of the Family Institute and was trying to steer it through a period of immense organizational transition. I was also trying to maintain my practice, write a book, do research, teach, and have a family. I was always short on sleep. I would hit the couch and unload all of my frustrations and tensions. Then I would fall silent. Then I would start to fall asleep. Since infancy, I had never been able to nap. As my eyelids became heavy, I would fight it. I'd start talking and "working." Good patients did not fall asleep, wasting time and money. My analyst did not interfere. He watched.

After many months of this struggle, I started to let myself doze off. I would shift into a very intense dream state and then pull myself back to reality. I'd report on the dreams. At least I was using my dozing off productively, not "just napping." Whenever I'd wake up, I'd glance over at my analyst to see if he too had dozed off. He would just be watching and patiently, if not lovingly, waiting. Finally, I let myself fall asleep and catnap. I would sleep for five to ten minutes and wake up refreshed and alert. He'd still be there. He didn't leave me when I stopped performing. It was a different sense of silence than the one I'd known sitting in the car with my father. I began to feel safe—that I could deeply relax in my sessions without being abandoned. He was like a good mother—interested in me no matter whether I was performing or just being.

As this process unfolded, two shifts started to occur in my life. I started to feel stronger within myself—less narcissistically vulnerable. I did not have to be on guard and vigilant all the time. I was not as easily hurt or threatened. I could go about my business less concerned about what others thought or said about me. The second was that I could catnap when I felt tired. I had developed the capacity to dip briefly into sleep (for five to ten minutes) and come back refreshed and alert. This new capacity was a gift I had discovered within myself. It was a gift with which I could comfort and refresh myself.

The analysis continued to strengthen and relax me. This process had very little, if anything, to do with words. It had to do with the relationship between my analyst and myself. The intensity and duration of the analysis—meeting three to four times a week for years—allowed my analyst to touch me at a deeper level than any therapist had ever touched me before. The analysis strengthened me sufficiently to tolerate and grow from the necessary changes that were to come in my marriage, ultimately making me a better husband and partner. I also believe that the analysis made me a better therapist, psychologist, and boss at the Family Institute. I became less vulnerable to the inevitable narcissistic injuries that are part of managing a relatively high-profile career and directing a major mental health institution linked to a leading research university. My emotional resilience increased substantially across all of the major domains of my life.

INTEGRATING THE PERSONAL AND
PROFESSIONAL—THE TAPESTRY

My multiple personal therapies—encompassing individual, marital, and family formats—over the past 40 years have profoundly impacted me, professionally and personally. My experience as a clinical psychologist, psychotherapy researcher, and family therapist over the past 28 years has also profoundly impacted me, professionally and personally. As an addicted integrationist, I have tried to weave these personal and professional experiences into a coherent and teachable theoretical framework for understanding and doing psychotherapy. As I mentioned at the beginning of this chapter, each of these experiences has contributed significantly to the creation of integrative problem-centered therapy, my model for how to use family therapies, individual therapies, and biological therapies with maximal effectiveness and efficiency.

Early on at McMaster, it became apparent to me that one of the keys to their success was their problem-solving orientation and their focus on the presenting problem. They were not trying to change every aspect of every patient or family but rather to help them resolve the problems for which they were seeking help. They were focused and pragmatic, trying the simplest and most direct interventions before trying more complex and indirect ones. After the psychoanalytic morass of my family-of-origin, this simple, direct, and focused approach made great sense and was very appealing. It has become a cornerstone of the problem-centered model. The model is centered on the presenting problems—the problems for which the patients are seeking help at this particular time. It is the place from which therapy typically begins.

Ultimately, I am most interested in the sequential contexts in which the problems occur—what I call the problem sequence. The transformation of the problem sequence into an alternative adaptive sequence is the primary process goal of the problem-centered therapy. In addition, analysis of the sequential context—what precedes and follows the emergence or intensification of the presenting problem—generally provides the best clues as to the nature of the underlying problem maintenance structure.

A key concept that emerged after I had moved back to Chicago was the idea of the problem maintenance structure. What struck me repeatedly during the first 10 years of practice was the impossibility of predicting which patients would respond in what way to my intervention. I saw patients labeled "borderline" respond rapidly and surprisingly to direct behavioral intervention. I saw high-functioning young couples seeking premarital counseling who were locked in a torturous struggle with each other that was unresponsive to everything but long-term, depth-oriented psychotherapy. Increasingly I began to think that the surface features of a presenting problem or disorder, as well as the surface features of a family, bore little relationship to what they would need in therapy. In fact, two cases that looked quite similar might end up requiring very different intervention.

Out of this thinking a set of principles began to emerge. Since I cannot know the problem maintenance structure in advance, the best place to start is with the simplest, most direct, and least expensive intervention. If that did not work, then I could get fancier (more complex, indirect, and expensive). In other words, I would presume that the patient system was healthy until proven otherwise. By "healthy" I mean able to respond to direct, straightforward intervention in a relatively brief time period. The burden of proof was on the patient system to prove to me that the patient needed more complex and indirect intervention. If I were to err, in contrast to my early experiences with the psychoanalytic model, I would err on the side of health, not pathology. Patients would have to convince me that they could not change.

As my thinking evolved, a conceptual matrix began to take shape (see fig. 12.1) with three vertical dimensions and six horizontal ones. The three vertical dimensions are: (a) family/community; (b) couple; and (c) individual. They represent the three primary *contexts* in which treatment occurs. The six horizontal dimensions are: (1) behavioral; (2) biobehavioral; (3) experiential; (4) Family-of-Origin; (5) Psychodynamic; and (6) self psychological. These dimensions or levels of the *matrix* each contain distinct theories about how problems develop, are maintained, and get resolved. Most significant, the levels and intervention contexts are sequenced according to principles of cost-effectiveness, simplicity, and directness. The arrow that goes from the top left of the matrix toward the lower right

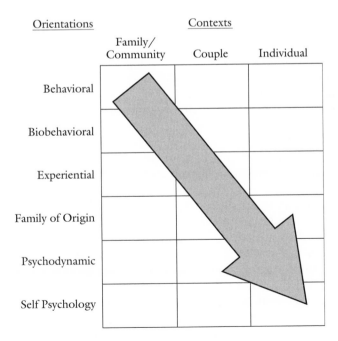

Figure 12.1.   Assessment/intervention matrix.

represents the gross or macro progression of interventions in problem-centered therapy. The sequential progression through the levels and down the matrix occurs in the face of the failure of the current level's intervention to resolve the presenting problem.

The matrix is called the assessment/intervention matrix because assessment and intervention within this model are inseparable and cooccurring activities that span the therapy from the first phone call to the last goodbye. Therapy is simultaneously (1) an intensive initiative to explore and transform the problem sequence and its underlying problem maintenance structure and (2) We learn about the problem maintenance structure, the set of constraints that prevent change, as we try to transform it. In fact, the efforts at transformation reveal the nature of the constraints. Therapy, for all patients, is both an educational and transformative endeavor.

The challenge of what to do when what you are doing does not work has been the transformative force in my personal and professional life. Unfortunately, in our society and in our educational systems we are not encouraged to try something and risk failing. Our innate capacity to fail and learn from failure is usually adulterated by the time we reach primary school. We need to learn to embrace our failures as learning and growth opportunities. There is no learning without failure. That message has been the driving force in the development of the problem-centered model, and it has been central to my growth as a person, husband, and father. We need to teach ourselves, our colleagues, our students, and our patients to welcome and learn from failure. That is true education and therapy.

THE THERAPIST'S THERAPY: DISTINCTIVE PROCESSES?

In reflecting on my experiences as a patient in psychotherapy over the years and in reflecting on my experience treating many mental health professionals, I ask myself the question: Is there anything particularly distinctive about the psychotherapeutic treatment of psychotherapists? My candid and somewhat surprising (to myself) answer is no. Mental health professionals are no different in their psychology and needs in and for therapy than anybody else. The mistake some therapists make is to think that therapists as patients are different—that they will have more insight, that they will be more resistant, that they will be more collaborative, or that they will be "better" or "worse" than other people.

The critical balancing act in treating psychotherapists is to not be seduced into believing that they are better or worse than anyone else, while communicating respect for their desire to help themselves and others. I know that when I selected my psychoanalyst, I selected him because I thought there was no way I could seduce him psychologically. I felt that he could see through my "bullshit," at the same time that he could respect and value me. He was not overly impressed with my impressive professional credentials, but his belief in my capacity to be a good person, psychologist, psychotherapist, and institutional leader sustained me.

Similarly, when we were in couples therapy, my couples therapist's willingness to take me on and make or help me address my contribution to our marital problems was essential to the success of that treatment. He was not seduced in the least by my growing reputation as a marital therapist and never colluded with me against my wife (despite my best efforts at times to work out such a collusive arrangement). At the same time, I felt that he respected me professionally.

In both of my major adult therapies (couples and analysis) I felt constructively challenged and taken on at the same time that I felt respected personally and professionally. That balancing act of support/valuing and confrontation was an essential therapeutic ingredient in my personal therapies. My analyst could confront my shockingly grandiose naivete in one session and refer a couple to me for therapy in the next. Similarly, my couples therapist would call me during the week with a referral after a session in which I had cried uncontrollably about the prospect of terminating our couples therapy and losing my relationship with him.

In my work with therapist-patients, my greatest error over the years has been to assume that they are any different from anyone else. I have been self-seduced by therapist-patients in countless ways—flattered that such an esteemed colleague would choose to seek me out as his or her therapist; sure that he or she would have integrated into his or her own life the insights in their own writings and teachings; sure that a therapist would never be able to act destructively and dangerously with his or her self or spouses, or with me.

A particularly dangerous pitfall to avoid is the creation of a pseudo-therapeutic alliance with a psychotherapist-patient who is a member of a couple or a family that I am treating. It is invariably a mistake to treat that family member as a cotherapist or special ally. On the other hand, it is crucially important not to depreciate or demean the therapist-patient in any way. The therapist's professional self-esteem must be protected, without creating a protection racket that impedes addressing his or her contribution to the problem. Frequently, family members will shame their therapist members for not practicing in their family what they teach their students or practice with their patients. Such shaming should be avoided at all costs, and the difficulty of practicing with one's spouse or children what one strives to accomplish with one's patients should be acknowledged.

SHAMANIC REFLECTIONS

In reflecting on the question whether there is something unique and/or special about the treatment of psychotherapist-patients, a somewhat shocking realization dawned on me. In thinking over my practice over the last 28 years in Chicago, I realized that for me, the most satisfying cases that I have worked with were couples in which one or both members were therapists, or individuals who were themselves therapists. I could easily

add that some of the least satisfying and most difficult were also psychotherapists. However, what was surprising to me was the recognition that
for me, something special and uniquely powerful had gone on in my treatment of therapists.

What were the qualities of those therapies that made them so powerful
and satisfying? Two qualities stand out particularly. The first is that in each
of these cases the therapist was struggling with a personal history of substantial childhood neglect and/or abuse, the legacy of which was imped-
ing his or her capacity to love and work effectively. The second was these
therapist-patients' intense desire to come to terms with and, if possible,
overcome this legacy of abuse and/or neglect. These patients wanted to be
able to love and work well and strove with great courage to do both. I think
this combination of a legacy of pain combined with high personal psychosocial aspirations offered me a very special and precious opportunity to
assist in the transformation of these peoples' lives. Invariably these treatments spanned many years and represented an opportunity for the patient-
therapists to use me and their relationship with me as a base or context for
their own personal transformation. At moments in these therapies, I was
their mother, father, brother, sister, supervisor, mentor, coach, and friend,
without ever leaving the well-defined and circumscribed role of therapist.
Ultimately, I felt immensely touched and privileged to have been privy and
party to this personal transformation.

In writing this, I find myself reflecting on my study of shamanism as a
history of religion major at Wesleyan. Usually, to become a shaman in a
so-called primitive or native culture, there had to be something wrong with
you. You were "chosen" by virtue of the fact that you had this special problem or vulnerability—you heard special voices, saw special things, felt great
pain, and knew suffering. But in addition to this "special vulnerability"
quality, shamanic candidates wanted to know about and to learn how to
work with the world of spirits, the underworld of normally unspoken forces,
entities, and events. They had this special combination of vulnerability and
psychosocial ambition. They suffered, and they wanted to understand and
come to terms with the causes of this suffering, so they could suffer less
and diminish the suffering of others.

The shamanic candidate's education involved the elder shamans teaching the shaman-in-training about himself or herself by taking him or her
on journeys to the underworld to do the work on self that was needed, as
well as to learn about the nature of this underworld so he or she could
help others. Perhaps it is the combination of vulnerability and ambition
in therapist-patients, and the opportunity of their therapists to help and teach
them about themselves and the obscure world of problem maintenance
structures, that makes these psychotherapies so special and powerful. And
it is intriguing to think that in creating and engaging in these psychotherapies, we are participating in a tradition of personal and professional transformation that has characterized our species from the beginning.

NOTE

1. The names and some identificatory information of all patients and some of the therapists in this chapter have been modified to protect their confidentiality and anonymity.

REFERENCES

Boszormenyi-Nagy, I., & Framo, J. (Eds.). (1969). *Intensive family therapy: Theoretical and practical aspects.* New York: Harper and Row.

Eliade, M. (1964). *Shamanism: Archaic techniques of ecstasy.* New York: Pantheon.

Kohut, H. (1971). *The analysis of the self.* New York: International Universities Press.

Kohut, H. (1984). *How does analysis cure?* Chicago: University of Chicago Press.

Lommel, A. (1967). *Shamanism: The beginnings of art.* New York: McGraw-Hill.

Pinsof, W. M. (1983). Integrative problem-centered therapy: Toward the synthesis of family and individual psychotherapies. *Journal of Marital and Family Therapy, 9,* 19–35.

Pinsof, W. M. (1995). *Integrative problem-centered therapy: A synthesis of biological, individual and family therapies.* New York: Basic Books.

Pinsof, W. M. (2002). Integrative problem-centered therapy. In J. Lebow & F. Kaslow (Eds.), *Comprehensive handbook of psychotherapy: Vol. 4. Integrative and eclectic* (pp. 341–366). New York: Wiley.

Watzlawick, P., Weakland, J., & Fisch, R. (1974). *Change: Principles of problem formation and resolution.* New York: Norton.

Research Findings: Undergoing Personal Therapy

13

THE PREVALENCE
AND PARAMETERS
OF PERSONAL THERAPY
IN THE UNITED STATES

JOHN C. NORCROSS & JAMES D. GUY

The vast majority of mental health professionals in the United States, independent of their professional discipline, have undergone personal treatment. Female, married, and insight-oriented therapists are most likely to seek therapy for themselves; behavior therapists and academics the least frequently and for the shortest duration. Psychotherapists have typically received personal treatment on several occasions; two or three discrete episodes tend to be the rule. A return to personal therapy following completion of formal training is also the norm. Personal therapy is routinely individual in format and private practice in location.

In what follows we detail these conclusions by reviewing the results of multiple studies conducted on the personal therapy experiences of psychologists, psychiatrists, social workers, counselors, and other mental health professionals practicing in the United States of America. Chapter 14 considers the prevalence and parameters of personal therapy among mental health professionals around the world.

METHODOLOGICAL CAVEATS

The data considered in this brief chapter are drawn from a series of published studies, all predicated on self-report. Every study employed a questionnaire or survey methodology, without independent verification of the veracity or accuracy of the self-reports. The studies are illustrative, not exhaustive, in scope. The response rates varied considerably, but it is safe to conclude that generally one-half of the number of potential professionals did not participate. Thus there is a definite possibility of response bias toward those psychotherapists whose personal history and theoretical orientation lead them to pursue personal treatment more frequently. Further, psychiatrists are relatively underrepresented in regard to sample size, due both to fewer studies conducted on this discipline and to their consistently lower response rate (Sudman & Bradburn, 1984). Psychologists, on the other hand, are overrepresented, since most of the research in this area has been conducted by psychologists on fellow psychologists. Finally and obviously, the results are entirely restricted to mental health professionals in the United States.

PREVALENCE OF PERSONAL THERAPY

General Estimates

Table 13.1 summarizes the prevalence of personal psychotherapy among mental health professionals in the United States across 14 studies. The universal finding is that the majority of responding professionals have received at least one episode of treatment themselves; in fact, the mean and median percentages cluster around 72% to 75%. The estimated prevalence is thus approximately three-quarters, with lows of 53% (for behaviorists) to 98% (for psychoanalysts).

The prevalence of personal therapy has not changed dramatically over time. Compare, for a direct example, the incidence estimate reported by Norcross, Strausser-Kirtland, and Missar (1988) to those obtained by Henry, Sims, and Spray (1973) almost 20 years earlier: 75% and 76% of psychologists, 67% and 67% of psychiatrists, 72% and 65% of clinical social workers.

Tellingly, the prevalence of personal treatment for mental health professionals is substantially higher than that for the general adult population in the United States. Best estimates, gleaned from national household surveys and national epidemiological studies (e.g., Kessler et al., 1994; Swindle, Heller, Pescosolido, & Kikuzawa, 2000), are that 25% to 27% of American adults have received specialized mental health care, a more inclusive category than psychotherapy. This lifetime utilization rate, assuming a far more inclusive set of services than psychotherapy, is one-third to one-half that of mental health professionals. Of course, these are general estimates. It is well established that proportionally more female, acutely distressed, and higher socioeconomic category patients receive more mental health care, and these characteristics aptly describe mental health professionals as a group.

Prevalence Following Training

The profession's collective silence on personal therapy has created an illusion that most mental health professionals do not experience need for personal therapy once they are in practice (Guy & Liaboe, 1986). However, the accumulating evidence rebuts any such illusion: most seasoned clinicians do in fact utilize the very services they provide.

The five identified studies that specifically addressed the prevalence of treatment following completion of formal training indicate that about half of seasoned mental health professionals returned to personal therapy. In his study of 141 psychoanalysts (77% response rate), Goldensohn (1977) found that 55% received personal treatment posttraining. Thirty-eight percent had additional psychoanalysis, and 43% had another form of psychotherapy (the most common being group therapy, couples therapy, and family therapy). In their study of 86 psychiatrists (77% response), Greden and Casariego (1975) reported that 43% had reinitiated personal therapy. Grunebaum (1983), in interviewing experienced psychotherapists, found that 55% returned to psychotherapy. In their study of 318 psychologists (44% response), Guy, Stark, and Poelstra (1988) noted that 62% had returned to personal therapy after receiving their terminal degree. In their study of 321 clinical psychologists (65% return rate), Darongkamas, Burton, and Cushway (1994) reported that 54% first sought personal therapy after completing their training.

In sum, several studies speak to reinitiating personal therapy following training, while others refer to initial participation in psychotherapy after completion of the terminal degree. But across studies and across disciplines, seasoned therapists in practice routinely seek psychotherapy for themselves.

As is so often the case, Freud anticipated the research findings many years ago. He recommended that the analyst reinitiate personal treatment in the recognition that practicing therapy continually exposes the clinician to the impact of patients' psychopathology and on the need to know and utilize one's own unconscious responsiveness in conducting therapy. "Every analyst," he wrote (1937/1964, p. 249), "should periodically—at intervals of five years or so—submit himself to analysis once more, without feeling ashamed of taking this step. This would mean, then, that not only the therapeutic analysis of patients but his own analysis would change from a terminable to an interminable task."

Prevalence as a Function of Theoretical Orientation

The prevalence of personal therapy varies systematically with theoretical orientation, as shown in the five representative studies presented in table 13.2. Examination of the studies, in toto, consistently reveals that insight-oriented mental health professionals are most likely to have undergone personal therapy. At the high end, 88% to 97% of self-identified psychoanalytic and 82% to 97% of psychodynamic clinicians have sought therapy for themselves. At the low end, about half of the behavior therapists acknowledge personal treatment. Behavior therapists do seek treatment—somewhere between 44% and 66%—but less frequently and for a shorter duration on average than their nonbehavioral colleagues (Gochman, Allgood, & Geer, 1982; Lazarus, 1971; Norcross & Prochaska, 1984; Norcross & Wogan, 1983; Orlinsky et al., chapter 14). In between these extremes were

Table 13.1 Prevalence of Personal Psychotherapy among Mental Health Professionals in the United States

Study	N	Profession	Response Rate	Prevalence	Length of Therapy
Deutsch (1985)	85 117 62	Psychologists Social workers Other therapists	42%	66% (for all)	Not reported
Guy, Stark, & Poelstra (1988)	318	Psychologists	44%	82%	M total hrs = 309.8 Mdn hours = 158 Range hours = 2–2000+
Henry, Sims, & Spray (1971)	1,465 733 1,154 638	Psychologists Psychiatrists Social workers Psychoanalysts	67% 46% 68% 54%	75% 65% 64% 98%	M episodes: Psychologists = 1.9 Psychiatrists = 1.6 Social Workers = 1.8 Psychoanalysts = 1.8
Holzman, Seawright, & Hughes (1996)	1,018	Psychologists in training	50%	75%	M weeks = 75.1 M sessions = 130.1
Kelly, Goldberg, Fiske, & Kilkowski (1978)	156	Psychologists	81%	60%	Not reported
Liaboe, Guy, Wong, & Deahnert (1989)	232	Psychologists Association for the Advancement of Behavior Therapy	46.4%	56% 53%	Not reported
Norcross, Strausser-Kirtland, & Missar (1988)	314 159 237	Psychologists Psychiatrists Social workers	65% 34% 50%	75% 67% 72%	M # episodes = 2.3 Mdn hours for: First therapy = 50 Second therapy = 49 Third therapy = 100

Study	N	Sample	%	%	Details
Norcross, Farber, & Prochaska (1993)	481	Psychologists	48%	80%	M hours = 336 SD = 321 hours Range = 3–2000+ hours Mdn hours = 200

Norcross, Geller, & Kurzawa (2000)	328	Psychologists	35%	89%	M and Mdn # episodes = 3
					SD = 1.6
					Mdn hours = 150
					M total hours = 370

Norman & Rosvall (1994)	78	Psychologists	43% (for all)	67%	Length of therapy:
	288	Social workers		56%	41% = 3 months or less 17% = 4–6 months 12% = 7–12 months 30% = 1 yr or greater
	20	Marriage and family therapists		65%	
Orlinsky et al. (chapter 14)	964	Mixed disciplines	Unknown	88%	22% currently in therapy 59% had > 1 therapy episode M = 4.4 years in therapy
Patterson & Utesch (1991)	51	Family therapists-in-training	90%	64%	M length = 7 months Range = 1 month–5 yrs
Prochaska & Norcross (1983)	410	Psychologists	41%	83%	M hours = 297 SD = 314 Mdn hours = 175 Range = 6–2,000 hours

Voigt (1998)	88	Clinical training directors	50%	78%	M # hours = 85
					Mdn # hours = 28
					Range = 0-600 hours

	230	Psychologists in practice	59%	94%	M # hours = 246
					Mdn # hours = 110
					Range = 0–1,200 hours

Table 13.2 Prevalence of Personal Psychotherapy by Theoretical Orientation

Study	Psychoanalytic	Psychodynamic	Humanistic	Eclectic	Cognitive	Behavioral	Systems
Norcross & Prochaska (1984)	97%	85%	84%	83%	NR	54%	NR
Norcross, Strausser & Faltus (1988)	88%	82%	58%	62%	69%	47%	85%
Norcross, Farber, & Prochaska (1993)	95%	97%	88%	78%	63%	66%	88%
Orlinsky et al. (chapter 14)	94%*	94%*	96%	92%	78%*	78%*	89%
Pope & Tabachnick (1994)	NR	94%	NR	87%	71%	NR	NR

*Theoretical orientations were combined. NR = not reported.

humanistic, systems, and eclectic respondents reporting at least one episode of personal therapy.

Prevalence as a Function of Professional Activities

Clinicians' activities definitely relate to the prevalence of personal treatment. The few studies that have empirically examined the matter have found similar patterns: mental health professionals conducting psychotherapy routinely have a higher tendency to have received personal treatment. In a classic study, Henry, Sims, and Spray (1971, 1973) conducted detailed interviews with psychiatrists, psychologists, social workers, and psychoanalysts. In all four professional groups, those who were practicing psychotherapy were more likely to have received personal therapy than those engaged in nontreatment roles. In another early study, Garfield and Kurtz (1976) found that psychologists in private practice and in outpatient clinics exceeded the overall frequency of personal therapy of 63% for the total group, with 70% and 77%, respectively. Of course, this variable is confounded with theoretical orientations, in that psychodynamically oriented clinicians are more likely to be employed in clinical positions.

The disparity in the incidence of personal therapy as a function of employment setting—or, more specifically, professional activities—is further reflected in the importance ascribed to personal therapy. Several studies have demonstrated that private practitioners more strongly endorse the importance of personal therapy than their colleagues in academic or administrative positions. In an article entitled "Practitioners and Academics Disagree," Voigt (1998) graphically explicates the divergence: 69% of psychotherapy practitioners but only 19% of training directors endorsed requiring students to undergo personal psychotherapy. Fully 94% of practitioners had undergone personal therapy, averaging 246 hours. By contrast, 78% of clinical directors had undergone personal therapy in their lives, averaging 85 hours.

Prevalence as a Function of Therapist Gender

Most published studies have not systematically examined prevalence rates separately for male and female therapists. Several smaller studies have found no link between experience in personal therapy and gender (e.g., Darongkamas et al., 1994; Prochaska & Norcross, 1983). However, at least seven studies suggest that slightly more female psychologists and social workers have engaged in personal therapy than male psychologists and social workers (Deutsch, 1985; Garfield & Kurtz, 1976; Norcross, Dryden, & DeMichele, 1992; Norman & Rosvall, 1994; Norcross, Strausser-Kirtland, et al., 1988; Orlinsky et al., chapter 14; Pope & Tabachnick, 1994). The difference appears to be on the order of 10%. For example, in the Norcross, Strausser-Kirtland, et al. (1988) study, 84% of female psychologists versus 71% of male psychologists and 79% of female social workers versus 58% of male social workers sought personal treatment. The data are not clear with regard to psychiatrists and family therapists, however.

Prevalence as a Function of Marital Status

Another factor impacting prevalence is marital status and marital history. Starting with the Henry et al. (1971) classic, several studies report that a larger percentage of married than single psychotherapists have undergone psychotherapy themselves. The difference may not be a result of age discrepancy; rather, it may be that personal treatment served to resolve the emotional and interpersonal difficulties that might have contributed to the dissolution of the marriage. As Norman and Rosvall (1994, p. 457) put it, "marital strain and the process of divorce may be an impetus for some individuals to enter personal therapy." Or, in the words of Henry et al. (1971, p. 141), "both marital disruption and remarriage appear to be strongly related to psychotherapy—a socialization experience that undoubtedly produces a more binding commitment to the psychodynamic explanatory system."

PARAMETERS OF PERSONAL THERAPY

Beyond the question of whether or not the clinician has ever received personal therapy/analysis lies the more complex and intriguing questions of its duration, format, frequency, and of course, outcome (the latter is taken up in chapter 17). Unfortunately, most studies either do not collect these data or do not present them in detail. Certainly, as shown in table 13.1, the length of personal treatment is not presented in any standardized manner. Different researchers gather and report the data differently—number of discrete episodes, number of hours, number of sessions, number of therapists, period of time, and so forth. Despite these limitations and vagaries, five consistent themes emerge.

First, the personal therapy of most mental health professionals is frequently lengthy, intensive work. The last column in table 13.1 presents the length of personal therapy for many of the studies. The mean number of therapy hours is in the hundreds. The mean number in these studies is invariably higher than the median number of hours, reflecting a skewed distribution. In one of our recent studies (Norcross, Geller, & Kurzawa, 2000), the median number of hours of individual personal therapy was 150, while the mean was 370. The large standard deviations reflect the large variability in length, ranging from a few hours to 5,200. In another of our studies (Guy et al., 1988), personal therapy ranged in length from 2 to 2,000 hours, but the mean was 309, hours and the median was 158. In examining the distributions of the total number of treatment hours, we typically find that it ranges from a low of 1 to 2 hours (2% of sample) to more than 1,000 hours (3% to 5% of the sample), the latter typically referring to psychoanalysis.

The length of personal therapy has also been expressed in time intervals, although this metric confounds the amount of treatment with its frequency. Nonetheless, the time estimates tend to corroborate the number of hours: lengthy therapy stretching over several years. Most estimates indicate a total, lifetime involvement in therapy spanning three or four years (Orlinsky et al., chapter 14; Pope & Tabachnick, 1994). There is some preliminary evidence that family therapists (Norman & Rosvall, 1994) and family therapists-in-training (Patterson & Utesch, 1991) might typically receive briefer therapy, at least compared to other mental health disciplines (also see chapter 6).

A second theme is that the length of personal therapy, like its prevalence, systematically varies as a function of theoretical orientation—both that of the therapist-patient and that of the treating therapist. Meaningful differences are regularly noted for differences in mean length, psychoanalysis being the lengthiest and behavioral the briefest. In one study (Guy et al., 1988) comparing the relative contribution of many variables to the length of personal therapy, the choice of a psychodynamic orientation accounted for the greatest amount of variance in the number of hours of personal psychotherapy received.

The statistical outliers are the behavior therapists in this regard. Systematic examination of the crossorientation data highlights the fact that, even when they seek personal therapy, behavior therapists do so for a shorter duration, on average at least. In two representative data sets (Norcross & Prochaska, 1984), 54% and 59% of behavior therapists reported personal therapy. The mean length was 88 hours (SD: 90; median: 60) in one set and 114 hours (SD: 193; median: 30) in the other. By contrast, the average and median lengths of personal treatment for nonbehaviorists were three to ten times more intensive.

Third, as a rule psychotherapists pursue personal treatment on more than one occasion. Across studies, the number of discrete episodes averages between 1.8 and 3.0. In one recent study (Norcross et al., 2000), 32% of psychologists sought personal therapy once, 32% sought therapy twice, and 22% three times, and the remaining 14% sought therapy on four or more occasions. Similarly, Orlinsky et al. (chapter 14) note that more than 59% of their large, multidisciplinary sample had more than one therapy experience. Pope and Tabachnick (1994) found the median number of therapists worked with was three, with a mode of two. Indeed, the length and multiple courses of personal treatment have led to the characterization of psychotherapists as "interminable patients" (Felton, 1986).

Fourth, the preponderance of personal therapy is individual therapy. For their only or most recent therapy, 80% of mental health professionals reported individual treatment, 6% couples/marital, 4% family, 4% group, and 6% some combination of these formats (Norcross, Strausser, et al., 1988; Norcross, Strausser-Kirtland, et al., 1988). Generalizing across two other studies (Guy et al., 1988; Norcross et al., 2000) on lifetime experiences with personal therapy, 95% to 96% of mental health professionals who undertook personal therapy received some individual therapy; 47% to 50% some couples/family therapy; and 34% to 48% group treatment.

Fifth, the available research consistently finds that independent practice is the primary location for the personal treatment of mental health professionals in the United States. Although the location of therapist's personal therapy is rarely investigated, when it is, it is overwhelmingly in independent practice. For example, Norcross and colleagues (Norcross, Strausser, et al., 1988; Norcross, Strausser-Kirtland, et al., 1988) report that 74% of personal therapy was conducted in independent practice, 6% in a psychoanalytic institute, 4% in a psychotherapy center, and just a smattering in other locations (e.g., college/student health center, community agency).

CONCLUDING COMMENT

All of the findings related to prevalence attest to the fact that a large proportion of mental health professionals in the United States frequently and, for some, repeatedly seek personal psychotherapy. We concur with Greenberg and Kaslows' (1984, p. 20) assertion that in doing so, psychotherapists "are, for the most part, consistent. They practice what they preach. When they have problems in living, significant degrees of anxiety or depression, or other neurotic symptoms they seek help from highly respected colleagues." Moreover, seeking personal treatment implies that "they believe in what they are doing and they perceive therapy as a constructive measure that not only relieves symptoms but also leads to personal growth."

Amid the bounty of statistics reviewed in this chapter is the overarching implication that the therapist's professional development and personal life are inexplicably intertwined. Although not all psychotherapy experiences are readily amenable to tabulation, it is apparent that psychotherapists struggle with the same psychological conflicts, life transitions, and existential questions as the clients they serve. Perhaps this is not only inevitable but as it should be. The clinician's fallibility, humanness, and own treatment experiences allow for a connection with clients. As true cotravelers with others on the journey, psychotherapists seek relief, fulfillment, and growth in much the same manner as those they assist. That practitioners should avail themselves of the benefits of personal psychotherapy over the course of years strikes us as both natural and reassuring.

REFERENCES

Buckley, P., Karasu, T. B., & Charles, E. (1981). Psychotherapists view their personal therapy. *Psychotherapy, 18*, 299–305.
Darongkamas, J., Burton M. V., & Cushway, D. (1994). The use of personal therapy by clinical psychologists working in the NHS in the United Kingdom. *Clinical Psychology and Psychotherapy, 1*, 165–173.
Deutsch, C. J. (1985). A survey of therapists' personal problems and treatment. *Professional Psychology: Research and Practice, 16*, 305–315.

Felton, J. R. (1986). The psychotherapist as the interminable patient. *Psychotherapy Patient*, *3*, 101–110.

Freud, S. (1937/1964). Analysis terminable and interminable. In J. Strachey (Ed. and Trans.), *Complete psychological works of Sigmund Freud* (Vol. 23). London: Hogarth Press.

Garfield, S. L., & Kurtz, R. M. (1976). Personal therapy for the psychotherapist: Some findings and issues. *Psychotherapy*, *13*, 188–192.

Gochman, S. I., Allgood, B. A., & Geer, C. R. (1982). A look at today's behavior therapists. *Professional Psychology*, *13*, 605–611.

Goldensohn, S. S. (1977). Graduates' evaluation of their psychoanalytic training. *Journal of the American Academy of Psychoanalysis*, *5*, 51–64.

Greden, J. F., & Casariego, J. I. (1975). Controversies in psychiatric education: A survey of residents' attitudes. *American Journal of Psychiatry*, *132*, 270–274.

Greenberg, S., & Kaslow, F. W. (1984). Psychoanalytic treatment for therapists, residents, and other trainees. In F. W. Kaslow (Ed.), *Psychotherapy with psychotherapists*. New York: Haworth.

Grunebaum, H. (1983). A study of therapists' choice of therapist. *American Journal of Psychiatry*, *140*, 1336–1339.

Guggenbuhl-Craig, A. (1971). *Power in the helping relationships*. Dallas: Spring.

Guy, J. D., & Liaboe, G. P. (1986). Personal therapy for the experienced psychotherapist: A discussion of its usefulness and utilization. *Clinical Psychologist*, *39*, 20–23.

Guy, J. D., Stark, M. J., & Poelstra, P. L. (1988). Personal therapy for psychotherapists before and after entering professional practice. *Professional Psychology: Research and Practice*, *19*, 474–476.

Henry, W. E., Sims, J. H., & Spray, S. L. (1971). *The fifth profession: Becoming a psychotherapist*. San Francisco: Jossey-Bass.

Henry, W. E., Sims, J. H., & Spray, S. L. (1973). *The public and private lives of psychotherapists*. San Francisco: Jossey-Bass.

Holzman, L. A., Searight, H. R., & Hughes, H. M. (1996). Clinical psychology graduate students and personal psychotherapy: Results of an exploratory survey. *Professional Psychology Research and Practice*, *27*, 98–101.

Kelly, E., Goldberg, L., Fiske, D., & Kilkowski, J. (1978). Twenty-five years later: A follow-up study of graduate students in clinical psychology assessed in the V.A. selection research project. *American Psychologist*, *33*, 746–755.

Kessler, R. C., McGonagle, K. A., Zhao, S., Nelson, C. B., Hughes, M., Eshleman, S., Wittchen, H., & Kendler, K. S. (1994). Lifetime and 12-month prevalence of DSM-III-R psychiatric disorders in the United States. *Archives of General Psychiatry*, *51*, 8–19.

Lazarus, A. A. (1971). Where do behavior therapists take their troubles? *Psychological Reports*, *28*, 349–350.

Liaboe, G. P., Guy, J. D., Wong, T., & Deahnert, J. R. (1989). The use of personal therapy by psychotherapists. *Psychotherapy in Private Practice*, *7*, 115–134.

MacDevitt, J. W. (1987). Therapists' personal therapy and professional self-awareness. *Psychotherapy*, *24*, 693–703.

Norcross, J. C., Dryden, W., & DeMichele, J. T. (1992). British clinical psychologists and personal therapy: III. What's good for the goose? *Clinical Psychology Forum*, *44*, 29–33.

Norcross, J. C., Farber, J. A., & Prochaska, J. O. (1993). Psychologists conducting psychotherapy: New findings and historical comparisons on the Psychotherapy Division membership. *Psychotherapy*, *30*, 692–697.

Norcross, J. C., Geller, J. D., & Kurzawa, E. K. (2000). Conducting psychotherapy with psychotherapists: I. Prevalence, patients, and problems. *Psychotherapy*, *37*, 199–205.

Norcross, J. C., & Prochaska, J. O. (1984). Where do behavior and other therapists take their troubles? II. *Behavior Therapist*, *7*, 26–27.

Norcross, J. C., Strausser, D. J., & Faltus, F. J. (1988). The therapist's therapist. *American Journal of Psychotherapy*, *42*, 53–66.

Norcross, J. C., Strausser-Kirtland, D., & Missar, C. D. (1988). The processes and outcomes of psychotherapists' personal treatment experiences. *Psychotherapy*, *25*, 36–43.

Norcross, J. C., & Wogan, M. (1983). American psychotherapists of diverse persuasions: Characteristics, theories, practices, and clients. *Professional Psychology*, *14*, 529–539.

Norman, J., & Rosvall, S. B. (1994). Help-seeking behavior among mental health practitioners. *Clinical Social Work Journal*, *22*, 449–460.

Orlinsky, D. E., & Ronnestad, M. H. (2001). *The psychotherapist's perspective: Experiences of work, development, and personal life.* Washington, DC: American Psychological Association.

Patterson, J. E., & Utesch, W. E. (1991). Personal therapy for family therapy graduate students. *Contemporary Family Therapy*, *13*, 333–343.

Pope, K. S., & Tabachnick, B. G. (1994). Therapists as patients: A national survey of psychologists' experiences, problems, and beliefs. *Professional Psychology: Research and Practice*, *25*, 247–258.

Prochaska, J. O., & Norcross, J. C. (1983). Contemporary psychotherapists: A national survey of characteristics, practices, orientations, and attitudes. *Psychotherapy: Theory, Research and Practice*, *20*, 161–173.

Sudman, S., & Bradburn, N. (1984). Improving mailed questionnaire design. In D. C. Lockhart (Ed.), *Making effective use of mailed questionnaires.* San Francisco: Jossey-Bass.

Swindle, R., Heller, K., Pescosolido, B., & Kikuzawa, S. (2000). Responses to nervous breakdowns in America over a 40-year period. *American Psychologist*, *55*, 740–749.

Voigt, H. (1998, August). *Practitioners and academics disagree: Personal therapy as a clinical training requirement.* Paper presented at the annual meeting of the American Psychological Association, San Francisco, CA.

14

THE PREVALENCE AND PARAMETERS OF PERSONAL THERAPY IN EUROPE AND ELSEWHERE

David E. Orlinsky, M. Helge Rønnestad,
Ulrike Willutzki, Hadas Wiseman,
Jean-François Botermans, and the
SPR Collaborative Research Network

In their extensive review of the research literature on the personal therapy of psychotherapists, Norcross and Guy (chapter 13) and Norcross and Connor (chapter 15) amply demonstrate two facts: first, that "the vast majority of mental health professionals in the United States have undergone personal treatment"; second, that virtually all of the studies done on this topic to date have focused on American therapists.

Our aim in this chapter is to add an international dimension to this research-based knowledge of personal therapy by drawing on an ongoing study of psychotherapists that has been conducted since 1990 by the Collaborative Research Network of the Society for Psychotherapy (Orlinsky et al., 1999; Orlinsky & Rønnestad, in press). Those resources include information about the characteristics, experiences, and practices of more than 5,000 therapists of diverse professions and various theoretical orientations in over a dozen countries. Part of the information provided by these therapists concerns their experiences of personal therapy.

METHODOLOGICAL CAVEATS

Before presenting our findings and comparing them with the studies reviewed by Norcross and Guy, a brief description of the methods by which they were obtained is in order. Our data on personal therapy were gathered with the Development of Psychotherapists Common Core Questionnaire (DPCCQ) (Orlinsky et al., 1999), which was designed by researchers (who were themselves practicing therapists) primarily to study the processes and correlates of development among psychotherapists over the course of their careers. Great care was taken to ask questions that made sense to us as therapists, and to translate those questions accurately into various languages (initially, French and German, but subsequently many others). The DPCCQ is a self-administered, mainly structured-response format instrument covering a wide range of topics, which usually takes from one to one and a half hours to complete.

A general methodological issue in survey research is the representativeness or *generalizability* of findings from the study sample, which depends both on the method by which a sample is drawn and the percentage of usable questionnaires that are actually returned. (That is the reason why Norcross and Guy cite "return rates" in their tabulation of survey studies.) In theory, if the sample is randomly drawn and the return rate is sufficiently high, then the findings based on the sample can be validly generalized to the population from which the sample was taken. To achieve this desired result, however, the nature and boundaries of the population one wants to study must be clearly defined. Unfortunately, when research focuses on therapists in general rather than on a specific group, such as members of an American Psychological Association (APA) division, it is far from clear who should be defined as a psychotherapist. Although there are many professional psychotherapists in the United States and elsewhere, there is no profession of psychotherapist per se, and there is no single professional association to which all therapists belong in this country or any other. The fact is that psychotherapy is practiced by members of different professions in different countries but nowhere by all or even most members of any given profession. Moreover, psychotherapists of the same professional background often have different theoretical orientations and belong to professional associations reflecting those orientations. Thus, it is virtually impossible to draw a representative sample because it is virtually impossible to define the population of psychotherapists as such.

A related and equally important methodological concern is *generality*. Findings from a randomly drawn sample from one of the APA practice divisions (e.g., clinical psychology, counseling psychology, psychotherapy, family psychology, psychoanalysis), even with a 100% return rate, would be generalizable only to members of that division, and not necessarily to members of other divisions or to psychological therapists who are not APA members, let alone to psychiatrists, clinical social workers, and other practitioners of psychotherapy. In other words, a study could have perfect *generalizability* but very limited *generality*.

In addition, return rates in the range of 35% to 45%, which typify a majority of the studies cited by Norcross and Guy, are equivalent to experimental attrition rates of 55% to 65%. Unless this attrition can be demonstrated or plausibly assumed to be random with respect to the phenomena under study, it seriously compromises the representativeness of a study, even if the sample initially was randomly drawn.

What sort of biases might be expected? One mentioned by Norcross and Guy (chapter 13, p. 166) is a "bias toward those psychotherapists whose personal history and theoretical orientation lead them to pursue personal treatment more frequently." This would be true of surveys that had the announced purpose of studying personal therapy but would not have been the case with the DPCCQ, since its title and introductory material gave no hint that the questionnaire deals with that topic. (In fact, the questions on personal therapy do not appear until the fifth page.) We would estimate the return rates of the various Collaborative Research Network data collections to range between 15% and 40%. Given the foregoing considerations, this probably is less significant than the fact that over 5,000 therapists have found it sufficiently rewarding to complete the DPCCQ and return it (often at their own cost). Given the title and the length of our questionnaire, we would suspect our findings may be biased toward therapists whose personal history and theoretical orientation lead them to believe in the importance of professional development and empirical research but not toward the importance of personal psychotherapy.

CURRENT SAMPLES OF PSYCHOTHERAPISTS

Because our aim in this chapter is to provide international data on personal therapy, we present our sample categorized by the countries where therapists reside. Currently there are 14 countries from which there are at least 100 therapists.[1] In descending order of sample size, the countries are Germany, the United States, Norway, South Korea, Switzerland, New Zealand, Portugal, Spain, Denmark, Sweden, Belgium, France, Russia, and Israel. All of the CRN data presented were collected during the last decade of the twentieth century.

The characteristics of these therapists are summarized in table 14.1.[2] On average, the countries with the most highly experienced therapists in our database (more than 10 years in therapeutic practice) are the United States, Switzerland, France, Spain, New Zealand, Norway, and Sweden; those with the least experienced therapists are South Korea and Russia. However, the large standard deviations indicate a broad range of career levels within each country.

In nine of the countries, psychologists are the most frequently represented therapists in our samples, ranging from 92% of the Norway sample (currently including about 70% of the population of psychotherapists among psychologists in Norway), 88% of the Denmark sample, and 83% of the Switzerland sample to 67% in the United States, 65% in the Portugal, and 59% in the Russia samples. On the other hand, medically trained psychotherapists (psychiatrists and, in Germany, specialists in the field of psychotherapy and psychosomatics) are most frequently represented in the France (82%), Korea (64%), and Germany (54%) samples. Other professions (e.g., social work,

Table 14.1 Samples and Therapist Characteristics

Sample	N	Years in Practice M	[SD]	Profession Medicine %	Psychology %	Other %	Gender F %	M %
United States	977	18.4	[12.8]	5.5	66.6	27.7	48.7	51.3
Germany	1,059	9.1	[7.2]	54.4	36.5	9.1	57.0	43.0
Switzerland	263	13.1	[6.6]	9.6	82.8	7.7	52.3	47.7
Norway	804	11.5	[8.2]	4.9	92.2	3.0	53.3	46.7
Denmark	158	10.2	[6.4]	2.5	88.0	9.5	68.4	31.6
Sweden	117	11.6	[6.5]	8.5	34.2	57.3	69.2	30.8
Portugal	188	10.1	[7.0]	28.2	65.4	6.4	63.6	36.4
Spain	182	12.1	[6.9]	17.0	73.6	9.3	54.7	45.3
Belgium	132	9.8	[7.1]	1.5	74.2	24.2	56.1	43.9
France	117	12.6	[6.7]	82.1	16.2	1.7	26.5	73.5
South Korea	538	5.6	[5.9]	64.3	13.0	22.7	34.9	65.1
New Zealand	254	11.9	[7.5]	8.7	31.1	60.2	25.2	74.8
Israel	101	11.1	[7.2]	6.9	73.3	19.8	75.8	24.2
Russia	110	6.1	[4.5]	28.2	59.1	12.7	71.8	28.2

Note. Medicine = psychiatry (and psychosomatics in Germany); Other = social work, counseling, nursing, and lay therapists.

Sample	N	Theoretical Orientation Ana/Dyn %	CogBeh %	Hum %	Sys %	BroadSpec %	NonSal %
United States	977	24.7	21.0	19.3	11.9	9.8	13.5
Germany	1,059	46.2	9.2	21.7	9.4	2.8	10.0
Switzerland	263	32.4	20.8	20.8	12.6	7.2	6.3
Norway	804	43.7	9.9	18.5	10.4	7.9	9.5
Denmark	158	45.0	2.3	27.5	10.7	6.1	8.4
Sweden	117	64.8	2.8	9.3	7.4	0.0	15.7
Portugal	188	29.4	32.7	10.5	13.7	7.2	6.5
Spain	182	46.9	18.5	11.1	17.9	1.2	4.3
Belgium	132	35.0	16.0	22.0	15.0	4.0	8.0
France	117	56.9	1.8	21.1	4.6	2.8	12.8
South Korea	538	18.1	11.0	21.1	1.5	5.8	42.5
New Zealand	254	21.0	28.0	15.0	10.5	13.0	12.5
Israel	101	64.3	4.8	13.1	7.1	9.5	1.2
Russia	110	26.9	6.4	42.3	3.8	5.1	15.4

Note. Ana/Dyn = salient analytic/psychodynamic; CogBeh = generally cognitive-behavioral; Hum = generally humanistic; Sys = generally systemic; BroadSpec = broad-spectrum eclectic; NonSal = no salient orientation (no 4 or 5 endorsement on any of the 0–5 orientation scales).

counseling, nursing) are most frequently represented in the samples from New Zealand (60%) and Sweden (57%).

Further substantial differences among the samples from these 14 countries can be seen in their gender ratios. Those with the largest proportion of women therapists were Israel, Russia, Sweden, Denmark, and Portugal. Those with the largest proportion of male therapists were New Zealand, France, and South Korea. However, gender ratios in the largest samples (Germany, the U.S., and Norway) were more evenly balanced.

Theoretical orientation was assessed by asking therapists "How much is your current therapeutic practice guided by each of the following theoretical frameworks?" This question is followed by 6 items, each of which is rated on a 6-point scale (from 0 ["Not at all"] to 5 ["Very greatly"]): Analytic/psychodynamic; Behavioral; Cognitive; Humanistic; Systemic; and Other (with instruction to specify the content). When allowed to rate the influence of multiple orientations in this way, 90% of the therapists in our database indicated more than one orientation. For analyses requiring a limited number of theoretical orientations, we categorized them in the following way. Ratings of 4 or 5 on the 0–5 scale for any given orientation was considered to indicate a strong or "salient" influence on the therapist's practice. When all the combinations of salient influences were inspected, six patterns included sufficient numbers of therapists to be useful for statistical purposes. These are saliently Analytic/dynamic, with no other salient influences; generally Cognitive-Behavioral, with inclusion of diverse salient influences other than Analytic/dynamic; generally Humanistic, with inclusion of other salient influences; generally Systemic, with inclusion of other salient influences; Broad-Spectrum Eclectic, indicating four or more salient orientations; and those whose theoretical orientations included no salient influences. Together these categories included 80% of the total sample.

Table 14.1 shows that therapists with saliently analytic/psychodynamic orientations were most frequently represented in 10 of our 14 countries, but were a majority in only three (Israel, Sweden, and France). Therapists with generally cognitive-behavioral orientations were most frequently represented in our samples from Portugal and New Zealand but were also well represented in our samples from the United States, Switzerland, Spain, and Belgium. The therapists in our samples from Russia and from South Korea most frequently were generally humanistic in orientation, as were substantial minorities in the United States, Germany, Switzerland, Belgium, and France. Finally, generally systemic and broad-spectrum therapists were not the most frequently in any of the samples, although there were substantial minorities of systemic therapists in Spain, Portugal, Belgium, New Zealand, the United States, and Germany. Therapists with no salient orientation typically were only small minorities in most countries but were the most common category in our South Korea sample[3] and were noticeable minorities in Sweden, Russia, the United States, France, and New Zealand. This finding evidently reflects the presence of large numbers of therapists in those countries who were still at an early stage of their careers.

PREVALENCE OF PERSONAL THERAPY

Table 14.2 shows the prevalence of personal therapy among therapists from the different countries in our sample. Despite many differences, it is clear that overwhelming majorities of therapists everywhere reported having had at least one course of personal psychotherapy, the sole exception being South

Table 14.2 Prevalence of Personal Therapy among Professional Psychotherapists

Sample	N	Any Ptx?	When in Ptx?			Courses		Total Years	
			Past Only	Past & Present	Present Only	M	[SD]	M	[SD]
United States	964	88.3%	72.4%	25.6%	2.0%	2.0	[1.0]	5.7	[6.0]
Germany	1,049	81.9%	55.2	26.3	18.5	1.7	[1.0]	4.7	[3.9]
Switzerland	261	95.5	74.7	21.1	4.2	2.1	[1.1]	6.5	[3.9]
Norway	800	79.9	67.8	27.4	4.9	1.5	[.94]	4.0	[3.2]
Denmark	156	90.4	60.7	37.1	2.1	2.2	[1.1]	5.0	[3.4]
Sweden	117	94.0	64.5	26.4	9.1	2.2	[1.0]	4.6	[3.0]
Portugal	187	65.8	74.2	18.3	7.5	1.5	[.88]	5.9	[3.9]
Spain	182	78.8	59.7	33.8	6.5	2.0	[1.0]	7.8	[4.6]
Belgium	132	83.3	60.4	29.2	10.4	2.0	[1.1]	6.6	[4.4]
France	91	98.9	na	na	na	na	na	na	
South Korea	535	36.1	66.2	23.4	10.4	0.8	[1.0]	2.2	[3.0]
New Zealand	249	83.5	78.3	21.3	0.5	2.1	[.89]	3.4	[3.6]
Israel	101	93.1	55.3	39.4	5.3	2.0	[.95]	5.2	[3.8]
Russia	110	71.8	50.6	32.9	16.5	1.7	[.86]	2.4	[2.6]
Total	5,224	79.2	65.5	26.8	7.7	1.8	[1.1]	5.1	[4.5]
Total [–Koreans]	4,709	84.1	65.5	26.8	7.7	1.8	[1.0]	5.2	[4.5]

Note. "Any Ptx?' asks about a therapist's status with respect to personal therapy. Percentages indicate the proportion of those who are currently having or have previously had personal therapy. "Course," or times in therapy, includes only Ss reporting having had personal therapy. "Total years" in therapy indicates cumulative total for up to three reported courses of treatment for Ss reporting having had personal therapy.

Korea. There, special circumstances prevail (Joo & Bae, personal communication)[4] that are similar to ones cited by Norcross and Connor (see chapter 15) as reasons therapists in the United States give for not entering therapy. Elsewhere, the rates of personal therapy range from a high of more than 90% (France, Switzerland, Sweden, Israel, Denmark) to a low of 72% (Russia) and 66% (Portugal).

The very fact that our national samples differ in so many other respects serves to underscore the generality of personal therapy as a common characteristic of psychotherapists worldwide. Including all therapists in our current database, the estimated prevalence is 79%. Including only therapists from countries of predominantly European culture (including, e.g., the United States and New Zealand), the estimated prevalence of personal therapy is to 84%. (These figures exceed the 72% to 75% prevalence estimated by Norcross and Guy for the United States on the basis of the 14 studies they reviewed, 13 of which had samples numbering less than 500. Another probable source of this discrepancy is the fact that several of the studies they reviewed included students or trainees who might not yet have entered therapy; see table 14.3.)

Table 14.2 also shows that more than a third of the therapists who reported having personal therapy were actually in therapy at the time they replied to the DPCCQ, either for the first time (about 8%) or for an additional course of treatment (about 27%). In fact, therapists from most of the countries reported an average of two courses of treatment (again with the exception of South Korea). Therapists with some experience of personal therapy had accumulated an estimated average of five years of therapy by the time they participated in our study, ranging from a low of two years among Koreans to a high of nearly eight years in Spain. Moreover, since the majority of therapists were still in the early and middle parts of their careers (see table 14.1), the total years of personal therapy accumulated by career end would most likely be even greater.

PARAMETERS OF PERSONAL THERAPY

To what extent do therapists' various characteristics influence the likelihood of their having personal therapy? Therapists are most typically described in terms of career level, professional background, and theoretical orientation. Therapist gender has also been reported to influence rates of personal therapy. We examine each of these in turn.

Career Level

Table 14.3 shows the impact of career level on rates of personal therapy for each country and for the database as a whole. As might be expected, novice therapists on average are somewhat less likely to have had personal therapy than their more experienced colleagues, but perhaps even more impressive

Table 14.3 Percentage of Therapists Reporting Personal Therapy by Career Level

Sample	N	Career Level					
		Novice %	Apprentice %	Graduate %	Established %	Seasoned %	Senior %
United States	921	79.0	79.3	85.5	91.0	91.1	90.8
Germany	981	71.4	79.5	88.5	83.7	78.9	69.2
Switzerland	258	(100.0)	(75.0)	96.0	96.7	94.0	100.0
Norway	766	67.3	82.9	86.6	76.8	77.9	93.2
Denmark	155	(66.7)	66.7	88.0	97.1	96.8	(83.3)
Sweden	108	(100.0)	(87.5)	86.7	97.6	94.9	(100.0)
Portugal	178	—	(72.7)	63.2	64.1	80.0	(83.3)
Spain	180	(50.0)	(70.0)	65.2	76.7	87.5	(100.0)
Belgium	128	85.7	92.0	76.0	87.2	75.9	(66.7)
France	83	—	(100.0)	100.0	96.8	100.0	(100.0)
South Korea	445	20.2	35.8	53.2	65.9	59.3	(75.0)
N. Zealand	242	(57.4)	85.7	87.2	88.0	78.0	80.0
Israel	100	—	(80.0)	92.6	97.6	89.5	(100.0)
Russia	110	81.3	69.2	74.1	67.6	(71.4)	—
Current Ptx	4,711	29.1	34.7	37.7	27.3	20.5	12.4
Total	5,037	60.2	70.5	82.0	82.9	84.9	89.4
Total [–Koreans]	4,586	71.8	80.0	85.1	84.7	85.6	89.5

Note. Career level categories: Novice (> 0 to < 1.5 yrs); Apprentice (1.5 to < 3.5 yrs); Graduate (3.5 to < 7 yrs); Established (7 to < 15 yrs); Seasoned (15 to < 25 yrs); Senior (25 to 45 yrs). Percentages in parentheses when cell $N < 10$.

is the fact that a great majority of even the youngest therapists (except Koreans) had already been in personal therapy. The fact that only 30% of the novices are currently in therapy indicates that they already had some therapy prior to becoming therapists themselves. More impressive yet is the fact that 21% of the seasoned therapists and 12% of the senior therapists actually were in personal therapy at the time they participated in the study. Those last two groups were well beyond the period of training—these therapists having been in practice at least 15 years, and some as many as 45 years—yet many of them were still (or again) involved in personal therapy.

The trends in prevalence across the career course vary somewhat from country to country. In some countries (e.g., the United States) the prevalence of personal therapy started very high (79% among novices) and soon reached a plateau (about 91% among established, seasoned, and senior therapists). In other countries (e.g., South Korea) the initial level was low (20% among novices) and gradually increased over the career course to a moderately high level (60% to 75% among established, seasoned, and senior therapists). Finally, in some countries there seems to be a curvilinear pattern, in which midcareer therapists were more likely to have had personal therapy than either novices or seniors. The latter pattern probably results from the interaction between a career-based trend, in which more experienced therapists typically have had more time and reason to undertake personal therapy, and a historical cohort–based trend, in which personal therapy has become progressively more acceptable and/or more available for younger therapists than it had been for their older colleagues. Russia may be a particularly good example of this interplay between career and historical patterns, which are often confounded in cross-sectional analyses of developmental trends.

Professional Background

Table 14.4 shows characteristically high prevalence of personal therapy among therapists of all professional backgrounds in those countries we have studied (South Korea again being a special case). Overall (omitting the Korean therapists), the therapists of diverse professions in our database report approximately equal rates of personal therapy, with all above 80%.

There is a tendency in some of our national subsamples (e.g., the U.S. and Russia) for medically trained therapists to have slightly lower rates of prevalence of personal therapy. However, in other countries (e.g., Germany, Norway, and Spain), psychologically trained therapists tend to have slightly lower rates of personal therapy. (This is particularly true among the Portuguese, who as a group also include the highest proportion of cognitive-behavioral therapists). Interestingly, therapists of other professional backgrounds (social workers, counselors, nurses, lay therapists) have as high or higher rates of personal therapy than medically and psychologically trained therapists.

Table 14.4   Percentage of Therapists Reporting Personal Therapy by Profession

Sample	N	Profession Medicine %	Psychology %	Other %
United States	962	61.1	91.1	86.9
Germany	1,049	84.0	76.2	92.6
Switzerland	260	92.0	94.9	100.0
Norway	800	94.9	78.8	87.5
Denmark	156	(100.0)	89.1	100.0
Sweden	117	(90.0)	100.0	91.0
Portugal	187	83.0	56.6	83.3
Spain	182	83.9	75.1	88.2
Belgium	132	(50.0)	79.6	96.9
France	91	98.6	100.0	(100.0)
South Korea	535	32.1	48.6	40.2
New Zealand	249	85.0	74.0	88.2
Israel	101	(42.9)	95.9	100.0
Russia	110	61.3	72.3	92.9
Total	5,238	69.9	82.0	83.6
Total [−Koreans]	4,703	82.5	82.8	90.3

Note. Medicine = psychiatry (& psychosomatics in Germany); Other = social work, counseling, nursing, and lay therapists. Percentages in parentheses when cell N < 10.

Theoretical Orientation

In their review of studies conducted in the United States, Norcross and Guy (see chapter 13) described a tendency for the prevalence of personal therapy to vary systematically with theoretical orientation, with psychodynamically oriented clinicians having the highest rates (82% to 97%) and behaviorally oriented therapists the lowest (44% to 66%). The findings from therapists in our international CRN database clearly confirm their conclusion. Table 14.5 shows for the database as a whole (omitting the Korean therapists) that 92% of saliently analytic/psychodynamic therapists and 92% of generally humanistic therapists reported having personal therapy, in comparison with 60% of the generally cognitive-behavioral therapists. (The figure for humanistic therapists is slightly lower when our Korean therapists are included but almost the same for analytic/psychodynamic and cognitive-behavioral therapists.)

Saliently analytic/psychodynamic therapists reported prevalence rates ranging from approximately 90% to 100% in 10 of 13 countries (excluding Korea) and about 88% in two others. Generally humanistic therapists reported prevalence rates between 90% and 100% in nine of those countries, and more than 75% in three others. Therapists who are generally systemic in orientation reported prevalence rates between 80% and 100% in 10 of 13 countries, and broad-spectrum therapists reported prevalence rates between 80% and 100% in 9 of 13 countries. By contrast, generally cognitive-behavioral therapists had the lowest prevalence rate in the Portugal and Spain

Table 14.5 Percentage of Therapists Reporting Personal Therapy by Theoretical Orientation

Sample	N	Theoretical Orientation					
		Ana/Dyn	CogBeh	Hum	Sys	BroadSpec	NonSal
United States	747	94.1%	78.3%	95.8%	88.9%	91.5%	76.8%
Germany	866	87.9	55.6	85.3	91.1	63.3	68.3
Switzerland	205	100.0	88.4	100.0	92.3	86.7	90.9
Norway	565	88.2	57.1	93.3	83.1	77.8	66.7
Denmark	129	89.7	(66.7)	100.0	92.9	(100.0)	(40.0)
Sweden	108	98.6	(66.7)	(80.0)	(100.0)	—	82.4
Portugal	152	93.3	20.0	87.5	81.0	(81.8)	(56.6)
Spain	162	97.4	33.3	100.0	58.6	(100.0)	(42.9)
Belgium	100	100.0	(43.8)	95.5	86.7	(75.0)	(62.5)
France	88	100.0	—	100.0	(100.0)	(100.0)	(88.9)
South Korea	462	48.2	39.2	50.0	(42.9)	59.3	19.4
New Zealand	197	92.9	62.5	90.0	71.4	100.0	95.7
Israel	84	96.3	(50.0)	100.0	(66.7)	(87.5)	(100.0)
Russia	78	61.9	(40.0)	75.8	(100.0)	(100.0)	(75.0)
Total	4,195	89.6	58.1	86.7	85.3	80.6	53.8
Total [−Koreans]	3,733	92.0	59.9	91.7	86.0	83.0	72.3

Note. AnaDyn = salient analytic/psychodynamic; CogBeh = generally cognitive-behavioral; Hum = generally humanistic; Sys = generally systemic; BroadSpec = broad-spectrum eclectic; NonSal = no salient orientation (no 4 or 5 endorsement on any of the 0–5 orientation scales). Percentages in parentheses when cell N < 10.

samples but nevertheless reported quite high rates of personal therapy in Switzerland and the United States, with prevalence rates of 50% or more in 9 of 13 countries. Even therapists who had no salient theoretical orientation reported prevalence rates of 50% or more in 11 of 13 countries. Thus, while the likelihood of having personal therapy is clearly influenced by a therapist's theoretical orientation, the most general finding is that it is a very common experience among therapists of all orientations.

Therapist Gender

Some of the studies on American psychotherapists reviewed by Norcross and Guy (see chapter 13) suggest that the prevalence of personal therapy may be somewhat higher among female than among male therapists. Our international data suggest that any differences between genders are very small and inconsistent. The overall percentage favoring females in the database shown in table 14.6 virtually disappears when the Korean therapists (predominantly male and atypical with respect to personal therapy) are removed.

The difference between men and women in the United States is only 2.4% and is little more than 1% in Germany, Switzerland, Sweden, Portugal, and South Korea. The most striking differences appear for Denmark (15%), Norway (9%), Israel (9%), and Belgium (8%). However, the differences favor females in Denmark, Norway, and Israel but favor males in Spain, Belgium, France, New Zealand, and Russia. These findings suggest that therapist gender, in and of itself, is not an important parameter of personal therapy.

PURPOSES OF PERSONAL THERAPY

Why do psychotherapists of both genders, all professional backgrounds, all career levels, and most theoretical orientations undertake personal therapy for themselves—many of them doing so more than once, and well into their later years?

Therapists reported on various aspects of their personal therapy, including the reasons they had entered into it, and were free to check any or all of the following three reasons: training, growth, or problems. Table 14.7 shows, for their first (or only) episode of personal therapy, that 60% gave personal growth, 56% personal problems, and 46% professional training as reasons for going into therapy. This supports and extends the five studies of United States therapists reviewed in this volume by Norcross and Connor (p. 198), who conclude that the majority entered treatment primarily for personal reasons.

Personal growth was the most commonly cited reason for undertaking therapy (or essentially tied for most frequent) among therapists from 10 of the 14 countries, and was mentioned by at least half of the therapists in 13 of the 14 countries. This fact is important for interpreting therapists' responses to our own and others' surveys. When therapists indicate they had personal rather than professional reasons for entering therapy, they are not

Table 14.6 Percentage of Therapists Reporting
Personal Therapy by Gender

Sample	N	Female %	Male %
United States	956	88.9	87.5
Germany	1,031	82.7	81.4
Switzerland	261	94.9	95.2
Norway	793	84.4	75.1
Denmark	156	95.3	80.0
Sweden	117	93.8	94.4
Portugal	186	66.1	66.2
Spain	179	75.5	81.5
Belgium	132	79.7	87.9
France	91	96.0	100.0
South Korea	530	37.0	35.8
New Zealand	241	72.1	87.2
Israel	99	96.0	87.5
Russia	110	70.9	74.2
Total	5,181	81.6	76.8
Total [–Koreans]	4,651	84.9	83.3

necessarily focusing on their problems in living or their psychopathology. There is also a more positive aspect to therapists' motivation for therapy: self-improvement, personal development, and enrichment.

The fact that the figures in table 14.7 add up to over 100% also indicates that many therapists checked multiple reasons for personal therapy. For example, the leading category of reasons cited for the first listed therapy

Table 14.7 Reasons for Entering Personal Therapy

Sample	N	Training %	Growth %	Problems %
United States	829	38.4	64.9	77.2
Germany	793	34.0	33.8	32.3
Switzerland	233	68.2	68.2	52.4
Norway	576	48.6	72.9	58.1
Denmark	139	66.9	81.3	56.8
Sweden	108	54.6	66.7	39.8
Portugal	118	67.8	76.3	45.8
Spain	140	72.9	68.6	57.1
Belgium	105	54.3	61.9	66.7
South Korea	110	62.7	50.9	41.8
New Zealand	254	36.2	54.3	53.1
Israel	92	33.7	75.0	76.1
Russia	79	72.2	78.5	64.6
Total	3830	46.4	59.8	55.5
Total [–Koreans]	3719	45.9	60.1	56.0

Note. Reasons cited for first listed therapy ($N = 3313$). Percentages are >100% because multiple reasons could be checked.

(25%) was the combination of training, growth, and problems, followed by growth and problems (18%), and growth and training (16%). Clearly, having multiple reasons for entering therapy is more persuasive than having just one.

CONCLUDING COMMENTS

The research presented in this chapter clearly confirms and broadly extends Norcross and Guy's (chapter 13, p. 165) summary of findings from prior studies that "the vast majority of mental health professionals in the United States . . . have undergone personal treatment." Based on our surveys that nearly double the combined number of therapists in all previous studies, we can say the same about mental health professionals in countries throughout Europe and elsewhere. In fact, it is difficult to imagine any other group, however defined, that utilizes psychotherapy more frequently and enthusiastically than psychotherapists themselves. While psychotherapists may be divided by theoretical orientation and professional background, one thing they have in common is their devotion to personal therapy.

One might wonder if this very high rate of utilization is not due at least in part to external circumstances rather than to the desire of therapists to avail themselves of the benefits that therapy can offer. Some therapists must undergo therapy as part of their training (e.g., in psychoanalytic institutes) or as a condition of licensure (e.g., under the new law in Germany). Nevertheless, even though it is not a required part of their training, rates of personal therapy were not generally lower for humanistic therapists or broad-spectrum therapists than for analytic/psychodynamic therapists, and in some countries not for systemic therapists as well. If training requirements were the main reason therapists sought personal therapy, one would expect to see very high rates among novices and apprentices, with a decrease at later career levels, whereas there actually is a steady increase in utilization of therapy by therapists in successive career cohorts. In addition, the variation in prevalence rates observed among therapists in our sample from different countries seems more a reflection of differences between these national groups in career level and proportions of various theoretical orientations than of differences in national regulations concerning licensure.

Clearly, therapy is viewed in some theoretical orientations mainly as a treatment for specific symptomatic conditions, whereas in other orientations it is viewed more broadly as a corrective for limitations and distortions in prior personality development or as a source of positive personal growth. Similarly, in some theoretical orientations therapy is generally viewed as a set of procedures in which the therapist's personality is largely irrelevant, so that personal therapy for therapists is not a crucial factor in their performance; whereas in other orientations, personal therapy is viewed as essential to a therapist's ability to engage in a constructive, emotionally meaningful relationship with patients. It makes sense that clinicians who view their work as a relatively impersonal procedure for treating symptomatic disorders would see personal therapy as relevant for themselves only if they themselves became symptomatic. It also makes sense that practitioners who take a broader, more relational view of therapy would feel that personal therapy could be of particular value to them, personally and professionally. Many more of the latter than the former are found in our sample. How much they felt they benefited from their personal therapy, both personally and professionally, is reported later in this volume (chapter 17).

ACKNOWLEDGMENT   The following colleagues collected data in the following countries. United States: D. Orlinsky, J. Norcross, L. Beutler, M. Silverman; T. Northcut, S. Stuart; Germany: U. Willutzki, J. Meyerberg, M. Cierpka, P. Buchheim, H. Ambühl, H. Kächele; Switzerland: H. Ambühl, N. Aapro; Norway: M. H. Rønnestad, A. von der Lippe; Denmark: E. Friis-Jorgensen; Sweden: D. Stiwne; Portugal: A. Branco Vasco; Spain: A. Avila Espada, I. Caro; Belgium: J-F. Botermans; France: P. Gerin, A. Dazord; South Korea: S. Bae, E. Joo; New Zealand: N. Kazantzis; Israel: H. Wiseman, G. Shefler; Russia: E. Kalmykova.

NOTES

1. Subsequent data collections in the United Kingdom, Canada, Norway, and elsewhere have added approximately 2,000 more.

2. Approximately 300 additional therapists from countries presently having fewer than 100 each in our database were not included in the analyses reported here.

3. The percentage of therapists in Korea who appear to have no salient orientation shrinks dramatically if the criterion used to define salience is 3 rather than 4 on the 0–5 scale, suggesting that a cultural emphasis on modesty in Korea may be influencing this result.

4. Our Korean colleagues, Drs. E. Joo and S. Bae, commented both on the relative scarcity of senior therapists in private practice to whom younger therapists would ordinarily go for personal therapy and on the relative lack of social acceptance regarding counseling and therapy until recently.

REFERENCES

Orlinsky, D. E., Ambühl, H., Rønnestad, M. H., Davis, J. D., Gerin, P., Davis, M., et al. (1999). The development of psychotherapists: Concepts, questions, and methods of a collaborative international study. *Psychotherapy Research, 9*, 127–153.

Orlinsky, D. E., & Rønnestad, M. H. (in press). *How psychotherapists develop: A study of therapeutic work and professional growth*. Washington, DC: American Psychological Association.

15

PSYCHOTHERAPISTS ENTERING PERSONAL THERAPY

Their Primary Reasons and Presenting Problems

JOHN C. NORCROSS & KELLY A. CONNOR

This brief chapter aims, within the context of the other research contributions to this compendium, to explicate the primary reasons and presenting problems for mental health professionals seeking their own treatment. For the purposes of this chapter we distinguish between personal reasons and training/professional reasons for seeking psychotherapy. The published literature we review consists primarily of studies conducted with mental health professionals living in the United States. This research has been conducted nearly exclusively on psychotherapists' voluntary pursuit of professional treatment. Of course, a few psychotherapists seek personal therapy under pressure from licensing boards, ethics committees, or organizations for impaired professionals. Typical charges concern sexual misconduct with patients, substance abuse, or nonsexual boundary violations (Freudenberger, 1986; Gabbard, 1995). This does not fall within the purview of our chapter but is covered elsewhere in this volume (chapter 22).

PRIMARY REASONS

At a foundational level, psychotherapists may seek personal treatment for personal reasons, for training/professional reasons, or for both reasons. Although oversimplified in a profession where the personal and the professional are nearly inseparable, the question does afford insight into psychotherapists' motivations for undergoing their own psychotherapy.

In discussing his experiences in treating psychotherapists as clients, Burton (1973, p. 94) says emphatically that his patients "do not come for training purposes or for credentialing, although this may be a peripheral value to the experience. They were all hurting badly and needed help to function in their customary way." The results of the available studies corroborate his personal experience.

Table 15.1 presents the results of five studies that asked mental health professionals whether they sought psychotherapy for personal reasons, professional reasons, or both. In all studies, the majority (50% to 67%) indicated that they entered treatment primarily for personal reasons. A minority (10% to 35%) replied that their treatment was largely for training reasons or professional purposes.

Several investigators asked about primary reasons in a different manner. Orlinsky et al. (chapter 14) extensively queried a large, multidisciplinary international sample of psychotherapists. When asked to check all of their reasons for involvement in personal treatment, 60% checked personal growth, 56% indicated personal problems, and 46% checked training. Interestingly, American therapists were far more likely than those from most other countries to give personal problems as their reason for treatment.

Similarly, Liaboe, Guy, Wong, and Deahnert (1989) examined the reasons for undergoing personal therapy among psychotherapists who pursued it after completing their formal training. The primary reason was not to counter the stress of practicing psychotherapy; on the contrary, the top two reasons were stress due to conflicts in personal life and, again, for personal growth. Before training or after training, the results are clear: mental health professionals largely enter psychotherapy to deal with "personal stuff."

Although there are small differences in the reasons advanced for entering treatment due to profession (Henry, Sims, & Spray, 1971), overall the pattern is remarkably consistent across discipline and orientations. Personal reasons predominate.

Table 15.1   Reasons for Entering Therapy

Reason	Wispe & Parloff (1965)	Henry, Sims, & Spray (1971)	Kelley, Goldberg, Fiske, & Kilkowski (1978)	Prochaska & Norcross (1983)	Norcross, Strausser-Kirtland, & Missar (1988)
Primarily for personal reasons	65%	50%	67%	61%	55%
Primarily for training or professional reasons	35%	18%	28%	11%	10%
Both personal and training	NR	32%	5%	28%	35%

REASONS FOR *NOT* ENTERING TREATMENT

In an early article, Arthur Burton (1973) summarized four major resistances that serve as reasons for healers not entering personal therapy. First is the paradox that those psychotherapists who are most firmly convinced of the efficacy of psychotherapy are also precisely those who have the most deeply rooted doubts about it. Second, psychotherapists believe that what was good enough for Freud is good enough for them: self-analysis will suffice. Third, psychotherapists are ever-fearful of personal regression and giving up power to another. The therapist's self-image and narcissism are such that he/she feels his self-knowledge and humanity are just a shade above that of other healers. And fourth, the final inhibitor to personal psychotherapy is shame—"a kind of damage that is done to a healer when he is forced to become a fellow sufferer of those he regularly treats, that is so subtle and intangible as to defy description" (Burton, 1973, p. 100).

The subsequent research in this area has largely confirmed Burton's clinical impressions. At least five studies took the interesting twist of asking mental health professionals for their reasons in *not* seeking personal therapy. While there are some differences evident in the results across studies, probably owing to methodological and sampling disparities, there is a robust consistency in the rationale for not undergoing personal therapy.

Deutsch (1985) asked a national sample of psychotherapists to identify reasons for not seeking personal therapy. The reasons were categorized into 11 clusters. The most commonly cited reason was that the psychotherapists found no acceptable therapist nearby that they respected or did not already know. Following closely were that the psychotherapists found help and support from other people (friends, family, coworker) and that the problem resolved before therapy was undertaken. The next three reasons were fear of exposure and confidentiality, a belief that therapists should be able to work out problems themselves, and that the therapists did not want to invest the energy in the undertaking.

Studying clinicians earlier in their careers, Holzman, Searight, and Hughes (1996) surveyed doctoral students who had never been in psychotherapy and asked for their reasons for having never entered personal treatment. The top five reasons were: no need for it (56%), finances (53%), no one had recommended it (17%), concern about confidentiality (10%), and lack of time (10%).

Farber (2000) surveyed 275 graduate students being trained to provide counseling and psychological services regarding their attitudes toward seeking psychotherapy themselves. Factor analysis of 26 items—the Trainees' Attitude Toward Seeking Psychotherapy Scale—revealed four underlying dimensions. The first reflected an affirmative, proactive duty to seek therapy in order to enhance individual growth and professional effectiveness. The three other dimensions—concern with professional credibility, concern with confidentiality, and need for self-sufficiency—predicted which trainees had not, in fact, sought personal therapy.

Further along the career path, Liaboe and colleagues (1989) asked seasoned practitioners to rank 13 reasons for not entering personal therapy following graduate school. In descending order, the top five ranked were: other sources of dealing with stress were adequate; it was too expensive; previous therapy was helpful; it was hard to find a therapist to be comfortable with; and the practitioner was not sure it would be helpful.

Norman and Rosvall (1994) also asked therapists why they were disinclined to enter personal therapy. Forty-five percent replied that therapy was not necessary at this time; 22% believed they dealt effectively on their own; 14% were concerned about confidentiality; 8% struggled with issues of professional credibility; and 3% did not know a "good" therapist for them.

Whether in graduate training, early in the career, or later in midcareer, mental health professionals offer similar reasons for not seeking personal therapy. These are, across studies, confidentiality concerns, financial expenses, exposure fears, self-sufficiency desires, time constraints, and difficulties in locating a good enough therapist outside of their immediate social and professional network. A sizable percentage also notes that they did not pursue personal treatment because other means proved effective in dealing with the inevitable burdens of life (and practicing psychotherapy).

These self-reported reasons for not entering personal treatment are corroborated and extended by one study (Norcross & Prochaska, 1986a, 1986b) that empirically compared psychotherapists who did initiate treatment to those who did not during a recent episode of psychological distress. Put another way, the study explored why some psychotherapists relied entirely on self-help whereas others pursued personal therapy. Four variables discriminated between the two groups. Clinicians seeking personal therapy (1) were more likely to have experienced personal therapy in the past; (2) were in personal treatment in the past for a greater number of hours; (3) suffered a longer (but not more severe) distress episode; and (4) rated their self-help (before seeking therapy) as less successful.

Seeking treatment after relatively unsuccessful self-change is not restricted to mental health professionals, of course. A study of college students' use of psychological services, for example, found that "the decision to actually use psychotherapy was likely to come only after ineffective attempts to cope with the problem one's self or with the help of a close friend or relative" (Farber & Geller, 1977, p. 306). Two noted psychologists (Goldfried & Davison, 1976, p. 9) put it a bit more directly: "to begin with, the very fact that the client has sought (professional) help is an open admission that he has been unable to adequately control certain aspects of his own life." Most therapeutic efforts are directed at unsuccessful self-changers.

PRESENTING PROBLEMS

Four published studies have directly inquired about psychotherapists' presenting problems or chief complaints for personal treatment—what troubles the troubleshooters. Holzman, Searight, and Hughes (1996) requested that clinical psychology graduate students (50% response; $N = 1,108$) rate their reasons from a list of 16 options and then calculated percentages based on the top four rankings. Mackey and Mackey (1994) interviewed 15 social workers about their precipitants for entering psychotherapy. Norcross, Strausser-Kirtland, and Missar (1988) studied psychologists, psychiatrists, and social workers (65%, 34%, and 50% return rates, respectively; total $N = 509$) and asked them to briefly describe their presenting problem for their most recent or only episode of personal therapy. Pope and Tabachnick (1994) asked a national sample of psychologists (60% return; $N = 476$) to reveal the major problem, distress, dysfunction, or issue they addressed in personal therapy. Although the samples and procedures differed across studies, the results follow a consistent pattern.

The three most frequent presenting problems are depression, marital/couple conflicts, and anxiety, as displayed in table 15.2. Family-of-origin conflicts represent a central theme, particularly for the graduate students in the Holzman et al. (1996) study, as do training purposes and personal/professional growth, when these responses were included in studies. Other frequent responses include feelings of loneliness, critical life events, substance abuse problems, and emotional depletion.

Psychotherapists' modal complaints for psychotherapy—depression, anxiety, and relationships—are consistent with the research in several other areas as well. First, the chief complaints for therapy generally parallel those of the population at large. Second, they are consistent with the evidence indicating that clinical practice exacts a negative toll on the practitioner, particularly in the forms of problematic anxiety, moderate depression, and emotional underinvolvement with family members (e.g., Bermak, 1977; Cray & Cray, 1977; Daniels, 1974; Dryden, 1995; Farber, 1983; Norcross & Prochaska, 1986a; Sussman, 1995). Third, anxiety, depression, and

Table 15.2 Presenting Problems for Psychotherapists' Personal Therapy

Problem	Mackey & Mackey (1994)	Holzman, Searight, & Hughes, (1996)*	Norcross, Strausser-Kirtland, & Missar (1988)	Pope & Tabachnick (1994)
Marital/relationship conflict	33%	32%	20%	15%
Depression	27%	38%	13%	19%
Anxiety/stress	7%	NR	12%	11%
Training purposes	NR	NR	5%	9%
Interpersonal conflicts	NR	6%	5%	NR
Need for self-understanding	NR	NR	4%	6%
Career or occupational problems	NR	9%	3%	1%
Family-of-origin conflicts	NR	25%	3%	7%
Personal or professional growth	NR	59%	NR	NR
Alcoholism or substance abuse	7%	1%	NR	NR
Other	27%	22%	35%	32%

*Each respondent was asked to give four reasons.

marital conflict are psychotherapists' chief presenting problems not only for personal treatment but also for their self-help efforts (Deutsch, 1985; Norcross & Prochaska, 1986b).

Psychotherapists' problems in living run the entire gamut of human concerns—abortions, affairs, divorce, alcoholism, murder of an old friend, a child's suicide, drug use, a sibling on trial for murder—to name just a few described by psychotherapists. But perhaps we should not see such malaise among therapists as anything unusual. Burton (1972, p. x) adds reassuringly: "but the point is that to meliorate the distinctive problems of living, one has also to be human, and that means to have problems like everyone else."

Despite the enormous responsibilities of the profession, few psychotherapists identify the presenting or precipitant problem for their personal therapy as a problematic patient. In two of our studies (Norcross et al., 1988; Norcross & Prochaska, 1986a), involving hundreds of seasoned practitioners, only *one* psychologist identified the precipitant as a client problem, in this case, a suicide attempt. The remaining 99% of therapists listed a nonpatient factor as the precipitant. Instead the occupational hazards were related to supervisors, policies, promotions, salaries, and similar organizational plights. In the context of a psychotherapist's total life, patient conflicts emerge as a moderate source of distress; it was much more likely to result from extratherapy life problems.

This finding may not startle many experienced clinicians. However, in contrast to the extensive research on in-therapy stress, it is perhaps a bit puzzling and ironic. Few studies have systematically studied the person of the psychotherapist qua person outside his or her professional world, thus underestimating real-life problems. Even the effects of therapists' personal characteristics are evaluated for their influence on clinical practice rather than for their impact on the total person.

In closing this section, we note a parallel between these empirical results and the notion of the wounded healer. In many societies healers have been associated with a weakness to which valuable properties are assigned. The mythological image of the wounded healer is widespread: not only does the patient have a therapist within himself or herself but also there lies a patient within the therapist. Primitive shamans, for instance, had a mixture of priestly and healing powers, but a requirement for the role was that they possess some defect, which in Western society would be recognized as an illness or disability (Bennet, 1979; Guggenbuhl-Craig, 1971; Rippere & Williams, 1985).

Many psychotherapists, we believe, choose the profession partly due to their affinity with the healer-patient archetype. Practitioners, medical and psychological alike, are accused of being more interested in pathology than health, more in the abnormal than the normal. This is a half-truth. Psychotherapists are attracted to the health-sickness polarity in others and in themselves. The image of the wounded healer thus symbolizes a painful awareness of our own limitations and the counterpole to health (Guggenbuhl-Craig, 1971).

Chessick (1978, p. 7) captured the essence of the wounded healer in saying: "Contrary to the popular misconception, it is the psychiatrist who seeks help for himself by consultation and further psychotherapy who shows best his capacity to help his patients; the psychiatrist who denies his needs and pretends to be self-sufficient may temporarily impress those around him but actually he is showing weakness rather than strength."

CONCLUDING COMMENT

In this focused research review, we have endeavored to highlight the reasons mental health professionals enter personal therapy, their reasons for not doing so, and the primary problems for their own treatment. There are no systematic or conclusive data about which variants of psychopathology are most prevalent among mental health professionals (Millon, Millon, & Antoni, 1986) or how distress is differentially manifested among practitioners. Still, we are struck by the robust and replicated findings that personal therapy is largely a personal endeavor—not a "training analysis"—aimed toward personal resolution and integration. For the most part, therapists' personal treatment is not, and indeed should not be, merely a required intellectual or training endeavor. Presenting problems are, by and large, nearly identical to those of the educated populace seeking mental health services. While we may be tempted to fantasize that seasoned psychotherapists are able to inoculate themselves against the ravages of life that beset their patients, a careful reading of the literature compellingly suggests otherwise. To paraphrase Freud, psychotherapists possess a special skill, but beyond that, we are inescapably human.

REFERENCES

Bennet, G. (1979). *Patients and their doctors: The journey through medical care.* London: Bailliere Tindall.

Bermak, G. E. (1977). Do psychiatrists have special emotional problems? *American Journal of Psycho-analysis, 37,* 141–147.

Burton, A. (1973). The psychotherapist as client. *American Journal of Psychoanalysis, 33,* 94–103.

Burton, A. (Ed.). (1972). *Twelve therapists: How they live and actualize themselves.* San Francisco: Jossey-Bass.

Chessick, R. D. (1978). The sad soul of the psychiatrist. *Bulletin of the Menninger Clinic, 42,* 1–9.

Cray, C., & Cray, M. (1977). Stresses and rewards within the psychiatrist's family. *American Journal of Psychoanalysis, 37,* 337–341.

Daniels, A. K. (1974). What troubles the trouble shooters. In P. M. Roman & H. M. Trice (Eds.), *The sociology of psychotherapy* (pp. 191–214). New York: Aronson.

Deutsch, C. J. (1985). A survey of therapists' personal problems and treatment. *Professional Psychology: Research and Practice, 16,* 305–315.

Dryden, W. (Ed.). (1995). *The stresses of counseling in action.* Thousand Oaks, CA: Sage.

Farber, B. A. (1983). Dysfunctional aspects of the therapeutic role. In B. A. Farber (Ed.), *Stress and burnout in the human service profession* (pp. 97–118). New York: Pergamon.

Farber, B. A., & Geller, J. D. (1977). Student attitudes toward psychotherapy. *Journal of American College Health Association, 25,* 301–307.

Farber, N. K. (2000). Trainees' Attitudes Toward Seeking Psychotherapy Scale: Development and validation of a research instrument. *Psychotherapy, 37,* 341–353.

Freudenberger, H. J. (1986). The health professional in treatment: Symptoms, dynamics, and treatment issues. In C. D. Scott & J. Hawk (Eds.), *Heal thyself: The health of health care professionals.* New York: Brunner/Mazel.

Gabbard, G. O. (1995). When the patient is a therapist: Special considerations in the psychoanalysis of mental health professionals. *Psychoanalytic Review, 82,* 63–79.

Goldfried, M. R., & Davison, G. S. (1976). *Clinical behavior therapy.* New York: Holt, Rinehart and Winston.

Guggenbuhl-Craig, A. (1971). *Power in the helping professions.* Dallas: Spring.

Henry, W. E., Sims, J. H., & Spray, S. L. (1971). *The fifth profession: Becoming a psychotherapist.* San Fransisco: Jossey-Bass.

Holzman, L. A., Searight, H. R., & Hughes, H. M. (1996). Clinical psychology graduate students and personal psychotherapy: Results of an exploratory survey. *Professional Psychology Research and Practice, 27,* 98–101.

Kelly, E. L., Goldberg, L. R., Fiske, D. W., & Kilkowski, J. M. (1978). Twenty-five years later. *American Psychologist, 33,* 746–755.

Liaboe, G. P., Guy, J. D., Wong, T., & Deahnert, J. R. (1989). The use of personal therapy by psychotherapists. *Psychotherapy in Private Practice, 7,* 115–134.

Looney, J. G., Harding, R. K., Blotoky, M. J., & Barnhart, F. D. (1980). Psychiatrists transition from training to career: Stress and mastery. *American Journal of Psychiatry, 137,* 25–32.

Mackey, R. A., & Mackey, E. F. (1994). Personal psychotherapy and the development of a professional self. *Families in Society, 75,* 490–498.

Millon, T., Millon, C., & Antoni, M. (1986). Sources of emotional and mental disorders among psychologists: A career development perspective. In R. R. Kilburg, P. E. Nathan, & R. W. Thoreson (Eds.), *Professionals in distress* (pp. 119–134). Washington, DC: American Psychological Association.

Norcross, J. C., & Prochaska, J. O. (1986a). Psychotherapist heal thyself I: The self-initiated and therapy-facilitated change of psychological distress. *Psychotherapy, 23,* 102–114.

Norcross, J. C., & Prochaska, J. O. (1986b). Psychotherapist heal thyself II: The self-initiated and therapy-facilitated change of psychological distress. *Psychotherapy, 23,* 345–356.

Norcross, J. C., Strausser-Kirtland, D., & Missar, C. D. (1988). The processes and outcomes of psychotherapists' personal treatment experiences. *Psychotherapy, 25,* 36–43.

Norman, J., & Rosvall, S. B. (1994). Help-seeking behavior among mental health practitioners. *Clinical Social Work Journal, 22,* 449–460.

Pope, K. S., & Tabachnick, B. G. (1994). Therapists as patients: A national survey of psychologists' experiences, problems, and beliefs. *Professional Psychology: Research and Practice, 25,* 247–258.

Prochaska, J. O., & Norcross, J. C. (1983). Contemporary psychotherapists: A national survey of characteristics, practices, orientations, and attitudes. *Psychotherapy: Theory, Research and Practice, 20*, 161–173.

Rippere, V., & Williams, R. (Eds.). (1985). *Wounded healers: Mental health workers' experiences of depression.* New York: Wiley.

Sussman, M. B. (Ed.). (1995). *A perilous calling: The hazards of psychotherapy practice.* New York: Wiley.

Wispe, L. G., & Parloff, M. B. (1965). Impact of psychotherapy on the productivity of psychologists. *Journal of Abnormal Psychology, 70*, 188–193.

16

THE SELECTION
AND CHARACTERISTICS
OF THERAPISTS'
PSYCHOTHERAPISTS

A Research Synthesis

JOHN C. NORCROSS & HENRY GRUNEBAUM

Remarkably few research studies focus on psychotherapists' experiences with their personal treatment (Clark, 1986; Macaskill, 1988; Macran & Shapiro, 1998). Even fewer empirical investigations tackle the selection and characteristics of the therapist's therapist. The silence is deafening.

In this brief chapter, we review the existing research on how mental health professionals select psychotherapists for their own psychotherapy and the concomitant characteristics of those therapists in terms of demographics, theoretical orientations, and professional disciplines. As with the other research chapters in this part of the book, the research studies considered are all published works in the English language, largely conducted in the United States.

SELECTION CRITERIA

In a pioneering article on therapist selection, Grunebaum (1983) interviewed 23 experienced, Boston-area psychotherapists (11 psychiatrists, 7 psychologists, 3 social workers, and 2 counselors) about how they had recently found a "good therapist" for themselves. The sample constituted an especially knowledgeable group with informed opinions about the quality of therapy and therapists. The therapist-patients in his sample said that they had four essential criteria in mind as they searched for their own psychotherapist. First, they sought a fellow psychotherapist who was professionally competent, based on general reputation and colleagues' recommendations. Related research (Darongkamas, Burton, & Cushway, 1994) documents, in fact, that psychotherapists begin the search for competent therapists by relying primarily on personal recommendations (55% of sample) and previous personal contacts (30% of sample). Second, the therapist-patients sought therapists outside their usual professional and social network in order to avoid extra therapeutic contact and hearing about them and their personal lives. Third was a warm, caring, and supportive disposition. In fact, 20 of the 23 interviewees spontaneously volunteered at least one of these adjectives in describing their therapists—the sense of being affirmed, appreciated, and respected as a person. Fourth, the therapist-patients sought a clinician with an active, talkative style.

Expanding on this study, Norcross, Strausser, and Faltus (1988) asked a national sample of psychologists (N = 509) to rate the influence of 16 factors on the selection of their therapists using a five-point, Likert-type scale where 1 was "not at all important," 3 was "somewhat important," and 5 was "very important. Table 16.1 presents the average ratings and rank orders of these therapist selection criteria, along with approximate ranks for Grunebaum's (1983) sample, calculated on the basis of his participants' frequency of nomination.

Table 16.1   Therapist Selection Criteria

			Rank Order	
	Ratings		Norcross, Strausser, & Faltus (1988)	Grunebaum (1983)
Criterion	Mean	SD		
Competence	4.68	.8	1	1 (Tie)
Clinical experience	4.33	.9	2	NR
Professional reputation	4.00	1.1	3	1 (Tie)
Warmth and caring	3.97	1.0	4	1 (Tie)
Openness	3.61	1.2	5	6
Theoretical orientation	3.56	1.2	6	NR
Reputation for being a therapists' therapist	3.36	1.4	7	NR
Flexibility	3.27	1.1	8	9
Not attributing everything to transference	3.25	1.4	9	8
Active (talkative) therapeutic style	3.03	1.2	10	1 (Tie)
Lack of criticism	2.98	1.3	11	7
Specific profession	2.94	1.4	12	NR
Being outside of my social/prof network	2.91	1.4	13	1 (Tie)
Success with similar patients	2.85	1.4	14	NR
Cost per session	2.51	1.2	15	NR
Research productivity	1.48	.9	16	NR

NR = not reported.
Ratings were made on a 5-point, Likert-type scale: 1 = not at all important, 3 = somewhat important, 5 = very important.

As can be seen, therapist-patients predicated their psychotherapist selection primarily on perceived competence, clinical experience, professional reputation, and interpersonal warmth. These top four criteria all received average ratings of at least 4.0 on the five-point scale. Six additional criteria received mean ratings of 3.0 or higher, indicating that they were at least "somewhat important": openness; theoretical orientation; reputation for being a therapists' therapist; flexibility; not attributing everything to transference; and active therapeutic style. Only the therapist's research productivity received an average score of less than 2.0.

These findings generally paralleled those obtained by Grunebaum (1983), with two exceptions. First, an active or talkative style was not rated in the larger study as highly as in Grunebaum's study, and second, the therapist's location outside of the clinician-patient's network was also not judged as as important a criterion. These two disparities may be partially explained by the fact that Grunebaum's sample was composed predominantly of older, psychoanalytically oriented psychotherapists who were practicing in the Boston metropolitan area. That is, the small disparities may be attributable to different cohorts. The Grunebaum sample was comprised entirely of experienced therapists who had one or more treatment experiences, almost always a psychoanalysis, obtained some 20 to 50 years ago. By contrast, the Norcross et al. sample was more heterogeneous and, as a rule, much younger, with far more opportunities in therapist selection.

The 16 selection criteria presented in table 16.1 were empirically evaluated across the therapist-patient's theoretical orientation and professional discipline. Four meaningful orientational differences were observed: (1) behavioral respondents were less influenced than psychoanalytic and eclectic respondents by their therapists' professional reputation; (2) eclectic respondents rated openness in a therapist more important than their psychoanalytic colleagues; (3) respondents of all persuasions were more wary of therapists attributing "everything to transference" than were their psychoanalytic counterparts; and (4) a therapist's specific orientation was rated more influential by psychoanalytic and humanistic therapists than behaviorists, who in turn rated it more important than eclectics.

Professional differences were also evident on the selection criteria, with the principal disparities existing between social workers on the one hand and psychologists and psychiatrists, on the other. In brief, social workers accorded more weight to treatment cost, therapist flexibility, interpersonal warmth, active style, and openness in their therapist selection. Psychologists rated a potential therapist's research productivity as more influential than either of the other two groups, although it still obtained the lowest mean score in all three professional groups. Finally, psychiatrists indicated that a specific profession exerted significantly more influence on their psychotherapist selection than psychologist or social workers.

The chosen therapist's gender was not considered in the foregoing research but has been implicated in other studies as exerting an impact, at least implicitly, on therapist selection. Considerable experience exists that same-gender matches are preferred and, as reviewed in the next section, are actively sought by mental health professionals in their own treatment.

Another selection factor may be the charisma or confidence of the therapist. The therapist's inner strength—or at least the public persona of it—is likely to play a key role. In writing of therapist selection, Burton (1973, p. 94) noted that "the best professionals have a kind of confidence and arrogance not warranted by reality, and a part of it is that they will not fall heir to the diseases they cure." Their charisma may place them "above the din of psychiatric battle" (p. 97).

In sum, psychotherapists of all disciplines and theoretical persuasions select their own therapists primarily on the basis of clinical acumen and interpersonal qualities. Competence, experience, reputation, warmth, and openness are accorded the highest consideration by therapist-patients. By contrast, the research productivity of the potential psychotherapist was rated as an unimportant, almost neglible, factor in selection decisions. This finding should remind us that academic standing and clinical expertise are probably orthogonal dimensions.

To echo Grunebaum's (1983, p. 1338) conclusion, "what we have learned that may be useful in conducting psychotherapy is that these therapist-patients seek a personal relationship with therapists—one in which they feel affirmed, appreciated, and respected by another human being whom they like, appreciate, and respect." That this holds true for psychologically sophisticated patients, as it has been shown to be for naive patients, corroborates the view that these factors are probably essential for effective psychological treatment (Greenberg & Staller, 1981). The therapist qualities of warmth, empathy, and mutual liking were central to positive outcome in psychotherapists' treatment experiences in at least three studies to date (Buckley, Karasu, & Charles, 1986; Norcross, Strausser-Kirtland, & Missar, 1988; Pope & Tabachnick, 1994; see also the review in chapter 17). It is also in total agreement with psychotherapy research generally (e.g., Orlinsky, Grawe, & Parks, 1994). Conversely the modal reason advanced for *harmful* treatment experiences among psychotherapists is a rigid, distant, and uninvolved therapeutic relationship (Grunebaum, 1986).

CHARACTERISTICS OF THERAPISTS SELECTED

Who do mental health professionals seek out for their own psychotherapy? Several research studies have asked psychotherapists to describe the characteristics of their chosen therapists, customarily in terms of demographics, orientation, and profession. In addition, one recent study (Norcross, Geller, & Kurzawa, 2000) investigated the features of psychotherapists who treat a large proportion of fellow mental health professionals—that, is "therapists' therapists."

Demographic Variables

A large, multidisciplinary study conducted in 1987 (Norcross, Strausser, et al., 1988) contained a series of items regarding the demographic characteristics of the therapist's therapist. Male therapists were chosen by 82% of the male respondents and by 67% of the female respondents; 33% of the women and 18% of the men received personal treatment from a female. However, these global figures represent historical artifacts. Analyses determined that an increasing proportion of women were seeking women as their personal therapists: 31% among an older group (10 or more years of clinical experience) but 43% among a younger group (fewer than 10 years). To a lesser extent, male respondents were also receiving more treatment from female therapists: 17% among the experienced and 22% among the inexperienced. This pattern was replicated across three different professional disciplines (psychologists, psychiatrists, social workers) and corresponds to the evolving demographics of the mental health professionals. Younger female therapists consistently received a higher proportion of personal treatment from women therapists than older female respondents: 41% versus 30% among psychologists, 33% versus 8% among psychiatrists; and 45% versus 35% among social workers. These demographic findings must be interpreted within the historical context in which they were collected; since 1987, increasing proportions of American mental health professionals are females and non-Caucasian.

Ninety-two percent of therapist-patients reported that their most recent or only psychotherapist was Caucasian. It was the rare Caucasian respondent indeed who did not receive treatment from a Caucasian clinician—only 3 percent received treatment from an American Indian, Black, or Hispanic. By contrast, fully one-half of the black respondents ($n = 8$) received treatment from a psychotherapist of minority racial heritage.

The gender and ethnicity of the therapist's therapist seem to exert greater influence than traditionally recognized. Although these factors were not specifically included in the study of selection criteria (table 16.1) and although none of Grunebaum's (1983) interviewees explicitly mentioned them, the chosen psychotherapist's demographics closely matched the respondent's. Even accounting for the historical underrepresentation of racial minority and women psychotherapists, these figures point to the ubiquitous practice of client-clinician demographic matching.

Theoretical Orientation

Several studies have examined the theoretical orientation of the therapist's therapist, especially in how it relates to the theoretical orientation of the therapist-patient. Of special interest—and of some controversy—has been the theoretical predilections of therapists chosen by behavior therapists. In what follows, moving from the general to specific, we review the central findings of these studies.

In general, the orientation choice for the therapist's therapy has been psychoanalytic or psychodynamic. The theoretical orientations of the therapists' psychotherapists, as depicted in table 16.2 for one large investigation (Norcross, Strausser, et al., 1988), show that this tends to be the case across multiple treatment episodes. Eclectic and humanistic therapists were also popular; however, there was no clear second choice for preferred orientation after the psychoanalytic or psychodynamic orientations. Fewer respondents chose psychoanalytic during the second therapy than during the first therapy, opting for more humanistic and psychodynamic therapists.

The results of other studies clearly bear these patterns out. Looking specifically at therapist choice posttraining, for example, Liaboe, Guy, Wong, and Deahnert (1989) identified the theoretical orientation of therapists following completion of formal training. Fifty-four percent chose a psychodynamic/psychoanalytic, 16% an eclectic, 8% a gestalt, and 7% an existential therapist. Only 6% selected a cognitive-behavioral therapist even though 14% of the therapists were themselves cognitive-behavioral. Norcross, Strausser-Kirtland, et al. (1988), for another example, reported that mental health professionals largely undertook personal treatment with psychoanalytic (41%) or psychodynamic (18%) psychotherapists. Eighty-seven percent of the respondents who reported psychoanalytic treatment indicated that their psychotherapist was a formally trained psychoanalyst. Sixteen percent of the total chose an eclectically inclined practitioner, but relatively few chose clinicians of behavioral or cognitive persuasions.

Therapist-patients' current theoretical orientations are related, not surprisingly, to their psychotherapists' orientation. This associative pattern for one study (Norcross, Strausser, et al., 1988) is presented in table 16.3 in the underscored diagonal. In nearly all of the cases (90%), psychoanalytic therapist-patients selected psychoanalytic (45%) or psychodynamic (34%) therapy for themselves. Behavioral therapist-patients were the least restrictive in their choices: 44% chose an eclectic, 19% chose a cognitivist, 19% a humanistic, 12% a psychoanalyst, and only 6% a behaviorist. Approximately one-third of the humanistic therapist-patients received personal treatment of the same humanistic orientation, but an even greater number (34%) received psychoanalytic or psychodynamic therapy. The eclectics tended to

Table 16.2 Summary of Personal Therapy Experiences

Variable	First Therapy	Second Therapy	Third Therapy
Average age of patient (years)	27.6	30.5	38.6
Treatment orientation			
Cognitive/behavioral	4%	9%	5%
Eclectic	11%	12%	13%
Humanistic	15%	20%	16%
Psychoanalytic	40%	29%	36%
Psychodynamic	21%	17%	17%
Systems	1%	5%	6%

Adapted from Norcross, Strausser & Faltus, 1988.

Table 16.3 Orientation—Choice of Personal Therapy

	Respondent's Orientation							
Therapist's Orientation	BEH (*n* = 16)	COG (*n* = 25)	ECL (*n* = 150)	HUM (*n* = 32)	PA (*n* = 71)	PD (*n* = 110)	SYS (*n* = 40)	*Total*
Behavioral (BEH)	6%	12%	4%	9%	3%	4%	5%	5%
Cognitive (COG)	19%	16%	4%	0%	0%	3%	5%	4%
Eclectic (ECL)	44%	28%	24%	22%	1%	6%	5%	16%
Humanistic (HUM)	19%	12%	17%	33%	1%	7%	10%	13%
Psychoanalytic (PA)	12%	20%	26%	19%	90%	45%	35%	41%
Psychodynamic (PD)	0%	0%	20%	15%	4%	34%	15%	18%
Systems (SYS)	0%	12%	5%	3%	0%	1%	25%	3%

Adapted from Norcross, Strausser & Faltus, 1988.

be more traditional still in their orientation choice, but almost a quarter received some sort of "eclectic" therapy.

With the exception of psychoanalysts, psychotherapists exhibit considerable theoretical variety in their personal therapy choice but favor the psychoanalytic persuasion. This pattern applies to behavior therapists as well.

Ekstein and Wallerstein (1972), among others, have addressed the conflicting motives for seeking personal therapy with someone of the same or similar theoretical persuasion. On the one hand, the professional usually assumes that the best psychotherapeutic experience would be one that is more or less based on the same theoretical principles that the practitioner will use herself or himself. Therapy with someone who belongs to the same school of thought fosters interpersonal modeling, identity formation, and theoretical socialization. On the other hand, undergoing personal treatment with someone of the same theoretical persuasion may well be an ideological or political commitment. The identification may slip into conversion, might preclude collaboration with different schools of thought, might discourage exchanges of opinion and experimentation, and might prevent the opening of minds. Ekstein and Wallerstein (1972) repeat the joke "In my father's house there are many mansions but it must be understood that my father is an analyst."

The Case of Behavior Therapists

In a brief 1971 article entitled "Where Do Behavior Therapists Take Their Troubles?" Lazarus articulated his anecdotal discovery that numerous behavior therapists were undergoing psychoanalysis, psychoanalytic psychotherapy, gestalt therapy, existential therapy, or some other form of nonbehavioral treatment. His article on therapy choice, which begat considerable controversy, indicated that three behavior therapists were in psychoanalysis, seven in psychoanalytic psychotherapy, five in gestalt therapy, three in bioenergetics, and four in existential therapy. In addition, many of the clinicians had experimented with or had become deeply involved with sensitivity training, T-groups, and marathon encounters. These findings underscore the fact that behavior therapy and insight-oriented therapy frequently have different aims and purposes. "May we sum it up by asking for *choices of treatment* rather than treatments of choice" (Lazarus, 1971, p. 350).

Subsequent and more systematic research has confirmed that considerable numbers of behavior therapists seek personal treatment—somewhere between 44% and 66% (see chapter 13)—but typically from nonbehavioral colleagues. Like Lazarus, Norcross and Prochaska (1984) found that the vast majority of behavior therapists did *not* choose behavioral treatment for themselves; only 6% to 8% in two different samples did so. Instead, psychoanalytic, psychodynamic, eclectic, and existential-humanistic therapies were the most prevalent therapy choices among the behavioral clinicians. Similarly, Darongkamas et al. (1994, p. 168), in a study of British clinical psychologists, report that "most cognitive-behavioral therapists chose therapists of orientations other than their own: 44% chose psychodynamic therapists, 22% chose eclectics and 22% other, and only 11% chose cognitive-behavioral therapists." Back in the United States, Norcross, Strausser, et al. (1988), in a large multidisciplinary study, found that less than one in ten behavior therapists chose behavioral treatment for themselves. Instead they preferred eclectic, psychoanalytic, and humanistic treatment by a margin of more than two to one over behavioral treatment. Concurrently, few *non*behavioral psychotherapists—5% to 10% depending on the study—elected behavior therapy for themselves.

Where, then, do behavior (and other) therapists take their troubles? For the most part, to mental health professionals of nonbehavioral persuasions. With the exception of psychoanalysts, psychotherapists exhibit considerable variety in their personal therapy choice. As Lazarus (1971) observed, psychodynamic systems of psychotherapy retain enormous appeal for those who can profit from intensive self-exploration. This seems to be particularly the case for psychotherapists, whose effectiveness is intimately related to their own awareness, esteem, and interpersonal skills. As with most of our clients, contemporary clinicians seek both behavior change and increased self-understanding from their personal psychotherapy (Buckley et al., 1981).

Joseph Wolpe, one of the founders of behavior therapy, took exception to these results. His letter to a journal editor (1988, p. 509) accused Norcross and colleagues of repeating "the outrageous allegation that the vast majority of behavior therapists do not choose behavioral treatment for themselves. If this were true it would bespeak unmatched cynicism and immorality. It would also show remarkable indifference, in the single context of their own needs, to the superior efficacy of behavior therapy that numerous studies have demonstrated."

Individual readers can judge for themselves whether the consistent results on this matter "bespeak unmatched cynicism and immorality" on the part of behavior therapists, but the empirical results are very consistent across studies. Several alternative explanations seem equally parsimonious and more likely to us. First, few behavior therapists—self-identified or Wolpe-approved—were available when clinicians sought personal treatment many years ago, and thus behavior therapy may indeed be underrepresented. Second, increased awareness and personal understanding are highly valued goals for a therapist's own therapy. Symptom alleviation per se was rated the least important of all outcome measures in one study of psychotherapists' treatment experiences (Buckley, Karasu, & Charles, 1986), although we readily appreciate that it may not be so for Wolpe. Increased awareness and personal understanding through self-exploration is a viable goal in and of itself, especially for relatively well-functioning behavior therapists.

Lazarus, whose initial article precipitated the controversy, has advanced a more moderate and evidence-based position. In personal correspondence, Lazarus (1971; see also Fay & Lazarus, 1984, p. 126) has summarized the matter as follows.

My 1971 paper on behavior therapists' penchant to select nonbehavioral therapists for their own treatment has been misquoted and misunderstood by more people than I have been able to keep track of. As you well know, the point was *not* that behavioral clinicians believe in the intrinsic superiority of psychoanalysis or any other nonbehavioral approach. The article did *not* say that behavior therapists are phonies who secretly recognize that nonbehavioral systems are better. Yet each of the forgoing allegations has been made in several different quarters. Nevertheless, if I was ordered to undergo personal therapy today, why would I not choose a behavior therapist? Because I *function* relatively well. But were I to develop specific fears, compulsions, sexual hangups, social deficits, or other nonfunctional patterns, I would rapidly rush to a behavior therapist for help. However, since I do not have these kinds of specific hangups, behavior therapy has little to offer me.

Professional Discipline

In contrast to the prodigious attention accorded to the theoretical orientation of the therapist's therapists, far less had been paid to the professional discipline. Indeed, we were able to identify only a single research article published in the United States that addressed the issue empirically.

Psychotherapists have historically received treatment from psychiatrists, psychologists, social workers, counselors, and lay analysts, in that general order (Norcross, Strausser, et al., 1988). There are definite preferences on the basis of professional discipline, however. Thirty-six percent of the psychologists received treatment from fellow psychologists, 35% from psychiatrists. Psychiatrists routinely sought out other psychiatrists—82% of the time. Social workers were the only group more likely to enter treatment with a therapist of a discipline different from their own. In fact, they chose psychiatrists (46% of the time) and psychologists (25%) much more frequently than fellow social workers (19%).

These findings, however, reflect the historical availability of psychotherapists, as opposed to more contemporary trends. In one study (Norcross, Strausser, et al., 1988; Norcross, Strausser-Kirtland, et al., 1988), the professional disciplines of personal therapists were examined across years to discern changes over time. The resultant analyses indicated that younger psychotherapists are increasingly seeking assistance from nonmedical psychotherapists, particularly from psychologists. Younger psychologists, for example, sought therapy from fellow psychologists more frequently (46%) than older psychologists (32%). In fact, the profession of choice for social worker's personal therapy of late has become psychology, not psychiatry. More recently, social workers sought out proportionally more psychologists (33% v. 25%) and social workers (30% v. 18%) but fewer psychiatrists (30% v. 52%).

The historical changes in clinicians' selections of their own therapists are impressive. The growing availability and professionalization of nonmedical psychotherapists are the obvious explanations, of course. In several respects, it is heartening to observe increasing proportions of mental health professionals being treated by members of their own gender and discipline. These treatment experiences can enhance personal validation and professional socialization. In other respects, however, this emerging pattern can promote professional indoctrination and theoretical "inbreeding." The ideal outcomes of personal psychotherapy, in our view, should not be compartmentalization or isolation but rather meaningful interpersonal exchanges and diverse learning experiences.

In the selection ratings of a personal therapist (table 16.2), the specific profession of the chosen psychotherapist was rated a mildly influential variable ($M = 1.94$ on a 5–point scale) and theoretical orientation moderately influential ($M = 3.56$). The actual data on profession choice and orientation choice bear out this influence. The profession and orientation of the selected therapist seem to hold more salience for certain subgroups, particularly psychiatrists and psychoanalysts, many of whom were historically restricted in their selection to approved analysts in training institutes. Insofar as psychiatrists sought fellow psychiatrists for personal treatment 82% of the time, it may well be that the prospective patient frequently limited himself or herself to choosing an experienced psychiatrist. In similar fashion, the psychoanalytically oriented patient typically restricted his or her therapist search to those of like orientation and *then* employed the criteria of acumen and concern.

CHARACTERISTICS OF THERAPISTS' THERAPISTS

A national study of psychologists conducting psychotherapy found that 16% definitely considered themselves a therapists' therapist and 25% probably did (28% maybe, 26% probably not, and 6% definitely not). A series of statistical analyses identified the demographic, professional, and caseload correlates of those psychologists who both designated themselves as therapists' therapists and whose caseload comprised a relatively high percentage (10% or more) of mental health professionals (Norcross, Geller, & Kurzawa, 2000).

In terms of demographics, psychologists routinely treating peers had significantly greater clinical experience (M of 23 years versus 19 years) and were significantly more likely to be fellows of their professional association (58% of fellows v. 29% of members). No differences were observed between the two groups on age, gender, or race/ethnicity.

In terms of professional variables, psychologists treating higher percentages of mental health professionals were significantly more likely to be employed in university departments and medical schools than in other settings. Theoretical orientation also bore a significant relationship to self-reported percentage of mental health professionals treated in the prior three years. Specifically, 41% of psychoanalytic/psychodynamic therapists, 36% of humanistic therapists, 32% of interpersonal, 23% of eclectic/integrative, and 17% of cognitive therapists related that 10% or more of their caseloads were comprised of peers.

In terms of caseload variables, psychologists treating a higher percentage of mental health professionals were distinguished by three variables. First, they reported a significantly higher percentage of psychologists (but not psychiatrists, social workers, counselors, or other therapists) in their mental health professional caseloads (M of 43% v. 33%). Second, they recorded a significantly lower percentage of behavior and cognitive-behavior therapists in their psychotherapist caseloads (M = 17% v. 29%). Third, and related, they treated significantly higher percentage of psychoanalytic/psychodynamic peers (M = 34% v. 17%). However, no reliable differences were found in terms of percentages of therapists hailing from other theoretical orientations or referral sources or therapy formats practiced.

Data gleaned from the perspective of the therapists' therapist support and extend the data collected from therapist-patients about their therapists. Therapists' therapists are, not surprisingly, older and more accomplished in their field. They are more likely to be employed in higher profile and academic positions, such as those at universities and medical schools. Therapists' therapists, at least by self-characterization, are significantly more inclined toward the psychodynamic and insight-oriented orientations. On the other end, therapists' therapists are far more likely to treat colleagues of the psychoanalytic persuasion and less likely to treat cognitive-behavior therapists. Although asked for in different ways and collected from different perspectives, these data coincide with the findings previously reviewed regarding the personal therapy choices of behavior and cognitive-behavior therapists.

CONCLUDING COMMENTS

In this chapter we have endeavored to examine the research evidence pertaining to the selection and characteristics of the therapist's therapist. While the results from the different studies are generally consistent with each other and with our clinical experiences, we are obliged to reiterate that the number of studies is small, largely restricted to the United States, and entirely dependent on self-reports. Moreover, the selection of a personal therapist—like that of a mate—may not be wholly conscious, and the reasons may be accessible only after many years of reflection. It may be, as Burton (1973, p. 96) asserted, that "the selection of a healer by healers is made on a dynamically preconscious or unconscious basis and then rationalized in terms of a few qualities." Whether this is true or not will only be known through additional research and probing discernment into the complex process of therapists selecting a personal therapist.

REFERENCES

Buckley, P., Karasu, T. B., & Charles, E. (1981). Psychotherapists view their personal therapy. *Psychotherapy, 18,* 299–305.

Burton, A. (1973). The psychotherapist as client. *American Journal of Psychoanalysis, 33,* 94–103.

Chessick, R. D. (1978). The sad soul of the psychiatrist. *Bulletin of the Menninger Clinic, 42,* 1–9.

Clark, M. M. (1986). Personal therapy: A review of empirical research. *Professional Psychology: Research and Practice, 17,* 541–543.

Darongkamas, J., Burton, M. V., & Cushway, D. (1994). The use of personal therapy by clinical psychologists working in the NHS in the United Kingdom. *Clinical Psychology and Psychotherapy, 1,* 165–173.

Ekstein, R., & Wallerstein, R. S. (1972). *The teaching and learning of psychotherapy.* New York: Basic Books.

Fay, A., & Lazarus, A. A. (1984). The therapist in behavioral and multimodal therapy. In F. N. Kaslow (Ed.), *Psychotherapy with psychotherapists* (pp. 123–146). New York: Haworth.

Greenberg, R. P., & Staller, J. (1981). Personal therapy for therapists. *American Journal of Psychiatry, 138,* 1467–1471.

Grunebaum, H. (1983). A study of therapists' choice of therapist. *American Journal of Psychiatry, 140,* 1336–1339.

Grunebaum, H. (1986). Harmful psychotherapy experiences. *American Journal of Psychotherapy, 40,* 165–176.

Lazarus, A. A. (1971). Where do behavior therapists take their troubles? *Psychological Reports, 28,* 349–350.

Liaboe, G. P., Guy, J. D., Wong, T., & Deahnert, J. R. (1989). The use of personal therapy by psychotherapists. *Psychotherapy in Private Practice, 7,* 115–134.

Macaskill, N. D. (1988). Personal therapy in the training of the psychotherapist: Is it effective? *British Journal of Psychotherapy, 4,* 219–226.

Macran, S., & Shapiro, D. (1998). The role of personal therapy for therapists: A review. *British Journal of Medical Psychology, 71,* 13–25.

Norcross, J. C., Geller, J. D., & Kurzawa, E. K. (2000). Conducting psychotherapy with psychotherapists: I. Prevalence, patients, and problems. *Psychotherapy, 37,* 199–205.

Norcross, J. C., & Prochaska, J. O. (1984). Where do behavior and other therapists take their troubles? II. *Behavior Therapist, 7,* 26–27.

Norcross, J. C., Strausser, D. J., & Faltus, F. J. (1988). The therapist's therapist. *American Journal of Psychotherapy, 42,* 53–66.

Norcross, J. C., Strausser-Kirtland, D., & Missar, C. D. (1988). The processes and outcomes of psychotherapists' personal treatment experiences. *Psychotherapy, 25,* 36–43.

Orlinsky, D. E., Grawe, K., & Parks, B. K. (1994). Process and outcome in psychotherapy. In A. E. Bergin & S. L. Garfield (Eds.), *Handbook of psychotherapy and behavior change* (pp. 270–376). New York: Wiley.

Pope, K. S., & Tabachnick, B. G. (1994). Therapists as patients: A national survey of psychologists' experiences, problems, and beliefs. *Professional Psychology: Research and Practice, 25,* 247–258.

Wolpe, J. (1988). Letter to the editor. *American Journal of Psychotherapy, 42,* 509.

17

OUTCOMES AND IMPACTS OF THE PSYCHOTHERAPIST'S OWN PSYCHOTHERAPY

A Research Review

DAVID E. ORLINSKY, JOHN C. NORCROSS,
M. HELGE RØNNESTAD, & HADAS WISEMAN

Previously in this book we have documented the extensive and intensive use of personal therapy by psychotherapists of various professional backgrounds and theoretical orientations, both in the United States and in other countries (see chapters 13–16). Now we may ask: "What does all this personal therapy do for psychotherapists?" Do the benefits therapists receive appear to warrant this widespread practice?

The rationale for therapists undergoing therapy is both personal and professional. On the personal side, therapists wish to have the help to live happier lives themselves and in that respect don't differ greatly from their patients. On the professional side, there is a longstanding view held by many authors that personal therapy is a desirable, if not essential, prerequisite for clinical work. In this chapter we shall review research evidence regarding the impact of the psychotherapists' own psychotherapy on their personal lives and their professional development. We shall also broaden the base of prior research by adding new findings from a large international study of psychotherapists.

PERSONAL OUTCOMES

Positive Benefits

Over the past decades, a number of published studies reported therapists' ratings of outcomes for their own personal therapy. Although the studies asked the question in different ways, the self-reported outcomes were consistently positive, as shown in table 17.1. Generally, the great majority of the practitioners surveyed—including more than 1,400 American and nearly 1,000 British therapists—reported that their personal therapy was helpful. Across six studies, 90% or more were satisfied with their treatment. The exception was the study of American mental health professions by Henry, Sims and Spray (1971), where only 68% to 71% reported satisfaction with personal therapy (due in part to lower rates of satisfaction among psychiatrists). Even when accounting for cognitive dissonance and rosy memories, the vast majority of therapists seem to have had very positive experiences. Moreover, psychotherapists report improvement in multiple areas: self-esteem, work functioning, social life, characterological conflicts, and symptom severity. The self-rated outcomes for improvement in behavioral symptoms, cognitive insight, and emotional relief are practically identical (Norcross, Strausser-Kirtland, & Missar, 1988), perhaps with symptom alleviation being slightly lower (Buckley, Karasu, & Charles, 1981).

Additional findings on the personal benefits of psychotherapy experienced by therapists come from the international study conducted by the Collaborative Research Network of the Society for Psychotherapy Research (Orlinsky et al., 1999; Orlinsky & Rønnestad, in press). As part of its focus on the factors associated with professional development, that study collected data on the personal therapy experiences of more than 5,000 therapists of diverse professions and various theoretical orientations in over a dozen countries.

Overall, about 80% of those surveyed reported having had at least one course of personal therapy, and those who did have therapy were asked to describe their specific treatments experiences. Part of the information

Table 17.1 Summary of Therapist Ratings on the Effectiveness of Their Personal Therapy

Study	*Sample*	*% Effective or Helpful*
Buckley, Karasu, & Charles (1981)	97 American psychotherapists	Between 94% (improved self-esteem) & 73% (symptom alleviation)
Henry, Sims, & Spray (1971)	117 American psychologists, psychiatrists, & social workers	68% to 71%
Liaboe, Guy, Wong, & Deahnert (1989)	232 American psychologists	95%
Norcross, Dryden, & DeMichele (1992)	993 British psychologists	90%
Norcross, Strausser-Kirtland, & Missar (1988)	508 American psychologists	92%
Patterson & Utesch (1991)	33 family therapists	97%
Pope & Tabachnick (1994)	476 American psychologists	99% (86% very or exceptionally helpful)

requested was the therapist's rating of the treatment's "value to you as a person" on a 6-point scale (from 0, "none," to 5, "very great"). This self-report measure is typical of "consumer satisfaction"–type outcome studies and is independent of outcome ratings made from other perspectives (see Orlinsky, Rønnestad, & Willutzki, 2004). On behalf of its use in the present study, we note that psychotherapists arguably are the most discriminating consumers of therapy one can imagine.

Table 17.2 summarizes the results of this rating for the first listed therapy reported by 3,629 therapists (which is not necessarily first therapy they had undergone). The results clearly support the high percentages of positive outcomes found in prior research. Overall, 88% reported positive outcomes, using the upper half of the 0–5 scale (i.e., 3, 4, or 5) to rate the personal value of their therapy. With a more stringent criterion (i.e., 4 or 5 on the 0–5 scale), 72% rated the personal value of their therapy as "great" or "very great."

Despite some variation in specific percentages, the results were generally consistent across countries. Positive benefit (> 3) was reported by more than 90% of the therapists in six countries (Spain, Portugal, Israel, Russia, Germany, Denmark), and by 80% to 90% in six countries (Switzerland, South Korea, Sweden, New Zealand, Norway, and the U.S.). Great or very great benefit (4–5) was reported by more than two-thirds of the therapists in 11 of 13 countries for which we have data.

It is sometimes said that what is most crucial about personal therapy is that therapists have at least one experience of great personal benefit, so that they acquire a sense of the potency of therapy that can be communicated

Table 17.2 Personal Benefits of Therapy: First Listed Treatment

		Personal Benefit		
Sample	N	*None*	*Positive*	*Very Positive*
United States	805	0.5%	88.0%	71.8%
Germany	771	0.8	92.2	75.9
Switzerland	228	0.4	88.2	72.8
Norway	549	2.0	84.9	65.4
Denmark	130	0.8	90.8	74.6
Sweden	102	1.0	87.3	68.6
Portugal	106	0.0	94.3	87.7
Spain	137	0.0	94.9	81.0
Belgium	98	8.2	78.6	63.3
South Korea	110	1.9	87.5	73.1
New Zealand	194	1.0	87.1	72.2
Israel	90	1.1	83.3	73.3
Russia	73	2.7	89.0	72.6
Total	3,629	1.2	88.4	72.2

Note. "None" = rating of 0 on a 0–5 scale of benefit (0 = Not at all; 5 = Very great); "Positive" = rating ≥ 3 on a 0–5 scale; "Very Positive" = rating of 4 or 5 on a 0–5 scale.

to their own patients. By this criterion, a better measure of the impact of personal therapy than the first treatment listed would be a review of outcomes based on the multiple therapies that therapists reported. Table 17.3 shows the percentages of therapists who had experienced at least one personal therapy which had great or very great value to them (4 or 5 on the 0–5 scale). Overall, 85% of more than 3,600 therapists reported having had at least one such very positive experience (and some of those who have not yet had it may be expected to do so eventually). The figures for different countries range from a low of 78% to 80% (South Korea, Norway, Russia) to a high exceeding 90% (Portugal, Spain, Sweden). If it is indeed crucial that therapists have at least one excellent experience in personal therapy, these data affirm that an overwhelming majority of therapists are very well prepared in this respect.

Most of the evidence presented thus far was based on therapists' self-conscious assessments of their personal therapy, and is thus vulnerable to various forms of bias. Less directly conscious, and thus less easily biased evidence, was found among 581 American therapists, and was replicated among 318 Norwegian therapists, by Orlinsky, Rønnestad, Wiseman, and Botermans (2002). In addition to questions about their personal therapy, those therapists were asked to rate the quality of their childhood experience by responding to the following questions: "Overall, when growing up, how much . . . Did you experience a sense of being genuinely cared for and supported? Did the family you grew up in function well, psychologically or emotionally?" The answers to those questions were combined to form a highly reliable scale of early life quality, which when analyzed was

Table 17.3 Percentage of Therapists Reporting One or More Highly Beneficial Personal Therapies

Sample	N	≥1 Highly Beneficial Personal Therapy
United States	808	85.4%
Germany	778	85.3
Switzerland	228	89.0
Norway	551	77.9
Denmark	130	87.7
Sweden	102	92.2
Portugal	107	93.5
Spain	137	92.2
Belgium	98	86.7
South Korea	104	77.9
New Zealand	195	89.2
Israel	90	88.9
Russia	73	79.5
Total	3,622	85.1

Note. "Highly beneficial" = rating of 4 or 5 on 0–5 scale (0 = Not at all, 5 = Very great). Percentages based on those who experienced personal therapy.

found to be moderately but significantly correlated with therapists' ratings of their current life satisfaction and well-being, with how they view themselves in close personal relationships, and with the quality of their therapeutic work experience. The quality of therapists' childhood experiences had a clear and pervasive influence on their current adult experience. However, the finding most important in the present context was that the apparent influence of childhood experience on current adult experience was notably lower among therapists who had experienced a highly beneficial personal therapy. For example, the correlation between quality of childhood experience and current life satisfaction was highly significant ($r = .25$, $P < .01$) for 149 respondents who did not have a highly beneficial experience in their personal therapy, but was much lower ($r = .07$, $P = $ n.s.) for 750 respondents who had a highly beneficial personal therapy. Similar differentials in correlations between childhood and adult experience were found for reliable measures of "warmth" and "openness" in personal self-image, and for "healing involvement" and "constructive coping" in therapeutic work experience.

These convergent findings suggest that a successful experience in personal therapy significantly attenuates the impact of remembered childhood experience on critical areas of adult functioning. It suggests that successful personal therapy helps therapists (and, presumably, other patients) to make peace with the past, and to experience adult life and work in terms of their current circumstances, relatively unburdened by the impact of childhood events.

Negative Effects

At the same time, as with all psychotherapy, a minority of mental health professionals did report null or even negative outcomes of their personal treatment. The precise percentages differ with the study sample and the response format. Nonetheless, the percentages in table 17.1 suggest that null or even harmful outcomes hover between 1% and 10%. Similarly, the percentages of unsatisfactory or nonbeneficial outcomes shown in table 17.2 range from 0% to 8%, although the figure exceeded 3% in just one country, and the overall mean for the sample was only 1%. These results compare favorably to the estimate of 9% to 11% negative outcomes made by Lambert, Shapiro, and Bergin (1986) for therapy studies in general.

Apart from global outcomes, a separate question is frequently posed in studies of this genre: Was your therapy/analysis harmful in any way? In four studies, this specific question elicits affirmative responses from 8% (Norcross et al., 1988) to 11% (Grunebaum, 1986), 21% (Buckley et al., 1981), and 22% (Pope & Tabachnick, 1994) of the samples. The level of self-rated harm in these studies was, for the most part, in the moderate range. In Pope and Tabachnick's (1994) study, for example, only 2% of the psychologists reported that their personal therapy experiences were very harmful.

We located five published attempts to identify covariates of harmful personal therapies. Buckley et al. (1981) found that "dreaming about the therapist" and "feeling that the therapist was the most important person in my life" were significantly correlated to ratings of harm, leading the authors to speculate that unresolved conflictual transference feelings play an important role in harmful therapy experiences. On the other hand, experiences of mutual liking and being understood by one's therapist correlated with most of the positive outcome factors.

Norcross et al. (1988) statistically evaluated the incidence of harm across characteristics of therapist-patients, their therapists, and treatment setting in a large study of psychologists, psychiatrists, and social workers in the United States. Psychologists were more likely to report negative effects of personal therapy than social workers (12% v. 4%; 7% for psychiatrists). Therapist-patients who reported negative outcomes were more likely to have had younger (and presumably less experienced) therapists, therapists whose profession was described as that of counselor, and therapists with an eclectic, systemic, or behavioral orientation. Finally, therapists who had been treated in a college/student health center (presumably when they were students, in settings where the therapists are often trainees) were more likely than others to report a negative outcome.

Norcross, Dryden, and DeMichele (1992), in a study of British psychologists, also found that therapist-patients of younger therapists reported significantly poorer outcomes; that behavior therapists perceived a disproportionate frequency of ineffective treatment; and that outcome was significantly related to therapist's profession—but in that sample, psychotherapy rendered by counselors was rated as *more* effective than that conducted by members of other professions.

Grunebaum (1986) summarized interviews with 47 therapist-patients who responded to advertisements in professional newsletters seeking persons who had experienced a "harmful" psychotherapy. Harmful therapy experiences clustered under five themes: distant and rigid therapists; emotionally seductive therapists; poor patient-therapist match; explicitly sexual therapies; and multiple involvements with the therapists.

Pope and Tabachnick (1994) asked their respondents (American psychologists) what caused the most harm in their personal therapy. Among the 25 categories into which response were sorted, the most frequent were a therapist's sexual or attempted sexual acts, incompetence, sadistic or emotionally abusive behavior, general failure to understand the patient, and nonsexual dual relationships and boundary violations. Subsequent statistical analyses revealed that ratings of harm were associated with therapist unkindness or error, therapist's manifestation of sexual interest, and patient-respondents' sexual attraction to the therapist.

In sum, a very large number of therapists in the United States and in more than a dozen other countries, surveyed in a number of independent studies, consistently reported experiencing high levels of personal benefit as patients in therapy. Reports of negative outcomes were relatively infrequent, and the factors associated with those reports are basically similar to the deficiencies and abuses that are generally found to cause patients harm.

PROFESSIONAL IMPACTS

Beyond the question of personal outcome, the therapist's own therapy often is also viewed as a desirable or even necessary prerequisite for clinical work. For instance, in "Analysis Terminable and Interminable," Freud (1937/1964, p. 246) asked about the person who wished to become an analyst: "where and how is the poor wretch to acquire the ideal qualifications which he will need in this profession? The answer is in an analysis of himself, with which his preparation for his future activity begins."

Of course, the relative importance attached to personal therapy varies with one's theoretical orientation (Garfield & Kurtz, 1976; Greenberg & Staller, 1981; Guy & Liaboe, 1986; Norcross et al., 1992; Wiseman & Shefler, 2001). At one end of the spectrum are those who claim that personal treatment is needed only when a clinician's dysfunction significantly impairs clinical services (see Kelly et al., 1978). At the other extreme are those like Fromm-Reichmann (1959, p. 42), who wrote that "any attempt at intensive psychotherapy is fraught with danger, hence unacceptable" when not preceded by personal analysis. In what follows, we examine evidence relating to the impact of personal therapy on the professional development and clinical effectiveness of psychotherapists.

Professional Development

In the foregoing quotation, Freud (1937/1964) advanced the view that personal therapy, experienced as a training analysis, is fundamental for the development of a trainee's therapeutic skill and capacity. The founder of modern psychotherapies also advised analysts to undertake additional personal therapy every five years or so, indicating his belief that personal therapy remains an essential resource for effective clinical practice and continuing professional development.

Although many therapists, including many psychoanalysts, no longer treat patients exactly in the way Freud prescribed, his wisdom on matters of therapeutic training and development has become an accepted part of conventional practice. For example, in their classic study of psychotherapists in America, Henry et al. (1971, p. 150) noted:

> Since competency in a highly specialized form of social interaction
> is required of all mental health professionals, it is not surprising
> that the types of [professional] socialization experiences most
> frequently mentioned as important are supervision, work experi-
> ences, contact with patients, field work, and personal psycho-
> therapy. Each of these aspects accounts for about 10 percent or

more of the first choices of the practitioners. Most of their respondents strongly valued experiential over didactic learning, and gave a relatively low rating to the influence of faculty members and course work on becoming a psychotherapist.

Similar results were reported in a recent study of 4,000 therapists from a number of countries (Orlinsky, Botermans, & Rønnestad, 2001). Personal therapy was consistently found to rank among the top three sources of positive influence on development, following direct experience with patients and formal case supervision. It was ranked clearly ahead of didactic experiences such as taking courses or seminars and reading professional journals (except by cognitive-behavioral therapists). For the most senior therapists, who had been in practice for from 25 to 50 years, personal therapy became the second most highly rated influence on development.

Overall, more than three-quarters of the therapists in the study reported that their personal therapy had a strongly positive influence on their own development as therapists, while fewer than 2% reported it having *any* negative impact (see table 17.4). A further analysis of these data by nation shows that at least three-quarters of the therapists in 12 of the 14 countries rated personal therapy as a strong positive influence on their development, and in the other two countries the figures were 71% (South Korea) and 65% (Norway). A small but notable proportion (5%) in a small sample of Russian therapists reported that personal therapy had some negative influence on their development, as did other smaller percentages in Belgium (2.8%), South Korea (2.4%), New Zealand (2%), and Norway (2%). These represent relatively few

Table 17.4 Influence of Personal Therapy on Overall Development as Therapist

Sample	N	Strong Positive Influence	Any Negative Influence
United States	745	76.9%	1.2%
Germany	841	75.4	1.5
Switzerland	248	82.7	1.2
Norway	604	64.9	2.0
Denmark	141	82.9	0.7
Sweden	105	92.4	1.0
Portugal	122	86.1	0.8
Spain	141	90.7	1.5
Belgium	109	86.3	2.8
France	89	91.0	1.1
South Korea	122	71.3	2.4
New Zealand	197	77.7	2.0
Israel	94	84.0	1.1
Russia	79	74.7	5.1
Total	3,868	77.6%	1.6%

Note. "Strong Positive Influence" = rating of 2 or 3 on a 0–3 scale of influence (0 = None, 3 = Very positive). "Any Negative Influence" = rating ≥ 1 on a 0–3 scale of influence (0 = None, 3 = Very negative). Percentages based on those who had experienced personal therapy.

individuals, and in most cases the negative impact was not strong—but, as with personal outcomes, the potential for negative effects of personal therapy cannot be ignored.

On the basis of reports of large numbers of therapists in many countries, it seems fair to conclude, as did Henry, Sims, and Spray (1973, p. 14), that "the accumulated evidence strongly suggests that individual psychotherapy not only serves as the focal point for professional training programs but also functions as the symbolic core of professional identity in the mental health field."

LASTING LESSONS

What specific lessons do therapists draw from their personal therapy? In two studies, Norcross and his colleagues asked psychotherapists in America and Great Britain to reflect on their personal treatment and to list any "lasting lessons" they acquired concerning the practice of psychotherapy (Norcross et al., 1988; Norcross et al., 1992). A multitude of diverse responses were content coded and are summarized in table 17.5 for both the American and British therapists. The most common responses all concerned the interpersonal relationships and dynamics of psychotherapy. These included: the centrality of warmth, empathy, and the personal relationship; the importance of transference and countertransference; the inevitable human-ness of the therapist; the need for more patience and tolerance in psychotherapy. Many British psychologists and American psychologists, psychiatrists, and social workers remarked that they personally discovered that psychotherapy could be effective and that change is possible, albeit gradual.

In another large survey, Pope and Tabachnick (1994) asked American psychologists to reflect on the most beneficial aspects of their personal therapy. The most commonly mentioned categories of benefit were enhanced self-awareness and self-understanding, followed by better self-esteem and improved skills as a therapist. Other benefits receiving frequent

Table 17.5 Lasting Lessons of Personal Therapy

Lesson	UK %	USA %
Centrality of the personal relationship, warmth, and empathy	16	12
Know what it feels like to be a patient	8	2
Importance of transference/countertransference	6	8
Need for personal treatment among therapists	6	4
Therapist's use of self is essential	5	4
Psychotherapy is effective	5	3
Change is gradual and painful, albeit possible	3	3
Need for more patience and tolerance	4	7
Therapist must be competent, reliable, committed	3	1
Importance of unconscious motivations and material	3	4

Note. Adapted from Norcross, Dryden, & DeMichele (1982) and Norcross, Strausser-Kirtland, and Missar (1988).

mention were better relationship with family of origin, support provided by the therapy, openness and acceptance of feelings, general improvement in relationships, decrease in depression, decrease in anxiety, personal growth, and improved sense of control.

Mackey and Mackey (1993) interviewed 30 social workers, half in training and half in practice, about the meaning personal therapy had for their professional roles. None of the interviewees had entered therapy to learn how to do clinical work. Coding of the interview transcripts produced three recurrent themes. The first theme, *therapist as model*, pertained to identification with the practice and person of the therapist. The second theme, *understanding therapeutic process*, spoke to how personal therapy enabled respondents to comprehend and master elements of clinical practice, with frequent references to the therapeutic relationship. The third theme, *integration*, included responses that addressed the interdependence of personal and professional life.

In intensive interviews with seven practicing therapists, Macran, Stiles, and Smith (1999) asked how their personal therapy affected their clinical work. Through systematic qualitative analysis of the interview transcripts, the authors identified three recurrent themes: orienting to the *therapist role* (e.g., humanity, power, boundaries), orienting to the *client* (trust, respect, patience), and orienting to the *relationship* (e.g., "listening with the third ear"). These clinicians felt they translated their experiences as clients into skills and attitudes that they used in their practice. Much the same themes were found by Wiseman and Shefler (2001) in their qualitative analyses of in-depth interviews with five experienced psychoanalytically oriented therapists in Israel.

These collective lessons, gleaned from intensive interviews and large surveys alike, are consistent with the results of the published process research and correlational studies on the psychotherapists' personal treatment, reviewed earlier in this chapter. It seems virtually impossible to have undergone personal therapy oneself without emerging with heightened appreciation of the interpersonal relationship and the vulnerability felt by patients.

Effect on Subsequent Performance

In addition to positive testimonials, however, a question that has been raised in several studies is whether therapists who have undergone personal therapy are more effective than colleagues who have not, as measured by their patients' outcomes. For example, Greenberg and Staller (1981) reviewed eight studies addressing this question and reported that two studies hint at a positive effect of personal therapy on clinical effectiveness, two studies show a negative effect, and four found no effect.

Clark (1986) reviewed eight overlapping (but not identical) studies and found only one study (Holt & Luborsky, 1958) with a trend supporting the hypothesis that personal therapy would improve the therapist's performance.

Five studies showed no relationship; and one study (Garfield & Bergin, 1971) tentatively concluded that therapy during formal training may even be detrimental to client outcome.

Macaskill (1988) also considered these studies, as did Macran and Shapiro (1998), who reviewed one additional recent study as well. All the reviewers concluded that there is no evidence that having personal therapy is positively or negatively related to client outcome. In other words, the research evidence is inconclusive. Macran and Shapiro (1998, p. 13) say that "whilst the majority of therapists feel that they have benefited professionally from personal therapy, there is very little empirical evidence that it has any measurable effect on client outcome."

More supportive evidence has been found when the effects of personal therapy on therapists' in-session behavior were examined. Macran and Shapiro (1998) reviewed a dozen studies on the general population of therapists, as well as studies on behavior therapists and psychoanalysts, and found the experience of personal therapy positively associated with observers' ratings and clinician's self-reports of their ability of display warmth, empathy, genuineness, awareness of countertransference, and increased emphasis on the therapeutic relationship. Greenberg and Staller (1981, p. 1470) similarly concluded that "personal therapy when combined with experience has been found to have some positive effects on the therapy relationship"— specifically, that a clinician's empathic ability may be facilitated and the occurrence of disliking a patient may be made less likely.

One criticism of this research is that studies often focused on whether therapists had personal therapy rather than on whether they felt they had benefited substantially from it. However, even if this more specific criterion had been used, there are grounds for questioning whether the results of a therapist's personal therapy can be judged from the impact that it has on the therapist's own patients. The cumulative and extensive evidence of half a century of scientific research on psychotherapy strongly suggests that the most important determinants of therapeutic success are the positive qualities or resources that patients bring to therapy and are able to mobilize and apply effectively in the therapeutic process (e.g., Lambert, 1992; Orlinsky et al., 2004). Therapists contribute to this process by providing a relationship in which patients feel an optimal balance of challenge and support, and by offering experiences through which patients can mobilize, develop, and apply the interpersonal, self-management, and problem-solving skills that will be most helpful in their lives. If the therapist cannot create a relationship that the patient feels is adequately supportive and stimulating, and cannot provide experiences from which the patient learns new skills, then the patient will be no better off than when he or she started therapy. Yet the therapist cannot create resources for the patient that the patient does not already have or have the capacity to develop.

Suppose, for the sake of argument, that 50% of the success of therapy is due to qualities and resources of the patient, that 35% is due to the relationship that develops interactively between patient and therapist, and that

15% is due to the therapist's individual qualities and resources. In this context, how much influence on client outcome can be due to the therapist's personal therapy? Successful personal therapy is just one of the therapist's resources, along with a basic therapeutic talent (Orlinsky et al., 1998), professional training, and skills honed through accumulated clinical experience (Orlinsky et al., 2001). As such, the therapist's personal therapy constitutes a relatively small part of a therapist's potential contribution to his or her patients' outcomes. Given the large amount of variance due to the patient's resources (which in studies would be virtually impossible to control) and the variability due to the vicissitudes of the developing therapeutic relationship, it is hard to imagine how a study could reliably detect the impact of the therapist's personal therapy on patients' outcomes.

Conceptually, we would propose that personal therapy contributes to the therapist's clinical work in three ways that may indirectly or occasionally influence a patient's outcome. First, viewed as a part of the therapist's training, personal therapy provides the therapist-patient with a model of therapeutic practice in which the therapist-patient observes the work of a more experienced therapist (Orlinsky & Rønnestad, 2002) and learns what is helpful or hindering from that (e.g., Norcross & Guy, chapter 13).

Second, a personally beneficial experience in personal therapy should further develop therapists' interpersonal skills so that they become more sensitive, more skillful, and more flexible in adjusting the impact of their behavior to the individual and evolving needs of their patients. In this regard, successful personal therapy should reduce the degree of pathogenic influence that a therapist, under stress, might inadvertently intrude into relationships with patients (e.g., Henry, Schacht, & Strupp, 1990) and generally should help therapists shield their patients from being influenced by the therapists' own unresolved personal issues.

Finally, successful personal therapy may well contribute to the therapists' ability to repair the ongoing stresses associated with therapeutic work (e.g., Guy, 1987) and to renew the energy they invest, session after session, in working with patients (Orlinsky et al., 1999). The first of these modes of potential influence of personal therapy on the therapist's clinical work focuses primarily on the therapist's individual skills; the second and third focus primarily on the therapist's contribution to engaging patients in an appropriately stimulating and supportive treatment relationship.

CONCLUDING OBSERVATIONS

The research findings reviewed in this chapter give ample evidence of the personal benefits and positive professional impact that psychotherapists derive from their personal therapy. For example, in the extensive international survey of therapists conducted by the Collaborative Research Network (Orlinsky & Rønnestad, in press), fully 85% of all who had undergone therapy reported having at least one experience of great or very great benefit to themselves personally, and more than 75% reported that having therapy had been a strong positive influence on their own development as psycho-therapists. Except for the indeterminate results of studies attempting to detect an effect of therapists' personal therapy on patient treatment out-comes, the accumulated evidence clearly supports the value of personal therapy.

Of course, many of the findings we have reviewed are based on thera-pists' own reports. Notwithstanding the fact that therapists are probably the most discriminating consumers of psychotherapy, better able than other patients to judge what is helpful to them, one might well wish to have evi-dence on the impact and outcomes of personal therapy based on other observational perspectives. For example, one could seek pre- and posttreat-ment assessments by other clinical experts (e.g., the therapist's therapist or independent raters) and by psychometric tests, as in any clinical outcome study. Yet any conclusions of such studies with respect to the outcomes and impacts of personal therapy assessed by therapist-patients would have to be drawn with caution, since there is strong evidence from outcome research indicating that judgments of therapeutic results from different observational perspectives are not necessarily very highly convergent (e.g., Orlinsky et al., 2004; Strupp & Hadley, 1977). There is a face validity to client assessments of therapy that cannot be easily denied even if they do not coincide with the judgments of others, especially when precautions are taken to minimize biases (e.g., anonymity for respondents) and when the findings are consis-tent across independent studies involving large numbers of therapists of different professional backgrounds, theoretical orientations, career levels, and nationalities.

Are the self-reported impacts on professional development of personal therapy sufficient to justify the widespread practice among therapists of undertaking extensive therapy for themselves? In our judgment, probably so. Norcross, Strausser-Kirtland, and Missar (1988, pp. 36–37), review-ing a number of earlier sources (e.g., Fleischer & Wissler, 1985; Fromm-Reichmann, 1959; Garfield & Kurtz, 1976; Nierenberg, 1972; Shapiro, 1976; Wampler & Strupp, 1976) formulated the reasons for this practice in the following way.

1. Personal treatment improves the emotional and mental func-tioning of the psychotherapist: it makes the clinician's life less neurotic and more gratifying in a profession where one's personal health is an indispensable foundation.

2. Personal treatment provides the therapist-patient with a more complete understanding of personal dynamics, interpersonal elicitations, and conflictual issues: the therapist will thereby conduct treatment with clearer perception, less contaminated reactions, and reduced countertransference potential.

3. Personal treatment alleviates the emotional stresses and burdens inherent in this "impossible profession": it enables practitioners

to deal more successfully with the special problems imposed by our craft.

4. Personal treatment serves as a profound socialization experience: it establishes a sense of conviction about the validity of psychotherapy, demonstrates its transformational power in their own lives, and facilitates the internalization of the healer role.

5. Personal treatment places therapists in the role of the client: it thus sensitizes them to the interpersonal reactions and needs of their clients and increases respect for their patients' struggles.

6. Personal treatment provides a firsthand, intensive opportunity to observe clinical methods: the therapist's therapist models interpersonal and technical skills.

However, we would also ask whether the foregoing reasons should be the only justification for therapists to have their own personal therapy. The answer, in our judgment, is probably not—if the matter is viewed in a broader context. The psychotherapist is first and foremost a person who, like all others, continually engages in constructing and maintaining a meaningful personal life, a process that occurs for the most part through interacting with significant others. Our common human condition dictates that the personal lives we construct are periodically threatened by crises (some of our own making), are susceptible to falling apart (at times due to our frailties), and when that happens need to be repaired (most readily with the help of others). A proper appreciation of the psychotherapist's professional role and functioning requires that they be viewed in this context. However thoroughly ingrained it may become, the role-identity of psychotherapist is just one aspect of the therapist's total self; one, moreover, that is acquired in adulthood and thus is necessarily grounded in a series of prior self-aspects that began in childhood. To the traditional proposition that "all men are mortal" may be added the modern insight that "no adult emerges from childhood without bearing some kind of emotional scar." At the core of the therapist's personality, to some extent still active in current life, is a vulnerable self-aspect that Whitaker and Malone (1954) referred to as the therapist's "patient vector." The therapist doesn't need to be seen as a "wounded healer" in the classical sense (e.g., Guggenbuhl-Craig, 1971). It is enough that therapists, like all other humans, have had to grow to adulthood through an extended period of relative helplessness and dependency. In whatever theoretical language they might formulate this, psychotherapists must understand and manage this patient-self within.

ACKNOWLEDGMENT   The following colleagues collected data in the following countries: United States: D. Orlinsky, J. Norcross, L. Beutler, M. Silverman; T. Northcut, S. Stuart; Germany: U. Willutzki, J. Meyerberg, M. Cierpka, P. Buchheim, H. Ambühl, H. Kächele; Switzerland: H. Ambühl, N. Aapro; Norway: M. H. Rønnestad, A. von der Lippe; Denmark: E. Friis-Jorgensen; Sweden:

D. Stiwne.; Portugal: A. Branco Vasco; Spain: A. Avila Espada, I. Caro; Belgium: J-F. Botermans; France: P. Gerin, A. Dazord; South Korea: S. Bae, E. Joo; New Zealand: N. Kazantzis; Israel: H. Wiseman, G. Shefler; Russia: E. Kalmykova.

REFERENCES

Bridges, N. A. (1995). Psychotherapy with therapists: Countertransference dilemmas. In M. B. Sussman (Ed.), *A perilous calling.* New York: Wiley.

Buckley, P., Karasu, T. B., & Charles, E. (1981). Psychotherapists view their personal therapy. *Psychotherapy, 18,* 299–305.

Burton, A. (1973). The psychotherapist as client. *American Journal of Psychoanalysis, 33,* 94–103.

Clark, M. M. (1986). Personal therapy: A review of empirical research. *Professional Psychology: Research and Practice, 17,* 541–543.

Deutsch, C. J. (1985). A survey of therapists' personal problems and treatment. *Professional Psychology: Research and Practice, 16,* 305–315.

Freud, S. (1937/1964). Analysis terminable and interminable. In J. Strachey (Ed. and Trans.), *The Standard edition of the complete psychological works of Sigmund Freud* (Vol. 23, pp. 216–253). London: Hogarth Press.

Fromm-Reichman, F. (1949). Notes on the personal and professional requirements of a psychotherapist. *Psychiatry, 12,* 361–378.

Garfield, S. L., & Bergin, A. E. (1971). Personal therapy, outcome and some therapist variables. *Psychotherapy, 8,* 251–253.

Garfield, S. L., & Kurtz, R. M. (1976). Personal therapy for the psychotherapist: Some findings and issues. *Psychotherapy, 13,* 188–192.

Gitelson, M. (1954). Therapeutic problems in the analysis of the "normal candidate." *International Journal of Psychoanalysis, 35,* 174–183.

Glass, J. (1986). Personal therapy and the student therapist. *Canadian Journal of Psychiatry, 31,* 304–312.

Glickauf-Huges, C., & Mehlman, E. (1995). Narcissistic issues in therapists: Diagnostic and treatment considerations. *Psychotherapy, 32,* 213–221.

Goldensohn, S. S. (1977). Graduates' evaluation of their psychoanalytic training. *Journal of the American Academy of Psychoanalysis, 5,* 51–64.

Greenberg, R. P., & Staller, J. (1981). Personal therapy for therapists. *American Journal of Psychiatry, 138,* 1467–1471.

Grunebaum, H. (1983). A study of therapists' choice of therapist. *American Journal of Psychiatry, 140,* 1336–1339.

Grunebaum, H. (1986). Harmful psychotherapy experiences. *American Journal of Psychotherapy, 40,* 165–176.

Guggenbuhl-Craig, A. (1971). *Power in the helping professions.* Dallas: Spring.

Guldner, C. A. (1978). Family therapy for the trainee in family therapy. *Journal of Marital and Family Therapy, 4,* 127–132.

Guy, J. D. (1987). *The personal life of the psychotherapist.* New York: Wiley.

Guy, J. D., & Liaboe, G. P. (1986). The impact of conducting personal therapy on therapist's interpersonal functioning. *Professional Psychology: Research and Practice, 17,* 111–114.

Guy, J. D., Stark, M. J., & Poelstra, P. L. (1988). Personal therapy for psychotherapists before and after entering professional practice. *Professional Psychology: Research and Practice, 19,* 474–476.

Henry, W. E., Sims, J. H., & Spray, S. L. (1971). *The fifth profession: Becoming a psychotherapist.* San Francisco: Jossey-Bass.

Henry, W. E., Sims, J. H., & Spray, S. L. (1973). *The public and private lives of psychotherapists.* San Francisco: Jossey-Bass.

Henry, W. P., Schacht, T. E., & Strupp, H. H. (1990). Patient and therapist introject, interpersonal process and differential psychotherapy outcome. *Journal of Consulting and Clinical Psychology, 58,* 768–774.

Holt, R. R., & Luborsky, L. (1958). *Personality patterns of psychiatrists* (Vol. 1). New York: Basic Books.

Lambert, M. J. (1992). Psychotherapy outcome research: Implications for integrative and eclectic practice. In J. C. Norcross & M. R. Goldfried (Eds.), *Handbook of psychotherapy integration* (pp. 94–129). New York: Basic Books.

Lambert, M. J., Shapiro, D. A., & Bergin, A. E. (1986). The effectiveness of psychotherapy. In S. L. Garfield & A. E. Bergin (Eds.), *Handbook of psychotherapy and behavior change* (3rd ed., pp. 157–211). New York: Wiley.

Liaboe, G. P., Guy, J. D., Wong, T., & Deahnert, J. R. (1989). The use of personal therapy by psychotherapists. *Psychotherapy in Private Practice, 7,* 115–134.

Macaskill, N. D. (1988). Personal therapy in the training of the psychotherapist: Is it effective? *British Journal of Psychotherapy, 4,* 219–226.

Macaskill, N., & Macaskill, A. (1992). Psychotherapists-in-training evaluate their personal therapy: Results of a UK survey. *British Journal of Psychotherapy, 9,* 133–138.

Mackey, R. A., & Mackey, E. F. (1993). The value of personal psychotherapy to clinical practice. *Clinical Social Work Journal, 21,* 97–110.

Macran, S., & Shapiro, D. (1998). The role of personal therapy for therapists: A review. *British Journal of Medical Psychology, 71,* 13–25.

Macran, S., Stiles, W. B., & Smith, J. A. (1999). How does personal therapy affect therapists' practice? *Journal of Counseling Psychology, 46,* 419–431.

Norcross, J. C. (1990). Personal therapy for therapists: One solution. *Psychotherapy in Private Practice, 8,* 45–59.

Norcross, J. C., Dryden, W., & DeMichele, J. T. (1992). British clinical psychologists and personal therapy: III. What's good for the goose? *Clinical Psychology Forum, 44,* 29–33.

Norcross, J. C., Strausser-Kirtland, D., & Missar, C. D. (1988). The processes and outcomes of psychotherapists' personal treatment experiences. *Psychotherapy, 25,* 36–43.

Orlinsky, D. E., Ambühl, H., Rønnestad, M. H., Davis, J. D., Gerin, P., Davis, M., et al. (1999). The development of psychotherapists: Concepts, questions, and methods of a collaborative international study. *Psychotherapy Research, 9,* 127–153.

Orlinsky, D. E., Botermans, J-F., & Rønnestad, M. H. (1998, June 27). *Psychotherapeutic talent is the skill that therapists have already when they start training: An empirical analysis.* Paper presented at the twenty-ninth Annual Meeting of the Society for Psychotherapy Research, Snowbird, UT.

Orlinsky, D. E., Botermans, J-F., & Rønnestad, M. H. (2001). Towards an empirically-grounded model of psychotherapy training: Four thousand therapists rate influences on their development. *Australian Psychologist, 36*(2), 139–148.

Orlinsky, D. E., & Rønnestad, M. H. (2002). *Therapists' therapists: Who they are and how they are distinguished.* Unpublished paper.

Orlinsky, D. E., & Rønnestad, M. H. (in press). *How psychotherapists develop: A study of therapeutic work and professional growth.* Washington, DC: American Psychological Association.

Orlinsky, D. E., Rønnestad, M. H., & Willutzki, U. (2004). In M. Lambert (Ed.), *Bergin and Garfield's handbook of psychotherapy and behavior change* (5th ed., pp. 307–389). New York: Wiley.

Orlinsky, D. E., Rønnestad, M. H., Wiseman, H., & Botermans, J-F. (2002). *The psychotherapist's own psychotherapy.* Unpublished manuscript.

Patterson, J. E., & Utesch, W. E. (1991). Personal therapy for family therapy graduate students. *Contemporary Family Therapy, 13,* 333–343.

Pope, K. S., & Tabachnick, B. G. (1994). Therapists as patients: A national survey of psychologists' experiences, problems, and beliefs. *Professional Psychology: Research and Practice, 25,* 247–258.

Seligman, M. E. P. (1995). The effectiveness of psychotherapy. *American Psychologist, 50,* 965–974.

Shapiro, D. (1976). The analyst's own analysis. *Journal of the American Psychoanalytic Association, 25,* 5–42.

Silverstone, S. (1970). On the mystique of training analysis. *Psychoanalytic Review, 57,* 283–284.

Strupp, H. H., & Hadley, S. W. (1977). A tripartite model of mental health and therapeutic outcomes *American Psychologist, 32,* 187–196.

Wampler, L. D., & Strupp, H. H. (1976). Personal therapy for students in clinical psychology: A matter of faith? *Professional Psychology, 7,* 195–201.

Wheeler, S. (1991). Personal therapy: An essential aspect of counselor training, or a distraction from focusing on the client? *International Journal for the Advancement of Counseling, 14,* 193–202.

Whitaker, C. W., & Malone, T. (1954). *The roots of psychotherapy.* New York: Blakiston.

Wiseman, H., & Shefler, G. (2001). Experienced psychoanalytically oriented therapists' narrative accounts of their personal therapy: Impacts on professional and personal development. *Psychotherapy: Theory/Research/Practice/Training, 38*(2), 129–141.

III

BEING A THERAPIST'S THERAPIST

Personal Experiences:
Firsthand Accounts
by Therapists'
Therapists

18

ON ANALYZING COLLEAGUES (TRAINEES INCLUDED)

Emanuel Berman

Of all the psychoanalyses conducted around the world, a considerable part are analyses of mental health professionals, themselves psychotherapists. Our literature has some difficulty in fully acknowledging and studying the impact of this phenomenon (Berman, 1995). Exploration has been limited so far, probably as a result of the view that sharing a profession is a superficial factor, marginal in its impact. This is an aspect of a theoretical tradition, in which "external" reality was viewed as a shallow layer mobilized for rationalization, allowing a defensive avoidance of deeper experiences, deflecting the analytic focus away from psychic reality. The "two realities," outer and inner, were seen as competing for our attention, and one needed to be pushed aside to allow the other space. A vivid example of this view is offered by Hurwitz (1986). When he told his first analyst that the analyst's style may influence his reactions to him, the analyst insisted: "You'd respond the same way no matter who was in this chair." Only his later experience with a second analyst made Hurwitz realize this was not so.

The actual importance of seemingly "external" factors has been gradually gaining recognition in the literature on training analyses. Psychoanalytic thinking in general has attempted to go beyond the dichotomy. Greenson's (1971) introduction of the concept "the real relationship" was a thoughtful attempt to correct the one-sided emphasis on transferential distortion. Yet, while acknowledging that "[a]*ll object relationships consist of different admixtures and blendings of real and transference components*" (p. 89), Greenson hastens to add that these ingredients "can and . . . should be separated from one another." In his examples he appears confident as to which perceptions of his patients are accurate and which are distorted. Such divisions preclude more dialectical conceptions, such as Winnicott's hypothesis that, once the object becomes real, "projective mechanisms assist in the act of *noticing what is there*, but they are not *the reason why the object is there*" (Winnicott, 1971, p. 106).

Gill's (1982) work reintroduces the impact of the analyst's actual personality and behavior as a crucial determinant in shaping the analytic process, now without any attempt to sharply separate it from the influence of the analysand's inner world; transference encompasses all determinants, plausibility replaces accuracy as an issue, the analyst strives for the same open-mindedness and suspension of judgment expected of the analysand. This framework, I believe, can be fruitfully integrated with our current tendency to view countertransference as ubiquitous, and with the exploration of the analyst's subjectivity as another reality influencing the analysand's transference. "Transference is the expression of the patient's relations with the fantasied and real countertransference of the analyst" (Racker, 1968, p. 131).

Viewing the analysand's experience as constantly interweaving past and present, perception and fantasy, attempted objectivity and unavoidable subjectivity, makes the impact of "external" realities—the analyst's character, age, gender, appearance, health, pregnancy, and other life events—quite crucial, although we can no longer attempt to put them "outside the brackets" of the exploration of transference (Simon, 1993). To the contrary, the way such realities are processed and given significance becomes in itself an intriguing issue in analysis. The capacity to explore "external" realities undefensively may be conceived as facilitating a greater acceptance of psychic reality, rather than as competing with, and taking away from, the importance of psychic reality.

In this context, the correlation between the acceptance of "inner" and "outer" reality appears central, both being seen as aspects of a capacity to confront complex—and at times painful—reality in all its levels. The capacity to bridge "external" reality (always colored by inner experiences) and psychic reality (always colored by actual events and persons) rather than experiencing them as competing opposites is a crucial element in the formation of transitional space, that intermediate area of experiencing which—in Winnicott's (1971) view—facilitates flexibility, creativity, playfulness, and change. "Transitional space breaks down when either inner or outer reality begins to dominate the scene, just as conversation stops if one of the participants takes over" (Phillips, 1988, p. 119).

When an analysand clings to concrete external details, in order to avoid threatening affects or fantasies, it is doubtful if his or her understanding of external reality could be profound. And when another analysand floods us with dreams in order to avoid painful issues in his or her family life, or because of "an essential lack of true relation to external reality" (Winnicott, 1958, p. 152), it is doubtful whether these dreams will lead to an in-depth understanding of this person's inner world. "Fantasy is only tolerable at full blast when objective reality is appreciated well" (Winnicott, 1958, p. 153).

The challenge we face, therefore, is not to push aside external reality, but rather to mobilize its understanding into the analytic process. It is not to deny our reality for the analysand—a hypocritical denial (Ferenczi, 1933) that may increase the analysand's defensiveness—but rather to take full responsibility for it. It is to avoid a shallow concrete representation of external reality, in order to reintroduce it into the analytic dialogue at a deeper level, aspiring to make the analysis fuller and more integrative (Berman, 2001).

The lack of fuller exploration of issues involved in analyzing therapists may also be influenced by the problem of confidentiality. Analysands who are colleagues, as well as their friends and acquaintances, come to conferences at which we present, and read journals in which we publish. The risk of exposure is greater.

It is probable that cases of analysand-colleagues are underrepresented in our literature in comparison to their actual higher representation in our practice. Also, their analyses may be presented under thick disguise, including an alteration of their professional identity. Such disguise naturally blocks any discussion of the place of this identity in the analytic process.

Radical disguise, we have come gradually to realize, may confuse and mislead the reader (Klumpner & Frank, 1991). Little (1951), for example, described an analysand's anxiety following a radio talk, shortly after the death of the analysand's mother. Lacan (1988, pp. 30–33), in discussing the case, interprets the radio audience as an anonymous audience, which could include the living and the dead, such as the analysand's mother. But this interpretation loses its ground when we learn (Little, 1990, p. 36) that the audience was anything but anonymous; the "radio" was Little's disguise, in an actually autobiographical episode, for a lecture she delivered to the British Psychoanalytic Society.

I will attempt to explore the impact of the professional affinity of analyst and analysand with all these challenges in mind. This chapter will outline central aspects of the object relations of therapists in treatment; discuss the unique significance such analysis may acquire, including the potential role of the analysand as the analyst's fantasied therapist or supervisor; and review incestuous elements in the situation, its influence on training, and dilemmas regarding its boundaries. Due to my concern for the confidentiality of my analysands, and to my reservations about "thick" disguises, I will limit my clinical examples to brief vignettes. The findings of empirical research—whenever available—will supplement my clinical impressions.

THE THERAPIST IN ANALYSIS: OBJECT RELATIONS

A central factor in the analysis of therapists is the appearance of the same emotional motives at the core of the analysand's vocational choice, and in the analytic situation. The same aspects of object relations appear, and a world of mirrorings, identifications, and comparisons is established. The dilemma of being a helper or needing help, of being therapist or patient, is omnipresent. Treating and being in treatment, giving and receiving, may be unconsciously equated.

In some cases neediness and the wish to be helped can only be experienced when projected out, onto a weak and needy "other," while the therapist clings to a sense of strength and mastery. This may be seen most clearly when a therapist enters a first analysis, or a first serious therapy, after several years of treating others. Such an analysis may prove to be very painful, because its success depends on "the return of the projected," on re-owning denied dependency needs, on shaking an overconfident self image.

A transparent example: My analysand comes late to his hour, explaining that he extended the session of his own patient, who "needs it much more badly." In extreme cases, the narcissistic blow of acknowledging the need for help may lead to a negative therapeutic reaction.

Another pattern is present when an analysand chooses to be trained as a psychotherapist as a response to a successful analysis. In principle, this could be a more promising sequence, although several questions have to be asked: Was the identification with the analyst worked through? Are idealization fantasies still active? Can the future therapist develop an autonomous identity, divorced from the wish to "become one's analyst"?

Gabbard (1995) describes therapist-analysands who crave the attention of both their patients (e.g., use transference interpretations excessively) and their analysts, hoping to be adored and idealized as a compensation for childhood lacks. At the other extreme, he suggests, therapists who survived adverse childhood situations by attempting to satisfy the narcissistic needs of others, may repeat this solution both with their patients and their analysts.

Isaacs-Elmhirst (1982–83) gives several examples of similar repeated patterns. In one of them, her analysand reports a dream in which Elmhirst's figure is merged with the figure of one of his patients. The combined figure represents the sick baby, while the dreamer appears as the reliable adult.

The reappearance of the same object relations in the analysand's transference to us and in his or her countertransference to patients is not limited, however, to direct equations. More complex connections may be undestood with the help of Ogden's (1983) conceptualization: the whole bipolar object relationship is internalized, and the subject can alternate in taking on one pole ("self" of childhood) or the other ("object" of childhood), while activating either complementary role in the other by projective identification.

A patient of mine was in treatment twice before, experiencing varying degrees of disappointment, feeling her needs were not sufficiently met. In spite of her intense conscious yearnings, many of our sessions were dominated by her lengthy monologues, which I interpreted as an unconscious blocking of any chance to receive, related to intense fears of rejection. She described great dedication to her patients and endless efforts to meet their needs. She shared with them many details of her personal life, and was disappointed I avoided such sharing. I felt she envied her patients for the warmth they received from her, which she kept seeking from her therapists, never feeling gratified.

This pattern has reminded me of some aspects of the Freud-Ferenczi relationship. Ferenczi attempted (through the "relaxation technique" and mutual analysis) to offer his patients the warmth and openness he felt lacking in Freud (Balint, 1969; Berman, 1996, 1999; Ferenczi, 1988; Haynal, 1988). Ferenczi (1933) criticized earlier stages of his own work (the "active technique" emphasizing authority and abstinence) as relying on identification with the aggressor, possibly also his own identification with Freud as an aggressor. Such trends also appear in analysand-therapists. The analysand may apply analytic anonymity and nondirectiveness in professional tasks in which they are ineffective—for example, supervising students, or dealing with a crisis on a psychiatric ward. Isaacs-Elmhirst (1982–83) gives another example: she is late to an analytic session, and subsequently her analysand is late to a session with his patient.

Some analysands avoid talking in analysis about their patients, out of anxiety regarding competition or judgment. Others may unconsciously express their own conflicts through describing patients. Unlike Gabbard (1995), I do not conceptualize this as resistance but rather as a valuable cautious communication. The conscious rationale may be an appeal for supervision. If the analyst mostly responds as a supervisor (focusing on the specifics of the treatment described) this may come at the expense of pursuing the fuller analytic goal, which requires relating such contents to the analysand's own inner life and transference. Yet the use by the analysand-therapist of the analyst's approach may in any case have intrinsic supervisory value, just as one may "borrow" supervisory experiences for inner goals that are substantially therapeutic. (For a detailed example, see Berman, 2000a, pp. 283–284).

The connection may at times be conscious, as in the following example. My analysand reports a dream, in which a patient he once interviewed, and did not accept for treatment because of her unbearable rage and bitterness, reappears in his clinic. I comment that in the dream the patient did come back. My analysand interrupts me: "Don't you encourage these feelings to come back here!"

Comparisons consciously made by analysands between the analytic process they go through and the treatment processes of their patients may have both an inhibiting and a facilitating influence: "When I heard you got married I felt hurt you didn't tell me. Then I realized I didn't tell my patients when I got married, so how can I complain?" Here, identification with me as a colleague blocks dependency needs and transferential fantasies approaching consciousness.

In another example, a comparison gradually leads toward greater insight and flexibility: "I am frustrated when you say nothing. My supervisor told me I must say something to my patient in every session. On the other hand, I realize how ambivalent this is. I recall my borderline patient, who always demands to know what exactly I think of her, but I actually know she only wants to hear good things."

At other moments, the analysand may turn to his or her self-image as a therapist as a rescue from the vulnerability of being a patient. For example, I comment on my analysand's tendency to put down my interpretations. He says this is related to his need for mastery. His next associations are his need for mastery as a therapist, and his work with a supervisee on the supervisee's need for control. I realize that the fast movement of identities—analysand, therapist, supervisor—indeed allowed him to regain mastery.

The fluidity of identities moves in the opposite direction in the following situation described by an analysand: "In the middle of a therapy session my patient told me her best friend is in therapy with you. I got all confused. In a split second I turned from therapist to patient."

DISCOVERY OF A NEW WORLD, OR AN INITIATION RITE?

For analysands who are not mental health professionals analysis may be a unique, unprecedented experience, completely different from their familiar world. They learn a new language, adopt a new outlook on life. This may be difficult but also exciting. The analyst may be the only actual representative (besides remote figures like Freud, or literary and cinematic analysts) of this new world.

In contrast, analysand-colleagues may experience analysis as a fateful initiation rite into a world they chose, a world now experienced as part of their personality. Studies, work, analysis, at times social life, are all part of the same integral whole. The same discourse dominates different segments of this universe. The analyst may be a model for internalization (or imitation?) in one's professional-personal identity. In our field, nothing can be purely professional. Still, the analyst is only one of many well-known representatives of the same world.

This situation invites comparisons and splits (Heimann, 1954). Transference may be split between the analyst and a significant supervisor: "When I feel depressed I'd rather meet my supervisor; it's easier for me to lean emotionally on a woman." There may be fantasies of being in analysis with a teacher or a supervisor, who may be the analyst of the analysand's friend (Berman, 1985). Yearnings unfulfilled with one's analyst may be achieved in displaced side transferences. For example, an analysand made great efforts to mobilize me into a "male alliance" against his mother and wife. While attempting to interpret this wish, I came to realize it was already gratified with a (male) supervisor to whom my analysand presented a highly resistant female patient who annoyed them both (Berman, 1988).

While our initial response may be to treat such splits as resistance, we may eventually utilize them to understand transference more fully, including its split-off extra-analytic branches. An attempt to base all our analytic work on the analysand's direct responses to us may be too narrow and misleading (Berman, 2001).

The attitude toward analysis and work as a fateful "package deal" becomes evident at moments of crisis. If analysis is experienced as stuck, this leads to doubts about one's vocational choice: "If I can't be helped, how can I help others?" The colleague-analysand does not have the option, available to other analysands, to retreat from the "new world" to the safer and more familiar "old world." Blaming the analyst is also harder, because putting one's analyst down necessitates putting down many colleagues who think of him or her highly. This may arouse a fantasy of being the child in "The Emperor's New Clothes"—a lonely, frightening position.

Another solution is masochistic-self devaluation. A colleague-analysand remarks: "If I don't progress in analysis, it proves my choice to become a dynamic psychotherapist was wrong. If my patients say I help them, and my colleagues respect me, this means I manage to fool them all. I am really an impostor."

Such expressions may be seen as a request for confirmation from the analyst, but they may convey a deeper and more painful experience. Professional knowledge may be mobilized for harsh self-diagnosis: "If you say I have a difficulty in trusting anybody, this means I am paranoid." Here the diagnosis is angrily projected onto me. (Gabbard [1995] speaks of therapists' fear of having a psychotic core.) In another case, without projection: "I identify in myself all the signs Kernberg lists for borderlines." The connotation is analysis can't help with such severe pathology.

In this case, a perfectionistic ego ideal was evident. Its contents were new (integration, insight, contact with affects, avoidance of splitting), but the perfection demanded, and the constant self-devaluation about failing to reach it, resembled the parents' attitudes around other ideals in the analysand's childhood (responsibility, honesty, conscientiousness, morality). In the inner world of this analysand there were two cores of superego demands, "professional superego" and "familial superego," with contrasts that made being "a servant of two masters" into a hopeless task. Expressing certain associations disappointed family values of avoiding gossip and slander, while withholding them meant failing professional ideals of openness and nondefensiveness.

Just as an experience of failure in analysis may lead to thoughts of abandoning the profession, so can professional failures arouse an impulse of quitting analysis. Failing a certification exam, being dismissed from a job, paucity of referrals, rejection by an institute—all may arouse a fantasy of "slamming the door." The analyst may be unconsciously seen as responsible for one's career. There may be several versions: anger at the analyst who doesn't help enough; concern that the analyst justifies what happened, maybe even influenced it ("I know your institute is nonreporting, but maybe your disappointment with me leaked to some members of the admissions committee?"); fear that the analyst is disappointed now, may be ashamed of the analysand, or concerned about being seen as responsible by colleagues; and apprehension that the analyst will now invest more in "successful children" who will glorify her or his name with their achievements.

Switching now to the countertransference side, I must say such fears may not be unfounded. The analysis of colleagues is conducted "in a fishbowl" (Gitelson, 1954). "Indirect countertransference," related to the imagined look of others (Racker, 1968), may be powerful. At times the analysand stimulates our anxieties directly, by mentioning hostile reports about our work to esteemed colleagues. But even without provocations, we may be disturbed by thoughts like "How does he talk about me with X or Y?" When one of our analysands is not admitted to our institute, we may wonder if this conveys a negative evaluation of our work. The tendency to blame therapists for their patients' problems is beautifully portrayed by Ekstein, Wallerstein, and Mandelbaum (1959).

When an analysand who is a colleague decides to terminate analysis one-sidedly, the unavoidable pain of any such rejection may be accompanied by the concern, "How will my colleagues see it?" We may be tempted to violate confidentiality by spreading our own version of what happened.

Treating colleagues unavoidably triggers our judgmental, evaluative look. Our professional concern is activated, and at some moments we cannot avoid the thought "God, and this person is going to treat others!" Gabbard (1995, p. 797) speaks of a fantasy of "policing the profession through analytic surveillance." Such reactions may appear between the lines of our interpretations and confirm the analysand's worst fears. Channeling such important countertransference reactions into effective, empathic work requires of us thorough working-through.

The presence of such judgments on both analyst's and analysand's mind may contribute to the lesser capacity for regression in these analyses (Balint, 1954). Certain forms of transference—psychotic, dependent, impulsive, perverse, seductive, for instance—may be artificially inhibited ("if *this* comes out it will be clear I can't be a therapist"), and covered up with more "acceptable," neurotic-oedipal dynamics.

THE INCESTUOUS DIMENSION

Several of my examples have already exposed the incestuous element in analyzing colleagues. In these analyses it is, as a rule, more intensive and widespread. Analyst and analysand cannot create a closed-off, intimate world that will function freely as a transitional space. Their relationship is part of a complex, three- or four-generational network (Berman, 1985), resembling an extended family or a tribe. In the genealogy, or "family tree," the analyst may be "second generation." The training analysts who analyzed and supervised him or her are "first generation." The analysand is "third generation," and if this analysand already treats students or younger colleagues, they become "fourth generation."

Our analysand may know other patients we see, our supervisees, our colleagues, as well as our past or present analysts or teachers. Analysands may become a student or supervisee of colleagues who play other important roles in our emotional life.

One result is that many figures in the analysand's interpersonal world are directly familiar to us. This makes it more difficult to respond to these figures on the level of internal object relations, to "translate" actual interactions into unconscious meanings. The actual acquaintance arouses concrete visual images and existing affective responses (Jacobs, 1983). We may find ourselves thinking, while listening in the session, "How accurately she describes him" or "How could he miss what's so evident about her?" We may be more sensitive to the pathology leading our analysand to fall in love with someone we despise, and be more tolerant when it's someone we care for.

In a parallel way, when an analysand who is a physicist tells us about a professional argument, it's easier for us to "translate" the contents of the confrontation into their deeper underlying significance. By contrast, an analysand who is a psychologist is debating issues that are close to our heart.

When analysands know we are acquainted with persons in their life, they talk about them cautiously and are often concerned we may identify with such persons more than with the analysand's experience of them. This situation may also threaten these persons, who become concerned about the way they are presented in the analysis. "X must be badmouthing me on your couch," I was told more than once. The analysand may feel a cautious attitude from some people since they found out who his or her analyst is. The experience could be of a loss of spontaneity in significant relations—a heavy price for the analysis.

Another solution the analysand's friends may choose is to ask the analysand to keep certain things secret from us. Such requests create a conflict of loyalties and burden associative freedom. They may be seen as attempts to sabotage analysis. Analysands differ in the degree they allow such requests or honor them. Making such alliances may be a way the analysand finds to avoid full exposure. Similarly, protectively concealing the names of individuals mentioned may convey the analysand's hesitation. How trustworthy is the analyst, how solid are the boundaries, can the analyst respond therapeutically or will she or he be tempted to abuse the analysis for the gratification of personal curiosity? Accepting the mystifying style of "someone said" may indicate not confronting a deep-rooted layer of mistrust.

Needless to say, we do face a realistic risk of being pushed by our curiosity to be excessively intrusive. Maintaining boundaries isn't always easy. When we are hurt by comments quoted on the couch, we may later meet the quoted person, and be unable to clarify things openly. Treating colleagues makes us lonelier and more vulnerable.

Another result of the incestuous situation is that the analysand is flooded with information and impressions about the analyst's personality, life, and functioning in various professional contexts. The degree of flooding depends on the extent of the overlap in the professional circles of analyst and analysand but also on the analysand's needs. These create a continuum. Curiosity and inquisitivenes, at one pole, may reflect a need for control, a fear of being caught by surprise, a struggle against the humiliation of one-sided exposure, at times infatuation or addictive preoccupation. The opposite, defensive pole is dominated by "turning a deaf ear" and a request not to be told things.

In most cases the available information is vast. Extensive exposure has a very different impact than the occasional exposure occurring in any analysis. It may create consistent inhibitions and blocks in associative flow, due to guilt over knowing "forbidden secrets" and over elaborating them in fantasy. These secrets rarely come to the foreground without a clear messege from the analyst encouraging their expression. Let us remember Klauber's (1981, p. 212) rhetorical question: "Is it really sound to act as though the patient had no knowledge of one's private life and family, or even of the severe blows that fate may deal one?" Stories absorbed confirm fears and hopes, inflame envy and anxiety, arouse scorn and admiration, constantly amplifying both conscious and unconscious transferential fantasies.

From stories about the analyst, the analysand crystallizes a picture of the analyst's general (transferential) attitude to the professional community, to colleagues, to students. This picture becomes meaningful for the analysand; no less meaningful than the analyst's direct behavior in their interaction. Following Racker's (1968) view that transference is always reactive to the analyst's countertransference, we may add a hypothesis. The general attitude of the analyst, even though it is not experienced firsthand in the sessions, also arouses transference feelings. These incorporate of course elements from the analysand's unique inner world.

For example, one analysand responded in particular—out of all she heard about me—to my image as independent and defiant of authority. She identified with this trait, and it encouraged the expression of her own rebelliousness, but it also aroused anxiety. Am I, her analyst, in danger? Is she endangering herself by following in my footsteps?

Another analysand responded much more to my active involvement in many professional settings, to my papers and public talks. This contrasted sharply with his passivity, with his fear of humiliating exposure. Early in analysis this contrast made him hopeless: I could never understand him. Later on, his ambition was aroused; a wish to "come out of the shadow" and assert his presence like me became prominent.

A third analysand was particularly sensitive to my tendency to become a mentor of promising beginners. She wished I could play such a role for her but feared this was hopeless, both because of the boundaries of analysis (she felt she got the short end of the stick, my inhibited and formal side) and because I came to see how disturbed she was.

In all these cases, the picture mirrored by the analysands was quite realistic and could by no means be defined as a distortion. Yet the pictures differed, and each was visibly influenced by the analysand's family background, life experiences, and dynamics.

Only when the verbalization of such impressions is seriously encouraged—only when we work on them nondefensively, and overcome the fear of our analysands' penetrating intelligent look—can we reach fully the intrapsychic needs and conflicts involved. Along the way, we may learn important new things about ourselves.

THE ANALYSAND AS THE ANALYST'S THERAPIST AND SUPERVISOR

Searles (1979) suggests that a therapeutic impulse of the patient toward the therapist is universal, as an outgrowth of the child's need to cure the parents of their shortcomings and limitations. He emphasizes that this tendency is not unique to patients who are therapists. I suspect, however, that the deeper roots of the choice to become a therapist guarantee the intensity of this motive in the analysis of therapists. In addition, the fuller knowledge the analysand-colleague may have about the analyst, and the diagnostic sensitivity cultivated by training, allow this analysand to identify even more astutely the analyst's Achilles' heel. We must remember Shapiro's (1976) finding, that most analysts in his study who were unhappy with the outcome of their own analysis attributed the difficulty to personal qualities or conflicts of their analysts.

An analysand I treated when I was still single told me once: "Because you have no children, you turn your students into your children. You must prefer brain children to flesh children."

My immediate experience was of insult and hurt. This was followed by an impulse to interpret her comment as resistance, as an avoidance of her own conflicts. But I soon realized this impulse was vindictive and defensive. I also noticed her tone was pained, not hostile. And, above all, I knew she was on to something, although the calm word "prefer" was far from the actual loaded conflictual emotions the topic carried for me.

Eventually, I interpreted mostly her fear that my own difficulties will prevent me from helping her to resolve her own conflicts around potential parenthood. Without confirming or denying her interpretation, I let her feel that her wish to help me was legitimate, and that I could perceive its empathic element, combined with her hope to make me a better analyst for her own sake.

Searles comments that the difficulty of the parent to treat the child's wish to "cure" him as legitimate and benign stems from hearing the child's voice as a scolding parental voice. The fact that the patient is a therapist increases this danger for the analyst. In the vignette I gave, my initial response to my analysand was as though to a parental figure. Her comment was close to comments my own analyst made around the same period. My aggression resulted from feeling under crossfire of two critical parents. It dissipated when I recognized the very different source of my patient's comment.

Isaacs-Elmhirst (1982–83) offers a Kleinian view of the same fantasy reversal. If in many analyses the analysands are experienced counter-transferentially as the analyst's damaged inner objects, the analysand-colleague may be seen more specifically as a parent who was damaged and became a helpless child. It is striking, however, that her article, which brilliantly interprets fantasies activated by the analysis of colleagues, does not explore the possibility that such analysands may actually recognize the analyst's inner damage.

A parallel issue: we may agree with Langs (1979) and others that every analysand is our supervisor, teaching us more than anyone else about the impact of our interventions. Most analysands do it implicitly. Analysand-colleagues may adopt a supervisory role much more explicitly. Whether they verbalize it or not (of course, things are easier when responses are verbalized), they can evaluate the analyst's interventions in comparison to standards internalized during training, out of identification with teachers, supervisors, and books.

This advantage involves a paradoxical risk. By assuming a supervisory stance, the analysand may become a less effective "supervisor." The competitive, judgmental side of this position (Gabbard [1995] even speaks of contempt and devaluation) reduces its emotional authenticity and pushes the analyst into a defensive corner.

For example, when an analysand tells me spontaneously, "for the past few minutes I feel very remote," I tend to reexamine my last intervention, before this phase. If I notice it was a rather intellectual interpretation, I may offer my analysand the hypothesis that my interpretation may have distanced him, and explore with him his emotional reaction to it.

If, on the other hand, an analysand-therapist tells me, "Your last interpretation was too intellectual, and it distanced me," I am more likely to feel uneasy because of his blaming tone. He may be correct, he actually "saved me work," but his professional formulation conveys that he is isolated now from the feelings of disappointment and loneliness possibly aroused by my heavyhanded intervention. He may have reacted to my distance with a defensive move into the role of a supervisor-critic who needs nothing. The professional identity is here mobilized defensively, and this process itself now requires interpretation. Still, in the long run, these analysands' criticism may become a valuable source of stimulation in improving our analytic skills!

A related issue, which I will only mention briefly, is analyzing therapists with a different theoretical orientation from our own, and dealing with their evaluative comments, which may be based on goals that we do not fully share. I will also just mention the important implications of treating therapists whose vocational background differs from our own. In such situations the tensions between the disciplines unavoidably enter the consulting room. As a psychologist, I may notice a psychiatrist flooding me from the couch with medical terms I do not understand, or a social worker triumphantly reminding me of Casement's similar background. This level too is interweaved, naturally, with personal dynamics.

UNIQUE ISSUES IN TRAINING ANALYSES

Starting with the classical discussions of the 1950s and 1960s (e.g., Balint, 1954; Bernfeld, 1962; Heimann, 1954; Kairys, 1964; McLaughlin, 1967), we came to realize how much the actual institute—its regulations, atmosphere, evaluation methods, reporting policies—is present in the consulting room during the candidate's analysis (see Wallerstein, 1993). An extreme example, reported by Lampl-de-Groot (1954) and others, are the cases (particularly in "reporting" institutes) in which anxiety immobilizes the training analysis, or makes it dishonest, so that only after graduation a second analysis becomes open and fruitful.

The tendency toward "pseudo-normality" among analytic candidates has been described by Sachs (1947) and Gitelson (1954), while Balint (1954, p. 161) speaks of instances of "covert, insincere, even hypocritical collusion." Shapiro adds: "training analyses tend to be pallid in comparison to the emotionally heated transference reactions that often arise in analysis under non-training conditions" (1976, p. 34).

A review of the literature on training analyses reveals that many of the issues are common to training analyses and to other analyses of mental health professionals: the more dramatic difference may be in comparing both groups to the treatment of individuals from outside the therapy field. Calef, in a followup study of his former analysands, concludes that the similarities between psychiatrists who were in analytic training while in analysis and those who were not (some of whom applied later on) "are more striking than the differences" (1982, p. 112).

The major difference, of course, is the impact of institute dynamics. There may be partial analogies to such dynamics outside analytic training as well, when the analyst—for example—is teaching in professional programs attended by the analysand; but most such programs do not arouse the awesome transference elicited by the psychoanalytic institute, and their impact on the analysis usually does not become that intense.

The study of institute dynamics has been pursued now for over half a century. Balint speaks of "submissiveness to dogmatic and authoritarian treatment without much protest" (1948, p. 167). Bernfeld describes how the enforcement of rules and regulations "takes the life out of psychoanalysis" (1962, p. 479). Kernberg suggests that "idealization processes and an ambience of persecution are practically universal in psychoanalytic institutes" (1986, p. 815). In my own work, I attempt to pinpoint several such idealizations, and relate the risks involved to a universal utopian fantasy of "molding a New Person" which in the specific case of analytic training may lead to the formation of a false analytic self (Berman, 2000b).

Where do institute dynamics penetrate the analytic process in the analysis of trainees? A major example is the practice of "reporting," where the candidate's analyst is expected to play a role in decisions about the candidate's progress: admission into training, starting supervised analyses, graduating. The growing criticism of the intrusiveness of this practice (e.g., Kairys, 1964; Kernberg, 1986, p. 817) led to its gradual abandonment by most psychoanalytic institutes. (The London institute remains a notable exception, in spite of internal debates about this policy.) Still, as I mentioned earlier, a reality of nonreporting cannot stop candidates from having anxious fantasies that what they say in analysis may leak out, influencing their evaluation and status informally.

While the dominant tendency in recent years has been "to remove the analysis of our candidates, as far as possible, from any institutional connection" (McLaughlin, 1967, p. 230), some institutes are still active in assigning personal analysts to their trainees. This practice is especially problematic in view of the consistent finding that the analyst-analysand match is crucial in influencing the success of the analysis (Kantrowitz, Katz & Paolitto, 1990; Shapiro, 1976, p. 36).

A major intrusion of the training structure into personal analysis occurs when an individual is admitted into training while already in analysis with an analyst who is not acknowledged as a training analyst by the institute. Some institutes require termination of the ongoing analysis and initiation of a new one with a training analyst, irrespective of the feelings of both trainee and original analyst. Such a policy may indicate that the idealization of training analysts comes at the expense of respect for the integrity, continuity, and natural course of the analytic process (Berman, 2000b, p. 49). The often painful experience may not be easy to work through in the subsequent analysis.

The few empirical followup studies of training analyses raise issues that are universal to the analytic process in general but also highlight some unique characteristics. Shapiro (1976), in his followup of 122 graduates of the Columbia Psychoanalytic Institute, speaks of the significance for the analysand of "finally joining his analyst as colleague, co-worker, or rival" (p. 5); of "halo responses from aspects of the educational and administrative milieu" (p. 13); of the impact of sibling rivalries and competitive pressures (p. 28) as well as of the hierarchical structure (p. 30). He emphasizes the way in which the setting, providing extensive feedback in supervision and in seminars, may also facilitate the development of insight (p. 35).

Schachter (1990, p. 478), in exploring analysts' reserved attitudes toward posttermination contact in comparison to its actual beneficial potential, notes the advantage of analysand-trainees, who often can continue contact with their former analysts without having to ask explicitly for additional help.

Martinez & Hoppe (1991), studying the experience of 214 American analysts, find that further therapy or analysis with one's analyst posttermination is significantly correlated with perceived benefit. Followup contact of a collegial or friendship nature is related to the experience of an ongoing intra-

psychic presence of one's analyst; and such an experience is in turn correlated with perceived benefit. Lack of posttermination contact, on the other
hand, is correlated with a lower experience of benefit.

Craige (2002), who analyzed the questionnaires of 121 respondents,
all American analytic candidates, and also interviewed 20 of them, emphasizes that they did not appear "a different breed from 'ordinary' patients",
and that "all reported having struggled with significant emotional pain."
Her focus on the mourning implicit in terminating analysis, and on different
patterns of handling it, indeed leads mostly to universal analytic issues,
emphasizing the crucial role of the analyst's availability and flexibility in
responding to posttermination crises.

ANALYSANDS AS COLLEAGUES: THE ISSUE
OF BOUNDARIES

At many moments, our analysand—whether undergoing training or not—
turns to us as a colleague, with professional questions, ideas, requests, or
comments. The dilemma—how much to acknowledge our professional
affinity and allow its expression—is not easy. Will answering or responding
concretely enhance or undermine analytic work? Each solution is problematic; each is loaded on a countertransferential level.

If we appear as refusing to accept our equality as adult professionals,
this may be experienced as infantilizing, humiliating. It may serve defensive needs:

> Many of us have particular difficulty with analysands' observations
> and judgments about our functioning as analysts and as members
> of the analytic community. The temptation to enjoy the narcissistic
> rewards inherent in our positions as analysts and educators . . .
> merges with the feelings of a parent who, with diminishing powers
> and shrinking time, is yielding up his or her future in every action
> of analyzing the patients' transference wishes. Is there any analysis
> in which the analyst is not at least partially a Lear awaiting the fate
> of being killed by the children? (Orgel, 1990, pp. 9–10)

On the other hand, a willingness to accept the analysand as a mature
colleague may complicate the effort to explore the immature parts of this
analysand's inner world. Personally, I do not see this risk as severe in some
of the minor daily examples, such as an analysand's question—sometimes
at the door—about the dates of a professional conference, or the reference
for a paper. In these situations we may apply Klauber's comment (1981,
p. 212) about analysts who do not reply to Christmas cards: "Is it really
sound to imagine that more is to be gained by rebuffing the patient in this
way than by reciprocating as a member of society with a common culture
and still analysing the motives when they come up?" Similarly, Etchegoyen
(1991, p. 320) explains his choice to let his analysand know (without
being asked) that a lecture the analyst planned to attend was canceled.

However, we must remember that the issue of boundaries may come up in more massive proportions, and have a much more profound impact on the nature of the analytic relationship. A clear example is situations where analysis and an actual comprehensive professional tie coexist. Is such an omnipotent attempt endangering the effective working-through of both transference and countertransference? Several historical examples of such "simultaneous" endeavors ended with bitter feelings on both sides: Freud and Ferenczi (Berman, 1996, 1999), Klein and Paula Heimann (Grosskurth, 1986), Fairbairn and Guntrip (Guntrip's personal notes convey more disappointment than his published account; Hughes, 1989).

I could imagine an attempt to rationalize such combinations as being based on a unique version of "the working alliance," mobilizing a "conflict-free ego sphere." However, Greenson's (1967) belief that such an alliance need not be interpreted was successfully challenged by Gill (1982). We now realize how a seemingly rational and unconflictual "alliance" may camouflage irrational needs, such as "the envy, competitiveness, and contempt that so often lie buried below" (Gabbard, 1995, p. 797), which actually require intensive interpretive work. When the analyst "strengthens the alliance" by turning the analysand into a student, disciple, co-worker, or political partner (Balint, 1948), this may unwittingly sabotage such interpretive work, and with it the full fruition of the analysis. Moreover, a combined analytic-supervisory-political alliance may lead to an exaggerated identification with *the* analyst-supervisor-mentor as a single parental figure, not allowing the painful but fruitful conflict of competing identifications in molding one's unique and autonomous professional self (Berman, 1999, 2000a).

Another issue in turning analysands into disciples and students (e.g., by inviting them to become supervisees after analysis will be over) is whether we are undermining the separation process and avoiding the need for mourning. Novick (1997) raises this risk as a major issue in the analyses of colleagues, and relates difficulties with termination to the unhappy outcome of some of them, including numerous historical cases. On the other hand, continued collaboration could enhance—as posttermination contact appears to enhance in general—the possibility of working out post-termination crises (Craige, 2002), of maintaining an experience of interest and concern without requiring that help must be explicitly requested (Schachter, 1990), and of strengthening the analyst's enduring intrapsychic presence as a helpful lively introject (Martinez & Hoppe, 1991).

We must take very seriously the risks in both directions. We should beware being seduced by a soothing closeness or a flattering discipleship into neglecting or undermining our analytic goals. Still, we must never forget two facts. In every analysis "the analyst and patient are also two real people, of equal adult status, in a real personal relationship to each other" (A.Freud, 1954, p. 373). In the cases discussed here we are also two real professionals, of potentially equal competence, in a real partnership with each other.

REFERENCES

Balint, M. (1948). On the psychoanalytic training system. *International Journal of Psychoanalysis, 29,* 163–173.

Balint, M. (1954). Analytic training and training analysis. *International Journal of Psychoanalysis, 35,* 157–162.

Balint, M. (1969). *The basic fault.* London: Tavistock.

Berman, E. (1985). Incestuous elements in psychoanalytic training. *International Psychoanalytic Studies Organization Bulletin, 7,* 9–10.

Berman, E. (1988). The joint exploration of the supervisory relationship as an aspect of psychoanalytic supervision. In J. M. Ross and W.A. Myers (Eds.), *New concepts in psychoanalytic psychotherapy.* Washington, DC: American Psychiatric Press.

Berman, E. (1995). On analyzing colleagues. *Contemporary Psychoanalysis, 31,* 521–539.

Berman, E. (1996). The Ferenczi renaissance. *Psychoanalytic Dialogues, 6,* 391–411.

Berman, E. (1999). Sandor Ferenczi today: Reviving the broken dialectic. *American Journal of Psychoanalysis, 59,* 303–313.

Berman, E. (2000a). Psychoanalytic supervision: The intersubjective development. *International Journal of Psychoanalysis, 81,* 273–290.

Berman, E. (2000b). The utopian fantasy of a New Person and the danger of a false analytic self. *Psychoanalytic Psychology, 17,* 38–60.

Berman, E. (2001). Psychoanalysis and life. *Psychoanalytic Quarterly, 70,* 35–65.

Bernfeld, S. (1962). On psychoanalytic training. *Psychoanalytic Quarterly, 31,* 457–482.

Calef, V. (1982). An introspective on training and nontraining analysis. *Annual of Psychoanalysis, 10,* 93–114.

Craige, H. (2002). Mourning analysis: The post-termination phase. *Journal of the American Psychoanalytic Association,* in press.

Ekstein, R., Wallerstein, J., & Mandelbaum, A. (1959). Countertransference in the residential treatment of children. *Psychoanalytic Study of the Child, 14,* 186–218.

Etchegoyen, R. H. (1991). *The fundamentals of psychoanalytic technique.* London: Karnac.

Ferenczi, S. (1933). Confusion of tongues between adults and the child. *International Journal of Psychoanalysis, 30,* 225–230.

Ferenczi, S. (1988). *Clinical diary.* (J. Dupont, Ed.). Cambridge, MA: Harvard University Press.

Freud, A. (1954). The widening scope of indications for psychoanalysis: Discussion. In *The writings of Anna Freud, 4.* New York: International Universities Press.

Gabbard, G. O. (1995). When the patient is a therapist: Special considerations in the psychoanalysis of mental health professionals. *Psychoanalytic Review, 82,* 709–725.

Gill, M. M. (1982). *Analysis of transference.* New York: International Universities Press.

Gitelson, M. (1954). Therapeutic problems in the analysis of the "normal" candidate. *International Journal of Psychoanalysis, 35,* 174–183.

Greenson, R. R. (1967). *The technique and practice of psychoanalysis.* New York: International Universities Press.

252   BEING A THERAPIST'S THERAPIST

Greenson, R. R. (1971). The "real" relationship between the patient and the psychoanalyst. In R. Langs (Ed.), *Classics in psychoanalytic technique*. New York: Aronson.

Grosskurth, P. (1986). *Melanie Klein*. New York: Knopf.

Hamilton, V. (1993). Truth and reality in psychoanalytic discourse. *International Journal of Psychoanalysis, 74*, 63–79.

Haynal, A. (1988). *The technique at issue*. London: Karnac.

Heimann, P. (1954). Problems of the training analysis. *International Journal of Psychoanalysis, 35*, 163–166.

Hughes, J. (1989). *Reshaping the psychoanalytic domain: The work of Melanie Klein, W.R.D. Fairbairn and D. W. Winnicott*. Berkeley: University of California Press.

Hurwitz, M. R. (1986). The analyst, his theory, and the psychoanalytic process. *Psychoanalytic Study of the Child, 41*, 439–466.

Isaacs-Elmhirst, S. (1982–83). Thoughts on countertratnsference (with reference to some aspects of the therapy. of colleagues). *International Journal of Psychoanalytic Psychotherapy, 9*, 419–433.

Jacobs, T. J. (1983). The analyst and the patient's object world: Notes on an aspect of countertransference. *Journal of the American Psychoanalytic Association, 31*, 619–642.

Kairys, D. (1964). The training analysis. *Psychoanalytic Quarterly, 33*, 485–512.

Kantrowitz, J. L., Katz, A. L. & Paolitto, F. (1990). Follow-up of psychoanalysis five to ten years after termination: III. The relation between the resolution of the transference and the patient-analyst match. *Journal of the American Psychoanalytic Association, 38*, 655–678.

Kernberg, O. (1986). Institutional problems of psychoanalytic education. *Journal of the American Psychoanalytic Association, 34*, 799–834.

Klauber, J. (1981). Elements of the psychoanalytic relationship and their therapeutic implications. In G. Kohon (Ed.), *The British school of psychoanalysis: The independent tradition*. London: Free Association Press.

Klumpner, G. H., & Frank, A. (1991). On methods of reporting clinical material. *Journal of the American Psychoanalytic Association, 39*, 537–551.

Lacan, J. (1988). *The seminar—Book I*. New York: Norton.

Lampl-de-Groot, J. (1954). Problems of psychoanalytic training. *International Journal of psychoanalysis, 35*, 184–187.

Langs, R. (1979). *The supervisory process*. New York: Aronson.

Little, M. (1951). Countertrasference and the patient's response to it. *International Journal of psychoanalysis, 32*, 32–40.

Little, M. (1981). *Transference neurosis and transference psychosis*. New York: Aronson.

Martinez, D. & Hoppe, S. K. (1991). The analyst's own analyst: Other aspects of internalization. Presented at the Twenty-Seventh Annual Meeting of the Society for Psychotherapy Research, Snowbird, Utah.

McLaughlin, F. (1967). Addendum to a controversial proposal: Some observations on the training analysis. *Psychoanalytic Quarterly, 36*, 230–247.

Novick, J. (1997). Termination conceivable and inconceivable. *Psychoanalytic Psychology, 14*, 145–162.

Ogden, T. (1983). The concept of internal object relations. *International Journal of psychoanalysis, 64*, 227–241.

Orgel, S. (1990). The future of psychoanalysis. *Psychoanalytic Quarterly, 69*, 1–20.

Phillips, A. (1988). *Winnicott.* London: Fontana.

Racker, H. (1968). *Transference and countertransference.* London: Maresfield.

Sachs, H. (1947). Observations of a training analyst. *Psychoanalytic Quarterly, 16*, 157–168.

Schachter, J. (1990). Post-termination patient-analyst contact. *International Journal of Psychoanalysis, 71*, 475–485.

Searles, H. (1979). The patient as a therapist to his analyst. In *Countertransference and related subjects.* New York: International Universities Press.

Shapiro, D. (1976). The analyst's own analysis. *Journal of the American Psychoanalytic Association, 44*, 491–509.

Simon, B. (1993). In search of psychoanalytic technique: Perspectives from on the couch and from behind the couch. *Journal of the American Psychoanalytic Association, 41*, 1051–1082.

Wallerstein, R. S. (1993). Between chaos and petrification: A summary of the Fifth IPA Conference of Training Analysts. *International Journal of psychoanalysis, 74*, 165–178.

Winnicott, D. W. (1958). *Through pediatrics to psychoanalysis.* New York: Basic Books.

Winnicott, D. W. (1971). *Playing and reality.* Harmondsworth: Penguin.

19

TREATING PSYCHOHERAPISTS WITH COGNITIVE THERAPY

Judith S. Beck & Andrew C. Butler

There is little difference in our cognitive therapy treatment of therapist-patients versus other patients. They have the same range of outpatient psychiatric disorders or psychological problems. They have the same kinds of difficulties at work, at home, and in relationships. They have the same kinds of automatic thoughts in and reactions to current situations. They have the same kinds of dysfunctional beliefs about themselves, their worlds, and other people and display the same kinds of dysfunctional coping strategies. They have the same kinds of strengths and weaknesses. They have the same kinds of goals. Like the others, our therapist-patients have the same kinds of religious, cultural, and racial backgrounds.

Our therapist-patients are male and female, old and young. As mental health professionals—psychiatrists, psychologists, social workers, and counselors—their average income, education, and social status is higher than the average of our other patients. They comprise between 10% and 30% of our current caseloads and have all kinds of therapeutic orientations. They report that they seek treatment with us because of the extensive research (over 350 outcome studies, Butler & Beck, in press) demonstrating the efficacy of cognitive therapy, dissatisfaction with previous therapy, and/or our personal reputations.

Although our therapist-patients have a small number of stressors unique to their profession (Kaslow, 1986; Sussman, 1995), most of our patients have work-related stressors (which are sometimes considerably more intense than those our therapist-patients experience). Regardless of the specific types of stressors patients experience, our cognitive therapy approach is generally the same.

GENERAL PRINCIPLES OF TREATMENT

Cognitive therapy treatment is based on a cognitive formulation of a patient's disorder(s) and on an ever-evolving cognitive conceptualization of that specific patient. The strategies we use in treatment do vary considerably from one disorder to another and from one patient to another but are not specific for therapist-patients. The principles of cognitive therapy, along with disorder-specific strategies, have been written about extensively elsewhere: for depression, see Beck (1995), Beck, Rush, Shaw, and Emery (1979); anxiety disorders, Beck and Emery (1985); substance abuse, Beck, Wright, Newman, and Liese (1993); and personality disorders, Beck and Freeman (1990).

Common to the treatment of nearly all patients is an emphasis on helping them to solve current problems, evaluate and modify their dysfunctional thoughts and beliefs, engage in productive behaviors, acquire needed cognitive and behavioral (including interpersonal) skills, and learn important strategies to minimize relapse (Beck, 1995). When an Axis II disorder is present, we often have to modify our style and use a wider range of strategies and techniques, including psychodynamic-like and experiential ones.

Some therapist-patients who are cognitive therapists (or other patients who have been in cognitive therapy previously) enter therapy with us having already changed their beliefs at an "intellectual" level. These patients are often able to move quickly to working at the "emotional" level in order to change their beliefs "in [their] gut." Another difference in treating mental health professionals is that they often require less psychoeducation. Usually it is not a problem when our therapist-patients come from a different therapeutic orientation, or they would not have self-selected cognitive therapy. At times it is more difficult for them to "buy" the model, so we help them translate their concepts into cognitive terms and vice versa.

Treatment takes place within a solid therapeutic relationship, which is generally as easy or as difficult to establish with therapist-patients as non-therapist-patients. We strive to be empathic, accepting, and caring while being actively engaged and fairly directive with patients so we can help them reduce their acute symptomatology as quickly as possible.

NATURE OF THE THERAPEUTIC RELATIONSHIP

With all patients, difficulties in the development of the therapeutic contract and in the power dynamics of the therapeutic relationship are minimized in cognitive therapy. Our work is highly collaborative. We provide rationales for what we do. We confirm our conceptualizations with patients. We jointly decide such matters as how often to meet, how long therapy should last, how to structure sessions, which problems we should work on in which order, what kind of "homework" is assigned. We teach them the skills they need to be their own cognitive therapists and present ourselves more as "guides," as part of a "team" with patients, rather than as experts (with its implication of superiority).

An important feature of cognitive therapy is eliciting patients' feedback during sessions to ensure that we are on the same "wavelength" and share the same understandings, which helps ensure that therapy makes sense and is useful. When patients start to look distressed in session, we elicit their immediate thoughts and feelings and deal with them on the spot. In addition, we elicit feedback at the end of each session. We check whether patients have perceived us as having misunderstood or having made mistakes, whether we have said anything that troubled them, and whether they feel we should alter therapy in some way in the next session.

A potential problem with therapist-patients (or any high-powered or high-status patient) can arise if we are too deferential and treat them differently from other patients. Similarly, as observed by Bridges (1993), identifying too strongly with the therapist-patient is one of the pitfalls facing the treating therapist. Hence we strive to maintain a consistent approach with all patients. For example, despite their diagnostic and clinical expertise, we still ask therapist-patients to complete our extensive evaluation forms and weekly mood scales. And despite their near-certainty that their thinking is accurate, we still assess the validity of their thoughts with them so we can both see to what degree their perceptions or conclusions are accurate.

DIFFICULTIES IN THE THERAPEUTIC RELATIONSHIP

The integral features of cognitive therapy just described help us to avoid many potential difficulties with therapist-patients and non-therapist-patients alike. Patients who enter therapy with relatively benign views about therapy, the therapist, and the likelihood of being helped are easier to engage in therapy than are those who begin treatment with negative beliefs. Those who have had a history of difficulty in relationships frequently have difficulty with the therapeutic relationship as well. Many of these patients have Axis II disorders or traits, and they bring the same dysfunctional beliefs to the therapeutic relationship that they bring to other relationships.

It is actually quite useful when the same pattern of dysfunctional thoughts and beliefs arises in our relationship with these patients. It affords us the opportunity to refine our conceptualizations and to help them identify, evaluate, and modify their distorted cognitions about *our* relationship. Once they change their distorted ideas about us, about themselves, or about themselves in relation to us, we help them generalize what they have just learned to improve other relationships.

These kinds of distorted perceptions and dysfunctional assumptions can occur with any patient. They may (or may not) take a particular form with therapist-patients. For example, several of our therapist-patients initially believed: "[My therapist] will think I'm a failure if I tell her how poorly I'm doing with my patients." As a result, a few minimized their work difficulties until their trust in us grew. The same difficulty does, of course, arise with other patients who incorrectly mind-read our view of their problems. In our clinical experience, a higher percentage of our therapist-patients come to therapy with the idea "I shouldn't have these problems" or "I should be able to handle my problems without help." Standard cognitive therapy techniques, including psychoeducation, allow them to respond to these thoughts.

Another difficulty arises when patients compare themselves unfavorably to us. The following transcript illustrates how we handled this difficulty with one therapist-patient:

> Therapist (switching topics when she notices the therapist-patient looking downcast): Rachel, how are you feeling right now?
>
> Patient (thinks): Sad. Heavy.
>
> Therapist: What was just going through your mind?
>
> Patient: I was thinking about how I'm just a "neighborhood" therapist. I'm not important like you.
>
> Therapist: Well, I'd disagree with that, but (establishing whether the patient is distressed enough to warrant further discussion on this topic) how sad are you feeling about this?
>
> Patient (sighs): Pretty sad.
>
> Therapist (collecting more information to see if they should continue in this vein): How often do you have thoughts like these, comparing yourself to me?
>
> Patient: I don't know. Pretty often, I guess.
>
> Therapist (assessing how well the patient responds to the thoughts, what degree of objectivity she has): And are you able to respond to the thoughts? What do you say to yourself?
>
> Patient: Nothing. They're true.
>
> Therapist: And what conclusion do you draw about yourself? What would it mean to you if I *were* more important than you?
>
> Patient (sighs): That I'm not good enough . . . Maybe I should stop being a therapist.

We then used standard cognitive therapy techniques to help the patient evaluate her dichotomous idea that if she isn't as "successful" or "important" as someone else it means she is "not good enough." Other patients also compare themselves (unfavorably) to us in terms of financial, social, or professional success, marital (and family) status, and so on, and believe they are, therefore, inferior.

Early in therapy some patients use compensatory strategies when they feel inferior. One therapist-patient, for example, asked us research and theoretical questions he thought we would not know to diminish his feelings of inferiority. Another patient continually tried to catch us making mistakes. A third therapist-patient kept reminding us of all the professional awards and honors that had been bestowed on him. These behaviors provided us with the opportunity to identify and modify their dysfunctional dichotomous beliefs about superiority and inferiority (which caused difficulty in their other relationships as well).

Another problem we have encountered occurs when therapist-patients derive significant benefit from cognitive therapy and blame themselves for not having used this approach with their own patients. Some of our non-therapist-patients are also self-critical for not having sought this kind of treatment earlier, especially when they have suffered significantly or believe others they care about have suffered because of them.

Some patients (therapist-patients or not) have difficulty establishing a sound therapeutic relationship because of control issues. They may believe: "If my therapist is in control, it means I'm weak" or "If I let my therapist control our therapy, I'll get hurt in some way." A subset of this problem occasionally arises with therapist-patients who have prescription privileges and self-medicate. Our suggestion to enter treatment with a psychopharmacologist sometimes provokes fears about confidentiality or being controlled by another person, which we deal with using standard cognitive therapy techniques.

MAKING MISTAKES IN THERAPY

Being human, we invariably make mistakes in treating patients (or they perceive us as making mistakes): misunderstanding what they have said, being too empathic or not empathic enough, forgetting information they have already told us, jumping to conclusions, making incorrect hypotheses. While we try to avoid mistakes, we also try to capitalize on them when they occur naturally. The following transcript illustrates one of our "mistakes" with a therapist-patient and how we handled it.

Patient (slowly):   I had such a terrible week. (sighs) It was so hard to get through the day, every day. (pauses) I just felt so overwhelmed. (pauses) I don't know what's wrong with me. I know I'm not the person I used to be. (pauses) I know I shouldn't feel that way, but . . .

Therapist (interrupting in order to set the agenda):   Can I ask you a question? It seems to me that one important problem to work on this week is your feeling so overwhelmed. Is that the most important problem? Are there other problems you also want to talk about today?

Patient (looking down, in a quiet tone of voice):   I don't know.

Therapist: John, how are you feeling right now?

Patient: I don't know.

Therapist: When I interrupted you just now, what went through your mind?

Patient (sighs):   Oh, just that you were getting down to business.

Therapist: Which meant?

Patient: Nothing, really . . . I know that's what we have to do.

Therapist: But . . . ?

Patient: I don't know. I guess it's irrational. I think I just wanted to get some stuff off my chest.

Therapist: I don't think that's irrational. It makes sense. Would you like to talk uninterrupted for a little while? When you've gotten more off your chest we can decide together what to do next.

Patient (sigh of relief): That sounds good.

We viewed this interaction as a change in strategy rather than a "mistake." In any case, it provided us with the opportunity to strengthen the therapeutic alliance as it showed the patient that we respected his desires, were willing to be flexible, were in tune with his emotional experience.

Other "mistakes," though, are out-and-out errors, as illustrated with a therapist-patient in the following transcript.

Therapist: What happened yesterday with Dr. Stone? (patient's psychiatrist)

Patient (in an angry tone): It wasn't very productive. (Accusingly) You know, you were supposed to call her at the end of last week, *before* my appointment.

Therapist: Oh, no. You're right. I *was* supposed to call her. I don't know what happened. I'm really sorry.

Patient: You know, it was practically a wasted visit.

Therapist: You must have been pretty upset with me. (long pause) What was the worst part for you—wasting the appointment? Something else?

Patient: (Shrugs)

Therapist: What did it mean to you that I didn't call the way I was supposed to?

Patient: You know, I thought I could count on you and now I know I can't.

Therapist: Which means?

Patient: You obviously didn't think I was very important.

This mistake enabled us to model straightforward apologizing and to identify and modify an important dysfunctional belief that interfered with many of the patient's other relationships, too.

Making mistakes with patients who are harshly self-critical can often help as they recognize that they make allowances for us, and that imperfection does not equal total incompetence. When they see how we are self-accepting about our mistakes, they sometimes become more willing to reveal their own imperfections.

PRACTICAL AND PRACTICAL/PSYCHOLOGICAL
PROBLEMS WITH THERAPIST-PATIENTS

Some difficulties with patients do not involve their dysfunctional beliefs but are practical in nature. Others are a combination of the practical and psychological. For example, some of our therapist-patients over-intellectualize. They may do so because that is their natural style or because they have learned to do so as a function of their theoretical orientation. Others overintellectualize for a psychological reason; for example, they believe"If I experience negative emotion, I'll be overwhelmed." The following transcript provides an example of over-intellectualization (as a practical problem) and illustrates one intervention with a therapist-patient.

Therapist: When were you feeling the most distressed this week?

Patient: I don't know. My mood didn't vary much.

Therapist (asking in a more concrete way, directed by data we had collected in previous sessions):   Did you have any negative interactions with your patients this week?

Patient (thinks):   Well, yes. I have this patient who always calls me in crisis, after hours, of course. We had a session earlier this week and she was mad that I had started the session a couple of minutes late but had to end on time. I'm always giving her extra time on all those phone calls, by the way. Anyway, she left me a voicemail message yesterday saying that she wasn't sure she wanted to see me again, that maybe I wasn't *experienced* enough to help her, that she was thinking of going back to her old therapist who had helped her so much in the past, stuff like that.

Therapist: How did you feel when you heard the message?

Patient (shrugs, as he often does when asked for the emotions he experiences)

Therapist: What was going through your mind?

Patient: Well, I knew at the time it was a narcissistic wound. (an interpretation, not his actual thoughts)

Therapist: Were you thinking something negative about yourself? Or about her?

Patient: I didn't have any specific thoughts.

Therapist (providing an automatic thought that was the probable opposite of what the patient *really* thought):   Let me put it another way. Were you thinking how wonderful it was that she left you that kind of message?

Patient: No! She's so ungrateful! And I might not have as much *experience* as her old therapist but she's not taking advantage of what I *do* have to offer. (these are his actual automatic thoughts)

Therapist: And her ingratitude and comment about your *lesser* experience made you feel how? Hurt, angry, sad, anxious?

Patient: Annoyed. She's so annoying!

Using this technique, we were able to elicit the patient's thoughts and emotion. Through additional questioning we identified an important belief underlying his annoyance, that he wasn't "good enough." We assessed the evidence, pro and con, of the validity of this belief and then examined alternative viewpoints.

Another practical or practical/psychological problem arises when a patient is overly detached during the therapy session, attending too much to process at the expense of content, as illustrated here, with a therapist-patient.

Therapist: And when your husband said, "You're spending too much time at work. You're neglecting the kids and me," what went through your mind?

Patient: I see what you're doing. You've got the situation, now you're going after my automatic thoughts and then you'll ask me what my emotional reaction was.

Therapist: Right! Hey, I see you've got the cognitive model.

Patient: Yeah . . . Not that I necessarily agree with it.

Therapist: That's okay. If I were in your place, I'd probably be skeptical, too. Is it okay if we go back to filling in the rest of the cognitive model so we can see if I can be helpful to you today?

Patient: Okay.

This particular problem is more common with our therapist-patients, though it arises occasionally with patients who have read about cognitive therapy or have previously had this kind of treatment.

A third practical problem, for many of our patients, is confidentiality. Some of our therapist-patients experience this concern more acutely than others. We elicit their specific concerns, detail our system for ensuring confidentiality, and, when needed, help them decatastrophize.

MAINTAINING BOUNDARIES

Prior to initiating treatment with therapist-patients, we discuss the advantages and disadvantages for them of entering into therapy with us and we review the limits of our relationship during and after therapy. When a problem arises anyway, and patients become upset, we use standard cognitive therapy techniques of helping them identify, evaluate, and modify their dysfunctional thoughts and assumptions. Typical beliefs include:

- "My therapist should do whatever I want (even if it means establishing a dual relationship)."

- "Since I am incapable, my therapist should solve my problems for me."
- "Since my therapist won't bend the rules [about dual relationships], it shows he doesn't really care about me."

Some nontherapist patients hold identical beliefs.

Maintaining boundaries with certain patients is more difficult than with others. Some (therapist-patients or not) expect to be treated in a special way, some demand entitlements, some believe we should take a primary caretaking, not just therapeutic, role. One therapist-patient, for example, believed we should treat her in a special way because of her professional status. She pressured us for appointments inconvenient to our schedule and expected unlimited phone access to us. Other patients believe they are entitled to special treatment by virtue of their professional or financial success, social status, or the like. Still others expect us to treat them specially because of their history of suffering.

At the start of treatment with therapist-patients, we clearly differentiate the therapeutic role from a supervisory one, declining to provide therapist-patients with direct advice in solving their difficulties with their own patients. (And we are especially careful to ensure they do not break their patients' confidentiality.) If a problem arises, we suggest that they seek supervision with others.

One therapist-patient, for example, asked us how he could get one of his own patients more behaviorally activated. He became angry when we suggested that this topic was a supervisory issue. First we dealt with his anger at us for "withholding" our help. When he recognized that we were trying to fulfill our ethical obligations, he became willing to discuss options for supervision.

A subtler and rather unique version of the same problem arose with a therapist-patient who seemed to linger in therapy. Initially he was quite focused and compliant with treatment and achieved a quick remission of acute symptomatology. In the following sessions he became rather unfocused and brought up a number of different, somewhat vague and unsubstantial problems to work on. When we pointed this out, he acknowledged his hidden agenda. He wanted to see what we would do with certain problems so he could do the same with his patients. This provided an opportunity for a discussion about the importance of openness and collaboration in the therapeutic relationship. We then collaboratively examined the advantages and disadvantages of trying to use therapy for training or supervisory purposes. On the plus side, his own therapy experiences provided firsthand knowledge about being a patient, which helped him empathize with his own patients. However, he came to see that trying directly to apply his therapy experiences to his patients had significant drawbacks and that explicit supervision with a supervisor would probably benefit him much more.

Occasionally, we have therapist-patients who wish to become trainees at our institute after they complete their therapy, often because they have come to value cognitive therapy and want to develop their competency in this approach. Others want to maintain a connection with us and feel special. In one case a patient-therapist felt entitled to special consideration: "I would think you could get me in since I've done so well with you." We handle such issues as we would with any patient who misinterprets the therapeutic relationship, providing a rationale for our policies (no special privilege) and then exploring the patient's reaction to what we have said. This kind of discussion can lead to significant therapeutic progress when patients are able to identify and modify relevant underlying beliefs, for example, "If others don't treat me as special, they don't respect me" or "If I'm not special, I'm worthless."

We avoid mentoring of our therapist-patients to avoid dual relationship problems. We do, however, intentionally self-disclose when relevant (about our own professional struggles along the way and how we resolved them, for example) to both therapist-patients and other patients.

COUNTERTRANSFERENCE ISSUES

As human beings we feel connection with all our patients. Most connections are on the positive side, a few on the negative. When we recognize we are having negative thoughts about a patient or ourselves in relation to a patient, we use cognitive therapy tools on ourselves. We also use such difficulties to provide ourselves with insight about how others in the patients' worlds probably react to them.

With some therapist-patients, we feel heightened concern if we think the well-being of their patients is compromised. We often feel significant self-induced pressure to help them so they can positively impact their patients. We often consult with our colleagues, and, sometimes, our state board of psychology, to discuss our ethical obligations when we believe a therapist-patient is professionally impaired.

Sometimes we have (rather pettier) concerns about what our therapist-patients say about us to other mental health professionals. Bridges (1995) describes the heightened perfectionistic beliefs and concerns about competence of some therapists who treat therapist-patients. Again, standard cognitive therapy tools (and, if necessary, consultation with a colleague) provide reality checks and allow us to decatastrophize so our own issues do not impinge on the therapy we provide.

SUMMARY

In cognitive therapy, we work from a cognitive framework with all patients but tailor treatment to the individual. Our treatment of therapist-patients, therefore, is usually no different from that of nontherapist-patients. The special issues one might think would arise only with therapist-patients (such as their feeling professionally inferior to us, fearing loss of confidentiality, seeking a dual relationship) do arise with our other patients as well (though sometimes in a modified form). Our treatment for all patients is based on a thorough evaluation, a continuously refined cognitive conceptualization, a treatment plan based on this conceptualization, and strategies designed not only to help them improve but also to teach them skills they can use themselves to reduce the risk of relapse.

Finally, rather than having our treatment of therapist-patients inform our work with other patients, the opposite is more frequently true.

REFERENCES

Beck, A. T., & Emery, G. (1985). *Anxiety disorders and phobias: A cognitive perspective.* New York: Basic Books.

Beck, A. T., & Freeman, A. (1990). *Cognitive therapy of personality disorders.* New York: Guilford Press.

Beck, A. T., Rush, A. J., Shaw, B. F., & Emery, G. (1979). *Cognitive therapy of depression.* New York: Guilford Press.

Beck, A. T., Wright, F. D., Newman, C. F., & Liese, B. S. (1993). *Cognitive therapy of substance abuse.* New York: Guilford Press.

Beck, J. S. (1995). *Cognitive therapy: Basics and beyond.* New York: Guilford Press.

Bridges, N. A. (1993). Clinical dilemmas: Therapists treating therapists. *American Journal of Orthopsychiatry, 63*(1), 34–44.

Bridges, N. A. (1995). Psychotherapy with therapists: Countertransference dilemmas. In M. B. Sussman (Ed.), *A perilous calling: The hazards of psychotherapy practice.* New York: Wiley.

Butler, A. C., & Beck, J. S. (in press). Cognitive therapy outcomes: A review of meta-analyses. *Journal of the Norwegian Psychological Association, 37*, 1–9.

Kaslow, F. W. (1986). Therapy with distressed psychotherapists: Special problems and challenges. In R. R. Kilburg, P. E. Nathan, & R. Thoreson (Eds.), *Professionals in distress: Issues, syndromes, and solutions in psychology* (pp. 187–209). Washington, DC: American Psychological Association.

Sussman, M. B. (1995). *A perilous calling: The hazards of psychotherapy practice.* New York: Wiley.

20

FEMINIST THERAPY
WITH THERAPISTS
Egalitarian and More

Laura S. Brown

Feminist therapy is a theory of psychotherapy that combines technical eclecticism with strong core principles informing the work and worldview of the therapist. These guiding concepts, which include as central the notion that therapy is a collaborative, egalitarian partnership of experts, would appear to make it particularly well suited for working with the psychotherapist-as-client. Many of the innovations and directions taken in feminist therapy during its three decades of existence have derived from the experiences of feminist therapists themselves in their personal therapy, both positive and problematic.

When the therapeutic paradigm is that of two experts working together, what happens when both parties define themselves as experts in the change process rather than having that expertise assigned only, or primarily, to the person currently sitting in the therapist's chair? Because the whole concept of egalitarianism is so open to interpretation, and so rife with inner contradictions, the practice of feminist therapy with other therapists can be extremely challenging. Therapists, like other clients, present to therapy with the full range of issues and problems. Therapists experience characterological twists and turns that can undermine the best efforts of the treatment provider. Therapists experience the aftereffects of trauma and interpersonal violence, impairing trust and the capacity to build relationships.

I have been practicing as a psychotherapist since 1979, and from the very beginning have worked with other mental health professionals. Several factors contributed to this happening so soon in my work. Although I was a young and inexperienced therapist when I opened my practice, I was in a unique position as one of the few openly lesbian and feminist therapists in my locale, and even more unique as the only openly lesbian licensed psychologist (read: the only one who could accept insurance payments). While there were a number of then-closeted lesbian and gay therapists in the area, few were practicing independently or were visibly and intentionally offering services to the lesbian community. My possession of a doctorate lent me what I now think was a spurious air of competence; people who might have thought twice about entrusting themselves to the care of a 25-year-old just out of graduate school saw those three magic letters after my name and came in the door.

Over the ensuing years, the reasons for therapists seeing me have changed to some degree. I am blessed with a plethora of proudly out-of-the-closet colleagues in psychology and other mental health disciplines, so I no longer reap the dubious benefit of being perceived as a scarce, and consequently overvalued, resource. Rather, as a senior therapist in the community, I now am seen as the wise, experienced person whose reputation has been bolstered by writing too much.

Ironically, as the years have gone by, I see therapists less, not because I am less sought out but because of changes in myself and my perspective on the role of a therapists' therapist. Early on, my own needs for validation and a sense of worth were being partially stroked by the presence of colleagues in my practice. More recently I have found that my desires for affiliation, colleagueship, and comfortable participation in social and professional events without worrying about boundaries have trumped the earlier needs for validation. I am less flattered by having a colleague approach me for treatment and, due to some painful experiences, more wary as well.

As the preceding paragraphs hint, I have primarily been a therapist for other therapists who define themselves as feminist practitioners. Most, although not all, of these people have been lesbian and bisexual women, although I have also seen a few heterosexual women and men who are psychotherapists as well. At the moment of my writing this article, only two of my active clients were themselves practicing psychotherapists. The majority of my therapist-clients have been psychologists and social workers, with a few doctoral students sprinkled into the mix. All of them have approached me for long-term, in-depth work, usually focused on the resolution of repeated interpersonal violence in childhood. This last factor describes the bulk of my psychotherapy practice over the past 15 years.

All of the work that I have done with other therapists has been feminist therapy. Since feminist therapy, although active for 30 years, is still not well understood by many who do not practice it, I will digress briefly to explain something about its theory and practice. As the theory of feminist therapy is central to the issues involved in working with other therapists as clients, this explication should assist the reader in making sense of the remainder of my chapter.

A BRIEF DESCRIPTION OF FEMINIST THERAPY

Feminist therapy is a technically eclectic approach to psychotherapy informed by feminist political theories and analysis, grounded in the multicultural feminist scholarship on the psychology of women and gender. The overarching goals of this approach are to lead both therapist and client toward strategies and solutions advancing feminist resistance to patriarchy, transformation, and social change in daily personal life, and in relationships with the social, emotional, and political environment (Brown, 1994); it is intentionally conceived of as something that will transform the therapist as well as the client. Feminist therapy requires a continual willingness to engage with oneself in a change process, and to do so not as the distant expert but a member of a system in which power is shared in increasingly equal portions between therapist and client. The feminist paradigm argues that individual change is unlikely when societal and environmental changes do not occur as well.

Feminist practice is not defined by the parameters of a population with whom the therapist works, or what specific interventions she or he uses, but instead by how she or he *thinks* about what is being done in therapy. Feminist practice attends to the power structure of the therapeutic relationship, and to the interaction between therapy and the larger social milieu. The therapist's epistemologies and strategies for engendering equality in therapy are seen as more important than specific therapeutic interventions.

Feminist therapy argues that the seemingly private and highly personal transactions of psychotherapy occur within a social and political framework that itself informs, transforms, or distorts the meanings given to individual experience, and to the very psychotherapeutic process itself. Therapy is conceptualized not simply as a discrete healing relationship between individuals but also as an experience that can potentially be socially transformative. Feminist therapy, like other critical models (Fox & Prilleltensky, 1997), questions such concepts as the possibility of a therapist being neutral or objective and challenges the regulation of ways of knowing and the limitation of received knowledge to positivist empiricist paradigms. Thus, it is open to a range of methodologies (Ballou, 1990) and heuristics (e.g., qualitative, quantitative, autobiographical, intuitive, etc.) (Brabeck & Brown, 1997) and to models for the therapeutic relationship itself that may differ, often radically, from the more standard paradigms for psychotherapy.

Feminist therapy, by being grounded in this critical and political analysis, aims to deprivatize the therapist's, and eventually the client's, understanding of human suffering by asserting that each life and each pain are manifestations of processes that are continuously extant in the layers of a larger social context. Yet feminist therapy requires that each life experience be viewed as valuable, unique, and authoritative. One of the more radical innovations of feminist therapy at the time it was first developed was the privileging of the client as an expert knower in the therapeutic relationship.

Clients are seen as expert sources of knowledge regarding both themselves and their cultural contexts. Because of this privileging of individual meaning and authority simultaneous with attention to public, political realities informing such meaning, feminist therapy straddles the theoretical gap between positivist and postmodernist views of human behavior and change, owing allegiance to neither. Feminist practice attends to both inner and outer worlds, blending dynamic and constructivist understandings of human behavior.

THE RELATIONSHIP IN FEMINIST THERAPY

While all forms of psychotherapy focus on the therapist-client relationship, feminist therapy has been especially emphatic in calling for an egalitarian relationship in therapy. This concept of egalitarianism in therapy reflects relationship paradigms emerging from feminist calls for radical rearrangements of social relationships. In addition, feminists both inside and outside of the world of therapy have analyzed and critiqued the meanings ascribed to caring and nurturance (Heyward, 1993; Noddings, 1984) and applied those critiques to the construction of the therapeutic exchange. Earlier critical analyses of power arrangements in psychotherapy (Chesler, 1972; Greenspan, 1983) led to attempts to develop a paradigm for an egalitarian, empowering therapy relationship.

Feminist theories have identified the importance of attending both to the symbolic relationship, that which usually is referred to in the psychotherapy literature as transference and countertransference, as well as the real in-the-world-now encounter. Feminist therapy has been especially sensitive to the way the internal, symbolic components of the interaction are shaped and colored by the signifiers of gender, race, class, and culture that obtain and give our actions meaning in the social world. From the start, feminist therapists have struggled to make sense of a relationship, psychotherapy, whose parameters as commonly defined appear to have an inherent poor fit with the goals of feminist social change.

Psychotherapy, like other social institutions of patriarchy, tends to embody a dominance-submission hierarchy of unequal power. Most models of therapy invest expertise and authority in one person, in this case the therapist. Hierarchy of power and value is embedded in these models. Much writing on therapy practice discusses the need for the therapist to manage and contain the client and the therapeutic process, reflecting a paradigm of therapy as one in which the therapist maintains power and unilaterally decides on the structure and boundaries of the therapy. From a feminist perspective, this paradigm is flawed at its core.

Power and its imbalances in therapy have proven to be especially thorny problems for feminist therapists, given the inherent imbalances in therapy itself. Therapy is, by its nature, an unbalanced relationship. The need to maintain boundaries, the desire to be helpful to the client and not use clients as sources of support no matter what their occupations outside of the treatment room, and the therapist's own desires for privacy and control—all conspire with the reality of clients' pain and needs to create a highly unequal allocation of certain types of interpersonal influence, even when that influence is explicitly defined as reciprocal or mutual in some way.

Because an analysis of power dynamics is so central to feminist theory (Brabeck & Brown, 1997; Brown, 1994; Lerman, 1987), the solution to the puzzle of power relationships in therapy is a core theoretical challenge for feminist therapy, both at the theoretical and practical levels. Strategies for addressing this often have run into the difficulties inherent in an attempt to merge two quite different ideologies. One, political feminism, sees the individual as living within a social context of political meaning and is concerned with the rearrangement of social and political power. The other, psychotherapy, has been almost entirely apolitical, viewing the transformation of individual lives as an end unto itself, with little concern or attention paid to social arrangements. Although not an overtly or intentionally political stance, it is one that represents a politics of upholding the status quo.

Egalitarianism and asymmetry form two important competing principles that create tensions in the construction of feminist therapy relationships. Feminist therapy interrogates and attempts to address the actual power arrangements present in the relationship as it exists in the here and now. In attempting to accomplish this goal, authors in the field of feminist therapy have described feminist therapy ideally as being an egalitarian relationship, although feminist therapists recognize that pure equality is not possible. The simple fact of who decides when to meet for therapy, and on whose turf and terms the transaction proceeds (always the therapist's decisions and settings), reveals the asymmetries lying beneath the surface of the exchange.

The concept of the egalitarian relationship represents an attempt to acknowledge the absence of equality while striving toward it as an ultimate goal. Egalitarian relationships are those structured so as to move toward equality of power, in which artificial and unnecessary barriers to equality of power are removed from the process. In this relationship, there is an equality of *value* between the participants and of respect for each person's worth. In an egalitarian psychotherapy relationship, a primary goal is for clients to come to know and value their own needs, voice, and knowledge as central and authoritative to their lives. Therapists are not to supplant this knowing with their own authority but rather to use their skills in order to resonate, mirror, and engage the clients in their own development and to assist clients in learning how such self-knowledge and self-value is obscured by patriarchal processes and institutions.

This egalitarian image sees therapists, by virtue of the role itself, as temporarily possessing certain kinds of greater power within that role. To satisfy feminist analysis of power, it is necessary to conceive of methods by which this power is shared and transmitted to the client in every aspect of the psychotherapeutic transaction. It also is important to strategize ways to respect personal power for the therapist, so that empowerment of the client does not simply become a matter of therapist compliance or abdication of personal agency. When the client is a psychotherapist, this can be particularly tricky, depending on the needs and dynamics the therapist-clients brings into play.

The temporary absence of equality of power between therapist and client is punctuated and made conscious in feminist practice by the therapist's analysis of the complex and subtle power dynamics in the exchange. This analysis requires close attention by the therapist in order to maintain the delicate balance, and not to accidentally garner to the therapist those powers that are typically ascribed to that role in dominant modalities but are eschewed in feminist methods (e.g., the power to define the other as pathological and the self as the norm). The methodologies for achieving this balance vary in their specifics across person and situation. Each such solution must take into account the powers of both therapist and client and challenge, in each, beliefs about what is meant by being and behaving powerfully. Examples of such strategies, which are preferred by although not unique to feminist therapists, have included the intentional use of self-disclosure by the therapist (Brown & Walker, 1990), the provision of flexible fee arrangements (Luepnitz, 1988), and a focus on the competencies of the client rather than her or his deficiencies (Brown, 1994, 2000).

WHEN THE CLIENT IS A PSYCHOTHERAPIST

All of these concepts underlying feminist therapy practice are usually known, to some degree or another, by the therapist-clients with whom I have worked. Several of them have read my work, which contains some of the major explications of feminist therapy theory. Others are at least familiar in passing with the notion that feminist therapy is supposed to be egalitarian. And it is definitely this issue of egalitarianism in therapy that has provided for some of the most interesting and productive, as well as painful and difficult, aspects of being a feminist therapist with other therapists, be they feminist or not.

Therapists-as-clients have not been particularly unique in their reasons for coming into treatment. As mentioned earlier, my therapist-clients have the same range of problems affecting the rest of my clients.

What differentiates the therapist-clients, if anything, is the degree of shame that they carry about their distress. Almost to a person, each suffers pain over her or his perception that the difficulties that brought her or him into treatment with me constitute evidence of fraud or impostership in the role of therapist. "If my clients only knew" is a common refrain. Marital therapists who cannot sustain intimate relationships, experts in treating incest who are themselves still in the grip of childhood sexual trauma, drug and alcohol counselors whose own abilities to maintain sobriety are constantly challenged, or simply garden-variety depression or anxiety—each of these is self-perceived by the therapist-client as a mark of professional unworthiness. Most of these clients have chosen the option, available in Washington State, to make a formal request that I keep no written records of their therapy with me. Few of those who have insurance that would still pay for therapy use it, and none of those with managed care coverage do. The issue of privacy and the heightened need for assurances of confidentiality seem to mark this group of clients, at least at the outset of therapy.

The fact that my office is in my home, and thus lacks the potential for encountering other therapists and clients in an office building, has often been perceived as a plus. (*Note*: In the two years since initially writing this article I have moved my home and located my office elsewhere. At least once therapist-client commented that she was glad that I had moved into a mixed-use building, containing the offices of everything from web developers to the local jazz society and very few other psychotherapy offices.) Needless to say, my level of caution in scheduling clients, which is already high, given the tremendous amount of social overlaps that occur among my clients, is heightened with this group. (For a further discussion of these issues, see Davis, Cole, & Rothblum, 1996.)

The power dynamics of therapy, which are so central in feminist practice, have undergone interesting twists and turns with my therapist-clients. I have found that many of them wish to give up more power to me than do clients in general. There is what I suspect to be a universal distrust of self in therapist-clients, a fear of outsmarting oneself with clever rationalizations and defenses. This fear appears to lead to overt and covert requests that I take over the therapy process and be in charge. These clients want to be more "client-like" in a traditional sense than many of my nontherapist clients, for whom respect for autonomy is often the paramount concern. The degree to which I am idealized by psychotherapist clients seems to be higher than what I encounter among clients in general. Some of this is clearly an artifact of my professional persona; a teacher, writer, and leader. But there also appears to be a heightened need on the part of therapist-clients to unthinkingly trust their therapist—at least, for the majority of these clients.

As a consequence, I must be more active in creating a space for therapist-clients to be clients. I must acknowledge more overtly the difficulties inherent in self-revelation, in vulnerability, in the development of a symbolic "transferential" relationship with me. I find myself using disclosure of my own experiences and fears in therapy, especially around regression and dependency, much more frequently with this group of clients, as a means of metacommunicating the safety of becoming young, small, and vulnerable with me. I also find myself referring more in a didactic manner to the paradoxes of vulnerability; how becoming emotionally competent, which I believe to be a sine qua non of therapy practice (Pope & Brown, 1996), is dependent on one's ability to be appropriately vulnerable, emotionally expressive, and able to let go of control. This definition of competence radically differs from general cultural constructions of competence as invulnerability and the ability to maintain a stiff upper lip.

Then there is the flip side of the equation. A small yet notable number of my therapist-clients seem to have come to therapy with me in search of a power struggle. They have read my work, and they quote it to me, usually out of context, in attempts to bend me to their desires, many of which fall far outside of my comfort zone. My ventures at analysis and interpretation are met with scorn, and reminders that in feminist therapy the client is *the* expert. (Omitting the notion that feminist therapy is allegedly a process of shared expertise!) Any attempts on my part to steer the direction of therapy are met with challenge, both to the direction and to my daring to claim authority.

BOUNDARY DILEMMAS

These variations on the construction of self-as-client among my therapist-clients can most easily be observed when negotiating boundaries. My own boundaries as a therapist have tended to be somewhat flexible. While I am adamant that I do not have sexual or intimate social relationships with my clients and former clients, I have long been of the persuasion that therapists and clients inhabit shared social realities and must find ways to negotiate those realities without rigidity. This phenomenon is certainly true in the social small towns of urban lesbian communities, where I reside, and feminist therapists have struggled from the outset with how to have personal privacy yet deal with the inevitable overlaps between our lives and those of our clients (Berman, 1985, 1990; Brown, 1988, 1991). The national organization of feminist therapists, the Feminist Therapy Institute (FTI), has struggled with the question of what to do when a therapist who is a client of a current member applies for membership herself; since the meetings of FTI are small, intimate gatherings where a fair amount of personal process is woven into the didactic component, some therapists view with discomfort the prospect of sharing that space with a current or former client, while others, including myself, have supported therapist-clients who would clearly fit in FTI to join.

In my own practice, I have attempted to balance clear personal boundaries with feminist inclusiveness. It's a work-in-progress. For most of my career I practiced from my home; although the office was separate from the rest of the house, clients knew where I lived. I utilize self-disclosure, both in my written work and in my therapy practice, attempting to exercise discretion. When I know that we will both be attending an extratherapy gathering, be it the local lesbian and gay synagogue, a concert, or a professional meeting, I take the initiative to discuss with clients how we will handle the boundaries. We talk about how I can best safeguard confidentiality in the outside world. Usually, all of these things are nonproblematic.

The special issues that have arisen with psychotherapist-clients have occurred in part around clients' shame and in part around the limits to the flexibility of my boundaries. When discussing extratherapeutic encounters with all clients, I communicate to them that they are in charge of initiating contact when outside the office, since the very fact of my knowing them is confidential. For psychotherapist-clients, this has led to some therapeutically very useful explorations of their shame-based interpretations of this offer. Variations on the theme of "You wouldn't want anyone to know that you knew me" have emerged. Clients who are extremely wary about anyone knowing that their relationship with me is one of a client want, at the same time, to be publicly known by me. Issues of personal worth, inclusion-exclusion, and coming under the positive halo of being a colleague who I know have all emerged.

These clients have struggled hard with initiating the contact. At first, several were unable to do so, and then experienced me as rejecting and cold, even while each one had insight that this was a projection arising from fears of what would happen should she or he initiate. At least one or two have gone counterphobic, making a point of sitting near me at meetings, and then facing anxiety over the possibility that they have been intrusive, an issue with which they were of course dealing in the therapy, and in life. I have had to resist rescuing people by varying this boundary. To me, it is extremely important to communicate in every possible way that therapy is private and confidential. Thus, for me to appear to assist the client by offering to be the one who initiates contact in public, while appearing to be a reasonable flex of the boundary, would in fact be a dangerous subtext about the flexibility of confidentiality as well.

There have also been some interesting individual boundary dilemmas. One therapist who I had treated many years previously was elected to follow me in office in a professional organization. We had had little contact between the end of therapy and that person's increasing involvement in our shared professional association. When it became apparent that this person was indeed very likely to be working closely with me for a number of years, I proposed that we meet to discuss how we would manage the lingering aftereffects of the therapeutic relationship, which, as Hall (1984) has noted, has a half-life longer than that of plutonium.

This therapist and I had parted with very positive feelings for one another. Our work had been very beneficial for the therapist-client, and I had come to like, admire, and respect this person for demonstrating courage, insight, and the willingness to work very hard indeed. Our distance over the years had been an unspoken acknowledgment of the awkwardness that lay in posttherapy relationships, as well as a reflection of my desire to honor this person's status as a colleague. So when we met we talked about how to handle the fact of our long knowing of one another and, in particular, how to make certain that any dynamics from our work as therapist and client that might emerge in our new close collegial relationship could be identified and dealt with. I suggested that, knowing this person, the dynamics would be those of tending to defer to me and not disagree with me, and to idealize me somewhat. All of these had been present in our therapy work. The former client added that given that I was more senior in the organization, and in a mentorship position, it would be difficult to entirely escape them. In addition, there were things I knew about this person from my role as therapist that I would need to put an ever-stronger firewall around in my mind. Personal details about prior relationships, children, and family and health issues, which might or might not be public knowledge to colleagues otherwise, went deeper into the inner file marked "confidential." We agreed that I would follow this person's lead in bringing such matters up in our now-shared public space.

We also talked about the changed boundaries around my life. How would we deal with the former client having more information about me, personally? What would it be like for this person to see me in my meeting-runner mode, where I am often abrupt, impatient, controlling, and irritable—in other words, quite different from how I am in a therapy room? What effect was it going to have on the client's inner construction of me, and of the therapy, to observe me in this way? While I am, I hope, relatively genuine as a person in my work as a therapist, the demand characteristics of running an all-volunteer organization of mental health professionals will perforce elicit different, equally genuine, behaviors than do those of the therapy office. How would this person feel when learning more about my personal life, which was beginning to include an increasingly troubled "marriage" with my (now former) partner?

Over the subsequent years, we discussed these points, both formally and informally. The relationship between us changed. The former client became more powerful and professionally acclaimed, to both of our joy and excitement, and in that growth we were able to work through a piece about how parents did or did not take pride in accomplishments, and did or did not compete, that could not have been addressed symbolically in therapy. My genuine pride in and active mentorship of the former client, which came easily and naturally to me, were also, for me, a chance to really experience referred joy (known in Yiddish as "naches") over the client's movement from a personal position of devaluation and timidity to one of strength, visibility, and leadership. As the relationship became less and less therapy and more and more collegial, we actually finished the work of therapy, even though formal therapy had been terminated years before.

There have also been a few more painful encounters with therapist-clients around boundaries. The concept of respecting the expertise of the client as a change agent in her or his own life has been distorted, on a few occasions, into a therapist-client's insistence on being a change agent in my life. I do not want my clients, no matter how skillful they are as therapists, to function in any sort of therapeutic role for me. My own needs for privacy and control, and my complete desire to maintain the roles as they are in therapy, are such to preclude that from happening. It has been difficult, at best, for me to acknowledge to clients when I am myself going through difficult personal straits, even when to do so was to allow them to correctly interpret my bad mood on a given day. It has usually been sufficient for me to say something along the lines of "I'm dealing with some difficult personal issues right now, so if you pick up sadness or discomfort, it's me, it's not about you."

But there have been a few therapist-clients who experienced my failure to accept their offers of help as insults. These individuals have, not surprisingly, been struggling with deep wounds to self and soul, and have had their entire sense of value rooted in their abilities to help others. They are often superb, highly intuitive therapists up to a point, possessing immense capacities for empathy with pain and the ability to be present with clients themselves in ways that I admire and can only aspire to. They are, however, uncomfortable with client autonomy and even more uncomfortable with my boundary around the acceptance of their help.

Ironically, these therapist-clients have had excellent, sometimes on-target insights about me. Their capacities for deep intuition, often honed in the searing fires of terrible childhood abuse, make them incredibly attentive to the dynamics of others, particularly so to the dynamics of someone on whom they are dependent for care. Yet were I to use those insights in the way they have been offered, I would violate my own privacy and boundaries. Worse, I would exploit clients' dependencies on me and avoid independently doing my own therapy work with my own therapist.

The struggles that have occurred at this nexus have been some of the most painful I have endured as a therapist. How to respond empathically, and in an empowering manner, to a client who tells me that she or he is profoundly hurt because I fail to value her or his expertise as a therapist, particularly when she or he is quoting (as is frequently the case at this juncture) something I have written about the egalitarian relationship and valuing client expertise, has been one of the truest challenges of my work as a feminist therapist. I can certainly relate to the pain of the client at this juncture. My acquaintance Carter Heyward (1993), a theologian and theorist of feminist theology, has written movingly and powerfully of her distress when her feminist therapist set and occasionally held the boundaries of their therapy, refusing to move more into mutuality.

And yet I cannot go that route. Mutuality occurs when both people wish it, not when someone forces herself to violate her own sense of what is right in order to accommodate another's desires. I have done this experiment in forcing myself into so-called mutuality, once, with a colleague who was not in therapy with me, whose words and pain were both persuasive enough for me to stop listening to my own voice. I regret that, deeply; it wounded me badly and for a long time undermined my ability to trust myself as a therapist, colleague, or friend. My boundaries became tighter and more rigid for a period of time.

This experience also clarified and refined my conceptualization of egalitarianism and mutuality, both in and outside of the therapy hour. As I said earlier, mutuality, although a desired goal of feminist practice, is not a technique to be applied on demand. It is, or should be, a natural outgrowth of how therapy works over time, as the roles shift and change. With the first therapist-client of whom I wrote, mutuality did occur, even though neither of us stated it as a goal. It arose from our mutual negotiations of the boundaries of our changing roles. With my colleague, mutuality never did occur, even though the conditions for it were theoretically more favorable than those extant in a psychotherapeutic context.

HOW IS THIS CLIENT DIFFERENT FROM
ALL OTHER CLIENTS?

In a word, not very. And in another word, profoundly. The mentorship function that occurs in feminist therapy with therapist-clients is, I believe, a unique component of therapy with this population. If a goal of an egalitarian relationship is the empowerment of the client, then how can such therapy take place without professional mentoring to one degree or another?

The trick of integrating mentorship into therapy is to make the mentoring a conscious aspect of the therapy issues already on the table. As someone whose only two completely unconflicted self-concepts throughout my lifetime have been my intelligence and my intellectual competence, it was a huge surprise to me to discover how many of my bright, capable colleagues deeply believed themselves to be stupid and fraudulent. The problem of impostorship, first described by Clance and Imes (1978) seems to be rampant among the psychotherapist-clients I have worked with. Mentoring these clients in their professional development and accomplishments, as a sort of lab in which the question of impostorship can be evaluated empirically, has been a frequent component of the therapy.

So, for example, supporting a therapist-client with a master's degree in applying to and then completing a doctoral program was one recent experience of combined mentorship and psychotherapy. As I frequently commented over the years during this person's successful pursuit of a Ph.D., while perhaps I could be fooled by my positive bias toward this person, it was unlikely that the entire faculty of a demanding doctoral program would or could be. The infinite and varied opportunities for the impostor dynamic to be triggered were marvelous grist for the therapeutic mill. My ability and willingness to lend some reality testing to the process (e.g., recalling out loud my own experience of getting a dissertation through committee) were some of the active mentoring components.

Such is frequently the case with psychotherapist-clients. The therapy becomes a place where they can discuss their fears of trying to write, in the presence of the therapist who is a much-published author and frequent book and journal editor; their desires to take leadership roles, with a therapist who has done so; and their struggles to grow professionally, with a therapist who can and does model encountering such struggles in her own life and practice. Because, in my writings, I have been relatively transparent as to much of my thinking as a therapist, I need not always make this information available directly in the therapy hour. But it is almost always a component of the work I do with psychotherapist-clients. Development of the professional self cannot, from a feminist perspective, be separated from the development of the personal self. If the personal is political and thus professional, then to create artificial dividing lines in the therapy of therapists would be inconsistent with feminist therapy's view of therapy and life being a seamless web, where each informs the other.

As such, psychotherapist-clients discuss their work in therapy. Of course, almost all of my clients, be they bus drivers or nurses or teachers or carpenters, discuss their work in therapy. Work is the bulk of the waking day, the place where conflicts and personal dynamics will perforce play themselves out. To artificially create a class of clients who are forbidden to process their work with me because it is therapy would seem ludicrous.

Once again, the job for me and my psychotherapist-clients is to carefully observe and respect the lines between therapy and supervision. I am aware that there have been a number of occasions over the years when the therapy hour of a psychotherapist-client did evolve into process supervision on a particularly painful or challenging case. In essence, I was treating in those sessions the therapist-client's symbolic, "countertransferential" relationship. At times, when a therapist-client found her or himself in a particularly thorny professional dilemma, the lines between therapy and supervision have blurred. I have made referrals to consultants, sent people home with books on the thorny issue, and made suggestions about where to get ongoing supervision resources. I construe this as an extension of the mentorship process. Therapy then becomes a forum in which the therapist-client can explore her or his fears and uncertainties about her or his work—a topic that almost every client in every occupation addresses at some point or another.

The serendipitous fact that I share an occupation with my therapist-clients means that there are two risks inherent. One is the risk that I, and my client, will think that I am more expert as a therapist on this work issue than I might otherwise be. And the other, complementary risk is that if and when the problem in the therapist-client's work is intrinsic to her or his defensive structures and unavailable to scrutiny at the moment, I may be deemed less valuable as a source of assistance on this work issue, given that whatever alleged insights I have to offer will be therapeutically premature for the therapist-client.

POSTTERMINATION AND PROFESSIONAL RELATIONSHIPS

Posttermination relationships with psychotherapist-clients are indeed unique. Although I may encounter other kinds of former clients at random in my life, many of my former psychotherapist-clients inhabit similar professional spheres. The bulk of my psychotherapist-clients have shared my feminist orientation and lesbian identity, and they are naturally drawn to some of the same professional organizations. Meetings of the Association for Women in Psychology and the Feminist Therapy Institute, of my state psychological association, and of various trauma-related professional societies, not to mention divisional social hours during the APA convention, are always opportunities to encounter people who once were in therapy with me. As noted earlier, I have had at least one occasion when a former client became a close colleague in a professional association.

The complexities of these posttermination relationships lie primarily, for me, in the constant need to maintain the firewall of confidentiality. My psychotherapist-clients may have repeatedly and publicly revealed the details that I must keep as confidential, but I cannot know that. So I have learned to act surprised, to ignore information that I know well, and to be attentive to the psychotherapist-client dynamic creeping into the collegial one. I have discussed with psychotherapist-clients the question of whether or not I would refer to them. To be known as someone who gets referrals from me has historically been a positive factor in my professional community. The ultimate tricky question is thus to be asked by a third party, who is ignorant of the relationship, if so-and-so, whom I know entirely as a client, is a good therapist to whom I would refer. I have resolved this question with the generic response that I don't know that person well enough to answer.

More troubling have been the few occasions when I knew a psychotherapist-client to be teetering on the edge of incompetence or impairment. I have used my power as the therapist to attempt to be persuasive as to the need to curtail or stop a practice. On a few occasions, psychotherapist-clients have gratefully taken this release from the burden of doing work that they could no longer handle and have used my support to get access to disability insurance or make a change to a job that they could tolerate well and do competently. On some other—much fewer—occasions, the messenger has had her head cut off, and I have been fired. This, too, is one of the more painful and difficult aspects of being a therapist with therapists. Although I believe that this challenge transcends theoretical orientations (unless one is a training analyst and thus in the position to stop the person's progress through analytic certification), I think that it is especially difficult in the context of feminist practice. The community of feminist therapists is small, and people know, and gossip about, one another. I have been in the position of hearing colleagues complain about the impairment of a former client, one of the "off-with-your-head" people, and feeling dread and worry, both for that person, and for my own reputation if my status as that person's former therapist became known. The necessity of confronting my own powerlessness as a therapist is enhanced in the small community of feminist practice, a fishbowl (Lyn, 1990) where both the private lives and the professional reputations of therapists are visible and often discussed.

CONTINUED SATISFACTIONS

With all of the challenges inherent in working as a therapist to therapists, I have for the most part enjoyed this aspect of my work. It has challenged me to think in new and more complex ways about the whole idea of an egalitarian relationship, and how to empower people to be as dependent and vulnerable as they wish to be, as well as to be as autonomous and functional. It has led me to learn more about my own boundaries as a therapist, and to appreciate the challenges of developing boundaries mutually when both therapist and therapist-client have their own set of boundary concerns.

Yet, as I mentioned earlier, I have chosen to do this work less and less as time has gone on. Initially, I received enormous ego gratification from being known as a therapist whom other therapists saw, marking it as an indicator of competence. I still see it as that. My need for such markers to appear from outside of me has diminished considerably over the years. I have less and less enjoyment in that aspect of being special. I found that the price I was paying in personal isolation felt too high. I wanted the people who were my close colleagues to be available to me as friends, as consultants, and, ultimately, as potential therapists for myself! As my friendship networks have matured and ripened, and the needs for collegial, consultative, and personal therapeutic relationships have been satisfied, I find myself open once again to working with other therapists. I sense that some of this is a function of my own developmental maturity as well (or at least, I hope this is the case).

Working with psychotherapist-clients has taught me incredible humility, both about my own skills as a therapist and about our profession in general. I firmly believe that it is the client, not the therapist, who makes the change happen in therapy. The therapist is the one who provides the necessary and sufficient conditions of emotional environment in which that change can take place. It is with my psychotherapist-clients, who utilize their own skills in the work they do as clients, that I can see this most vividly, and be most powerfully reminded that I am not the one who makes change happen.

My work as a therapist for therapists has also informed my own choices around psychotherapy. I have learned that a similarity of theory may not always be conducive to good work happening in therapy. At times, my feminist therapist-clients and I have been able to collude in avoidance and defenses, using our shared language and constructs, in ways that did not happen when the therapist was either not a feminist or not as enmeshed in the theory of feminist practice. My clients could outsmart themselves, and me, less effectively when neither of us were smartly quoting the same theory. Being off the same page, having to negotiate the discontinuities between my and a therapist-client's theories of themselves and the world, was often extremely productive, because we both were required to stretch past our comfort zones. Thus, my own choices of personal therapist were broadened in very productive ways.

So what advice do I have to offer to colleagues contemplating this endeavor? First, be solid in your sense of yourself. Competition with a client can be deadly, as can the unspoken requirement that clients adulate us in order to fill the holes in our professional self-worth. I have been better and more effective with these, and all my clients, when I needed no feedback about the value and alleged brilliance of my insights! While this might seem self-evident, my experience as a client has shown otherwise. Too many therapists to whom I have gone have tried to prove their worth on the back of mine, and I know that this is not a unique experience for therapists in therapy.

Second, have a clear and strong colleague network. I almost foreclosed my own early on by choosing to work with a number of therapists who were potential peers and colleagues. Isolation is a problem for therapists in general; becoming the therapist's therapist, especially if you are a member of a small social community, can be deadly.

And finally, remember that the therapist-client is a client, first, last, and in between. This seems obvious, but experience would suggest otherwise. The dangers inherent in our identification with clients who share some or all of our own characteristics—be it religion, culture, sexual orientation, or occupation—is that we make the client special in ways that preclude our ability to see her or him clearly as the suffering human being in search of assistance and a place to experiment with personal change. Our countertransferences to clients who are therapists will be, like all such relationships, complicated critters (Brown, 2001), reflecting our similarities and differences of race, class, and culture, as well as the impacts of our social contexts. Our greatest challenge is to remember that this individual, no matter how like us, no matter how skillful she or he may be in her or his own practice of therapy, is with us for her or his own process of healing and transformation. When this is lost sight of, therapy for therapists can become destructive to the client and to the integrity of the process. When we are able to maintain this vision, and to rest firmly in our role as healer, the potentials for an exciting, powerful therapeutic experience are all present.

REFERENCES

Ballou, M. (1990). Approaching a feminist-principled paradigm in the construction of personality theory. In L. S. Brown & M. P. P. Root (Eds.), *Diversity and complexity in feminist therapy* (pp. 23–40). New York: Haworth.

Berman, J. S. (1985). Ethical feminist perspectives on dual relationships. In L. B. Rosewater & L. E. A. Walker (Eds.), *Handbook of feminist therapy* (pp. 287–296). New York: Springer.

Berman, J. S. (1990). The problem of overlapping relationships in the feminist community. In H. Lerman & N. Porter (Eds.), *Feminist ethics in psychotherapy* (pp. 106–110). New York: Springer.

Brabeck, M., & Brown, L. S. (1997). Feminist theory and psychological practice. In J. Worell & N. Johnson (Eds.), *Shaping the future of feminist psychology: Education, research and practice* (pp. 15–36) Washington, DC: American Psychological Association.

Brown, L. S. (1988) From perplexity to complexity: Thinking about ethics in the lesbian therapy community. *Women and Therapy, 8,* 13–26.

Brown, L. S. (1991). Ethical issues in feminist therapy: Selected topics. *Psychology of Women Quarterly, 15,* 323–336.

Brown, L. S. (1994). *Subversive dialogues: Theory in feminist therapy* New York: Basic Books

Brown, L. S. (2000). Feminist therapy. In C. R. Snyder & R. Ingram (Eds.), *Handbook of psychological change: Psychotherapy process and practices for the Twenty-first century.* New York: Wiley.

Brown, L. S. (2001). Feelings in context: Countertransference and the real world in feminist therapy. *In Session/Journal of Clinical Psychology, 57,* 1005–1012.

Brown, L. S., & Walker, L. E. A. (1990) Feminist therapy perspectives on self-disclosure. In G. Stricker & M. Fisher (Eds.), *Self-disclosure in the therapeutic relationship* (pp. 135–156). New York: Plenum.

Chesler, P. (1972). *Women and madness.* Garden City, NY: Doubleday.

Clance, P. R., & Imes, S. (1978). The impostor phenomenon in high-achieving women: Dynamics and therapeutic intervention. *Psychotherapy: Theory, Research and Practice, 15,* 241–247.

Davis, N., Cole, E., & Rothblum, E. (1996). *Lesbian therapists and their therapy: From both sides of the couch.* New York: Haworth.

Fox, D., & Prilleltensky, I. (Eds.) (1997). *Critical psychology: An introduction.* London: Sage.

Greenspan, M. (1983). *A new approach to women and therapy.* New York: McGraw-Hill.

Hall, M. (1984, May). *Counselor-client sex and feminist therapy: A new look at an old taboo.* Paper presented at the Third Advanced Feminist Therapy Institute, Oakland, CA.

Heyward, C. (1993). *When boundaries betray us.* San Francisco: HarperCollins.

Lerman, H. (1987). *A mote in Freud's eye.* New York: Springer.

Luepnitz, D. A. (1988). *The family interpreted.* New York: Basic Books.

Lyn, L. (1990). *Life in the fishbowl: Lesbian and gay therapists' social interactions with their therapists.* Unpublished master's thesis, Southern Illinois University at Carbondale.

Noddings, N. (1984). *Caring.* Berkeley: University of California Press.

Pope, K. S., & Brown, L. S. (1996). *Recovered memories of abuse: Assessment, therapy, forensics.* Washington, DC: American Psychological Association.

21

LISTENING TO THE LISTENER

An Existential-Humanistic Approach to Psychotherapy with Psychotherapists

MYRTLE HEERY & JAMES F. T. BUGENTAL

In this chapter we will address the issue of psychotherapists who, after practicing psychotherapy for some time, turn to psychotherapy not as a requirement but out of a genuine life need. We will explore some of the myths about being a psychotherapist, four human givens that propel the need for psychotherapy, and two clinical cases in which the clients themselves were therapists, demonstrating the process of existential-humanistic psychotherapy.

WHEN WOULD A PSYCHOTHERAPIST ENTER PSYCHOTHERAPY?

While training for a career as a psychotherapist, one often undergoes psychotherapy oneself. Sometimes this therapy may not be fulfilling; its outcome is measured in terms of hours toward a requirement instead of personal growth.

Nevertheless, good psychotherapy is a process that may elicit growth for the student. The trainee is likely to find that his or her issues as a client parallel to some degree those of the clients he or she will later see in his or her own practice. Equally he or she will discover the many individual variations on similar issues. The journey of students in psychotherapy is well known to many psychotherapists, but the journey of licensed clinicians in psychotherapy is not. In fact, the literature on therapy for therapists is al-most nonexistent, despite being much needed, given the consistency of referrals we have experienced.

In Dr. Bugental's practice of over 50 years, increasingly and consistently he had two to three types of therapists (clinical psychologists, psychiatrists, marriage, family therapist, social workers) as clients at any given time. This consistency of therapists as clients developed through name recognition in the psychology profession: publications of books and periodicals, presenta-tions at psychological conferences such as the APA, trainings offered to psy-chotherapists, and teaching positions at various university settings. Dr. Heery has seen a similar development in her practice of over 25 years.

THE MYTH OF THE PSYCHOTHERAPIST—LOSING FACE

Every profession has its myths. For the psychotherapist, one such myth is that of "having it all together," the myth that a practicing psychotherapist has crossed some threshold and is now above needing help himself or her-self. How does the myth of "having it all together" affect the psychothera-pist? As psychotherapists in the therapy room, we must carefully discern with each client how much of our own inner experience to disclose. Many parts of us are moved in the process of giving psychotherapy, naturally pro-pelling us into searching deep within our own beings as we are being present with the client. This myth can serve as an obstacle to self-disclosure—and rightfully so in the context of a therapy session. If seeing clients brings up a continued sense of inner unrest, then a psychotherapist might not only consider consultation but individual psychotherapy.

So you lose your psychotherapist's face and wear the face of the client. Where will you arrive then? We know from experience that we are unfold-ing and that it is desirable to choose help in our growth process. Life is a process rather than a destination. Holding onto the mask of "knowing it all" distances the therapist from himself or herself and his or her relation-ship with the client. Allowing not-knowing to be a part of one's life brings human vulnerability into the moment. A psychotherapist is not a god who knows all but rather an individual accompanying others on a full—and often painful—human journey. The therapist's own pain needs attention in per-sonal psychotherapy, not in psychotherapy with the client.

FOUR EXISTENTIAL GIVENS

Existential-humanistic psychotherapy holds that all human experience is predicated on certain inescapable givens of the human condition. How an individual deals with these givens is at the root of the distresses he or she brings to psychotherapy. Different theorists in this school (Bugental, 1965; Yalom, 1980) expound on these givens. Here we will explore four givens of-fered by Bugental (1987): embodiedness, finitude, choicefulness, and being a part of and apart from.

Embodiedness

Everyone has a body, a vehicle through which to experience life. This is the given of *embodiedness*. From moment to moment, we experience the dualities of hunger and satiation, pleasure and pain, illness and injury, high or low energy. Over time our bodies grow, mature, and age. Our bodies continually remind us that life is change. Our bodies also remind us that each life is unique, even as each body is unique: one to a customer.

Human nature wants to cling to permanence, but life continually presents us with impermanence. We see this everywhere, including therapy practice. We know that the client we see on the first visit will also have a last visit. The client we saw last week in many respects is not the same person we are seeing this week. A diagnosis we make at the beginning of a session may not be the one we make at the end of the same session. Some of the potentials latent in each of us emerge, while others retreat. Life is in *process*, it is not stagnant, and our changing bodies continually mirror this.

Some people spend much time caring for and enhancing their bodies. This can become an obsession, a desperate act to pretend to permanence in the face of inexorable change. Psychological distress often arises when one denies or confronts the impermanence of the body. No one is immune to this, including psychotherapists.

Finitude

As each now-moment slips away into next moment, we continually experience the given of *finitude*: the limitedness of life. We must deal with loss, with situations beyond our control, and with continual change. As therapists, we realize that we can only do so much; we can only see so many clients, and we will only practice this profession so long. Finitude influences us daily. We seek certainty in a variety of ways: by training to become a therapist, passing exams for a license, or purchasing insurance for our practice. We try to avoid unwanted contingencies, but there are always circumstances beyond our control.

The awareness of death is the ultimate experience of finitude. Therapists listen to some clients grieving for lost ones and other clients facing their own deaths. Listening to concerns of death is a reminder of one's own death (Heery, 2001). We do not know when, where, or how we will die. The simultaneous certainty and uncertainty of death impacts us powerfully. Each one of us is impacted differently in the way we live our lives. Some of us seek certainty by purchasing insurance policies and saving money while others buy lottery tickets or risk losing money, on the stock market.

We can view all of this—risking as well as seeking security—as attempts to deal with the ultimate finitude of death. Everyone lives accompanied by the shadow of death. For therapists this confrontation can be intensified. We face it in our own lives and hear our clients exploring all manner of variations of it as well.

Choice

Life presents us with choices on every front, from what to eat for breakfast to what to do with the rest of our lives. This is the given of *choicefulness*. It is paradoxically and inextricably interwoven with our experience of finitude: the choices available to us may not be endless; nonetheless, even declining to choose is making a choice.

Entering psychotherapy is also a choice. Psychotherapists see individuals coming into the office in distress; many leave with new perspectives and with a larger view toward living their lives. For some therapists, facilitating the growth of others is sufficient fulfillment in itself. For others, facilitating and repeatedly watching these changes in others can become an impetus to making changes in one's own life; thus, one makes the choice to become the active participant.

This is not simple countertransference, an out-of-proportion reaction to the client, but rather the cumulative effect of watching people receive the benefits of psychotherapy and wanting some of the benefits for oneself. One therapist said to me,[1] "I wanted the goodies I was giving. I wanted to be in psychotherapy." The wanting is an essential step from the subjective world to the objective world, so that doing psychotherapy becomes a reality. I often ask psychotherapists "What brought you here?" I hear a variety of answers, but one consistent theme is the desire to receive the same benefits that they are giving, thus to enlarge their own lives with meaning and purpose.

The choice to seek psychotherapy for oneself as a therapist raises many questions: "Who will I see? How will this be seen by the therapist I work with and by the community in which I live?" Our freedom of choice here can be limited by the situation we find ourselves in and the belief systems we operate under. In some milieus the myth of the psychotherapist "having it all together" may hold one back: it is looked down on for a psychotherapist to be in psychotherapy. It is shameful and proof that that person must not have it all together. So seeking out therapy for oneself flouts the myth that the psychotherapist has life all worked out at all times.

In other milieus, the prevailing myth might be just the opposite: that it is absolutely necessary that a therapist be in psychotherapy. *This* version of the myth holds that there must be something wrong with the therapist who is *not* in psychotherapy. After all, anyone who is conscious is in psychotherapy, and if you are not then you must be in denial or on some ego trip.

Being a Part of *and* Apart From

Being *a part of* and *apart from* is another given of the human condition that existential-humanistic psychotherapy recognizes. Just as life continually presents us with choices, so we continually face the experience of feeling *a part of* some situations and *apart from* others. As with the other givens, this involves a paradox: we can no more feel connected with everyone and everything around us than we can feel disconnected from them. We connect with humanity all the time, yet we are each uniquely apart from it at the same time.

During the process of existential-humanistic psychotherapy, the therapist has the experience of being simultaneously a part of and apart from the client. Knowing that this is a limited relationship enforces the experience of being *apart from*. We certainly do not know the client outside of the psychotherapeutic setting, and when the therapy ends, the relationship ends. Yet while the therapy is in process, the relationship can be intense and moving. The therapist frequently has the experience of being *a part of*. We join many times with the client's human experiences. We are companions in a powerful process of change and possibility.

A psychotherapist can be enriched by being a part of another person's journey in living. When a client leaves or finishes therapy, we may sharply experience the aloneness of our own lives. The client walks into the office alone and leaves alone. I also walk into my office alone and leave alone. Life is with others, yet each of us is ultimately alone.

Being with this ultimate separateness can create a tension inside us, referred to as existential anxiety (May, 1969). This tension appears in relationship both to others and to self. It is an unavoidable part of the human condition. Everyone, including psychotherapists, can build defensive patterns against this anxiety-producing given. Yet certain situations in our professional or personal lives can bring our way of being with this given into question.

THE PARADOX OF LISTENING—A GIVEN IN PSYCHOTHERAPY

The experience of these human givens can impel anyone, including a psychotherapist, to desire being listened to professionally. We are not speaking of listening by friends or lovers but rather clinical listening, professional listening. Listening is a multidimensional process, and listening *to* a professional listener has many aspects which we are just beginning to recognize and verbalize. There is a difference between listening to someone who has professional listening skills—that is, a therapist—and listening to someone without this training. Knowledge of the therapeutic process can work both for and against the client who is a therapist by profession. In working with psychotherapist-clients, the therapist meets a client who is usually eager to commit and work deeply, which can be an exciting and rewarding experience for both (Bugental, 2001).

On the other hand, one aspect we have recognized is the often-present "inner critic" in both the listener and the listened to. This inner critic can be both a help and a hindrance, requiring vigilance on the part of the listener. For the psychotherapist-client, it is a great help to be the recipient of a process he or she trusts and knows so well. Yet, this very familiarity can turn into a hindrance. He or she will probably meet her own inner "subtherapist" or "professional critic" during sessions, through perceptions such as "Gee, Doctor, that was a great intervention you just made with me," or the opposite: "Gee, Doctor, your intervention was way off the mark." Whether the psychotherapist-client speaks this evaluation or thinks it, this activity of the "subtherapist" becomes part of the resistance to the work.

In this critical voice of the psychotherapist-client, we will often hear competition. What is the inner experience of this competitive voice in the client? How does the therapist receive this competition? The focus in our work is on the process of the client, the subjective experience. We are focusing on process, not the content of the statements made. This type of competition will not be unique to a psychotherapist-client, but at the same time clients from various professions will frequently explore competition issues during psychotherapy.

This focus on the resistance activates transference and countertransference, a necessary positive force to the forward movement of in-depth existential-humanistic psychotherapy. The psychotherapist-client will sometimes make attempts to become buddies with the therapist by alluding to their status as colleagues or inviting collusion through implied criticism of other therapists. "Oh, you know how *they* are," one psychotherapist-client said dismissively of attendees at a professional conference. In another instance, a psychotherapist-client said with a laugh (and an implied challenge), "We both know I am just resisting you now."

From the therapist's side, the invitation to join in the laugh might be tempting and modulated by countertransference activated in the therapist. Most therapists have unmet personal needs to be acknowledged professionally; therefore, we support exploring countertransference through supervision. It does not serve the client for the therapist to join the buddy system.

A unique caring and caution can arise inside the therapist around performance anxiety and "doing it right" and around being evaluated and judged as a therapist working with a therapist. Sometimes self-disclosure by the therapist is in order. This has to be done with great care and sensitivity to timing, but therapist self-disclosure is sometimes necessary to explore the client's impact on another; for example, "We are both psychotherapists by profession. I know, on occasion, I have joined your laughter concerning our shared profession, yet I find myself hesitating to laugh with you now." Such self-disclosure requires tremendous care. The therapist must feel and evaluate each situation closely. Working through the transference and countertransference relationship with a psychotherapist-client requires vigilance by the psychotherapist.

For the therapist, helping other therapists may give rise to a sense of being recognized and appreciated. On the other hand, it can as easily aggrandize the professional ego with a sense of honor and pride in becoming known as a "therapist's therapist."

The issue of balance arises here; the psychotherapist needs to monitor this helping activity with careful vigilance. Dr. Heery experienced performance anxiety when first seeing therapists as clients when her inner critic would say, for example, "Boy, that was sure an unnecessary thing to say!" and similar self-criticisms. This anxiety eased through supervision and consultation, as well as through the lived experience of seeing more therapists as clients.

During Dr. Bugental's half-century of private practice, he has had many individual and collective honors, such as teaching psychiatric residents and seeing well-known psychologists and psychiatrists as clients. All of these honors have certainly been accompanied with pride. The years have also shown Dr. Bugental the great value of seeking consistent consultation with peers to monitor and keep close guard against a sense of feeling like the "superknowing therapist." It is crucial to remember that the work of psychotherapy is for the client rather than for the aggrandizement of the psychotherapist. Peer consultation groups can serve delicious humble pie, and we highly recommend them.

MIXING THERAPY MODELS—THE CASE OF LAURA

Just as there are many different individuals, there are many different forms of psychotherapy. Existential-humanistic psychotherapy is concerned with the uniqueness and irreducibility of human experience. There are no universal laws of behavior in this school.

There is certainly a major difference in style of psychotherapy between our work and that of many public mental health agencies. We offer long-term in-depth psychotherapy while most public mental health agencies offer short-term therapy, primarily cognitive-behavior based. The clinicians in these venues are often limited to five to ten sessions with any one client. We find it valuable to explore the journey of a psychotherapist from one of these agencies who came to Dr. Heery for psychotherapy.

Laura, as we shall call her, had been working in a public mental health agency for the past 20 years, and now she is calling for an appointment for herself. She raises many questions about privacy in her initial phone call to me. Is the waiting room shared with anyone else? Would anyone see her entering and leaving my office? Her tone is cautious. Laura needs assurance that others would not know she was seeing me. I can make no absolute promises, but I can certainly give her some assurance that her actual visits to me would be private.

When Laura comes to our first interview, I hear the anxiety in her voice. I do not focus on her words but on the music behind the words. I hear a cry in her voice. In this short contact she seems very much apart from her therapeutic world. She is stepping outside her professional domain to seek for herself a type of psychotherapy that is quite different from her own practice. My assurance of physical privacy temporarily appeases her tension, and our work has already begun.

Transformative Potential of Anxiety

Laura finds herself in a very ambiguous situation in her life. She practices a form of psychotherapy that she has begun to believe is not helping her clients. She feels restricted by the requirements for short-term psychotherapy. Her clients want to continue, but she is unable to allow them to do so. She is overwhelmed by the unthinkable—the suspicion that she is failing to help others. *What will I do?* she wonders. *I have no other training, and the training I have is not helping people. They come for a few sessions, and then, sure enough, they need to come back. I am not permitted to help them again. They are not given a second chance, nor am I.*

Laura's dilemma arises from the conflict between a given and a chosen condition. She has chosen to be a psychotherapist working at this agency, yet she finds herself constrained by the agency's rules. This paradoxical condition calls Laura's authenticity into question. She can no longer depend on what and how she thinks. In spite of her efforts to remain true to her training, she finds that she cannot.

It is important for me not to join Laura in her perception of how limited the type of therapy she practices has become. Her dissatisfaction is a call for her to seek more authentic living; this dissatisfaction enlivens the moment, and I reflect it for her.

"Laura, I hear your dissatisfaction with your job. What are you willing to do?"

"Well, I thought you could help me decide what to do. I know you practice a different type of therapy—long-term—so I am hoping you can help me."

She stops and drifts off into silence. I feel into this moment with her. I feel we are both traveling in space for a moment going nowhere, just drifting.

"Laura, where are you?"

"Oh, just drifting, not really anywhere. Do you think you can help me?"

Laura has just clearly shown me her ambivalence. I will call her attention to this ambivalence; we will visit it many times over the course of her therapy. We are now confronted with Laura's ambivalence about doing her work in the moment. She has asked me to do her work for her while she drifts along. This is her "resistance," and this is our present work: looking at her ambivalence toward her life in this moment (Bugental, 1999).

"Laura, for a moment we were both drifting. Is that helping you?"

"Well, I certainly did not ask you to drift with me, but can you help me?"

Now our client-therapist relationship is the focus. This human relationship, rather than ideas or explanations, will be the ground for any transformation Laura makes. It creates the opportunity for her to have a new experience in relating. The focus is the moment, not the past or the future but now (Heery & Bugental, 1999). Discovering how Laura is actually choosing to be in the moment is our journey together, which lasts several years.

"Laura, when I asked you what you are willing to do concerning your work, you chose to drift, and I accompanied you. This is an important moment in our relationship. You did not directly ask me to drift with you, but I joined you where you chose to go. We are drifting together."

Thus our work begins on an important note: drifting. We explore often what drifting does and does not do for Laura and how this contributes to the choices she is making with her life. This moment of drifting is a hint of much to come in Laura's future therapy sessions. My participation with Laura ranges through instructional, silent, mirroring, empathic, pressing, and more; it covers much of the spectrum of being human in the client-therapist relationship. This work is like a musician playing an instrument that yields many possible frequencies. The therapy has to be tuned each time. It is spontaneous yet also disciplined, as any artistry requires.

In this process of Laura's long-term therapy, many resistances come up, as is appropriate. Her resistance often takes the form of drifting, of abdicating responsibility for her life by expecting me to fix her and blaming the agency for her inability to practice therapy as she actually wants to.

Laura needs resistances to function, just as she needs her skin to contain her organs. Resistance is a part of the human condition. Laura will never be without resistance. Our work together calls into question the present resistances, makes room for new resistances, and moves toward accessing untapped potential in Laura.

By continuing to focus inwardly, Laura reaches new horizons of her latent potentials and uses them, consciously choosing how to be *a part of* and *apart from*. Inwardly she begins to feel at home inside of herself, allowing herself to be different in an environment that does not mirror her beliefs. Slowly, when she drifts she becomes more focused on what she actually wants to do with her talents, not only as a therapist but as a person living fully here and now. Inwardly she accesses her ability to listen to herself and chose from inside. Outwardly she starts a part-time private therapy practice using an eclectic approach. She remains at her government-based job on a part-time basis with a renewed sense of being herself in spite of restraining conditions.

A Psychotherapist Faces a Life-Threatening Illness:
The Case of Sara

For many psychotherapists, retirement is a time for appreciation of life. After helping others for years, we see retirement as a time when we can give to self, family, and friends. To some extent we can now choose the level of emotional concern we will hold for others and hopefully limit it during retirement. And, of course, retirement confronts us with a host of self-concerns: aging, health, money, loss of loved ones, and searching for new meanings in life.

Sara, as we shall call her, retired from a successful psychotherapy practice years before seeing me. She enjoyed excellent health and filled her days caring for her grandchildren and living out many other well-kept dreams.

A couple of months before she came to see me, she began having pain in her throat. Concerned, she sought medical advice. Initial tests showed nothing wrong. Very soon, though, this benign first diagnosis was followed by a diagnosis of life-threatening throat cancer.

When Sara comes for her first session, she looks shocked. Her eyes are wide, as if headlights are shining in them. In fact, life *is* shining headlights on her. She has been given what she considers a death sentence: a diagnosis of cancer. Her wide, moist eyes move me. I am acutely aware of her and my own reactions as she tells me the story of her diagnosis. A life-threatening diagnosis may enliven and intensify a therapeutic relationship.

Sara's experience brings back to me feelings associated with my husband. Within the last five years, he had been diagnosed with cancer and survived. I am not only a psychotherapist but the spouse of a cancer survivor. Does Sara know this? I do not know if she does, but *I* know. I have accompanied my husband and many clients on their journey with cancer. Some have survived, some have not. I have never accompanied a therapist on this journey before. Sara's arrival in my office moves me. It moves me out of my comfort zone of imagining life going on forever. My attention is drawn to Sara as she speaks.

"I am so frightened. My brother died from cancer. This diagnosis is a nightmare for me."

I settle into my chair, knowing and feeling Sara's fear. She has begun her therapeutic work. Her eagerness to search is palpable. Sara's illness is pushing her into difficult memories and prodding her into the present moment with fear. The emotions seem propelled by an intense search for meaning. What could this diagnosis mean? Sara has given a life of service to others, and now less than a year into retirement she receives a death sentence?

Sara's situation impacts me. My husband is not dead; in fact he is presently in excellent health. I have not been diagnosed with cancer. Will I be? Perhaps. True, I will die, but I do not know when or how. These thoughts cross my awareness as Sara reveals more of herself. She says, "I do not want the pain of this disease. I cannot believe I have this disease; I will not believe it."

Naturally Sara resists the diagnosis. Her anger is audible as her voice rises when she speaks. I bring her attention to her physical body.

"Sara, your eyes are alert and your voice is forceful as you describe your diagnosis."

We have begun to live the moment by drawing attention to what is actual: the language of her body in the moment. Sara is doing her therapy work by bringing her full presence into the moment. I am aware that I am doing my work by being present and by mirroring what she brings into the moment and by remembering that Sara is a colleague as well as a client. I trust that she can respond with self-exploration to my statement about her physical expression. She does not ask why we are not exploring her diagnosis but allows her awareness to expand into her body. "I know I must look very alert," she says. "I feel so frightened inside and angry. It feels right that my body is saying what is true for me inside. So many feelings are emerging. I cannot begin to say all of them."

"You have made a beginning."

We sit in silence. Yes, I am accompanying Sara on her journey. The silence has sealed our knowingness that we are on this journey together. In this moment I am aware that she is easy for me to reach. Sara's years of experience as a therapist give her immediate access to her own subjective world. Being in her presence is challenging, and I feel honored that she has chosen me to accompany her through this life-threatening experience.

I know well that Sara's journey could be my journey one day. Of course, it is not my journey *now*, but the similarities are there: I too am an aging therapist looking into my retirement years. I seem to have missed Sara's loss—the loss of a husband to cancer—but death is always in my awareness on some level, and it comes forward as I continue meeting Sara. I feel gratitude for Sara's arrival in my office. The moment is rich with aliveness and full awareness of the possibility of life being taken away.

Unique to This Therapy

From the beginning, we see that Sara and her situation call for the therapist to respond with a presence that is willing to travel into unknown territory. This is true for many clients, of course, but particularly so in a life-threatening situation. Sara in turn recognizes and openly accepts responsibility for self-exploration in this situation, probably in part from her training and experience in psychotherapy.

What is unique to this form of psychotherapy? What does this vignette show us about existential-humanistic psychotherapy? In it we see in action the ten commandments to the psychotherapist (Bugental, 1999) that form the foundation of existential-humanistic work:

1. Be there.
2. Insist that the client be there.
3. Listen and hear . . . more than you talk.
4. Don't let the words obscure the music.
5. When you do talk, keep it brief and uncluttered.
6. Always monitor the alliance.
7. Fit whatever you do to the context in the moment.
8. Don't ask for what can't be said.
9. Insist that the client be there.
10. Be there yourself.

It is no typo that these last two commandments are the same as the first two. They form the bedrock on which all the others are founded. These ten commandments provide a framework within which the therapist lives with the client in the moment. It is part of a stand we make with and for the client. In Greek this is called a *pou sto*, "where I stand."

My *pou sto* with Sara—in addition to these ten commandments—is that I believe she has the ability and resources within herself to face this diagnosis. I know that at times Sara will try my belief with resistance and self-doubts. My job—my *pou sto*—is steadfastly to hold this belief in her inner potential, even in the face of her possible death. Not only do I hold this belief myself, I help Sara access her own potential over and over and in a variety of situations. Thus we work through her resistance and access her latent potential to deal with this threat to her life.

We have touched Sara's potential in these brief few minutes, and we have met very little resistance. We have formed an alliance based on trust. It becomes the cornerstone of our work together.

Therapist Helps Therapist

Working with Sara is full of paradoxes. Who is helping whom? Are we helping each other to die? It certainly feels that way. Because we are close in age and I am looking at retirement, her situation continues to touch me in ways that are more mysterious than frightening. It seems I am being shown the opportunities of a life-threatening illness without actually having one. I am living it, yet I am not living it.

In the first stages of our work, I keep having a nagging sense that Sara does not really have the throat cancer she had been diagnosed with. Dealing with this sense is tricky. If I explore this nagging with my mind, it feels like wishful thinking or denial. In a feeling sense, though, the nagging has a larger knowing to it—larger because it keeps presenting itself to me with great certainty. I continue to feel from inside that this is not the right diagnosis. I decide to voice my concern.

"Sara, I am consistently feeling that there is something about your diagnosis that is not clear."

"Yes, I feel that way also. I think it is wishful thinking though. It is interesting that you have been having the same sensing about it."

"Yes, it is."

"My husband and I are going for a second opinion very soon to make sure this diagnosis is correct."

"Have you already scheduled this appointment?"

"Oh yes, we will be going next week."

In due time we find out that Sara has indeed been misdiagnosed. But now she has a diagnosis of a different terminal disease, but one that is far less threatening and has a longer life expectancy. With this diagnosis in place, the doctors are advising her to wait and see what may develop. This new diagnosis opens Sara into relief and a deep sense of mystery.

"Now I truly do not know what to think. Perhaps, if there is a lesson here, I should not think." Sara throws her head back and laughs infectiously, and I join her. We stop.

"What is happening, Sara?"

"It is funny, and it is not funny. I feel I am now placed in the very center of not knowing, not only with myself but now with the medical community. I feel alone and frightened."

"What is It?"

"It is my life, my life."

Suddenly, Sara is wide-eyed as if an alarm has gone off inside her. Her life expectancy is limited—or is it? We sit in another profound silence. In that silence my mind is full of unspoken questions. Perhaps Sara's mind is just as full in the same way, but I don't know that. I do know that the processes of both therapist and client are deeply interwoven at times. Somehow, we both knew the diagnosis was wrong. We both knew something was amiss. We both know we are dealing with the unknown.

The Case of the Missing Anger

Sara is beginning to assert her own life during her sessions, but she unwittingly slides into the role of the good client. She seems very attuned to her searching process and to expressing her inner world. Yet she expresses her right to be here only minimally. She appears excessively caring, a quality that is often well developed in therapists. She even understands why the doctors made the misdiagnosis. This caring as a therapist is becoming the resistance to her own untapped potential.

"Sometimes I wonder what I will do if this disease gets hold of me slowly and I end up losing my voice."

"So?"

"Well, not speaking will certainly cut short our sessions."

"So?"

Sara pauses and looks deeply into my eyes. She seems lost, not knowing what to say or do. This is the exact moment that holds a deep potential for Sara. She has mentioned her own personal loss and the potential loss of her therapy and now confronts the seeming loss of my kindness. Can she meet this moment with the vitality of her anger? Her pattern of care-taking others now breaks as she takes a deep breath and lets her anger come forth center stage.

" What do you mean 'so?' Does it matter to you at all that I will not be able to speak one day?"

"Does it matter to you? This is the important question."

"Of course it matters. My voice, my life matters to me, of course. I do not know how you see me, but my life matters a lot to me. My voice has been my profession in many ways for years. My voice is the way I express my inner self. If I lose that, I lose a lot. A lot, I tell you."

She is fighting now, ostensibly fighting me yet beginning to fight for her life. Her life is what truly matters to her. She is asserting her own desire to live, to live with a voice. She stops to see my response and continues.

"You know, I am not going to play my pleasing game with you. I do it all the time. What matters is me and my life, not you and how you might be responding to me. Yes, what we do here is important but not nearly as important as I am. I need to tell you that I am here for me. My life is important to me."

She is sitting straight and clearly in her own space as she speaks. In this moment Sara is not allowing herself to be subordinated in this therapy relationship. She is putting herself first, which is unusual for her, as it is for many therapists. Yes, she has lived the therapeutic relationship from both sides and knows the potency of pleasing. She is choosing her life in the moment, not in the future. Her voice is strong and clear. She is alive and present to this moment with the force of her anger helping her to fully be.

Sara has found herself in the unavoidably ambiguous state common to all persons in therapy. They must fight for their lives, and often they must fight the therapist. I want this vital force in the room. If Sara lives now, she must mobilize all the power she has, and anger is a part of her vital force—anger for what she's been handed: a disease that could take her voice, her discarded dreams, all the unknown moments she must now hold and live, and the possibility of losing her life. And there is always more.

Listening with a Third Ear

If I listen to the music of Sara's words, not just the words, I am listening with a "third ear," the ear that hears through the subtle realms of existence. I no longer focus on the notes of the music; I hear the melody and feel the emotions it awakens in me. Here is a woman who has devoted her life to helping others and now must help herself by facing her possible death. How she deals with her diagnosis touches both of us.

Facing death is a part of the human condition; we all know it, especially as we go for our annual physicals or mammograms. Death is not a popular subject in the halls of academia, yet it is a reality underlying our lives as we pore over books and attend seminars to gain insight into helping others.

I review Sara's case in a consultation with Dr. Bugental. He listens closely as I describe her, looks at me, and asks, "Have you considered how it will be for you if she dies?"

I stop and take a deep breath. Tears begin rolling down my face.

"Yes, I have. I will miss her. She is so very real. She touches me deeply."

He says nothing. He waits in that manner I have grown to know so well from our two decades of working together. I move deeper into the moment. "I am also aware that I will miss you when you die. You are also real and have helped me to be real with myself and others. Thank you."

To be real, what more can we ask from each other as therapists—or as human beings? Sometimes we must travel far to discover what is near.

ACKNOWLEDGMENT   To protect the identities of the clients mentioned in this chapter, all clients are disguised and all statements attributed to them are paraphrased.

NOTES

1. Unless otherwise indicated, all first-person singular pronouns refer to Dr. Heery.

REFERENCES

Bugental, J. F. T. (1965). *The search for authenticity*. New York: Holt, Rinehart, and Winston.
Bugental, J. F. T. (1987). *The art of the psychotherapist*. New York: Norton.
Bugental, J. F. T. (1999). *Psychotherapy isn't what you think*. Phoenix, AZ: Zieg, Tucker.
Heery, M. (2001). A humanistic perspective on bereavement. In K. J. Schneider, J. F. T. Bugental, & J. Fraser Pierson (Eds.), *The handbook of humanistic psychology*. Thousand Oaks, CA: Sage.
Heery, M., & Bugental, J. F. T. (1999). Unearthing the moment. *Self and Society*, *27*, 25–27.
May, R. (1969). *Love and will*. New York: Norton.
Yalom, I. (1980). *Existential psychotherapy*. New York: Basic Books.

22

CONDUCTING MARITAL AND FAMILY THERAPY WITH THERAPISTS

Harry J. Aponte

Marital and family therapy is essentially systemic in approach to people problems (Goldberg & Goldberg, 1996). It views clients in the context of family life and the social environment. The therapist is considered part of the therapeutic milieu, "an acting and reacting member of the therapeutic system" (Minuchin, 1974, pp. 90–91). When the client is another therapist, the salient dimension of the therapy is that therapist and client share a common professional identity and, often, a common professional community. This closes the personal distance between them, creating a delicate emotional situation for both therapist and client.

Moreover, in marital and family work, therapist-clients bring into the context their marriage partners and children and consequently enter the therapeutic relationship more vulnerable than they would be as individual patients. A colleague (the therapist) is looking behind the screen of the client's public role directly into the latter's domestic circumstances. Over and above the common anxiety of clients that their psychological flaws will expose them as dysfunctional to their therapists, these clinician-clients confront the prospect that in the eyes of the therapist their domestic problems will reflect on their professional competence. For the clinician-clients the worries may take the form not only of "What will my therapist think of me personally?" but also of "Will I look incapable of helping others if my own family life is so troubled?"

Further complicating treatment, on the other side of this therapeutic relationship, therapists may feel their reputations are on the line when they treat a colleague. In that sense, they too may experience a unique kind of vulnerability. Both therapist and clinician-client may feel some pressure to look good to the other in their counseling encounter.

THE PERSON OF THE THERAPIST

For therapists, the single most significant factor affecting the treatment of other clinicians is the therapist's own person. Today's marital and family therapy is active, drawing therapists into a dynamic engagement with their clients. Therapists use themselves with all their life experience in their healing role (Aponte & Winter, 2000; Satir, 2000). Their empathic identification with the humanity of their clients helps them understand and relate to their clients' struggles. When working with other clinicians, therapists take on the added challenge of sharing a professional identity. This additional dimension challenges therapists to be well grounded personally and secure professionally as they venture into the world of their fellow professionals.

Identification

Therapists encounter themselves at multiple levels in their clients' lives as they work with the domestic difficulties of their clients' family lives (Aponte, 1994b). In particular, when *joining* in the therapeutic relationship within family therapy (Aponte & VanDeusen, 1981) it is necessary that therapists allow themselves to walk and feel with their clients. In the case of therapists' sharing a professional identity with clients, they are open to many possible points of common professional experiences and personal emotions—so much so that family therapists worry about being connected too closely with the clinician-client over other family members. On the other hand, therapists may experience so much need to look competent before their colleague-clients that they risk feeling competitive with them, finding themselves in a one-upmanship game. Therapist-clients are inclined to feed this competitive environment if they overfunction in the therapy because they fear looking incompetent in the presence not only of another therapist but also of their own families. For therapists, this same-trade identification on top of the human connection presents an opportunity to see and understand because of a shared experience but also a dangerous trap for overidentifying and emotional overinvestment.

Vicariously Experiencing Our Wounds

All therapists come close to their own personal and family wounds in the hurts and failures of their clients (Aponte, 1998a). To relate to their clients' hurts, they need to permit themselves to recall and feel their own. This means that therapists are called to exercise their skills while standing in emotional currents of their own vulnerabilities. With therapist-clients, they are also likely to encounter clients' troubles that touch on their own clinical triumphs and failures, past and present. The chances are that in their

clients' family lives, they will come upon those common personal/profes-
sional issues of competing careers between spouses, and upon clinical schedules that rob evening time from spouse and children. They may even meet
children, much like their own, who complain that their parents talk more
like therapists than like parents to them. At the purely human level, they
come face-to-face with therapist-clients' failing marriages, or clients'
acting-out, troubled youngsters—all possibly touching on their own family
troubles, even as they must be grounded in their personal competence.
Therapists are drawn into their same-trade clients' experiences at deeper
and multiple levels. Their task as therapists is to be open and connected to
their own domestic and professional difficulties in ways that foster empathy with their clients' struggles and, paradoxically, their own therapeutic
competence. With therapist-clients they will need to utilize this empathy
along with their own human vulnerability at a highly challenging professional level in a sensitive and complex therapeutic relationship.

Intensity of Therapeutic Relationships

Therapists relate to clients at a human level within their professional roles.
They engage with their clients at a people level. In so doing they inevitably
reveal parts of themselves, if only traces of their thinking, emotions, values,
and history (Aponte, 1994a, pp. 147–168). They like and dislike them;
agree and disagree with them; cry with and struggle for control with them.
While exposing something of their own humanity, therapists are aware
that their colleague-clients are also taking measure of their performance
in their professional roles. Therapists come up against the task of balancing the personal engagement with their clinician-clients with an alertness
to the simultaneous professional role-taking. This is an especially delicate
multidynamics factor when the therapists practice in the same community, where reputation matters.

On the professional level, clinician-clients may or may not share the
same professional discipline or adhere to the same school of therapy.
Therapists encounter their clients' similar or opposing ideas about what
is pathological or healthy living, what is therapeutically helpful or not. It
is impossible for their clinician-clients not to think as therapists at various points in their personal treatment. These clients inevitably think and
react like fellow therapists.

Clinician-clients, more often than not, also feel a need to be acknowledged for their skill status by their therapists, especially in the presence of
their families, even as they expose their human frailties. Therapists have to
relate to clinician-clients with spouse and family as people in trouble, but
always with an awareness of the clinician-clients' professional and personal
self-esteem. The presence of their families intensifies the emotional charge
of these interactions. This extra dimension of relating to the client's occupation presents another opportunity to reach the patient but also a potentially troublesome obstacle to a successful therapeutic relationship.

BEING CENTERED

There is no greater challenge for therapists of therapists than to be grounded within their own professional and personal lives. All therapists are faced with the need to both identify and differentiate with clients (Bowen, 1972). The work with therapist-clients and their families adds layers of complexity to identifying and differentiating in the therapeutic relationship, and calls for therapists to be particularly well centered within themselves. What, then, does it mean to be so centered in therapy?

First, therapists to be grounded in their designated helping roles are called to articulate for themselves an inner sense of their spiritual, philosophical and professional values (Aponte, 1994a, 1995, 1998b). These values identify, define and set the standards for therapists' views of the objective reality of human experience, the functions of social structures like family, and morally appropriate ideals for human behavior. Postmodern constructivist philosophy questions contemporary views about reality (Held, 1995). Radical feminism raises doubts about the value of marriage and family (Goldner, 1985). Today's perspectives on circularity in therapy potentially undermine the significance of the individual's moral responsibility (Aponte, 1994a). All therapists conduct therapy from a philosophical base, however conscious or explicated. Clarity about values facilitates their remaining well-anchored within themselves as they navigate through their clients' moral struggles about life's choices and familial relationships. Knowing their value base helps therapists speak from their philosophical convictions while also differentiating from their clients' values, no matter how otherwise identified with them.

A second and essential base to being grounded is therapists' connection to their own trade and personal life struggles. On a professional level, therapists are always confronting new techniques and theories that profess to improve on what they already practice. Therapists question their own treatment approaches as they are exposed to novel ideas. Moreover, all therapists face ambiguous outcomes or outright failure in the therapy they conduct. These working vicissitudes help shape their self-perception and self-esteem in the role of therapist. The issue is of special relevance when therapists try to hold onto a sense of competence in light of the challenge that therapy with therapists and their families represents.

Therapists are also on their own individual life journeys. Their own positive growth and neurotic hangups, their family triumphs and failures, all color how they think about their clients' lives and use themselves strategically with clients. Their life philosophies toward their own domestic challenges will affect how they relate to their clients' efforts to deal with their personal and family problems. Therapists' honesty with themselves about their own issues and the clarity of their approach to these life themes, as well as how energetically they contend with their difficulties, keep them grounded within their individual boundaries as they engage with their clients' struggles.

In each clinical encounter, therapists also find direct personal challenges to themselves in their relationships with clients. Because of the close identification with other professionals, interactions with their families are more highly charged. Therapists are called to manage themselves actively and therapeutically within their interactions with clients. To so manage themselves they need to observe themselves from within, and be in touch with the associations bestirred by what they see and hear in session.

Family therapists know that with couples and families they do not have as much control of the therapeutic environment as in individual therapy. In an individual therapy, they relate to clients in a single, two-way interactional street. In marital and family situations, many paths are trekked at once among family members and the therapist. Therapists who are well plugged into their own journeys will not get lost on the paths they walk with their clients. Therapists aware of and consciously committed to their own journeys are better able to accept their clients' freedom to choose their own answers.

There is mystery in the human heart, and certainly in the human relationship. In a marriage or family where there is the intention of a lifelong commitment, people's destinies are linked at the root of the human connection (Aponte & DiCesare, 2000). Therapists may view the individual heart and the intimacy of marriage and family from outside but never quite from within. Therapists' roles mandate that they foster differentiation and clients' freedom to determine their own destinies. To do so therapists must have some connection to the mystery in their own lives. Pursuing meaning in the pain and struggles of their own journeys allows them to empathically identify with their craft-fellows and speak from their particular convictions while relating to clients with the freedom of differentiation.

THIS THERAPIST

Other therapists are apt to consider an experienced psychotherapist such as myself, with decades supervising, training, and presenting workshops, safe enough for them to consult with. And a solo practice such as mine offers those therapists the prospect of a more private and confidential environment. They are risking much in taking their families to therapy and look for assurances of both therapeutic competence and emotional safety.

We all have encountered our shares of vicissitudes working with therapist-clients. However, age and experience foster confidence in dealing with colleagues. During our own raw youth we feel more acutely the stresses and pulls of treating other therapists and their families. Working with their families, in particular, feels close and engenders emotional vulnerability. When therapists' families participate, it is not as easy to make allowances for the client's professional sensitivities. Family members not directly involved in the therapist-client's clinical practice are initially often more disposed than the professional family member to engage frankly around difficult domestic issues. Therapeutic work with other clinicians and their families, especially those we have known in some other context, can turn out to be some of the most demanding therapeutic challenges we face as therapists to therapists.

My philosophy is that there is no greater asset for this challenging task than the evolution of a therapist's own spirituality. Nouwen (1975) speaks to the ability "to perceive and understand this world from a quiet inner center" (p. 38). Frankl addresses spirituality from the perspective of *meaning* (1963). Finding meaning in one's own life allows a therapist "the inner freedom and personal value," as Frankl puts it (p. 79), to remain rooted within one's own self while also being able "to grasp another human being in the innermost core of his personality" through the act of love (p. 176). Caring about a troubled client means to me being prepared to suffer with the client, by genuinely caring about the client's pain while also empathizing through an inner connection with one's own journey of tears, *the wounded healer* (Nouwen, 1972, pp. 87–89). For this suffering to serve the purpose of caring, we reach into its *deepest meaning* (Frankl, p. 178), in the meaning our spirituality lends it. This "selfless outgoing love" (Nouwen, 1992, p. 126) forms the basis of Nouwen's (1975) notion of hospitality that cares with freedom, "not a subtle invitation to adopt the life style of the host, but the gift of a chance for the guest to find his own" (pp. 73–74).

The challenge of the intimate (Aponte, 1998a) work of therapy with those who are most like us and share some facet of life with us lies in the paradox of identifying closely with them while remaining well grounded in the identity and meaning of our own lives.

Some Examples

José is a social worker and family therapist who shares my Puerto Rican ethnicity as well as life in the same South Bronx neighborhood. He comes with a troubled marriage. His wife is also a therapist. José suffers from the downside of having to hustle on one's own as a kid, depending too much on one's self, and not knowing how to lean on others. The son of migrant parents, whose native tongue is not English, he may have to represent himself when negotiating life with the community, for example, at his school. Living in a neighborhood like the South Bronx means that he may have to maneuver around turfs, and pick and choose with whom he will hang out not just for friendship's sake but also for personal safety. If he has personal tastes that do not fit with his crowd, like a serious interest in art, he may have to make trips on his own to the Metropolitan Museum of Art. He learns to manage on his own. Problems at home may mean that he keeps it all to himself. In later years, this background may not help intimacy in his marriage.

I can readily empathize with José's wife's criticisms of him because I understand all too well the chisel marks on one's personality of having to depend on one's self to overcome a tough early life plus minority status. The shared background with José allows me to know all too well how he is struggling and to speak to it in such a way that he knows in his gut he is understood. There is no hiding here. Yet, while I have been there, I am also somewhere else now, and can challenge his rationalizations and avoidances.

The trust built on shared identity permits strong confrontations, but the presence of his wife in such an exposure by a fellow therapist and paisano also strips him to a level of vulnerability he might not have with another therapist. This is a Latin man, and there is some pride of manhood here. Will he feel humiliated? The wire this therapist must balance on is very thin and very high above ground. I can only expose him in the presence of his wife if I also expose my own similar struggles so that we identify publicly not only in the common heritage of which we are proud but also in our common flaws. Both our struggles with our pasts are exposed in the presence of his wife. Wife, therapist-client, and therapist must all work within the tensions of our flaws and strengths, our handicaps and our accountabilities. I muddle around in these paradoxes while reminding myself that they will need to decide what to do with all they are understanding and experiencing in the therapeutic process. My experience is my own, and the decisions I have made around these same insights are my own. His marriage is distinct and his own. As much as therapist and client share in common, they are different, and their destinies will be played out in their distinctly separate paths. Learn to identify but also to let go.

David is another family therapist who came with some marital troubles but with a principal concern about his adolescent daughter, who was emotionally impulsive and prone to becoming involved in injudicious relationships with young men. David and I shared almost nothing in terms of our ethnic backgrounds, families of origin, and home communities. However, we had known each other professionally through a number of professional coincidences. David was experienced, competent, and competitive. His wife was not a therapist. Both his wife and his daughter had felt the intrusiveness of David's professional views on their personal lives. Now David faced a therapist he had chosen because he trusted his competence, but also someone who might challenge him openly in the presence of his family. Wife and daughter would not know whether the therapist would be able to see their viewpoints when they saw things differently from David, whom they knew had some vague professional association with the therapist.

I knew much was expected of me by the various members of the family. I also knew that I would need to monitor my own competitiveness, having deep roots more in the old habit of striving to survive more than in any need to shine professionally. In addition, the subtle theme of dealing with ethnic and socioeconomic difference of a white family with a middle-class background from this Puerto Rican from a New York barrio. Moreover, this was a spiritually secular family who held more liberal moral standards than I. These differences would come to a head when questions came up about the kind of freedom to give their daughter around sex and boys, but also about responsibility and accountability about the girl's use of money. The parents were less inclined to set black-and-white expectations than I was. Yet my clinical bias, influenced by my own cultural and religious background, was that this young woman needed less negotiation of rules and conditions and more structure with clearer consequences. The girl herself complained to me that I was too conservative in my moral views, which she was smart enough to perceive even when I did not explicitly profess them.

My dilemma was how to be myself with them where I believed it could help them, and when to leave them to their own devices. I needed first to allow myself to reach into my own life, and draw from the common themes of also being married and having a daughter who had not long ago passed through her adolescence. They all needed to feel that common humanity with me because I would also be challenging their child-raising standards and practices. Before proposing my child-rearing values, however, I needed to listen to them as they were, and not through the thick filter of my own life experience. I had to listen and to ask and to communicate a real understanding. Then I could run what I was hearing through my personal (ethnic and religious background) and professional filters (because my structural orientation to family therapy also inclined me to attend to rules and structure). Next I needed to be sure that the tentative conclusions I was reaching about what the family needed were well grounded in clinical goals, not in my preferences. When, finally, I was to communicate my observations and suggestions, I led with my clinical assessment that not just the therapist father could make sense of but also his wife and daughter. These comments were then followed by a disclaimer—that these opinions were influenced by my own personal and professional biases. It was for them to weigh my views and decide whether they fit for them. They would have to decide what to do because they must live with the consequences of their decisions. The father said he was relieved that I did not hold back with him. He wanted a therapist who would be direct with him. His own strength of personality and professional reputation discouraged dissenting views to his own. An environment that encouraged free expression of views and values supported the wife/mother to assert her perspectives with both her husband and her daughter. The daughter had repeatedly voiced the criticism that her mother was too accommodating to her father's thinking. The daughter still complained that I was trying to restrict her but then threw in a story about a girlfriend of hers who was getting herself in trouble with guys because her therapist was too easy with her.

CONCLUSION

The challenges to the person of the therapist that therapy presents are compounded by the added level of shared professional identity and community when therapists work with therapist-clients and their families. The call to be able to identify at both personal and professional levels is essential. So is the need to differentiate so that clients can connect with us even as they make their own choices about their lives within the context of the close relationships and work they are doing with their colleague therapists. Therapists face the ever-repeated call to know themselves. They are also to have such a grasp on their own personal life struggles that, from a well-centered place, they are able to empathize while also challenging their therapist-clients within their family contexts. All this implies allowing a personal and professional vulnerability on the part of therapists, coupled with a security about their personal journeys and professional identities that make for openness with well-defined boundaries.

ACKNOWLEDGMENT   Theresa Romeo-Aponte helped in the preparation of this chapter.

REFERENCES

Aponte, H. J. (1994a). *Bread and spirit: Therapy with the new poor.* New York: Norton.

Aponte, H. J. (1994b). How personal can training get? *Journal of Marital and Family Therapy, 20,* 3–15.

Aponte, H. J. (1995, Fall). Political bias, moral values, and spirituality in the training of psychotherapists. *Bulletin of the Menninger Clinic, 60,* 488–502.

Aponte, H. J. (1998a). Intimacy in the therapist-client relationship. In W. J. Matthews & J. H. Edgette (Eds.), *Current thinking and research in brief therapy: Solutions, strategies, narratives* (Vol. 2, pp. 1–27). Philadelphia: Taylor and Francis.

Aponte, H. J. (1998b). Love, the spiritual wellspring of forgiveness: An example of spirituality in therapy. *Journal of Family Therapy, 20,* 37–58.

Aponte, H. J. (1999). The stresses of poverty and the comfort of spirituality. In F. Walsh (Ed.), *Spiritual resources in family therapy* (pp. 76–89). New York: Guilford.

Aponte, H. J., & DiCesare, E. J. (2000). Structural theory. In F. M. Dattilio & L. Bevilacqua (Eds.), *Comparative treatment of couples problems.* (pp. 45–57). New York: Springer.

Aponte, H. J., & VanDeusen, J. M. (1981). Structural family therapy. In A. S. Gurman & D. P. Kniskern (Eds.), *Handbook of family therapy* (pp. 310–360). New York: Brunner/Mazel.

Aponte, H. J., & Winter, J. E. (2000). The person and practice of the therapist. In M. Baldwin (Ed.), *The use of self in therapy* (2nd ed., pp. 127–165). New York: Haworth.

Bowen, M. (1972). Toward a differentiation of a self in one's family. In James L. Framo (Ed.), *Family interaction* (pp. 111–173). New York: Springer.

Frankl, V. E. (1963). *Man's search for meaning.* New York: Washington Square Press.

Goldenberg, I., & Goldenberg, H. (1996). *Family therapy: An overview* (4th ed.). Pacific Grove, CA: Brooks/Cole.

Goldner, V. (1985). November/December). Warning: Family therapy may be hazardous to your health. *Family Therapy Networker, 9,* 18–23.

Held, B. S. (1995). *Back to reality.* New York. Norton.

Minuchin, S. (1974). *Families and family therapy.* Cambridge, MA: Harvard University Press.

Nouwen, H. J. M. (1972). *The wounded healer.* New York: Doubleday.

Nouwen, H. J. M. (1975). *Reaching out.* New York: Doubleday.

Nouwen, H. J. M. (1992). *The return of the prodigal son.* New York: Doubleday.

Satir, V. (2000). The therapist story. In M. Baldwin (Ed.), *The use of self in therapy* (2nd ed., pp. 17–28). New York: Haworth.

23

GROUP THERAPY FOR THERAPISTS IN GESTALT THERAPY TRAINING
A Therapist-Trainer's Perspective

PHILIP LICHTENBERG

The therapy that I am describing here is group therapy with trained and practicing psychotherapists. Some of these folks are in the early stages of their careers, but most have been active for some time and are now planning to acquire a new skill or a new orientation. They are interested in learning about Gestalt therapy with the intention of becoming Gestalt therapists or enhancing their work by learning how to conduct Gestalt therapy. Since I retrained as a Gestalt therapist nearly 20 years ago after studying, practicing, and teaching psychoanalytic therapy for the previous 20-odd years, I have a sense of affinity for the joys and challenges of such an undoing and rebuilding process. Similarly, because I trained as both a clinical and a social psychologist, worked for a decade in interdisciplinary research, and taught for 35 years in social work and psychology departments, I can relate easily to psychologists and social workers who make up the bulk of our trainees at the Gestalt Therapy Institute of Philadelphia, where this group therapy proceeds. Between this group therapy inside our training program, on which I will elaborate, and my part-time private practice working with individuals and couples, I estimate that 70% of my current work is devoted to therapy with persons who are themselves psychotherapists. It was not always so, obviously, and I can attribute this current situation to age and experience as much as to anything else.

The composition of the groups is much like that of the professions of psychology and social work: mostly women, mostly white, ages ranging from thirties to sixties, and orientations varying from behavioral to family systems to psychoanalytic.

307

As one of four trainers[1] who deal with these groups, I can say only why *I* believe they select us as therapists. My colleagues may have other ideas about this. One factor is our reputation as a training program. Like a good university, we benefit from having had excellent trainees who spread the word about their experience in the program. Many of the trainees have already experienced one or more of us: in classrooms where we teach; in our private practices; in professional programs we sponsor; in introductory faculty workshops over a weekend, in which we demonstrate how we conduct our groups; and in other continuing education workshops and seminars. Very few persons come into our program without some previous contact with us. Thus, the individuals who participate in this group therapy have had extensive forecontact with us. They will have been oriented to how we work, how we ask them what they want, how we examine jointly whether we can work together, and so on.

MIXED EMOTIONS

While many of our participants are committed and primed for therapeutic work, they are also, like clients in general, significantly ambivalent about entering the process. They are probably even more open and vocal in their ambivalence, since part of our orienting them is to invite difference and criticism of us. We will ask: "What don't you like about what you have seen or heard of us?" The ambivalence persists through the whole three-year training. Members come in on Friday night when they are tired. They give up a whole weekend a month when they would otherwise be with family and friends. Family members may resent their absence, their excitement, or what they learn is happening in the therapy.

Probably most significant for the ongoing ambivalence is the deep and powerful work that takes place in the therapy. For any therapy to be effective, I believe, it must arouse strong emotions—anxiety, rage, love, jealousy, distrust, nausea, and disgust—and the anticipation of intense times with unpredictable sessions rouses ambivalence.

Most weekends begin with one or many members voicing their negative concerns during the check-in period. The simple, quiet acceptance of negative feelings, indeed the expectation that some members will not fully want to be present, affects the psychotherapy in two important ways. First, we are supporting the "no" function of the individual, which is promoting the development of ego function. In Gestalt therapy, healthy ego function is conceived as significantly alienating and extruding what is unwanted and identifying and approaching what is desirable in the present moment. Second, we are fostering the person's comfort with and ability to stay with strong feelings, negative feelings as well as positive ones. To experience and say one's strong emotions and to stay in contact with an other when that person is experiencing emotions intensely are both viewed as positive, growth-making activities. Group therapy especially facilitates each of these processes, since what one person in the group experiences is usually shared by others; support is never far away.

Most Sunday evenings of the training find the participants tired and full of a new sense of possibility. When sessions formally end, members do not usually leave quickly but instead gather in small groups and finish more privately.

GROUP CHARACTERISTICS

The size of the therapy groups ranges from 7 to 16 persons, sizes optimal for small group functioning. Groups smaller than six or seven persons, we have found, require too much from the members in the way we do the training. For example, with a smaller group than this, participants feel compelled to perform at each meeting, which minimizes choice and presents problems of its own. With groups larger than this, some individuals would remain invisible beyond what is both challenging and useful for them. The optimal small group size promotes diversity as well as intimacy, the opportunity for dealing with various kinds of difference as well as intense closeness and ongoing mutual support. Since both autonomy and homonomy, separateness and togetherness are vital components of lively relationships in the view of the theory of Gestalt therapy (Angyal, 1965, Lichtenberg, 1991), group size is an important element of the training and the therapy. The ability to invent, create, and define oneself in social relationships *and* the ability to lose oneself as part of a larger entity depend on the possibility that such a group size presents.

THE TRAINING PROGRAM

The training program is three years long. The group meets one weekend a month for nine months each year. Two-thirds of the sessions include Friday nights, and all involve six hours of session on Saturdays and Sundays. The work is divided into three main segments: theory presentation on Friday nights and Saturday mornings; practice, in which trainees function as therapists, clients, and observers on Saturday afternoon, or present cases from their practice; group experiential—the group therapy of this chapter—all day Sunday. Because Gestalt therapy is derived in part from the progressive education of John Dewey, the experiential and cognitive learning with the therapy are interwoven. In his discussion of education for democracy, Dewey (1916) placed a heavy emphasis on building understanding on top of experience. Similarly, he tied growth to developments in the realm of direct experience. Thus, in the times of focus on theory, exercises and experiments are often conducted to illustrate the theory under study. And in the experiential sessions on Sundays, the leader will often respond to questions and interests concerning the theory that guided the work the leader has done with an individual, with several members, or with the group as a whole. These discussions of the theoretical underpinning of the work some-times add a cognitive component to the experience of the individual who has worked or that of the group as a whole.

The intermixture of theory and experience means that the group therapy within an educational program is somewhat different from group therapy in a Gestalt therapy mode more generally. We do not usually tell our cli-ents about the theory we use in meeting them, though we could do so; maybe we should even think of doing this more often as a method of keep-ing to the equality of client and therapist that guides our efforts. If one does this, care must be taken not to depersonalize one's actions as a therapist. In individual therapy outside the training program, I often do use theory explicitly.

Another aspect of this connection between experience and theory is our view that changing experience in the present is more vital to growth than understanding the origin and nature of one's problems. If *this time* the therapist/trainee experiences differently around a pattern that had been created earlier by that person in a perceived emergency—if he or she envi-sions new alternatives to a locked-in way of being—that person may assimi-late the experience, feel more an agent of his or her life, and grow into a new faith in self and the world.

To say that experience is more productive of growth than is understand-ing is not to be antiintellectual or antitheoretical. Some folks in the early days of Gestalt therapy, both inside the field and as observers of it, were indeed antiintellectual, but the founders and best practitioners of Gestalt therapy were and are sophisticated in the theories of psychotherapy. Psy-choanalysts and New York intellectuals who were educators, philosophers, social thinkers, and poets—Frederick Perls, Laura Perls, Elliot Shapiro, Paul Weitz, Paul Goodman, and Isadore From—created Gestalt therapy, and they grounded the therapy very much in the theory of the time.

Because the theory and experiential work are ever connected, when participants come to a Sunday experiential session, they are often quite ready to work on expanding their awareness and experimenting with new ways of being in the sessions. The exercises in theory presentation and being a client in abbreviated sessions with fellow trainees engage the individuals personally and act as forecontact and ground for the Sunday sessions. The group therapy experience builds on a priming background.

Because Gestalt therapy centers on how people experience regulating themselves in social life and influencing their contact with others, rather than on solving a given personal problem, the group sessions are less tied to exploring something decided on before the therapy ensues. The prim-ing of the previous days is just that: readiness to engage in learning about one's awareness, that is, one's modes of experiencing and constructing experiences. We say to the therapists/trainees that they do not need to come with a trouble or problem to work with a leader or the group, although they may bring such a matter with them. Simply following one's experi-ence or a group process will invariably lead to moments when people limit their experience (to a temporary loss of ego function) and thus to an opportunity to do otherwise with added support and challenge. Probably more than in a typical group therapy, then, trainees are prepared for personality change rather than solutions to the problems in their lives. The therapy is aimed at providing them with a fuller use of their own resources. With fewer or less intrusive losses of healthy ego function, the self-regulating propensities of individuals are trusted in their solving of problems they face.

THERAPISTS IN THERAPY

This readiness for change in personality is correlated with the fact that most psychotherapists are relatively healthy in a psychological sense. While the members of this group therapy endeavor vary considerably in their emotional well-being, the bias is toward the upper range of functioning. Some members of the group have serious problems, though none are psychotic, and even the most highly functioning individuals carry significant limitations to creative living. The therapy process does not lack for challenges to participants and leaders alike. Abuse, molestation, rape, eating disorders, panic attacks, suspiciousness, and so forth are common issues that arise in the work. Yet, possibly because a significant number of these persons have had extensive therapy in their past, or maybe because *relatively* healthy people enter the field of psychotherapy, or even because only well enough individuals self-select into this program, the tendency is to have effective persons interacting in the therapy.

In respect to this bias, three further comments can be made. First, psychotherapists in this group therapy who are more troubled have a better-than-average holding environment. Second, change from the beginning to the ending over three years (162 hours) of the therapy is often profound. Third, boundary issues between therapist and client can be treated more in terms of ongoing relationship rather than from strict rules developed by outside authorities.

Because all members experience intense feelings and undergo strong challenges to established patterns of behavior, more unstable individuals do not appear as exceptional within these groups as they do in everyday life. Being less outside the norms sometimes weakens felt shame and allows these persons to stay with their ways of behaving over longer periods. Further, they are the recipients of considerably more support than they are accustomed to receiving. While some of these folks leave the group prematurely, and others are often tempted to leave, and some are caught in scapegoating processes, the attention to group process and the willingness of group members to own their reactions combine to make this a unique holding environment. Much of the isolation and despair of troubled persons in the everyday world arises because most persons around them are not prepared to deal openly with either group relations in the here and now or their own reactions to stormy behaviors.

Psychotherapists are not only themselves objects of projections; they frequently project upon their clients as well (Gibbons, Lichtenberg, & van Beusekom, 1994). Dealing with their own projecting tendencies brings those who are more emotionally mature into greater equality and community with those less mature. The successes of therapeutic community in the past (Jones, 1968) can be attributed to such a supportive holding environment. The presence of highly functioning individuals, accordingly, is a critical element in the therapeutic work.

One of the great sources of pride and pleasure for a therapist is being witness to the growth and unfolding of clients, particularly those who are not only clients but also psychotherapists. That persons who are relatively well off make excellent use of psychotherapy is an established observation. They are more trusting and hopeful, more willing to risk, and more able to assimilate and utilize the experiences of the therapeutic process. Typically, our therapist-patient participants can remember several memorable, transforming moments over long periods of time. Remembering such moments is itself a further assimilation of the experience. Gestalt therapy is built around the creation of a "safe emergency" (Perls, Hefferline, & Goodman, 1951). The quality of *emergency* recapitulates the time when habitual coping patterns that were once appropriate became locked in and, now aroused anew, are less than fully adapted to the ongoing, present situation. The past sense of emergency is brought back to life. The quality of *safe* means that this time there is enough support to create an opportunity for a more age-appropriate, value-consistent, ego-syntonic response to the challenging context. Since some of what makes the present situation safe derives from the already developed self-support of the participant, the therapeutic process is effective in enabling significant personal growth.

COLLEGIALITY AND BOUNDARIES

Boundary issues are a main concern in all therapeutic endeavors. Because Gestalt therapy focuses explicitly the nature and quality of the contact between client and therapist, attention to these issues is a regular component of the therapy. The contexts of contacting and the possibilities and limitations of contacting are not set by rules and regulations but rather are matters of negotiation and open communication. (The anarchist background of Gestalt therapy that came directly from Paul Goodman and indirectly from the radical experience of Fritz Perls is relevant here.) As already indicated, training and psychotherapy overlap in this program. Some participants are in individual therapy with one or another of the faculty members; others are in supervision or consultation groups or in classes.

Gestalt therapists regularly disclose their own experiences, whether these are reactions to the client's work or matters that naturally come into play in the process. Rather than being hidden or mysterious figures, Gestalt therapists tend to be transparent and available. For example, Isadore From, one of Gestalt therapy's founders, would deal with what he considered a projection in the following way. "You seem to experience X thusly, while I experience it in this other way. Let us see how and why our experiences differ (personal communication, 1983). He did not pose his own experience as superior; it was considered to be simply different. Connections at social events between clients and therapists are common. After the training program ends, therapist and client may have continuing encounters as colleagues and friends.

The critical elements in dealing with boundary issues are openness, directness, meeting as equals, avoiding exploitation, and mutual respect. These elements cannot be legislated but must be newly created in the contacting process. Living by externally imposed rules limits the creative adjustments that come from personal contact. That said, we pay significant attention to ethical issues around boundary concerns throughout the training. We emphasize living out the critical elements just noted not to conform to laws so much as to practice respectful, honorable therapy.

In order for therapists who are therapist-patients in a therapy/training group to become collegial with me, their therapist, a developmental process must typically happen. This process extends over the several years of therapy and beyond it, and the process has some ironic qualities. Early on, the therapist-patients function as clients/trainees. They must bracket their customary role as authority as professional therapist and adopt the position of one who is ready to be influenced. In my experience, it is the most accomplished therapists, those furthest along in the profession, who seem most ready to open themselves to the therapeutic encounters. They come into the program primed to be affected by it, whereas clients in general and relatively new therapists are reserved, if not defensive. Accordingly, a significant part of the early work consists of orientation toward being a client, a position not usually seen as collegial.

Because this is a group therapy in which individuals are working separately in the group with the therapist, as well as through interaction with the group as a whole, a special issue in the orientation process involves the individual-therapist dyad in relation to the rest of the group. The group members are asked to attend to and reflect on their own reactions during an individual's work and to use the awareness they have if they wish to learn from that work. They may also think about how they would conduct the therapy if they were in the role of therapist. This is a preliminary way of being collegial with me when they are observing me working with one of their peers. They are asked, however, not to continue the therapeutic work when the individual-therapist dyad has completed a piece of work. The individual is to be allowed to assimilate the experience.

Gestalt therapy is viewed by many of its practitioners as a way of living as well as a form of psychotherapy. Thus, to become a client and a Gestalt therapist is to enter a new culture of sorts. Since equalitarianism is one characteristic promulgated by Gestalt therapists, collegiality is fostered through the way the therapist does the therapy.

Nothing is more important to this activity than disclosure by the leader of his or her own experience. Among the revelations that are most influential in promoting equality are those in which I acknowledge or display strong feelings and moments of great vulnerability. Following Hellmuth Kaiser (1965), who insisted that the therapist must not ever leave the client emotionally, I as a Gestalt therapist go to where the therapist/trainee is emotionally engaged and stay with that person in that experience. Not to solve my client's depression but to be with the client in that depression is a method for supporting the client and trusting that his or her creativity will find a way out of the depression. To be this time sad as the client is sad and to assure the client that both of us will be all right is one form of help that promotes feeling equal and ready to be colleagues. Or to stay emotionally attuned with the client, though not experiencing exactly what the client feels, can be another form of support.

More directly engaging the therapist/trainee as a colleague is the evaluation process used in the eighth of every nine sessions. Each participant is called on to evaluate every other member of the group, including me as group leader. Members are asked to speak both to the strengths and gains they have observed and to those matters where there is room for improvement. Learning to provide thoughts on other persons that are true and useful and that can be assimilated by the others is a development in ego function and also a ground for collegiality with peers and group leader. This task is customarily anticipated and carried out with significant anxiety. We are not accustomed, even as psychotherapists, to the mutual evaluation of each other in the fullness of our strengths and limitations. Such a level of intimacy as a two-way street is not the typical coin of psychotherapy, though again this was central to Jones's (1968) conception of therapeutic community.

In the third year of the group therapy, the therapists/trainees and I function on an equal level in additional ways. Trainees take on the role of group leader in their peer group for some of the sessions. When I am present, I function as a participant-observer in the activity. Similarly, in the third year, trainees may colead other groups in the program with me. In this situation we are partners in the work, helping each other, questioning each other, and so forth. On occasion I have coled groups outside the program with one of the members of the training program.

This unfolding as a junior colleague occurs not only during the group therapy experience but also for some years subsequently. Becoming a Gestalt therapist takes time, and during the years they are developing this way of life, trainees increasingly give over authority to me while also taking on more authority in their own work.

MENTORING

In the same way that, under healthy child-rearing, one's children become one's friends in adulthood, so too one's therapists/trainees become one's peers as part of the developmental process by which they become Gestalt therapists. Mentoring is a significant component in this process. Since I encourage each Gestalt therapist to rely on his or her own special qualities and interests, mentoring in this group therapy centers on supporting the therapists/trainees in finding and inventing who they are. The therapists/trainees are also supported in relying on this self-definition in the therapy work they practice outside the training. Some participants prefer to rely on the use of language in dialogic encounters, while others are body-centered and still others are inclined toward nonverbal communication. While each Gestalt therapist utilizes all of these modes of contact, dependence on one's own strengths is facilitated in the mentoring activity. To be a successful mentor in this context, I, as a group leader, must follow my own bent and use my own ego functions to the fullest while supporting the therapist/trainee in doing the same.

If the therapist/trainee has come with a dramatically different theoretical orientation, I do not focus on the differences between that orientation and Gestalt therapy. Instead, I pay attention to the ways of being embedded in that perspective and how these can be realized in the practice of Gestalt therapy. While Gestalt therapy is not directly aimed at changing behavior or creating different cognitive patterns, the trainee's expertise in observing behavior or cognitive style can be used in exploring the structure of his or her own client's experience. Interruptions of contact via behavioral or cognitive methods can be observed and worked with. Gestalt therapy in its origins was eclectic, so it is not intolerant of alternative approaches to psychotherapy, though it has its own internal structure. Accordingly, having therapists/trainees with substantially different orientations is no problem in the group therapy.

At the same time, one's theoretical perspective may reflect the way one lives. Theory may justify the therapist's limitations as well as guide his or her practice. Thus, cognitive-behavioral theory *may* privilege thought over feeling. Classic psychoanalysis *may* foster the analyst's inclination to interpret rather than empathize with the patient, and *may* thus inadvertently lead to projecting by the analyst and faulty introjecting by the patient. Old-style behaviorism *may* place the therapist in a superior position as expert with respect to the client, rather than as an equal. Insofar as a theoretical persuasion fosters distortions in experiencing and contacting on the part of the therapist, the background of the therapist/trainee may enter the group therapy as an issue to be addressed. We seldom have direct theoretical debates in the therapeutic activity, but the therapy itself often affects attitudes toward a given theoretical orientation.

Given that the training program is broader than the group therapy, the therapist/trainee brings his or her work as a therapist into the training in other segments of the training weekend. While there is minimal opportunity for the direct expression of the trainee's work as a therapist in the group therapy, there is considerable space for the trainee to use and appreciate acquired skill. I have already mentioned that trainees function as group leaders or coleaders. They also have occasion to do case presentations from their outside work with the Institute's faculty providing supervision within a Gestalt therapy perspective and method of supervising. In this supervision, the therapist/trainee can see how his or her own tendencies and those of the Gestalt therapist supervisor mesh or differ. In these several ways the therapist/trainee's theoretical orientation is a part of the therapy while not an explicit focus.

When I reflect now on how trainees react to mistakes, technical errors, and empathic failures on my part during group sessions, I am addressing their ego functioning and mine. I invite criticism, difference, challenge as part of orientation and of the therapy itself. Accordingly, reactions to errors are a natural part of the therapy, and phrasing one's concerns is a growing capability. Most of the questions are from within interest about Gestalt therapy rather than coming from attempts to apply other theoretical perspectives. In addition, in my judgment, the reactions are usually supportive of both fellow group members and the group leader. The context of this group therapy as a learning environment probably contributes to the quality of these reactions.

The trainees are close observers of the work that is taking place. They are caught up in the experience of the individual working or in the group process, so that attention to mistakes is more likely to surface during discussion of what has taken place. During the work itself, the trainees are experiencing, not analyzing, what is happening. I stimulate their analysis of errors more by discussing my efforts, and I am open to their observations and suggestions, knowing that it is easier to see possibilities when one is an observer of a process than when one is immersed in it.

In addition to being observers of mistakes on my part, the trainees are the direct recipients of these. In this role the trainees react as clients, as opposed to fellow therapists. For example, early in a training year with new trainees, as an experiment in the therapy, I asked the participants to look at each other and to register for themselves who they liked the most, who the least, and what positives and negatives they could imagine about each of the others. Because they were still in the initial phases of getting to know each other and learning how the group therapy would proceed, they were not eager to do this experiment and yet not ready to tell me I was being inappropriate. Accordingly, they did the easy part—who do I like the most, though I'll not say it aloud—and resisted the rest. The only negative that surfaced was criticism of the experiment and, implicitly, of me. They tried to be "good" clients, cooperative and agreeable, and when I acknowledged my error, they were relieved and forthcoming about their resistance. I was bringing them to distance from me in my error, while bonding further with each other. When I admitted my mistake openly and without shame, the trainees came closer to me and to the therapeutic process.

When the therapists/trainees are further along in therapy, they know that they are unlikely to be alone in the group when they feel burdened by an empathic failure of the therapist. They have been encouraged to express their concerns and told that if they have a negative reaction it is very likely that someone else in the group feels similarly. Because this is commonly demonstrated, group therapy more than individual therapy enables challenge to the therapist by the client. The client's support is not limited to the therapist. It follows that mistakes by the therapist are more often directly addressed and dealt with when they are impacting most presently. This characteristic of the therapy and the training is useful in developing ego function, that is, the capacity to identify what is congenial for them and to alienate that which is not desired at a given time. A basic theme in Gestalt therapy, derived from educational theory, is that challenge must be geared to support.

RESPONDING TO THERAPY

Do therapists/trainees respond to different facets of the therapeutic process from persons who are not therapists? I think so, at least in this context. The group therapy is part of a training program, and the trainees, therefore, have a dual focus. They are seriously occupied with their own experience and growth, as is true for clients in general. Yet they are also highly attentive to me as a therapist, not only from the development of transference—projections on me as therapist, which we try to minimize in Gestalt therapy—but also from their wish to see how a Gestalt therapist works. The trainees continually evaluate me, and they choose to adopt those practices that they find fruitful and valuable.

Isadore From's (personal communication, 1983) discussion of handling a projecting client, which I have previously described, was tied to his view that in the meeting of persons it is vital to have a distinct "I" and a distinct "You." The client should be aware of self as a distinct person and of the therapist in his or her particularity as a distinct other. So, too, the therapist should be aware of the client as a distinct person and of self as a distinct individual. This group therapy, because it involves participants who are themselves therapists, is the ground for a special instance of the leader/therapist to be distinct to the therapists/trainees. I am not only someone who focuses on the trainee and in that posture one who can be vague or clear given the client's disposition to include a "You." I am also a therapist representing the Gestalt therapy that is to be learned and in that respect a particular "You" to them. If the therapist/trainee is to learn this type of therapy, he or she will look closely at how I carry out the role of therapist.

Related to this special case, as a therapist of therapists I try hard not to be introjected or imitated, even though I know this is very likely with novice therapists. Therapists/trainees should neither become like me nor act just like me. Early in the history of Gestalt therapy this was a problem, and those who imitated the leaders relied excessively on techniques and seemed too often to use gimmicks. The aim of Gestalt therapy is to have each person become individuated according to his or her unique tendencies. Therapists/trainees are encouraged to find their own special nature in general, as well as their own style as therapist. If they introject the leader, they cannot grow into their fullness, so I pay attention to how the therapists/trainees discriminate and assimilate what they take from me in the therapy process. Such discriminating of what is coming toward them is part of the healthy aggression that Gestalt therapy encourages My challenge as a therapist of other therapists is to be this distinct "You" while not fostering their being more like me than they naturally are, or less different from me than they naturally are.

When I consider how the therapists/trainees include me in their fantasies, I am aware that there is more space for me in their lives than is usual with other clients. I tend to appear not only in their particular problem areas but also, quite naturally, in their work lives. While they may not have introjected my way of doing things if I have been successful in limiting that, they do hold my support of them in being true to their bent and in relying on their creativity. As they take pride in themselves as therapists, they hold images of my pride and pleasure in *their* way of working as therapists. Other than the fact that we do the same kind of work, roughly, my presence in their fantasy life does not seem to differ significantly from how I live on in the lives of other clients.

CONCERNS AND WORRIES

What are the heavy, the burdensome or troublesome, experiences and concerns in conducting therapy with partners in the mental health profession? I do worry at times about the thin line between challenging the trainees and shaming them. If I do not challenge therapists at their growth points—and I consider myself more gentle than challenging, though I have heard that I am sometimes perceived as "intimidating"—then they will not develop further their ego functions and their therapy will be limited. If I do not challenge well, I may shame the trainee, who in turn may very well shame his or her clients. As I reflect on this, I am aware that I have on occasion shamed a trainee, though this has occurred in supervising a practicum rather than in the group therapy itself. Upon learning of the shame, I have used the group therapy setting to encourage and support the criticism of me on the one hand and to explore and own what was going on in me that I should have been hurtful on the other. I have also enlisted a fellow faculty member to work with the trainee and me in meeting and reconciling around the shame event.

In addition, I fret about how good the trainees will be as Gestalt therapists. My colleagues and I believe that group therapy is vital to the unfolding of the trainees in the Gestalt therapy context. Yet I am also cognizant of the fact that it takes many years to evolve into a full-fledged Gestalt therapist. Since I am often connected with these folks in the early years of that evolution, I do not know how they will turn out in the long run. This becomes a concern for me in two directions: will they do their clients justice or harm? And will they bring honor to the field of Gestalt therapy? As a longtime professor, I know that I am only a small part of an individual's growth and performance, but I worry about this anyway. I do not carry this preoccupation to the point where I demand that the trainees meet exacting standards in the program and in the therapy, since I believe that heavy evaluation is itself destructive in its authoritarian bias. Accordingly, I trust that the mutual evaluations we use each year will serve their purpose and, in the process, lighten my sense of burden.

As the reader may note, my colleagues and I both discriminate between supervision and psychotherapy while still using the combination. We do supervision with the therapists/trainees explicitly the day before the group therapy. And, as I have mentioned, issues such as shaming in supervision enter into the dialogic aspect of the psychotherapy. Since we are invested in what goes on in the therapist/trainee when that person is doing psychotherapy, and we make this a central component of supervision, we may contribute to a blurring between the therapist as supervisee and as client. However, our conscious distinction in definition between these two functions seems to keep the differences clear. Some trainees are accustomed to having the focus of supervision on the case rather than on their part in the transaction with clients. For them, the supervision can arouse more anxiety than usual, but over time, given the place of therapy for dealing with matters of anxiety, this dissipates as an issue.

The same open clarification and discussion takes place when our trainees function as professionals in our community. One complication is that many of our graduates want referrals, and we cannot accommodate all of them. We follow our mandate of contacting each other in a direct, mutual way in this domain too. When a graduate asks for referrals, I may suggest what sorts of clients I am tempted to refer to them. Others I may encourage to seek to attract clients through public presentations or contact with physicians who might refer clients to them. If I am uncomfortable with sending clients to a given graduate, I try to say that too.

PLEASURES IN THE PROJECT

I consider Gestalt therapy to be a philosophical stance, a theory of human functioning, a theory of psychotherapy, and a guide to living as an individual in families, groups, or institutions. Accordingly, the rewards from doing group therapy with therapists pertain not only to these group members, though their growth and unfolding are a source of clear pleasure for me. I see many of these people beyond the three years they are in the group, and I am thus privileged to see their deepening as persons and their development as therapists. Since I consider that these folks undergo the equivalent of a change in culture, I find their enhanced vitality wondrous to behold. My own life takes on greater meaning from their increasing capacity to live and work in creative fashion.

More indirectly, of course, is my sense of their enabling others to move in this same direction. As they practice Gestalt therapy effectively themselves, they assist their clients to function according to the more democratic, equalitarian, agentic, and healthy aggressive mode that underpins Gestalt therapy. Because we focus on contact in social living, those affected by the therapy are inclined to influence the groups and institutions in which they are embedded in directions consistent with the stance of Gestalt therapy. Some of the therapists do this directly by working in institutions.

The result, I believe, is that the social orientation to which I am committed and about which I have written (Lichtenberg, 1990/1994; Lichtenberg et al., 1997), is promulgated far beyond the group in which the therapy takes place. If it does not spread as strongly and widely as a wildfire, it does venture far beyond the time and place of the therapeutic endeavor.

One other pleasure should not be overlooked. We say that Gestalt therapy is a serious and profound psychotherapy; it impacts persons deeply if well carried out. As a consequence, we are able to know our trainees on an intimate level. To meet another person intimately is not a frequent occurrence in modern life, and yet it is an honor to be cherished. That this takes place in many psychotherapies does not mean that it is any the less a source of great gratification for me. That therapists are more likely than the general run of clients to be open to such intimacy, I believe, means that there are more occasions for such intimacy to be experienced. This intimacy, moreover, proceeds in two directions, since the therapist in contacting the client must be open to self-disclosure of a personal nature. While not using the client for the solution of personal problems, the therapist must be able to be open personally without undue defensiveness.

Finally, conducting therapy with therapists/trainees is a process that builds a community. Many of these therapists/trainees work in the region in which the therapy takes place. They become colleagues. They attend the continuing education and other meetings that I go to. They are resources for referrals, sending clients to me and receiving clients from me. They are coorganizers of professional organizations for the ongoing development of Gestalt therapy and Gestalt therapists. Given the notion that this therapy informs how people interact in community, I find myself in a social milieu that is lively, challenging, inclusive, and respectful of all kinds of difference.

Because the participants are themselves therapists, they try out some of the ideas that are percolating and bring back their own experience with the application of new theoretical formulations. This is a kind of practical validation that does not count for much in the "scientific" view of psychology, but it is a validation of theory that I prize highly.

My further growth as a psychotherapist has been nurtured by work with therapists/trainees for two main reasons. First, these individuals are always thinking about what works for them, and they share these thoughts with me. They also are direct about what is less useful and open to my correcting or modifying what I have done. They are, after all, partners in the therapy world, and want the best for themselves as well as for others. Second, they are more likely to be psychologically minded and ready to deal with matters that others may keep to the periphery. For example, therapists must deal often with projecting within the therapeutic process, tendencies of the clients but also of themselves. As objects of projections by their clients, therapists must learn how to discriminate what is theirs from what is being imposed on them. And all too often therapists are prone to project on clients, especially those who make them uncomfortable. Concentrated work on such projecting inclinations with these therapists/trainees has advanced my capacity as a group therapist.

Finally, I think being a therapist to other therapists is best done during the later stages of one's career. Inevitably, one becomes a mentor as well as a therapist, and being a mentor one relies on additional personal resources beyond therapeutic skill. While I am careful to alert therapists/trainees not to introject without discrimination what I am offering them, I often use my past experience as something that guides me and might be useful for them. Since I no longer need to prove myself, acquire new esteem, or struggle on the upward climb of building a career, I can be relaxed about certain problems and be humble or modest in my claims.

For example, when clients choose not to continue working with me, I can always see the positive in this. They are exercising their ego function either in deciding they have gotten enough from me or extruding me as giving them less than they desired. I may still look to see if I have been mistaken somewhere, but my relaxation in the matter turns out to be positive for the client as well as for me. On occasion, when a client has announced a wish to terminate at the point of anxiety about what is coming next in our work (as I see it), my attention to their ego function and support of their choosing has served to motivate them to continue their effort. Either way, stopping or continuing is fine with me, and that has had effects. I can pass this truth along to the therapists/trainees as my mentor, Isadore From, gave it to me early in my retraining as a Gestalt therapist.

So I recommend to those who are therapists to other therapists that they not eschew the overlap of therapy and mentoring but use it mindfully and with care. It may be easier in group therapy such as that which I have described, since other therapists in the group can contribute and support the process as well as modulate what the leader provides. Yet it may as well be fruitful in individual work with a therapist. Walking the line of being equal with the other and having something special to contribute is democratic authority at its best.

NOTE

1. My colleagues are Mary Lou Schack, Ph.D., Joyce E. Lewis, L.S.W., and David Henrich, L.S.W.

REFERENCES

Angyal, A. (1965). *Neurosis and treatment: A holistic theory*. New York: Wiley.
Dewey, J. (1916). *Democracy and education*. New York: Macmillan.
Gibbons, D., Lichtenberg, P., & van Beusekom, J. (1994). Working with victims: Being empathic helpers. *Clinical Social Work Journal, 22*(2), 211–222.

Jones, M. (1968). *Social psychiatry in practice: The idea of the therapeutic community.* Baltimore: Penguin Books.

Kaiser, H. (1965). *Effective psychotherapy: The contribution of Hellmuth Kaiser* (Louis B. Fierman, Ed.). New York: Free Press.

Lichtenberg, P. (1990/1994). *Undoing the clinch of oppression.* New York: Lang. Reissued in 1994 as *Community and confluence: Undoing the clinch of oppression.* Cleveland, OH: GIC Press.

Lichtenberg, P. (1991). Intimacy as a function of autonomy and merging. *Gestalt Journal, 9,* 27–43.

Lichtenberg, P., van Beusekom, J., & Gibbons, D. (1997). *Encountering bigotry: Befriending projecting persons in everyday life.* Northvale, NJ: Aronson.

Perls, F., Hefferline, R. F., & Goodman, P. (1951). *Gestalt therapy: Excitement and growth in the human personality.* New York: Julian Press.

24

TREATING IMPAIRED PSYCHOTHERAPISTS AND "WOUNDED HEALERS"

GARY R. SCHOENER

I n this chapter I will review the concept of professional impairment in
the psychotherapy professions. It is a concept that has undergone some
changes and reformulation over the past two decades. Although at one time
it was synonymous with substance abuse or alcoholism, today it connotes a
wide range of personal problems. As such, the treatment of professionals
in the psychotherapy fields who are experiencing some impairment in their
ability to perform their duties may take many forms. I will examine a variety of approaches to treatment of the impaired professional and also discuss a number of challenges when one is seeking to help a wounded healer.

DISTRESS AND IMPAIRMENT IN THE
PSYCHOTHERAPY PROFESSIONS

In the 1980s the field of psychology became concerned with the *distressed
practitioner* (Kilburg, Nathan, & Thoreson, 1986; Thoreson, Miller, &
Krauskopt, 1989) as well as the impact of stress on clinicians (Guy, Poelstra,
& Stark, 1989). In other health care fields, such as medicine and nursing,
the focus had traditionally been on practitioners who were alcoholic or
substance addicted, and *impairment* was often synonymous with addictions.
Impaired practitioner programs and *colleague assistance committees* in these
professions focused on addictive disorders (Schwebel, Skorina, & Schoener,
1991). A substantial literature evolved concerning treatment approaches
geared for health care professionals (e.g., Bissell & Haberman, 1984; Crosby
& Bissell, 1989).

Well in advance of these efforts, a self-help organization, International Doctors in Alcoholics Anonymous (IDAA), was founded in upstate New York in 1949 by a group of doctors and one psychologist; IDAA has well over 6,000 members today. It can be found on the internet at http://www.idaa.org/. In addition, over the past 25 years many programs have developed that specialize in treating the chemically addicted health care professional. One example, the Talbott Recovery Campus (http://www.talbottcampus.com) provides outcome research on its website. Large numbers of physicians, nurses, and other health care professionals have received treatment for addictions in these programs.

Lacking prescriptive authority and ready access to medications, substance abuse was not seen as a major problem in psychology. Alcoholism was considered a significant problem by some, and Psychologists Helping Psychologists was created to join the parallel organizations in other professions which were part of IDAA. Although not as extensive as work focused on other health care professions, a growing body of research was focused on the alcoholic psychologist (e.g., Skorina, Bissell, & DeSoto, 1990; Thoreson, Nathan, Skorina, & Kilburg, 1983).

Moving away from the concept of the *distressed practitioner*, an American Psychological Association advisory committee recommended focus on the *impaired practitioner* with the following definition, which would apply to impairment in most mental health fields.

> *Impairment* refers to *objective* change in a person's professional
> functioning. An impaired psychologist is one whose work-related
> performance has diminished in quality. This may be manifested in
> one or more of the following ways: work assignments are typically
> late or incomplete; conflict with colleagues has noticeably in-
> creased; clients, students, or families have registered complaints; or
> the amount of absenteeism and tardiness has markedly increased.
> (Schwebel, Skorina, Schoener, 1994, p. 2)

Studies of impairment have increased dramatically over the past two decades (Schwebel et al., 1991, 1994). Several studies have been conducted by state psychological associations (e.g., Brodie & Robinson, 1991; Mukherjee, 1991), whereas others have involved national surveys (e.g. Sherman & Thelen, 1998). In the field of psychology there has been some development of colleague assistance committees, but most states do not have them, and many of the existing ones have limited roles (Barnett & Hillard, 2001).

Although in nursing, law, medicine, and many other fields such committees are virtually universal, in the psychotherapy professions (marriage and family therapy, counseling, psychiatry, psychology, and social work) the efforts have been far more limited (Schwebel et al., 1994). The field of social work, for example, lacked any national task force through the 1990s, although a manual was produced to aid states who wished to establish programs. A survey done in 1994, to which 42 chapters (approximately three-quarters of all) responded, found that only 29% had programs, and a full 50% had no program and no plans for one (Negreen, 1995). Reamer (1992) noted that a chapter of Social Workers Helping Social Workers, a self-help group, was not established until 1980, and as of 1987 it had only 65 members—an infinitesimal percentage of the hundreds of thousands of members of NASW. Yet survey data had clearly indicated a substantial incidence and prevalence of such problems in the field (Fewell, King, & Weinstein, 1993).

Thus, currently it is difficult to obtain a comprehensive view of this type of intervention with impaired colleagues. Most practitioners seem to either not seek help or to do it individually and privately. This also creates a significant barrier to research and the development of models of care.

It should be noted that in a broad range of health care fields there has been pressure for the impaired practitioner programs to become more holistic in approach and to move from their focus on alcoholism or substance abuse and include the treatment of depression, anxiety, sexual impulse control disorders, and adjustment disorders in general (e.g., Bennett & O'Donovan, 2001). In addition, research has also focused on unique aspects of abuse by health care professionals (e.g., Coombs, 1997). One study of a group of doctors, nurses, dentists, and pharmacists, for example, found professional pride and a feeling of immunity, optimism about drugs as a cure for various ills, and use of chemicals to manage stressful career demands were as important as easy access in the patterns developed by these professionals (Coombs, 1996).

But the diversity of impairment and its impacts is so great that it is fundamentally impossible to research the psychotherapy of the *impaired practitioner* per se. However, several bodies of research connected to impairment are germane to some unique issues for psychotherapy professionals. Employers and regulatory bodies and "wounded healers" themselves have for some time been asking for the design and evaluation of the rehabilitation of individual practitioners (Gartrell et al., 1989). In fact, more recent books on troubled practitioners have focused on the rehabilitation of those who violate boundaries (Bloom, Nadelson, & Notman, 1999; Irons & Schneider, 1991).

As a practical matter, while depression and other emotional disorders play a role in some complaints about professionals, in the psychotherapy professions the most common complaints to agencies, training programs, ethics committees, and regulatory bodies such as licensing boards relate to failure to maintain professional boundaries and to sexual contact with patients or members of their families. In at least one study where psychologists were asked to rate frequency of problems in other psychologists, the top five problems observed (percentages indicate percentage of psychologists listing it) were: depression (84%), burnout/overwork (81%), relationship problems (78%), dual relationship/poor boundaries (76%), and mishandled countertransference (68%). Sexual contacts with clients or supervisees were listed by 53%, and alcohol/chemical use by 52% (Brodie & Robinson, 1991).

So the issue of how to effectively treat an impaired psychotherapy professional cannot be viewed as being apart from the issues of problems in practice. The psychotherapist must be concerned with functioning on the job—not just personal distress or generic difficulties in functioning. Furthermore, the implementation of the Americans With Disabilities Act, which requires that employers make *reasonable accommodations*, has challenged organizations to determine how to assess rehabilitation success related to return to work. This also applies to professionals who are still in training. More recently the problems of impairment in students and trainees has been studied (Forrest, Elman, Gizara, & Vacha-Hasse, 1999; Schoener, 1999a). The longstanding practice of simply sending students for psychotherapy, or disciplining them and providing them with tighter supervision, is being replaced with a model focused on *impairment* and *rehabilitation*. A key issue is the safe return to work without compromise to services provided to clients.

RESEARCH ON THERAPISTS AND BOUNDARIES

The maintenance of professional boundaries has always been a problem and a challenge in psychotherapy (Epstein, 1994; Gabbard & Lester, 1995; Jehu, 1994). While one might prefer to see people with boundary problems as a handful of poorly trained or ethically limited persons, this ignores some of the history. The early analytic circle in Vienna was rife with dual relationships, violations of confidentiality, and poor boundaries (Grosskurth, 1991; Kerr, 1993).

Borys (1988) compared social workers, psychologists, and psychiatrists who admitted to sex with clients to those who did not on a number of self-reported boundaries issues. Despite the fact that 40 of her 44 offenders had *only a posttermination* sexual relationship (which one would have expected to have brought about agreement on a number of items on her scale), she could only correctly classify 55% of the erotic practitioners and 79% of the nonerotic when comparing them on her Social Involvement Scale. Borys (1988) also found considerable variability within the psychotherapy disciplines as to what is deemed acceptable in a number of areas, such as accepting a gift, inviting clients to an open house, treating an employee, becoming friends with a former client, and disclosing one's own stresses to a client.

Lamb and Catanzaro (1998), in a national study of American psychologists, compared a group that acknowledged sexual boundary violations with either clients or students and supervisees with a group that did not acknowledge such violations. Nonsignificant differences were found between the two groups on a great many questions, including initiating touch with a client, discussing details of a *current* personal stressor with a client, and attending a client's special social event. Some significant findings of differences also reveal relatively high numbers of *both* offenders and nonoffenders admitting having had significant social contact with clients.

As the concern about professionals who engage in boundary violations has increased, a growing number of programs provide some form of boundaries retraining, in tandem with psychotherapy or other forms of treatment (e.g., Schoener, 1999b; Spickard, Swiggart, Manley, & Dodd, 2002) As a result, in most communities the intervention options have gone well beyond the traditional addictions program.

PROFESSIONALS WHO VIOLATE OR FAIL TO MAINTAIN BOUNDARIES

The failure to maintain professional boundaries or the violation of boundaries can take a great range of shapes and occur for a great variety of reasons. This can involve all types of overinvolvement with clients, including social contacts outside of the professional relationship, involving oneself in the client's life, confidentiality violations, excessive anger, physical contact, romantic game-playing, erotic talk, sexual contact, and numerous other things.

Based on consultation in more than 3,000 cases over a quarter of a century, and also reviewing the literature including cases reports, the following list represents a number of factors that have appeared frequently enough in clinical experience or case reports to be significant in *more than a handful of cases.*

1. *Inadequate training.* This may reflect a general lack of training relative to boundaries or a specific lacunae in the training as regards relationships with clients or patients.

2. *Poor training for the particular role or job.* The professional may have good training, but not for the role that has been undertaken. He or she may be in over his or her head in terms of the demands of the job. Some practitioners from large urban settings have great difficulty functioning in rural settings, where they are expected to perform a much wider range of functions. They may also encounter their clients or patients more frequently outside of the office.

3. *Inadequate job description or poor orientation to job role.* Some workers get into trouble in situations where the lack of good job and role definition and lack of orientation and supervision sets the stage for compromising situations. This is commonly seen in church settings but is surprisingly common also in health care settings.

4. *Lack of or failure to use the supervision that is available.* Some job situations lack the necessary supervisory backup to help staff cope with difficulties and challenges. While in and of itself this does not "cause" boundary violations, it can help set the stage, or fail to provide for early intervention.

5. *Lack of awareness of transference/countertransference in general, or in a given situation.* Some professionals are not aware of their areas of vulnerability and lose their boundaries with certain clients.

6. *Excessive need for client approval.* Professionals who are insecure and who will do anything to gain client approval have great difficulty setting

limits. Some very solid practitioners will experience periods in their life where the loss of important relationships, or even problems at work, will undermine their self-esteem and lead to an excessive need for client approval.

7. *Naivete and lack of good social judgment.* Some workers appear to lack the "social intelligence" necessary to be a professional, or do not wish to be in the professional role. They deny the power differential and responsibility that goes with the professional role and would like to function more like a friend. In some severe cases the practitioner is diagnosed as having Asperger's Disorder.

8. *Organic impairment.* Although it is uncommon, some professionals are impaired due to brain injury or other organically based impairment. Organic disorders in more senior practitioners can have an impact on professionalism. Such impairments may represent a problem that cannot be repaired by supervision.

9. *Impaired judgment secondary to addiction or alcoholism.* Substance abusers and alcoholics may have judgment that is impaired due to their varying mood states or intoxication.

10. *Psychopathology.* Beyond the psychopathology inherent in some of the previous categories, it may turn out that the worker has a disorder of mood, thinking, or impulse control.

11. *Emotional neediness and dependency.* Low self-esteem and high dependency needs, which lead to needs for client, patient, or parishioner acceptance on a long-term or chronic basis.

12. *Situational neediness or impairment—the "wounded healer."* Due to acute situational depression, a life crisis, or other more transitory problems, a professional becomes situationally needy and at risk to cross boundaries.

13. *The professional as a superhero.* Practitioners who are driven to be "perfect" or do everything for clients, ironically, may begin taking risks while rationalizing that they need to try "everything" that might help.

14. *Surrender to the client.* As in Gabbard's (1994) description of *masochistic surrender*, the practitioner has a history of being dominated in relationships and feeling frustrated about it, allows a client to manipulate and dominate, and then is consumed by resentment about this fact. Again, this situation is often created when a client or patient is continually resistant to change or "cure."

These categories are not mutually exclusive. In most cases there are multiple determinants. The key is to determine what the pattern is, if any, and why it occurred. Note also that many of these determinants are *not treatment issues per se* but would be very relevant to a decision by a treating therapist about return-to-work recommendations.

TREATMENT OF PROFESSIONALS WHO VIOLATE BOUNDARIES

Prior to the last decade, sexual misconduct and related boundary violations by therapists and other health care professionals were often treated with an attitude of tolerance. Offending professionals received mild discipline, and returned to practice, while receiving some sort of psychotherapy and possibly supervision of their work. It was often assumed that they would not repeat. Typically no formal assessment was done to determine rehabilitation potential. A number of psychotherapists were apparently willing to undertake the treatment of such cases with only limited knowledge of the original offenses and without a clear plan for how a repeat of the behavior was going to be prevented. The focus of such therapies was whatever the offending professional wanted to discuss. Often the professional misconduct received little or no attention. The etiology of the unprofessional conduct might not even be identified. Professionals often were deemed "cured" after a course of therapy that largely addressed distress and/or depression that was secondary to having faced discipline.

Even when a more targeted approach was taken to the planning of a rehabilitation effort, a subsequent employer, board of licensure or registration, or colleague might undermine the plan. It is quite common, even today, for example, for a practitioner to be required to obtain a clinical internship or a very formal type of supervision but be unable to do so. The practitioner then appeals to the licensing or regulatory authority, which relents and allows a lesser level of training or supervision. For example, the following case was described by Bates and Brodsky (1989, p. 80).

> But the board did not hold to the original five mandates. The results of the psychological evaluation ordered in the first mandate may not have offered great promise for rehabilitation. The second mandate had to be altered: Dr. X could find no clinical internship program that would admit him. . . . They lifted the requirement of a clinical internship. In its place, they set out a requirement that Dr. X practice under the supervision of a licensed psychologist for 2 years, or at least 1500 hours per year.

In many situations in the United States and elsewhere, licensure and regulatory boards have designed rehabilitation plans without an independent assessment. Thus, it is difficult to judge situations in which some sort of therapy and/or retraining and supervision have been prescribed and failed to prevent a reoccurrence of the offense. In addition, in recent years regulatory bodies in North America have been experimenting with "boundaries training" and and ethics coursework to supplement, or replace, personal therapy for offenders (e.g. Schoener, 1999a, 1999b). Debate as to the value and efficacy of this practice became a public issue in the *New York Times Magazine* story "Dr. Smith Goes to Sexual-Rehab School" (Abraham, 1995).

MISUSES OF REHABILITATION

While it might seem reasonable to presume that rehabilitation involves an attempt to alleviate conditions that led to the original misconduct so that the likelihood of a repeat offense is greatly lessened or eliminated, the term is often used to mean other things. It has been noted that rehabilitation as it is sometimes now practiced serves more as a minor form of punishment, perhaps to expiate the guilt of the offending therapist and, maybe even more, of the sanctioning committee or court (Brodsky, 1986, p. 164). We use it to mean a planned attempt to return a psychotherapist to previous levels of functioning and competence and to lessen or eliminate the likelihood of misconduct, boundary crossings, or substandard work.

COGNITIVE-BEHAVIORAL APPROACHES

Until recently little has been published on the extensive work with professionals who have engaged in sexual misconduct by traditional sex offender treatment programs. Typically they tend to focus their evaluation on identification of sexual impulse control disorders as presented in the *DSM-IV*. Since some professionals who have offended against clients do not show the same compulsive behaviors as other sex offenders, these programs take into account the behavioral circumstances of the offense(s) in an effort to devise a rehabilitation strategy. Thus, work such as that of Abel and colleagues focuses on developing skills to decrease arousal, including the development of safeguards to attempt to prevent the professional from ending up in a high-risk situation again (Abel, Osborn, & Warberg, 1995) paralleling the authors' work with other types of sex offenders but extending it considerably (Abel & Osborn, 1999). Cognitive-behavior therapy is also utilized widely in the treatment of other conditions that impair professionals, from depression to substance abuse.

Cognitive-behavior therapy has been researched extensively, although its application to professionals who have offended is more recent and not well researched. Typically a period of evaluation and intensive treatment is followed by a structured aftercare program, including cognitive-behavioral therapy, reeducation, and a strong emphasis on relapse prevention. Sometimes a client satisfaction or quality assurance–type questionnaire is given to patients to attempt to assess whether violations are continuing. Monitoring by colleagues and the use of the polygraph are common aspects of posttreatment surveillance in cases involving sexual misconduct.

PSYCHODYNAMIC APPROACHES

Strean's (1993) book *Therapists Who Have Sex with Their Patients: Treatment and Recovery* presents case studies. One of the cases involves a sadomasochistic social worker who makes his female ex-patients suffer. The overall approach is psychodynamic and individualized. One of the three cases involves a female therapist. Claman (1987) and others have also presented cases analyzed from a dynamic or psychoanalytic perspective. Gabbard (1999) has done the most extensive writing on the psychodynamic approach to these problems.

Gabbard (1994), based on extensive clinical experience with offenders at the Menninger Clinic in Topeka, Kansas, sorts offenders into four groups: (1) psychotic disorders; (2) predatory psychopathy and paraphilias; (3) masochistic surrender—a "giving in" to a challenging or difficult client, hoping to mollify the client by being flexible with boundaries; (4) *lovesick*—within the "lovesick" category he notes a number of issues or dynamics that singly, or in multiples, play a role in the misconduct. Treatment efforts are focused on the "lovesick" category as well as those in the "masochistic surrender" grouping, which includes therapists with masochistic and self-destructive tendencies who essentially allow clients to intimidate or control them. The psychotics and the predators are not deemed good subjects for rehabilitation.

SEXUAL ADDICTION

Another approach to assessment and treatment of those who cross sexual boundaries has grown out of the work on sexual addiction. This literature has been rapidly expanding in recent years (Irons & Schneider, 1999). While the typical sexual addiction program seeks to identify addictive or compulsive aspects of sexual behavior and classifies a wide range of individuals into this single category, a more complex theoretic base has been developed by Irons. This model presumes that some professionals who engage in sexual misconduct do not have a paraphilia or psychosexual disorder as defined in *DSM-IV*. The model takes into account the parallels with incest in such relationships and relates the acting-out behavior to an attempt to cope with inner wounds. (They report a high percentage of abuse victims among the professionals they evaluate.) They also frequently find other addictions to be present (Irons & Schneider, 1999).

Extending the addictions approach, Irons presents a set of "archetypal categories" that are reminiscent of a Jungian approach to personality and attempts to use them to further describe offenders. Irons and Schneider (1999) found the following when they applied these categories to a sample of 88 sexually exploitative health care professionals. They found different percentages fell in each group, and that the percentage in each category who were diagnosed with sexual addiction also varied considerably.

The naive prince—early in career, feels invulnerable, tends to develop "special relationships" with certain types of clients, and blurs boundaries (7.9% overall but none of the sex addicts in this category).

The wounded warrior—overwhelmed by demands, overly dependent on professional mantle for validation; patient involvement is temporary escape (21.6% overall, with 37% in this category judged to be sex addicts).

The self-serving martyr—middle or late career; work is primary; withdrawn, angry, and resentful (23.9% overall, with 62% in this category judged to be sex addicts).

The false lover—enjoys living on the edge, the "thrill of the chase"; a risk-taker who desires adventure (19.3% overall, but with 94% in this category classed as sex addicts).

The dark king—powerful and charming; successful, manipulative; sexual exploitation as an expression of power (12.5% of sample, but 91% in this category were diagnosed as sex addicts).

The wild card—erratic course in personal and professional life; significant difficulties in functioning—has major Axis I disorder (14.8% of the total sample, with only 23% judged to be sex addicts).

The assessments done utilizing this approach are inpatient assessments for the most part. The presumption is that the intensity of the evaluation and milieu will penetrate denial and other defenses and reveal the underlying problems. This approach can be utilized with a resistant person who does not fully acknowledge the degree of dysfunction. Irons and Schneider have collaborated on a fine book, *The Wounded Healer* (Irons & Schneider, 1999) which is the best summary of this work and this approach.

COMMON FEATURES OF ASSESSMENTS

Despite the substantial differences in approach, as compared with traditional psychological evaluation, each of these assessment methodologies involves the collection of far more background data from persons other than the person being assessed. Each involves obtaining behavioral description of the events in question, and each one requires a good deal of cooperation. Each approach recognizes that some offenders lie or minimize, and also that some will seek these assessments in order to attempt to avoid consequences. Each believes that some offenders cannot be rehabilitated and recognizes the need to counsel some people out of the field.

Each pays some attention to the dynamics of the professional relationship and assumes multiple determinants in the typical case. Each presumes that public safety is a key issue, and each involves an initial diagnostic decision, a treatment plan, and an eventual evaluation after treatment is concluded to assess whether it was successful.

All of these approaches presume that professional retraining of various types may be necessary and that skill and training issues may be as important as psychopathology in some cases. But "knee-jerk" referrals for retraining or supervision are no more useful than referrals for therapy. One needs to be quite specific as to what deficits in skills or training are present and why the specified course of retraining is expected to remedy the situation.

Each involves the use of supervision and the development of a reentry plan with possible practice limitations. However, all stress the importance of clearly defining the supervision. It is critical that its goals and requirements are spelled out in detail, and that case consultation (voluntary sharing of clinical material, often termed "supervision") be differentiated from true supervision, wherein the supervisor is legally responsible for the practice oversight.

In recent years some licensure boards have taken to requiring "ethics consultation," which involves regular meetings, often monthly, with an "ethics consultant." It is unclear what this is expected to accomplish, in that in most misconduct cases there was no lack of understanding of professional ethical standards. We have seen this required of professionals who teach ethics or have served on ethics committees, and in situations where *knowledge of ethics* was in no way lacking—that is, in situations where the practitioner was completely clear as to what was being violated. "Boundaries training" has also been added to rehabilitation plans (Abraham, 1995), but again this is often not clearly connected to why the misconduct occurred. Even referrals for ethics coursework, meetings with an ethics consultant, or boundaries "training or coaching" should have their justification in the findings of an independent assessment. No less rationale is needed for such a referral than for a referral for therapy.

PSYCHOTHERAPISTS' UNIQUENESS

There is a very useful literature on the frequency of various historical factors in the lives of psychotherapists, and those who treat them would do well to be familiar with what is known about them (e.g., Guy, 1987; Guy et al., 1989; Pope & Tabachnick, 1994). A good deal is known about their self-care strategies (e.g., Guy & Norcross, 1999; Mahoney, 1997). Less is known about their marriages, although there is a considerable literature on physician's marriages (e.g., Myers, 1994; Sotile & Sotile, 2000a).

But the most unique thing about providing treatment to a psychotherapist is the potential for projective identification in the form of either, or both, transference and countertransference. Gonsiorek (1989) has described this in therapy with professionals who have engaged in sex with one of their clients. He describes things he does to challenge the client's tendency to overidentify with him by, for example, raising a theoretical point on which he and the client are likely to disagree.

Gabbard (1995) has written on the transference/countertransference issues involved in treatment of professionals who have been sanctioned by boards of licensure or employers for sexual boundary violations. He provides the following vignette (p. 102).

> Dr. A came to his first session of psychotherapy after being referred by a state licensing board. He began the session by asking me if it would be okay if he called me by my first name. I suggested to him

that because he was seeing me in a professional relationship, it would probably be more appropriate for him to call me Dr. Gabbard. He acceded to my request, but went on several times in the session to use my first name, only to apologize afterwards.

As the therapy went on, he told me he had heard that I had written a book on this subject and asked if he could borrow the book from me to read up on the kind of problems he had. He assured me he would return it in a couple of weeks. I told him that while I really had no doubts about his returning the book, I nevertheless felt it was not a good idea for me to loan him books because it was another variant of the professional boundary problem that had gotten him into difficulty in the first place. He then asked if I could buy one of the books at the author's discount price and he would reimburse me. Again, I told him that I thought that the financial transgressions between us should only be related to the fee.

During another therapy session, while he was describing how he had fallen in love with a patient, he told me that he was aware that all therapists became sexually excited by certain patients, and he asked me if that ever happened to me. I stressed to him that the focus of psychotherapy was on him and his countertransference difficulties rather than on mine. Late in therapy, Dr. A told me he thought he was getting better and wondered if we could switch from psychotherapy to supervision. I responded that I felt he needed me as a psychotherapist and that there were other people available as supervisors.

Gabbard (1995) notes that among the challenges of doing psychotherapy on practitioners who have crossed boundaries with their own clients are the struggle to avoid being put in various roles, as follows.

1. *Therapist as policeman.* To the degree that the therapist is an extension of the licensure board or the disciplinary activities of an employer, there can be a perception of, or a drift into the role, being of a disciplinarian and watchdog.
2. *Therapists as rescuer and absolver.* Many disciplined professionals come for therapy in a traumatized state. Therapy may be seen as a place for confession and absolution. Seeing the professional/ client as a victim, at least in part, is an easy step, as are rescue fantasies.
3. *Therapist as authoritarian parent.* Many professionals who violate boundaries have a longstanding resentment of authority and a rebellious streak that is easily triggered in some settings. In therapy they can bring about an authoritarian response from the therapist. In the case of those with a history of self-destructive and masochistic relationships, they may pity them-

selves sufficiently to bring on frustration in the supervisor, eventually leading to some punitive interaction.

4. *Supervisor as corruptible object.* Practitioners who have trouble managing boundaries in general will challenge the therapeutic boundaries. To the degree that they can undermine these boundaries, they may show that the therapist too has boundaries problems.

REPORTING DUTIES AND OTHER ETHICAL/LEGAL ISSUES

If the professional who is being treated is on probation, the therapist is likely to have reporting duties involving a licensure board or employer. So privacy is always limited in these relationships, something that can be troubling to both the professional/client and the treating therapist.

In at least two jurisdictions, the State of Minnesota and the Province of Ontario, there are reporting duties under existing laws that supersede the client's privacy. In Ontario the reporting of sexual misconduct by regulated health care professionals is mandated, even if the information was gained solely from a treatment relationship with the offending practitioner. This would include a situation in which, during psychotherapy, a practitioner admits to offenses not yet discovered by the regulatory board (called a professional college in Canada).

In Minnesota the rules are more complicated. In the case of licensed psychologists, only other psychologists are mandated reporters, and there is an exception granted if the information was learned in the context of a professional relationship with the psychologist who might be disciplined. However, with other licensed psychotherapy professionals, they *and the psychologists* have a duty to report any behavior that might lead to board discipline, and there is no exception granted if it was learned in a psychotherapy context. The only alternative is that the professional in question can be referred to a program for impaired health professionals and he or she may receive treatment in a diversion type program if this is the first offense.

There is an exception to any reporting duties in the case of a professional receiving treatment for substance abuse or alcoholism. The privacy of such conversations and records is covered by a federal law and the Code of Federal Regulations, Chapter 42, which makes them immune to even the invasion of a search warrant. Only a court order can unseal them. However, regular psychotherapy has no such protection (Brooks, 1997).

It is absolutely critical to define all of the limits of confidentiality prior to beginning either evaluation or treatment. The therapist must address hypothetical situations such as ones in which the therapist believes client safety is at issue. This goes well beyond the routine issues of disclosure of (1) reporting duties; (2) any reports required to the employer or board; or (3) the fact that a court order can open the records over the client's objections.

But beyond the complexity of these duties lies another challenge—that of how to ethically handle a situation in which you believe that clients may be at risk. This can be an issue during psychotherapy and also at its conclusion when recommendations are expected. The highly publicized crisis in 2002 about the return to the pulpit of priests who have abused children has helped create a national debate about the responsibilities of special programs that evaluate and treat impaired clergy (e.g., Investigative Staff of the Boston Globe, 2002). Under what circumstances could a treating therapist be held accountable for harm done, during or following treatment of an impaired professional? The reader is referred to some useful discussions, which have concluded, in short, that some liability could exist under certain fact situations (e.g., Bisbing, Jorgenson, & Sutherland, 1995; Jorgenson, 1995).

RETURN TO PRACTICE

While the licensure board or employer makes the final determination about practice reentry and what limits or supervision are necessary, the treating therapist normally makes a key recommendation. Most psychotherapists do not have experience with this sort of "return-to-work" recommendation. In order to respond to such a request, it is necessary to have a clear picture of the workplace, clientele, and duties of the client/professional and to understand what his or her job actually entails. If the therapy is purely voluntary and not part of a disciplinary intervention, the therapist can only attempt to coach or convince the client to exercise good judgment and voluntarily limit work to areas in which safe practice is possible.

When the psychotherapy is part of a formal rehabilitation plan, the therapist is likely to be asked to determine if the goals set out were accomplished. This can be done by an independent assessor, including the original assessor. It is important to remember that even if the professional proves to be a cooperative client, a number of outcomes are possible, as follows.

1. The professional agrees to rehabilitation, but then goes back and tries to get the requirements changed by the licensure board or employer.
2. Professional begins the psychotherapy, but says that he or she is finished prematurely and drops out.
3. The professional becomes disenchanted with the field during the psychotherapy and asks for vocational counseling into another field of work.
4. The professional makes considerable change, but not enough to be deemed to be a safe practitioner. A variant on this is that he or she would be safe in a different job with a different level of supervision, but not in the job he or she has.
5. Treatment is not successful—either the problems are not solved or newly identified ones make it clear that safe practice is not likely.

Certainly some of the issues involving questions of return to practice are the ability to maintain practitioner wellness—an issue receiving considerable attention in the literature (e.g., Norcross, 2000; Sotile & Sotile, 2000b) and the popular press (e.g. Abramson, 1995; Wendling, 1999). Regarding the ability to maintain professional boundaries, there is a growing literature which the treating therapist needs to master, since this is likely to be an issue at some point in the psychotherapy of any impaired professional (e.g., Epstein, 1994; Gabbard & Lester, 1995; Pope, Sonne, & Holroyd, 1993).

CONCLUSION

Over the past several decades the concept of the *impaired professional* has been broadened by the psychotherapy fields to reach far beyond the original concept of the substance-abusing health care professional. While alcoholism and substance abuse are still hazards in all health care fields, the expanding focus has embraced a variety of other disorders, including mood disorders and other personal problems that might well interfere with a practitioner's work.

Although structured programs and some specialized support groups may at times be of assistance, many impaired psychotherapy professionals are treated with outpatient psychotherapy rather than in a specialized program. Those who undertake such work need to familiarize themselves with the growing body of knowledge about psychotherapy professionals and how they function.

Furthermore, the concept has also been applied to professionals who come to the attention of a regulatory board or employer because of problems in their work, including, but not limited to, boundary violations with clients. While the quality of service to clients and client safety is an issue with all types of impairment, it has become increasingly clearer that the psychotherapy of impaired professionals needs to be done in the context of ethical and possibly legal duties to the community at large.

Along the same lines, it is critical that the psychotherapist recognize that a recommendation regarding any return to work, or any level of work and supervision, needs to be informed by more detailed knowledge of the professional/client's job and workplace. That role and duty is one that may be unfamiliar to many psychotherapists.

REFERENCES

Abel, G., & Osborn, C. (1999). Cognitive-behavioral treatment of professional sexual misconduct. In J. Bloom, C. Nadelson, & M. Notman (Eds.), *Physician misconduct* (pp. 225–246). Washington, DC: American Psychiatric Press.

Abel, G., Osborn, C., & Warberg, B. (1995). Cognitive-behavioral treatment for professional sexual misconduct. *Psychiatric Annals, 25*, 106–112.

Abraham, L. (1995, November 5). Dr. Smith goes to sexual-rehab school. *New York Times Magazine*, 44–49.

Barnett, J., & Hillard, D. (2001). Psychologists distress and impairment: The availability, nature and use of colleague assistance programs for psychologists. *Professional Psychology: Research and Practice, 32,* 205–210.

Bates, C., & Brodsky, A. (1989). *Sex in the therapy hour.* New York: Guilford.

Bennett, J., & O'Donovan, D. (2001). Substance misuse by doctors, nurses and other health care workers. *Current Opinion in Psychiatry, 14,* 195–199.

Bisbing, S., Jorgenson, L., & Sutherland, P. (1995). *Sexual abuse by professionals: A legal guide.* (With 1997 and 1999 supplements) Charlottesville, VA: Michie.

Bissell, L., & Haberman, P.W. (1984). *Alcoholism in the professions.* New York: Oxford University Press.

Bloom, J., Nadelson, C., & Notman, M. (1999). *Physician sexual misconduct.* Washington, DC: American Psychiatric Press.

Borys, D. (1988). Dual relationships between therapist and client: A national survey of clinicians' attitudes and practices. Unpublished doctoral dissertation, University of California, Los Angeles.

Brodie, J., & Robinson, B. (1991, July). MPA distressed/impaired psychologists survey: Overview and results. *Minnesota Psychologist, 40,* 7–10.

Brodsky, A. (1986). The distressed psychologist: Sexual intimacies and exploitation. In R. R. Kilburg, P. Nathan, & R. Thoreson (Eds.), *Professionals in distress: Issues, syndromes and solutions in psychology* (pp. 153—171). Washington, DC: American Psychological Association.

Brooks, M. (1997). Legal aspects of confidentiality. In J. Lowinson, P. Ruiz, R. Millman, & J. Langrod (Eds.), *Substance abuse: A comprehensive textbook* (3rd ed., pp. 884–899). Baltimore: Williams and Wilkins.

Claman, J. M. (1987). Mirror hunger in the psychodynamics of sexually abusing therapists. *American Journal of Psychoanalysis, 47,* 35–40.

Coombs, R. H. (1996). Addicted health professionals. *Journal of Substance Misuse, 1,* 187–194.

Coombs, R. H. (1997). *Drug impaired professionals.* Cambridge, MA: Harvard University Press.

Crosby, L. R., & Bissell, L. (1989). *To care enough: Interventions with chemically dependent colleagues.* Minneapolis, MN: Johnson Institute Books.

Epstein, R. S. (1994). *Keeping boundaries: Maintaining safety and integrity in the psychotherapeutic process.* Washington, DC: American Psychiatric Press.

Fewell, C. H., King, B. L., & Weinstein, D. L. (1993). Alcohol and other drug abuse among social work colleagues and their families: Impact on practice. *Social Work, 38,* 565–570.

Floyd, M., Myszka, M. T., & Orr, P. (1998). Licensed psychologists' knowledge and utilization of a state association colleague assistance program. *Professional Psychology: Research and Practice, 29,* 594–598.

Forrest, L., Elman, N., Gizara, S., & Vacha-Hasse, T. (1999). Trainee impairment: A review of identification, remediation, dismissal, and legal issues. *Counseling Psychologist, 27,* 627–686.

Gabbard, G. (1994). Sexual misconduct. In J. Oldham & M. Riba (Eds.), *Review of psychiatry* (Vol. 13, 433–456). Washington, DC: American Psychiatric Press.

Gabbard, G. (1995). Transference and countertransference in the psychotherapy of therapsits charged with sexual misconduct. *Psychiatric Annals, 25,* 100–105.

Gabbard, G. (1999). Psychodynamic approaches to physician sexual misconduct. In J. Bloom, C. Nadelson, & M. Notman (Eds.), *Physician sexual misconduct* (pp. 205–223). Washington, DC: American Psychiatric Press.

Gabbard, G., & Lester, E. (1995). *Boundaries and boundary violations in psychoanalysis.* New York: Basic Books.

Gartrell, N., Herman, J., Olarte, S., Feldstein, M., Localio, R., & Schoener, G. (1989). Sexual abuse of patients by therapists: Strategies for offender management and rehabilitation. In R. D. Miller (Ed.), *Legal implications of hospital policies and practices* (pp. 55–66). San Francisco: Jossey Bass.

Gonsiorek, J. (1989). Working therapeutically with therapists who have become sexually involved with clients. In G. Schoener, J. Milgrom, J. Gonsiorek, E. Luepker, & R. Conroe, *Psychotherapists' sexual involvement with clients: Intervention and prevention* (pp. 421–433). Minneapolis, MN: Walk-In Counseling Center.

Gonsiorek, J. (Ed.). (1995). *Breach of trust: Sexual exploitation by health care professionals and clergy.* Thousand Oaks, CA: Sage.

Gonsiorek, J., & Schoener, G. (1987). Assessment and evaluation of therapists who sexually exploit clients. *Professional Practice of Psychology, 8,* 79–93.

Grosskurth, P. (1991). *The secret ring: Freud's inner circle and the politics of psychoanalysis.* Reading, MA: Addison-Wesley.

Guy, J. (1987). *The personal life of the therapist.* New York: Wiley.

Guy, J., & Norcross, J. (1999). Therapist self-care checklist. In G. Koocher, J. Norcross, & S. Hill III (Eds.), *Psychologists' desk reference* (pp. 387–392). New York: Oxford University Press.

Guy, J., Poelstra, P.L., & Stark, M.J. (1989). Personal distress and therapeutic effectiveness: National survey of psychologists practicing psychotherapy. *Professional Psychology: Research and Practice, 20,* 48–50.

Investigative Staff of the Boston Globe. (2002). *Betrayal: The crisis in the Catholic Church.* Boston: Little, Brown.

Irons, R., & Schneider, J. (1999). *The wounded healer: An addiction-sensitive approach to the sexually exploitive professional.* Northvale, NJ: Aronson.

Jehu, D. (1994). *Patients as victims: Sexual abuse in psychotherapy and counselling.* Chichester, UK: Wiley.

Jorgenson, L. (1995). Rehabilitating sexually exploitive therapists: A risk management perspective. *Psychiatric Annals, 25,* 118–122.

Kaslow, F. (1984). *Psychotherapy with psychotherapists.* New York: Haworth Press.

Kerr, J. (1993). *A most dangerous method: The story of Jung, Freud, and Sabina Spielrein.* New York: Knopf.

Kilburg, R., Nathan, P., & Thoreson, R. (1986). *Professionals in distress: Issues, syndromes, and solutions in psychology.* Washington, DC: American Psychological Association.

Lamb, D., & Catanzaro, S. (1998). Sexual and nonsexual boundary violations involving psychologists, clients, supervisees, and students: Implications for professional practice. *Professional Psychology: Research and Practice, 29,* 498–503.

Mahoney, M. J. (1997). Psychotherapists' personal problems and self-care patterns. *Professional Psychology: Research and Practice, 28,* 14–16.

Milgrom, J. (1992). *Boundaries in professional relationships: A training manual.* Minneapolis, MN: Walk-In Counseling Center.

Mukherjee, A. (1991, July). MPA distressed/impaired psychologists survey: Summary of responses to open-ended questions. *Minnesota Psychologist, 40,* 10–12.

Myers, M. (1994). *Doctor's marriages: A look at the problems and their solutions.* New York: Plenum.

Nace, E. P. (1995). *Achievement and addiction: A guide to the treatment of professionals.* New York: Brunner/Mazel.

Negreen, S. E. (1995). *A chapter guide on colleague assistance for impaired social workers.* Washington, DC: National Association of Social Workers.

Norcross, J. (2000). Psychologists self-care: Practitioner-tested, research-informed strategies. *Professional Psychology: Research and Practice, 31,* 710–713.

Pope, K., Sonne, J., & Holroyd, J. (1993). *Sexual feelings in psychotherapy: Explorations for therapists and therapists-in-training.* Washington, DC: American Psychological Association.

Pope, K., & Tabachnick, B. G. (1994). Therapists as patients: A national survey of psychologist' experiences, problems, and beliefs. *Professional Psychology: Research and Practice, 25,* 247–258.

Reamer, F. G. (1992). The impaired social worker. *Social Work, 37,* 165–170.

Schoener, G. (1999a). Practicing what we preach. *Counseling Psychologist, 27,* 693–701.

Schoener, G. (1999b). Preventive and remedial boundaries training for helping professionals and clergy: Successful approaches and useful tools. *Journal of Sex Education and Therapy, 24,* 209–217.

Schoener, G., Milgrom, J., Gonsiorek, J., Luepker, E., & Conroe, R. (1989). *Psychotherapists' sexual involvement with clients: Intervention and prevention.* Minneapolis, MN: Walk-In Counseling Center.

Schwebel, M., Skorina, J., & Schoener, G. (1991). *Assisting impaired psychologists: Program development for state psychological associations.* Washington, DC: American Psychological Association.

Schwebel, M., Skorina, J., & Schoener, G. (1994). *Assisting impaired psychologists—Revised edition: Program development for state psychological associations.* Washington, DC: American Psychological Association.

Sherman, M. D. (1996). Distress and professional impairment due to mental health problems among psychotherapists. *Clinical Psychology Review, 16,* 199–315.

Sherman, M. D., & Thelen, M. H. (1998). Distress and professional impairment among psychologists in clinical practice. *Professional Psychology: Research and Practice, 29,* 79–85

Skorina, J., Bissell, L. C., & De Soto, C. B. (1990). The alcoholic psychologist: Routes to recovery. *Professional Psychology: Research and Practice, 2,* 348–351.

Sotile, W., & Sotile, M. (2000a). *The medical marriage.* Chicago: American Medical Assn.

Sotile, W., & Sotile, M. (2000b). *The resilient physician.* Chicago: American Medical Assn.

Spickard, A., Swiggart, W., Manley, G., & Dodd, D. (2002). A continuing education course for physicians who cross sexual boundaries. *Sexual Addiction and Compulsivity, 9,* 33–42.

Strean, H. (1993). *Therapists who have sex with their patients.* New York: Brunner/Mazel.

Thoreson, R. W., Miller, M., & Krauskopf, C. J. (1989). The distressed psychologist: Prevalence and treatment considerations. *Professional Psychology: Research and Practice, 20,* 153–158.

Thoreson, R., Nathan, P., Skorina, J. K., & Kilburg, R. (1983). The alcoholic psychologist: Issues, problems, and implications for the profession. *Professional Psychology: Research and Practice, 14*, 670–684.

Wendling, T. (1999, December 5, 6, 7). When psychologists cross the line. *Cleveland Plain Dealer*. Available in reprint form by contacting the paper at (216) 999-4213, or the author, Ted Wendling, at twendling@plaind.com.

*Research Findings: Providing
Personal Therapy to
Other Therapists*

25

RESEARCH ON CONDUCTING PSYCHOTHERAPY WITH MENTAL HEALTH PROFESSIONALS

Jesse D. Geller, John C. Norcross, & David E. Orlinsky

This chapter has two primary purposes. The first is to present a practice-friendly research review on such basic questions as: How frequently do psychotherapists treat other therapists? What are the characteristics of these therapist-patients? Who are the therapists' therapists? What treatment modalities are typically offered? What distinguishes the treatment of mental health professionals compared to lay persons? The second purpose is to contribute to the development of an organized body of knowledge that can effectively guide the work of therapists who are therapists of fellow mental health professionals.

Only a handful of therapists have written about their experiences conducting psychotherapy with fellow therapists. They have come largely from psychodynamic and psychoanalytic backgrounds (e.g., Berman, 1995; Bridges, 1993, 1995; Burton, 1973; Fleischer & Wissler, 1985; Freudenberger, 1986; Gabbard, 1995; Glickauf-Hughes & Melman, 1995; for an exception, see Kaslow, 1984). Their thoughtful writings converge with respect to the following generalizations. First, they all share the view that treating colleagues is characteristically difficult, even for seasoned clinicians. Second, every author has acknowledged that there are indeed idiosyncratic aspects and special considerations in treating psychotherapists. Third, the clinical dilemmas specific to the psychotherapy of psychotherapists tend to derive from several interrelated sources—unusual pressures to maintain therapeutic boundaries, confrontations with intense countertransferential

345

feelings, and unique problems around the recognition and management of identification issues.

Despite the clinical, educational and theoretical importance of these challenges, scant empirical attention has been given to the experience of conducting therapy with therapists and therapists-in-training. In fact, excluding research specifically devoted to training analyses or the personal analyses of psychoanalytic candidates (see Curtis and Mazier, chapter 26), the two empirical studies reviewed and integrated in this chapter are the only ones we found that have systematically investigated the psychotherapy of therapist-patients.

The procedures, participants, and instrumentation for what we shall refer to as the SPR and Division 29 studies are detailed in previous reports (Norcross, Geller, & Kurzawa, 2000, 2001; Orlinsky et al., 1999). Following are sketches of the methodological features of each study.

THE SPR PROJECT

Over the past decade, the SPR Collaborative Research Network (Orlinsky & Ronnestad, in press) has been conducting an international study of the development of psychotherapists. To date, more than 5,000 therapists of different countries, different professions, varied theoretical orientations, and all career stages, from novices to seniors, have self-administered the project's basic measure—the Development of Psychotherapists' Common Core Questionnaire (DPCCQ). In this chapter, we draw primarily on the respondent's answer to the question "How many other therapists have sought you to be their personal therapist?" and their ratings of how they perceived themselves in relation to patients, how frequently they experienced various types of difficulty in treating patients, as well as the coping strategies they have employed when difficulties have arisen.

THE DIVISION 29 PROJECT

Norcross, Geller, and Kurzawa's (2000, 2001) study was designed to address the following questions.

- Do psychotherapists believe that certain aspects of the process of therapy are more or less specific to working with patients who are themselves therapists?
- Are there particular stressors and satisfactions associated with the work?
- What advice would psychotherapists give their colleagues to help them conduct more effective therapy with therapist-patients?
- Do the personal and professional histories of psychotherapists

influence the manner in which they treat fellow mental health professionals?

- Do psychotherapists treating larger numbers of fellow mental health professionals and those treating fewer do this work differently?
- What are the correlates of identifying oneself as a therapists' therapist?

We constructed a self-administered questionnaire, including Likert scales and open-ended questions to address areas of inquiry. One section of the questionnaire concerned the mental health professionals seen by the respondent in terms of their career status, gender, professional discipline, theoretical orientation, source of referral, and the modality of therapy implemented. Another section asked psychotherapists to rate the extent to which they used 78 clinical practices the same, less, or more with psychotherapists than with laypersons of comparable intelligence, socio-economic status, and diagnosis. The questions were clustered into six domains. Treatment formats (9 items), therapeutic style (14 items) in terms of four dimensions, based on the factorially derived findings of Orlinsky et al. (1999); process of therapy (31 items); subjective experiences of therapists, including those that are commonly referred to as countertransference reactions (17 items); the termination process (3 items); and posttherapy contacts (4 items). Two items reflecting the distinction between symptom relief and enhanced self-understanding were used to assess treatment outcome. Item ratings were made on a five-point, Likert-type format (1 = much less frequently with psychotherapists, 3 = the same frequency with psychotherapists, 5 = much more frequently with psychotherapists).

The questionnaire concluded with two open-ended questions. Psychotherapists were requested to nominate their leading stressor and their leading satisfaction when conducting psychotherapy with psychotherapists in a free-response format. And in the last section of the questionnaire, the psychotherapists were asked to "offer two brief pieces of advice for fellow psychotherapists to help them conduct effective psychotherapy with psychotherapists."

The questionnaire was mailed to 1,000 randomly selected members and fellows of the APA's Division of Psychotherapy. In all, 349 responded, a total response rate of 35%, and 328 provided usable questionnaires, a functional return rate of 33%. The sample was representative of the entire Division of Psychotherapy in regard to membership status in the organization, gender, ethnic/racial background, age, highest academic degree, and geographic area. The sample was made up largely of experienced therapists. The average number of years of clinical experience was 20 (SD = 10). The modal respondent was a middle-aged, Ph.D. psychologist who conducts therapy within a private practice.

PREVALENCE OF CONDUCTING THERAPY
WITH MENTAL HEALTH PROFESSIONALS

In both studies, one research question was to identify how many therapists have provided personal therapy to other therapists. In the Division 29 study, the psychologists estimated the percentage of psychotherapy clients, over the past three years, who have been mental health professionals, defined as master's- or doctoral-level professionals in mental health or those in training for the profession. Twenty-seven percent estimated that 1% to 5% of their caseloads consisted of mental health professionals and professionals-in-training. Fifteen percent and 14% estimated 5% and 10%, respectively. Seventeen percent estimated that more than 10% of their psychotherapy clients were mental health professionals or professionals-in-training. The remaining 26% reported that they had not treated any mental health professionals during this time. The resulting median was 3% and the mean 7% (SD = 9.4).

In the SPR study, approximately half of the 5,000 therapists reported having had at least one other therapist as a patient. The largest group of those who have treated other therapists in the SPR study reported having treated only one to three therapists. Fourteen percent reported having treated 10 or more therapist-patients, and 7% had treated more than 15.

These are surprisingly high proportions and stand in stark contrast to the puzzling silence that surrounds the psychotherapy of psychotherapists. What other population of psychotherapy clients, accounting for this sizable proportion of therapists' daily work, has been so neglected in the literature and in training? Gabbard (1995) describes this state of affairs as an "unfortunate void."

These findings must be taken into account as the profession thinks through such policy issues as: How do we ensure that the services provided to therapist-patients fulfill the ethical requirement of working within one's area of competence? Does solid competence in working with adult nontherapist patients automatically qualify one to treat therapist patients?

Mental health professionals rarely receive formal training and supervision in treating fellow mental health professionals. In one sense this is not surprising or disconcerting, since graduate education does not focus on treating any particular occupational group. In another sense, however, it is not clear when it is ethically and professionally appropriate for a mental health professional to accept the responsibility of treating a colleague in the absence of specific training or supervision.

CHARACTERISTICS OF PSYCHOTHERAPIST-PATIENTS

Practically all of the therapist-patients in the Division 29 study were voluntary and self-referred; 75% of the respondents indicated that essentially all of their therapist caseload was voluntary. The median was 100% and the mean 88% (SD = 26). An average of 7% (SD = 18.2; Mdn = 0) of the thera-

pist-patients were strongly encouraged but not required by training programs, licensing boards, or professional organizations to obtain personal
treatment. Very few (M = 4%, SD = 16, Mdn = 0) were mandated to obtain
personal treatment.

The career status of their own therapy-patients was wide ranging—26%
of the mental health professionals were, on average, in training, 39% were
in their early careers, and 29% were in their middle or late careers. Far less
is known about the contribution of personal therapy to the development
of experienced therapists than to those who are beginning their careers. The
majority of therapist-patients were fellow psychologists (37%) and social
workers (29%). Counselor-therapists and psychiatrists constituted most
of the remaining clients. The predominant theoretical orientations endorsed by these mental health professionals were eclectic-integrative (25%),
psychodynamic-psychoanalytic (24%), and behavioral-cognitive (23%).

PARAMETERS OF PERSONAL THERAPY

In terms of the percentage of psychotherapy devoted to various formats,
the respondents in the Division 29 study indicated that individual therapy
was the rule with mental health professionals. Fully 85% of the treatment
time was individual therapy (SD = 22); in fact, 64% of the responding psychologists related that they essentially conducted only individual therapy
with mental health professionals over the past three years. Less than 10%
saw mental health professionals within the context of couples or family
therapy. Group (3.6%) and couples/family (9.7%) therapy was relatively
rare.

IDENTIFYING THERAPISTS' THERAPISTS

It is one thing to treat mental health professionals rarely or infrequently. It
is quite a different matter to be known as a "therapists' therapist." Acquiring this role and identity bestows a special status on a clinician. Particular
expectations and meanings are attached to this identity by patients and
therapists alike. For example, therapists' therapists unavoidably become role
models, powerfully and implicitly influencing how their therapist-patients,
especially those who are in training, conduct themselves as practitioners.

Various strategies can be used to identify therapists' therapists. In the
Division 29 study, therapists' therapists were identified on the basis of self-
characterization. Practitioners rated themselves on a 5-point, Likert-type
scale on the degree to which they considered themselves "a therapist's therapist" (1 = yes, definitely; 5 = definitely not). Sixteen percent responded that
they definitely considered themselves a therapists' therapist, 25% said probably, 28% said maybe, 26% said probably not, and 6% said definitely not.
For the purposes of the study, only those who answered "yes, definitely"
were classified as therapists' therapists. Congruent with their self-designation, these therapists' therapists reported treating about twice the number

of fellow therapists in their caseloads compared with the other respondents (m = 14.2% v. 7.3%).

In the SPR study, the sample's therapists' therapists were identified on the basis of the therapists' estimate of the number of other therapists who sought them out to be their personal therapist. In order to examine the descriptive characteristics and clinical practices of therapist's therapists in the SPR study, Orlinsky and colleagues formed three groups of "senior" (highly experienced) therapists: the 27 (or 27%) who had treated many other therapists (16–25+); the 218 (47%) who had treated some other therapists (4–15); and the 120 (or 26%) who had treated none or very few therapists

CHARACTERISTICS OF THERAPISTS' THERAPISTS

In the SPR study, each of these comparison groups had an average of more than 30 years in practice and were about 60 years old. Even at this highest level of seniority, those most likely to have treated other therapists had a little over two more years of experience and were a little more than two years older than the seniors who had treated few or no other therapists. In fact, a stepwise multiple regression analysis indicated that a therapist's experience level, measured simply by the number of years in therapeutic practice, is by far the most important predictor of the number of therapist-patients treated, accounting alone for nearly 27% of the total variance and 87% of the predicted variance. With the variance attributable to experience level removed, the next most important predictor of experience as a therapist's therapist was number of hours per week in private practice.

Those who were most specialized as therapist's therapists tended to be more strongly influenced by humanistic theories of psychotherapy. Therapists indicated their theoretical orientation on the DPCCQ by rating the extent to which their practice was influenced by each of the following, with multiple ratings allowed: analytic/psychodynamic, behavioral, cognitive, humanistic, systemic, and "other." Most therapists rated being influenced in varying degrees by combinations of orientations.

A reanalysis of the SPR database for the largest national subsamples (U.S., Norway, Germany, and South Korea), yielded identical findings. In each subsample, having treated more therapist–patients was significantly associated with having a more humanistic orientation, as was seniority, and having a more extensive private practice.

In the Division 29 study, psychologists reporting 10% or more of their caseloads were mental health professionals (31% of the sample) and those reporting 9% or less were compared. Here, too, the percentage of mental health professionals treated in the past three years bore a significant relationship to years of clinical experience. Psychologists who routinely treated fellow therapists had significantly greater clinical experience (M of 23 v. 19 years). In addition, they were significantly more likely to be fellows of the APA (58% of fellows v. 29% of members) and significantly more likely to be employed in university departments (56%) or medical schools (50%) than in other settings than those who reported treating few other therapists.

Self-designation as a therapist's therapist also bore a significant relationship to espoused theoretical orientation. Congruent with the SPR findings, 35% of the humanistic therapists responded as such, with a low of 9% cognitive therapists and 10% interpersonal therapists. In between were 14% of eclectic/integrative and 11% of psychoanalytic/psychodynamic therapists. Theoretical orientation bore a somewhat different but still statistically significant relationship to self-reported percentage of mental health professionals treated in the prior three years.

THE PERSONAL THERAPY OF THERAPISTS' THERAPISTS

Freud viewed personal therapy as an essential part of the education and training of psychoanalysts. He also recognized the need for periodic or ongoing therapy for experienced analysts. It appears that American therapists, like their European counterparts, share this view.

In the Division 29 study, as in previous studies of psychologists, (e.g., Norcross, Strausser-Kirtland, & Missar, 1988; Pope & Tabachnick, 1994), the mean and median number of discrete episodes of receiving personal therapy was three (SD = 1.6). Almost all (96%) had undergone some individual therapy, with a median of 150 hours and a mean of 370. Sixteen percent said they were currently in therapy or analysis. Exactly half of the respondents underwent couples/family treatment, and 34% had been patients in a therapy group.

The majority of the respondents characterized their therapy as moderately to very helpful, replicating previous findings (e.g., Guy & Liaboe, 1986; Henry, Sims, & Spray, 1971; Norcross, Strausser-Kirtland & Missar, 1988; Pope & Tabachnick, 1994). Relative to their colleagues, self-ascribed therapists' therapists reported (even) more successful outcomes in their own personal therapy. Two percent of the therapists in the Division 29 study characterized the outcome of their only or most recent therapy as harmful (very, moderately, or somewhat). An additional 3% reported no change, and 12% rated their therapy as only somewhat helpful. In keeping with these findings, 2% of the American psychologists surveyed by Pope and Tabachnick (1994) reported that therapy had been "very" or "exceptionally" harmful; 22% reported that their experiences with therapy, taken as a whole, had been at least somewhat harmful.

A collateral line of research (Geller, 1999; Orlinsky & Geller, 1993) strongly supports the conclusion that the internalized representations that therapist-patients construct of communicative exchanges with their current and former therapists have, for good or ill, the power to concretely shape and organize their perceptions of and responses to patients, whether they be therapists or nontherapists.

Although no reliable differences were observed in the Division 29 study between psychologists with high- and low-percentage psychotherapist clientele in the frequency with which they experienced personal therapy themselves or their self-reported outcomes of such experience, psychologists who treated large proportions of their peers rated the importance of personal therapy significantly higher as both a prerequisite for clinical work and an opportunity for ongoing development during their careers.

CLINICAL PRACTICES—SPR STUDY

A comparison of the clinical practices of senior therapists with extensive, moderate, and scant experience as therapist's therapists yielded a number of significant relationships. The results, presented in table 25.1, indicate that therapists who have extensively treated other therapists perceive themselves as exhibiting significantly more "warmth" in relating to their patients generally (not just to therapist-patients) than do seniors who have had few, if any, therapist-patients. (The multiitem scale of "warmth" is composed of separate self-ratings on the degree to which one is accepting, warm, friendly, and tolerant in relating to patients.) This corresponds well with the qualities that therapist-patients report they want when selecting a personal therapist (see Norcross and Grunebaum, chapter 16). There was no significant difference between the groups of senior therapists in how "reserved" (detached, guarded, and reserved) they feel they are with patients.

The most experienced therapists' therapists rated themselves significantly more "skillful" (determined, effective, skillful, and subtle) in sessions and significantly more "invested" (committed, involved, and intuitive) in working with patients than those who have had few, if any, therapist-patients.

Senior therapists with extensive or moderate experience treating other therapists reported encountering less frequent difficulties overall (on a scale composed of 18 specific types of difficulty) than those who have had few, if any, therapist-patients. Therapist's therapists reported less frequently feeling "uneasy that [their] personal values make it difficult to maintain an appropriate attitude towards a patient" and less frequently feeling "in danger of losing control of the therapeutic situation to a patient."

In coping with difficulties that do arise, seniors who have most extensively treated other therapists were significantly more likely than those with few, if any, therapist-patients to "attempt to solve the problem collaboratively with the patient" and significantly less likely to "reframe the therapeutic contract" by redefining the roles and goals of treatment. There were no significant differences between groups in the tendency to utilize other constructive coping strategies, to seek consultation, or to be avoidant/critical with troublesome patients.

In terms of their overall career development, senior therapists who have treated many or moderate numbers of therapist-patients were significantly higher than those who had treated few in their own "sense of therapeutic mastery." This composite scale includes ratings on the following questions. "How much mastery do you have of the techniques and strategies involved in practicing therapy?" "How well do you understand what happens

Table 25.1 Therapists' Therapists: Process Experiences of Highly Experienced Nonproviders and Providers

Process Experiences	Number of Therapists Treated			Differences
	(1) 0–3	(2) 4–15	(3) 16–25+	
Relatedness (0–3 scale)				
Warmth***	2.45	2.56	2.67	3>1
Directiveness*	1.02	1.19	1.08	2>1
Reserve with patients	0.84	0.81	0.70	ns
Agency (0–3 scale)				
Skillfulness in sessions*	1.88	2.04	2.05	3>1
Sense of investment***	2.32	2.46	2.58	3>1
Difficulties (0–5 scale)				
Total difficulties*	1.30	1.17	1.04	3,2<1
In danger of losing control of the therapeutic situation to a patient*	1.06	0.84	0.78	3,2<1
Uneasy that your personal values make it difficult to maintain appropriate attitude toward a patient*	1.09	0.92	0.73	3,2<1
Troubled by moral or ethical issues that have arisen in your work with a patient	1.10	1.05	1.05	ns
Disturbed that circumstances in your personal life are interfering in your work with a patient	.98	1.05	.96	ns
Conflicted about how to reconcile obligations to a patient and equivalent obligations to others	1.12	1.07	1.01	ns
Coping strategies (0–5 scale)				
Constructive coping	2.29	2.95	2.85	ns
Seek consultation	2.52	2.49	2.27	ns
Reframe helping contract*	1.82	1.73	1.51	3,2<1
Problem-solve with patient*	3.12	3.34	3.41	3>1
Avoid problem/criticize patient	1.20	1.20	1.12	ns
Career development (0–5 scale)				
Sense of therapeutic mastery***	3.92	4.16	4.29	3,2>1
Overcame limitations as therapist***	3.60	3.75	4.06	3>2,1

Note: All therapists with 25 to 50 years in practice *p < .05 **p < .01 ***p < .001

moment-by-moment during therapy sessions?" "How much precision, subtlety, and finesse have you attained in your therapeutic work?" and "How capable do you feel to guide the development of other psychotherapists?" Finally, senior therapists who had extensive experience as therapists' therapists were significantly higher than both other senior groups in the degree to which they felt they had "succeeded in overcoming [their] past limitations" as psychotherapists.

CLINICAL PRACTICES—DIVISION 29 STUDY

To provide a context for examining how self-designation as a therapists' therapist might influence the manner in which fellow mental health professionals are treated, let us first consider how the respondents of the Division 29 sample, in its entirety, compared their therapeutic approach with psychotherapists to their approach with lay persons of comparable intelligence, socioeconomic status, and diagnosis.

The respondents rated a series of 78 questions comparing the therapy conducted with therapists and laypersons on a 5-point Likert scale (where 1 = much more frequently with psychotherapists, 3 = the same frequency with psychotherapists, and 5 = much more frequently with psychotherapists). "Equivalent" practice was operationally defined as an average response between 2.76 and 3.24, with response hovering around the 3.0 scale midpoint identified as the same frequency. Items receiving a group mean of 2.75 or lower were designated as "less frequent," whereas those receiving a mean score of 3.25 or higher were designated as "more frequent." Table 25.2 summarizes the mean responses for all items both graphically and numerically.

As shown in table 25.2, the sample as a whole reported that in terms of treatment format, therapist-patients are more likely to be offered individual therapy. Concomitantly, relative to lay persons of comparable education and diagnosis, therapist-patients are less likely to be offered couples therapy or group therapy. Moreover, responding psychologists indicated that therapist-patients are less likely to be medicated, referred to support groups, recommended to self-help books as part of their ongoing treatment, or hospitalized.

With respect to therapy process, table 25.2 indicates that at one and the same time there are deep similarities and important differences in the ways therapists conduct psychotherapy with therapist and nontherapist patients. For example, therapists do not appear to be more or less task centered, advice giving, self-disclosing, encouraging of affective expression, or likely to use humor or therapeutic touch with one group of patients than the other. As they reported it to us, therapists allow no variations in regard to the ground rules of psychotherapy (e.g., confidentiality, length of sessions), boundary decisions (e.g., patient contact outside of sessions), the payment of fees (e.g., negotiating a lower fee, charging for missed sessions), or the expression of personal feelings (e.g., expression of caring for or anger toward patient). Neither do they discern differences in the content of the communicative exchanges they have with therapist and nontherapist patients. For example, work stressors, sexual issues, choice of career, and shame or guilt about seeking therapy regularly and equally surface as themes with both groups.

An examination of the clinical practices in the categories designated as more or less suggests that what distinguishes the psychotherapy of therapist-patients may be operative primarily at an experiential-emotional level.

Table 25.2   Clinical Practices with Psychotherapist-Patients Relative to Practices with Lay Persons of Comparable Intelligence, Socioeconomic Status, and Diagnosis

Less Frequent (M<2.76)	*Equivalent Frequency* M=2.76–3.29	*More Frequent* (M>3.24)
Treatment formats	**Therapeutic style**	**Treatment formats**
Conduct couples/family therapy	Challenging, Demanding	Conduct individual therapy
Conduct group therapy	Determined	Conduct long-term therapy
Refer for medication	Directive, Effective	
Use hospitalization	Friendly	**Therapy process**
Recommend a support group	Guarded, Involved	Share the responsibility for creating a therapeutic contract
Suggest a self-help book	Nurturant, Reserved	Limit information in treatment notes
Conduct short-term therapy	Skillful, Warm	Wonder about the boundaries between my personal and professional roles
Therapeutic style	**Therapy process**	Conscious of the "techniques" I use
Authoritative	Talk about sexual issues	Attend to counter-transference reactions
Detached	Feel competitive with patient	Discuss current issues and research in the field
Therapy process	Feel concerned about confidentiality	Worry about treatment effectiveness
Number of canceled sessions	Disclose my own personal therapy	Concerned patient may be critical of my work
	Examine patient's choice of career	Enjoy being with the patient
	Ambitious in therapeutic goals	**Outcome**
	Have contact with patient outside of sessions	Positive therapy outcome in terms of self-understanding/enhanced insight
	Tell the patient I am angry with him or her	
	Address the patient's shame or guilt about seeking therapy	**Posttermination**
	Tell the patient I care about him or her	Frequency of contact with patient posttherapy
	Use humor in the session	
	Use therapeutic touch	
	Negotiate a lower-than-customary fee	
	Encourage expression of affect	
	Recommend between-session tasks	
	Experience difficulty balancing distance and closeness	
	Reveal personal problems I have experienced	
	Pride in contributing to patient's well-being	
	Experience a turbulent therapeutic relationship	

(continued)

Table 25.2   continued

Less Frequent (M<2.76)	Equivalent Frequency M=2.76–3.29	More Frequent (M>3.24)
	Aware of gender issues in therapy	
	Aware of the power dynamics in therapy	
	Focus on transference reactions	
	Number of canceled sessions	
	Feel like emotionally withdrawing from patient	
	Aware of the difficulty of meaningful change	
	Give advice	
	Conversational	
	Offer a diagnosis	
	Address the client by his or her first name	
	Accept a hug from the client	
	Apologize for my mistakes or errors	
	Scrupulous about the length of our sessions	
	Termination issues	
	Mutually agreed-on termination	
	Frequency of externally imposed endings	
	Experience strong feelings about termination	
	Outcome	
	Positive therapy outcome in terms of behavior change/symptom relief	
	Posttermination	
	Enter into a professional relationship with patient	
	Enter into a social relationship	
	Return of patient for further therapy	

As they experienced it and reported to us, the therapists enjoy being with therapist-patients more than with nontherapist patients. A related difference is the finding that therapists felt less detached from and friendlier toward their therapist-patients. A variant on these states of relatedness is implied by the finding that therapists are more likely to discuss research and professional matters with their therapist-patients. Intellectual intimacy affirms the collegial connection between patient and therapist.

The participants report using the same techniques with both categories of patients, but they are aware, at the same time, of being more self-conscious of their techniques and more likely to attend to their countertransference reactions when the patient is a mental health professional. The therapists relate feeling comparably effective and skillful with their therapist and nontherapist patients, but they are more likely to "worry about treatment effectiveness" and are more concerned about the patient "being critical of their work" when the patient is a fellow therapist.

While equally concerned with protecting the confidentiality of all of their patients, therapists are more likely to limit the information contained in their therapist-patients' therapy notes. Breaching confidentiality represents the violation of an ethical mandate. By contrast, the decision to exclude certain types of information from a therapist-patients' clinical records is based on personal considerations rather than published moral codes. Any of several explanations can be evoked to account for the motivational underpinnings of this decision. One plausible interpretation is that therapists feel more "protective" toward and identified with their therapist-patients, having once been therapist-patients themselves. According to Gabbard (1995), in psychoanalytic circles, fears of public exposure and shame are shared by both therapist-patients and their therapists.

Another possible domain in which the psychotherapy of psychotherapists may stand apart from the psychotherapy of lay patients is in the indices of positive therapy outcomes. On the one hand, the results of the Division 29 study suggest that therapists do not discern differences in the extent to which therapist and nontherapist patients realize positive therapeutic outcomes in terms of behavior change and symptomatic relief. On the other hand, they are more likely to discern positive outcomes in terms of self-understanding and insight among their therapist-patients.

There are many interpretations for this difference. Although psychological mindedness is a desirable trait in all patients, seeking self-knowledge is one of the principle motives for choosing to become a psychotherapist (Farber & Golden, 1997). Moreover, a heightened capacity to continue self-analysis, following termination, constitutes a vital tool of the effective therapist, especially if he or she views himself or herself as a participant observer in the therapeutic dialogue. In other words, the capacity to reflect on and interpret one's experiences, rather than act on them, figures prominently in the professional and personal aspects of therapist-patients' lives. Consequently, it is possible that therapists make a greater effort to strengthen their therapist-patients' capacities for self-reflection.

In terms of posttherapy experiences, the respondents acknowledged having a greater frequency of contact with their therapist-patients than with lay persons following termination, but that this increased posttermination contact with therapist-patients was not accompanied by increases in the probability of entering into a social relationship or the former patient returning for further psychotherapy.

In the Division 29 study, practitioners' self-characterization as a therapists' therapist was clearly associated with the manner in which they treated mental health professionals. A comparison of the self-designated therapists' therapists and the other respondents yielded statistically significant differences on 16 of the 78 items related to clinical practice. In terms of treatment format, therapists' therapists were less likely to conduct short-term therapy. From the standpoint of affective involvement, they characterized themselves as *less* guarded, detached, likely to emotionally withdraw, and likely to have patients cancel sessions. Concomitantly, they perceived themselves as feeling more effective with their therapist-patients than did their colleagues.

In terms of therapy process, self-designated therapists' therapists related that they were *more* likely to: share the responsibility for creating a therapeutic contract, show warmth, apologize for mistakes or errors, attend to countertransference reactions, be task centered, discuss current issues and research in the field, disclose information about their own personal therapy, and arrive at a mutually agreed-on termination.

In sum, the differences observed in the entire sample in the Division 29 study emerged with greater clarity and intensity in the responses of the self-designated therapists' therapists. In other words, the qualities and clinical practices that the therapist sample, as a whole, ascribed to itself were even more fully realized in the subsample of therapists' therapists. Moreover, there was considerable similarity in clinical practices between the American psychologists who characterized themselves as therapists' therapists and the therapists in the SPR study who had extensive experience treating therapists.

The data accumulated in both studies are consistent with the hypothesis that the relationships therapists' therapists establish with therapist-patients are embedded within emotional atmospheres (Geller, 1984) that are qualitatively different than those established by other therapists. Insofar as their self-appraisals are accurate, therapists' therapists, relative to other therapists, feel more efficacious with their therapist-patients. At the same time, their depth of involvement with therapist-patients is more capable of withstanding threats to their feelings of efficacy. In addition, they appear to be better prepared to nondefensively use the rise and fall of their feelings of efficacy and involvement as interpretive resources in their work with therapist-patients.

It remains to be seen whether those who have attracted more therapist-patients are, in fact, more proficient. Unfortunately, information directly relevant to this question is neither in the Division 29 nor the SPR study. What the findings of both studies do indicate is a significantly greater self-confidence among those who characterize themselves as therapists' therapists and among those who have treated many other therapists. It is unclear how much they have gained of this greater sense of confidence by having treated many other therapists and, on the other hand, how much they have attracted so many therapist-patients by being the most confident and charismatic of senior therapists. It also remains to be seen how much the differential self-perceptions of those senior therapists accurately reflect their qualities as clinicians. If they are indeed accurate, that could well explain why so many other therapists have sought them for personal therapy. What we wish to highlight here is that combining the various findings suggests that the emotional atmospheres created by therapists' therapists can be described as more lively, spirited, and natural.

SATISFACTIONS AND STRESSORS

In the Division 29 study, therapists generated 236 responses by the request to nominate one satisfaction of conducting psychotherapy with psychotherapists, beyond that associated with conducting psychotherapy in general. These were subsequently coded into 13 mutually exclusive categories, including an "other category" consisting of singular responses, by a process of iterative, recursive coding. The percentage of responses that were assigned to the eight most frequent categories of satisfactions are displayed in table 25.3.

By far the most prominent satisfaction reported was that the psycho-therapist-patients were experienced as "better" clients, with whom one could establish a "better" therapeutic relationship. This finding dovetails with the therapists' ratings of their clinical practices. Here they reported "enjoying being with" therapist-patients more than with nontherapist patients. These sources of satisfaction arise while doing the work. As can be seen in table 25.3, far greater prominence was given to the sources of satisfaction that derive from the consequences of doing the work successfully and not to the pleasures inherent in more immediate sources of satisfaction. These included helping therapist-patients enhance their clinical effectiveness,

Table 25.3   Most Frequent Satisfactions of Conducting Psychotherapy with Psychotherapists

Satisfaction	N	% of Total
Better clients/better relationships	72	30.5
Helping therapist-patients be more effective	39	16.5
Acknowledgment by peers	20	8.5
Contributing to the profession	19	8.0
Indirectly helping clients of therapist-patients	15	6.4
More challenging group of patients	9	3.8
Working with someone with similar qualities	9	3.8
Watching the client grow	9	3.8

thereby contributing indirectly to the welfare of the clients of the therapist-patient. They also included earning the praise or acknowledgment
of one's colleagues and contributing to the advancement of the profession. None of these ("narcissistic") rewards is as available when treating
nontherapists. They bring sharply into focus the danger of turning one's
therapist-patients into "disciples" or "professional offspring" who will carry
on one's message.

A parallel question regarding the stressors of conducting psychotherapy netted 230 intriguing responses. These, too, were coded by a similar process into 13 discrete categories, including "other," and the most
frequent are presented in table 25.4. As can be seen, the emphasis here is
on the therapist's relationship to his or her therapist-patients and not on
the extratherapeutic consequences of the relationship. The primary stress
associated with treating fellow mental health professionals appears to be
the activation of anxieties and doubts about one's own abilities as a therapist. Less prevalent, but related to the primary concern, was the experience
that fellow psychotherapists were more challenging or resistant to change
(than nonpsychotherapist patients) as well as more critical consumers of
psychotherapy. Another 17% wrote of the burdens of feeling a greater sense
of responsibility when working with therapist-patients. Concerns about
boundary violations, such as entering into a dual relationship, were cited
with comparable frequency. Further, the boundary-challenging experience
of encountering patients outside of therapy was noted by 6% of the sample.

An integrative summary of the most frequent satisfactions and stressors
associated with conducting psychotherapy with therapists supports the view,
previously expressed by a handful of therapist's therapists in clinical case reports, that treating therapist-patients tends to be experienced simultaneously
as a privilege and as a burden. Our initial results reaffirm their shared view
that treating a colleague increases the probability that psychotherapists will
feel more anxious and self-conscious about their techniques, preferences, and
emotional reactions to the potential conflicts of the treatment situation.

The satisfactions and stresses of doing therapy stand in a dynamic,
ever-changing relationship to one another. At any given moment one may

Table 25.4 Most Frequent Stressors of Conducting
Psychotherapy with Psychotherapists

Stressor	N	% of Total
Activates therapist's anxieties regarding ability	62	27.0
More challenging/more resistant to change	38	16.5
Clients tend to be more critical	26	11.3
Feel greater responsibility	17	7.4
Boundary concerns/dual relationships	16	7.0
Encounter clients outside of session	14	6.1
Elitist attitudes of patients	8	3.5
Competitive feelings in therapy process	8	3.5

be figural, the other ground. What is of importance is the capacity to nondefensively direct an investigatory attitude toward all emotional reactions to and affective judgments toward patients. We take the position that therapists who are unable to engage in such self-exploration and collaborative inquiry are ill equipped to grasp and deal with the common clinical dilemmas that are brought into existence or intensified by the fact that a patient is also a therapist, especially if he or she suffers from characterological difficulties.

ADVICE TO FELLOW PSYCHOTHERAPISTS

Parallel findings can be discerned in the advice the therapists gave about treating mental health professionals. A generous amount and an impressive variety of advice to help others conduct effective treatment with fellow therapists was offered. The total number of pieces of advice was 415, and these were content-coded into 28 mutually exclusive categories. Coding was completed by two of the authors; when disagreement surfaced, it was resolved by mutual discussion.

The most frequent advice is summarized in table 25.5. As can be seen, the modal advice was to treat all patients in an equal and consistent manner. As one respondent put it, "A patient is a patient is a patient." Recommendations that could be construed as equally applicable to the psychotherapy of all patients, such as "listen empathically, "be respectful," "clarify the treatment contract and goals early on," were, however, in the minority. The majority of the advice offered dealt with and was linked to the previously noted stressors that were nominated as more or less specific to conducting psychotherapy with psychotherapists.

Two interrelated themes can be extracted from these offerings. Much of the advice dealt with boundary-challenging aspects of the therapy of

Table 25.5 Most Common Advice for Conducting Psychotherapy with Fellow Psychotherapists

Advice	N	% of Total
Treat all patients equally and consistently	68	16.4
Maintain clear boundaries and avoid dual relationships	46	11.1
Avoid overidentifying with therapist-patients	27	6.5
Remember that therapist-patients are not immune to problems of other patients simply because they are therapists	23	5.5
Don't be intimidated or overwhelmed by performance anxiety	20	4.8
Listen empathically	20	4.8
Anticipate and attend to countertransference reactions	19	4.6
Clarify the treatment contract and goals early on	14	3.4
Avoiding diluting therapy by converting it into supervision or by chatting about professional topics	10	2.4
Be respectful	9	2.2
Consult with colleagues and seek supervision as needed	9	2.2

therapists, such as the dangers of overidentification, the pitfalls of dual relationships, and the temptation to convert psychotherapy into supervision. The other theme was to anticipate and attend to potentially problematic feelings, for example, envy, self-aggrandizement, intimidation, and competitiveness with one's therapist-patients. The overall similarity in these findings suggest that coordinating the formal and contractual role relations that separate the positions of patient and therapist is an ongoing tension that is inherent to the psychotherapy of fellow therapists. The overriding message is that in our role as therapists' therapists, we are neither impartial scientists nor unbiased helpers.

METHODOLOGY AND ITS DISCONTENTS

Caution is essential in interpreting the research findings presented in this chapter. Both studies await replication. It is unclear how the experiences of Division 29 members would compare with those of psychologists or psychotherapists generally. The response rate (35%) in the Division 29 study suggests that people with histories of personal therapy or treating psychotherapists in their practices may be overrepresented in this sample. The sample of the SPR study similarly is of unknown representativeness. There is a possibility that there is a socially desirable pull toward identifying oneself as a "therapists' therapist."

And, of course, there are the inescapable virtues and limitations of anonymous self-reports. Is there any reason to believe that psychotherapists are more accurate and reliable observers of their own behavior than lay persons? Most of the questionnaire items involve enormously complex issues. The research to date is suggestive and preliminary. Although inconclusive, the overall findings suggest that if a therapist is to achieve competence in treating therapist-patients, he or she must be prepared to be more collaborative and egalitarian throughout the course of therapy, as well as more flexible in his or her management of the role boundaries that separate the positions of patient and therapist during treatment and following termination (see Geller, chapter 27).

CONCLUDING COMMENTS

We conclude with a call for the scientific study of such researchable questions as: What particular aspects of their personal therapies are therapists most likely to repeat with their own patients? What distinguishes the treatment of therapists who undergo therapy at different stages of their careers? What criteria can a therapist rely on to distinguish countertransference-based doubts about professional competence from the reality of overextending oneself? What are the consequences of not benefiting from a particular approach to therapy early in one's career? What is the legacy of finding the clinical practices of a particular school of therapy harmful? What special considerations, if any, attend to the decision to medicate or hospitalize a mental health professional? Are there normative aspects of the subjective experience of encountering the resisted aspects of therapist-patients' experience of therapy? How can a therapist best prepare for the day when he or she will begin treating a fellow therapist? And what are the additional burdens and special problems posed by therapists mandated to receive treatment by professional authorities?

REFERENCES

Berman, E. (1995). On analyzing colleagues. *Contemporary Psychoanalysis, 31,* 521–539.

Bridges, N. A. (1993). Clinical dilemmas: Therapists treating therapists. *American Journal of Orthopsychiatry, 63,* 34–44.

Bridges, N. A. (1995). Psychotherapy with therapists: Countertransference dilemmas. In M. B. Sussman (Ed.), *A perilous calling.* New York: Wiley.

Burton, A. (1973). The psychotherapist as client. *American Journal of Psychoanalysis, 33,* 94–103.

Farber, B. A., & Golden, V. (1997). Psychological mindedness in psychotherapists. In M. McCallum & W. E. Piper (Eds.), *Psychological Mindedness.* Hillsdale, NJ: Erlbaum.

Fleischer, J. A., & Wissler, A. (1985). The therapist as patient: Special problems and considerations. *Psychotherapy, 22,* 586–594.

Freud, S. (1937/1964). Analysis terminable and interminable. In J. Strachey (Ed. and Trans.), *The Standard edition of the complete psychological works of Sigmund Freud* (Vol. 23, pp. 216–253). London: Hogarth Press.

Freudenberger, H. J. (1986). The health professional in treatment: Symptoms, dynamics and treatment issues. In C. D. Scott & J. Hawk (Eds.), *Heal thyself, the health of health care professionals.* New York: Brunner/Mazel.

Gabbard, G. O. (1995). Transference and countertransference in the psychotherapy of therapists charged with sexual misconduct. *Journal of Psychotherapy Practice and Research, 4,* 10–17.

Geller, J. D. (1984). Moods, feelings, and the process of affect formation. In C. Van Dyke, L. Temoshok, & L. Zegans (Eds.), *Emotions in health and illness: Applications to clinical practice.* New York: Grune and Stratton.

Geller, J. D. (1999). What does it mean to practice psychotherapy scientifically? *Psychoanalysis and Psychotherapy, 10,* 187–214.

Glickauf-Hughes, C., & Mehlman, E. (1995). Narcissistic issues in therapists: Diagnostic and treatment considerations. *Psychotherapy, 32,* 213–221.

Grunebaum, H. (1983). A study of therapists' choice of therapists. *American Journal of Psychiatry, 140,* 1336–1339.

Guy, J. D., & Liaboe, G. P. (1986). Personal therapy for the experienced psychotherapist. A discussion of its usefulness and utilization. *Clinical Psychologist, 39,* 20–23.

Henry, W. E., Sims, J. H., & Spray, S.L. (1971). *The fifth profession: Becoming a psychotherapist.* San Francisco: Jossey-Bass.

Kaslow, F.W. (Ed.). (1984). *Psychotherapy with psychotherapists.* New York: Haworth.

Macran, S., & Shapiro, D. (1998). The role of personal therapy for therapists: A review. *British Journal of Medical Psychology, 71,* 13–25.

Norcross, J.C. (1990). Personal therapy for therapists: One solution. *Psychotherapy in Private Practice, 8*, 45–59.

Norcross, J. C., Farber, J. A., & Prochaska, J. O. (1993). Psychologists conducting psychotherapy: New findings and historical comparisons on the Psychotherapy Division membership. *Psychotherapy, 30*, 692–697.

Norcross, J. C., Geller, J. D., & Kurzawa, E. K. (2000). Conducting psychotherapy with psychotherapists: I: Prevalence, patients and problems. *Psychotherapy, 37*, 199–205.

Norcross, J. C., Geller, J. D., & Kurzawa, E. K. (2001). Conducting psychotherapy with psychotherapists II: Clinical practices and collegial advice. *Journal of Psychotherapy Practice and Research, 10*, 37–45.

Norcross, J. C., Strausser, D. J., & Faltus, F. J. (1988). The therapist's therapist. *American Journal of Psychotherapy, 42*, 53–66.

Norcross, J.C., Strausser-Kirtland, D., & Missar, C. D. (1988). The processes and outcomes of psychotherapists' personal treatment experiences. *Psychotherapy, 25*, 36–43.

Orlinsky, D. E., & Geller, J. D. (1993). Patients' representations of their therapists and therapy: New measures. In J. Miller, J. P. Lubovsky, J. Barber, & N. E. Doeherty (Eds.), *Psychodynamic treatment research* (pp. 423–466). New York: Basic Books.

Orlinsky, D., Ambuhl, M., Ronnestad, M. H., Davis, J. D., Gerin, P., Davis, M., Willutzki, U., Botermans, J. F., Dazord, A., Cierpka, M., Aapro, N., Buchheim, P., Bae, S., Davidson, C., Friis-Jorgensen, E., Joo, E., Kalmykova, E., Meyerberg, J., Northcut, T., Parks, B., Scherb, E., Schroder, T., Shefler, G., Stiwne, D., Stuart, S., Tarragona, M., Vasco, A. B., & Wiseman, H. (1999). The development of psychotherapists: Concepts, questions, and methods of a collaborative international study. *Psychotherapy Research 9*, 127–153.

Orlinsky, D. E., & Ronnestad, M. H. (in press). *How psychotherapists develop: A study of therapeutic work and professional development*. Washington, D.C. American Psychological Association.

Pope, K. S., & Tabachnick, B. G. (1994). Therapists as patients: A national survey of psychologists' experiences, problems, and beliefs. *Professional Psychology. Research and Practice, 25*, 247–258.

26

TRAINING ANALYSES
Historical Considerations
and Empirical Research

REBECCA C. CURTIS & MAZIA QAISER

I n the last century, psychoanalytic training has evolved both theoretically and practically from the classical discoveries of Freud in the early
1900s. Regardless of the theoretical orientation of a psychoanalytic institute, the training analysis has been cited as the most important and crucial
component for the analytic candidate (Benedek, 1969; Bibring, 1954;
Limentani, 1974, 1992; Torras de Bea, 1992). Yet the empirical research
dedicated to understanding and uncovering the unique dynamics of the
training analysis is relatively sparse.

As we enter a new millennium in the understanding of the analytic
process as an interactive merging of an analyst's experience with that of her
or his training analyst, we hope to encourage more quantitative studies on
the single most important part of the analytic candidate's study—the training analysis. We psychoanalysts also require further research on how change
can be measured within the psychoanalytic process.

This chapter begins with a brief historical account of theoretical writings about the training analysis. We then review the empirical research on
outcomes of training analyses and discuss suggestions for future research.

A HISTORICAL PERSPECTIVE ON TRAINING ANALYSIS

Early in the development of psychoanalysis, Freud (1910/1968) expressed
the need for personal analysis for those who wanted to apply psychoanalytic technique. He continued his elaborations on "training" analysis in his
work "Analysis Terminable and Interminable" (1937/1968), suggesting

that self-analysis should occur throughout one's life and career as an analyst, and not at termination of one's training analysis (see chapter 2). The best knowledge of what took place in early training analyses comes from reports such as those of Kardiner (1977) regarding his analysis with Freud (see Lohser & Newton [1996] for reports of other early training analyses with Freud) and Menaker (1989) regarding her analysis with Anna Freud.

Sachs (1947), the first appointed training analyst at the Berlin Institute, wrote about the importance of the Institute's selection process—in choosing proper candidates. He said that the purpose of the analysis is to remove resistances obstructing development of a freely functioning ego.

Balint (1954) reviewed five periods in the history of the training analysis. In the first period, the analysis was purely instructional in nature. The candidate read about psychoanalytic theory from books and then underwent an analysis lasting from several weeks to several months in order "to experience in his own mind the validity and force of the main findings" (p. 157). In the second period, the training analysis was for the purpose of demonstration. The informality of the training analysis at that time was evident in an unpublished letter by Freud to Ferenczi in 1909 that Balint quotes and translates within his article. In the letter, Freud referred to the walks twice a week after dinner with Eitingen during which Eitingen had his analysis. The third period was one of "proper analysis." Ferenczi had argued that it was untenable that patients were better analyzed than their analysts and that their analyses should be as long and as deep as a therapeutic analysis. In 1922 at the Berlin Congress it was agreed that only those persons would be authorized to practice psychoanalysis who "had submitted to a training-analysis conducted by an analyst appointed by the society at that time" (Kovacs, 1936, p. 349). Ferenczi also instigated the fourth period. He believed that training analyses should achieve more than therapeutic analyses. In 1927, a new doctrine was declared: that analysts should be more fully analyzed than their patients (Kovacs, 1936). During this period analyses became longer and longer. During the fifth period the training analysis also had the goal of research and became a kind of "super-therapy" (Balint, 1954, p. 159). The analysis was intended to go beyond the Oedipus conflict "into the pre-oedipal states, which means that they must express in words mental experiences of a non-verbal or even pre-verbal period" (p. 159). Of special importance were the "aggressive-destructive urges of the mind" (p. 159).

A number of analysts have written about the pressures on the training analyst. The result of the analysis was obvious to the analyst's colleagues (Heimann, 1954) and created anxiety about judgment about his or her work (Kairys, 1964). Many authors (e.g. Calef & Weinshel, 1973; Greenacre, 1966; Kairys, 1964; McLaughlin, 1973) remarked on the incompatible roles of analyst and evaluator if analysts reported to the training committee on the analytic candidate's progress. The general practice in many institutes was for the analyst to comment on the candidate's readiness to see patients and readiness to graduate. Kairys (1964) recommended that the training analysis be separated from the institute, and McLaughlin (1973) recommended a nonreporting training analysis.

Limentani (1974) highlighted more of the specific problems associated with the training analysis. He specifically discussed interferences from the candidate, playing the dual role of patient and student, and from the Institute, the context in which the training analysis takes place. This point was further elaborated by Pfeffer (1974, p. 79), who said that "the training analyst is confronted with a student-patient who not only wants to be analyzed but also wants to be an analyst. In different students the relative degree of motivation may vary between these two aims." Special problems of identification arise because the training analyst is probably the student's first model of an analyst. In addition, the student is what Pfeffer refers to as a "captive patient" who does not have the ability to stop the analysis because it is a requirement. Moreover, the student is caught between the analyst's allegiance to him or her and the analyst's allegiance to the Institute.

Limentani (1992) framed the aims of the training analysis as being "good enough," borrowing from Winnicott's (1965) phrase for the adequate care-giving needed in order for solid ego development. He said that analytic training is a unique and controversial facet of analytic training but that "it could also lead to denial on the part of the analyst that this is a very *special* situation" (p. 133). Sachs (1992) focused his attention on the syncretistic problems of combining training and therapy, echoing earlier discussions. In a training analysis, the patient's/candidate's countertransference becomes more layered with feelings toward the Institute to which he or she belongs and toward the Institute's role in the success of training. Limentani supported Sachs's assertion at a 1965 conference (cited in Limentani, 1992, p. 135) that artistry is necessary "to name and frame issues which serve as a balance to the endless ambitions of reductionism and . . . unfulfillable ambitions of human beings." These conflicts continue to reverberate throughout the field, suggesting that empirical work may help us to "name and reframe" some of the unique issues surrounding the training analysis.

In a recent article, Gerber (2001, p. 14) asserted that "something is wrong with the relationship between psychoanalysis and research." He recommended that (1) trainees should learn research from day one, alongside theory and practice, (2) clinicians should cite research within the theoretical and clinical classroom, and (3) researchers should develop a standard battery to measure important patient and therapy parameters, allowing for a consistent procedure for measurement.

In *Unfree Associations*, Kirsner (2000) examined the inner workings of several psychoanalytic training institutes. He mentions "the tripartite division in analytic education that most institutes adopt—training analysis, seminars, and supervision" and says that "the training analysis is regarded as the most important" (p. 4). It is here where psychoanalytic teachings are handed down, and "training analysts anoint their analysts through the medium of training analysis" (p. 4). Since a training analyst has the right to conduct analysis with the candidate as part of the training, power and control tensions are paramount.

Later in his book, Kirsner describes the reformist movement, which occurred at the Boston Psychoanalytic Society and Institute, where a director proposed a structural change allowing candidates to choose a reputable member for their training analysis. This change ensured that the analyst would never be contacted for a report on the candidate. Members of the Institute wanted a nonreporting training analysis, and this led to controversy in Boston's analytic community. The question of reporting versus nonreporting is central to analytic training. In his concluding remarks, Kirsner suggests that the position of the training analyst be dropped and recommends abolishing the mandatory training analysis altogether.

Kirsner subsequently suggested a series of less radical solutions: that candidates' analyses should be kept entirely separate from the institute; candidates should be able to choose their analyst; the training analyst should not be associated with the assessment process; and no reports of the progress of the analysis should be given to the institute. These solutions, he believes, will eliminate the power currently given to training analysts and help to lift what he characterizes as the "basic fault in analytic institutes": qualification "on the basis of an unwarranted claim to knowledge" (p. 248). Some institutes, of course, never had reporting analyses or abandoned the practice over time.

RESEARCH ON TRAINING ANALYSES

There have been only a few published empirical studies on training analyses (Craige, in press; Curtis, Field, Knaan-Kostman, & Mannix, in press; Martinez & Hoppe, 1991; Shapiro, 1974, 1976), although there have been a couple of studies of therapists who experienced psychoanalysis as part of their training, prior to it, or subsequent to it. In what follows we summarize the major findings of these studies in chronological order.

Shapiro (1974) sent a questionnaire to all 198 living graduates of the Columbia University Psychoanalytic Center for Training and Research. Sixty-two percent of the questionnaires were returned, 121 complete and two more partially completed. Anonymity was guaranteed, with only four respondents choosing to sign their questionnaires. It was noted that there was a higher return rate among graduates from the last 10 years. In addition to questions about such issues as the length of the analysis and seeking subsequent analysis, the respondents were asked which of three factors represented significant problems for the analysis: (a) your own problems; (b) difficulties stemming from your analyst; and (c) difficulties "related to undertaking personal analysis in the context of the Institute psychoanalytic training program" (Shapiro, 1976, p. 39).

Six out of every seven respondents rated the outcome as satisfactory. This occurred although the training analyses had all been reporting analyses at that institute up until the time the survey was conducted. Thirty-two percent of the analysts rated their treatment as "highly satisfactory," 53% as "generally satisfactory," 12% as "somewhat unsatisfactory," and 2% as "very unsatisfactory." The highly satisfied analysts by their own self-reports appeared "to have entered treatment initially with less severe character and symptomatic pathology" (Shapiro, 1976, p. 15). The questionnaire did not ask for a self-assessed diagnosis. One in 12 reported struggling with substantial problems derived from excessive admiration of the training analyst. Only one in 10 of these graduates later reentered analysis, and almost all did so with their former analysts. They said that the reason for wanting additional analysis was the existence of new problems or new life situations.

Of the "generally satisfactory" outcome group, two-fifths reported major difficulties and slightly less than a third reported one or more severe and insoluble problems. Significant character pathology was identified in a third of the group—difficulties resolving such pathology perhaps increased by the evaluative and reporting role of the analyst or countertransference reactions of the analyst. One-fifth of this group sought further analysis.

Of the 28% who acknowledged severe difficulties in the analysis, 25% believed the difficulties arose from their personality alone, 28% from their personality, that of the analyst, and the context combined, 23% from the training context alone, 18% from the training analyst alone, and 6% from the training context and the training analyst together.

Of the group that was dissatisfied (15%) with the outcome of the training analysis, nearly half (44%) reported significant personal pathology, whereas of those satisfied with their gains only 8% reported such pathology. One-fourth thought the major difficulties were due to the training analyst's personality or behavior. Of those who were dissatisfied with their therapeutic outcome, 17 of 18 viewed their major problems as coming at least in part from the training analyst. In three-fifths, these problems were insurmountable. Shapiro noted that it was surprising that there was little feeling expressed that the assignment of the analyst by the Institute may have hampered the success of these analyses. Although all of the respondents had graduated from the Institute, the questionnaire did not ask if the training analyst had prevented the trainee's progression in training at any point, such as beginning to see patients or graduating.

Goldensohn (1977) conducted an evaluation of the overall training experience of graduates of the William Alanson White Institute, including a rating of their experience in their training analysis. Of the 183 graduates, 7% returned the questionnaire. When asked to rate various aspects of their training experience, 89.5% reported that the training analysis was helpful or somewhat helpful. A system of weighting what was most helpful in the training was devised. The supervisory experience (rated 3.64 on a four-point scale) was weighted most highly, with the training analysis next in importance. Because few analysts returned the questionnaire, it is unclear if these results were representative of the attitudes toward the training experience.

In addition to these studies on psychoanalytic training, Buckley, Karasu, and Charles (1981) conducted a study of 97 practicing psychotherapists who had experienced intensive psychotherapy (24%) or psychoanalysis (76%). Of these 97, 71 (74%) returned the questionnaire. Positive benefits of treatment involved improvements in self-esteem (94% of the respondents), work function (86%), social/sex life (86%), character (89%), and alleviation of symptoms (73%). Improvement in all areas (self-esteem, work function, social/sex life, character change, and alleviation of symptoms) was correlated positively with the feeling of being liked by and liking the therapist. Twenty-one percent reported that their treatment was harmful in some way. The data suggested that unresolved transference issues were central to a negative effect.

Meisels (1990) reported on the applications for membership of the psychologist/psychoanalyst section of the Psychoanalytic Division of the American Psychological Association. Membership in this section requires training at a psychoanalytic institute, so all of the respondents should have experienced an analysis before or during their training. He was privy to the application forms for membership that included the personal analytic histories of hundreds of applicants. Most of the applicants had seven or eight years of analysis, with one-quarter to one-third having had more than 10 years of treatment. He noted that therapists could learn a great deal about the therapeutic action of psychoanalysis by systematically studying themselves.

WILLIAM ALANSON WHITE INSTITUTE/OSLO INSTITUTT FOR PSYKOTERAPI STUDY OF TRAINING ANALYSES

Curtis et al. (2004) posed questions to analysts about what they believed led to most change in their own analysis. The analysts were instructed to report on one analysis, which could be the training analysis, but were not required to indicate which analysis they chose. The study investigated what analysands experienced as most helpful and most hurtful in their analyses.

The researchers sent questionnaires to all of the graduates of the William Alanson White Institute and the Institutt for Psykoterapi in Oslo, Norway (over 300 analysts altogether), both members of the International Federation of Psychoanalytic Societies with nonreporting training analyses. Seventy-five questionnaires were returned. The questionnaires contained demographic questions, 68 analyst behaviors (with ratings of frequency and degree of helpfulness/hurtfulness), and 79 questions regarding the changes of these psychoanalysts when they were patients. There was also a question asking for the analysands' report of their perceived overall change.

Virtually all (98%) of these patient-analysts gave themselves diagnoses, with the most common being a depressive character style (49%) and obsessive-compulsive style (14%). Overall, 87% of the analysts reported a moderate or high degree of positive, overall change, with only 1% reporting deterioration during treatment.

The data from the Norwegian and American analysts did not differ significantly in regard to what they found helpful and hurtful in their analyses. They did differ in that these analysts as patients believed that their analysts held an interpersonal orientation in a majority of the cases from the White Institute and a Freudian orientation in a majority of the cases from the Oslo Institute.

First, the mean ratings of helpfulness and hurtfulness were examined. The individual analyst behaviors rated most helpful were of support and acceptance (e.g., "open to my ideas, experiences, and feelings," "was nonjudgmental and noncritical," and "validated my experience.") Other most helpful behaviors related to insights such as the item "asked questions to help me think and feel in new ways." The analysts' affective expression and liveliness were very important to patients, as was reflected by high ratings on "was genuine," "showed warmth," and "had a sense of humor."

Next, correlations of helpful/hurtful ratings with reported change were conducted. Forty-four of the 68 items were significantly correlated with overall reported psychological change. The item "helped me become aware of psychological experiences I was avoiding" was the item most highly correlated with overall change. These 44 significant items were entered into a factor analysis, revealing five factors: the first related to acceptance, support, and mirroring; the second to positive, active interventions; the third to frame issues and negative affect; the fourth to self-disclosure and mutuality; and the fifth to suggestion and advice-giving. Interestingly, the best predictor of change was the active interventions factor, followed by the acceptance and support factor, and finally the self-disclosure and mutuality factor (as indicated by a multiple regression analysis). The other two factors were not significantly correlated with overall perceived change.

These results are important in that they show that it is not simply the therapeutic relationship that is most related to outcome but that specific interventions on the part of the therapist play the most important role in change. Curtis et al. (2004) assert that for analysts to be "as helpful as possible, we need to be more than genuine, warm, and empathic. We need to gain more knowledge about the specific interventions that are most effective in leading to change and those that may be practiced frequently, but do not actually facilitate much movement."

In this study, the analysts also responded to questionnaires about their own changes as patients in psychoanalysis. Seventy-nine possible ways of changing were examined, including questions eliciting changes appropriate for a very high-functioning group, along with some SCL-90 type items. Most respondents (58%) reported a moderate degree of benefit overall, 29% a large amount of benefit, and 9% a small amount of benefit, with only one person reporting deterioration during the analysis.

On a 13-point scale from "greatly deteriorated" to "greatly improved," mean changes ranged from 0.19 to 3.46. A cluster analysis revealed four factors, in order of predicting overall self-reported change: (1) confidence and acceptance of feelings and impulses; (2) improvement in relationships and physical functioning; (3) serious symptoms; and (4) food-related symptoms. The individual items receiving the highest ratings of change regarded the capacity for intimacy, concerns with being rejected, the ability to link past and present experiences, having a wider range of options, comfort with one's own power, the ability to put feelings into words, and fewer self-doubts. The items changing the least regarded eating disorders and depersonalization.

As mentioned previously, three analyst behavior factors significantly predicted overall change—specific interventions, supportive relationship, and mutuality, in that order. In examining correlations of analyst behaviors and patient change factors, the analyst's "supportive relationship" factor and "advice-giving" were correlated with changes in "confidence and acceptance of feelings," whereas the analyst's "active interventions" were correlated with both the patient's "improvement in relationships" and "confidence and acceptance of feelings." Once again, overall results indicate that specific interventions in the context of a supportive relationship are most predictive of experienced change, not simply a supportive alliance (or the relationship). If the changes these analysts reported in their feelings toward others apply to their relationships with their patients, they are capable of more intimacy and a wider range of emotions, able to tolerate more uncomfortable feelings, and much more.

Craige's Work on Posttermination Mourning

Craige's (2002) recent study investigates how analysands who are psychoanalytic candidates in a training analysis experience the analytic relationship after termination. According to Craige, only a few writings discuss the fate of the analysand and the completion of the analytic process after termination.

Craige mailed a questionnaire to all candidate members of the American Psychoanalytic Association. Of the 642 candidates who received the mailing, approximately 57% responded. While two-thirds of the respondents were still in analysis, 121 respondents had terminated their training analyses. These 121 candidates completed the questionnaire on posttermination experience reported in the study. Training analyses ranged from one to 16 years, with the length of time elapsed since termination ranging from one month to 21 years (the median was two years). Fifty-seven candidates (47% of the 121 respondents) consented to be interviewed. The majority of candidates (76%) experienced a *sense of loss* (italics in original) after termination that lasted more than a few days. On the average, respondents who experienced a "sense of loss" reported that their experience of loss lasted between 6 months and a year. According to Craige, this finding indicates that if the termination phase has been painful, the posttermination phase is likely to be painful as well. Her conclusion from this is that one's understanding and feeling the loss of the analyst as it is anticipated during the termination phase does not necessarily protect the candidate from experiencing painful feelings of loss after termination.

The sense of loss of the unique analytic relationship after termination was positively correlated with all of the dimensions related to the candidates' overall experience during their training analysis: a positive experience, a successful experience, a strong working alliance, an intensely experienced transference, and a warm relationship. It was also positively correlated with a sense of having achieved something valuable and of taking *a* step forward in adult development after termination. This finding highlights the importance of the working alliance in a successful analytic outcome and corroborates the results of Buckley et al. (1981) where outcomes were positively correlated with a positive, warm emotional "tone" in the treatment relationship. A surprising result for Craige was that neither the sense of painful loss nor the loss of the unique analytic relationship was significantly correlated with significant emotional loss in childhood or adulthood. Nor was the sense of loss related to the emergence of loss, separation/individuation, or trauma as important issues during the training analysis.

According to Craige, the second group also had a "good-enough analysis" that reached termination with mutual agreement because a reasonable resolution of personal concerns had been achieved. However, these members reported that they experienced difficulty after termination, including feeling depressed, lost, angry, and abandoned. Painful feelings evoked by the final separation from the analyst surprised these candidates and strained their self-analytic capacities. These posttermination feeling states were painful enough to send two of these candidates back for a brief period of therapy and prompt the other two to enter a second brief analysis. With additional treatment, all members of this group reached a successful termination and established the presence of an internal image of the analyst that was predominantly positive.

As Craige asserts, "the most sobering finding of this study is that 28% percent of candidates rated themselves as disappointed with the results of their analysis." Disappointed candidates scored themselves significantly lower than other respondents on all measures of experience during analysis and were more likely to end their analyses in a state of impasse or stalemate. She suggests that these findings signal a need for further study.

Craige asserts that the positive quality of this new object, however, is not immutable. During the posttermination phase, the affective coloration of the internal image of the analyst may change from good-enough to bad, spoiling the results of a good analysis when the analysand experiences the loss of the analyst as a repetition of earlier, traumatic losses or as a rupture of an unanalyzed, self-object transference. Therefore, the posttermination phase should be viewed as a period of vulnerability in the life of the analysand. She asserts that an analysand who successfully navigates through this potentially dangerous phase may gain an enhanced sense of resilience and accomplishment. Craige's ideas are an important contribution in our understanding of the training analysis along a continuum that extends past the termination date, and into Freud's "interminable" landscape of understanding.

Martinez and Hoppe Studies

Additional studies of training analyses by Diane Martinez and Sue Keir Hoppe (1998) focus on the analysand's internalized representation of his or her own analyst as the point of perceived therapeutic benefit. Their study asserts that a lack of such an internalized presence was more common to those who felt untouched or hurt by their analytic experience. Their questionnaire explored the nature of the internalized presence of the analyst postanalysis and the relationship of this presence to perceived outcome. Outcome items included gender of analyst and postanalysis contact. Martinez and Hoppe mailed 600 randomly selected members of the American Psychoanalytic Association. The response rate was 36%.

The principal results are as follows. Some 78% of the respondents said that they derived "very much" or "tremendous" benefit from their training analysis. Sixty-three percent of men and 72% of women reported that their training analyst is an ongoing intrapsychic presence, as either "a person in my head" (33%), "observing" (29%), or "nurturing or soothing" (27%). Seventy percent have "loving, warm" feelings toward their training analysts. Three variables significantly correlated with perceived benefit were (1) the experience of an ongoing intrapsychic presence; (2) having further therapy or analysis with one's analyst postanalysis; and (3) follow-up contact of a collegial or friendship nature. Consistent with Kantrowitz's (1992, 1993,1995; Kantrowitz et al., 1989; Kantrowitz, Katz, & Paolitto, 1990) findings, there were no significant correlations between perceived benefit and length of analysis. In addition, respondents who reported no posttermination contact with their analysts reported low benefit from analysis, "current aversive/angry feelings" toward the analyst, and an "authoritative/judgmental" intrapsychic presence (if one existed).

These results coincide with Geller's psychotherapy outcome research (Geller, Cooley, & Hartley, 1981; Geller, 1999) with his Therapy Representation Inventory. Namely, the internal representation of the therapist and the use of this representation for continued dialogue are significantly correlated with self-perceived improvement (see chapter 27.)

Of note are the disappointing results of the analyses of 22% of the trainees in the Martinez and Hoppe study (1998), 28% in the Craige (2002) study, and 14% in the Shapiro (1974, 1976) study. Given the time and expense of these analyses, these results are disturbing and might reflect the practice of assigning analysts who then reported to a training committee. In contrast, only one of the analysts in the White and Oslo institutes study, where analysts clearly were not assigned and were nonreporting, felt no benefit. Together, the studies by Martinez and Hoppe and Craige suggest that it is very important that analysis be terminated with a predominantly positive internal image of the analyst, if possible.

San Francisco Psychoanalytic Institute Studies

Bush (2004) of the San Francisco Psychoanalytic Institute is conducting ongoing research on how psychoanalysts view their own analysis in terms of effectiveness. Bush cites two broad objectives for his project: (1) to develop a comprehensive outcome questionnaire that can be used as a research instrument to study the effectiveness of psychoanalysis, to test different explanations of how change occurs, and to investigate whether different components of psychoanalytic technique and process contribute to different dimensions of outcome; and (2) to obtain retrospective assessment of graduate analysts on the effective ingredients in their own analyses.

Bush's goal is to fuel future comparative studies comparing psychoanalytic outcomes of analysts in training with lay patients in both long- and short-term therapy, as well as to track changes in how one experiences oneself, one's analyst, one's parents, and one's progress over the course of an analysis.

His measure, the Psychoanalyst Feedback Questionnaire (PFQ), solicits detailed information about (1) how the analysand changed as a result of his or her analysis, (2) what components of the analysts' technique, manner, and relationship with the analysand contributed positively to the changes that were made or negatively to the changes that were not made, (3) what childhood relationships influenced how the analysand reacted to the analyst, and (4) how theoretical orientation and family history affected the "match" between the analysand and analyst.

SUMMARY AND CONCLUSIONS

Overall, the studies on training analyses are consistent with those regarding the therapy of therapists (see chapter 25). The findings of the percentage of analysts (75%–87%) finding benefit from their training analyses is similar to that reported by Orlinsky and Norcross for therapists in general. The analysts, like therapists in general, saw themselves as gaining in self-awareness and openness to their feelings. They also saw themselves as improving in their relations with others and as having fewer symptoms. None of the published studies, however, examined whether their analysis helped them to do better work with patients or about their liking for or their tolerance of their patients. For psychoanalysis, dreaming about the analyst is expected and was not related to a negative outcome. The intrapsychic presence of the analyst after termination was an important benefit of treatment for many analysts. Although psychoanalysts in an unsatisfactory reporting analysis experienced problems with the personality of the training analyst, they were not asked specifically whether the analyst was sexualized or sadistic, as was asked in other studies of therapists. The problems seemed to be related often to the evaluative role of the analyst, the analyst's ability to hinder progress in one's steps toward graduation, and termination when there is not a predominantly positive internal image of the analyst. Composite studies also showed that helpfulness of specific interventions on the part of the analyst, and not only the warm, understanding quality of the relationship itself, was related to the self-reported outcome of the training analysis.

FUTURE RESEARCH

The training analysis continues to be regarded as the most important part of psychoanalysts' education. In spite of this belief, there is little research on what happens in these analyses or in other analyses. In their review of major international research programs on psychotherapy, Beutler and Crago (1991) found that 18 out of 40 are psychoanalytically oriented. Since the training analysis is part of psychoanalytically oriented work, it is unfortunate the more research is not dedicated to this critical part of an analyst's education. There is simply a lack of research on the outcomes of psychoanalysis in general and of training analyses in particular, although a body of research dealing with the process of training analysis is beginning to develop.

We leave the reader with some research questions and ideas, which may be of interest to the current generation of training analysts and the analysands with whom they work. Some of these questions are as follows: (1) Which factors distinguish training analyses from other analyses? (2) How does the analyst's theoretical perspective or the orientation of an institute affect the outcome of training analyses? (3) What personal qualities in the analyst, and the match between analyst and patient, relate to outcome? (4) What constitutes an effective outcome for training analyses? (5) What is the effect of nonreporting versus reporting during training analyses? (6) For those analysands who are disappointed by the experience, what are the major sources of the disappointment? (7) Are the changes experienced by analysts in their training analyses corroborated by their analysts, patients, and others? (8) Do changes in the analyst-patient result in subsequent benefits for his or her own patients? (9) Do psychoanalytic interventions that are most helpful to mental health practitioners differ from those most helpful with lay persons with similar problems? (10) Do training analysts deviate from analytic technique less in training analyses than in other analyses?

REFERENCES

Balint, M. (1954). Analytic training and training analysis. *International Journal of Psychoanalysis, 35,* 157–162.
Benedek, T. (1969). Training analysis—past, present, and future. *International Journal of Psychoanalysis, 50,* 437–445.

Beutler, L. E., & Crago, M. (Eds.). (1991). *Psychotherapy research*. Washington, DC: American Psychological Association.

Bibring, G. (1954). The training analysis and its place in psychoanalytic training. *International Journal of Psychoanalysis, 35*, 169–173.

Buckley, P., Karasu, T. B., & Charles, E. (1981). Psychotherapists view their personal therapy. *Psychotherapy: Theory, Research, and Practice, 18*, 299–305.

Bush, M. (2004). *How psychoanalysts view their own analyses: An effectiveness study*. San Francisco: San Francisco Psychoanalytic Institute. Unpublished paper.

Calef, V., & Weinshel, E. M. (1973). Reporting, non-reporting, and assessment in training analysis, *Journal of the American Psychoanalytic Association, 21*, 714–726.

Craige, H. (2002). Mourning analysis: the post-termination phase. *Journal of the American Psychoanalytic Association, 50*, 507–550.

Curtis, R., Field, C., Knaan-Kostman, I., & Mannix, K. (2004). What 75 psychoanalysts found helpful and hurtful in their own analyses. *Psychoanalytic Psychology, 29*, 183–202.

Freud, S. (1968a). Analysis terminable and interminable. In J. Strachey (Ed. and Trans.), *The standard edition of the complete psychological works of Sigmund Freud* (Vol. 23, pp. 216–253). London: Hogarth Press. (Original work published 1937.)

Freud, S. (1968b). The future prospects of psycho-analysis. In J. Strachey (Ed. and Trans.), *The standard edition of the complete psychological works of Sigmund Freud* (Vol. 11, pp. 141–151). London: Hogarth Press. (Original work published 1910.)

Geller, J. D., Cooley, R., & Hartley, D. (1981–82). Images of the psychotherapist: A theoretical and methodological perspective. *Imagination, Cognition, and Personality, 1*, 123.

Geller, J. D. (1999). What does it mean to practice psychotherapy scientifically? *Psychoanalysis and Psychotherapy, 10*, 199–205.

Gerber, A. (2001). A proposal for the integration of psychoanalysis and research. *Psychologist/Psychoanalyst Newsletter of Division 39*(21, 3), 14–17.

Goldensohn, S. S. (1977). Graduates' evaluation of their psychoanalytic training. *Journal of the American Academy of Psychoanalysis, 5*, 51–64.

Greenacre, P. (1966). Problems of training analysis. *Psychoanalytic Quarterly, 35*, 540–567.

Heimann, P. (1954). Problems of the training analysis. *International Journal of Psychoanalysis, 35*, 163–168.

Kairys, D. (1964). Training analysis: A critical review of the literature and a controversial proposal. *Psychoanalytic Quarterly, 33*, 485–512.

Kantrowitz, J. (1992). The analyst's style and its impact on the analytic process: Overcoming an analyst-patient stalemate. *Journal of the American Psychoanalytic Association, 40*, 169–181.

Kantrowitz, J. (1993). The uniqueness of the patient-analyst pair: Approaches for elucidating the analyst's role. *International Journal of Psychoanalysis, 74*, 893–904.

Kantrowitz, J. (1995). The beneficial aspects of the patient-analyst match. *International Journal of Psychoanalysis, 76*, 299–313.

Kantrowitz, J., Katz, A., Greenman, D., Morris, H., Paolitto, F., Sashin, J., & Solomon, L. (1989). The patient-analyst match and the outcome of psychoanalysis: A study of 13 cases. *Journal of the American Psychoanalytic Association, 37*, 893–920.

Kantrowitz, J., Katz, A., & Paolitto, F. (1990). Follow up of psychoanalysis five to ten years after termination: III. The relation between the resolution of the transference and the patient-analyst match. *Journal of the American Psychoanalytic Association, 38*, 655–678.

Kardiner, A. (1977). *My analysis with Freud: Reminiscences.* New York: Norton.

Kirsner, D. (2000). *Unfree associations.* London: Process Press.

Kovacs, V. (1936). Training and control analysis. *International Journal of Psychoanalysis, 17*, 346–354.

Limentani, A. (1974). The training analyst and the difficulties in the training psychoanalytic situation. *International Journal of Psychoanalysis, 55*, 71–77.

Limentani, A. (1992). What makes training analysis "good enough." *International Review of Psychoanalysis, 19*, 133–135.

Lohser, B., & Newton, P. M. (1996). *Unorthodox Freud: A view from the couch.* New York: Guilford.

Martinez, D., & Hoppe, S. (1998). *The analyst's own analyst: Other aspects of internalization.* Paper presented at the Society for Psychotherapy Research Twenty-Seventh annual meeting, Snowbird, Utah.

McLaughlin, J. T. (1973). Non-reporting training analyst, the analysis and the institute. *Journal of the American Psychoanalytic Association, 21*, 697–712.

Meisels, M. (1990). The personal analysis. In M. Meisels & E. R. Shapiro (Eds.), *Tradition and innovation in psychoanalytic education* (pp. 111–124). Hillsdale, NJ: Erlbaum.

Menaker, E. (1989). *Appointment in Vienna: An American psychoanalyst recalls her student days in pre-war Austria.* New York: St. Martin's Press.

Pfeffer, A. (1974). The difficulties of the training analyst in the training analysis. International Journal of Psychoanalysis, 55, 79–83.

Sachs, D. (1992). What makes training analysis "good enough": Syncretistic dilemma. *International Review of Psychoanalysis, 19*, 147–158.

Sachs, H. (1947). Observations of a training analyst. *Psychoanalyst Quarterly, 16*, 157–168.

Shapiro, D. (1974). The training setting in training analysis: A retrospective view of the evaluative and reporting role and other "hampering" factors. *International Journal of Psychoanalysis, 55*, 297–306.

Shapiro, D. (1976). The analyst's own analysis. *Journal of the American Psychoanalytic Association, 24*, 5–42.

Torras de Bea, E. (1992). Towards a "good enough" training analysis, *International Review of Psychoanalysis, 19*, 159–168.

Winnicott, D. W. (1965). *The maturational processes and the facilitating environment.* London: Hogarth Press.

27

BOUNDARIES AND INTERNALIZATION IN THE PSYCHOTHERAPY OF PSYCHOTHERAPISTS

Clinical and Research Perspectives

JESSE D. GELLER

The word "boundary" has been used as a metaphor by individual, group, couples, and family therapists, of varying theoretical persuasions, to serve multiple and overlapping ends (e.g., Bowen, 1978; Epstein, 1994; Framo, 1982; Gabbard & Lester, 1995; Greene & Geller, 1985; Gutheil & Gabbard, 1993, Hartmann, 1991; Johnston & Farber, 1996; Minuchin, 1976, Ruttan & Stone, 1993; Smith & Fitzpatrick, 1995). "Boundaries" has been used to describe and understand (1) the discontinuities of time, space, and task definition that separate psychotherapy, as a social system, from the rest of the interpersonal environment; (2) the role requirements that are specific to the positions of patient and therapist; (3) the ethical standards and codes of conduct that arise out of therapists' efforts to protect patients from harm and exploitation; and finally, (4) as the mental activities that enable individuals to construct and preserve personally significant distinctions between self and nonself, fantasy and reality, "inside" personal space, and "outside" extrapersonal space and other aspects of personality functioning that affect the course and outcome of psychotherapy.

This research-informed chapter brings to the foreground the relevance of these interrelated figurative applications of the notion of boundaries to the psychotherapies offered to and experienced by psychotherapists and therapists-in-training. Experience and science support two propositions that shall serve as the primary focus of this chapter. First, there are "reality" factors that are more or less specific to the psychotherapy of therapist-patients that must be taken into account when dealing with the contractual, interpersonal, ethical, and intrapersonal boundaries that arise during the beginning, termination, and posttermination phases of the process of therapy. Second, internalization-based models of the therapeutic action of psychotherapy offer an illuminating vantage point from which to examine the ways psychotherapy contributes to the personal and professional development of psychotherapist-patients.

Our research (e.g. Geller 1988, 1998) has focused primarily on those internalization processes that transform the patterns of listening and talking, seeing and being seen, feeling and being-with that recurrently characterize the communicative exchanges that occur during the course of therapy into aggregates of enduring representations of interactions-with-the-therapist. It is a central tenet of this chapter that patients are likely to benefit from therapy—and maintain these gains following termination—to the extent that they construct, preserve in long-term memory, use, and identify with positively toned representations of the "self-in-relation-to-my-empathic therapist." I further assume that the processes that bring these benignly influential representations into existence are operative in all therapies in which patients and their therapists communicate responsibly and creatively within the context of an increasingly collaborative and intimate relationship.

Unless otherwise specified, I shall be writing about long-term expressive-exploratory individual therapy. Some time in my fifties, I sensed that I was selectively integrating existential-humanistic and psychodynamic ideas into my own uniquely derivative blend (Geller, 2003b). If I am feeling glib, I will refer to myself as a "Gellerian." Concurrently, I began treating therapist-patients with greater regularity. For the past seven years, I have usually had three to five therapist-patients in my caseload at any one time. Although there are important exceptions, the majority of these individuals are in their early thirties and aspire to becoming competent and autonomous therapists. One of my first therapist-clients was a 72-year-old retired clinical social worker. At termination, she left me with an indelible remark: "How great it is to peak in my seventies." I think of her when I need to be reminded about the ongoing possibilities of adult development.

THERAPISTS AND NONTHERAPISTS AS PATIENTS

There is obviously a great deal of overlap between patients who are therapists and those who are not. Perhaps most saliently, therapist and nontherapist patients are subject to the same agents that contribute to therapeutic change. Like lay patients, therapist-patients vary widely in their estimates of the relative amounts of catharsis, guidance, cognitive restructuring, reassurance, coaching, mentoring, role modeling, confrontation, and self-exploration they will "need." They vary, too, in their fears as to what they might not receive. Therapist- and nontherapist-patients are also subject to the same forces that can interfere with therapeutic progress. For example, no matter how intellectually well prepared therapist-patients may be to view themselves as actively implicated in their own difficulties, or to rationally cooperate with their therapists, unconsciously motivated resistances intrude into the therapy of therapist-patients as pervasively as they do in the psychotherapy of lay patients.

Nevertheless, it is also true, that therapist- and nontherapist-patients can differ in ways that are clinically relevant, and that such differences often bear upon boundary-related issues (see chapter 25). For instance, whatever their original reasons for seeking therapy, their choice of therapist is based on sources of information that are more readily available to mental health professionals. Therefore, therapist-patients are likely to know more about their prospective therapists' personal characteristics, professional reputation, and theoretical orientation, and what these factors imply about what will or should occur during the course of therapy, than equally well-educated patients drawn from the general clinical population. They are more familiar with the physical settings in which therapists work, and have more detailed information about the contractual arrangements of therapy prior to becoming patients. Therapist-patients begin their own treatments with greater awareness of the customs, conventions, and language of psychotherapy than do lay patients. Thus, they are more likely to detect those moments when their therapists deviate from accepted practices. At the same time, they are also more likely to be aware when they themselves deviate from behaving like a "good patient."

Lay patients frequently know very little about their therapists' private lives. They are also less likely than therapist-patients to encounter their therapists outside of therapy, especially if they live in large urban areas. By comparison, in small cities like New Haven, extratherapeutic contact between patient/therapists and their therapists is often "unavoidable." In places like these, therapist-patients have the opportunity to observe their therapists at seminars, parties, academic conferences, and organizational meetings.

Even if both therapist and patient strictly avoid social or professional contacts during the course of treatment, therapist-patients are often privy to "gossip" about their clinicians. The upshot is that many therapist-patients begin treatment knowing more about their therapist's reputation, status in professional organizations, and lifestyle than either may be willing to consciously admit. For example, in departments of psychiatry, junior faculty often select therapists from the senior members of their departments. In contrast, it is not uncommon for lay patients to complain about not knowing enough about their therapist "as a person."

Most therapies end with the understanding, implicit or explicit, that the patient is free to recontact the therapist if the need arises (Schachter, 1992). For those lay patients who do not avail themselves of this opportunity, the termination of therapy represents a total and permanent separation. By way of contrast, when patient-therapists and their former therapists continue to live and work in the same community, there are often many opportunities for posttherapy contact. In some communities, mental health professionals transform therapeutic relationships into supervisory relationships, and vice versa. Analytic candidates are destined to become the colleagues of their training analysts. Gestalt training programs are similarly organized (see Lichtenberg, chapter 23).

DO THESE DIFFERENCES MAKE A DIFFERENCE?

Clearly, the therapy of therapists takes place in interpersonal and organizational contexts that are potentially quite different from those that are encountered with lay patients. The cumulative effect of these differences is at least twofold. When the patient is also a therapist, one expectable consequence would be a heightened awareness of the therapeutic tasks that revolve around the temporal, spatial, and interpersonal boundaries woven into the work structure of psychotherapy. The second major consequence would be the introduction of an interpersonal boundary that is missing when the patient is a nontherapist. This boundary is created by the dynamic tension between the formal roles of therapist and patient and the collegial aspects of the relationship. Treating a therapist-patient effectively requires protecting and preserving the professional therapeutic relationship while honoring shared membership in the same profession. Reconciling the sometimes competing claims of these dual imperatives further complicates therapeutic tasks that are in themselves quite thorny. These include locating the optimal placement of the boundaries that separate the therapist-patient's and therapist's "professional" and "personal" selves, and choosing a clinical stance regarding the poles of expertise and egalitarianism. Not surprisingly, the therapists we surveyed ranked understanding and managing boundary issues as one of the most challenging aspects of their work with therapist-patients (see chapter 25).

INTERSUBJECTIVITY

Earlier generations of psychoanalytic therapists downplayed the influence of sharing the same profession on training analyses and personal analyses (Fleming, 1987). This view is a particular instance of a more fundamental assumption. According to classical psychoanalytic theorizing, as long as analysts fulfill the principles of abstinence, anonymity, and neutrality, transference reactions will start with and reside solely in the patient (Freud, 1940).

My approach to the therapy of therapists rests on an opposing point of view. I believe that sharing the same profession as one's patient influences the interactive processes reverberating in both patient and therapist in much the same way that gender, age, race, and social class shape the day-to-day and transferential aspects of the therapeutic relationship. I presume that, like these self-evident sociopsychological realities, the importance of sharing the same profession as one's patient to the course and outcome of therapy varies from patient to patient and from time to time with a particular patient.

This perspective is compatible with converging trends in the psycho-analytic (e.g. Gabbard, 1995; Mitchell, 1993), existential (see Heery and Bugental, chapter 21), and feminist (see Brown, chapter 20) psychotherapy literatures. Today's therapists take it as an a priori assumption that inter-personal and intrapersonal processes affect each other and cannot be sharply separated (e.g., Aron, 1991). In this vein, transference reactions and resis-tances have come to be regarded as interactive processes that go on between patient and therapist; their activation depends, in part, on the personal "re-ality" of the therapist, including his or her personal experience of a therapy relationship (e.g., Ehrenberg, 1992, Hoffman, 1998).

Nothing is more characteristic of contemporary theorizing than chal-lenges to the notions of "objective reality" and the reality of "objective truth" (Shevrin, 1995). For example, it would appear from debates about the evi-dential status of "case histories" that it has become increasingly difficult to locate the boundaries that separate imaginative literature from scientific writ-ing (Spence, 1993). The emerging consensus is that "interbeing" (Mahoney, 1991) or what Atwood and Stolorow (1980) call "intersubjectivity" is the fundamental context for human knowing.

In keeping with an increased emphasis on the interdependent aspects of the therapeutic relationship, such basic principles as mutuality, reciprocity, symmetry, and optional responsiveness are coming to be regarded as the proper baselines for participation in the therapeutic relationship (e.g., Aron, 1996, Bacal, 1985, Greenberg, 1995, Mitchell, 1993). These methodologi-cal ideals, like the orthodox Freudian triumvirate of anonymity, abstinence, and neutrality, to which Freud himself evidently did not adhere (Lohser & Newton, 1996), can be interpreted more or less restrictively. Nevertheless, their endorsement tends to encourage therapists to be both more emotion-ally expressive and self-disclosing of feelings and attitudes toward patients. This shift has intensified heated debates about what a therapist should and should not reveal to a patient and has heightened ambiguities regarding the optimal placement of the boundary between therapeutic intimacy and personal intimacy.

Concurrently, an emphasis on the precise timing of transference inter-pretations is being subordinated to the establishment of a "healing" rela-tionship in psychoanalytic theories of technique (e.g., Renik, 1993). An important manifestation of this conceptual shift is the increased emphasis being given to the sequence of empathy, failures of empathy, and their repa-ration by therapists who conceive of the processes of internalization as making an independent and positive contribution to the outcome of therapy (e.g., Blatt & Behrends, 1987; Dorpat, 1974; Kohut, 1971; Loewald, 1962; Mitchell, 1988). For example, Kohut (1984) has hypothesized, and we concur, that empathizing with a patient's negative reactions to narcissis-tic injuries activates the processes of internalization that will strengthen his or her self-esteem, vitality, sense of coherence, and continuity. What will be emphasized in the pages that follow is the hypothesis that clinical strategies designed to harness the therapeutic potential of the processes of internalization gain effectiveness to the extent that they are informed by an empathic appreciation of the nature and functioning of a patient's psychological boundaries.

THE IDEA OF PSYCHOLOGICAL BOUNDARIES

As defined by the dictionary, a boundary is that which delineates one entity as separate from another (*Webster's Unabridged Dictionary of the English Language*, 5th ed., 1990). I have chosen the term "psychological boundaries" to refer to the complex network of intrapersonal processes that presumably underlie and regulate the ability to make distinctions between various domains of experience and to establish linkages among them. In other words, I designate as psychological boundaries the representational capacities that provide the nonverbal substrate for such experience-based distinctions as inside and outside; self and nonself; the past, present, and future; remembering and imagining; fantasy and perception.

Some psychological boundaries operate at the juncture between the interpersonal and intrapersonal domains of experience. I infer their existence from individual differences in the distinction between the physical body and ever-present "body image" or "body schema" (Fisher, 1979) and from variations in what anthropologists refer to as "personal space" (Hall, 1966).

Each of us constructs and maintains, unconsciously, a psychic image that envelops, more or less cohesively, one's entire body (e.g., Fisher, 1979). This body image is quite separate from what we know, objectively, about our physicality. Were it not so, eating and body dysmorphic disorders would not be so prevalent. Introspective inquiries indicate that body images vary along multiple continua, for example, size, shape, and three-dimensionality, as well as their "penetration" and "barrier" characteristics (e.g., Bloomer & Moore, 1979). In complex combinations these attributes form the basis for the sense of there being an "inside me" and an "out there." And to anticipate a later point, they create a containing or symbolizing space, like the "mind," in which psychological experiences can occur.

Anthropologists were first to discover the existence of a psychological boundary that further differentiates "out there" into "inside" personal space and "outside" extrapersonal space (Hall, 1966). Apparently, without necessarily being aware of it, we locate ourselves within an intangible and invisible boundary that extends beyond and surrounds our psychic image of our bodies. The experiential reality of this interpersonal boundary is most acutely sensed when an uninvited other trespasses or intrudes on our "personal space." Research indicates that there are cultural, characterological, and situational differences in the distances at which individuals feel that they are "too close to" or "too far away" from others with whom they are interacting (e.g., Hall, 1966; Sommer, 1969).

Equally important to adaptation are the psychological boundaries that operate when interacting with internalized others, most notably when they are not physically present. It falls to these psychological boundaries to serve differentiating, integrating, and dedifferentiating functions vis-à-vis the representations of self and nonself that emanate from *within* us. One of the primary functions of the psychological boundaries that reside within "the representational world" (Sandler & Rosenblatt, 1962) is to subdivide experiences taking place "inside me" into those that are "lived bodily" and those that are known cognitively. This function manifests itself in the deeply ingrained tendency to treat the mind as if it actually had an "inside" that holds and contains thoughts, feelings, and all the persons within us. As the following common expressions indicate, we tend to un-self-consciously speak of the mind as a more or less enclosed "place" of its own from which subjective experiences leave and enter; for example, "My mind is too filled up to take in any more," "I can't get my mind around it," "My mind feels like a sieve," "I couldn't get you out of my mind," "I put her in the back of my mind." As the last two statements illustrate, varying degrees of "spaciousness" can separate the others who are represented in interaction with the subjectively grasped sense of self.

Apart from their content and the functions they serve, representations of human interactions can be described in terms of the "forms" in which they take shape in conscious and preconscious experiences (Geller, 1984). Any single instance of remembering or fantasizing about an absent other varies in the extent to which it finds expression in pictures, sounds, a flow of word meanings, tastes, odors, body sensations, and enactments. My work has been deeply influenced by Bruner's (1964) model of cognitive growth. The conceptual starting point of his model is the assumption that psychological boundaries are laid down between the sensory-motor, imagistic, and verbal symbolizing systems during the course of development by the processes of representational differentiation and integration. A person is psychologically advantaged insofar as he or she can travel back and forth freely across the boundaries that separate these functionally differentiated modes of organizing, storing, and expressing knowledge. Early on I try to learn whether a patient is equipped with the representational capacities that will enable him or her to keep apart or establish linkages between concrete, physicalized, and affect-laden memories and fantasies and abstract and verbalizable ideas about the interactions to which they refer—depending on the clinical needs of the moment. The work of exploratory-expressive therapy is facilitated when a patient's psychological boundaries function like the synaptic connections that make possible the transmission of information across the spaces that separate adjacent neurons. Inferences from clinical data suggest that this work will be stifled if the boundaries separating a patient's analytical intelligence and his or her sensuously-receptive modes of knowing function more like the fortified geographical borders that encircle countries at war.

Individuals appear to vary widely in their ability to separate these varied incarnations of psychological boundaries from everything that accompanies and surrounds them. The psychological boundaries that keep self-representations, and representations of others, separate yet related are integral aspects of subjective experiences. But they typically operate at a prereflective level of symbolic functioning. Their phenomenological properties are rarely brought into focal awareness.

Preliminary research (Geller, 2003a) indicates that if consciously thought of, the boundaries that structure the experience of "inner space" tend to be described primarily in terms of visual images and metaphors. As for my patients, they tend to draw on the same metaphors when describing experienced variations in the boundaries that define and delineate their psychic images of their minds and their bodies. Those aspects of psychological boundaries that are potentially reportable tend to be described as varying with respect to such properties as their location, size, hardness, intactness, fluidity, permeability, transparency, and capability of expanding or contracting or of being moved backward and forward. Furthermore, qualitative changes in these properties tend to be understood as occurring in a range between opposite extremes. Rigidity-flexibility, fluidity-stability, transparency-opaqueness are three such polarities. If the pitfalls of reification can be avoided, these metaphors provide a useful vocabulary for thinking and talking about the boundary-related issues that may arise during the course of therapy.

THE BOUNDARIES BETWEEN PSYCHOTHERAPY AND PSYCHOTHERAPY SUPERVISION

Whatever their presenting complaints, and however reluctant they may be to take on the identity of patient, therapists typically conceive of personal therapy as operating on two fronts simultaneously—the therapeutic and the educational, (e.g., Geller & Schaffer, 1988). Many of the analysts Shapiro (1976) interviewed cited identifications and counteridentifications with their therapists' approach as the single most important determinant of their attitudes toward what it means to *be* a therapist and *do* the work of therapy. Similarly, it has long been recognized by psychoanalytic educators that "teaching and healing are not clearly differentiated dichotomies, but tend to cross their ill-defined boundaries" (Wolf, 1996, p. 253). Furthermore, our research indicates that many therapist-patients use internalized representations of their therapists as models to be imitated, perhaps only in fantasy, when they are experiencing difficulties in coping with the unscripted, stressful, novel, and unpredictable aspects of practicing therapy (Geller & Farber, 1993). Whether they are experienced as comforting or threatening, or serve as stimuli for conformity or rebellion, representations of one's therapist's conversational style appear to have direct functional significance for a therapist's choices regarding expressivity, spontaneity, and the limits of self-disclosure.

A POTENTIAL FOR CONFUSION

Quite understandably, the teaching methods of psychotherapy supervisors who focus attention on the understanding of problematic countertransference reactions tend to be regarded by student therapists as models of the ways therapy is conducted. This is particularly true when a supervisor goes so far as to explore the ways a supervisee expresses indirectly or reenacts, within the supervisory relationship, temporary identifications or unresolved and unarticulated issues he or she has with the patient under consideration (Doehrman, 1976). The learning that takes place when such "parallel processes" (Caligor, 1981) are subject to inquiry can be as affectively, as compared to cognitively, based as the experiential and interpersonal learning that takes place in exploratory therapy. Consequently, within this supervisory context, an educational enterprise itself can begin to feel like a therapeutic undertaking. When such conditions prevail, a therapist-patient may unconsciously equate the experience of being in therapy and being in supervision.

Given the potential for confusion, early in therapy I listen for opportunities to achieve mutual understanding of the similarities and differences between the learning and self-exploration that take place in psychotherapy and psychotherapy supervision, especially if the therapist-patient is in training and has never been in personal therapy.

There are limits to what a supervisee will tell a supervisor about his or her problematic emotional reactions and attitudes toward particular patients (Yourman & Farber, 1996). Therapists-in-training tend to reveal to their therapists what they "hide" from their supervisors. This includes their difficulties understanding and managing patient "enactments" that evoke defensiveness, hostility, and withdrawal. Trying to understand, in therapy, the difficulties of conscience involved in making this choice can prompt very useful discussions about the boundaries that separate privacy and secrecy. Even if brought into supervision, such countertransference reactions are not as likely to be as thoroughly explored as they would be in psychotherapy.

The importance of clearly distinguishing between psychotherapy and psychotherapy supervision is particularly urgent when a therapist seeks "supervision" with a former therapist in a state of crisis regarding his or her emotional overinvolvement with a particular patient. If the former therapist-patient's psychopathology renders him or her vulnerable to "boundary violations" (Gabbard & Lester, 1995), it is essential to propose that the contract be one of purchasing psychotherapy and not supervision. Otherwise, a clinician is at risk of being held equally responsible for any ethical misconduct of which his or her patient might be accused.

PREPARING PATIENTS FOR THERAPY

Research conducted in the early 1960s strengthened my conviction that socializing individuals into the role of patient and educating them about how to use therapy for personal benefit promotes positive outcomes (e.g., Hoehn-Saric et al., 1964). To prepare "naive" patients for the exploratory work to come, I will try to underscore the courage it takes to speak truthfully about one's "vulnerable selves." I will also emphasize the inevitability of reluctances about speaking "truthfully," given the degree of candor and affective freedom required of patients. I will often find occasion to mention that so-called resistances and negative transference reactions are inevitable and that they may bring to light otherwise inaccessible knowledge of fears and defenses against hostility and hatred.

From the opening moments of the first session, I can implement these clinical strategies with therapist-patients in ways that convey another message—I accept our shared professional identity. For example, I can phrase my comments by making reference to persons only a fellow therapist would recognize. I draw on the quotes and anecdotes that are parts of the largely undocumented "oral history" of our profession. To illustrate the interdependence of transference and countertransference, I might quote a statement a supervisor of mine attributed to Jung: "The therapy has not begun until it is problematic for both participants." If the patient is an inexperienced therapist struggling, for the first time, with a "negative transference reaction," I might quote what a teacher told me H. S. Sullivan said: "God save me from a therapy that is going well."

Quoting our intellectual ancestors is a way of affirming that we share membership in a professional community, and a common history passed on from one generation of therapists to the next. This clinical strategy isn't always successful. A therapist-patient of mine informed me that my Jung quotation was, for him, an "empathic failure, because it could be applied to many others besides myself." Another patient betrayed his displeasure with my choosing an anecdote from my own career to illustrate a point. Thinking he was going to say "I hate your anecdote," he found himself saying "I hate your antidote." I take these as examples of the repeatedly obtained finding that acceptance of a therapist's comments depends not only on their accuracy or truthfulness but also on how well these communications integrate with a patient's stylistic and aesthetic preferences.

With respect to matters of style, investigations of the "fit" between therapists and patients (Kantrowitz et al., 1989) and autobiographical accounts of analysts who have been treated by two or more analysts (e.g. Couch, 1995; Guntrip, 1973; Hurwitz, 1986; Simon, 1993), plus my own experiences as a patient, converge with respect to a variety of generalizations. The foremost of these is that both therapists and patients inevitably possess distinctive and potentially quite different conversational styles. Second, from a patient's point of view, it may be difficult to distinguish between a therapist's perceived competence and one's positive or negative feelings about his or her conversational style. Third, a distinctive feature of therapeutic competence is the ability to speak in "a voice" that is attuned to a patient's communicative requirements. Fourth, giving thoughtful attention to a patient's communicative requirements with regard to matters of style is experienced as an affirmative and empathic answer to questions that frequently thematize interactions between therapist-patients and their therapists. "Is my therapist able to recognize and respond flexibly to my individuality?" "Can he or she understand my concrete and immediate experiences?" "Is he or she available and prepared to learn from and with me?" "Is he or she insistent on controlling the entire therapy?" "How powerful should each of us be in deciding what needs changing, and how these changes should be brought about?"

THE POWER DYNAMICS OF THERAPY

There is more power and authority inherent in the role of therapist than in the role of patient. This emotionally charged fact is clearly evident in the following potentially potent sources of frustration and gratification. Therapists are in charge of defining and controlling where and when therapy will take place. They have the legitimate authority to impose geographical restrictions and temporal limitations on their availability. Therapists also have the primary responsibility for conceptualizing and assigning the tasks and division of labor required to accomplish the goals of therapy.

Early on, in any course of therapy, it is important to gauge how a patient's reactions to the power differentials that separate the positions of patient and therapist will influence the separation-reunion cycles woven into the work structure of therapy and the establishment of a therapeutic alliance (Geller, 1988). For some patients, clarity regarding the boundaries that separate "inside" and "outside" of therapy sessions has an organizing influence in regard to their feelings of safety and expressivity. For others, the temporal and spatial arrangements of therapy engender ambivalence. As a therapist-patient of mine put it, "I experience the therapeutic situation as equal parts cage and sanctuary." For still others, issues of "leadership" and "followership" provoke power struggles, some fueled by unresolved conflicts with "authority figures."

I am most keenly aware of the power dynamics that are inherent in psychotherapy when attempting to differentiate between requests for technique modifications that organically flow from a seasoned therapist-patient's theory of therapeutic change and efforts to induce conformity with transference-driven motivations. This challenging task has arisen most frequently while working out a "therapeutic contract" (Orlinsky & Howard, 1986) regarding the use of self-disclosure as a therapeutic technique. It is a quite negative thing to share personal information with a therapist-patient who views self-disclosure as a form of acting out that contaminates the transference and subverts the therapeutic process. It is quite another if a therapist-patient believes the indications for self-disclosure are ever present during the course of therapy.

Among other considerations, I take a therapist-patient's basic position along this continuum into account when deciding whether to voluntarily reveal personal information to achieve a therapeutic goal (Geller, 2003b). I believe that as long as there will be "levelers" and "sharpeners" (Witkin & Goodenough, 1981), there will never be agreement regarding the precise location of the place beyond which one should not self-disclose. Reconciling divergent views regarding matters of technique in the direction of the therapist-patient is a subtle way of introducing greater "symmetry" into the relationship.

Moreover, patients often benefit from recognizing that their therapist believes that learning to learn with another through the medium of dialogue is as important for the therapist as it is for the patient. As an example of these principles, I accommodated a Jungian analyst's request that we focus primarily on the interpretation of his dreams, and that I share my associations to his dream images. These are standard practices among Jungian therapists. To express respect for his approach, I extended the limits beyond which I characteristically self-disclose. Not to have done so, he later told me, would have been a "mistake" and an "empathic failure."

A QUESTION OF TECHNIQUE

Seventy-nine percent of the participants in Pope and Tabachnick's (1994) sample of therapist-patients reported that they felt their therapists had made clinical and therapeutic errors. Comparable norms are not available for lay patients. Whatever the global percentage may be, both lay patients and therapist-patients' evaluations of their therapists' competence range from complete admiration to utter disdain. It is, however, specific to the therapy of therapist-patients that they can voice their positive and negative judgments in the language of the profession.

Empathizing with a therapist-patient who is complaining in the language of "science" or "ethics" about what one is doing or not doing is perhaps the greatest technical challenge of all. Sometimes it is the first step toward helping such patients develop the capacity to speak about hateful feelings in a constructive and responsible manner. Working toward this therapeutic goal is a predominant focus in some therapies, less so in others, but it is of some importance in all therapies. In my experience it is a particularly powerful therapeutic tool when the therapist-patient has considerable conflicts about his or her critical/sadistic impulses or tends to be masochistic and underentitled. Patients suffering from these characterological problems begin therapy with a reduced ability to recognize and accept their therapist's empathic understandings. Working through reactions to the disappointing, enraging, and frustrating aspects of the process of therapy prepares them to take pleasure in the actuality of their therapist's caring concern.

In the next two sections, I illustrate how I apply these ideas. For the sake of confidentiality and continuity, I have blended clinical examples that actually occurred with different therapist-patients into working clinical models of two protypical therapist patients.

THE HANDLING OF EMPATHIC FAILURES

A patient can feel that a therapist has taught him or her new "truths" about himself or herself without feeling empathically understood by that therapist. This was the legacy of K.'s first therapy. Like other therapist-patients who have had previous therapies, K., a brilliant 33-year-old clinical psychologist and self-diagnosed "obsessive compulsive with schizoid tendencies," arrived with an elaborate psychodynamic formulation of his presenting complaints. He came to therapy knowing that his unwanted, but irresistible, "perfectionism" and "diminished capacity for loving" were the result of growing up with a mother who "didn't enjoy being nurturant." But his hard-won insights had not led to behavioral change, and he felt neither liked nor respected by his former therapist.

During the initial stage of therapy he could not release himself from the burden of being "the responsible one," "the rational one," "the one-in-charge," nor could he explicitly reveal his "disowned dependency needs." He wanted to be a "good" patient but could not avail himself of the regressive inducements of patienthood. As a compromise, he defensively clung to the therapeutic alliance. He acted "as if" we could work together as "equal partners" to bring about therapeutic change, but it quickly became clear to both of us that he was unable to continue collaborating with me if I started a session two or three minutes late. He reacted to these occasional lapses of punctuality as if they signified "incompetence and a lack of integrity." He took my policy of extending the length of such sessions beyond the prearranged ending as further evidence of my "flagrantly careless mismanagement of the therapeutic frame." He quoted Langs (1976) to impress on me that even minor departures from the maintenance of invariant temporal boundaries represented a failure to live up to the ego ideals and values of the profession. His eloquent critiques collapsed the distinction between the technical principles and the moral norms that regulate the professional boundaries between patients and therapists. Moreover, he experienced his explanations single-mindedly, as if they were factual and concrete realities.

At the time of intake, he could only tolerate hearing echoes of the meanings inherent in what he said. Efforts on my part to make inferences beyond the meanings he gave for our problematic interactions were resentfully disregarded. Initially, even my questions were experienced as "interruptions" and "disruptive." It wasn't until the second year of treatment that he could turn his curiosity to issues that I deemed in need of exploration. As we were to learn, needing help in making meaning of his experiences induced in him a humiliating sense of being "foolish" and "stupid." He was guided by the belief that I only listened to find out what was "wrong" with him and what he "didn't know" about himself.

His unflattering interpretations of my handling of the beginnings and endings of sessions provoked in me a great deal of soul-searching. What sustained me was the hypothesis that responding nondefensively to his criticisms would ultimately strengthen his ability to recognize, tolerate, and benefit from being empathically understood. To do this, I found a way of conducting therapy that allowed for and upheld his need to discover his own personalized meanings for the problematic aspects of our relationship. This required choosing comments that highlighted the limits of my understanding. I restricted myself to questions that could be asked by both patient and therapist—"How do you want to use the time today?" "How do you understand this?" Another way of avoiding narcissistic injuries was to invite him to elaborate on *how* he experienced *what* he experienced. Dealing respectfully with his communicative requirements entailed giving priority to interventions that widened and deepened the immediacy of what he heard, thought, saw, and felt.

Our work together was not so much about adding new insights to those he had taken away from his first therapy but rather about concretizing and energizing insights that had previously remained disembodied. Along the way he gained access to his imaginative capacities. He extended "bridges" across what were once the barriers to awareness that separated his verbal and imagistic modes of knowing. Establishing meaningful connections between these distinct spheres of experiencing proved to be the gateway through which he could enter a new and transformative stage of therapy. It laid the groundwork for a major turning point in his therapy. This transition took place during a session in which he both recalled how his mother alternated between being withdrawn and verbally abusive, and realized that he expressed his disavowed longings to be dependent on me in the form of criticisms. His lists of "shoulds" for me were thereafter seen as "enactments of desire." A correlated step forward was taken when he also acknowledged that questioning and complaining about my techniques—"Why are you doing it that way?" "What are you trying to do?"—were driven as much by aggressive competitiveness and by the need to cover up his own searing doubts about how best to conduct therapy as by the high value he placed on scientific skepticism. From that time forth, he found the "intellectual courage" to begin talking about how his morally perfectionistic orientation was exerting a restrictive influence on his functioning as a therapist and compromising his own sense of "goodness."

BALANCING SELF-CONCERN AND CONCERN FOR OTHERS

In diverse vocabularies, mystics, Zen Buddhists, poets, parents, lovers, and therapists have offered boundary-based explanations of variations in the ability to give and receive empathy (e.g., Rogers, 1975). They all share the assumption that trying to understand what another person feels, empathically, is one of the most mature variants of the capacity to enter into relationships in which there is a movement toward the experience of two persons becoming "one." Phenomenologically speaking, empathy is a mode of knowing the other that comes about by softening or blurring the boundaries separating self and nonself without actually losing awareness of the distinction. Similarly, mature dependency requires a certain level of comfort in reexperiencing "symbiotic" modes of relatedness on one's own behalf.

A basic tenet of "relational" perspectives on psychoanalytic theory (e.g., Blatt & Behrends, 1987) is that the acquisition of the psychological boundaries that support feeling secure in one's identity as well as the ability to function independently and the freedom to relax the burdens of self-determination and self-other differentiation tend to develop more or less simultaneously in an interactive dialectic. Under ideal circumstances, the two coincide—a person possesses representational capacities that both uphold the sense that he or she is clearly separate, autonomous, and unique in relation to others and yet enable him or her to take pleasure and help from experiences of "merging" or "fusing" with valued others.

A particularly poignant variant of the inconsistencies possible involves therapist-patients whose capacity to give their patients empathy far exceeds their capacity to receive empathy from their own therapists. Sometimes the very boundary-related personality characteristics that enable therapists to be empathic with their patients may leave them vulnerable to difficulties regulating the distinction and distance between self and nonself in other intimate interpersonal contexts. In listening to my own therapist-patients, and those discussed by supervisees and colleagues, I have been struck by the frequency with which these inconsistencies surface during the course of therapy when the therapist-patient is struggling with the conflict between unselfish sacrifice of personal desires, selfishness and healthy self-interest. To illustrate, I turn next to B., a 32-year-old psychoanalytically oriented therapist for whom psychological matters and questions of value often merged into one another.

PRIDE AND RESPECT

The statement "I want my therapist to be proud of me" received the highest degree of endorsement in my study with Farber of the themes that organize therapist-patients' involvements with mental representations of their therapists (Geller & Farber, 1993). The polar principles of admiration/pride and disillusionment have been key affective components of my experiences treating therapists who have struggled in an ongoing way with serious "mental illnesses." However talented these individuals may have been as therapists, they all began therapy fearful that I would regard them as "unfit" to be therapists. To the contrary, their intimate familiarity with terror, despair, futility, and chaos seemed to have prepared them to "stay with" patients who are in the throes of such awful experiences.

Patient B. was further burdened by what he called "maturity morality"—the superego-driven conviction that he had to be "healthier" than his patients. Shame was the penalty he paid for having failed to profit from the year-and-a-half-long psychoanalytic therapy he had undergone while in graduate school. His reasons for coming to therapy this time included guilt about not "coming out" and "joining the gay pride movement."

The following communicative exchange took place during the ninth session:

Patient: I've been thinking a lot about coming out. I have a lot of guilt for not doing my part.

Therapist: Guilt?

Patient: I feel like I'm passing . . . like a light-skinned black person who is pretending to be white. It's like I'm going against my people.

Therapist: It feels cowardly keeping your homosexuality a secret . . . especially in professional circles?

Patient: Yeah, I'd like to be more courageous. It would help a lot of people too, give them hope. I could be used as a resource. People could pick my brain. But I just don't know if I could bear the shame. What is this fear of what other people think? Why do I wrestle with it?

Therapist: Let me add another question. Are you worried about what I will think of you and your sexuality, and the choice you are trying to make?

Patient: Yes. I am afraid you will see all my behavior through that lens . . . and that you'd view parts of my personality as part of my pathology.

In therapy, as elsewhere, B. was hyperaware of the gap that separated the public image he sought to project "out there," and his "insider's view" of what was "really going on." He was troubled, morally, by his ability to "simulate authenticity." His facade of normalcy had been created so that he would not appear effeminate, but it alienated him from his body and diminished his capacity for pleasure. K. had likened his body to that of "the Tin Man" in *The Wizard of Oz*. By contrast, B. likened his "false self" to a "wall that separates public from private spaces."

Building on this metaphor, we arrived at the realization that he spent a great deal of time "looking at" himself, evaluatively, but rarely "looked in" on his own thoughts and feelings, contemplatively. Although very curious about the subjective experiences of others, he felt "immodest" whenever he devoted himself to self-exploration. During the initial phase of therapy, without being conscious of it, he avoided feeling "selfish" by rapidly applying what he learned about himself in therapy to his work as a therapist.

Responsiveness to nonverbal cues, the ability to project oneself in to the consciousness of others, sensitivity to people's stated and unstated needs—these attributes strengthen one's access to the empathic mode of knowing. B. was abundantly endowed with them. They enabled him to excel as a therapist, but they also made it difficult for him to retain his own perspective while entering the point of view of others. His interpretive bias was to identify with the other person's view of a problematic situation. If he himself was dealt with hurtfully, he tended to "blame" himself and to believe that he must have "done something wrong or bad."

B. said of himself "I feel like a cliché . . . the therapist who is masochistic because of the caretaking role he adopted in his family." But it eventually proved liberating when he discovered that his felt inability to join the gay pride movement was directly related to and analogous with his generalized inhibitions about carving out an identity separate from his family of origin. Following this insight, he began to relinquish the burdens of defining himself as an "outsider" or "displaced" person, as had his parents, who felt like "devalued exiles." He no longer felt compelled to protect them by remaining silent when they drew sharp and repugnant distinctions between "them" (e.g., homosexuals and "the goyim") and "us" (e.g., heterosexuals and Jews).

Before B. arrived at the point where he could "come out," a major focus of our conversations was his deep shame about his own dependency needs. In truth, B. was raised to be a provider, not a recipient of caring concern. From early childhood he had adopted a parental role vis-à-vis his Eastern European immigrant parents and his mentally retarded younger sister. Besides valuing himself almost exclusively for what he could do to protect his family, B. feared he would be regarded as "childish," "infantile," and "clinging" if he risked expressing his unsatisfied yearnings to be empathically understood. Saying "I want" made him feel like a "helpless child."

We devoted ourselves to expanding the range of desires that could be articulated with those with whom he wished to be intimate or aggressive. Within the microcosm of the therapeutic situation, we took special notice of how and why he disavowed negative reactions to my mistakes and empathic failures. Allowing himself to "complain" about the ways I didn't meet his needs advanced the work of therapy in several ways. On these occasions he benefited from the experience of "truth-telling," from confrontations with his wishes to devalue my idealized qualities, and he came to a greater understanding of the meanings of his fears and defenses against expressing anger. In a previous therapy, B. had learned that his intense conflicts about his own aggressive strivings had developed as a result of defensive counteridentifications with his competitive, combative, and intermittently rageful father.

As his wishes became more fully known to himself, B. became more comfortable experiencing my actual physical presence and his previously dissociated hope of finding a therapist who could serve as an idealized model of the therapist he hoped to become. A major turning point occurred when he was finally able to tolerate looking at me when my silent presence gave evidence of patience and compassion. The listening presence of the empathically responsive therapist communicates tender emotions that may never be put into words. A great deal of what we regard as being empathic is only conveyed through gestures, postures, and facial expressions.

Expanding the range of perceptual capacities B. brought into therapy made it more possible for him to "take in" those aspects of my empathy that were carried by my nonverbal contributions to the therapeutic dialogue. The cumulative impact of these changes started a ripple effect that brought together the "supportive" and "exploratory" aspects of his therapy. Generally speaking, once this kind of integration has been consolidated, there is no end in sight to the potential collaborative and intimate conversations that are possible.

THE TERMINATION PHASE OF THERAPY

Knowing when and how to end a lengthy and ambitious therapy that is going well is a most difficult task for both therapist and patient. If patient and therapist have shared a close and productive relationship, there will be intimations of arbitrariness in their (final) goodbye. With respect to assessing termination, most therapists are likely to reply that multiple and patient-specific criteria should be used (Firestein, 1978). I have found a variety of markers to be sensitive indices for recognizing a patient's progress in therapy and readiness to enter the termination subphase of the therapeutic process.

Among the most important intratherapy markers are (1) the ability to work together with the therapist in exploring personal qualities that present obstacles to change; (2) the ability to use language responsibly and constructively when feeling hateful toward the therapist; (3) an enhanced sense of competence about one's participation in therapy; (4) the ability to oscillate between regressive and progressive forms of mental activity; (5) the fullest and freest expression of previously unacknowledged and unmourned losses; (6) the ability to smoothly exchange the positions of listener and speaker; (7) the ability to choose what to "take in" and what to "keep out" of what the therapist has to offer; and finally, (8) the ability to place the bodily experience and not merely the eyes and the ears at the center of the perceptual and representational experience of therapy.

In varying combinations, these diverse achievements seem to go hand in hand with the approaching realization of a patient's "life goals" (e.g., symptomatic relief and enhanced self-esteem). At the same time they seem to indicate that the therapy will also have an "afterlife" in the form of evocative and benignly influential representations of therapy-with-the-therapist. At this juncture, the patient is growing increasingly capable of continued self-analysis.

THE CAPACITY TO ENGAGE IN SELF-ANALYSIS

From the perspective of the processes of internalization, one can distinguish between introjective and identificatory forms of self-reflexiveness (Orlinsky & Geller, 1993). At the introjective level of internalization, patients symbolically reconstruct the therapeutic dialogue in order to reflect on and interpret their own experience. The research cited earlier in this chapter found that therapist-patients are most likely to engage in imaginary conversations with the "felt presence" of their therapist for the purposes of self-reflection when carrying out the tasks of therapeutic work and organizing the experience of being a therapist. At the identificatory level of symbolization, the manner in which a patient engages in self-analysis is modeled on representations of the therapist's abilities and personal qualities but excludes conscious representations of what has been shown or given to them by their therapists. Who is listening when you talk to yourself?

In the classical psychoanalytic tradition, the received wisdom has been that self-analytic abilities that derive from constructive identifications associated with altered functioning are more "mature" than those based on calling forth introjected representations-of-the-self-in-relation-to the therapist. This essentially untested assumption is of more than theoretical interest to psychoanalytic therapists who wish or need to interact with personifications or introjected representations of their analysts following termination. The psychoanalyst Martinez (Martinez & Hoppe, 1998) tells us she felt ashamed of her inclination to interact intermittently with her "analyst introject" because she had been taught that doing so implied "immaturity," the prolongation of a dependent relation to the analyst, and therefore cast doubt on the completeness of her analysis. Obviously, such theoretical subtleties are of little or no concern to nontherapist patients, or for that matter, to nonanalytic therapist-patients.

THE POSTTERMINATION PHASE OF PSYCHOTHERAPY

At every stage of therapy, distinctions must be made between those personal attributes that are role relevant and those aspects of the self that must be suppressed in the interest of successful task accomplishment. In the psychotherapy of therapist-patients, this task is complicated by the inherent tension created by straddling the interpersonal boundary between the formal roles of patient and therapist and the collegial aspects of the relationship. Nowhere are the ambiguities posed by these tasks more apparent than in the therapist's efforts to deal with the largely unexamined question: How can I continue to interact with my former patients in ways that fulfill my therapeutic and ethical responsibilities to them following the termination of therapy?

All major mental health professional codes of ethics contain proscriptions against so-called boundary violations (Pope & Vasquez, 1998). The American Psychological Association (1992) did not classify having sex with a former patient as a boundary violation until 1977 (Pope & Bouhoutsos, 1986). Currently, there are no explicit guidelines regarding the ethics of nonromantic and nonsexual relationships following the discontinuation of therapeutic services, other than those that are clearly exploitative and destructive. Moreover, professional codes still have little to say about a question that is of particular concern to therapists' therapists. Beyond termination, are standards of conduct regarding "dual relationships" equally applicable to lay patients and members of the same professional community? Dual or multiple relationships are those in which additional role relations are established in conjunction with or in succession to the professional therapeutic relationship.

The extreme position is that the restrictions on extratherapeutic contact that applied during therapy should extend to the posttermination phase of the relationship. A major reason given for this policy is that to do otherwise would make it difficult for a former patient to resume therapy at some point in the future. Most therapies do, in fact, end with the agreement that the patient is free to return to therapy whenever his or her judgment indicates its usefulness (Schacter, 1992). Hartlaub, Martin, and Rhine (1986) found that it is not uncommon for former analysands to recontact their former analysts for a brief or even for an extended therapy. Such contacts tended to increase as time elapsed after termination, irrespective of the patient's diagnostic category or age.

Unless a lay patient renews professional contact with his or her therapist, termination of therapy potentially represents a total and permanent separation. Psychotherapists who continue to live and work in the same professional group as their former therapists markedly diverge from lay patients in this respect. Treating a fellow therapist significantly increases the possibility that a social or professional relationship will "replace" the therapeutic relationship after termination. Hence the question, following termination, of how one can continue to interact with one's former patients in ways that fulfill one's therapeutic and ethical responsibilities to them arises more frequently in the psychotherapy of therapists than in the psychotherapy of lay patients.

ONCE A PATIENT, ALWAYS A PATIENT

When I unavoidably encounter former patients in public settings, I aspire to behave in ways that are disciplined by attentiveness to the following questions. Is the person still mourning the loss of the therapeutic relationship? Will my behavior confirm or disconfirm his or her preexisting mental models of our relationship? Does he or she use representations of the therapeutic dialogue to continue the work of therapy in the privacy of consciousness? Are these representations still transference laden? Did the therapy leave behind a legacy of malevolent and persecutory introjects? Does he or she call me forth like an "imaginary companion" (of childhood) to avoid or curb anxiety and loneliness? How ready is he or she to reexperience the transferential aspects of our relationship? Will he or she view my behavior as deviating from the standards that define the ideals of our profession?

The standards I hold myself to when interacting with former patients at such events as seminars, parties, and professional meetings have been heavily influenced by the convergent findings of clinical research on the persistence of transference reactions after termination (Kantrowitz et al., 1990; Oremland, Blacker, & Norman, 1975; Pfeffer, 1963; Schlessinger & Robbins, 1974) and empirical studies of the form, content, functions, and affective coloration of the internalized representation of the therapeutic relationship that lay and therapist-patients retain and recall after termination (Arnold, Farber, & Geller, 2004; Orlinsky & Geller, 1993; Wyzontek, Geller, & Farber, 1995). Both lines of inquiry strongly support the conviction that a posttermination phase (Rangell, 1966) of the therapeutic relationship must be considered to be an integral part of the therapeutic process itself, and not just as the time after therapy ends.

Studies of the transformations that representations of the therapeutic relationship undergo after termination are few. Our studies indicate that former therapist-patients are apt to recall representations-of-therapy-with-my-therapist more frequently and vividly than former nontherapist patients (Wyzontek et al., 1995). As previously noted, representations of the missed or yearned-for former therapist can appear in awareness in various forms. They can be "visualized." They can be "heard." They can materialize in consciousness in the form of verbal thought. They can also include proximal imagery, that is, kinesthetic, proprioceptive, and tactile representations. Initial findings suggest that former therapist-patients' evocative memories of their therapists are more highly saturated with proximal imagery than are those of lay patients.

Therapist-patients' written descriptions of their former therapists, in comparison to those authored by lay patients, tend to give greater emphasis to the therapists' "inner life." The lay patients focused their portraits primarily on their therapists' observable behaviors, especially those that gratified or frustrated their needs. Far more than lay patients, former therapist-patients' portraits expressed greater interest in their therapists' feelings, values and attitudes.

With respect to the ability to use representations of the therapeutic dialogue for adaptive and reparative purposes, lay patients and therapist-patients have not differed significantly in our studies. We have obtained significant positive correlations between ratings of self-perceived benefits from therapy and two representational activities. These are the tendency to use representations of the therapeutic dialogue to continue the work of therapy into the future, and the tendency to use representations to give expression to missing therapy and the therapist. By way of contrast, the tendency to evoke representations of the therapist to engage in sexual and aggressive fantasies has been found to correlate negatively with self-perceived improvement.

These findings are consistent with the results of the previously referenced followup research interviews with therapist and nontherapist analysands. On the one hand, these studies support Loewald's (1960, 1962) contention that the ending of a beneficial analysis ushers in a gradual relinquishment or "mourning" of the relationship and its internalization. On the other hand, they indicate that successful terminations do not result in the complete resolution of transference reactions but in their modulation to the point that the patient can deal with them more effectively. Remaining mindful that transference wishes and dispositions persist beyond termination can go a long way toward easing the awkwardness and ambiguities of etiquette that arise during contacts with therapist-patients after the discontinuation of regularly scheduled sessions.

From the point of view of the processes of internalization, therapy can make people "worse" to the extent that the experience leaves behind a legacy of disappointing, malevolent, or persecutory images of the therapist. On a case-by-case basis, this outcome can be assessed by scheduling therapist-initiated "followup" (as compared to therapeutic sessions) visits with patients during the posttermination phase of the relationship. Schachter (1992) has been experimenting with planned-for patient-analyst posttermination contact to review how the patient has fared and to reevaluate the gains and limitations of the analytic process. He has found the risk/benefit ratio for such contact to be highly favorable, and that patients do benefit from experiencing a reaffirmation of the therapeutic alliance. These followup sessions might prove to be an ideal "anthropological laboratory" (Kundera, 1984) for studying the fate of the transference residues that linger after termination, the work of mourning, the afterlife of the therapeutic process, and relapse prevention strategies.

CONCLUSION

In this chapter, I have attempted to identify some of what is unique about the psychotherapy of therapists from the standpoint of the complex interplay between the notion of psychological boundaries and the processes of internalization. I have drawn on the concepts and data of body image theorists, anthropologists, cognitive developmental psychologists, and psychoanalysts to develop a framework that therapists could use to think and talk about the psychological boundaries that are operative in interpersonal contexts and in the privacy of consciousness. I have cited clinical experiences and psychotherapy research findings that support the hypothesis that internalization-based models of the therapeutic action of therapy offer an illuminating vantage point from which to examine whether there are clinically significant differences in the therapies offered to and experienced by therapist and nontherapist patients. At the end of it all I have arrived at the conclusion—to paraphrase Kluckhohm and Murray (1949, p. 53)—that every psychotherapist-patient is in certain respects (a) like all other patients, (b) like some other patients, and (c) like no other patient. To be continued . . .

REFERENCES

American Psychological Association. (1992). Ethical principles of psychologists and code of conduct. *American Psychologist, 49,* 1597–1611.

Arnold, E. G., Farber, B. A., & Geller, J. D. (2004) Termination, post-termination, and internalization of therapy and the therapist: Internal representation and psychotherapy outcome. In D. P. Charman (Ed.), *Core processes in brief psychodynamic psychotherapy* (pp. 289–308). Hillsdale, NJ: Erlbaum.

Aron, L. (1991).The patient's experience of the analyst's subjectivity. *Psychoanalytic Dialogues, 1,* 29–51.

Aron, L. (1996). *A meeting of minds: Mutuality in psychoanalysis.* Hillsdale, NJ: Analytic Press.

Atwood, G., & Stolorow, R. (1980). Psychoanalytic concepts and the representational world. *Psychoanalysis and Contemporary Thought, 3,* 267–290.

Bacal, H. A. (1985). Optimal responsiveness and the therapeutic process. In A. Goldberg (Ed.), *Progress in self psychology* (pp. 202–206). New York: Guilford.

Blatt, S. J., & Behrends, R. S. (1987). Internalization, separation-individuation, and the nature of therapeutic action. *International Journal of Psychoanalysis*, *68*, 279–297.

Bloomer, K. C., & Moore, W. M. (1977). *Body, memory, and architecture.* New Haven, CT: Yale University Press.

Bowen, M. (1978). *Family therapy in clinical practice.* New York: Aronson.

Bowlby, J. (1973). *Attachment and loss. Vol. 2. Separation.* New York: Basic Books.

Bruner, J. (1964). The course of cognitive growth. *American Psychologist*, *19*, 1–15.

Caligor, P. C. (1981). Parallel and reciprocal processes in psychoanalytic supervision. *Contemporary Psychoanalysis*, *17*, 1–27.

Couch, A. S. (1995). Anna Freud's adult psychoanalytic technique: A defense of classical analysis. *International Journal of Psychoanalysis*, *76*, 153–171.

Doehrmann, M. (1976). Parallel processes in supervision and psychotherapy. *Bulletin of the Menninger Clinic*, *40*, 9–110.

Dorpat, T. L. (1974). Internalization of the patient-analyst relationship in patients with narcissistic disorders. *International Journal of Psychoanalysis*, *55*, 183–191.

Edelson, M. (1988). *Psychoanalysis: A theory in crisis.* Chicago: University of Chicago Press.

Ehrenberg, D. B. (1992). *Extending the reach of psychoanalytic interaction.* New York: Norton.

Epstein, R. S. (1994). *Keeping boundaries: Maintaining safety and integrity in the psychotherapeutic process.* Washington, DC: American Psychiatric Press.

Firestein, S. K. (1978). *Termination in psychoanalysis.* New York: International Universities Press.

Fisher, S. (1979). *Body experience in fantasy and behavior.* New York: Appleton Century Croft.

Fleming, J. (1987). *The teaching and learning of psychoanalysis.* New York: Guilford.

Framo, J. (1982). *Explorations in marital and family therapy.* New York: Springer.

Freud, S. (1940). An outline of psychoanalysis. In J. Strachey (Ed. and Trans.), *The standard edition of the psychological works of Sigmund Freud* (Vol. 23, pp. 139–207). London: Hogarth Press. (Original work published 1964.)

Gabbard, G. O. (1995). When the patient is a therapist: Special challenges in the psychoanalytic treatment of mental health professionals. *Psychoanalytic Review*, *82*, 709–125.

Gabbard, G. O., & Lester, F. P. (1995). Boundaries and boundary violations in psychoanalysis. New York: Basic Books.

Geller, J. D. (1984). Moods, feelings, and the process of affect formation. In L. Temoshuk, L. S. Zegans, & C. Van Dyke (Eds.), *Emotions in health and illness: Foundations of clinical practice* (pp. 171–186). Orlando, FL: Grune and Stratton.

Geller, J. D. (1988). The process of psychotherapy: Separation and the complex interplay among empathy, insight and internalization. In J. Bloom-Feshbach & S. Bloom-Feshbach (Eds.), *The psychology of separation through the life span* (pp. 459–514). San Francisco: Jossey-Bass.

Geller, J. D. (1994). The psychotherapist's experience of interest and boredom. *Psychotherapy*, *3*, 3–16.

Geller, J. D. (1996). Thank you for Jenny. In B. Gerson (Ed.), *The therapist as a person* (pp. 119–141). New York: Analytic Press.

Geller, J. D. (1998). What does it mean to practice psychotherapy scientifically? *Psychoanalysis and Psychotherapy, 47,* 187–215.

Geller, J. D. (2003a). My personal Tiresias: A geographer of the inner world. In R. Landy (Ed.), *Symbolization and desymbolization* (pp. 511–533). New York: Other Press.

Geller, J.D. (2003b). Self-disclosure in psychoanalytic-existential psychotherapy. *Journal of Clinical Psychology/In Session, 59,* 1–14.

Geller, J. D., & Farber, B. A. (1993). Factors influencing the process of internalization in psychotherapy. *Psychotherapy Research, 3,* 166–180.

Geller, J. D., & Schaffer, C. E. (1988, June 23). *Internalization of the supervisory dialogue and the development of therapeutic competence.* Paper presented at the Twenty-first Annual Meeting of the Society for Psychotherapy Research, Santa Fe, NM.

Geller, J. D., Smith-Behrends, R., & Hartley, D. (1981–82). Images of the psychotherapist: A theoretical and methodological perspective. *Imagination, Cognition and Personality, 1,* 123–146.

Greenberg, J. R. (1995). Psychoanalytic technique and the interactive matrix. *Psychoanalytic Quarterly, 64,* 1–22.

Greene, L. R., & Geller, J. D. (1985). Effects of therapists' clinical experience and personal boundaries on termination of psychotherapy. *Journal of Psychiatric Education, 7,* 31–35.

Guntrip, H. (1973). *Psychoanalytic theory, therapy and self.* New York: Basic Books.

Gutheil, T. G. & Gabbard, G. O. (1993). The concept of boundaries in clinical practice: Theoretical and risk management dimensions. *American Journal of Psychiatry, 150,* 188–196.

Hall, E. T. (1966). *The hidden dimension.* Garden City, NY: Doubleday.

Hartlaub, G. H., Martin, G. C., & Rhine, M. W. (1986). Recontact with the analyst following termination: A survey of seventy-one cases. *Journal of the American Psychoanalytic Association, 34,* 885–910.

Hartmann, E. (1991). *Boundaries in the mind: A new psychology of personality.* New York: Basic Books.

Hoehn-Saric, R., Frank, J. D., Imber, S., Nash, E. H., Stone, A. R., & Battle, C. C. (1964). Systematic preparation of patients for psychotherapy. 1. Effects on therapy, behavior and outcome. *Journal of Psychotherapy Research, 2,* 267–281.

Hoffmann, I. Z. (1998). *Ritual and spontaneity in the psychoanalytic process.* New York: Analytic Press.

Hurwitz, M. R. (1986). The analyst, his theory, and psychoanalytic process. *Psychoanalytic Study of the Child, 41,* 439–466.

Johnston, S. H., & Farber, B. A. (1996). The maintenance of boundaries in psychotherapeutic practice. *Psychotherapy, 33,* 391–402.

Kantrowitz, J. L., Katz, A. L., Greenman, D. A., Morris H., Paolitto, F., Sashin, J., & Solomon, L. (1989). The patient-analyst match and the outcome of psychoanalysis: A pilot study. *Journal of the American Psychoanalytic Association, 37,* 893–920.

Kantrowitz, L. I., Katz, A. L., & Paolitto, F. (1990). Follow-up of psychoanalysis five to ten years after termination. *Journal of the American Psychoanalytic Association, 38,* 637–654.

Kluckhohn, T., & Murray, H. (1949). *Explorations in personality*. Cambridge, MA: Harvard University Press.

Kohut, H. (1971). *The analysis of the self*. New York: International Universities Press.

Kohut, H. (1984). *How does analysis cure?* (A. Goldberg & P. Stepansky, Eds.). Chicago: University of Chicago Press.

Kundera, M. (1984). *The unbearable lightness of being*. New York: Harper and Row.

Langs, R. (1976). *The bipersonal field*. New York: Aronson.

Loewald, H. (1960). On the therapeutic action of psychoanalysis. *International Journal of Psychoanalysis, 41*, 1–18.

Loewald, H. W. (1962). Internalization, separation, mourning, and the super-ego. *Psychoanalytic Quarterly, 31*, 483–504.

Lohser, B., & Newton, P. M. (1996). *Unorthodox Freud: The view from the couch*. New York: Guilford.

Mahoney, M. J. (1991). *Human change processes: The scientific foundations of psy-chotherapy*. New York: Basic Books.

Martinez, D., & Hoppe, S.K. (1998). The analyst's own analyst: Other aspects of internalization. Paper presented at the Twenty-seventh Annual Meeting of the Society for Psychotherapy Research, Snowbird, UT.

Mitchell, S. A. (1988). *Relational concepts in psychoanalysis*. Cambridge, MA: Harvard University Press.

Mitchell, S. A. (1993). *Hope and dread in psychoanalysis*. New York: Basic Books.

Minuchin, S. (1976). *Families and family therapy*. Cambridge, MA: Harvard University Press.

Oremland, J. D., Blacker, K. H., & Norman, H. F. (1975). Incompleteness in "successful" psychoanalyses: A follow-up study. *Journal of the American Psychoanalytic Association, 23*, 819–844.

Orlinsky, D. E., & Geller, J. D. (1993). Patients' representations of their therapists and therapy: New measures. In J. Miller, J. P. Luborsky, J. P. Barber, & N. E. Docherty (Eds.), *Psychodynamic treatment research* (pp. 423–466). New York: Basic Books.

Orlinsky, D. E., & Howard, K. I. (1986). Process and outcome in psychotherapy. In S. L. Garfield & A. E. Bergin (Eds.), *Handbook of psychotherapy and behavior change* (3rd ed., pp. 311–381). New York: Wiley.

Pfeffer, A. (1963). The meaning of the analyst after analysis. *Journal of the American Psychoanalytic Association, 11*, 229–244.

Pope, K. S., & Bouhoutsos, N. (1986). *Sexual intimacy between therapists and patients*. New York: Praeger.

Pope, K. S., & Tabachnick, B. G. (1994). Therapists as patients: A national survey of psychologists' experiences, problems, and beliefs. *Professional Psychology: Research and Practice, 25*, 247–258.

Pope, K. S., & Vasquez, M. J. T. (1998). *Ethics in psychotherapy and counseling*. San Francisco: Jossey-Bass.

Rangell, L. (1966). An overview of ending an analysis. *Journal of the American Psychoanalytic Association, 11*, 229–244.

Renik, O. (1993). Analytic interaction: Conceptualizing technique in light of the analyst's irreducible subjectivity. *Psychoanalytic Quarterly, 62*, 553–571.

Rogers, C. (1975). Empathic: An unappreciated way of being. *Counseling Psychologist, 5*, 1–10.

Ruttan, J. S., & Stone, W. N. (1993). *Psychodynamic group psychotherapy.* Toronto: Coll Amore Press.

Sandler, J., & Rosenblatt, B. (1962). The concept of the representational world. *Psychoanalytic Study of the Child, 17,* 128–145.

Schachter, J. (1992). Concepts of termination and post-termination patient-analyst contact. *International Journal of Psychoanalysis, 73,* 137–154.

Schafer, R. (1959). Generative empathy in the treatment situation. *Psychoanalytic Quarterly, 28,* 342–373.

Schafer, R. (1968). *Aspects of internalization.* New York: International Universities Press.

Schlessinger, N., & Robbins, J. (1974). Assessment and follow-up in psychoanalysis. *Journal of the American Psychoanalytic Association, 22,* 542–567.

Shapiro, D. (1976). The analyst's own analysis. *Journal of the American Psychoanalytic Association, 24,* 5–42.

Shevrin, H. (1995). Psychoanalysis as science. *Journal of the American Psychoanalytic Association, 43,* 963–986.

Simon, B. (1993). In search of psychoanalytic technique: Perspectives from on the couch and behind the couch. *Journal of the American Psychoanalytic Association, 41,* 1051–1081.

Smith, D., & Fitzpatrick, M. (1995). Patient-therapist boundary issues: An integrative summary of theory and research. *Professional Psychology: Research and Practice, 26,* 499–506.

Sommer, R. (1969). *Personal space.* Englewood Cliffs, NJ: Prentice Hall.

Spence, D. P. (1993). *Narrative truth and historical truth.* New York: Norton.

Witkin, H. A., & Goodnough, D. R. (1981). *Cognitive styles: Essence and origins.* New York: International Universities Press.

Wolf, E. S. (1996). How to supervise without doing harm: Comments on psychoanalytic supervision. *Psychoanalytic Inquiry, 15,* 252–267.

Wzontek, N., Geller, J. D., & Farber, B. A. (1995). Patients' post-termination representations of their psychotherapists. *Journal of the American Academy of Psychoanalysis, 23,* 395–410.

Yourman, D. J., & Farber, B. A. (1996). Nondisclosure and distortion in psychotherapy supervision. *Psychotherapy, 33,* 567–575.

EPILOGUE

The Patient Psychotherapist, the Psychotherapist's Psychotherapist, and the Therapist as a Person

DAVID E. ORLINSKY, JESSE D. GELLER, & JOHN C. NORCROSS

I magine us, in these final pages, discussing the chapters of our book with an intelligent but professionally untrained Impartial Person—perhaps a descendant of the very one with whom Freud (1926/1959) conversed in his book on "lay analysis." We can imagine such an individual asking, with some sense of puzzlement:

> Why should psychotherapists themselves, as a routine matter, need
> or want to undergo psychotherapy, many of them more than once
> if the researchers are to be believed? After all, physicians don't
> generally submit to medical treatments unless compelled to do so
> by a specific illness, nor do dentists have their teeth drilled or
> extracted in order to have had the experience. Are psychotherapists
> so disturbed that they really need to have personal therapy? And, if
> they are, doesn't it imply that they're unfit to be treating others in
> need of psychological help?

We readily concede that this question by our Impartial Person makes a valid if limited point. A minority of psychotherapists do at times succumb to the same types of emotional and psychological disorders that their patients present for treatment, through some combination of their own vulnerabilities and the stresses of their personal or professional lives. When that occurs to therapists, their personal disorders may not only require treatment but may also significantly impair their ability to provide effective and ethical treatment to patients. The impaired psychotherapist is of great concern to the profession for two reasons: ethically, to protect patients and the public at large from mistreatment; and, humanely, to ensure that colleagues who are in trouble obtain appropriate help. In the same way, physicians and other health care workers who are ill may infect or otherwise harm their patients, an occurrence that suitable measures should prevent from happening; and health care workers certainly deserve to receive adequate care themselves when they fall ill.

Yet this concern about impaired psychotherapists, serious as it is, really applies to a fairly small minority of cases, a fact that indicates the great majority of psychotherapists who undergo personal therapy do so for other reasons. Our Impartial Person's question is misdirected because the analogy between psychotherapy and medicine or dentistry is only partially correct. As Freud took great pains to clarify to his Impartial Person many years ago, psychoanalytic treatments—and, in these later days, other forms of psychotherapy as well—differ significantly from biological medicine. Moreover, as Freud argued, and as the advocates of most other psychotherapies would agree, there are significant differences between the professional and personal qualities that enable clinicians to practice psychological or physical modes of treatment effectively.

Conceptions of this difference vary somewhat according to the proponents of the various psychotherapies, as illustrated in part I of this book. However, we think all those authors would agree that the interpersonal relationship between therapist and patient plays a much greater role in the psychological therapies than in physical medicine (also see Norcross, 2002). In physical medicine, the treatment is essentially biochemical, mechanical, or surgical in nature, while the relationship between doctor and patient is viewed as incidental—an adjunct to the treatment that may usefully encourage compliance with the prescribed regimen. The traditional doctor's long familiarity with individual patients and their families and the prized "bedside manner" that once functioned as a source of support have virtually disappeared in the current age of intensely specialized, bureaucratically organized, productivity-driven medical practice.

In the psychological therapies, by contrast, a positive patient-therapist relationship is of the essence, whether it is conceptualized as a precondition for the effective delivery of interventions (e.g., in cognitive and behavioral treatment), as a source of strategic leverage for modifying a larger nexus of relationships (e.g., in systemic family treatment), as a vital context of personality change (e.g., through the psychoanalytic interpretation and working-through of transference reactions), or in its own right as a supportive and growth-facilitating influence (e.g., in experiential and group psychotherapies). These different conceptions of the relationship between therapist and patient are not logically incompatible but rather emphasize and illustrate the varied therapeutic potentials inherent in that relationship. It is the salience of the interpersonal or "interhuman" element (Buber, 1965) in all psychotherapies that really explains the prevalent and important custom of personal therapy for psychotherapists.

The varied therapeutic potentials of the doctor-patient relationship just noted may be plausibly viewed as sources of the traditional physician's bedside manner's healing influence—often the only healing influence available to physicians prior to the still relatively recent development of scientific medicine. The potency of this psychological influence is attested by the strenuous and generally only partially successful efforts of medical researchers to control the so-called placebo factor when attempting experimentally to evaluate physical interventions. It is even quite plausible to view the historical development of the modern psychotherapies from psychoanalysis onward as the evolution, specialization, and progressive refinement of therapeutic potentials that were inherent in the traditional physician's bedside manner.

As the Impartial Person in our imagined conversation seems ready to grasp this point, we shall try to make our reasoning more explicit. The fact that interpersonal relatedness is such a central aspect of the psychotherapies means that psychotherapists' *personal* qualities—their social perceptiveness, emotional resonance and responsiveness, motivation to help, compassion, self-understanding, and self-discipline—are integral parts of their therapeutic work with patients, along with the more generic *professional* qualities of technical competence, probity, and objectivity. Those personal qualities need to be developed and maintained at a high level of sophistication and refinement—a higher level, in fact, than most people are normally required or expected to have in their close personal relationships. Because of patients' heightened vulnerability—due both to their experiences of past harm, and to their current dependence on their therapists—the psychotherapeutic relationship generally is more easily damaged by moments of misunderstanding, intemperate emotional expression, and wittingly or unwittingly given hurt than are the close family relations that are governed by a norm of "love" in our society (e.g., Bellah, Madsen, Sullivan, Swidler, & Tipton, 1985; Schneider, 1968). The personal psychotherapy undertaken by so many therapists may be viewed in large measure as the means for developing, refining, and maintaining their interpersonal qualities and skills at the highest level.

Yet, however refined their personal qualities may be, and however egalitarian their self-concepts vis-à-vis their patients, psychotherapists always also bear a responsibility as managing partners in their professional work with patients. As such, they are obligated to apply their technical knowledge and exercising their professional judgment objectively and solely for their patients' benefit. These impersonal professional qualities, which psychotherapists share with other health care and human service professions as well as other fiduciary professions (e.g., accountants, attorneys), differ markedly from the highly personal qualities that psychotherapists need in order to perform their specific function.

Thus another critical challenge for psychotherapists is the need to integrate and effectively balance the personal and impersonal qualities required of them by their "impossible profession." This challenge is all the greater when therapists provide therapy for other psychotherapists, since the natural sense of identification with the patient, based on their shared vocation, may significantly strain the balance between necessary personal and impersonal qualities, though it may be strained in other ways as well. Achieving and maintaining this balance is another major function of the personal therapy that is so often sought and used by therapists of varied theoretical orientations.

At this point, our Impartial Person, who has been listening attentively, nods in apparent agreement but is clearly ready to pose a further question:

> If the reasons given thus far for psychotherapists to have their own personal therapy are valid (as they seem to be), and if they apply more or less similarly to all therapists (as, by your argument, they should), then why do therapists of differing theoretical orientations—for example, those writing in parts I and II of the book—choose such different ways to implement the functions attributed personal therapy? Some writers require that it be done in one specific way and for a certain length of time, while other writers seem less stringent in their requirements or recommend different procedures. In fact, some writers seem not to talk about "personal therapy" at all but instead prefer terms like "facilitative relationship training," "growth-work," or "self-exploratory group encounters." Granted, as you have said, that personal therapy is essential or at least highly valuable for psychotherapists, why is there so much variation in the recommendations they offer for psychotherapists?

The answer to our Impartial Person's reasonable question rests in the different conceptions that therapists hold about psychopathology, its nature, and its prevalence—even among those therapists who are, as Freud described himself, "approximately normal" (Freud, 1900/1953, p. 105)—and the extent to which relationships with other persons are affected it. These concepts are rather intricately interwoven, but we shall try our best to make our meaning clear by comparing the differences between theoretical perspectives.

Viewed from a broadly behavioral perspective, pathology typically is identified for practical purposes with the appearance of overt symptoms that significantly impair the patient's functioning and also generally cause emotional distress to the persons involved or to their close associates. These symptoms themselves are not seen as manifestations of some unobserved "underlying" disorder reflecting the patient's character or personality. Pathological symptoms are believed to arise through faulty or maladaptive learning and, although they can be quite serious and debilitating, are viewed as incidental rather than integral to the patient's core personal identity. The same may be said of the cognitive-behavioral and cognitive therapies, with the exception that the source of symptoms is seen not so much as due to conditioning or instrumental learning as to unrealistic or irrational beliefs and the faulty cognitive habits from which they arise, such as all-or-nothing reasoning or untested overgeneralization of situationally specific experiences.

Behavioral and cognitive-behavioral therapies are largely directed toward the removal or amelioration of specific symptoms, and patients are considered to be cured when those symptoms have been removed. In addition, therapies that are more specifically cognitive in focus aim to correct the unrealistic beliefs and faulty reasoning that are held to give rise to symptoms. In both cases, however, the absence of manifest symptoms implies that there is no reason to suspect the presence of pathology or to prescribe a course of treatment. Logically, it follows that there is no reason to recommend personal therapy for therapists if they do not themselves currently experience or manifest overt symptoms.

Nevertheless, therapists of this theoretical persuasion increasingly recognize that their interpersonal behavior with patients can have a significant impact on the course and outcome of treatment, and that therapists (like persons generally) normally view their own behavior and its effects from a somewhat egocentric or subjective perspective. For these reasons, training experiences that help therapists become more accurately aware of, and better able to control, the impact of their behavior on others are a valuable asset for any therapist. However, such training experiences do not constitute therapy in the strict sense, and often are not so labeled, even though the procedures may resemble those that are used in other forms of psychotherapy.

In contrast to the behavioral therapies, which focus on patients' symptoms and not their personalities, existential and humanistic theories tend to view individuals' problems principally as limitations or distortions in their self-realization or personal development; that is, as essential and integral to their being. Traditionally, many humanistic approaches (e.g., client-centered and experiential therapies) deemphasized psychopathology as such, typically preferring to call persons in therapy "clients" rather than "patients" and generally avoided categorizing clients in diagnostic terms. Theoretically, the main source of clients' distressing and problematically limited self-realization is attributed to the absence of growth-facilitating conditions such as warmth and empathy in their primary relationships, resulting in self-defeating or distorted self-attitudes, rather than to conditioning of specific dysfunctional responses or maladaptive instrumental learning in particular stimulus situations. However, just as the insufficiency of growth-facilitating conditions once impeded the clients' development as "fully-functioning persons" (Rogers, 1959), so can the provision of growth-facilitating conditions experienced in therapy now lead to the belated renewal of personal growth. For most clients, and especially for those who are not too seriously impaired, the experience of growth-facilitating conditions in an interpersonal relationship *is* the core therapeutic experience. Whether these growth-facilitating conditions are understood as the genuine, empathic, and unconditional acceptance of the client as defined by Rogers (1957), or as the apposite and astute balance of challenge and support designed to confront clients with a "safe emergency" in the Gestalt manner (Perls, 1976), humanistic therapies aim to stimulate and support the process of self-development that is viewed as inherent in personality.

In this context, personal therapy or analogous experiences of personal encounter are important to therapists for two reasons. The first, primarily professional reason is to refine the therapist's ability to sensitively meet the needs of individual clients for optimally growth-facilitating relationships; that is, to be consistently empathic, personally authentic, constructively affirming, and appropriately challenging with a broad range of clients. The second, primarily private (though not unrelated) reason is that personal growth or self-realization is an ongoing, never wholly completed process of response to the challenges of living on which well-being depends. From the humanistic perspective, a therapist's commitment to the personal growth of clients, to be wholly authentic, must be matched by a parallel commitment to his or her own personal growth. This commitment may take the form of personal therapy if therapists experience significant impediments to growth reflected in a lack of well-being, or it may occur through less formal means such as participation in periodic training workshops and ongoing encounter groups.

Historically, of course, the tradition of having therapists undergo personal psychotherapy originated in psychoanalysis with Freud's (e.g., 1912/1958) prescription that an essential component of a psychoanalyst's training must take the form of a training analysis, which ideally should be periodically supplemented with additional treatment. In psychoanalytic theory, as in the humanistic approaches, psychopathology is rooted in disturbances of development, only in ways that appear at once more inevitable, more universal, more influential, more intractable, and more pervasive (Freud, 1917/1963). They are more *inevitable* because they are rooted in the unresolved and generally unresolvable conflicts of childhood (e.g., the Oedipus or "family" complex), which no one can escape, no matter how benign one's early interpersonal environment. They are more *universal* because, just as all people put on their trousers one leg at a time, so every adult has inevitably survived many years of childhood immaturity and dependence, which effectively precluded resolution of developmentally significant conflicts. They are more *influential* because the residues of unresolved childhood conflicts constitute the deepest core of an individual's personality. They are more *intractable* because the residues of unresolved childhood conflicts are largely unconscious, wrapped in layers of defensive resistance, and so are beyond the individual's normal self-awareness and voluntary control. Finally, the forms taken by those conflicts are more *pervasive* because the individual tends to repeat them compulsively, unwittingly, and more or less insidiously as unconscious transferences in subsequent relationships.

Whether major symptoms arise from these conflicts or not is, theoretically at least, almost a secondary consideration, although clinically of course it is a serious issue. In psychoanalytic and psychodynamic theory, the same conflicts are manifested in minor symptoms such as the eponymous mental malfunctions of everyday life known as "Freudian slips" and such normal experiences of waking and sleeping life as private fantasies and dreams.

Psychoanalysts and psychoanalytically oriented therapists typically are called on to deal only with more serious conflict-residues (e.g., neurotic symptoms, inhibitions, and character problems), but in so doing they must be prepared to deal both with their patients' and their own unconscious processes. To be effective, they must have extended their own self-awareness and self-control over the unconscious tendencies that would otherwise result in blind spots that would impede the patient's therapeutic progress and in unconscious countertransferences that would distort the therapeutic relationship. At the same time, where there is sufficient openness and communication between conscious and unconscious modes of experience, the therapist's unconscious can be an advantageous source of therapeutically creative engagement with the patient, in which the therapist "can turn his own unconscious like a receptive organ towards the transmitting unconscious of the patient" (Freud, 1912/1958, p. 115). This creative aspect of the unconscious is also emphasized and elaborated in Jungian analysis.

Of all the varied approaches to psychotherapy represented in this book, psychoanalytic theory projects the direst and most somber view that would require psychotherapists to have an extensive and effective experience of personal therapy. Nevertheless, we remind our Impartial Person that, however influential it may have been historically, it is not a prospect shared by all theoretical approaches. We have already mentioned how cognitive-behavioral and humanistic perspectives on therapy, which are clearly quite different from that of psychoanalysis and from each other, also lead therapists to have an experience of personal therapy (or some highly similar procedure) as a vital part of their clinical training and practice. The systemic approach to therapeutic work is further case in point.

Systemic therapies differ from other therapeutic approaches with regard to the understanding of psychopathology by viewing its principal source as the network of primary relationships in which the identified patient participates. For the most part, those primary relationship networks involve family groups, particularly the individual's family-of-origin (the relational network in which he or she lived through childhood), although the adult's current marital and family relationships may in fact be the focus of treatment. In systemic therapies, the disturbances of behavior, thought, and emotion that are generally identified as psychopathology are viewed basically as properties of the family system itself rather than as internal properties of individual family members—although the symptoms of that systemic pathology may be manifested primarily through one member of the group or one specific relationship within the larger network. This emphasis on the interpersonal and group context in understanding pathology (and personality more broadly) contrasts dramatically with the individualistic perspectives of other therapeutic approaches, which focus either intrapsychically on conflicts and interactions between personality components (psychodynamic theories), on self-realization of the individual as a whole person (humanistic theories), or on the learned adaptations and maladaptations of individuals to their environment (cognitive-behavioral theories).

Although therapy informed by systemic theory can be conducted with individual patients, systemic therapists typically prefer to work with family groups or family subsystems (e.g., parent-child pairs, marital couples) and focus their interventions directly on those relationships. Systemically oriented therapists work to transform the "patient" family or family subsystem by joining in it actively (if temporarily) as participant-observers, with the aim of helping the system become a less conflictful, more benign milieu for the system's resident participants. However, to join and participate therapeutically in "patient" families or subsystems, therapists must be able to negotiate the turbulent currents of emotional interaction characteristic of those systems, withstand the emotional pressures generated by them, and manage to operate effectively in the intense interactive flow between family members. To do this, therapists must be clearly aware and in control of the vulnerabilities and propensities in family contexts they themselves have developed as members of their own families of origin. Personal therapy is probably most relevant specifically for systemic therapists in this connection, in addition to the general benefits of personal therapy that may be shared with clinicians of other orientations.

In sum, we conclude our answer to the Impartial Person's second question by suggesting that personal therapy (along with similar procedures designed to enhance personal and professional growth) is important to therapists across a broad theoretical spectrum but that it is important for different reasons to different types of psychotherapist. Each theoretical orientation finds good reasons for requiring or recommending that therapists undergo personal therapy, even if those reasons do vary from one orientation to another.

Since this conversation with our Impartial Person is a construct of our imagination, we take the liberty of averting further questions about the reasons for the great diversity among psychotherapists' theoretical orientations. However, our Impartial Person, who has graciously accepted our answers thus far, will still not let us escape without asking one final question:

> I understand now that personal therapy is truly important for psychotherapists, and that psychotherapy differs in this respect from other health care professions. I also understand that diverse theories view the question of personal psychotherapy from different angles and recommend it for different purposes. But, from what I have read and been told, it seems that personal therapy has not been much discussed in the professional literature. Why hasn't it been discussed more, and why isn't it more frequently recommended in training programs?

Once again, our Impartial Person has rather astutely identified a significant issue. To this question, we offer the following reply. Psychotherapists themselves literally rave about (most of) their personal therapy experiences. They overwhelmingly report high satisfaction with and salutary outcomes from their personal therapy. They do so privately and individually, but for reasons of confidentiality few mental health practitioners publicly discuss their personal psychotherapy. Unfortunately, this understandable unwillingness to discuss highly personal experiences more openly results in a state of pluralistic ignorance. Hence, knowledge of the varied benefits of personal therapy for psychotherapists tends to be part of an underground therapeutic culture (Wachtel, 1977)—something that virtually all psychotherapists know but do not publicly disclose.

Only rare and courageous psychotherapists publicly and professionally expose their own history of personal therapy, because doing so entails revealing the most personal, sensitive, and conflictual aspects of their private lives both to a potential audience of professionally uneducated lay persons and to an audience of professionally educated but potentially overcritical colleagues. The former may just be further convinced of the impression, first voiced more politely by our Impartial Person, that "All shrinks are nuts." Even more feared is the likelihood that overcritical professional colleagues will weigh in with damaging diagnoses of the therapists who discuss their experiences in personal therapy.

For similar reasons, many training programs are also unwilling to publicly require that students and graduates undergo personal therapy. This is a matter of appearance as well as choice. Requiring therapy for initiates (outside of psychoanalytic institutes) may convey the impression that students and trainees are typically disturbed or impaired as individuals, which would significantly compromise their credibility as help-givers. Furthermore, to require personal therapy of trainees would impose a significant cost on young persons who are not yet professionally employed and must already find means of support during their student years. Most important, perhaps, requiring personal therapy would preclude students and graduates from making the individual choice and personal commitment to therapy that are essential for gaining real benefit from it and from other growth-enhancing experiences.

Indeed, one of our prime objectives in compiling and editing this book is to bring together and discuss the personal therapy experiences of psychotherapists in a public and professionally respectful forum. Having done what we can to realize this goal, we will take the liberty of addressing a few final thoughts to our Impartial Person and to other readers.

Every person who enters psychotherapy hopes, at some level, to find a perfect therapist—one who is unfailingly understanding, ever available, consistently caring, and always able to provide the exact balance of support and challenge that will make the therapeutic experience an ideal "safe emergency." Every person who enters psychotherapy deserves no less. Yet no psychotherapist is or can be a perfect therapist; only (at best, perhaps) a "good enough" therapist—available most of the time, understanding most of the time, responsive and caring most of the time. The sad though obvious fact is that we psychotherapists are human too, which means that while often good enough we not infrequently are not quite good enough to meet our patients' needs, and we sometimes are—on the evidence, relatively rarely—bad enough to do harm.

The psychotherapist's need for his or her own personal therapy is created, first and foremost, by our ethical obligation to do no harm, hopefully by helping the occasional bad therapist to become good enough; and, ultimately, by our professional obligation to keep trying against all odds to bridge the unspannable gap between being the good enough therapist that most of us can be most of the time and the perfect therapist that our patients deserve but must learn to live without. As therapists we need to improve constantly, not only in our work as therapists but (strange as it may seem) also in our work as patients. We must keep our patient-selves sitting beside us when working as therapists for others, partly to keep a watchful eye on our patient-selves so that they do not interfere, but also to call on our patient-selves sometimes for advice and continuously as a source of compassion. So it is that we need to become better and better patients *as well as* better and better therapists, *in order* to be better and better therapists.

Who can meet our inevitable need for personal therapy except other psychotherapists, imperfect in principle but good enough in practice, who thereby carry a double burden as therapists' therapists? Thus we see the psychotherapist as a person who is both a therapist, a patient, and a psychotherapist-and-patient: at work in a hall of mirrors in which one tries to remain clear-sighted while inevitably also seeing oneself as one sees the other, and seeing the other as one sees oneself. It may in some respect often be easier work to have other therapists as patients, since they tend (by and large) to be healthier, better-put-together persons than the average, and they bring their therapist-selves with them to potentially assist in the process. Yet working with other therapists also is work done on a more slippery slope with persons whose patient-selves have more complex if less drastic needs, and whose therapist-selves can interfere as well as aid—a slippery slope where a misstep can be easier and the consequences of a misstep can be harder to correct.

To confront the special challenges involved in the psychotherapist's personal therapy, we have tried in this book to create a space of common discourse among psychotherapists as patients (many of whom are therapists' therapists), among therapists' therapists (all of whom are likely to have had personal therapy), and among therapy researchers (most of whom are also therapists) who have studied therapists as patients *and* therapists' therapists. To promote this common discourse, we have brought together understandings of the therapist's personal therapy from diverse theoretical perspectives. Now in this last chapter, which we expect and certainly hope will not be the last word on this subject, we have tried, by answering the imagined questions of our Impartial Person, to draw together some of the lines of discourse presented in previous chapters, to map their patterns of convergence and difference, to define the current frontier of knowledge and ignorance on the subject, to find what practical wisdom there that we may, and to propose where next to turn in search of wider and deeper understanding. To our professional colleagues and readers, we close by paraphrasing the French poet Charles Baudelaire, who wrote (1861/1954, p. 82): "—Hypocrite lecteur,—mon semblable,—mon frère." *Therapist-reader, our likeness, our kin!*

REFERENCES

Baudelaire, C. (1861/1954). Au lecteur. In *Les fleurs du mal.* In Y.-G. Le Dantec (Ed.), *Baudelaire: Oeuvres completes.* Paris: Librairie Gallimard.

Bellah, R. N., Madsen, R., Sullivan, W. M., Swidler, A., & Tipton, S. M. (1985). *Habits of the heart: Individualism and commitment in American life.* Berkeley: University of California Press.

Buber, M. (1965). Elements of the interhuman. In M. Friedman (Ed.), *The knowledge of man: Selected essays* (pp. 72–88). New York: Harper and Row.

Freud, S. (1900/1953). *The interpretation of dreams.* In J. Strachey (Ed. and Trans.), *The standard edition of the complete psychological works of Sigmund Freud* (Vol. 5). London: Hogarth Press.

Freud, S. (1912/1958). Recommendations to physicians practising psychoanalysis. In J. Strachey (Ed. and Trans.), *The standard edition of the complete psychological works of Sigmund Freud* (Vol. 12, pp. 109–120). London: Hogarth Press.

Freud, S. (1917/1963). *Introductory lectures on psycho-analysis.* Lecture 23. In J. Strachey (Ed. and Trans.), *The standard edition of the complete psychological works of Sigmund Freud* (Vol. 16, pp. 358–377). London: Hogarth Press.

Freud, S. (1926/1959). *The question of lay analysis: Conversations with an impartial person.* In J. Strachey (Ed. and Trans.), *The standard edition of the complete psychological works of Sigmund Freud* (Vol. 20). London: Hogarth Press.

Norcross, J. C. (Ed.). (2002). *Psychotherapy relationships that work: Therapist contributions and responsiveness to patient needs.* New York: Oxford University Press.

Perls, F. (1976). *The Gestalt approach and eye witness to therapy.* New York: Bantam Books.

Rogers, C. R. (1957). The necessary and sufficient conditions of therapeutic personality change. *Journal of Consulting Psychology, 22,* 95–103.

Rogers, C. R. (1959). A theory of therapy, personality, and interpersonal relationships, as developed in the client-centered framework. In S. Koch (Ed.), *Psychology: A study of a science* (Vol. 3, pp. 184–256). New York: McGraw-Hill.

Schneider, D. M. (1968). *American kinship: A cultural account.* Englewood Cliffs, NJ: Prentice-Hall.

Wachtel, P. L. (1977). *Psychoanalysis and behavior therapy: Toward integration.* New York: Basic Books.

APPENDIX

Guidelines for
Firsthand Accounts

CONTENT TO BE ADDRESSED IN THERAPISTS'
THERAPIST CHAPTERS

Thank you for your interest in contributing a chapter for *The Psychotherapist's Own Therapy: Patient and Clinician Perspectives*. We are asking each author to keep in mind a core set of issues when writing the chapter. Addressing the following content in your chapter will (1) promote continuity among the chapters in this section of the book, (2) afford convergence between your first-person account and the subsequent research-oriented chapters in the book, and (3) permit comparative analyses between the complementary experiences of therapists conducting personal therapy (part III) and those receiving it (part II). Toward these ends, we request that you address the following domains in whatever form and sequence that suits you best. The Representative Questions are intended only to be evocative; we do not request that you respond to each.

    1. Your history and experience in treating mental health professionals. Representative Questions: How many years have you been providing personal therapy or analysis? What proportion of your current practice is devoted to providing therapy for other therapists? What types of mental health professionals in terms of gender, ethnicity, profession, and orientation do you generally see? What types of therapy do you usually provide for other therapists? If you were asked to speculate, why do psychotherapists select you as their therapists?

2. Your experiences of what, if anything, distinguishes the psychotherapy of patients who are themselves psychotherapists from the psychotherapy offered to nontherapists. Representative Questions: Do you notice any differences in your treatment experiences with fellow psychotherapists or therapists-in-training in:

- Presenting problems and treatment goals
- The treatment format/modality you choose
- The power dynamics of the therapeutic relationship
- Negotiation of the therapeutic contract
- Modifications in technique
- Maintaining boundaries
- The termination process
- Posttermination relationships
- The essential determinants of the success of psychotherapy.

3. Your observations on the distinctive process of treating mental health professionals. Representative Questions: What has been your experience in treating therapists whose theoretical orientation is substantially different from your own? How you give therapists the freedom to be patients while respecting the collegial aspects of the relationship? Are therapist-patients selectively responsive to different facets of the process than nontherapist patients? Is mentoring an important component of your work with therapist-patients? What role does discussion of the patient's work as a therapist play in their treatment? How do therapist-patients react to your technical errors, empathic failures, and minor violations of the therapeutic frame? Are the roles you play in the fantasies of your therapist-patients different from those imagined by nontherapists?

4. Your burdens and stressors in conducting psychotherapy with fellow mental health professionals (beyond those associated with conducting psychotherapy in general). Representative Questions: What are the most difficult features of treating psychotherapists? Are there cases in which psychotherapists make the worst patients? On what occasions do you become most aware that you are treating a psychotherapist? Do you feel increased pressure to be "successful" when the patient is also a therapist? How do you avoid the blurring of psychotherapy and supervision? What are the complications—and how do you handle them—of former psychotherapist-patients becoming professionals in the same locale?

5. Your satisfactions and rewards in conducting psychotherapy with mental health professionals (beyond those associated with conducting psychotherapy in general). Representative Questions: What are the most rewarding features of treating psychotherapists? What are the gratifications of being considered a "therapist's therapist"?

6. Your lessons from treating fellow psychotherapists for improving psychotherapy in general, and psychotherapy with psychotherapists in particular. Representative Questions: How much have your experiences providing therapy for other therapist influenced your own development as a psycho-therapist? In what ways, positively and negatively? What, if anything, does the therapy of therapists tell us about how to treat nontherapist patients? What advice would you offer fellow clinicians to help them conduct effective psychotherapy with other therapists?

CONTENT TO BE ADDRESSED IN THERAPIST-PATIENT CHAPTERS

Thank you for your interest in contributing a chapter for *The Psychotherapist's Own Therapy: Patient and Clinician Perspectives*. We are asking each author to keep in mind a core set of issues when writing the chapter. Addressing the following content in your chapter will (1) promote continuity among the chapters in this section of the book, (2) afford convergence between your first-person account and the subsequent research-oriented chapters in the book, and (3) permit comparative analyses between the complementary experiences of therapists conducting personal therapy (part III) and those receiving it (part II). Toward these ends, we request that you address the following domains in whatever form and sequence suits you best. The Representative Questions are intended only to be evocative; we do not request that you respond to each.

In addressing these matters, we invite you to write in a comfortably disclosing manner. We understand that you may elect to be selective in the autobiographical material you will include.

1. Your history and experience in receiving personal therapy/analysis. Representative Questions: How many different times have you been in therapy, with how many different therapists? What types of therapy have you received by theoretical orientation and by treatment modality? Overall, how many hours or years of personal therapy have you had? What were the most salient considerations in selecting your therapist(s)? Who was your personal therapist(s) in terms of gender, ethnicity, profession, and orientation? Did any of the matches or mismatches in gender, ethnicity, profession, or orientation pose difficulties? Were your reasons for seeking therapy mainly training, personal growth, or personal problems? What were your chief complaints and treatment goals? Were these related to your career choice as a psychotherapist?

2. Your experiences of what, if anything, distinguishes the psychotherapy of patients who are themselves psychotherapists from the psychotherapy offered to nontherapists. Representative Questions: Did you notice or infer any differences in your treatment experiences in

- Presenting problems and treatment goals
- The treatment format/modality offered
- The power dynamics of the therapeutic relationship
- Negotiation of the therapeutic contract
- Modifications in technique

- Maintaining boundaries
- The termination process
- Posttermination relationships
- The essential determinants of the success of psychotherapy.

3. Your observations on the distinctive process of receiving psychotherapy as a mental health professional. Representative Questions: How did you take, as a professional (or professional-in-training), to being in psychotherapy yourself? How did your therapist give you, as a therapist-patient, the freedom to be a patient while respecting the collegial aspects of the relationship? What else might accomplish this purpose? What role did discussion of your work as a therapist play in your treatment? How did you react to your therapist's technical errors, empathic failures, and minor violations of the therapeutic frame? What were your fantasies about your therapist?

4. Your burdens and stressors in receiving psychotherapy as a mental health professional. Representative Questions: What were the most difficult features of being in psychotherapy? What were your concerns about maintaining proper boundaries with your therapist? How did you and your therapist avoid the blurring of psychotherapy and informal supervision? How did you handle the complications of you, as a former patient, becoming a professional?

5. Your satisfactions and rewards in receiving psychotherapy as a mental health professional. Representative Questions: How much value/benefit has personal therapy had for you in your personal life? What were the best and worst outcomes? Was mentoring an important component of your therapy? What was the impact on your personal and professional development?

6. Your lessons from undergoing personal psychotherapy for improving psychotherapy in general, and psychotherapy with psychotherapists in particular. Representative Questions: How much have your experiences undergoing personal therapy influenced your development as a psychotherapist? What are your "lasting lessons" about psychotherapy from your personal treatment experiences? What, if anything, does the therapy of therapists tell us about how to treat nontherapist patients? What advice would you offer fellow clinicians to help them select effective psychotherapists?

INDEX

abandonment, 75, 127
abstinence, 90, 382, 383
acting out, 19, 22, 331
adult development theory, 8
age-associated tasks, 8
Albert Ellis Institute, 111
alcoholism, 324, 335
ambivalence, 15, 308
amnesia, 64–66, 70, 73–74
"Analysis Terminable and
    Interminable" (Freud), 6, 220,
    365
analytical psychology, 28–29
analytic ego, 25
analytic superego, 25
anchored instruction, 35
anger, 136–37, 294–95
anonymity, 90, 382, 383
anti-Semitism, 93
anxiety
    over death, 115, 123
    and empathy, 23
    of novice therapists, 126
    as presenting problem, 196
    provoked by patients, 21
    transformative potential of, 289–90

Aponte, Harry J., 297
archetypal images, 27
assessment/intervention matrix, 158
asymmetry, 269
Atman, 117
Atwood, G.E., 114
authenticity, 87–88, 394
authority, 389
autobiographical narratives, 7, 96

bad-object relations, 66–67, 71–72,
    74–75, 79
Bassui (Zen master), 123
Beck, Judith S., 254
behavioral family therapy, 54
    See also cognitive-behavioral
        therapy; family therapy
behavioral therapy, 131, 208–10
Berman, Emanuel, 235
Bible, 129
Blatt, Sid, 89
body awareness, 92–93
body image, 384
bond, 104
Bordin, E., 102, 103, 104
Botermans, Jean-François, 177

boundaries
  and analysands as colleagues, 249–50
  clear, 125, 134
  in cognitive therapy, 261–63
  definition of, 379, 384
  within family, 149
  in feminist therapy, 272–75
  in Gestalt therapy, 312–14
  interpersonal, 382
  psychological, 384–86
  between psychotherapy and
    psychotherapy supervision, 386
  in psychotherapy of
    psychotherapists, 379–400
  sexual, 326–37, 397
  in therapy, 32, 141
  violations of, 22, 397
Bowen, Murray, 55, 56
bravery, 83
British Association for Counselling, 98
British Psychological Society, 98
Brown, Laura S., 265–80
Bruner, J., 385
Bugental, James T., 117–28, 282,
  288, 295
Butler, Andrew C., 254

career level, 183–85
change
  dealing with continual, 284
  goals for, 103, 104
  through therapeutic interventions,
    142
childhood conflicts, 410
children, 65, 149
choicefulness, 283, 285
client-centered therapy, 36, 131
clinical practices, 352–59
cognitive-behavioral therapy, 408–9,
  411
  for couples and families, 54
  Dryden on, 111
  personal therapy in, 41–49
  for sexual misconduct, 330
  terminology of, 43
cognitive growth, 385
cognitive therapy, 254–64, 408–9
Collaborative Research Network of
  the Society for Psychotherapy
  Research, 215, 225

collective responsibility, 30
collective unconscious, 27
communicative intimacy, 86
competence, 388, 390
competition, 287
concern for others, 392–93
confidences, 125
conflict, 19, 21–23, 24, 25, 410–11
connectedness, 283, 285–86, 290
Connor, Kelly A., 192
conversational style, 388
counteridentification, 22, 96
countertransference
  and analysis of colleagues, 242
  in analytical psychology, 29
  in cognitive therapy, 263
  in existential-humanistic
    psychotherapy, 287
  and family therapy, 54, 56
  in feminist therapy, 268
  interdependence with transference,
    388
  and sexual boundary violations,
    333–34
  in training analysis, 22, 23, 24
couples conflict, 196
couples therapy, 54, 56, 57, 159
courage, 82, 83
Craige, H., 372–74
Curtis, Rebecca C., 365

dark king archetype, 332
death
  anxiety, 123
  dealing with, 284, 295
  early, 82, 83
  inevitability of, 115–17
  Wittine on, 115–17, 119, 123
defense mechanisms, 115
defensive needs, 249
defensive resistance, 410
depression, 149, 196
developmental approach, 29
developmental task, 93
  Development of Psychotherapists'
    Common Core Questionnaire
    (DPCCQ), 178, 179, 183, 346,
    350
Dewey, John, 309
distance violations, 94–95

distant father, 117
distressed practitioners, 323–37
Division 29 Project, 346–51, 362
doctor/patient relationship, 406–7
DPCCQ. *See* Development of
　Psychotherapists' Common Core
　Questionnaire
dreams, 28–29, 91–92, 136, 141, 390
Dryden, Windy, 6, 8, 98–113
dual relationships, 397

Eastern mystics, 123
Edelson, Marshall, 89
egalitarianism, 265–80
ego, 16, 22, 67, 79, 308
Eisner, Rona, 133–37, 141
Eitingon model, 17
Elliott, Robert, 34
Ellis, Albert, 102, 105, 111–13
embodiedness, 283, 284
emotional healing, 36
emotion coaching approach, 39
emotions, mixed, 308–9
empathy
　ability to give and receive, 392–93
　and anxiety, 23
　experiential learning of, 36
　failures of, 383, 390–92
　for patient, 21
　and personal therapy and growth
　　work, 35, 37
　and transient identification, 24
encounter groups, 131–32
Epstein, Nathan, 147–49, 150
Erikson, Erik, 89
ethics, 333, 335, 397, 414
ethnicity, of therapist's therapist, 205
existential-humanistic psychotherapy,
　114–28, 282–96
existential liberation, 38
existential psychotherapy, 38, 115
experience, 34, 384, 385
experience-near learning, 35
experiential-humanistic therapies, 34–39
explicitness, 102–3
extraversion, 29

failure
　of empathy, 383, 390–92
　of family-of-origin work, 152

of family therapy, 149
and growth, 145–46
to maintain boundaries, 327–28
of marital therapy, 149–51
of psychoanalysis, 146–49
of psychodynamic therapy, 154–55
Fairbairn, W.R.D., 63–70, 72–74, 76,
　78, 79
Fairbairn-Guntrip metaphor, 65
false lover archetype, 332
family-of-origin, 55, 149–52, 411
family relationships, 412
family therapy
　behavioral, 54
　definition of, 52
　and failure of psychoanalysis, 146–
　　49
　role of personal therapy in, 52–57
　with therapist's therapist, 297–305
fears, 83
feedback, 256
feeling, 29
feelingful awareness, 118
fees, 8, 90, 126, 137
feigned illness, 107
Feldenkrais method, 92
felt presence, 396
feminist therapy, 265–80
Feminist Therapy Institute, 272
Ferenczi, S., 239, 366
finitude, 283, 284
Fordham, M., 31–32
Framo, James, 55
free association, 118
Freud, Anna, 21
Freud, Sigmund
　as "approximately normal," 408
　on difference between
　　psychoanalysis and biological
　　medicine, 406
　and Ferenczi, 239, 366
　free association technique, 118
　Geller's study of, 84–85
　Guntrip on, 73, 79
　"mainstream" model, 15–25
　on personal therapy, 5–6, 167, 220,
　　365
　on training analysis, 27, 31, 410
　views on unconscious, 15, 16
Freudian psychodynamics, 115

Freudian slip, 85, 411
From, Isadore, 312

Gabbard, G., 333–34
Geller, Jesse D., 3, 81–96, 345, 379, 405
gender
   and prevalence of personal therapy, 171–72, 188, 189
   and therapist's therapist, 205
   and training analysis, 31
generality, of study samples, 178
generalizability, of study samples, 178
Gestalt therapy
   collegiality and boundaries, 312–14
   concerns in conducting, 318–19
   group therapy for therapists in, 37–38, 307–21
   mentoring in, 314–17
   response to, 317–18
   training program, 309–11
Gestalt Therapy Institute (Phila., Pa.), 307
goals
   for change, 103, 104
   of feminist therapy, 267
   and individual therapies, 105
   of personal therapy, 9, 389
God, 117, 121, 122, 129
Goodman, Paul, 312
Gormally, James, 130, 138
Great Britain, 98, 99
group format
   in cognitive-behavioral therapy, 45
   in Gestalt therapy, 38, 307–21
   one year of group therapy, 106–8
   personal development groups, 108–10
   rational emotive-behavior therapy, 108
   in understanding pathology, 411
growth
   cognitive, 385
   and failure, 145–46
   in Gestalt therapy, 37
   with good psychotherapy, 282
   work, 34–39
Grunebaum, Henry, 201
Guntrip, Harry, 63–80
Guy, James D., 165

Haley, Jay, 53
Harper, Robert, 102, 105
healing, 154–55, 383
Heery, Myrtle, 282, 288
helpfulness/hurtfulness ratings, 371
helping skills, 130–31
Hill, Clara E., 129–43
Holocaust, 93
homosexual panic, 23
Hoppe, Sue Keir, 374
human encounter movement, 55
humanistic approaches, 409, 411, 412
   See also existential-humanistic psychotherapy

idealizing selfobject transference, 126
identification
   with patient, 22, 23–24, 298, 408
   with therapist, 96
   of therapist's therapist, 349–50
   transient, 24
impaired practitioners, 323–37, 405–6
impermanence, 284
individuality, 30
individual therapy, 132–33, 173, 301, 380
individuation, 8
inferiority, 102, 105, 257
informed consent, 102
inner critic, 286
inner searching, 117–25
institute dynamics, 247–48
Institutt for Psykoterapi (Oslo, Norway), 370–71
integrative approaches, 131
integrative problem-centered therapy, 145–46, 156–58
internalization, 240, 379–400
International Association for Analytical Psychology, 28, 29
International Doctors in Alcoholics Anonymous, 324
interpersonal boundary, 382
intersubjectivity, 382–84
introspection, 81, 129
introversion, 27, 29
intuition, 29

I-process, 117, 122, 126, 127
irony, 88

Judaism, 93
Jung, Carl, 27–28
Jungian analysis
    and dream images, 28–29, 390
    Dryden on, 110, 111, 112
    Kirsch on, 27–32
    role of personal therapy in
        formation of Jungian analyst, 27–
        32
    and unconscious, 27, 411
    Wittine on, 115, 116, 117, 127

Kaiser, Helmuth, 86–87, 314
Kaiserian therapists, 87, 88
Kirsch, Thomas B., 27
Kirsner, D., 367–68
Klein, Melanie, 69
Kohut, H., 7

Laireiter, Anton-Rupert, 41
Lasko, Al, 119
Lasky, Richard, 15
Lazarus, Arnold, 103, 208–9
learning, 34, 36, 145
Lebow, Jay, 52
lesbian women, 266
Lichtenberg, Philip, 307
life stages, 8
life-threatening illness, 290–96
Limentani, A., 367
limits. See boundaries
listening, 104, 131, 134, 286–88,
    295
Lofgren, Borge, 89
long-term psychotherapy, 142, 288,
    380
loss, 372

Maharshi, Ramana, 123
marital conflict, 196
marital status, 172
marital therapy
    behavioral, 54
    failure of, 149–51, 154
    of Hill, 137–39
    with therapist's therapist, 297–305
Martinez, Diane, 374, 397

meaning, 302
meditation, 93, 116, 121
memories, 81, 91
Memories, Dreams, Reflections (Jung),
    27
Menninger, K., 90
mentoring
    of Ellis, 111
    in feminist therapy, 276, 277
    in Gestalt therapy, 314–17
    of men, 117
midlife crisis, 110
mind, 384, 385
Minnesota, 335
Minuchin, Salvatore, 54
mirror analyst, 64, 67
Morse, Stephen, 65
multiple analyses, 28, 31
mutuality, 275, 383

naive prince archetype, 331
narcissism, 194
narrative therapy, 7, 56
neutrality, 90, 382, 383
New Guide to Rational Living, A
    (Ellis and Harper), 102, 105
Norcross, John C., 3, 165, 192, 201,
    214, 345, 405
note-taking, 100, 104

objective reality, 383
objective truth, 383
object relations, 152–54, 237–40
    See also bad-object relations
oedipal phase, 23, 66–67, 68–69,
    410
Ontario (Canada), 335
optional responsiveness, 383
Orlinsky, David E., 3, 177, 214, 345,
    405

pacing, 106
parental depression, 149
parenting, 139
Partyka, Rhea, 34
Perls, Fritz, 118, 312
personal agency, 35
personal becoming, 36
personal development groups, 108–
    10

personal encounter, 410
personal growth. *See* growth
personality
  basic pattern of, 64
  and conflict, 410
  Geller on, 83
  Guntrip on, 64, 79
  of psychoanalyst, 21, 24
  theory, 114
  unknown aspects of, 83
personal space, 384
personal therapy, 3–10, 411
  in cognitive-behavioral therapy,
    41–49
  definition of, 5
  effect on subsequent performance,
    223–25
  evolution of, 5–7
  Freud on, 5–6
  functions of, 35–36
  goals of, 9, 389
  and growth work in experiential-
    humanistic therapies, 34–39
  importance of, 410, 412
  lasting lessons of, 222–25
  length of, 172–73
  limits of, 32, 141
  methodological caveats on studies
    of, 165–66, 177–79
  multiple yet singular purpose of, 9–10
  negative effects of, 218–20
  outcomes and impacts of, 214–27
  parameters of, 165–74, 177–91, 349
  positive benefits of, 214–18
  presenting problems, 195–98
  prevalence and parameters
    internationally, 177–91
  prevalence and parameters in U.S.,
    165–74
  prevalence with mental health
    professionals, 348
  professional impact of, 220–22
  psychotherapists entering, 192–98
  purposes of, 188–90, 192–93, 406
  reasons for not entering, 194–95
  as requirement for therapists, 413
  research findings on undergoing,
    163–227
  role in formation of Jungian
    analyst, 27–32

  in systemic/family therapy, 52–57,
    412
  and theoretical orientation, 207,
    408, 412
  therapists' need for, 414
  of therapists' therapists, 351–52
person-centered concepts, 34
person-centered therapy, 36–37, 99
physical medicine, 406
Pinsof, William M., 8, 145–61
post-termination contact, 381–82
post-termination mourning, 372–74
post-termination phase, 397–99
post-termination relationships, 277–
  78
power dynamics, 389–90
practice-centered concepts, 45, 46
presence, 125, 126, 396
pride, 393–96
primordial images, 27
privacy, 7, 30, 288, 387
prizing, 35
problem-centered therapy, 146, 156–
  58
problem maintenance structure, 156–
  58
problem sequence, 156, 158
problem solving therapy, 53
process-experiential therapy, 39
professional background, 185–86
professional development, 220–22
professional discipline, 210–11
professional impairment, 323–37
proximal imagery, 399
pseudo-normality, 247
psychiatry, 100
psychoanalysis, 15, 17, 21, 89
psychodrama, 100, 103
psychodynamic therapy, 131, 142,
  154, 330–31, 411
psychological boundaries, 384–86
psychological types, 29, 31
Psychologists Helping Psychologists,
  324
psychopathology, 408, 409, 410
psychotherapist(s)
  advice to, 361–62
  boundaries and internalization in
    psychotherapy of, 379–400
  choice of, 381

decision to become, 86
decision to enter psychotherapy, 282–83
impaired practitioners, 323–37, 405–6
myth of losing face, 283
personal qualities, 381, 407
presenting problems of, 195–98
professional qualities, 407
relationship with patient, 406
vicariously experiencing wounds, 298–99
See also therapist's therapist
Public and Private Lives of Psychotherapists (Henry et al.), 3
public speaking, 101

Qaiser, Mazia, 365

radical disguises, 7
rational emotive-behavior therapy (REBT), 98, 101–2, 105–6, 108, 111–13
REBT. *See* rational emotive-behavior therapy
reciprocity, 383
regressed ego, 67
regression, 73
rehabilitation, 329–30
Reich, Wilhelm, 118
relationships
  doctor/patient, 406–7
  dual, 397
  family, 412
  with family-of-origin, 55, 149–51
  in feminist therapy, 268–70
  "natural fit," 64
  post-termination, 277–78
  power, 269
  sexual, 326–37
  symbolic, 268
  therapist/patient, 406
  See also therapeutic relationship
religion, 129–30
resistance
  to analysis, 16, 388
  confronting and analyzing, 88
  defensive, 410
  in existential-humanistic psychotherapy, 287

feminist, 267
Freud on, 6
of Guntrip, 66
as interactive process, 383
of therapist-patients, 6, 381
respect, 393–96
retirement, 290–91
Rogers, Carl, 102, 104, 105
Rolf method, 92
Rønnestad, Michael Helge, 177, 214

San Francisco Psychoanalytic Institute, 29–30, 375
Satir, Virginia, 55
Schafer, Roy, 89
Schizoid Phenomena, Object-Relations and the Self (Guntrip), 72
Schoener, Gary R., 323
searching, 117–25
secrecy, 243–44, 387
self-acceptance, 105–6
self-analysis, 17, 194, 396–97
self-awareness, 34, 411
self-concern, 392–93
self-disclosure, 112, 119, 126, 134, 283, 287, 389–90
self-exploration, 44, 45–47
self-identity, 122–23
self-image, 194
self/Self, 117, 120–21, 127, 128, 385
self-serving martyr archetype, 332
sensation, 29
sense of loss, 372
sense of place, 82
sensory experiences, 92–93
separateness, 283, 285–86, 290
sexual addiction, 331–32
sexual relationships, 326–37
shamanism, 145, 160
spirituality, 116, 302
SPR Collaborative Research Network, 346, 348, 350, 352–53
standards, 398
Stolorow, R.D., 114
stream of consciousness, 124
stressors, 360
structural theory, 16, 65
structural therapy, 54
subjectivity, 125–26, 128

substance abuse, 324, 335
Sullivan, H.S., 388
supervisor and supervision
  and analysand as analyst's therapist,
    245–47
  boundaries between psychotherapy
    and psychotherapy supervision,
    386–87
  as corruptible object, 335
  and feminist therapy, 277
  and transference, 240
symbolic approach, 29
symmetry, 383
systemic therapies, 52–57, 411–12

technique-related models, 45, 46
termination of therapy
  abrupt, 101, 104
  criteria for, 396
  Dryden's, 101, 104
  Geller's, 95–96
  Hill's, 135
  planning for, 104
  post-termination mourning, 372–74
  post-termination phase, 397–99
  post-termination relationships,
    277–78, 381–82
  premature, 126–27
theoretical orientations
  and choice of personal therapy,
    207, 408
  and Gestalt therapy, 315
  and prevalence of personal therapy,
    167, 171, 186–88
  of therapist's therapist, 205–8
  therapist's therapy in different, 13–
    57
  and varying reasons for personal
    therapy, 412
therapeutic contract, 389
therapeutic environment, 125
therapeutic massage, 92
therapeutic relationship, 141, 406–7
  difficulties in, 256–58
  intensity of, 299
  in marital and family therapy, 297
  nature of, 255–56
therapist-patient(s), 59–227
  characteristics of, 7, 348–49
  Dryden as, 98–113

firsthand accounts by, 61–161
  Geller as, 81–96
  Guntrip as, 63–80
  Hill as, 129–43
  Pinsof as, 145–61
  practical and practical/
    psychological problems with,
    260–61
  preparing patients for role as, 387–
    89
  psychotherapy of, 4, 7, 61–161
  research findings on, 163–227
  resistance of, 6, 382
  Wittine as, 114–28
  See also personal therapy
therapist's therapists, 231–415
  advice to, 361–62
  analysis of colleagues and trainees,
    235–50
  characteristics of, 204–12, 350–51
  clinical practices of, 352–59
  and countertransference, 242, 268
  demographic variables in choosing,
    205, 211
  existential-humanistic approach,
    282–96
  feminist therapy with, 265–80
  firsthand accounts, 233–337
  identification with patients, 408
  identifying, 349–50
  impaired practitioners, 323–37
  incestuous dimension of, 242–45
  lack of training for, 4
  marital and family therapy with,
    297–305
  personal therapy of, 351–52
  person of, 298–99, 381
  research on psychotherapy with
    mental health professionals, 345–
    63
  satisfactions of, 3–4, 278–80, 359–
    60
  selection criteria for, 201–4
  stressors of, 360
  and transference, 240, 268
  treatment with cognitive therapy,
    254–64
  well-centered, 300–301
  See also psychotherapist(s);
    therapist-patient(s)

therapy models, 288–96
thinking, 29
Thomas, Ross, 86
training analysis
  current issues, 30–31
  definition of, 5
  as educational, 16–17
  first model of, 17
  and formation of Jungian analyst,
    27–32
  Freud on, 27, 31, 410
  hiding from analyst, 20
  historical perspective on, 365–68
  Institutt for Psykoterapi (Oslo,
    Norway), 370–71
  Jung on, 27
  limits of, 32
  in "mainstream" Freudian model,
    15–25
  reporting aspect of, 18–19, 20, 248
  research on, 368–76
  and specific content of work, 18
  unique issues in, 247–49
  U.S./European training guidelines,
    29–30
  William Alanson White Institute,
    370–71
training-related stress, 35
training therapy models, 45, 46
transference
  and analysis of colleagues, 240
  in analytical psychology, 29
  beyond termination, 399
  in classic theory, 382
  in existential-humanistic
    psychotherapy, 287
  of Fairbairn/Guntrip, 68, 69, 72
  in feminist therapy, 268
  idealizing selfobject, 126
  influence of in therapy, 142
  as interactive process, 383
  interdependence with
    countertransference, 388
  during marital therapy, 138–39, 154
  and multiple analysis, 31

  negative reactions, 388
  and sexual boundary violations,
    333–34
  and training analysis, 18, 24–25
trauma, 64–67, 73–75
trusted companion, 82
"Two Analyses of Mr. Z., The"
  (Kohut), 7

unconscious
  collective, 27
  Freud's views on, 15, 16
  Jung on, 27, 117
  self-control over, 411
unformulated experience, 83
Unfree Associations (Kirsner), 367–68

violations
  boundary, 22, 327–29, 397
  distance, 94–95
  sexual, 326–37, 397
vocational guidance, 82, 130
vulnerability, 35, 407

Wasserman, Harvey, 86
Wheelwright, Joseph, 28
Whitaker, Carl, 54–55
wild card archetype, 332
William Alanson White Institute,
  370–71
Willoughby, Alan, 86
Willutzki, Ulrike, 41, 177
Winnicott, D.W., 63–65, 67–70, 73–
  79
Wiseman, Hadas, 177, 214
Wittine, Bryan, 114–28
Wolff, Toni, 28
Wolpe, Joseph, 209
working alliance, 104, 250
wounded healers, 302, 323–37
wounded warrior archetype, 331
writer's block, 95
writing, 93–94, 276

yoga, 92, 93